Primary and Secondary Qualities

Primary and Secondary Qualities

The Historical and Ongoing Debate

EDITED BY
Lawrence Nolan

OXFORD
UNIVERSITY PRESS

OXFORD
UNIVERSITY PRESS

Great Clarendon Street, Oxford OX2 6DP

Oxford University Press is a department of the University of Oxford.
It furthers the University's objective of excellence in research, scholarship,
and education by publishing worldwide in

Oxford New York

Auckland Cape Town Dar es Salaam Hong Kong Karachi
Kuala Lumpur Madrid Melbourne Mexico City Nairobi
New Delhi Shanghai Taipei Toronto

With offices in

Argentina Austria Brazil Chile Czech Republic France Greece
Guatemala Hungary Italy Japan Poland Portugal Singapore
South Korea Switzerland Thailand Turkey Ukraine Vietnam

Oxford is a registered trade mark of Oxford University Press
in the UK and in certain other countries

Published in the United States
by Oxford University Press Inc., New York

First published 2011

British Library Cataloguing in Publication Data
Data available

Library of Congress Cataloging in Publication Data
Data available

Typeset by SPI Publisher Services, Pondichery, India
Printed in Great Britain
on acid-free paper by
MPG Books Group, Bodmin and King's Lynn

ISBN 978–0–19–955615–1

1 3 5 7 9 10 8 6 4 2

In memory of Paul Hoffman

Acknowledgements

I would like to thank those who advised me at various stages of this project, especially Alex Byrne, Gary Hatfield, Nicholas Jolley, Peter Momtchiloff, Alan Nelson, Lex Newman, Bob Pasnau, and Al Spangler. I am also grateful to two anonymous referees commissioned by the press and several other referees that I enlisted to comment on particular chapters. Last but not least I would like to acknowledge the students in my graduate seminar in metaphysics in fall 2009, especially John Clevenger. Their questions and insights have shaped my own views about the nature of the primary–secondary quality distinction.

Contents

Notes on Contributors

MICHAEL AYERS is Emeritus Professor of Philosophy, University of Oxford and Fellow of the British Academy. He is the author of *Locke: Epistemology and Ontology* (1991) and co-editor (with Daniel Garber) of *The Cambridge History of Seventeenth-Century Philosophy* (1998).

ALEX BYRNE is Professor of Philosophy at the Massachusetts Institute of Technology, and works primarily in philosophy of mind and epistemology. He edited the two-volume *Readings on Color* (1997) with David Hilbert, and they have also co-authored many papers on the subject.

MARTHA BRANDT BOLTON is Professor of Philosophy at Rutgers University. She writes on various figures in seventeenth- and eighteenth-century philosophy. Her recent articles include 'Leibniz's *Nouveaux Essais*: a Contest by Dialogue', in *Leibniz and the English Speaking World*, ed. Phemister and Brown, and 'Locke and Leibniz on the Structure of Substance and Powers: the Metaphysics of Moral Subjects', *Studies on Locke: Sources, Contemporaries, and Legacy*, eds. Hutton and Shurman.

LISA DOWNING is Professor of Philosophy at the Ohio State University. Her articles (on Locke, Berkeley, and Malebranche, among others) focus on mechanist conceptions of body and their justification, debates surrounding gravity/attraction, and changing conceptions of scientific explanation in the early modern period. She is working on a book on empiricism and Newtonianism, among other projects.

GARY HATFIELD is Professor of Philosophy at the University of Pennsylvania. He is the author of *The Natural and the Normative: Theories of Spatial Perception from Kant to Helmholtz* (1990), *Descartes and the Meditations* (2003), and *Perception and Cognition: Essays in the Philosophy of Psychology* (2009), as well as numerous articles and book chapters in the history of modern philosophy and the philosophy of psychology. He translated Kant's *Prolegomena* (2004).

DAVID HILBERT is Professor of Philosophy at University of Illinois at Chicago and works primarily on issues concerning color and vision. He is the author of *Color and Color Perception* (1987) and he edited a two-volume anthology on the philosophy and science of color, *Readings on Color* (1997), with Alex Byrne. He is the author of several papers on color with Byrne and is currently working on perceptual constancies.

DAVID LANDY is Assistant Professor of Philosophy at San Francisco State University and specializes in modern philosophy.

MI-KYOUNG LEE is Associate Professor of Philosophy at the University of Colorado at Boulder. She is the author of *Epistemology after Protagoras: Responses to Relativism in Plato, Aristotle and Democritus* (Oxford 2005), as well as numerous articles in the history of ancient Greek philosophy, especially epistemology.

ANTONIA LOLORDO is Associate Professor of Philosophy at the University of Virginia. She is the author of *Pierre Gassendi and the Birth of Early Modern Philosophy* (2007) and numerous papers in modern philosophy.

EDWIN MCCANN is Associate Professor in Philosophy at the University of Southern California. He is the author of numerous articles in modern philosophy and is currently writing a book on Locke.

BARRY MAUND is a Senior Research Fellow in Philosophy at the University of Western Australia. He is the author of *Colours: Their Nature and Representation* (1995) and *Perception* (2003). He has written articles and chapters in philosophy of perception, philosophy of science, and the history of modern philosophy. He is the author of the entry on 'Color' in the *Stanford Encyclopedia of Philosophy*.

ALAN NELSON is Professor of Philosophy at the University of North Carolina at Chapel Hill. He has written numerous essays in early modern philosophy and the philosophy of science, and is the editor of *A Companion to Rationalism* (2005).

LAWRENCE NOLAN is Professor of Philosophy at California State University, Long Beach. He is the author of numerous essays in early modern philosophy and is currently editing the *Cambridge Descartes Lexicon*.

ROBERT PASNAU is Professor of Philosophy at the University of Colorado. He is the editor of the *Cambridge History of Medieval Philosophy* (2010), and the author of various books and studies in the history of philosophy, including *Metaphysical Themes 1274–1671* (2010).

JAMES VAN CLEVE is Professor of Philosophy at the University of Southern California. He is the author of *Problems from Kant* (1999) and of many articles in epistemology, metaphysics, and the history of modern philosophy. His next book will be entitled *Problems from Reid*.

KENNETH P. WINKLER is Professor of Philosophy at Yale University. He is the author of *Berkeley: An Interpretation* (1989). A collection of his essays, *Matters of Reason: Essays in Early Modern British Philosophy*, is forthcoming. His other books include *The Cambridge Companion to Berkeley* (2005) and an abridgment of Locke's *Essay concerning Human Understanding* (1995). From 2000 to 2005 he was editor, with Elizabeth Radcliffe, of the journal *Hume Studies*.

Introduction

Lawrence Nolan

I. The nature of the primary–secondary quality distinction and the aims of this volume

The objects that we experience with our senses appear to have various properties, including extension (or spatial dimension), size, shape, motion, and position, on the one hand, as well as color, sound, taste, odor, heat, cold, etc., on the other hand. However, the seventeenth-century revolution in science ushered in a radically new conception of the nature of physical objects that sought to revise this common-sense picture. Known as "mechanism", the new science conceived the universe on the model of a machine and tried to explain all physical phenomena in terms of the mechanical properties of the insensibly small parts of matter. If the universe is like a machine, then the only salient properties for the purpose of scientific explanation are those that enable one object to causally affect another through direct contact, just as one explains the operation of a clock by appealing exclusively to the size, shape, and motion of its gears. The color of the clock or the sound it makes when it chimes on the hour are irrelevant to understanding how it keeps time and thus do not figure in such explanations. As a consequence, the new science restricted the "real qualities" of bodies to those that can be understood in mechanical or geometric terms, and treated qualities such as sensuous red as mere appearances. Another way of expressing these points is to say that the "mechanical philosophers" drew a distinction between primary and secondary qualities and that this distinction was at the heart of the new science. The primary qualities were so-called because of their privileged role in scientific explanation, in contrast to the secondary qualities. There were fierce disagreements about the precise nature of both types of quality but the mechanical philosophers concurred in holding that secondary qualities are in some way derivative and/or dependent on the primary. Many such thinkers also tried to explain why, prior to engaging in philosophical reflection, one is tempted to treat colors and the like as qualities on a par with size and shape.

The primary–secondary quality distinction has its roots in ancient Greek and medieval Scholastic thought, as some of the papers in this volume will attest. However, the formulation in the modern period (roughly the seventeenth and eighteenth centuries) is rightly regarded as definitive. Although we associate this distinction most commonly with Locke and Boyle, versions of it had many defenders, including Galileo, Hobbes, Gassendi, Descartes, Spinoza, Malebranche, Newton, Leibniz, Hume, Reid, and Kant. The doctrine of qualities has also been extremely influential over the past two centuries, and a new debate about the nature of the distinction raged at the end of the twentieth century, especially among Australian philosophers such as David Armstrong and J. J. C. Smart. It is sometimes asserted that the primary–secondary quality distinction is the product of an outmoded science,[1] but I take it that, with some qualifications, most contemporary philosophers would endorse a version of it.[2] Various attempts have been made to reduce qualities that have been traditionally categorized as secondary—such as heat—to primary qualities, and, in light of these efforts, one contemporary philosopher has predicted that the class of secondary qualities is subject to a career of declining membership.[3] But such predictions are premature. Moreover, even if these efforts at reduction were completely successful, there would still be an important distinction between the primary qualities of objects and qualities such as heat *as it is experienced or felt.*[4] Leaving aside the other qualities traditionally categorized as secondary, the nature of color is presently one of the most contentious topics in metaphysics. The physicalist account of color, which attempts to reduce it to a primary quality, is merely one among several theories and there is nothing even approaching a consensus. The distinction between primary and secondary qualities thus appears alive and well.

The central aim of this collection of essays is to trace the historical development of the distinction between two types of quality and, to a lesser extent, understand its impact on contemporary philosophy. Our focus will be on the modern period since the classic formulation is to be found there. But the volume begins with chapters on ancient Greek and medieval Scholastic accounts of qualities in an effort to pinpoint the distinction's origins. The next ten chapters are devoted to philosophical reflections on qualities from the seventeenth through the nineteenth centuries. Virtually every major figure is represented from Gassendi to Kant, and special attention is paid to figures such as Locke and Descartes, who merit two chapters each, given the complexity of their views and their central role in promoting the aspirations of the new science. The last two chapters are devoted to the contemporary debate over the status of color, but their respective authors self-consciously link their discussions to early modern disputes about the nature of secondary qualities. All fourteen essays were specially commissioned for this volume and are appearing in print for the first time. Many of the authors have

[1] See e.g. J. J. Macintosh 1976, 102, and A. D. Smith's response (1990, 228f).

[2] This conjecture is shared by Robert Pasnau 2006, 568, and Smith 1990, 221, among others. Smith opines that the reason most philosophers would endorse the distinction is because "science tells them so" (1990, 231).

[3] John Campbell 1972, 226.

[4] In this case, the distinction would be a version of the objective–subjective distinction.

written on the primary–secondary quality distinction (or on the nature of color) in other contexts, and all were selected for their expertise on a given figure, historical period, or topic.

2. The beguiling character of the distinction

There are few philosophical doctrines, if any, which are more familiar than the distinction between primary and secondary qualities. Most philosophers cut their teeth on it as part of their undergraduate training in the discipline, and for good reason. Studying the doctrine of qualities introduces one to a wide swath of issues in metaphysics, epistemology, philosophy of mind, philosophy of perception, and semantics. It also forces one to confront questions about the relation between philosophy and science, and about the nature of scientific explanation. It offers an especially useful vantage point on the mechanical philosophy of the seventeenth century, exposing the revolutionary character of the new science and showing how it differed from that of its Scholastic-Aristotelian predecessor.

In addition to being familiar, the doctrine of qualities also seems intuitively simple, perhaps in part because it is often characterized as an appearance–reality distinction: there are certain qualities that objects in the world have intrinsically, independent of our perception of them, while there are others that we ascribe to objects only in relation to our perceptual apparatus or sensibility. For example, the world in itself consists of objects that are extended and shaped but not colored, at least not in the way that we experience color. Color as perceived is merely a subjective consequence of the way that objects affect our sensory faculties.[5]

But the primary–secondary quality distinction is also very beguiling: despite its intuitive character, it is notoriously elusive. There are several difficulties here. First and foremost, it is extremely difficult to identify the central ground of the distinction. Asserting that it is based on the more fundamental distinction between appearance and reality does not take us very far, for that is consistent with a broad range of ways of being distinct. What remains to be specified is whether it is a distinction between essential vs non-essential properties of objects, intrinsic vs extrinsic, objective vs subjective, perceiver-dependent vs perceiver-independent, dispositional vs categorical, etc. Second, there are familiar lists of primary qualities (extension, size, figure, motion, force, etc.) and of secondary qualities (colors, sounds, tastes, odors, heat, cold, etc.), but what are the criteria for membership in each class, and how do we determine whether the lists are complete? I suggested above that the criterion for being a primary quality is explanatory basicality: unlike secondary qualities, primary qualities play a crucial role in providing intelligible explanations of natural phenomena. Although this claim

[5] For more on the relation of the primary–secondary distinction to the appearance–reality dichotomy, see Barry Stroud 2000, 3f.

continues to have a great deal of currency both among historical commentators[6] and contemporary proponents[7] of the primary–secondary quality distinction, it is controversial. Third, is the distinction between primary and secondary qualities supposed to be exhaustive of all properties? It is sometimes noted that the distinction is restricted to simple properties (which in turn causally produce, or at least correspond to, simple ideas in us).[8] But if that is true, at least among the mechanical philosophers who recognize a metaphysical distinction, then it complicates efforts to categorize the distinction using a standard framework for discriminating types of property such as those mentioned above ("dispositional vs categorical", etc.). Fourth, what is the nature of secondary qualities? Are they mind-dependent entities such as mental qualia, powers or dispositions of external objects, or the causal bases of such powers? One problem with the second view is that early modern mechanical philosophers associated irreducible powers with Scholastic occult qualities, which they abhorred because of their obscurity and vacuity in developing scientific explanations of natural phenomena. Within an early modern context, this makes it tempting to hold that secondary qualities qua powers ultimately reduce to primary qualities or to an arrangement of such qualities (what Boyle and Locke call "textures"). But reducing secondary qualities to primary ones effectively collapses any metaphysical distinction between them, or so it would seem.

3. Synopses of the essays in this collection

As noted above, the primary aim of this volume is to trace the historical development of the distinction between primary and secondary qualities and to understand its various incarnations. Thus, we begin with chapters on ancient Greek and medieval Scholastic accounts of qualities before turning to the mechanical philosophers of the modern period with whom the distinction is traditionally associated, and then to contemporary theories of color to assess its influence. It is sometimes suggested that, like many seminal philosophical ideas, the distinction has its roots in ancient Greek thought. In chapter 1, Mi-Kyoung Lee examines this suggestion by surveying the views of a variety of ancient philosophers, while reserving special treatment for Democritus, Plato, Aristotle, and Epicurus. She argues that certain strands of modern thinking about the distinction were indeed present in several classical philosophers but that Aristotle and, as one would expect, the ancient atomists, come closest to anticipating their seventeenth-century counterparts.

6 Michael Ayers attributes this view to Locke; see chapter 6 of this volume.

7 See Smith 1990.

8 See chapter 9 of this volume and Smith 1990, 228. The authors of the former (Alan Nelson and David Landy) assert this of the empiricists, while Smith applies it to rationalists such as Descartes, who treats primary qualities such as shape and size as examples of 'simple natures'. Locke recognized a third class of quality ('tertiary qualities') whose members should also be regarded as simple, as he conceived of them as being on a par with secondary qualities.

In a famous fragment, Democritus says that tastes, colors, heat, and cold exist only "by convention", while atoms and the void exist "in reality". Some scholars deny that Democritus is drawing a primary–secondary quality distinction here and claim instead that he is simply distinguishing between the intrinsic properties of atoms and the derivative properties of composites. The latter distinction is of course crucial to Democritus' atomism, but Lee takes him to be engaged in the passage in question in an attack on the senses and not to be making any claims about the properties of atoms. He is merely drawing an epistemic distinction between the senses, which report only about how things appear, and reason, which is able to divine the truth about reality. However, Lee maintains that this epistemic distinction does correspond to a metaphysical distinction between primary and secondary qualities. She compares and contrasts Democritus' views on qualities to those of Plato in the *Timaeus*, where he too espouses a type of atomism. Like their seventeenth-century counterparts, Democritus and Plato both regard sensible qualities as depending on the fundamental primary qualities of matter. They also recognize the perceiver-dependent character of sensible qualities. However, whereas Democritus leaves it unclear whether qualities such as colors and smells are 1) merely appearances in the minds of perceivers or 2) powers that belong to aggregates of atoms to cause certain effects, Plato clearly regards such qualities as real properties of objects.

Like Democritus and Plato, Aristotle and Epicurus are concerned to identify the basic principles of nature and to distinguish them from derived properties, of which sensible qualities such as color constitute a special category. But Lee argues that the latter two philosophers go further than their predecessors in insisting upon the reality of such qualities (despite their relational status) and their causal efficacy. It is the latter claim (among others) that the seventeenth-century mechanists found so offensive, but Lee notes that there is much in Aristotle and Epicurus that the former could embrace, including the attempt to explain all other qualities in terms of the primary ones, which are taken to be universal.

Lee's paper shows that it would be a mistake to suppose that the distinction between primary and secondary qualities was the invention of early modern philosophy. Even if they did not use this exact terminology, and even if not all of the strands of the distinction were always present, the ancient Greeks shared many of the same concerns as the seventeenth-century mechanists. In chapter 2, Robert Pasnau argues that the distinction was also alive and well in the Scholastic tradition of the late Middle Ages. As in the modern period, the Scholastics treat the primary qualities as the fundamental causal agents in the natural world and regard them as inseparable from all bodies. They also hold that secondary qualities depend on the former for their being. In addition to showing how the Scholastic distinction prefigures its modern counterpart, Pasnau pinpoints the important differences between them. More notably, he argues that the term "primary qualities" has a very different extension in each tradition. The Scholastics bracket the mechanical qualities of bodies (which they regard neither as primary nor secondary) and instead privilege the four qualities (Hot, Cold, Wet, Dry) that give rise to Aristotle's four elements (earth, air, fire, and water). These qualities play a crucial role in Scholastic science but—unlike size, shape, extension, etc. in the modern tradition—are not explanatorily exhaustive.

In the second half of his essay, Pasnau attempts to dispel some of the myths associated with Scholastic accounts of sensible qualities. In particular, he is concerned to correct the assumption that the Scholastics regard secondary qualities such as color as primitive, *sui generis* features of the world that exactly resemble our experience of them. Scholastic thinkers are often accused of "projecting" their sensations onto the world, but Pasnau argues that they are instead committed to "Revelation", a somewhat weaker doctrine according to which sensory experience reveals the true nature of sensible qualities.

One expects that the primary–secondary quality distinction would find a natural home within every variety of mechanistic atomism. After all, atomism holds that the only things that exist are atoms and their spatial properties (i.e. their "primary qualities"). All the other properties that we attribute to bodies are merely appearances that depend on the former, and hence qualify as "secondary qualities." And, as we have seen, among the ancient atomists, Democritus, Plato, and Epicurus are committed to some version of the distinction. However, Antonia LoLordo argues in chapter 3 that the early modern atomist Pierre Gassendi does not draw such a distinction because he conceives all qualities (of composite bodies) as textures, that is, as arrangements of atoms. Qualities traditionally categorized as primary, such as shape, and qualities traditionally categorized as secondary, such as color, are merely epistemically distinct in that we are able to hypothesize about the texture of bodies that constitutes their macroscopic shape, but cannot do this in the case of color. She also observes that Gassendi and Walter Charleton both turn almost all qualities, including those of macroscopic bodies, into occult qualities in the sense that they have a hidden nature. We do not know in most instances what texture constitutes a given sensible quality. In discussing Gassendi's endorsement of the texture view of all qualities, LoLordo also explains why he rejected the two competing alternatives in the seventeenth century—namely, the appearance view and the power view—which one associates with Galileo and Locke's respective accounts of secondary qualities. LoLordo locates the source of Gassendi's heterodox position among the mechanical philosophers in the qualitative nature of his physics, which eschews quantitative explanations of phenomena such as gravity and magnetism. For him, "the traditional primary qualities of macroscopic bodies are not used for explanatory purposes in physics. They are mere *explananda*, just like color and taste."

Descartes has been saddled with perhaps every possible account of the status of so-called secondary qualities that was available in the seventeenth-century. Depending on whom one reads, Descartes is said variously to treat colors, sounds, odors, etc. as 1) sensations, 2) dispositions to produce sensations in human perceivers, or 3) the micro-physical structures that underlie those dispositions. This scholarly tradition reaches its high-water mark in a prominent essay by Margaret Wilson, who argues that Descartes (and, for that matter, several early modern philosophers) vacillate on the ontological status of secondary qualities. In chapter 4, I challenge the shared realist assumption of all these readings by arguing that Descartes is in fact a nominalist about secondary qualities: colors, etc. are merely names for either 1) the properties of bodies that cause our sense perceptions or 2) the perceptions themselves, considered abstractly. I frame my argument with a much-neglected expression. In almost every passage in which he is purported to affirm a realist thesis about color, Descartes speaks of "what we call color" (or "what we call red", etc.). Typically, when using this expression, he is referring to the properties of bodies that we ordinarily refer to as "colors." He is not speaking in his own voice or claiming, in light of philosophical reflection, that we *ought* to call such and such properties "colors." In short, he is best read as making a semantic point, rather than a metaphysical one, about how the term "color" is used in ordinary discourse. As he sees it, this general term and particular color terms (such as "green") serve as placeholders in everyday parlance for whatever it is in bodies that causes our visual sensations, in the absence of a complete scientific story. Rather than offering a metaphysical theory of secondary qualities in such passages, Descartes sees himself as attacking the Scholastic Resemblance Thesis, according to which our sense perceptions resemble their external causes.

In the second half of the paper, I locate the source of Descartes color nominalism within his general account of how much is given in sensory experience or, in his terms, "taught by nature." He maintains that most of what we take to be given in experience is in fact the product of false judgments formed in our early childhood and exacerbated by Scholastic philosophical training. These false judgments include not only the Scholastic view that "colors" are qualities in objects, but also the more fundamental assumption that "colors" are qualities—an assumption that involves reifying mental abstractions. On the basis of this discussion, I conclude that Descartes is not a friend of qualia, contrary to a myth too long associated with his philosophy.

Setting aside the debate over the ontological status of secondary qualities, one issue is clear: Descartes and the other early modern mechanical philosophers deny that color, taste, odor, heat, cold, etc. are in bodies in any way that resembles our sensory experience of them. Indeed, it is crucial to their scientific program to show that the only real and intrinsic properties of material objects are geometric and kinematic ones. But this raises an important question. How do they establish this result, especially if our senses seem to teach us otherwise? In chapter 5, Lisa Downing tackles this question for both Descartes and Robert Boyle, who, as she notes, are the two most influential modern proponents of strict mechanism. She argues that most of Descartes' arguments appeal to Ockham's razor. Having shown that matter can be conceived without qualities such as hardness or color, and that we can explain all natural phenomena via geometric properties alone, he shifts the burden of proof onto the Scholastic to show that we must posit anything else. Downing, however, thinks this argument fails precisely because Descartes' physics does not explain all observable phenomena. In an attempt to find something better, she reaches deep into the text in search of an a priori argument for the same conclusion. Unfortunately, the only such argument to be discovered depends on a controversial premise about the intelligibility of assigning sensible qualities to bodies. After assessing several possible strategies for justifying this premise, Downing ultimately concludes that the argument fails, but provides a helpful lesson about one of the ways in which Descartes' physics leans on his metaphysics.

Downing believes that Boyle's efforts to banish secondary qualities from the physical world are more successful, but only because his aims are more modest. Boyle holds that the primary–secondary quality distinction is part and parcel of the mechanistic hypothesis, whose truth can be established only as probable on the basis of experimental success. If there is one point upon which Descartes and Boyle agree it is that reflection reveals the unique explanatory status of mechanism.

One of the most important recent debates among commentators on Locke's philosophy is whether, in distinguishing primary and secondary qualities, Locke sees himself as drawing out the consequences of seventeenth-century corpuscularian science or, instead, as marshaling arguments based upon "reflective common sense." On the first reading, he does not have independent arguments for the distinction apart from a specific scientific theory; on the second, he does. In chapter 1, Michael Ayers maintains that these two readings find their source in an ambivalence in Locke's own position but argues that an argument independent of corpuscularian assumptions is implicit in Locke's discussion. He thinks that Locke mounts a single argument for both corpuscularianism and for the primary–secondary quality distinction that appeals to the prominent role that observable primary qualities play in intelligible explanations of how material objects behave. "Corpuscularianism was not a theory plucked from the air, but was founded on intelligible observable processes." One attraction of Ayers' discussion is that it offers a novel explanation of the role that corpuscularian speculation plays in Locke's argument. It also delineates the sense in which mechanical explanations of natural phenomena are (partially) "intelligible" for Locke.

Ayers tackles two other related tensions in the *Essay*, the first between Locke as a sceptic and Locke as corpuscularian. Even while defending the new science, Locke deflates its explanatory pretensions by denying that we can know the real essence of matter or are close to understanding such basic physical phenomena as cohesion and gravity. The second tension is between two models for understanding sensory ideas—one that treats them as inherently representational and the other that treats them as "blank effects." Ayers draws important lessons from these tensions which, while not leaving Locke completely unscathed, highlight his insight that the perception of bodies in space (along with their primary qualities) is fundamental to the way all higher animals apprehend the world. Secondary qualities such as colors, by contrast, are not fundamental, but tied to the sensory apparatus of particular classes of animal.

A formidable challenge facing proponents of the new seventeenth-century mechanical science, with its austere conception of the universe as consisting merely of matter and motion, is that it seems to defy common sense. This fact makes it difficult to accept. By contrast, Scholastic-Aristotelian science, which teaches that the colors, sounds, odors, etc. of our everyday experience are real qualities of bodies, seems to vindicate common sense. As Edwin McCann sees it, the main goal of Locke's argument for the primary–secondary quality distinction is to overturn this judgment by showing that, in fact, mechanism better accords with our ordinary, pre-scientific notions of body and its causality than its Scholastic competitor. In defending this interpretation, McCann rejects a tradition of scholarship that sees Locke as trying to provide justificatory arguments for the primary–secondary quality distinction, and as making robust metaphysical claims. By McCann's lights, Locke's goal is more modest, in keeping with his self-description as an under-laborer to the great scientists of his day and the empiricist constraint of not going beyond the dictates of experience. Indeed, like Ayers, McCann stresses Locke's deep doubts about the possibility of ever understanding some of the main underpinnings of mechanism, such as the transmission of motion by impulse or contact. Such conceptual gaps stand in the way of ever achieving knowledge that the primary–secondary quality distinction applies to nature.

McCann frames his discussion with an important distinction that he finds implicit in the *Essay* between two types of primary quality—the mechanical affections of the insensibly small parts of matter, and the mechanical affections of macroscopic objects that we experience with our senses. He amasses a wealth of textual evidence for this distinction, but his main argument for it derives from the important interpretive results that follow from seeing how it is at work in the *Essay*. Using this distinction, McCann develops novel solutions to many of the vexed interpretive difficulties pertaining to Locke's famous claims about resemblance, the inseparability of primary qualities from bodies, and the status of secondary qualities as bare powers.

A common theme of a few essays in this volume is whether there is a metaphysical, or merely an epistemic, distinction between primary and secondary qualities. In chapter 8, Martha Bolton argues that for Leibniz the distinction is merely epistemic: primary and secondary qualities differ only in our manner of knowing them. Although Leibniz sides with other early modern mechanists on issues concerning scientific explanation, there are two features of his philosophical system that set him apart and preclude him from affirming a metaphysical distinction between types of quality. The first is his phenomenalism, according to which material things are merely the intentional contents of perceptual states. This means that, like Berkeley, Leibniz holds that primary and secondary qualities have the same status: both are relative and dependent on the imagination. The second feature is his dynamical physics, which makes physical forces more basic than the canonical primary qualities.

In the second half of the chapter, Bolton attempts to identify the distinctive feature of Leibnizian secondary qualities and, in the process, reveals other ways in which his treatment of qualities differs from that of fellow mechanists. Leibniz identifies secondary qualities with microphysical structures, but holds that we could never produce a theoretical reduction because bodies are endlessly divided and heterogeneous, and thus beyond the purview of scientific theories, which are intelligible and explanatory only insofar as they abstract from complexity. Given this complexity, all of our perceptions of bodies are confused to some degree (but, surprisingly, veridical!); however, our perceptions of secondary qualities are particularly confused. Leibniz takes this confusion to account for their distinctive character. Primary qualities, by contrast, are intelligible because our concepts of them are innate and because the qualities themselves are common to several sense organs. They thus depend, not on the constitution of some particular organ, but on the nature of body itself. Some early modern mechanists such as Locke appear to have held that what sets secondary qualities apart is that our sensations of them are intrinsically non-intentional. Such sensations are merely "blank effects" or mental qualia that in no way resemble their mechanical causes (see chapter 6 on Locke, as discussed above). Bolton argues that, for Leibniz, sensations of warmth, etc. *are* intentional, and that there is even a kind of structural resemblance between the sensation and the physical quality, even if we are not aware of it. Perceptions of secondary qualities are more complex and carry more information than they seem to, contra Locke and others.

In a curious passage in the *Essay Concerning Human Understanding*, Locke claims that all ideas enter the mind "simple and unmixed" and defines a simple idea as "one uniform Appearance, or conception in the mind" (II.ii.1). This remark seems to imply that one could experience a particular shade of red, for example, divorced from all other qualities, including extension and shape. But is this really possible? Berkeley famously thinks not. In chapter 9, Alan Nelson and David Landy investigate Hume's answer to this question as part of a general inquiry into the relation between ideas and qualities. They see Hume as developing Berkeley's insight, and argue that simple ideas are never perceived as simple, but are instead theoretical posits within his science of human nature. As part of this argument, they offer an account of the phenomenology of sense perception that attempts to show that such perception is always unavoidably complex. For example, any effort to focus one's attention on a putatively simple quality requires one to discriminate that quality from the rest of our experience. But the very act of discriminating results in the experience of a complex, relational idea. Nelson and Landy are keenly aware of the air of paradox here, and much of their essay is devoted to dispelling it. They also address several other challenges to their view. For one thing, Hume seems committed on textual grounds to the perception of simple ideas as *minima sensibilia*. He also holds an empiricist theory of meaning, according to which the meaning of a word is an idea. If we never perceive a simple idea as such, then what is the meaning of the term "simple idea", which bulks large in Hume's theory of ideas?

The issue of whether one could perceive a simple idea *as* simple has important implications for the distinction between primary and secondary qualities. Nelson and Landy contend that within Berkeley and Hume's theories of ideas, simple qualities *are* simple ideas. This claim alone, if true, provides a deep ground for concluding that the primary–secondary quality distinction, like the simple–complex idea distinction, is pragmatic rather than metaphysical in nature.

In the *Treatise of Human Nature*, Hume asserts that the "fundamental principle" of modern philosophy is that colors, sounds, tastes, smells, heat, and cold are "nothing but impressions in the mind". This claim raises several questions. First, the status of the so-called "secondary qualities" was one of the most fiercely debated issues in the modern period and there were at least three competing theories, the subjectivist account being only one of them. Why, then, does Hume ignore this debate and write as if there was a consensus among modern philosophers on this topic? Second, what is Hume's own attitude toward this principle? Does he endorse it? Third, does he offer different assessments of it in the *Treatise* and the *Enquiry*? Finally, Hume famously compares vice and virtue to secondary qualities. But is he entitled to this comparison? In chapter 10, Kenneth Winkler addresses all of these interpretive questions, while focusing primarily on the second.

After some fascinating preliminaries about the origins of the terms "sensible qualities" and "secondary qualities", and the subtle semantic differences between them, Winkler begins by discussing Hume's argument in the *Treatise* for the fundamental principle. Hume thinks that the only credible way to defend this principle is by appealing to considerations of perceptual relativity, but here he distinguishes three uses of relativity, only one of which he takes to be characteristically modern. Winkler discusses several difficulties involved in trying to assess Hume's attitude toward these uses of relativity, especially the one he associates with modern philosophy. Winkler also thinks that the argument Hume marshals for the fundamental principle is uncharacteristically weak. In an effort to make sense of these difficulties he analyzes two competing conceptions of the objectivity of a quality that he finds in the text, one in terms of causal relevance and another in terms of conceptual compulsoriness. Here one can hear the echoes of seventeenth-century debates about what makes some qualities primary and others secondary. Is it that only the former are causally efficacious and play an explanatory role in physics, or is it that only the former are inseparable from our idea of body? Winkler proposes three ways of resolving the conflict between these two conceptions, but believes that they all fail. He reluctantly concludes that Hume cannot be completely satisfied by any theory of sensible qualities that he is in a position to provide.

The topic of James Van Cleve's essay in chapter 11 is the foundation or underlying principle of Thomas Reid's distinction between primary and secondary qualities. Some recent commentators have urged that Reid treats it as an epistemological distinction, but Van Cleve argues that he regards it as metaphysical. The debate between Van Cleve and his opponents hinges on whether Reid takes secondary qualities to be dispositions or their causal bases. If the latter, then they would be reducible to primary qualities or to their combinations, and hence the distinction between the two types of quality would be merely in how we know them. But if secondary qualities were dispositions to produce sensations in perceivers, then they would be extrinsic properties, and hence differ metaphysically from primary qualities. Van Cleve defends the dispositional view. Incidentally, some commentators have argued that Locke regards secondary qualities as powers (rather than causal bases or textures) for this very reason: if secondary qualities were textures then the distinction between primary and secondary qualities would collapse *as* a metaphysical distinction.[9]

[9] See Samuel Rickless 1997.

One intriguing feature of Van Cleve's discussion is his comparison of Reid's views with those of a variety of historical and contemporary figures, including Locke, Berkeley, Hume, Mill, Smart, Armstrong, Putnam, and Harman. In an effort to pinpoint the significance of Reid's thought on qualities, he also discusses four views that are opposed to his: 1) naïve realism, 2) the claim that all properties are secondary qualities, 3) the Berkeleyean claim that no object could have primary qualities exclusively, and 4) the position, championed by many contemporary color theorists, that sensations are completely transparent and thus lack intrinsic features.

In the course of articulating his transcendental idealism in the *Prolegomena to Any Future Metaphysics*, Kant famously speaks of space as an appearance and compares it to the status of color on Locke's account of secondary qualities. While this comparison seems to involve a misunderstanding of Locke, who treats secondary qualities as powers in bodies rather than as the subjective effects of such powers, it also seems to imply that Kant himself did not distinguish between primary and secondary qualities. In chapter 12, Gary Hatfield argues that, in fact, Kant did draw such a distinction in his critical period, but restricted it to the realm of appearances: whereas color is merely the subjective effect of sensory stimulation on human sensibility, the primary qualities are explanatorily basic in describing and accounting for the empirically known effects of bodies on the senses. As a child of a post-Newtonian world, Kant treats spatialized forces—rather than extension, motion, shape, etc.—as the primary qualities of bodies. Nevertheless, the role that he conceives for these qualities in the explanatory program of the natural sciences is the same as that envisaged by the pre-Newtonian mechanists. Kant can even say, in a Lockean vein, that the spatial structure that we perceive (and intuit a priori) "resembles" the spatial structure of physical forces. But neither primary nor secondary qualities resemble things in themselves—the noumenal objects whose properties are beyond our ken.

As an illustration of Kant's influence on nineteenth-century thought, Hatfield devotes the second half of his paper to a comparison between Kant and Hermann Helmholtz, the German physicist and philosopher known for his perceptual theories of space and color. Like Kant, Helmholtz distinguishes color as a secondary quality from spatial qualities, but his attitude toward the latter changes over time: he begins as a realist but, under the spell of Kant's philosophy, ultimately comes to view space as the subjective form in which forces and relations appear, while at the same time offering an empiricist and psychological twist on the notion of a subjective form. Kant and Helmholtz diverge on the status of secondary qualities, and they do so in a way that mirrors the difference between Galileo and Locke, respectively: Kant regards color as a subjective sensation in the mind, whereas Helmholtz views color as a power to cause sensations in perceivers.

One of the legacies of early modern philosophy is that our perception of external objects is indirect. We are immediately acquainted only with the sensory effects that bodies cause in us, and must determine their qualities on the basis of these effects.

Thomas Reid calls this the "natural sign theory": our sensations are "signs" for the qualities of bodies that cause them but which they in no way resemble, just as words bear no similitude to what they signify.[10] On the basis of this theory, it seems plausible to suppose that sensible qualities such as color, insofar as they are in objects, are merely dispositions to produce sensations in us (or, more precisely, in standard viewers under standard viewing conditions). As noted above, Van Cleve argues just that on Reid's behalf.

Some contemporary color theorists have resurrected dispositionalism, which they sometimes call the "secondary quality theory" of color so as to distinguish it from recent attempts to reduce color to a primary quality. In chapter 13, Alex Byrne and David R. Hilbert argue that all of the major arguments for dispositionalism, in both its historical and contemporary forms, fail. Thus, they conclude, the secondary quality theory is philosophically unmotivated. Dispositionalism is often criticized on the ground that it is impossible to specify the "standard viewing conditions" and "standard viewers" in a principled manner. Some forms of dispositionalism—namely those that identify a property (say, green) with a disposition (say, to look green)—are also alleged to be circular. Byrne and Hilbert attempt to refute the second objection, but see the first as a genuine problem. However, they set it aside in order to uncover what they regard as deeper difficulties. The main source of these difficulties is the natural sign theory, which they take to be explicit in early modern dispositionalists such as Reid, and at least implicit in contemporary defenses of dispositionalism. Against this theory, Byrne and Hilbert argue that we have better than indirect epistemic access to the properties of external objects. They grant that certain objects are disposed, for example, to look red, but deny that the property red *just is* a disposition. Dispositionalism is neither a conceptual (or self-evident) truth, nor something we should accept on pragmatic grounds.

Barry Maund's essay in the final chapter of this volume complements that of Bryne and Hilbert. Whereas they attempt to undermine dispositionalism, he directs his attack against color realism more generally. Maund argues for color eliminativism, or the view that ordinary physical objects such as peaches, starfish, and glasses of wine do not have the colors they appear to have. He is careful to distinguish different forms of eliminativism, and advocates the ontological variety while rejecting conceptual eliminativism. He believes that there are important reasons for retaining the ordinary concept of color, even if it is not instantiated, and so urges us to adopt a "fictionalist attitude", which consists in treating a wide range of statements about color "as if they were true".

The strategy of Maund's argument for color eliminativism is simple. He enumerates four principles that colors purportedly obey according to our common-sense

[10] As Byrne and Hilbert observe (see note 16 of chapter 13), some early modern proponents of this theory such as Descartes take the signs to be the causes of our sensations rather than the sensations themselves.

understanding of them. He then argues that there are no physical properties that satisfy all four of these principles, especially the following two:

1) Colors are qualities that play a causal role in the perception of objects as having those colors.
2) Colors stand in certain structural relationships of similarity and difference (e.g. orange is more similar to red and yellow than to blue or green).

The argument depends on establishing that colors, should they exist, would have to satisfy these four principles, and Maund responds at length to those color realists who would deny this. Among other things, this discussion raises questions about how our color-naming practice works, and Maund defends a different account from Reid's natural sign theory, which he, like Byrne and Hilbert, rejects. According to Maund's diagnosis, the main failing of color realism (or, more specifically, color physicalism) is that it is unable to explain the phenomenal character of color experience (what it is, for example, to look red), either in terms of the intrinsic features of the experience or the representational content. He proposes a hybrid account of phenomenal character that commits him to projectivism, or the view that the perceiver projects the subjective features of his experience onto external objects. He concludes his essay by comparing and contrasting his theory with that of Descartes and Locke, whom he takes to be kindred eliminativists of a sort, even if their account of our color concepts and our color-naming practices must be rejected.[11]

Lawrence Nolan
Long Beach, California

Bibliography

Campbell, John. 1972. "Primary and Secondary Qualities," *Canadian Journal of Philosophy* 2: 219–32.

Macintosh, J. J. 1976. "Primary and Secondary Qualities," *Studia Leibnitiana* 8: 88–104.

Pasnau, Robert. 2006. "A Theory of Secondary Qualities," *Philosophy and Phenomenological Research* 73: 568–91.

Rickless, Samuel C. 1997. "Locke on Primary and Secondary Qualities," *Pacific Philosophical Quarterly* 78: 297–319.

Smith, A. D. 1990. "Of Primary and Secondary Qualities," *Philosophical Review* 99: 221–54.

Stroud, Barry. 2000. *The Quest for Reality: Subjectivism and the Metaphysics of Color*. New York: Oxford University Press.

[11] I gratefully acknowledge comments on previous drafts of this Introduction by Margaret Atherton, Alan Nelson, and Al Spangler.

1

The Distinction between Primary and Secondary Qualities in Ancient Greek Philosophy

Mi-Kyoung Lee

1. Introduction

It is natural to ask whether the distinction between primary and secondary qualities that one finds among the mechanical philosophers of the seventeenth century has antecedents in ancient Greek philosophy.[1] But this question is difficult to answer for at least two reasons. First, the ancient Greeks did not possess terms corresponding to "primary quality" and "secondary quality", and hence did not have a terminology neatly marking the distinction as we do. They did have terms such as *aisthēta* ("those things that can be perceived"), *ta phainomena tais aisthēsesi* ("what appears to the senses"), and *aisthētai poiotētes* ("sensible qualities"), among others, which are often used to refer to the "secondary" qualities, but can also be used more broadly to refer to such things as dogs and horses, or the properties of being such. The primary–secondary quality distinction, however, is a distinction *within* the genus of sensible qualities, and hence these Greek terms fail to pick out the relevant distinction.

Second, though we moderns have terms marking a distinction, there is some confusion even for us about what exactly is intended by the distinction; depending upon how we understand the distinction, we will answer the question about the Greeks differently. It is generally agreed that the *locus classicus* for such a distinction is in the mechanical philosophy of Galileo, Descartes, and Boyle, as well as in Locke. Galileo seems to have drawn a distinction between "primary" and "secondary" qualities as part of an argument rejecting Scholastic-Aristotelian ways of understanding

[1] In this chapter, I use the following translations: for the Pre-Socratics with the exception of Democritus, Barnes 1987; for Democritus (and testimony about Democritus, including Theophrastus'), Taylor 1999a; for Plato, Cooper ed. 1997; for Aristotle's *De Generatione et Corruptione*, Williams 1982. References to the Pre-Socratics include the fragment or testimonium number in Diels-Kranz 1951–2; references to Democritus include the corresponding fragment number (e.g. "D16 Taylor") or testimonium number ("46a Taylor") in Taylor 1999a, which is much superior to Diels' collection, but does not include the Greek.

matter. On that view of matter, hot, cold, wet, and dry are the fundamental qualities of matter—to which Galileo responds by arguing that these are not primary qualities of matter at all, but *secondary* qualities, along with the other objects of sensation. The "primary and real properties" of body are shape, size, number, motion, spatio-temporal location, and contact. Primary qualities are those qualities which all bodies have necessarily: what makes qualities "primary" is that they are essential and necessary to body. "Secondary" qualities are all those (sensible) qualities that are not primary: being a brick and being a horse, as well as being red or sweet, would presumably count, on this criterion, as "secondary" qualities. Galileo and Descartes seem to have thought that matter has primary qualities, but not secondary qualities: secondary qualities are not "real" (since, for example, they are not causally efficacious). Locke by contrast, thought that bodies *do* have secondary qualities, and characterized those qualities as powers of bodies to produce certain effects in observers; hence, they are by definition relational, that is, are to be defined in relation to perceivers or minds. They are properties of bodies, but not fundamental properties—unlike the primary qualities, they are defined as "mere powers". In addition, he notoriously held that our ideas of the primary qualities "resemble" the primary qualities themselves which cause them, whereas our ideas of the secondary qualities do not resemble their causes—our ideas of color, for example, are caused by complex configurations of the primary qualities, which when characterized as powers to produce those ideas, are called secondary qualities. In any case, what makes secondary qualities "secondary" is that their existence and nature can be explained in terms of the primary qualities of bodies.

This distinction has become quite ordinary and familiar, and there is some agreement in popular usage about the extension of the terms "primary quality" and "secondary quality"; usually properties such as size, shape, solidity, etc. are referred to as "primary", and properties such as color, smells, tastes, objects of touch, and sounds (i.e. the objects of sensory experience, narrowly construed) are taken to be "secondary" (which is what I shall refer to as "secondary qualities" in the remainder of this chapter). However, there is little certainty about what the real basis of the distinction is supposed to be. First, one could have in mind a distinction based on a theory about what are the essential attributes of matter, and in particular, of pieces of matter, namely, bodies. One might argue that shape, weight, size, and solidity are essential to body, since no matter how many times one divides matter, it continues to retain these qualities, whereas, if one divides bodies past a certain point they lose their color, smell, etc. Secondary qualities are then simply all the other qualities of body, where this encompasses both non-relational properties (such as being human), and relational properties (such as being sweet). What unifies secondary qualities, on this understanding, is the fact that all of them can be explained in terms of the primary qualities of bodies. Hence, we expect some kind of account of the relation that secondary qualities bear to primary qualities—for example by assigning secondary qualities to groupings of certain kinds of bodies and their primary qualities, or by showing that changes in secondary qualities depend on changes in primary qualities in such a way that the secondary qualities supervene on the primary ones. Following Pasnau in his chapter on the Scholastics, one might look for some of the following theses in order to establish the causal priority of the primary qualities over the secondary qualities: (i) the primary qualities are the fundamental explanation of natural change, (ii) the primary qualities are present in all bodies, (iii) the primary qualities, not the secondary qualities, are the primary causal agents (Ch. 2 pp. 45–6).

Alternatively, secondary qualities can be marked off from the primary ones by their subjectivity and causal relations to minds, in contrast with the primary qualities, which are objective and non-relational. For one can make mistakes about "secondary" qualities, and experience conflicting appearances with respect to them, without any change occurring in the objects themselves. For example, the wine appears both sweet to me and dry to you, while it remains the same in itself, undergoing no changes. Thus, its being sweet appears to be a matter of how it affects us, with our particular physical conditions and temperaments, not a matter of how the body constituting the wine is in itself. So understood, the primary–secondary quality distinction is a version of the distinction between appearance and reality.

Thus, the primary–secondary quality distinction can be understood in two ways: (1) it is a way of marking off a metaphysical distinction between essential and non-essential properties of matter and of bodies. As such, it promises to be a basic feature of any materialist ontology, and hence one would expect any theory of matter to have commitments on such a question. (2) In another sense, it is a way of marking off those sensible qualities which seem to be particularly subjective, that is, dependent on the responses that perceivers have to them. Qualities like colors and flavors give rise to conflicting appearances in different perceivers, and this in turn seems to have something to do with the epistemic facts about our sense-modalities and modes of perception.

Once we are clear about the fact that there are these two strands of thinking involved in the so-called primary–secondary quality distinction, we can both recognize the perils of anachronism in asking the question "did the ancient Greek philosophers draw the distinction?"—as though failure to combine these two strands of thought in a single distinction would be evidence of some kind of philosophical primitivism—but also answer it fairly straightforwardly by considering the ways in which they dealt with one or both strands of thinking.[2] In my view, the ancient Greek philosophers were concerned with both distinctions, though most of them did not combine them in the particular way that is distinctive of the seventeenth-century thinkers. Not surprisingly, it is the atomists of antiquity, Democritus, Plato, and Epicurus—the predecessors of the early modern corpuscularians—who seem to have come closest to drawing the

[2] These complications explain why there isn't much scholarly literature on the primary quality-secondary quality distinction in ancient Greek philosophy; discussions tend instead to focus on different ancient opinions about the nature of sensible qualities.

primary–secondary quality distinction in the way now familiar to us. But there are good reasons to view Aristotle himself—the target of the early modern mechanists—as having himself argued for a version of the primary–secondary quality distinction as well.

In the remainder of this introductory section, I shall give a brief overview of the entire period, with some comments about how the ancient Greek philosophers line up on these questions, and then I shall turn in subsequent sections to the views of the most interesting candidates: Democritus, Plato, Aristotle, and Epicurus.

Because many ancient Greek philosophers were concerned, from the very beginning, to explain what the nature of things really is, and which "beings" are most fundamental, we find evidence of the first strand of thinking about "primary qualities" throughout the period. Many of the so-called Pre-Socratic philosophers, including Thales up through Democritus, seem to offer competing theories of matter—thus, for example, one might say that when Thales said "the all is water", he was arguing that water is to be identified as the basic matter underlying all things (and similarly with Anaximander's *apeiron*, Anaximenes' *aer*, Empedocles' elements (earth, air, water, and fire), and Anaxagoras' so-called "roots").[3] Thus, many of them do offer explanations of change and alteration in observable things in terms of more basic substances and their qualities. And though they do not put it this way, some of them can be described (admittedly anachronistically) as distinguishing between primary, that is, essential, qualities of matter, and secondary, that is, derivative, qualities of material things. Thus, Empedocles, for example, argues that things like animals and plants are made up out of the four basic elements; famously, he says that

> Another thing I will tell you: there is no birth for any mortal thing, nor any cursed end in death. But there is only mixing and interchange of what is mixed—but men name these things birth.
> (Plutarch, *Against Colotes* 1111F = DK 31B8, trans. Barnes in Barnes 1987)

That is, what people call "coming into being"—for example, the birth of a baby—is not really anything other than a "mixing and interchange" of what already exists and does not in itself change.

However, with the exception of Democritus, none of the Pre-Socratics seem to have singled out the secondary qualities more narrowly construed (i.e. colors, sounds, smells, tastes, etc.) for special treatment, or attempted to show specifically how to derive them from the primary ones. Thus, for example, Anaxagoras' theory of elements includes stuffs-cum-qualities such as the sweet, the bitter, blood, bone, the hot, the red, etc.; he has what we would call "secondary" qualities mingling happily with "primary" qualities.

The second strand of thinking we identified above—the one which marks sensible qualities off as subjective and perceiver-dependent—makes its first appearance in

[3] This reading of the Pre-Socratics goes back to Aristotle (*Metaphysics* I 3). For texts translations and commentary, see Kirk Raven and Schofield 1983. Guthrie 1962 and Guthrie 1965 are still classic treatments of the earlier and later Pre-Socratics respectively. See also Kahn 1960, and more recently, Graham 2006.

some of the Pre-Socratics who made use of conflicting appearance arguments, in the service of the thesis that things are not as they seem, and that our means of discovering the truth are highly fallible.[4] Thus, for example, Xenophanes famously points out that if cows could draw pictures of the gods, they would give them cow-attributes; this seems to suggest that our conception of the gods is fallible (Clement *Strom.* V, 109, 3 = DK 21B15). And Heraclitus offers arguments of the form "things are F and not-F", either in order to emphasize how fallible human modes of understanding are, or in order to emphasize that things may have the appearance of confusion and diversity, though there does, in fact, exist an underlying order. Such arguments culminate in Protagoras' conflicting appearance arguments: he is said by Plato and other sources to have argued that things appear F and not-F, and thus are F for some and not-F for others (Plato, *Tht.* 152a2–4 = DK 80 B1; see also Sextus *M* VII 60, DL IX 51, and *Tht.* 161c3). While Protagoras' aim seems to have been to argue for some kind of thoroughgoing relativism or infallibilism (the position that no one ever has false beliefs), Plato regards the argument as being particularly plausible in, and relevant to, cases of sensible qualities (such as sweetness, bitterness, etc.) and value properties (such as goodness, beauty etc. *Tht.* 171d–172b). That is, such properties seem particularly prone to giving rise to conflicting appearances and disagreement, even when the objects involved do not change in themselves. Plato should therefore be credited, in the *Theaetetus*, with being the first to point out, in antiquity, that perceptible properties along with value properties seem to be the most likely to be observer-dependent and subjective. Plato goes on to develop—in the "secret doctrine" of the *Theaetetus*, where Plato develops Protagoras' ideas on his behalf—a radically perceiver-dependent theory of sensible qualities, where things are *F* (e.g. colored) if and only if they appear so to someone (*Tht.* 153–160).[5] (Of course, he himself goes on to reject as untenable both the metaphysical and epistemological doctrines he develops on Protagoras' behalf.)

The conflicting appearance arguments which Plato and Aristotle associate with Protagoras went on to have a long history in the Hellenistic period when they were collected by the Pyrrhonist skeptic Aenesidemus in the so-called Ten Modes of Aenesidemus.[6] Whereas the conclusion of these arguments for Protagoras was that "things are as they seem to each", the Pyrrhonists seem to have concluded, variously, that "all things are relative" (to how they seem), or that, given the equal strength of arguments on both sides, it is impossible to tell how things really are (or how they are in themselves), from which suspension of judgment follows. Sextus Empiricus, the second to third century AD Pyrrhonist doctor, and an important source for Pyrrhonist

[4] For a very helpful introduction to epistemology in the Pre-Socratics, see Hussey 1990, and also Hussey 1972; on the Greek tradition of *ou mallon* ('no more this than that') arguments, see DeLacy 1958.

[5] See Burnyeat 1979, Burnyeat 1982 for two seminal papers on this part of the *Theaetetus*, as well as McDowell 1973 and Burnyeat 1990; some recent responses to Burnyeat include Fine 1996 and Lee 2005.

[6] See Striker 1983, Annas and Barnes 1985.

skepticism, is arguably aware that it is sensible qualities and value properties in particular that are vulnerable to these kinds of skeptical arguments.

Thus, there is throughout the history of ancient Greek philosophy a rich tradition of thinking about sensible qualities and their distinctively subjective, relative, or observer-dependent status. However, it is really only the philosophers of the late fifth and fourth centuries BC, Democritus, Plato, and Aristotle, who for the first time attempt to develop theories about the nature of sensible qualities, and ask whether these number among the fundamental qualities of all bodies—thus linking the first strand of thinking about the primary–secondary quality distinction with the second. That these thinkers were the first to consider sensible qualities in any detail is confirmed by Theophrastus (*c*.372 to 286 BC), who was a student of Aristotle's and successor to him as head of the Peripatetic school. In his treatise *De Sensibus* or "On the Senses", he sets out an account of pre-Aristotelian views about the senses and the sensible qualities.[7] By way of introduction to the second half of the treatise where he deals with sensible qualities, he says that Plato and Democritus were the only ones (among Aristotle's predecessors) to go into the sensible qualities in any detail. He goes on to discuss Plato and Democritus critically, implicitly pointing forward to what he no doubt regards as Aristotle's more consistent and tenable position on sensible qualities in the *De Anima* and the *De Sensu*. In the remainder of this chapter, I shall follow Theophrastus by focusing on Democritus and Plato, before turning to Aristotle and Epicurus.

The topic of sensible qualities in antiquity is a huge one; my treatment will necessarily have to be selective and abbreviated for the purposes of this volume. One major school which I will mention only in order to set aside is that of the Stoics, who are notable for avoiding the distinction. The Stoics are foundationalists in their epistemology, and argue that all *kataleptic* or "cognitive" impressions are true;[8] these perceptual impressions are not confined to awareness of colors, sounds, and smells, say, but include such perceptions as perceiving *that there is an egg in front of me*, or perceiving *that this is not Socrates but his double*. They do not seem to have picked out colors, sounds, and smells as special in any way, but included them among the qualities of sensible objects.[9] Their lack of interest in the specific mechanics of perception and in the ontological status of so-called secondary qualities is notable; this is perhaps because Chrysippus and the other Stoics were ultimately more interested in locating qualities like virtue and vice in nature, than in investigating questions of metaphysics

[7] For the text see Diels 1879; for a translation and commentary, see Stratton 1917, which is badly outdated. But at least for Theophrastus' treatment of Democritus, we have the excellent translation and commentary in Taylor 1999a; Long 1996 is very helpful on the question of Theophrastus' reliability as a source for Plato's views.

[8] For Stoic epistemology, see Long and Sedley 1987 chapters 39–41, Frede 1987, and Hankinson 2003.

[9] See Long and Sedley 1987 chapters 27–29 (on Stoic metaphysics). The fourth genus "relatively disposed" in the Stoic theory of "categories" seems to have included qualities such as sweetness, but the category is certainly not limited to the so-called secondary qualities; see also Sedley 2005.

and natural science for their own sake. At any rate, they do not seem to have made a significant contribution to our topic.

2. Democritus

We begin with the atomist Democritus (*c.*460 to 356 BC), who despite his traditional classification as a "pre-Socratic" was a younger contemporary of Socrates'. Democritus espoused the doctrines of his predecessor Leucippus, according to whom there are two fundamentally basic and distinct kinds of realities in the natural world, atoms and void. The atoms move around in the void, colliding or entangling with each other. But they are in themselves unchanging and indestructible. The macroscopic objects that we see are simply the products of the interactions of the atoms in the void. They are various compounds consisting of arrangements of different kinds of atoms; the changes in arrangements give rise to what we see as qualitative alteration and substantial generation and corruption.[10]

Democritus regards the atoms as having certain properties, but there are many controversies surrounding the details of his theory. Atoms possess intrinsic properties, such as shape, size, impenetrability, motion, ordering, arrangement, and maybe weight. All other properties besides these are apparently properties of aggregates of atoms, and can be characterized in terms of the intrinsic properties of the atoms making up an aggregate.[11] Thus, Aristotle reports Democritus' memorable analogy between atoms and the letters of the alphabet, which can produce a multitude of different words from a few letters in combination: the differences between words can be explained by differences in shape (*schēma*) of atoms (e.g. as A differs from N); differences in arrangement (*taxis*), as AN differs from NA; and differences in positional orientation (*thesis*), as N differs from Z (Aristotle, *Metaphysics* 985b4–22 = DK 67A6 = 46a Taylor). The bulk of the remaining fragments and reports about Democritus have to do with his "aitiologies", where he shows how to explain, in terms of his atomist theory, various kinds of macroscopic properties and phenomena.[12]

Aristotle criticizes Democritus at length for making heat an intrinsic property of spherical atoms—Aristotle regards this as an arbitrary exception (*GC* I 8. 324b35–326b6 = DK 67A7 = 48a Taylor). As Taylor notes, however, this is probably unfair to Democritus, since Democritus may very well have intended to say that heat is a

[10] For translations and commentary on Democritus, including excellent treatments of Democritus' atomism, theory of perception, and sensible qualities, see Taylor 1999a; for a briefer introduction to Democritus, see Taylor 1999b. Sedley 1992 contains an invaluable discussion of Sextus Empiricus' report on Democritus' epistemology. The treatment of Democritus and Theophrastus here depends heavily on Lee 2005.

[11] Difficulties include the question of whether the atoms are necessarily microscopic or whether as one fragment has it there could be atoms as big as a cosmos (DK 68A47); whether atoms are conceptually or only physically minimal (Furley 1967); and whether atoms have weight and move because of this, or whether their movement is entirely due to collision (cf. O'Brien 1981, Furley 1989, McDiarmid 1956, Balme 1941).

[12] Morel 1996 is an extended study of these aitiologies.

property of *aggregates* of spherical atoms, not of these atoms individually.[13] If so, then heat is not an exception to the thesis that shape, size, motion, and arrangement are the only intrinsic properties of atoms; all others are attributes of aggregates of atoms.

What about the other so-called secondary qualities? Does Democritus pick these out for special treatment? One famous fragment makes it appear that he does:

By convention (*nomōi*) sweet and by convention bitter, by convention hot, by convention cold, by convention colour; but in reality (*eteēi*) atoms and void.

(Sextus Empiricus *Against the Mathematicians* [*M*] VII 135 = DK 68 B9 = D16 Taylor; also Diogenes Laertius IX.72; Galen *On Medical Experience* 15.7 = DK 68B125; Galen *On the Elements according to Hippocrates* I.2; and in slightly different form Plutarch, *Against Colotes* 1110E-F = 206 Taylor)

Democritus seems to be marking a distinction between two types of qualities: (i) sweet, bitter, hot, cold, color, etc., which seems to correspond to what we would call secondary qualities, and (ii) the basic qualities of atoms and void, which he does not name here, but would presumably include shape, size, and motion. But at the same time there are a number of questions about what Democritus has in mind. First, there is some question of how to fill in the "etc."; he lists flavors, temperatures, and colors. But if the list is meant to go on, then what else is supposed to be on the list? Maybe smells? But Theophrastus says that Democritus didn't have much to say about them. Sounds? But Sextus seems to think Democritus did not include them, though he should have: sensible qualities are by *nomos*; sounds are a sensible quality; hence sounds must be by *nomos* (Sextus *M* VI 53 = 123b Taylor).

The uncertainty surrounding the list suggests that Democritus did not then go on to spell out exactly what this putative class of "secondary qualities" would include. This then leads to the second question: what is the point of this distinction for Democritus—indeed is he drawing a distinction at all? Is Democritus saying of the atoms themselves that they have their own intrinsic properties, but are not sweet, bitter, hot, cold, or colored—they only have these properties "by convention" (*nomōi*)? But what does it mean to say that these exist "by convention"? Perhaps what's meant is that things are red "by convention" in the way that we say that this arrangement is to be called "dog" and this arrangement of atoms is to be called "cat": there is something arbitrary and conventional about calling this arrangement of atoms "red" and this arrangement of atoms "sweet". But if that were the rationale, then it would appear that he's not distinguishing between primary and secondary qualities, but rather distinguishing between intrinsic properties of the atoms, and properties that belong to them in combination. The point, then, would be that atoms individually and by themselves are no more colored than they are dogs: being a dog is a property that belongs to a certain combination of atoms, and so too, being red is a property that belongs to a certain combination of atoms. If this is the thought, however, then it appears that Democritus is simply alluding

[13] Taylor 1999a: 75n63.

again to a distinction between microscopic and macroscopic properties, and saying that *all* macroscopic qualities are conventional.[14]

At least some readers in antiquity read Democritus this way. Plutarch, for one, paraphrases him as follows:

> But even more in his second charge he [i.e., Colotes the Epicurean who has attacked Democritus] fails to see that he is expelling Epicurus from life along with Democritus. For he says that Democritus' statements *that colour and sweetness and the compound and the rest are by convention, but the void and the atoms in reality contradict the senses, and that someone who abides by this theory and applies it would not consider that he is a man or that he is alive.*
>
> (Plutarch, *Against Colotes* 8, 1110e–1111c = 206 Taylor)

Thus Plutarch thinks that Democritus is saying that not only the secondary qualities (i.e. sweet, bitter, hot, cold, etc.) exist *nomōi* or "by convention", but also that atomic compounds and aggregates do. The thought is that aggregates are no more real than sweet and bitter are: they are nothing other than groupings of what is real. The point of saying that these things exist "by convention" is, then, to indicate that it is only a convention, an observer-dependent construction, to think that this grouping exists as opposed to that one. None of these groupings exists in reality: it is a mere "convention" on our part to talk as though such aggregates really exist—over and above the atoms that constitute such groupings. On this reading of fragment B9, Democritus is endorsing a sweeping form of anti-realism about all properties of aggregates and the aggregates themselves, in contrast with atoms and their essential properties. This claim could be given additional support with evidence that he thought that nothing is causally efficacious except for atoms and their essential properties. So understood, Democritus is not so much making a distinction between primary and secondary qualities, but rather denying that anything exists besides atoms and void.

On the other hand, there is another way of interpreting fragment B9, and Democritus quite generally, which understands his point, not to be about intrinsic properties of atoms in contrast with "conventional" properties at the macroscopic level, but more specifically about a subset of the latter, understood as the objects of the senses. On this reading, which I favor, Democritus is worried about the ability of the senses to discover the nature of reality: the senses seem to report only about what we would call secondary qualities, whereas reason (*logos*) is able to divine the truth about reality, namely, that it is composed out of atoms and void. Democritus' worry is epistemological in nature: perception of a certain class of sensible qualities is ultimately uninformative about the true nature of the things they belong to. For when one is perceiving color, the perception simply registers how one's eyes have been affected by some

[14] Pasnau 2007 argues along these lines, concluding that Democritus did not intend to draw a distinction between primary and secondary qualities; others who read Democritus as an eliminativist (who is then led however reluctantly to skepticism) include Sedley 1988: 298–9, Wardy 1988, Purinton 1991.

external object, and so one has not ultimately found out anything about what that external object is like in itself.[15]

This is how Theophrastus, Sextus, and Galen read Democritus; they present him as raising in fragment B9 a problem specifically about the senses.[16] They tend to paraphrase the Greek terms *nomos* and *eteē*, translated above as "by convention" and "in reality", which indicates that by the late fourth-century BC and later, these terms—certainly "*eteē*", which is rare, but perhaps also "*nomos*"—were felt to be somewhat archaic, or at least in need of explanation; they paraphrase him as meaning that according to the senses, things *appear* to be sweet, bitter, hot, cold, etc., but in reality there are atoms and void. Democritus is not here talking about which properties do or do not belong to atoms; rather, he is engaged in an attack on the senses. The problem is that they do not tell us about what things are in reality, namely atoms and void, but instead tell us about things like the hot, the cold, the sweet, etc.

What exactly is so objectionable about reports like "this is sweet, bitter, hot, cold, etc."? Democritus thinks these are only reports about how things appear to us, that is, how they affect us and how they are "for us", not reports about how things are in themselves. As far as the senses go:

> In fact we know nothing firm, but what changes according to the condition of the body and of the things that enter it and come up against it.
>
> (Sextus, *Against the Mathematicians* VII 136 = DK 68B9 = D17 Taylor)

And again:

> This argument too shows that in reality we know nothing about anything, but each person's opinion is something which flows in.
>
> (Sextus Empiricus, *Against the Mathematicians* VII 137 = DK 68B7 = D20 Taylor)

When the senses tell us "this is hot" or "this is red", they are reporting how they have been affected by the atoms and void (in aggregate), not reporting how anything is in itself. And because hotness, sweetness, and redness turn out to be nothing other than

[15] There are reasons for dismissing Plutarch's testimony, and with it the eliminativist reading. First, Plutarch is the only source among many ancient philosophers who quote B9/125 who includes the phrase "and by convention compound" (*nomōi sungkrisin*); the other sources (Theophrastus, Galen, and Sextus) are more careful and limit the clause to secondary qualities (see also Taylor, p. 152 n. 141). And Plutarch is almost certainly not looking at a text of Democritus, but rather discussing and relying on the Epicurean philosopher Colotes, whom we have independent reasons for distrusting as a source for Democritus' views. Second, some scholars have argued that it would be implausible to attribute to Democritus the anti-realist position described above on the basis of Plutarch's testimony alone, since there is a large body of evidence that Democritus did think that atomic aggregates, and macroscopic bodies, have causal efficacy (Furley 1993, Morel 1996, Taylor 1999: 152 n. 141). Thus, while he was certainly a reductionist of one kind or another, he was not an *eliminativist* who thought that the only things that exist and have causal powers are atoms, void, and their essential properties. Rather, he was happy to assign causal responsibility for a wide range of phenomena to atomistic aggregates.

[16] See Lee 2005 (chs. 8–9) on Democritus for supporting evidence and arguments; for other interpretations which also read Democritus as focusing on secondary qualities narrowly construed, see Furley 1993, O'Keefe 1997, Ganson 1999, Taylor 1999.

affections of the senses, we can conclude that things are intrinsically no more hot than not hot, no more sweet than not sweet, etc. (*Outlines of Pyrrhonism* I 213). Our senses thus systematically mislead us by representing things as having properties that they do not really have in themselves.

Theophrastus is an especially important source for Democritus because he fills out our picture about the reasons why Democritus was concerned about sensible qualities. He says that Democritus' considered view about sensible qualities is that at least some of them do not "have their own nature"; sensible qualities are relational properties of objects having to do with the power that aggregates of atoms have to affect objects with sense organs. Among the sensible qualities, heavy, light, hard, and soft can all be identified with aggregates of certain types of atoms; hence, presumably, these are *not* sensible qualities that are "by *nomos*". But, as Theophrastus says, "None of the other sensible qualities has any nature of its own, but all are states of the sense when it is altered so as to give rise to an appearance. For there is no nature belonging to hot or cold, but change in shape [sc. of the thing perceived] brings about alteration in us; a concentrated effect dominates each individual, whereas an effect which is spread out over time is not noticed" (*De Sensibus* 63 = 113 Taylor). Thus, flavors (including the sour, sweet, astringent, bitter, saline, pungent), colors, sounds, smells, and temperatures are properties that aggregates have in virtue of their ability to affect things with certain kinds of sense-organs in certain ways. Consider, for example, sharp flavor: "sharp flavour consists of small, fine-grained atoms of an angular zigzag shape. Because these are pungent they penetrate everywhere, and because they are rough and angular they compress and contract, thus creating empty spaces in the body and heating it; for the more void a thing contains, the hotter it becomes" (*DS* 65). Democritus thinks that sharp flavour is to be identified with a preponderance of a certain type of small, fine-grained zigzag shaped atom, precisely because such atoms have the power to produce a certain effect on tongues. For it turns out that tongues themselves are constituted in such a way that only certain shapes and sizes can enter in and produce certain effects, whereas others cannot enter and thus have no effect, or at least not the relevant kind of effect, on it.

If this is correct, then we can conclude that Democritus, like Plato as we shall see, is worried about the status of a certain subset of sensible qualities, precisely because they cannot be defined except in relation to perceiving subjects. This subset seems to correspond roughly to what we would call secondary qualities, although its membership does not seem to be very well defined. Democritus' concern here is not, evidently, to distinguish crisply between primary and secondary qualities, but rather to argue that the senses tell us about sensory experiences and affections, rather than how things are in themselves. Galen (*c.*129–200 AD) thus presents Democritus as concerned with the nature of evidence: the senses basically give us reports about how we are affected by the atoms that impinge upon our bodies—but this does not tell us anything about what the atoms in objects themselves are like (*On Medical Experience* 15.7, p. 114 Walzer = DK 68 B125/T179c Taylor). For that, we need to turn to the evidence of reason—in particular, the kind of reasoning that leads us to the hypothesis of the existence of atoms and void, and to the explanatory work that such a hypothesis can do. This strongly suggests that the shape, size, and motion that belong to atoms are not, for Democritus, *sensible* in nature at all—these are qualities that are discerned by the intellect alone, along with the very existence of atoms and void. If Democritus thinks that the shape, size, and motion that we attribute to macroscopic objects are grasped by the senses, this leaves it unclear what relation there is between the size, shape, and motion belonging to atoms, and the corresponding sensible qualities of shape, size and motion belonging to macroscopic objects.[17]

Consider the following line of thought: (1) atoms are imperceptible because of their smallness, (2) secondary qualities are perceptible qualities; hence (3) atoms don't have secondary qualities (Taylor 1999: 175). This is supported by the fragment preserved in Sextus: "Of knowing there are two forms, the one genuine, the other dark. And of the dark kind this is the complete list: sight, hearing, smell, taste and touch. The one which is genuine, but separated from this one . . . [*then Sextus remarks "Then, by way of judging the genuine one superior to the dark one, he adds these words:"*] . . . is when the dark one is no longer able either to see in the direction of greater smallness, nor to hear nor to smell nor to taste nor to sense by touch other things in the direction of greater fineness" (Sextus *M* VII 139 = DK 68B11 = Taylor D22, trans. after Sedley 1992: 35–6). The idea is that atoms are imperceptible because they are so small, and hence *cannot* have qualities such as color, taste, or smell. But this suggests that the atoms themselves have no sensible qualities at all; the size, shape, and weight that they have must also be imperceptible, by the same argument. If so, then Democritus is distinguishing between two modes of cognition, the intellectual (by which we can grasp what features matter has) and the perceptual (which is a mode of affection by groupings of atoms and void)—but correspondingly to a distinction between the intrinsic qualities of atoms (whose nature is discerned by means of inference to the best explanation) and the non-intrinsic qualities of compounds (which are grasped by the senses). This then looks very much like a distinction between primary qualities of atoms and secondary qualities of macroscopic bodies.

Even so, Theophrastus accuses Democritus of inconsistency because he says that the attack on the senses—in particular the claim that the sensible qualities which the senses tell us about are nothing other than affections of the senses—is elsewhere contradicted by Democritus' account of sensible qualities. He writes, "In general, the greatest contradiction, which pervades the whole theory, is his both making them states of perception and at the same time distinguishing them by their shapes, and saying that the same thing appears bitter to some, sweet to others, and different to yet others. For it is

[17] Presumably size, shape, and solidity cannot be explained just in terms of the size, shape, and solidity of atoms alone, since a large mug, for example, could be made up of many small-size atoms or fewer larger-size atoms. Only in the case of location and weight of macroscopic objects is there a direct correlation with the location and weight of the atoms constituting them.

impossible for the shape to be a state, or for the same thing to be spherical to some and differently shaped to others (yet perhaps that is how it has to be, if it is sweet to some and bitter to others), or for the shapes to change according to our dispositions. It is simply the case that shape is intrinsic, but sweet and sensible qualities in general are relative and dependent on other things, as he says" (*DS* 69). According to Theophrastus, Democritus wants to explain sensible qualities that objects have in terms of their atomic constitution (hence, as he says, things have sharp flavors when they are constituted out of small, fine-grained zigzag atoms which easily penetrate the surfaces of the tongue), but that seems to be inconsistent with the view that sensible quality is really to be identified with the effect that is produced on the tongue—where some people might taste one mixture as being sharp flavored, and others might taste it as being mild.

Theophrastus' charge of inconsistency is probably an artifact of an overly literal reading of Democritus:[18] he thinks it is inconsistent to (A) identify particular sensible qualities with intrinsic qualities of the atoms, but at the same time to (B) define sensible qualities quite generally as affections of the senses (as part of his attack on the senses). Theophrastus is probably mistaken to read the passages where Democritus says, for example, that sweetness is round, good-sized atoms as stating strict identities. Rather, Democritus means that there are consistent correlations between something's being sweet and its having round, good-sized atoms in it; he may even think that it is impossible for round, good-sized atoms to produce the sensation of bitterness (say), even in someone ill. Thus, the presence of round, good-sized atoms is a necessary condition for something's appearing sweet to perceivers. However it is not a sufficient condition: as Theophrastus reports, Democritus is very attentive to the importance of environmental and physiological factors in determining the kind of perceptual experience someone will have. And since objects are composite aggregates of different kinds of atoms, it is easy to explain why something can appear both sweet and bitter—to different perceivers, or in different environments—even when they remain the same. In sum, Democritus probably endorses (B), the thesis that sensible qualities are affections of the senses, not (A), the thesis that particular sensible qualities are identical with certain kinds of intrinsic qualities of atoms.

In any case, whether Theophrastus is correct to charge Democritus with inconsistency, his criticisms do strongly suggest that Democritus was not very clear about whether sensible qualities, because they are not intrinsic properties of atoms, but rather relational properties belonging to aggregates, (i) do not really belong by nature to anything at all (as Theophrastus suggests), or (ii) are real but non-intrinsic properties of aggregates. The latter option is open to Democritus, that is, to maintain that sensible qualities are relational, causally efficacious properties of macroscopic bodies. Thus, just because sharpness is the disposition that small zigzag atoms have of producing a certain effect in tongues, it doesn't follow that things aren't "really" sharp in flavor, or that

18 This is a very condensed version of my argument at Lee 2005: Ch. 8.3.2.

there can't be an objective answer as to whether or not a thing is sharp in flavor. And part of the reason why things *are* really sharp in flavor is precisely because there is a systematic relationship between atomic composition and effects on other objects. This is the kind of view that Theophrastus favors—and which we see Aristotle and Epicurus develop.

3. Plato

In the so-called middle period dialogues like the *Phaedo* and the *Republic*, Plato notoriously holds that perception is systematically misleading about a systematically misleading part of reality. And so one might think that he would be an unlikely figure to turn to for the primary–secondary quality distinction, or at least for any close analysis of the nature of sensible qualities. But people forget about the importance of the *Timaeus* both in antiquity and later (when it was the only book of Plato's that was translated into Latin until the Renaissance). And the *Timaeus* contains what appears to be Plato's own attempt to offer a *Peri Physeōs* or "Physics" of his own. In it, he draws a kind of distinction between primary and secondary qualities.[19]

In the *Timaeus*, we find a triple account of the cosmos from three different points of view: once viewing it purely as the product of Reason (29e–47e), once viewing it purely as the product of Necessity (48b–68d), and once viewing it as the joint production of Necessity and Reason together (69–92). In the account of the world viewed as the product of "Necessity" alone, that is, viewed purely in terms of the material which the Demiurge was given to work with, we are told that at the most fundamental level, there is something which is exceedingly hard to grasp, but can be understood by employing metaphors and analogies—something which doesn't have a name, which Plato initially calls "the receptacle (*hypodochē*) of all becoming" (*Ti* 49a5-6) and subsequently calls "space" (*chōra*, 52a8, d3). This is a kind of matter which does not have any qualities of its own, but is the "receptacle" in which all other qualities are reflected. There is considerable scholarly debate about whether Plato's "receptacle" is a material substratum (in particular, a kind of ultimate prime matter underlying the primary bodies or elements), a kind of spatial field (see e.g. *Ti* 52b "We say that whatever is must necessarily be in some place"), or perhaps both. Aristotle, at any rate, regards his own theory of matter as an improvement upon Plato's (*De Generatione et Corruptione* II 1).

Having hypothesized the existence of this "receptacle" or as we might think of it, basic matter, Plato then offers an account of the elements. On his view, the elements are the parts of the receptacle that form regular solids. Beginning with a variety of shapes of regular solids, Plato explains the four primary bodies in terms of those basic shapes: particles of fire are tetrahedra, that is, pyramids, which are the most mobile regular solids; particles of air are octahedra; particles of water icosahedra; and particles

[19] Not much has been written on the secondary qualities in Plato's *Timaeus*, but for a very helpful treatment of Plato's theory of colors, see Ierodiakonou 2005.

of earth cubes (*Ti* 55d6–57d6). He goes on to explain how transformation of these primary, elemental bodies is possible; he also tries to explain how the varieties of physical bodies—for example, different kinds of liquids, metals, and other kind of compounds—come to be from the four primary bodies.

What is of great interest to us is what Plato does next. Before he turns to his account of what we would call the sensible qualities, which will be the last topic in his account of the properties of basic matter, he says:

> We have now pretty much completed our presentation of the kinds of bodies that are distinguished by their multifarious shapes, their combinations and their intertransformations. Now we must try to shed some light on what has caused them to come to have the properties they do. First, we need at every step in our discourse to appeal to the existence of sense perception, but we have so far discussed neither the coming to be of flesh, or of what pertains to flesh, nor the part of the soul that is mortal. It so happens, however, that we cannot give an adequate account of these matters without referring to perceptual properties, but neither can we give an account of the latter without referring to the former, and to treat them simultaneously is all but impossible. So we must start by assuming the one or the other, and later revisit what we have assumed. Let's begin by taking for granted for now the existence of body and soul. This will allow our account of these properties to succeed the account we've just given of the elemental kinds.
>
> (*Timaeus* 61c–d, trans. Zeyl in Cooper 1997)

The reason for Plato's worry is that the qualities he's about to describe cannot be described purely in terms of the primary bodies and their basic properties which he's already described, but also require one to assume the existence of perceivers and the nature of their sense organs. But the account of perception, sense organs, and perceivers is not given until the third part of the *Timaeus*, where he describes the world as a joint product of Reason and Necessity. One cannot really give an account of perceptual properties apart from perception, but at the same time, one cannot give an account of perception without referring to perceptual properties. That is, perceptual properties cannot strictly speaking be dealt with purely in terms of the fundamental properties of matter: any account dealing with them has to also refer to the fact that perceptual properties are those properties which have a certain effect on perceivers constituted in a certain way. Plato is clearly worried about the fact that some properties of body cannot properly be characterized without referring to the fact that they have the power to produce certain effects on perceiving subjects. We might put the point by saying that they are relational properties, unlike the intrinsic properties of matter and of the elements which he has been discussing so far.

With this prelude, Plato then goes on to talk first about tactile qualities which affect the whole body (61c–64a), as well as pleasure and pain (64a–65b), and then about the perceptual properties that affect particular parts of the bodies, that is, the sense organs (65b–68d): tastes, smells, sounds, and colors. Throughout, the account is meant to show how the fundamental properties of the primary bodies (i.e. fire, earth, water, air) can explain what we would call the secondary qualities of those bodies. Fire is *hot*, for example, because the particles making it up act on our perceiving bodies by dividing and cutting it (61d–62a). Something is *hard* because it is what our flesh gives way to (62bc); things that are composed of quadrangles are "the least liable to being displaced because [their] bases are very secure" (62bc). Likewise, color is "a flame which flows forth from bodies of all sorts, with its parts proportional to our sight so as to produce perception" (67c–68d).

Plato is explaining why objects are hot, hard, or colored by appealing both to the primary elements out of which they are composed *and* to their effects on perceivers and sense organs. This then explains why Plato thinks there is something problematic about these properties—not that they are derivative of the primary ones, since in his view many macroscopic objects, such as wine, or saps, or types of frost, are derivative in this sense, but that some properties make an essential reference to the existence and nature of perceivers. Note that this worry is rather different from the familiar old complaint from the middle dialogues that things in the sensible world are variable and unstable: it has specifically to do with the perceiver-dependent nature of some sensible qualities.

There is strong support for this reading of Plato from Theophrastus. After praising Plato and Democritus for going into the topic of the sensible qualities more fully than any others (*DS* 59), he then makes the claim that will be the theme of his discussion of the two:

> Democritus and Plato discussed them [i.e. *ta aisthēta*, 'the objects of sense'] the most fully, for they distinguish them in detail; except that Plato does not deprive the objects of sense (*ta aisthēta*) of their own nature, whereas Democritus reduces them all to states of sense. We shall not discuss which of these views is true, but let us try to set out how far each pursued the topic and what distinctions he made, having first given an outline of each view in its entirety. Democritus does not give a uniform account of them all, but differentiates some by size, some by shape, and some by order and arrangement. Plato ascribes almost all to states and [i.e., states of] the sense. So each seems to contradict his assumption (*hypothesis*), as Democritus makes them out to be states of the sense but distinguishes them with respect to their own nature, while Plato makes them out to be things in their own right but ascribes them to states of the sense
>
> (*De Sensibus* 60–61 = 113 Taylor)

Plato "contradicts" himself when, by including sensible qualities in his account of the fundamental properties of matter, he implicitly "assumes", as Theophrastus puts it, that sensible qualities are "things in their own right" (since he includes them in his treatment of material necessity and basic matter), but in the details of his explanation of each sensible quality he ends up making them nothing other than affections of the sense. (In my view, "depriving them of their nature" is Theophrastus' way of saying that an account has rendered a property in relational terms, in particular, the relation a perceiver has to an object, instead of describing it in intrinsic terms, purely in terms of the body and its non-relational properties.) The idea is presumably that Plato is not an anti-realist about sensible qualities, since after all he analyzes such qualities as powers enjoyed by elements and the complexes they can form, and he includes them in his basic theory of matter and material necessity. But at the same time, he ends up undermining their status by defining the sensible qualities in terms of their effects on the senses. Thus, for example, color is nothing other than the effect that certain (fire) particles have on the sense organs. Theophrastus thinks that there is an implicit tension in both Democritus' and Plato's accounts of sensible qualities—between regarding sensible qualities as being a part of an account of the basic and derivative natural features of matter, and regarding them as not really belonging to matter by nature. Whether Theophrastus is correct about there being an inconsistency in each view is not something we can go into here. His criticism, however, raises exactly the right questions about both philosophers: both Democritus and Plato seem to regard sensible qualities as depending in some sense upon the fundamental, primary qualities of matter (atoms and void, or the elements, respectively). Thus, for example, Democritus correlates flavors with atoms of a certain shape and size; Plato includes his account of sensible qualities under the rubric of the basic and derived properties of matter. But at the same time, both of them, in different contexts, recognize that sensible qualities are distinct from properties like texture or being heavy because an account of them requires one to make essential reference to the effect that such qualities have on perceivers. Thus, Democritus rejects perception as misleading because it only reports about how things are "for us". And Plato defines the sensible qualities as properties things have to affect the sensory organs in specific ways; for example, "things that rinse the vessels and wash the entire area around the tongue are all called bitter *when they do so to excess and so assault the tongue as to dissolve some of it*, as soda actually can do" (*Ti.* 65d). For both philosophers, this raises the question of whether such qualities belong to the nature of things—or whether things are in themselves no more bitter than not. They do not squarely answer this, however, because their concerns lie elsewhere. It remains for later thinkers—such as Aristotle, Epicurus, and their followers—to try to formulate their answers more precisely.

4. Aristotle

Aristotle draws much more precisely than his predecessors two different sets of distinctions between sensible qualities, both of which are relevant to the distinction between primary and secondary qualities.

The first place where Aristotle draws something that looks like a primary–secondary quality distinction is in the *De Anima* (II 6, III 1), where he distinguishes broadly between intrinsically sensible qualities (*aisthēta kath' hauta*), and coincidentally sensible qualities (*aisthēta kata sumbebēkos*). Roughly speaking, this is a distinction between those qualities which we perceive because they affect the sense organs, and those qualities which are coincidental to, that is, happen to belong to (or follow upon), the sorts of qualities which *are* capable of affecting the sense organs. Hence, color is the sort of thing that directly affects the eye; it is therefore intrinsically sensible. By contrast, when I see Socrates, it is not insofar as he is Socrates that he is visible to my eye, but rather because he is colored. Hence, his being Socrates is coincidentally sensible. Aristotle goes on to make a second distinction, within the class of intrinsically sensible qualities, between (i) the "proper sensibles" (*idia aisthēta*) and (ii) the "common sensibles" (*koina aisthēta*). The proper sensibles include colors, sights, sounds, smells etc., whereas the common sensibles include shape, size, motion, etc. His distinction here actually provides us with a very sensible basis for making a distinction between primary and secondary qualities, understood as a distinction between those sensible properties such as size and shape that can be detected through various sense modalities, and those to which we have access only through a distinctive sort of sensation produced by a specialized sense modality.[20] Aristotle's purpose here is not, of course, to distinguish between the more and less fundamental properties of matter, but simply to explain what sorts of properties are capable of "moving" (*kinein*) the senses. (He defines color, for example, as what is able to move (*kinētikon*) the transparent (*DA* II 7. 418a26–b2); the property of being able to be seen belongs to color not as part of its essence, but as a necessary (*kath' hauto*) accident of color.[21]) Thus, historically, when seventeenth-century philosophers put forward the primary–secondary quality distinction as a way of criticizing Aristotle's view of the fundamental properties of matter, this is not the doctrine that they had in mind.

Rather, what they had in mind is the distinction made in the *De Generatione et Corruptione* Book II 1–6, where Aristotle turns to describing the very lowest-level of matter, i.e. the "elements", the primary qualities of matter, which are the Hot, the Cold, the Wet, and the Dry. These two pairs of contraries can be combined to form the so-called simple bodies:

Earth is Cold and Dry.
Air is Hot and Wet.
Fire is Hot and Dry.
Water is Cold and Wet.

Hot–Cold are active forces, Hot being "that which aggregates things that are of the same kind" and Cold being "that which gathers and aggregates indiscriminately things that are related and things that are not of the same type" (*GC* II 2. 329b24–31). Wet–Dry are passive qualities having to do with the capacity to be affected: "wet is that which is not bounded by any boundary of its own but is easily bounded; dry is that which is easily bounded by a boundary of its own, but is hard <for other things> to bound" (*GC* II 2. 329b31–33, trans. Williams). All other qualities are in some emergent way from, or supervenient on, the mixtures which can be formed from

[20] On this as the basis for making a distinction between primary and secondary qualities, see Pasnau 2006: esp. 579ff.

[21] Aristotle does not define color as a subjective-dispositional property—that is, he does not define color simply as the disposition to produce a certain experience of color; see Silverman 1989. There is a huge literature on Aristotle's theory of perception, in particular, on Aristotle's perceptual realism, and on the question of what exactly he thinks happens in the eye, for example, when someone sees color (cf. Sorabji 1979, Burnyeat 1992, Nussbaum and Putnam 1992, Broadie 1992, Burnyeat 1995, Menn 2002, Caston 2004).

the simple bodies and their basic qualities.[22] Though he does not systematically try to show how all the other qualities can be explained in terms of the primary ones, he is arguably committed to the claim that (i) primary qualities are the fundamental explanation of natural change; changes in secondary qualities occur because of changes in primary qualities in the constituents making up an aggregate or mixture. Furthermore, he is arguably committed to (ii) the thesis of universality, according to which the primary qualities are in all bodies; that is, they continue to exist, and are not supplanted via mixture. (Claim (ii) is not entailed by claim (i) since there could be primary qualities that only belong to certain kinds of beings, e.g. living beings.)

Did Aristotle also endorse the claim—often made by proponents of a primary–secondary quality distinction—that (iii) the primary qualities, not the secondary qualities, are the only causally efficacious agents in nature? That is, did he think that the only causal agents are the primary qualities: Hot, Cold, Wet, Dry? No, he did not. On the contrary, he seems to have held that sensible qualities, such as sounds and colors, are to be identified as the causal bases of powers things have to produce perceptions. Colors, for example, are causally responsible for our perceptual experiences of them (*DA* II 7). But at the same time colors, and the things that have them, possess these causal powers because of lower-level facts about the presence of the Hot, the Cold, the Wet and the Dry in them. This at any rate appears to be the project of the *De Sensu*: to show what kind of physical facts ground the ability of colors (ch. 3), flavors (ch. 4), and odors (ch. 5) to have causal effects on, and set in motion the senses. Thus, in the *De Sensu*, Aristotle offers an account of what colors, flavors, and odors are, in order to show how they are able to have causal effects on perceivers, as discussed in the *De Anima*.[23]

If Aristotle did indeed argue that sensible qualities are causally efficacious—that is, productive of causal effects on perceivers that are revealed in their perceptual experiences—then this sets the stage for the attacks that would follow in the sixteenth century and later on Scholastic Aristotelianism and on the idea that qualitative "forms" have any place in a science. Why Aristotle felt compelled to argue for this claim is probably partly to be explained by his response to his predecessors, Plato and Democritus. Recall that Theophrastus reviewed their theories of sensible qualities, accusing both of them of an inconsistency: "each seems to contradict his assumption (*hypothesis*), as Democritus makes them out to be states of the sense but distinguishes them with respect to their own nature, while Plato makes them out to be things in their own right but ascribes them to states of the sense" (*DS* 61). He reveals his own stance when he elaborates his criticism of Plato as follows:

[22] See Williams 1982 *ad loc.*, especially pp. 158–161; for difficulties in Aristotle's account of mixture, see Cooper 2004.

[23] See Ganson 1997 for this interpretation of Aristotle, which he frames as a kind of reply to Galileo's understanding of Aristotle.

With respect to the nature of the flavors, he <Plato> does not say what each is . . . ; rather, he makes clear the effects (*ta pathê*) which come about from them. For <he claims> that the harsh or astringent flavor contracts the pores, and that the saline flavor cleanses them, which just is an affection (*pathos*) of us; similarly with the other flavors. But we seek their essence (*tên ousian*) more and why they do these things, since we observe the effects (*DS* 89).

Thus, Theophrastus thinks that by studying Plato and Democritus' theories one can learn from their mistakes—in particular, one can see that it is a mistake to simply characterize the sensible qualities in terms of their effects on perceivers. They are not simply *relational* properties of bodies in the sense that they have the ability to produce "an effect of this kind in a body of this kind", for that ability should be grounded in bodies' intrinsic properties as well. Hence, for Plato and Democritus, that means describing sensible qualities in terms of the particular shape, size, and grouping of particles or atoms that enable an object to affect a perceiving eye and produce the impression of redness. Aristotle's own view is set out in the *De Sensu*: there, he offers an empirical, scientific account of the physical basis of the colors, smells, flavors, etc., relating these to the primary qualities of hot, cold, wet, and dry. But showing this is simply a part of saying why they have causal efficacy: it is not Aristotle's intention to try to eliminate the so-called secondary qualities altogether from a scientific account of the properties of bodies and matter.

5. Epicurus

In the Hellenistic period, Epicurus (341–271 BC) develops—in reaction to Democritus—a defense of the reality of sensible qualities. Though he endorses many of the same atomist doctrines as Democritus, he goes to great lengths to distance himself from him, often stressing the internal tensions and problems in Democritus' theories that his own can overcome. Epicurus and his followers tend to read Democritus as a skeptic, one who thinks that nothing exists besides atoms and void. Whether or not Epicurus is correct in reading Democritus as a skeptic,[24] he develops his own views expressly in order to counter what he correctly regards as the self-stultifying consequences of such a skepticism—as he puts it, life becomes impossible if one believes that nothing exists besides atoms and void. Rather, Epicurus thinks that, even if atoms and void are ontologically primary, other things too are real, including secondary qualities.[25] In his view, sensible qualities are relational properties, but no less real for that.

Epicurus contributes to the debate by gaining clarity about how to think about this relational aspect of sensible qualities. He distinguishes per se substances—bodies and space—from the entities that depend on them: permanent attributes, accidental properties, and time. But he is at pains to emphasize that, despite the parasitic nature of the latter on the former, they are nonetheless real. Permanent attributes of body include

[24] Barnes 1982 reads Democritus as a skeptic, but for arguments against, see McKim 1984 and Curd 2001.

[25] For more on Epicurus' physics, see Bailey 1928, Furley 1976, Long and Sedley 1987, chapters 4–15, especially ch. 12 'Microscopic and macroscopic properties', Sedley 2005.

tangibility, shape, size, and weight. They are permanent because they are inseparable from anything considered as body; they are the only essential qualities that atoms have at the microscopic level. At the macroscopic level, however, some secondary qualities, such as temperature and color, may be essential to body, as for example heat is essential to fire, and yellow color is essential to gold, and may be regarded as its permanent attributes. Accidents, that is, non-essential attributes, exist not at the atomic level, but at the macroscopic level (Epicurus *Letter to Herodotus* 54–5 = LS 12D; Lucretius *De Rerum Natura* 2.730–833 = LS 12E); they can include relational and dispositional properties. Thus, Lucretius gives as examples of accidental properties servitude and poverty, both of which belong to things not per se but in virtue of complex relations that hold between people (*DRN* I 455–6).

Polystratus, who was the third head of Epicurus' school, the Garden, in the third century BC, defends the reality of relation and dispositional properties in the course of defending value properties like "fair" and "foul". He puts the point exactly: just because a predicate is relative, and just because a thing is F only in relation to something else, does not mean that F-ness is not real (Polystratus *On Irrational Contempt* 23.26–26.23 = LS 7D).[26] Relational properties are not intrinsic properties of objects, and so one might mistakenly conclude that these properties do not really belong to objects. But this would be a mistake. Consider, for example, being bigger. A thing is not per se bigger: "bigger" is a relational predicate, and hence a thing can only be bigger than something else. But it does not follow from this that things are not really bigger or smaller at all. And the fact that something is both bigger than X and smaller than Y does not show that it is not really bigger or smaller at all.

The same point can be applied, Polystratus argues, to powers, which are also relational properties. Consider for example, the properties of being nourishing or deadly. Peanuts (to use O'Keefe's example) can be nourishing or deadly to different people—nourishing to some, but deadly to those with a peanut allergy. Its deadliness is relational, but it does not follow that deadliness is not a real property of peanuts at all—that it is somehow conventional or subjective for that reason. The Epicureans thought we should regard sensible qualities like colors and flavors as relational in the same way. Colors are not intrinsic but relational properties of bodies—for they are powers of certain bodies to produce certain sensory affections in the bodies of perceivers, which in turn produce certain effects in their minds. Whether bodies have those colors depends on the atomic constitution of those bodies; whether they produce those effects on a given perceiver depends very much on the atomic constitution of their bodies, in particular, their sense organs. Thus, the same object may give rise to different impressions in different perceivers who are differently constituted. It does not follow, however, that colors are not real properties of objects for Epicurus. Like the property of being deadly, the property of being sweet or red is a dispositional property that objects

[26] See Striker 1983: 110ff. and O'Keefe 2009: 36–38.

have in relation to other objects under certain conditions. Proper understanding of the nature of relations can thus help Epicureans to make the point that, even if atoms do not possess in themselves any other attributes besides size, shape, weight, and motion, and even if sensible qualities only belong to macroscopic objects in virtue of complex relations they have with other objects, sensible qualities should still be regarded as real, existent properties of things, powers that they have to cause effects in other objects. Thus, like Aristotle, Epicurus appears to have endorsed a view of sensible qualities that makes them dependent upon the primary qualities of matter, but at the same time no less real, causally efficacious attributes of the bodies to which they belong. In this way, their theories look forward to developments in the Scholastic and seventeenth-century debates concerning the nature of primary and secondary qualities.

6. Conclusion

None of the ancient Greek philosophers used terminology exactly corresponding to our terms "primary" and "secondary" qualities, but as we have seen, that fact by itself is not very interesting. For we see that many of them did concern themselves with (i) the question of what properties are essential to matter, and to bodies, (ii) the question of whether any non-intrinsic properties of body are causally efficacious, and (iii) in particular, the special causal connection that the so-called secondary qualities have with our sense-modalities and sensory experiences. We started with Democritus and Plato who each posit a mechanistic theory to explain natural change and movement; both philosophers start with a theory of elements—atoms and void, and triangular solids, respectively—which have a limited set of intrinsic properties. This then raises for both the question of how to explain the properties of macroscopic objects, including the qualities that are the objects of the senses. Both recognize, though in different ways, the relational nature of the objects of sense. Democritus thinks that qualities like colors, smells, and flavors belong to objects insofar as they affect perceivers in certain ways; he seizes on this to attack the senses as uninformative about the true nature of things. His treatment makes it clear that sensible qualities do not belong to the atoms themselves; it is uncertain however, whether he thinks that sensible qualities are relational powers of aggregates to cause certain effects in certain objects under certain conditions, or whether he thinks sensible qualities are little more than appearances produced in the minds of perceivers. Plato clearly regards sensible qualities like colors and smells as real properties of objects, and yet he seems to think that they are different from qualities like texture and weight because they make an essential reference to perceivers.

The very existence of Aristotle's *De Anima* and *De Sensu*, and Theophrastus' treatise *De Sensibus* indicates that by the late fourth century BC, Aristotle and his students were focusing on the topic of sensible qualities. Aristotle distinguishes between those qualities like color, sound, and smell, that are the objects of a single sense-modality—which he calls the "proper sensibles"—and those qualities like size and shape that are the objects of more than one modality—which he calls "common sensibles". The extension of these terms—"proper" vs "common" sensibles—corresponds roughly to what we usually think of as primary and secondary qualities. However, Aristotle's objective here is not so much to draw a metaphysical distinction between more and less fundamental properties, but rather to analyze the sense in which these properties are sensible; only some of these are "sensible" in the strict sense, that is, those to which we have access only through a specialized kind of sensation produced in a special sense.

Like Democritus and Plato, Aristotle has a view about the basic principles of nature, that is, the "elements", set out in the *De Generatione et Corruptione*, where he argues that the four primary bodies, earth, air, water, and fire, are characterized by four basic properties, the Hot, the Wet, the Cold, and the Dry. These are not actually sensible qualities, but rather are active and passive powers that in combination through mixture produce higher-level qualities. Aristotle seems to think that sensible qualities—color, flavors, and smells—can be explained in terms of the elemental constitution of objects. And yet at the same time, they cannot simply be identified with combinations or mixtures of elements, since they are clearly causal powers themselves—powers to move and set in motion the senses.

Finally, Epicurus, like Democritus, thinks that atoms and void have a limited number of primary qualities: size, shape, motion, and weight. All other qualities are either accidental or essential qualities of bodies. Among the accidental qualities of bodies are the sensible qualities like color, smell, flavor, and sound. Epicurus regards these qualities as relational properties of bodies; they consist of the power that these bodies have to produce certain effects in perceivers under certain conditions. Epicurus stresses—in what is presumably meant to be a rebuke to Democritus—that the fact that they are relational should not be taken to mean that they are merely appearances. That is, relational properties—like being bigger than, or being deadly (to human beings)—do not belong intrinsically to objects, but they are at the same time real properties with real causal effects. Thus, both Epicurus and Aristotle seem to have (i) developed a theory of the basic qualities of matter or of the elements, (ii) distinguished from other derived properties of bodies a special category of sensible quality, that is, those qualities whose definition requires some reference to perceivers, and (iii) regarded these qualities as non-primary qualities of bodies, but at the same time very real properties with causal powers.

Claims of influence by these thinkers on later philosophers clearly depend upon what among their writings later philosophers read, and how they read them. Be that as it may, the ancient Greek philosophers as a group bequeathed a number of fruitful and interesting ideas concerning primary and secondary qualities to the Aristotelian Scholastics of the medieval period and to the seventeenth-century mechanists inspired by Epicurus and the ancient atomists.[27]

[27] I gratefully acknowledge helpful comments and suggestions I received from the editor Lawrence Nolan, from Dominic Bailey, Peter Hunt, and Robert Pasnau, as well as from two anonymous referees for Oxford University Press.

Bibliography

Annas, Julia and Jonathan Barnes. 1985. *The Modes of Scepticism: Ancient Texts and Modern Interpretations*, Cambridge: Cambridge University Press.

Bailey, Cyril. 1928. *The Greek Atomists and Epicurus: A Study*, Oxford: Clarendon Press.

Barnes, Jonathan. 1982. *The Presocratic Philosophers*, revised edition, London: Routledge & Kegan Paul.

—— 1987. *Early Greek Philosophy*, Harmondsworth: Penguin.

—— Algra, Keimpe and Malcolm Schofield (eds.). 2005. *The Cambridge History of Hellenistic Philosophy*, Cambridge: Cambridge University Press.

Broadie, Sarah. 1992. "Aristotle's Perceptual Realism," in John Ellis (ed.), *Ancient Minds*, 137–59, Spindel Conference, Memphis State University, October 1992. (*The Southern Journal of Philosophy* 31 (1992), supplement.)

Burnyeat, M. F. 1979. "Conflicting Appearances," *Proceedings of the British Academy*, London, 65: 69–111, Oxford: Oxford University Press.

—— 1982. "Idealism and Greek Philosophy: What Descartes Saw and Berkeley Missed," *Philosophical Review* 91/1: 3–40.

—— (ed.). 1990. *The Theaetetus of Plato*, trans. M. J. Levett, rev. M. F. Burnyeat, with an introduction by M. F. Burnyeat, Indianapolis, IN: Hackett Publishing Co.

—— 1992. "Is an Aristotelian Philosophy of Mind still Credible? (A Draft)," in Nussbaum and Rorty (eds.), *Essays on Aristotle's De Anima*, Oxford: Clarendon Press.

—— 1995. "How Much Happens When Aristotle Sees Red and Hears Middle C?: Remarks on De anima 2 7–8," in Martha C. Nussbaum and Amélie O. Rorty (eds.), *Essays on Aristotle's De Anima*, paperback edition, Oxford: Clarendon Press/New York: Oxford University Press. Originally published as "Aristote voit du rouge et entend un 'do': Combien se passe-t-il de choses? Remarques sur le 'De Anima', II, 7–8," *Revue Philosophique de la France et de l'étranger* 118/2 (Ap.–Jun. 1993), 263–80.

Caston, Victor. 2004. "The Spirit and the Letter: Aristotle on Perception," in Ricardo Salles (ed.), *Metaphysics, Soul, and Ethics: Themes from the Work of Richard Sorabji*, Oxford: Oxford University Press, 245–320.

Cooper, John M. (ed.). 1997. *Plato: Complete Works*, Indianapolis, IN: Hackett Publishing Co.

—— 2004. "Two Notes on Aristotle on Mixture," in his *Knowledge, Nature, and the Good: Essays on Ancient Philosophy*, Princeton and Oxford: Princeton University Press, 148–173.

Curd, Patricia Koenig. 2001. "Why Democritus was not a Skeptic," in A. Preus (ed.), *Before Plato: Essays in Ancient Greek Philosophy*, vi (Albany, NY: SUNY Press), 149–69.

DeLacy, Phillip. 1958. "*ou mallon* and the antecedents of ancient scepticism," *Phronesis* 3: 59–71; reprinted in John P. Anton and George L. Kustas (eds.), *Essays in Ancient Greek Philosophy*, Albany: State University of New York Press 1971, 593–606.

Diels, Hermann. 1879. *Doxographi Graeci*. Collegit, recensuit, prolegomenis indicibusque instruxit Hermannus Diels, Berlin: G. Reimer.

—— 1951–2. *Die Fragmente der Vorsokratiker*, 6th edn., revised by Walther Kranz, 2 vols. and Index, Zurich and Hildesheim: Weidmann.

Fine, Gail. 1996. "Conflicting Appearances: *Theaetetus* 153d–154b," in C. Gill and M. M. McCabe (eds.), *Form and Argument in Late Plato*, Oxford: Oxford University Press, 105–133.

Frede, Michael. 1987. "Stoics and Skeptics on Clear and Distinct Impressions," in his *Essays in Ancient Philosophy*, University Minnesota Press; reprinted in *The Original Sceptics: A Controversy*. Indianapolis, IN: Hackett Publishing Co. 1997.

Furley, David, 1967. *Two Studies in the Greek Atomists*, Princeton: Princeton University Press.

—— 1993. "Democritus and Epicurus on Sensible Qualities," in J. Brunschwig and M. C. Nussbaum (eds.), *Passions and Perceptions: Studies in Hellenistic Philosophy of Mind*, Proceedings of the Fifth Symposium Hellenisticum, Cambridge: Cambridge University Press, 72–94.

Ganson, Todd Stuart. 1997. "What's Wrong with the Aristotelian Theory of Sensible Qualities," *Phronesis* XLII/3: 263–282.

—— 1999. "Democritus against Reducing Sensible Qualities," *Ancient Philosophy* 19: 201–215.

Graham, D. W. 2006. *Explaining the Cosmos: The Ionian Tradition of Scientific Philosophy*, Princeton: Princeton University Press.

Guthrie, W. K. C. 1962. *A History of Greek Philosophy*. Vol. I: *The Earlier Presocratics and the Pythagoreans*, Cambridge: Cambridge University Press.

—— 1965. *A History of Greek Philosophy*. Vol. II: *The Presocratic Tradition from Parmenides to Democritus*, Cambridge: Cambridge University Press.

Hankinson, R. J. 2003. "Stoic Epistemology," in Brad Inwood (ed.), *Cambridge Companion to the Stoics*, Cambridge: Cambridge University Press, 59–84.

Hussey, Edward. 1972. *The Presocratics*, London: Gerald Duckworth & Co.

—— 1990. "The Beginnings of Epistemology: From Homer to Philolaus," in S. Everson (ed.), *Companions to Ancient Thought*, i. *Epistemology*, Cambridge: Cambridge University Press, 11–38.

Ierodiakonou, Katerina. 2005. "Plato's Theory of Colours in the Timaeus," *Rhizai: A Journal for Ancient Philosophy and Science* 2: 219–233.

Irwin, T. H. 1988. *Aristotle's First Principles*, Oxford: Clarendon Press.

Kahn, Charles H. 1960. *Anaximander and the Origins of Greek Cosmology*, New York: Columbia University Press/London and Oxford: Oxford University Press.

Kirk, G. S., J. E. Raven and M. Schofield. 1983. *The Presocratic Philosophers*, 2nd edn., Cambridge: Cambridge University Press.

Lee, Mi-Kyoung. 2005. *Epistemology After Protagoras: Responses to Relativism in Plato, Aristotle, and Democritus*, Oxford: Clarendon Press.

Long, A. A. and David Sedley. 1987. *The Hellenistic Philosophers*, vol. 1, Cambridge and NY: Cambridge University Press.

Long, A. A. 1996. "Theophrastus's *De Sensibus* on Plato," in K. A. Algra, P. van der Horst and D. T. Runia (eds.), *Polyhistōr: Papers offered to J. Mansfeld on the Occasion of his Sixtieth Birthday*, Leiden: Brill, 345–62.

McDowell, John. 1973. *Plato: Theaetetus*, trans. with notes, Oxford: Clarendon Press.

McKim, R. 1984. "Democritus against Scepticism: All Sense-Impressions are True," in Linos G. Benakis (ed.), *Proceedings of the First International Congress on Democritus*, Xanthi 6–9 October 1983, 2 vols., Xanthi: International Democritean Foundation, i. 281–290.

Morel, Pierre-Marie. 1996. *Démocrite et la recherche des causes*, Préface de Jacques Brunschwig, Paris: Klincksieck.

Nussbaum, Martha and Hilary Putnam. 1992. "Changing Aristotle's Mind," in M. Nussbaum and A. O. Rorty (eds.), *Essays on Aristotle's De Anima*, Oxford: Clarendon Press.

O'Keefe, Timothy. 1997. "The Ontological Status of Sensible Qualities for Democritus and Epicurus," *Ancient Philosophy* 17: 119–134.

—— 2009. *Epicureanism*, Berkeley: University of California Press.

Pasnau, Robert. 2006. "A Theory of Secondary Qualities," *Philosophy and Phenomenological Research* LXXIII/3: 568–591.

—— 2007. "Democritus and Secondary Qualities," *Archiv für Geschichte der Philosophie* 89: 99–121.

Purinton, J. 1991. "Epicurus' Libertarian Atomism," Ph.D. dissertation, Princeton University.

Sedley, David. 1988. "Epicurean Anti-reductionism," in J. Barnes and M. Mignucci (eds.), *Matter and Metaphysics*, Naples: Bibliopolis, 295–327.

—— 1992. "Sextus Empiricus and the Atomists' Criteria of Truth," *Elenchos* 13: 19–56.

—— 2005. "Hellenistic Physics and Metaphysics," in Barnes, Algra and Schofield (eds.), *The Cambridge History of Hellenistic Philosophy*, Cambridge: Cambridge University Press.

Silverman, Allan. 1989. "Color and Color-Perception in Aristotle's *De Anima*," *Ancient Philosophy* 9: 271–92.

Sorabji, Richard. 1979. "Body and Soul," *Philosophy* 49: 63–89; repr. with revisions in J. Barnes, M. Schofield, R. Sorabji (eds.), *Articles on Aristotle*, Vol. 4: *Psychology and Aesthetics*. London: Duckworth 1979.

Stratton, G. M. 1917. *Theophrastus and the Greek Physiological Psychology before Aristotle*, trans. with commentary, London: Allen & Unwin.

Striker, Gisela. 1983. "The Ten Tropes of Aenesidemus," in Myles Burnyeat (ed.), *The Skeptical Tradition* (Berkeley, CA: University of California Press), 95–115; reprinted in her *Essays on Hellenistic Epistemology and Ethics*, Cambridge and New York: Cambridge University Press 1996.

—— 1990. "The Problem of the Criterion," in S. Everson (ed.), *Epistemology: Companions to Ancient Thought* 1, Cambridge and New York: Cambridge University Press), 143–60.

Taylor, C. C. W. 1999a. *The Atomists, Leucippus and Democritus: Fragments*, a text and translation with a commentary, Phoenix Presocratics series, 5, Toronto: University of Toronto Press.

—— 1999b. "The Atomists," in A. A. Long (ed.), *The Cambridge Companion to Early Greek Philosophy*, Cambridge and New York: Cambridge University Press, 181–204.

Wardy, R. B. B. 1988. "Eleatic Pluralism," *Archiv für Geschichte der Philosophie* 70: 125–46.

Williams, C. J. F. 1982. *Aristotle's De generatione et corruptione*, translated with notes, Clarendon Aristotle series, Oxford: Clarendon Press.

2

Scholastic Qualities, Primary and Secondary

Robert Pasnau

1. Fundamentals of the Scholastic theory[1]

The distinction between two kinds of qualities, primary and secondary, is one of the core doctrines of Scholastic natural philosophy. Far from being an invention of the modern era, it is something to which any student of Aristotelian philosophy—which is to say anyone who studied philosophy in a European university up until the eighteenth century—would have been introduced at a tender age. The distinction is, moreover, every bit as important for Scholastic philosophers as it would become in the seventeenth and eighteenth centuries, since the primary qualities, on the Aristotelian tradition, are the fundamental causal agents of the natural world.

The *locus classicus* for the Scholastic idea is the beginning of Book II of *On Generation and Corruption*, where Aristotle attempts to tease out the fundamental qualities of the natural bodies around us. Considering Empedocles's proposal that there are four basic elements—Earth, Water, Air, Fire—Aristotle argues that this thesis can be proved correct by establishing that there are four basic qualities:

Hot, Cold, Wet, Dry.

These qualities, in their various possible combinations, give rise to the four elements. For generations of later Aristotelians, these are the primary qualities, and the secondary qualities are those further features of things—texture, color, flavor, odor, etc.—that the primary qualities explain.

The basic thesis behind the distinction is that the primary qualities, after prime matter, are the most basic principles of the natural, sublunary world (see *Gen. et Cor.* II.1, 329a32–34). The restriction to the realm beneath the moon is necessary, because the Scholastics held that the heavenly bodies are made of a fifth kind of stuff, and work

[1] There is almost no literature on Scholastic theories of the primary and secondary qualities. The best extended discussion remains Maier, *An der Grenze*, pp. 3–22 (translated in Sargent, *On the Threshold*, ch. 6).

in fundamentally different ways. If we confine our attention to the bodies around us, however (as I will hereafter tacitly do), then we arrive at prime matter as the most basic explanatory principle, inasmuch as it lies beneath all change. Beyond prime matter lie the four primary qualities, which are the most basic principles responsible for shaping matter. These are prior even to the four elements inasmuch as they explain those elements, according to the following scheme:

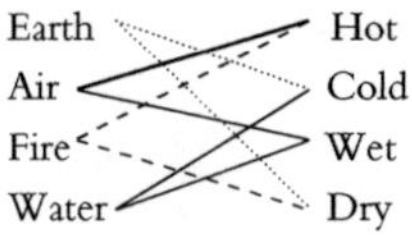

Earth is Cold and Dry.
Air is Hot and Wet.
Fire is Hot and Dry.
Water is Cold and Wet.

Fig. 2.1 The four elements and the four primary qualities

This is not to say that the primary qualities define the four elements, or (equivalently) constitute their essence. The standard Scholastic view was that these qualities are accidents of the elements, and that the elements have some further substantial form, unknown to us, that gives rise to these qualities. Still, the four qualities are explanatorily basic, for it is in virtue of them that the elements function as they do. And since these elements are the building blocks of the natural world—as Thomas Aquinas puts it, they are "the cause of generation and corruption and alteration in all other bodies" (*In De gen. et cor.* prooem., n. 2)—the primary qualities get pride of place in an account of the natural world.

To say, as Aquinas does, that the elements cause "generation and corruption" and "alteration" is to make them explanatorily basic with regard to both substantial and accidental change. ("Alteration" is the technical term for qualitative accidental change, whereas "generation and corruption" refers to substantial change). Hence the primary qualities are explanatorily basic in two sorts of ways: with respect to both substances and other qualities. Eustachius a Sancto Paulo puts the first idea quite clearly in his early seventeenth-century textbook: "these qualities are called primary because from their blending (*temperie*) results the nature of a mixed body, and when this blending is dissolved, the mixed body is necessarily dissolved" (*Summa philosophiae quadripartita* III.2.2.1.1, II:208). Several factors make this aspect of the account less straightforward than it initially seems. First, although bodies are always the result of a mixture of the four elements, and their associated primary qualities, there are other factors at play in the natural realm, such as substantial forms, spiritual qualities, occult qualities, and the heavenly bodies (see below). All of this, to be sure, serves to make the account less austerely reductive in its explanatory character. Second, it was controversial whether the elements, or even their qualities, continue to exist within the mixture. It was commonly claimed instead that, having been mixed together so as to constitute a body of a certain kind, the elements merge together so as to become such a body, and no longer themselves actually exist. Third, the elements are never found in isolation. Of course we do find ordinary earth, air, fire, and water existing separately, but these are mixed bodies, each one a composite of the four elements. The elements, therefore, as Aristotle makes clear, are distinct from (albeit similar to) the ordinary bodies that we customarily refer to as *earth* etc. (*Gen. et cor.* II.3, 330b22–25). (To mark this difference, it is useful to capitalize the names of the elements and their attendant qualities.) An important consequence of this last point is that both the elements and the elemental qualities, since they never appear separately, have the status of a theoretical postulate, and so were vulnerable to the seventeenth-century charge of obscurity, and to their attempt to replace these universal qualities with primary qualities of a very different sort.

The primary qualities are also explanatorily basic with respect to other qualities. As Albert the Great puts it, "the primary qualities of tangible things are the cause of all the other sensible qualities" (*In Gen. et cor.* II.1.1). Walter Burley puts the same claim this way: "secondary qualities are caused by a mixture of primary qualities" (*De formis* pars post. p. 65). This notion of two classes of qualities—one basic and the other dependent on the first—was a commonplace of Scholastic discussions from the thirteenth into the seventeenth century, to be found in virtually any Scholastic discussion of the elemental composition of bodies. According to the late sixteenth-century Coimbran commentary on *Generation and Corruption*, for instance, "colors, flavors, smells, and other secondary qualities arise from the various temperaments and proportions of the primary qualities" (I.10.4). The Protestant Christoph Scheibler, writing in the early seventeenth century, holds that primary qualities do not depend on others, whereas "after the primary qualities follow the secondary qualities, which arise from the primary" (*Philosophia compendiosa* III.13.1).

Whereas it is a straightforward task to list the Aristotelian primary qualities, it is more difficult to say what the secondary qualities are. As a first approximation, we might say that the secondary qualities are the non-primary sensible qualities. But this is liable to mislead and is only roughly correct. First, it is liable to mislead, because Scholastic authors do not count as qualities—primary or secondary—any of the various geometric–kinetic properties. These are not *qualities* at all, inasmuch as they fall into some other genus in Aristotle's category framework, whether that be Quantity or Action or some other category (see §3 below). Second, this rough account admits of a much more fine-grained taxonomy, inasmuch as there are many kinds of qualities. Scholastics authors routinely accept the following broad division:

a. the four basic, elemental, primary qualities: Hot, Cold, Wet, Dry;
b. the non-basic tactile qualities: heavy, lightweight, hard, soft, viscous, brittle, rough, smooth, course, and fine (cf. *Gen. et cor.* II.2, 329b20);
c. the other sensible qualities: color, sound, smell, taste;
d. occult qualities, such as magnetism;
e. the so-called spiritual or intentional qualities, such as light or color as it exists in a medium or sensory organ;
f. wholly immaterial qualities, such as thoughts and volitions.

Although one sometimes finds other usages, the most common practice is to treat (b–c) as secondary qualities. The list in (b) comes straight from Aristotle, and he is perfectly clear (329b33) that all of these can be derived from (a). (Even here, however, there is doubt regarding heavy and lightweight. For despite their inclusion on Aristotle's canonical list, they are in other contexts treated as basic, active powers, toward or away from the center of the Earth.) The sensible qualities in (c) are also standardly described as secondary qualities. (Or, at any rate, color, smell, and taste are. I discuss sound in the following section.) We have already seen the Coimbrans claiming as much, and it is easy to find the claim in earlier authors. Here, for instance, is Albert of Saxony in the fourteenth century:

> The other sensible qualities, pertaining to the other senses—such as color, flavor, and odor—do not belong to the pure elements. This is proved, because such qualities are caused by a mixture of the primary qualities of the tangible qualities. But there is no such mixture of contraries, neither formal nor virtual, in a pure element—otherwise it would not be simple. Therefore etc. (*In Gen. et cor.* II.1, p. 184)

Hence the four elements, if they were to exist in isolation, could not have any color or other such sensible qualities, because that would require them to have a mixture of all four primary qualities.

The remaining qualities (d–f) are not usually described as secondary, and do not arise from the primary qualities. Those in (f) obviously do not, since they lie outside the realm of body altogether. The occult qualities (d) are likewise famously resistant to any sort of more fundamental explanation.[2] The qualities in (e) are yet another story. Despite their name, intentional/spiritual qualities are a part of the physical world, and interact with bodies in a straightforward way. In contrast to the case of the occult qualities, however, Scholastic authors in this case take themselves to have something of an idea of how the process works. Light (*lumen*) in the air, for instance, is the product of the light (*lux*) of the sun or a flame. (Latin usefully distinguishes between a light source [*lux*] and light in a medium [*lumen*].) Colors and other sensible qualities in the air (*species in medio*) are caused by the sensible qualities on the surfaces of objects. Still, despite being relatively well understood, these cannot be wholly explained in elemental terms.[3]

[2] Scheibler refers to occult qualities as "tertiary qualities" and offers this useful definition: "The tertiary or occult qualities are said to be certain hidden (*absconditae*) powers by which natural things act or are acted on by something, but whose character (*ratio*) cannot be given by primary or secondary qualities" (*Philosophia compendiosa* III.13.4).

[3] See Nicole Oresme: "Those accidents are called material that follow the conditions of matter, as are the primary qualities and those that follow them, and whose transmutation gives rise (*disponit*) in its own right to generation and corruption, and that have a contrary. The others, which do not follow the primary qualities nor have a contrary nor give rise to generation and corruption are said to have spiritual existence—for example, light (*lumen*), influences, the species of color in the air and in the organ, acts of the soul, and such things" (*In De anima* III.13, p. 412).

2. Three Scholastic theses

The main idea behind the Scholastic primary–secondary distinction is that of explanatory priority: the primary qualities are the fundamental explanation of natural change, both substantial and accidental. After prime matter, they are the most basic level of explanation in natural philosophy. There are three further theses, however, that are extremely important for understanding the Scholastic distinction. The first is the thesis of *universality*, that the primary qualities are present in all bodies. This is to say that, in the sublunary realm, all bodies are a mixture of the four elements and their attendant qualities. The universality thesis had been articulated explicitly by Aristotle (*Gen. et cor.* II.8), and was, so far as I can find, maintained without exception by Scholastic authors. To be sure, given the familiar (and eventually notorious) Scholastic commitment to the separability of qualities from their subjects, the universality thesis can obtain only as a matter of natural, rather than metaphysical necessity. Yet it is far from clear why the thesis should hold of necessity, even in this weaker sense. For even granted that the primary qualities are explanatorily basic, it seems clear that there could be a certain primary quality that occurs only in certain sorts of entities—a special basic quality, for instance, that is found only in living beings. This, however, was not the Scholastic view. Following Aristotle, they supposed that each and every body would contain each of the primary qualities.

A second core thesis is *supervenience*: that no change is possible to secondary qualities without a change to the primary qualities. Here, for instance, is Boethius of Dacia from around the start of our period:

> In the case of these last states there can be no alteration unless there is an alteration in the primary qualities, and the primary qualities are the causes of these. For instance, this body is soft, because it is half Dry and twice Wet. If this were always to be so, then that body would not become hard. The same is evident for young and old: unless there is a change in primary qualities, a body is not changed from young to old (nor vice versa); rather, that mixed body would always remain at the same point. (*In Gen. et cor.* I.16c)

And here is Giles of Orleans, from around the same time, on the consequences of denying that there is change at the level of the primary qualities:

> It would also follow that there could be no alteration in secondary qualities—that is, in colors, flavors, white and black, etc The reason is that every alteration in secondary qualities is caused by some alteration made in the primary qualities. But there is no alteration in primary qualities, or so we are supposing. Therefore there could not be alteration in secondary qualities. (*In Gen. et cor.* I.6c)

What both passages make explicit is that no change is possible to the secondary qualities without a change to the primary qualities. This is what, in modern parlance, we can describe as the supervenience of secondary on primary qualities.

Although supervenience, all by itself, is not a causal relationship, it reflects in the present case the degree of Scholastic commitment to the explanatory priority of the primary qualities. Even so, Scholastic authors do not suppose that the secondary qualities can be *reduced* to the primary qualities, if by that one means that to have a color is nothing more than to have a certain mixture of primary qualities. Although the Scholastics believe that objects have colors because of the way their primary qualities mix, they think that to have a color is to have a further, secondary quality: a real accident from the Aristotelian category of Quality.

The third and most significant thesis is that of *causal primacy*: that the primary qualities are the primary causal agents in the physical realm. This is an aspect of how Aristotle had conceived of the elemental qualities from the start: Hot and Cold, he thought, are the two qualities in virtue of which bodies act on the world, and Wet and Dry are the two qualities in virtue of which bodies are acted on (e.g. *Meteor.* IV.5). What seems to have inspired Aristotle to give Hot and Cold this special status is that they, unlike other qualities, transfer their likeness to other bodies: a pink surface does not make other nearby surfaces pink, but a hot or a cold body does pass its temperature onto other nearby bodies. As doubtful a theoretical foundation as that is, it became unquestioned orthodoxy among Scholastic authors that the elemental qualities are the primary agents in nature. Thus, according to Albert the Great, "the primary qualities are primarily active and passive, and it is in virtue of them that whatever acts acts, and whatever is acted on is acted on" (*De praed.* 5.6; ed. Jammy I:162a). Eventually, it became common to treat all four elemental qualities as active, and it is in this form that the doctrine endured all the way through the Scholastic era. Here, for instance, is Benedictus Pererius in the late sixteenth century:

> the four primary qualities [are] Cold, Hot, Wet, and Dry. From the alteration that occurs in these primary qualities results every alteration in the secondary qualities, which are based on the mixture of the primary qualities—namely, colors, odors, flavors, health, sickness, and others of this kind. The alteration of other things, which is properly change (*motus*), should be treated as that alone that occurs in virtue of the primary qualities alone, since it is here that there is properly acting, being acted upon, and contrariety. (*De communibus principiis* XIV.2, pp. 736–37)

This is a perfectly ordinary statement of standard Scholastic thinking in this area, and yet the doctrine expressed is quite extraordinary and underappreciated. It holds that the world as we perceive it is not the locus of causal efficacy: that change occurs in virtue of four underlying primary qualities on which the remaining sensible qualities supervene. The secondary qualities are epiphenomenal, involved in the spiritual–intentional processes that lead to sensation, but not otherwise playing a causal role in the natural world.

Since these claims were not particularly controversial among Scholastic authors, they were not subject to the sort of detailed scrutiny that one finds concerning vexed topics such as the status of prime matter or quantity, and the subject was particularly remote from the concerns of the theologians who have received the lion's share of attention from modern scholars. Perhaps the best place to find a discussion of these issues is in authors whose interests in natural philosophy were more practical, and hence required serious attention to causal mechanisms. Consider, for example, Paul of Taranto, the late-thirteenth-century alchemist who authored the influential *Summa perfectionis* (traditionally ascribed to "Geber," Jabir ibn Hayyan).[4] In the theoretical prologue to his *Liber tam theoricae quam practicae veritatis in arte alkimica*, Taranto provides a sketch of standard Aristotelian theory, so that readers will understand the proper method of attempting alchemical transformations. He begins with the claim—characteristic of Aristotelian thought but so antithetical to seventeenth-century mechanism—that "every power in nature is a certain quality" (p. 7). This leads to the now-familiar division between primary and secondary qualities, and then the crucial claim:

> The aforesaid secondary qualities are not of themselves properly active on a given nature except *per accidens*... Taste acts on nature only through something else, namely Hot, Cold, Dry, and Wet, which are in the flavorful thing. Nor can any of the secondary qualities act within the nature and essence of anything, except through the primary qualities.... [In contrast,] Hot, Cold, Dry, and Wet are nature's hands, as it were, and principle powers, through which nature transforms and makes all generable things. (*Liber veritatis* pp. 8–9)

Like most Scholastic authors, Taranto treats all four primary qualities as active, rather than following Aristotle's claim that Wet and Dry are merely passive. These are "nature's hands," an idea that leads Taranto to his main conclusion about how the alchemist should proceed:

> The aforesaid points to the cause of defect and error in certain unskilled, fraudulent, and false artificers, who either have not arrived at the true arrangement of things or who through sophistry compose solely for external appearance. Whoever either does not know how or cannot use such powers (other than those of the secondary qualities) will never produce, through color and superficial operations, anything other than external accidents through vain appearance, and will arrive at no truth regarding these. But he who knows these capacities of nature lying in the pure elements through Earth, Water, Air, and Fire, and recognizes how to grasp them with the power of art–and knows how to join the mineral principles to the said powers..., will most truly be able to transform and bring about natural forms through art, ...just as nature herself brings these things about in mines. (pp. 12–13)

If one wants to change the nature of things—to make true gold, for instance, and not just the appearance of gold—one must harness the primary qualities. Otherwise, one is simply scratching at the surface.

3. The mechanical affections

Viewed in a certain light, there is something thoroughly modern, or at any rate seventeenth-century, about Paul of Taranto's proposal. A forerunner to Robert Boyle, Taranto wants to reform scientific practice in accord with a clearer theoretical

[4] Paul of Taranto is the recent discovery of William Newman—see, e.g. his *Atoms and Alchemy* ch. 1.

understanding of the foundations of nature. The alchemists he criticizes have relied, unwittingly or perhaps deceitfully, on faulty philosophical presuppositions, and their project has accordingly been doomed to failure. By taking seriously the true causal forces at work in the world, we can use nature's own tools to transmute natural kinds. Of course, viewed in a different light, Taranto's ideas could not be farther from Boyle's, inasmuch as they disagree utterly on what those true causal forces are. Boyle rejects Aristotelian qualities across the board, primary and secondary. Taranto, meanwhile, does not even mention the "mechanical affections" that Boyle would make so much of. How could Taranto and the other authors we have considered simply ignore the geometric–kinetic properties that seventeenth-century authors would elevate to the status of primary qualities?

It is not exactly the case that Scholastic authors ignore the geometric–kinetic properties. Such properties are, instead, bracketed off as cases not subject to an account in terms of primary qualities. One can see this sort of bracketing strategy at work even among the sensible qualities themselves, in the case of sound.[5] Although one might suppose that Scholastic authors would count sound as a paradigmatic secondary quality, they do not. For whereas the color, odor, and flavor of a body supervene on the primary qualities, no one could suppose this about sound. Even if primary qualities play a role in the sound a body emits when struck, the sound itself depends on motion. It depends, first, on the motion of the body that emits the sound, which in turn is usually produced by the motion of another body, which strikes it. And since it was standardly supposed that sounds exist in the air or other medium, rather than in the body itself, the sound further depends on the motion of that medium, as it is put in motion by the vibrating object. Hence, in several ways, sound depends on motion, not just on qualitative features of a body. Few authors went so far as to identify sound with a certain sort of motion. But it was commonplace to describe sound as arising from motion, which is to say that it does not fit the usual paradigm of a secondary quality. Buridan makes this explicit, when he qualifies his account of secondary qualities by saying that "I do not speak of sounds, which are made not through Heat, Cold, Wet, etc., but through the local motion of the air" (*In Gen. et cor.* II.1c). It was up to the terminological preferences of a given author whether to conclude that sound should therefore not be a secondary quality, or whether the lesson instead is that some secondary qualities do not arise from primary qualities.

Sound is standardly assimilated to a larger set of cases. Here is Oresme, attempting to sort out the question of what counts as a secondary quality:

> If all other qualities [beyond the four primary ones] are said to be secondary then a distinction must be drawn. There are some that follow from the primary qualities and their alteration—for example, whiteness and perhaps some flavors. Then there are others that, as it were, do not

[5] I have discussed the case of sound in some detail in "Sensible Qualities."

pertain to these, because they neither are those primary qualities nor do they follow from them—light (*lumen*), for example, and also rarity or shape, which follow local motion and are not properly called *secondary*. Also in this way, as was said, sound is not properly a secondary quality because it does not follow alteration but rather local motion with regard to velocity.

(*In Phys*. II.5 ad 3)

On Oresme's usage, then, the true secondary qualities are only those that follow from the primary qualities. Other important qualities—light, rarity/denseness, shape, and sound—count as secondary qualities only in an improper sense. For each of these exceptions, some other account must be provided. Light—that is, *lumen*, the light propagated in a medium—is treated as spiritual quality, and rarity as a product purely of local motion.[6] Shapes, in contrast, although perplexingly located by Aristotle in the category of Quality (*Cat*. 10a11), plainly cannot be explained by the primary qualities. Hence they have to be excluded from the ranks of the properly secondary qualities.[7]

Paralleling the case of shape are the cases of size and motion. Clearly none of the three can be explained reductively in terms of the primary qualities, and so room has to be made for them somewhere else. If not quite ignored, then, the mechanical affections certainly were sidelined. This is to say that they were not only given a separate ontological status, but also regarded as derivative aspects of explanation in natural philosophy. We have seen this already, by implication, in the above-quoted passages identifying the Aristotelian primary qualities as the fundamental causal and explanatory principle in the natural realm. The case of Paul of Taranto is particularly clear: to bring about real changes in nature one must wield "nature's hands"—meaning not the size, shape, and motion of particles, but their four elemental qualities. Franciscus Toletus, to take another example, regards shape as even less of a causal agent than the secondary qualities, for whereas the secondary qualities are at least indirectly active, inasmuch as they are a product of the active primary qualities, "shapes are in no way active, neither in their own right nor in virtue of anything belonging to them, because they are not composed of the primary qualities" (*In Phys*. VII.3.3, IV:198rb). The Scholastics were so thoroughly persuaded that qualities are the primary natural causal agents that they could not accept identifying sound with motion: for if sound were motion then it would not be a quality, and in that case could not have the appropriate causal impact on the senses. More generally, this is why Scholastic authors never seriously considered

[6] It was controversial among Scholastic authors whether rarefaction and condensation could be explained purely in terms of local motion. Others would invoke accidents in the category of Quantity. Even on that view, however, it would not seem promising from the Scholastic perspective to reduce *quantitative* accidents to the primary *qualities*. I discuss quantitative accidents in considerable detail in my forthcoming *Metaphysical Themes 1274–1671*.

[7] Different authors try to handle geometric properties in different ways. Boethius of Dacia simply excludes from his supervenience claim those properties "caused by an external cause, such as that a body is square" (*In Gen. et cor*. I.16c). Paul of Venice argues that shapes are a distinct kind of real quality, distinct not just from the primary and secondary qualities, but also from the substance and the spatial structure of its parts (*Summa philosophiae naturalis* VI.20).

eliminating real qualities from their ontology. As the primary causal agents in the natural world, they were utterly indispensable.

From a seventeenth-century perspective, all of this may seem quite incredible. Given the post-Scholastic confidence in the explanatory power of the geometrical properties of bodies, how could Scholastic authors not just embrace irreducible real qualities, but even allow them to overshadow size, shape, and motion? Again, it is useful to focus on a figure whose concerns are decidedly practical. Hieronymus Fracastorius was an early sixteenth-century Paduan physicist whose account of a germ theory of disease ought to have made him as famous today as his contemporary, Copernicus. (As it happens, we value the history of astronomy more than the history of medicine.) In a crucial chapter from his masterpiece *De contagione*, Fracastorius attacks the dismissive view that the spread of contagious disease is simply the result of occult properties. This is nothing more than an excuse to avoid dealing with the question, Fracastorius declares, since to appeal to occult properties is nothing more than to say that we do not know what the cause of contagion is. So he proposes to work through the various *possible* causes:

> We must suppose that, although there are ten genera of all things, the only active principles are Substance and Quality. For it is evident that neither Quantity nor Relation nor Where nor, in short, any of the other categories produces any effect, except *per accidens*. Moreover, it is evident that substance produces nothing *per se* except for local motions up or down, rarefaction and condensation, and circular motions; for these motions are produced by the [substantial] form of things. All other actions come from qualities. (I.6, p. 22)

Although the scant literature on Fracastorius often describes him as a corpuscularian,[8] his philosophical views here are those of a mainstream Scholastic Aristotelian. Given the theoretical presuppositions he describes, there are only two possibilities for how diseases can spread: either by substance, or by quality. But all a substance itself can do is bring about locomotion, and Fracastorius goes on to dismiss this sort of causal explanation almost out of hand, remarking that "contagion is not *per se* a local motion, but rather the corruption of certain things and the generation of other things" (p. 24). The mechanistic explanations that would become ascendant in the following century strike Fracastorius as non-starters, and so he focuses on quality as the only viable kind of explanation. Here he draws the distinction registered earlier between ordinary material qualities and the spiritual qualities that pass through air and water.

> It is clear that material qualities can bring about many things, for the so-called primary qualities generate and alter all things, whereas the so-called secondary qualities—light (*lux*), odor, flavor, and sound—bring about nothing among themselves, since they are not contraries, but still they move the senses by means of those qualities that are called spiritual. It is also clear that these spiritual qualities have many actions and are a power in nature. (pp. 23–24)

[8] See e.g. the bio-bibliography in the *Cambridge History of Renaissance Philosophy*, which remarks that Fracastorius "favoured a Democritean corpuscular theory."

Which of these explains contagious disease? Not the secondary qualities, obviously. The spiritual qualities are plausible candidates, but Fracastorius argues that spiritual qualities are dependent on their sources in a way that the spread of contagion is not: the light in the medium ceases, for instance, when the light source is turned off, and odors fade as distances grow greater, whereas contagions endure without their source, and can spread "even across the sea" (p. 24). This leaves the primary qualities:

> If they say that contagion is brought about by some material quality, then they will appeal to nothing that is unknown unless perhaps they invent some unknown kind of quality that is neither Hot, nor Wet, nor Dry. But this certainly cannot be imagined. (p. 24)

Fracastorius concludes that contagion must be explained in terms of the familiar primary qualities. But since such qualities cannot naturally float free of substances, these qualities must inhere in some kind of substance, a *seminarium* or germ, which is capable of generating further such germs and thereby spreading. The distinctive mix of primary qualities found in a given kind of germ acts on the germ's host, thereby causing disease.

From our perspective, Fracastorius is indefensibly precipitate in holding that new primary qualities "cannot be imagined." This is what it looks like, in retrospect, when one pins one's theory to the best fundamental science of the day. When that science collapses—as sciences are prone to do—one's theory collapses with it. Even so, by following the Aristotelian framework of the elemental qualities, Fracastorius was able to arrive at the germ theory of disease.

4. Projection

In contrast to at least some seventeenth-century formulations, the Scholastic distinction between primary and secondary qualities is completely unrelated to the appearance–reality gap. This has given rise to a great deal of nonsense about what the Scholastics thought about the relationship between our sensations and the sensible qualities of objects. Admittedly, it is hard to know exactly what they thought in this area, because they hardly ever talk about phenomenal experience. They talk about acts of sensation and thought, to be sure, and they talk about the representational content of those acts, but the what-it-is-like of the experience itself is not usually a subject of interest. Even so, two sorts of quite erroneous claims have frequently been made about Scholastic thought in this domain: first, that color and the other secondary qualities are primitive, *sui generis* features of reality; second, that they are exactly like our experience of them.[9]

[9] For primitiveness, see Peter Alexander, *Ideas, Qualities and Corpuscles* p. 41: "Questions such as 'What makes this substance yellow?' were likely to be regarded as the most fundamental kind of question about natural phenomena and as representing the point at which questioning had to stop because we are at the limits of observation." For exact resemblance to experience, see Robert Adams, "Flavors, Colors, and God" p. 246: "We do not think there is any quality in physical objects that resembles the peculiar qualities or qualia that make the difference between experiencing red and yellow, or between the taste of sugar and salt. . . . But the

The first of these can be dispelled quite quickly. Although it is true, as we will see in §6, that Scholastic authors were hardly ever even tempted to deny the reality of the secondary qualities, they certainly did not treat those qualities as primitive in the sense of being explanatorily basic. Instead, as we have seen, it is the Aristotelian primary qualities—Hot, Cold, Wet, and Dry—that are basic. The secondary qualities were so-called precisely because they are causally dependent and supervenient on those elemental qualities. (Even heat, as we perceive it, can be explained in terms of an elemental mixture in which the primary quality of Heat is particularly prominent.) Moreover, and for the same reason, the secondary qualities were as far from being *sui generis* as is possible within the Aristotelian scheme. To categorize them as qualities was to group them with the primary causal agents in the natural, sublunary world, the elemental qualities that underlie all alteration, generation, and corruption. Color and the rest were therefore given as naturalistic a treatment as one could hope for at the time, embedded squarely within the best available natural science.

The second misunderstanding is trickier. The usual term for the thesis that the secondary qualities are exactly like our experiences of them is *Projection*. Ordinarily, Projection is understood as an error theory in the philosophy of perception: it is the view that we erroneously project characteristics of our sensory experiences out onto the external world. But the Scholastics are often charged with holding Projection as an affirmative thesis: that we rightly project features of experience out onto the world, because the world really does possess the various phenomenal characteristics of our sensory experiences. One possible basis for what we might call Veridical Projection is the standard Scholastic thesis that all cognition requires a likeness between cognizer and cognized. The likeness thesis was a frequent target of criticism in the seventeenth century.[10] Yet for it to yield Veridical Projection, it would have to be construed in a very strong and implausible way. When a perceiver sees color, for instance, and so has a phenomenal experience of a color, the color would have to resemble the phenomenal experience itself: the colors would then be exactly as the experience is. The word "exactly" here can mean only one thing: that the qualities in the world are like our sensations all the way down to the phenomenal experience itself: that the experience

typical opinion of Aristotelian Scholastics was that phenomenal qualia are similar to, and produced by, physical qualities that we perceive in bodies by means of the qualia. There is a qualitative 'form' in the sugar that is like the quality of the taste of sugar that makes it different from the taste of salt. The quality of the appearance of red that makes it different from the appearance of yellow resembles a form or quality that is present on the surface of a typical ripe apple." John Cottingham, "Descartes on Colour" p. 238, gets both these notions into the same sentence: "What is denied is the inherence of redness *qua* redness—redness construed as a certain sort of *sui generis* quality supposed to inhere in objects in a way that exactly matches our sensory awareness of it."

[10] Locke's attack on resemblance seems to describe the doctrine of Veridical Projection exactly: "Flame is denominated hot and light; snow, white and cold; and manna, white and sweet, from the ideas they produce in us: Which qualities are commonly thought to be the same in those bodies that those ideas are in us, the one the perfect resemblance of the other, as they are in a mirror; and it would by most men be judged very extravagant, if one should say otherwise" (*Essay* II.8.16).

itself is somehow in the external world. If less than that is meant—if the claim is merely that our experiences in some respect or another resemble the sensible qualities they represent—then the thesis is far from being implausible, and may even be true. The Scholastics, however, were committed only to this weaker thesis, not to exact resemblance. We can see as much by looking more closely at the likeness thesis as they formulated it. First, it is motivated not by a theory of what the secondary qualities are, but by a general Aristotelian principle about causality: that all effects resemble their causes. That this is the motivation is clear from how authors defend the likeness thesis, and also from their willingness to apply the likeness thesis to all cognition, sensory and intellectual. Second, the very fact that the likeness thesis gets applied to intellectual cognition should make us extremely wary about understanding it in a crude and literal fashion: what would it be for the essence of horse to be exactly like our idea of horse? Third, many Scholastic authors make it clear that they understand likeness in very broad terms that do not require the cognition itself to be exactly like the thing it represents. Suárez, to take just one example, while accepting that the objects of cognition are a formal likeness of the intentional species in the cognitive faculty that represents them, denies that these species have to be "of the same kind" as objects in the world. Ordinary resemblance may require sameness of kind, but "representational likeness" is special, and can obtain between very different sorts of entities (*In De an.* 5.2 concl. 2).

Creating a *sui generis* category of representational likeness is doubtless unhelpful if one is trying to explain mental representation in terms of some better-understood concept. Even so, the passage makes it clear that Scholastic talk of likeness between cognizer and cognized does not require supposing that the secondary qualities are exactly as they appear to be. Admittedly, here, as always, one has to be cautious in overgeneralizing about Scholastic views. Suárez is responding to Durand of St. Pourçain, who did insist that likeness requires sameness of kind. Durand was probably the inspiration for William Crathorn, a few years later in the early fourteenth century, who notoriously insisted that we can perceive colors and other sensible qualities only if the sensory faculty literally takes on the quality in question, becoming red and round, for instance.[11] But even these authors who take likeness quite literally are not endorsing Veridical Projection. Crathorn thinks that the visual power becomes red when it sees red, but this does not mean that phenomenal experiences are projected out onto the world. On the contrary, for Crathorn, the world's sensible qualities are projected into the mind. In general, then, the

[11] Durand of Saint-Pourçain relies on his insistence on sameness of kind to show that angels do not have intelligible species (*Sent.* II.3.6 n. 17), and that human beings cannot perceive God through any species that serves as a likeness of God (ibid., IV.49.2 n. 13). For Crathorn, see *Sent.* I.1 (tr. Pasnau, *Cambridge Translations* pp. 285–90; see also my *Theories of Cognition* pp. 101–5). Aquinas, like Suárez, insists that the resemblance found in cognition is distinct from ordinary resemblance (see, e.g. *Quaest. de veritate* 2.3 ad 9). Brower and Brower-Toland, "Aquinas on Mental Representation," have recently argued that he treats cognitive resemblance as "primitive or *sui generis*."

Scholastic commitment to analyzing mental representation in terms of likeness provides no evidence for the thesis that they endorse Veridical Projection.

There is, however, more than just a lack of evidence here; there is also a kind of pragmatic impossibility. We could justly ascribe the thesis of exact likeness—that is, Veridical Projection—to the Scholastics only if we could find an author who sets the thesis out in reasonably explicit terms. But Veridical Projection is a thesis that, as soon as it is set out in explicit terms, shows itself to be incoherent. Anyone who gets far enough along to distinguish phenomenal experiences from things in the world, and then considers whether the latter might be exactly like the former, has to see immediately that the thesis is impossible. There could certainly be isomorphic elements between sensation and object—that is what the likeness thesis in its weak and plausible form must maintain—but it is simply incoherent to think that inanimate objects could be exactly like phenomenal experiences. George Berkeley surely put it too strongly when he famously remarked that "an idea can be like nothing but an idea; a colour or figure can be like nothing but another colour or figure" (*Principles* I.8), but the claim is manifestly true when directed at the sort of exact likeness that Veridical Projection insists on. Inanimate objects cannot be characterized in terms of phenomenal experiences—that follows directly from their being *inanimate*. So not only is there no evidence that the Scholastics endorsed Veridical Projection, but it is actually impossible that they could have explicitly done so. This is not to deny that many people throughout history have been implicitly under the spell of Projection: no doubt there are many who, failing to grasp the appearance–reality gap, have treated the appearances as if they were reality. Perhaps even some philosophers have been under the spell. But there is a pragmatic impossibility in ascribing Veridical Projection to someone as a philosophical thesis, because even to articulate the thesis requires enough sophistication to see immediately that the thesis is incoherent.

5. Revelation

Although it is not plausible to suppose that any Scholastic authors defend Veridical Projection, I think it can be shown that they often defend a different thesis, *Revelation*. I use this label in the same way it is used in modern discussions, as the thesis that sensory experience reveals the very nature of the sensible qualities.[12] To have a standard visual experience of red, for instance, is to know essentially what red is. One might suppose that the only way to believe Revelation is to embrace either Veridical Projection or Anti-Realism, where the latter is the thesis that sensible qualities do not exist in the external world. If sensible qualities either are nothing other than sensory experiences, or else exactly resemble those experiences, then Revelation might plausibly be maintained. Could it be maintained otherwise? I believe that Scholastic authors commonly

[12] The classic statement of Revelation is in Mark Johnston, "How to Speak of the Colors."

supposed so. The idea would be that while the senses do not reveal everything about the secondary qualities of material objects, they reveal enough to give us a clear sense of what those qualities are.

From the Scholastic perspective, there is a great deal that the senses could not conceivably reveal about the secondary qualities. They could not, for instance, reveal that these qualities are accidents, or that they belong to the Aristotelian category of Quality. These are metaphysical, not empirical results. The senses also could not reveal that the secondary qualities are caused by, and supervene on, the primary qualities, or that the different hues of color are caused by black and white intermingling in different degrees (see Aristotle, *De sensu* ch. 3). These are theses of natural philosophy that are not immediately revealed to sensation. One might well wonder just what content that leaves for the thesis of Revelation. What it leaves, most notably, is that the senses reveal the quality spaces of the different secondary qualities. This is to say, for instance, that although vision does not show anything about the metaphysical status or causal bases of color, it does show everything there is to be shown about the differences among the colors. Orange is similar to red; red is similar to purple; purple is more similar to blue than to green. These are important facts about color that anyone knows just by looking at the colors; indeed, it is plausible to say that they are in some sense the essence of the colors. No doubt there are other facts about color that sight reveals, but these seem the best candidates for supporting Revelation.

These remarks regarding Revelation are somewhat speculative, because Scholastic authors do not discuss the issue in enough detail to get very clear about their view. Why, then, should we think they endorsed Revelation at all? One reason is their treatment of the secondary qualities as paradigmatic examples of manifest qualities. To be manifest involves more than simply being immediately observable; if that were all it meant, then magnetism—the paradigmatic occult quality—would count as manifest. The secondary qualities are manifest, then, because in seeing them one sees not just *that* they are, but further one sees *what* they are. Thus Aquinas remarks that "if there are things that are known to us in their own right—such as heat, cold, whiteness, and the like—these are not denominated by other things. Hence in such cases that which the name signifies is the same as that through which the name is imposed to signify" (*Summa theol.* 1a 13.8c). Most things get their reference fixed via some sort of accidental or extrinsic feature, but in the case of the secondary qualities we grasp immediately their very nature.

Further evidence comes from discussions of the Aristotelian dictum that one who lacks some sense must lack some corresponding knowledge (*Post. an.* I.18, 81a38). Scholastic authors understand this to mean that someone who lacks vision, say, will also lack knowledge about colors. But then the question arises of whether someone would truly be barred from knowledge of a certain secondary quality without the corresponding sense. If the secondary qualities were primitive, *sui generis* properties, then the answer might seem to be clearly yes. But given that this is not the Scholastic view, and that instead we understand their underlying causes, one might think that one *could* grasp the secondary qualities without being able to perceive them. Thus John Buridan remarks:

> The entire difficulty in this question is why through a knowledge of the [primary] tangible qualities we cannot come to a knowledge of [e.g.] flavors or odors, since these are their causes, just as in many other cases we go from knowledge of causes to knowledge of effects, and conversely. (*In Post. an.* I.28c)

Buridan goes on to allow that this is possible: even someone blind from birth can acquire knowledge (*scientia*) about color. Such knowledge will be "confused," however, in the technical sense of failing to discriminate between cases of different kinds. So Buridan's final conclusion is that "if we lack a sense from birth then it is impossible for us, with respect to the sensibles proper to that sense, to acquire naturally a knowledge of the quidditative concepts of those sensibles" (ibid.). That is, only someone who has known what it is like to see colors can know what colors essentially are. This conclusion would seem to depend on Revelation. Although Buridan does not attempt to characterize these "quidditative concepts" of the secondary qualities that we grasp through the senses, his point is that the senses, and only the senses, show us the secondary qualities as they are.

The same idea is spelled out somewhat more, two centuries later, in Domingo de Soto's treatment of this same question. De Soto's discussion, although quite different in its details, reaches essentially the same conclusion as Buridan's. The congenitally blind can know something about colors: they can know, for instance, that one color dilates sight whereas another contracts it, that the stuff that is known by taste as milk is white, and that white is what dilates sight. Still, the congenitally blind cannot have knowledge of colors "through proper and quidditative concepts":

> This is proved, because the blind do not properly understand what it is for whiteness to dilate sight and for blackness to contract it,[13] but through a comparison to sound or taste. Nor do they understand the difference between white and black, red and green; instead, they have concepts of these that are just like those that I have when I discuss some sixth sense—whether, that is, God could make another sense by which I would perceive another sensible distinct from the five kinds of sensibles. (*In Post. an.* I q. 6, p. 388a)

De Soto mentions two shortcomings in a non-visual grasp of color. First, the knowledge that whiteness "dilates sight" (line 1) is not "proper" in the way it would be if one could actually sense whiteness. Second, a non-visual grasp of the colors does not reveal the differences between them. Given these remarks, however, which are all De Soto gives us, one might suppose that the blind *could* acquire a proper and distinctive grasp of the colors. Dilation and contraction are evidently mechanical events that can be grasped in all of their details without any visual information: why, then, couldn't someone blind grasp the distinctive event that occurs when white acts on sight?

[13] See Plato, *Timaeus* 67d–e. (I owe this reference to Mark Smith.)

Similarly, given that the secondary qualities supervene on the primary qualities, why couldn't one arrive at a perfectly "proper" understanding of a given color by coming to grasp just what mixture of elemental qualities gives rise to it? What De Soto must be supposing, although he does not say so explicitly, is that even these sorts of determinate, uniquely specifying accounts would leave out the essence of what the colors are. One can specify just how much a given color dilates sight, but without having the experience, one is not grasping the "quiddity" of the color itself. Similarly, one could know what elemental mixture causes a given color, but a proper, quidditative grasp of color requires grasping the visual differences between the colors.

More would need to be said to make this line of thought plausible, but even in their schematic form, these passages are extremely good evidence for the doctrine of Revelation. Indeed, the texts are so suggestive that they might seem to betray a commitment to the much stronger doctrine of Veridical Projection. For why would one suppose that the essence of the secondary qualities is revealed only by perception, unless one thought that the perceptual experience itself is something that the quality in the world possesses? Admittedly, it is possible that this incoherent notion is what motivates either Buridan or De Soto. But this is something that they neither say nor are committed to, inasmuch as there is room to defend Revelation without Veridical Projection. One can think that the phenomenal features of experience display the essential features of the secondary qualities—the space of similarities between them—without taking the further, incoherent step of supposing that the secondary qualities *possess* the phenomenal features of experience. Accordingly, if charity is to count for anything as a principle of interpretation, it should lead us to read these authors as committed to Revelation, not Veridical Projection.

6. Realism

Realism, as I will use the term here, is the doctrine that the secondary qualities exist in the external world. (Anti-Realism is simply the denial of Realism.) Before Galileo, Anti-Realism is virtually unheard of—one needs to go all the way back to Democritus to find a defense of it. According to the usual misunderstandings of the Scholastic theory of the secondary qualities, it would have been quite inconceivable for the Scholastics to have taken an Anti-Realist position, inasmuch as the senses show the world to be populated with irreducible qualities that are exactly as they seem to be. In fact, however, Anti-Realism was a more tempting option for Scholastics authors than is ordinarily realized, and the reasons why they nevertheless resisted it are worth examining.

It is useful to distinguish two motivations for Anti-Realism. The first arises from the appearance–reality gap, and relocates the secondary qualities, moving them from external bodies into the mind. This is, in effect, a response to Projection: it amounts to supposing that we have been confusing the mental and the physical, and proposes to untangle the mess by relocating the secondary qualities. The second form of Anti-Realism is eliminativist. It takes its inspiration from a reductive account of the secondary qualities in terms of other, primary qualities, and then decides that, in truth, there are no secondary qualities at all.

Although Scholastic authors were aware of both of these possibilities, the second option was by far the more tempting, inasmuch as various analogous cases made eliminativism look plausible. The four elements, for instance, along with their substantial forms, were usually thought to cease existing when mixed together. Within a mixture, according to the standard view, there is only the mixed body and its substantial form (gold, for instance, and the substantial form of gold). There are no further substantial forms for the elements, because the elements do not actually exist within the mixed body. The details here were hotly disputed, but the basic view was widely accepted. A similar sort of reduction was often proposed for the elemental qualities: that they too, being accidents of the elements, could no longer exist once the elements themselves were corrupted by mixture. Here too there was considerable disagreement, and some authors held that the elemental qualities do remain within a mixed body, but the issue was at any rate widely debated.[14]

If mixture results in the elements and their qualities ceasing to exist, then it is natural to wonder how much further this might go. No one proposed eliminating the primary qualities altogether, given their vital causal role in natural philosophy. But might the secondary qualities be reduced, or even eliminated, so that instead of supervening on the primary qualities they would, in fact, be nothing more than a mixture of primary qualities? Although this question was not widely discussed, authors with strong inclinations toward parsimony were sometimes tempted. Richard Fitzralph reports in his *Sentences* commentary (*c.*1328) that he himself had once succumbed:

> Some say that every color is light (*lux*), that every flavor is a mixture of primary qualities, and that odor is flavor. Indeed I at one point did not believe that anything exists other than substance or the five qualities—namely, the four elemental qualities and light (*lux*)—supposing there to be a small number of things. The reason was that I was focused on these few things, and I could preserve those by this stance. Hence I believed it to be true, in accord with that principle stated above [that if something can be done through few just as it can through more, then it is better than it be done through few rather than more]. And in this way those who have been well trained in logic err in recognizing too few things, whereas others who are ignorant of logic ascribe to every statement a new entity (*res*), postulating more entities than God has ever established as real. (*Sent.* II.1.2, in Maier, *An der Grenze*, p. 16n)

Anti-Realism is here depicted as a natural consequence of the sort of parsimonious ontology that would come to be associated with nominalism. And indeed, once one gets down to an ontology of substances and qualities, the natural next step is to think

[14] For Scholastic disputes over mixture see Wood and Weisberg, "Interpreting Aristotle on Mixture."

about whether one can make do with fewer kinds of qualities. Given that the secondary qualities both supervene on the primary qualities and yield almost all causal activity to the primary qualities, it is no wonder that Fitzralph was tempted to go farther and simply eliminate them.

Ultimately, Fitzralph changed his mind about this, and I have found no one else before the seventeenth century who comes so close to Anti-Realism. The main reason would seem to be that they played a limited but important causal role that was mentioned briefly earlier: they give rise to intentionally existing species in the surrounding medium, which in turn give rise to our sensations of those qualities. Here is Paul of Taranto, the late-thirteenth-century alchemist, in a passage already quoted in part:

> The aforesaid secondary qualities are not of themselves properly active on a given nature except *per accidens*, for they are properly active of themselves on sense through their species. according to the spiritual and intentional existence that these species have, and not according to their natural existence, except *per accidens*. For color moves sight according to the intentional existence that it has in the transparent medium, and not according to the natural existence it has in natural things, and taste as taste, of itself, moves the sense and not nature, for a similar reason. And it is not taste that nourishes, but food and drink—namely, the substance that *has* the taste. Thus taste acts on nature only through something else, namely Hot, Cold, Dry, and Wet, which are in the flavorful thing. Nor can any of the secondary qualities act within the nature and essence of anything, except through the primary qualities. (*Liber veritatis*, pp. 8–9)

This was the standard Scholastic view: the secondary qualities do not act naturally on the world, but do act through spiritual/intentional qualities. This causal role is incompatible with Anti-Realism. For Scholastic authors, the principal test for the reality of any accident is whether the supposed accident does anything in the world, such that its elimination would leave a causal void. Applying this test to the case of the secondary qualities, Scholastic authors were universally realists.

The result is that color and other secondary qualities, just as much as the four elemental primary qualities, take their place among the real accidents that would be the subject of such ferocious criticism in the seventeenth century. In reading those criticisms, it is important to understand that the distinction between primary and secondary qualities is not being invented out of whole cloth. It is instead a familiar, even famous, Scholastic doctrine, which the seventeenth-century critics of Scholasticism would neither wholly accept nor wholly reject, but rather tailor to their own purposes.[15]

[15] The material in this chapter appears in a somewhat different form in *Metaphysical Themes 1274–1671*, where I go on to discuss the rejection of qualities in the post-Scholastic era. I owe thanks to Larry Nolan and an anonymous reader for helpful comments.

Bibliography

Albert of Saxony. *Questiones subtilissime in libros de generatione* (Venice, 1505; repr. Frankfurt: Minerva, 1970).

Albert the Great. *Opera Omnia*, ed. P. Jammy (Lyon, 1651).

Alexander, Peter. *Ideas, Qualities and Corpuscles: Locke and Boyle on the External World* (Cambridge: Cambridge University Press, 1985).

Adams, Robert M. "Flavors, Colors, and God," in *The Virtue of Faith and Other Essays in Philosophical Theology* (Oxford: Oxford University Press, 1987) 245–47.

Aristotle. *The Complete Works of Aristotle: The Revised Oxford Translation*, ed. J. Barnes (Princeton: Princeton University Press, 1984).

Benedictus Pererius. *De communibus omnium rerum naturalium principiis et affectionibus* (Paris, 1579).

Berkeley, George. *Berkeley's Philosophical Writings*, ed. D. M. Armstrong (New York: Macmillan, 1965).

Boethius of Dacia. *Opera*, ed. J. Pinborg et al. (Copenhagen: DSL/Gad, 1969–).

Brower, Jeffrey and Susan Brower-Toland. "Aquinas on Mental Representation," *Philosophical Review* 117 (2008) 193–243.

Collegium Conimbricense. *Commentarii Collegii Conimbricensis in libros de generatione et corruptione Aristotelis* (Cologne, 1606; repr. Hildesheim: G. Olms, 2003).

Cottingham, John. "Descartes on Colour," *Proceedings of the Aristotelian Society* 90 (1989–90) 231–46.

Domingo de Soto. *In Porphyrii Isagogen, Aristotelis Categorias, librosque De demonstratione absolutissima commentaria* (Venice, 1587; repr. Frankfurt: Minerva, 1967).

Durand of St. Pourçain. *In Petri Lombardi Sententias theologicas commentarium libri quatuor* (Venice: ex typographia Guerraea, 1571; repr. Ridgewood, NJ: Gregg, 1964).

Eustachius a Sancto Paulo. *Summa philosophiae quadripartita* (Cambridge, 1648) [first ed. 1609].

Francisco Suárez. *De anima: Commentaria una cum quaestionibus in libros Aristotelis De anima*, ed. S. Castellote (Madrid: Sociedad de Estudios y Publicaciones, 1978).

Franciscus Toletus. *Opera omnia philosophica* (Cologne: Birckmann, 1615–16; repr. Hidesheim: G. Olms, 1985).

Giles of Orleans. *Quaestiones super De generatione et corruptione*, ed. Z. Kuksewicz (Amsterdam: B. R. Grüner, 1993).

Hieronymus Fracastorius. *De contagione et contagiosis morbis et eorum curatione libri III*, ed. W. C. Wright (New York, Putnam, 1930).

John Buridan. *Quaestiones super De generatione et corruptione*, ed. M. Streijger (Leiden: Brill, forthcoming).

—— "Quaestiones in duos Aristotilis libros Posteriorum Analyticorum," ed. H. Hubien (unpublished manuscript).

Johnston, Mark. "How to Speak of the Colors," *Philosophical Studies* 68 (1992) 221–63.

Maier, Anneliese. *An der Grenze von Scholastik und Naturwissenschaft*, 2nd ed. (Rome: Edizioni di Storia e Letteratura, 1952).

—— *On the Threshold of Exact Science: Selected Writings of Anneliese Maier on Late Medieval Natural Philosophy*, tr. S. Sargent (Philadelphia: University of Pennsylvania Press, 1982).

Newman, William R. *Atoms and Alchemy: Chymistry and the Experimental Origins of the Scientific Revolution* (Chicago: University of Chicago Press, 2006).

Nicole Oresme. "Quaestiones super libros Physicorum," ed. S. Caroti et al. (unpublished draft).

Pasnau, Robert. "Sensible Qualities: The Case of Sound," *Journal of the History of Philosophy* 38 (2000) 27–40.

—— *Cambridge Translations of Medieval Philosophical Texts. Volume 3: Mind and Knowledge* (New York: Cambridge University Press, 2002).

—— *Metaphysical Themes 1274–1671* (Oxford: Clarendon Press, 2011).

Paul of Taranto. *Liber tam theoricae quam practicae veritatis in arte alkimica*, ed. W. R. Newman, in *The Summa Perfectionis and Late Medieval Alchemy: A Study of Chemical Traditions, Techniques, and Theories in Thirteenth-Century Italy* (Ph.D. dissertation: Harvard University, 1986).

Paul of Venice. *Summa philosophiae naturalis* (Venice, 1503; repr. Hildesheim: Olms, 1974).

Scheibler, Christoph. *Philosophia compendiosa*, 6th ed. (Oxford, 1639).

Schmitt, Charles and Quentin Skinner (eds.). *The Cambridge History of Renaissance Philosophy* (Cambridge: Cambridge University Press, 1988).

Thomas Aquinas. *In Aristotelis libros De caelo et mundo, De generatione et corruptione, Meteorologicorum expositio*, ed. R. M. Spiazzi (Rome: Marietti, 1952).

—— *Summa theologiae*, ed. P. Caramello (Rome: Marietti, 1950–53).

Walter Burley. *De formis*, ed. F. Scott (Munich: Verlag der Bayerischen Akademie der Wissenschaften, 1970).

William Crathorn. *Quästionen zum ersten sentenzenbuch*, ed. F. Hoffmann (Münster: Aschendorff, 1988).

Wood, Rega and Michael Weisberg, "Interpreting Aristotle on Mixture: Problems about Elemental Composition from Philoponus to Cooper," *Studies in History and Philosophy of Science* 35 (2004) 681–706.

3

Gassendi and the Seventeenth-Century Atomists on Primary and Secondary Qualities

Antonia LoLordo

1. Introduction

Many different kinds of atomism were available in the seventeenth century. Gassendi and followers like Walter Charleton argued for a roughly mechanist version of atomism on which atoms had only the qualities size, shape, solidity and motion, and all other qualities of bodies supervened on the qualities of atoms.[1] Others opted for Galileo's mathematical point-atoms; atoms endowed with forms; atoms for each of the distinct elements, whether chemical or Aristotelian; and so on.[2]

One can fairly easily reconstruct something like the primary–secondary quality distinction for each of these various forms of atomism. If you treat the determinable properties whose determinants atoms possess as the primary qualities, then everything else is a secondary quality that must derive from those primary qualities. Thus someone who thinks there are four types of atoms, one for each of the four Aristotelian elements, would identify the primary qualities as heat, cold, wetness, and dryness, and treat all other qualities as secondary. Indeed, Gassendi uses the term 'primary quality' as a synonym for 'elemental quality' in precisely this way (1.494a).[3]

Here, however, I shall limit my discussion to the primary–secondary quality distinction as it arises in mechanical atomism. Limitations of space preclude examining how all

[1] Two caveats. First, Gassendi distinguishes motion from motive power, and ascribes both motion and motive power to atoms. But while this is important for other reasons, it plays no role here: hence I shall simply speak about motion. (For more on motive power, see LoLordo 2008a.) Second, Gassendi—like many other atomists—allows the possibility of superadded powers, for example the power involved in animal generation. But he insists that, if there are such powers, they must be superadded *by God*: it takes divine intervention for there to be anything in body that does not supervene on the qualities of atoms. For more on this, see LoLordo 2007, chapter 7.

[2] For a variety of atomism that involves forms, see Sennert 1636. For a variety that has atoms for each of the five chemical elements, see van Helmont 1648.

[3] See Goclenius 1980, 980 (article "Qualitas").

the different forms of seventeenth-century atomism treat qualities. Moreover, we begin to lose our grip on the primary–secondary quality distinction quite quickly once we step away from roughly mechanist philosophies. As philosophers now commonly think of it, the primary-secondary quality distinction has a number of components. Both primary and secondary qualities are types of sensible qualities.[4] However, they are ontologically—not merely epistemically—different in some important ways. The primary qualities are size, shape, solidity and motion. The secondary qualities are color, taste, smell and the like. The primary qualities are used in scientific explanation; the secondary qualities are not.[5] Abandoning too many of these components makes us lose our grip on the distinction.[6] Mechanical atomism is the only form of atomism for which a primary–secondary quality distinction with these components is even a contender, so I shall limit my discussion to it.[7]

However, discussing the primary–secondary quality distinction in mechanical atomism is a somewhat odd thing to do. Gassendi does not explicitly distinguish primary and secondary qualities, and I shall argue that none of the various ways he carves up qualities amounts to such a distinction. One of my goals is to clarify the ontology Gassendi assigns to the qualities that are paradigmatically thought of as secondary. This will show that they are more like primary qualities, as traditionally understood, than secondary qualities. The lack of a primary–secondary quality distinction in Gassendi may seem somewhat surprising to twenty-first-century readers. For it strikes us as a very natural distinction for a mechanical atomist to draw. Thus, my second main goal is to explain why Gassendi draws the distinctions between qualities he does, and why he does *not* draw any clear distinction between the traditional primary and secondary qualities.

I shall proceed as follows. I begin, in section 2, with the problem atomists face. Since atoms lack all qualities except size, shape, solidity, and motion, we must explain the various macro-level qualities as categorical features deriving from the configuration or

[4] More precisely, both primary and secondary qualities are determinants of a determinable at least some of whose determinants are sensible. There are obviously some bodies whose size, shape, and perhaps color are too small for us to see.

[5] I do *not* claim that part of the primary–secondary quality distinction is that use in scientific explanation is a criterion for distinguishing primary qualities from secondary qualities. That would be too strong. For scholars argue about whether Locke derives his primary–secondary quality distinction from corpuscularianism, or whether he takes himself to have independent arguments for it—arguments that depend merely on ordinary experience. And if use in scientific explanation must be a criterion for distinguishing primary qualities from secondary qualities, the second way of interpreting Locke would be prima facie absurd.

[6] However, our grasp on the distinction can survive *some* change in its components. Certain contemporary philosophers argue that color is a primary quality. See e.g. Jackson 1996. However, Jackson is careful to note that his view that colors are physical properties "is sometimes known as the primary quality view of color, although the idea is not that colors are identical with complexes of primary qualities in a sense tied to Locke's famous list, but rather that they are identical with complexes of properties the physical sciences appeal to in their causal explanations" (199).

[7] For instance, a form of atomism on which there are atoms for each of the three chemical elements makes the primary qualities—and perhaps some of the secondary qualities as well—insensible, and alters the list of primary and secondary qualities drastically.

arrangement of atoms; as powers; or as appearances in the mind. When Gassendi speaks of the configuration or arrangement of atoms, he typically speaks of the *contextura*—the way in which atoms are woven together.[8] I translate this term as 'texture'. For although this is an archaic usage, Locke and Boyle used 'texture' to speak of the arrangement of corpuscular parts.[9]

An important question is which of these three views Gassendi adopted and why. Contemporaries such as Descartes and Galileo held that primary qualities are categorical features of bodies while secondary qualities exist only in the mind. A generation later, Boyle and Locke agreed that primary qualities are categorical features, but argued that secondary qualities are better thought of as powers. The texture view, the power view, and the appearance view were all live options for Gassendi.

In section 3, I outline the various distinctions Gassendi draws between types of qualities, and in section 4, I look at his overarching argument that qualities are modes of bodies and consider why he rejects the Galilean appearance view. I consider his reasons for favoring the texture view over the power view in section 5. In section 6, I consider a puzzling passage that seems to suggest the Lockean claim that there is nothing in bodies resembling the heat we feel. This is a problem for my interpretation because it is naturally read as contrasting ideas of color and heat with ideas of shape and solidity, which *do* resemble something in bodies. In section 7, I draw on the distinction between appearance and reality and on Gassendi's Epicurean claim that the appearances are always true to show that he draws no such contrast. In section 8, I argue that because he holds that qualities like color and heat are textures, Gassendi in effect rejects the primary–secondary quality distinction. For an implication of his view is that while there is an important *epistemic* difference between qualities like size and shape on one hand and qualities like heat and color on the other, there is no real metaphysical difference. Finally, in section 9 I conclude by suggesting a reason why Gassendi may not have distinguished between primary and secondary qualities in the way many of his seventeenth-century contemporaries did.

2. Three possibilities

Seventeenth-century philosophers were familiar with the description of Democritean atomism provided by Diogenes Laertius:

> The first principles of the universe are atoms and empty space . . . the atoms are unlimited in size and number . . . and thereby generate all composite things . . . The qualities of things exist merely by convention; in nature there is nothing but atoms and void space.[10]

[8] From the verb *contexo*—to weave, entwine, join or bind; secondarily, to compose, construct, or put together.

[9] See e.g. *Essay* 2.8.10: "by their *primary qualities*, *i.e.* by the bulk, figure, texture, and motion of their insensible parts", and Boyle, "Origin of Forms and Qualities" 4 (Boyle 1979, 30): "a certain disposition or contrivance of parts in the whole, which we may call the *texture* of it".

[10] Diogenes Laertius 2000, IX 44–45.

Not all scholars agree that 'by convention' is an accurate translation of Diogenes' Greek. But in his *Physiologia Epicuro-Gassendo-Charletonia*, Charleton translates the relevant part into Latin as follows: "Lege enim color, lege amaror, lege dulcor"—"For color exists by law, bitterness by law, sweetness by law."[11] He goes on to explain that

> [Q]ualities... [ought] to be reputed not as absolute and entire Realities, but simple and occasional Appearances, whose specification consisteth in a certain modification of the First Matter, respective to that distinct Affection they introduce into this or that particular sense, when thereby actually deprehended. Not that *Democritus* meant, in a litteral sense, that their production was determinable *ex institutio hominum*, by the opinionative laws of mans Will... but in a *Metaphorical* [sense], that as the justice, injustice, decency, turpitude, culpability, laudability of Human actions, are determined by the Conformity or Difformity they bear to the Constitutions Civil, or Laws generally admitted, so likewise do the whiteness, blackness, sweetness, bitterness, heat or cold, of all Natural Concretions receive their distinct essence, or determination from certain positions and regular ordinations of Atoms.[12]

Set aside how odd it is to find an early modern philosopher suggesting that moral qualities are qualities human actions bear in relation to the civil law. Another oddity is more significant: in this brief passage, Charleton appears to suggest three different ontologies of the qualities of macroscopic bodies:

(1) *The appearance view*. Qualities are appearances: very roughly, mind-dependent entities rather than "absolute and entire Realities".[13] On this view, bodies do not really possess qualities at all: qualities belong only to minds.
(2) *The power view*. For a body to have a given quality is for it to have a certain causal power—the ability to "introduce" an "Affection" into the senses and thereby to affect the mind of the perceiver in a particular way.[14] Bodies possess their powers to affect us in virtue of having certain textures, that is, by being composed of certain atoms arranged in a certain way.
(3) *The texture view*. For a body to have a given quality is just for it to have a certain texture or arrangement of atoms. We pick out the relevant texture by identifying the one that causes a certain effect on us.[15]

[11] Charleton's *Physiologia* is a free partial translation of Gassendi, with some of Charleton's own remarks tossed in. The discussion of qualities is fairly close to Gassendi's, although some of the examples are different. Charleton's *Physiologia* is important as one of the main vehicles by which knowledge of Gassendi was transferred to later English philosophers.

[12] Charleton 1654, 129.

[13] Charleton neither defines the term "appearance" precisely nor uses it particularly frequently. However, that appearances are in the mind is suggested by the following passage: "An Apparence we term it, because the *Quale* or Suchness of every sensible thing, receives its peculiar determination from the relation it holds to that sense, that peculiarly discerns it: at least from the judgment made in the mind according to the evidence of sensation". In any case, it does not matter much for current purposes whether Charleton intends to suggest the possibility that qualities are mental: it is a live option for early modern philosophers in any case.

[14] More precisely, a power to cause a certain effect on the sense organs of a certain kind of perceiver under certain specified conditions. From now on I will simply say "the power to affect us in a certain way", as shorthand. The reader should insert an implicit clause about normal perceivers and normal circumstances.

[15] I make this view more precise in section 5 below.

Despite these complications, the basic picture Charleton lays out is clear enough. Bodies have a certain texture. In virtue of possessing this texture, they have the power to affect human sense organs in certain regular ways. (They do this either by direct contact, in the case of touch and taste; through corpuscular emissions; or through modifications of light.) When the sense organs are affected, the perceiver senses, or becomes aware of, some aspect of the thing sensed. The three different possibilities are simply different ways of identifying what, within this picture, is the quality.

Why is this philosophically significant? Why was it important for early modern philosophers to decide between these three views? One way to get a handle on this is by looking at the disagreements that took place over the ontology of qualities in the early modern period. Boyle, Descartes, Galileo, and Locke all agreed that the primary qualities are categorical properties that are intrinsic to bodies and depend on their micro-level constituents. This is as close as you can get to holding that primary qualities are textures without actually being an atomist. However, they disagreed about the ontology of secondary qualities. On the standard reading, Galileo and Descartes locate colors and the other secondary qualities in the mind, while Locke and Boyle hold something more like the power view.[16] I discuss their differing philosophical motivations in sections 4, 5, and 6 below.

Which solution did seventeenth-century mechanical atomists adopt, and why? It turns out that answering this question is less than straightforward. One reason is that Gassendi does not draw any clear distinction between the primary and secondary qualities of macroscopic bodies. While he distinguishes the various sorts of qualities in a number of different ways, none of these distinctions is straightforwardly the distinction between primary and secondary qualities. To see this, let us begin by looking at his account of qualities as presented in the *Syntagma Philosophicum*.

3. Gassendi's taxonomy

Gassendi's *Physics* begins by laying out the fundamental entities of atomism: atoms—which possess only the properties of size, shape, solidity, and motion—moving in absolute space and time. Once this material is in place, he moves on to discuss the nature of qualities. The basic question is simple. If everything in the world is composed of mechanical atoms, how do qualities arise?

Gassendi answers this question in several stages. He begins the chapter "What Qualities Are" by noting that

> Since Atoms are the whole matter or corporeal substance that bodies consist in, if we conceive or notice something else in bodies, it is not a substance but a mode of a substance, that is, a certain texture [*contexturam*] of the material principle (1.372b).

[16] See Lisa Downing's chapter in this volume.

Bodies consist just in atoms. Thus, whatever we perceive in bodies must either be the atoms themselves or a way of being of those atoms—in other words, a way in which those atoms are arranged. From this it follows trivially, he seems to think, that qualities must be ways in which atoms are arranged. Where are the other two options suggested by Charleton, qualities as appearances and qualities as powers? What has led Gassendi to think that the texture view simply follows from atomism? Answering this question will have to wait until we know a little more about what Gassendi's texture view involves.

After asserting that all qualities are modes or textures, Gassendi goes on to discuss the various qualities. His aim in this discussion is twofold: first, to begin investigating what texture constitutes what quality; and second, to show how it is even *possible* for a quality to be constituted by a texture. Given the generally speculative nature of Gassendi's atomist explanations—a feature consonant with the general early modern articulation of atomism as a research program rather than a complete science—the second is rather more important to him. Certainly the second will concern us more.

The discussion begins with chapters on rarity, density, perspicuity and opacity; magnitude, figure, subtlety, coarseness, smoothness and roughness; motion or the motive power; and heaviness (*gravitas*) and lightness. Then—remarking that he will now move from qualities that depend on the properties of individual atoms to "those qualities that depend on the properties of many atoms joined together" (1.394b)—he goes on to discuss heat and cold; fluidity, firmness, wetness and dryness; and softness, hardness, flexibility, tractability and ductility. A subdivision of these are "the qualities by which the various senses are affected" (1.409b): taste and odor; sound; light; color; and *simulacra* or intentional species. Finally, he turns to those qualities called occult: magnetism, electricity and the like.

A few observations about this method of proceeding are worth making. First, by starting with rarity and density—qualities that can be possessed by composite bodies but not by individual atoms—Gassendi provides a clue that his discussion is aimed just at the qualities of composite bodies. He distinguishes between size and shape as they apply to atoms, and size and shape as they apply to composite bodies, much more clearly than most early modern writers.[17] Second, both the location of the book on qualities within the overarching structure of the *Syntagma* and the fact that it mixes together sensible qualities with Lockean "secondary qualities mediately perceived" like flexibility and ductility, suggest that Gassendi's discussion will focus on what exists in bodies rather than what the mind perceives. This is a very different approach from the Lockean one, which discusses qualities by way of clarifying discussion of ideas, and which in any case Locke explicitly advertises as a digression. I shall argue that this difference in approach is significant for understanding the very different ontologies that Gassendi and Locke end up with.

[17] I suggest below that this flows from his interest in the perceptual relativity of the qualities of macroscopic bodies.

A number of distinctions are made in the course of Gassendi's discussion. One is straightforward: the distinction between the qualities of atoms and the qualities of composite bodies. Atomic qualities are fundamental; composite qualities somehow flow from them. A second distinction—that between essential (*coniuncta*) and accidental (*eventa*) properties—is also relatively straightforward. The size, shape, and motive power of atoms are essential properties: atoms cannot persist without their size, shape, and motive power persisting. Position, on the other hand, is an accidental property of atoms. It is obviously a substantive metaphysical question what properties of composite bodies are essential, but we can put that aside for current purposes. For the distinction between primary and secondary qualities is pretty clearly not the distinction between essential and non-essential properties: size and motion are no more intuitively essential to composite bodies than color and heat.[18]

The third distinction between types of qualities is the most important for current purposes:

(1) "[Q]ualities depending on or adjunct to the properties of individual [atoms], of which sort are magnitude or quantity and consequently subtlety and coarseness: and similarly figure, and what follows from it, like smoothness and roughness" (1.375a).

Rarity and density are also qualities of this type.

(2) Qualities that are "adjunct to things as composite, or taken all at once: of this sort are, foremost, those that pertain to the various senses, as in respect of touch the qualities heat, cold, fluidity, firmness, humidity, dryness; and then, arising from them hardness, softness, flexibility, ductility, malleability and similar others . . . In respect of taste, flavor; in respect of smell, smell; in respect of hearing, sound; in respect of sight, light, color and . . . Intentional species" (1.375a).

This sort of quality can be subdivided into two types: sensible qualities and qualities that are made manifest only indirectly, by sensing their effect on other bodies. But some qualities—such as heat, which causes both felt heat and changes in other bodies—are both sensible and otherwise manifest.

The distinction between type 1 and type 2 qualities, then, is the distinction between qualities that are "adjunct to the properties of individual [atoms]" and qualities that are "adjunct to things as composite, or taken all at once". The fact that rarity and density are type 1 rather than type 2 is a useful clue for understanding what this means.

[18] One way of drawing the primary–secondary quality distinction is, however, related. It is sometimes suggested that the primary qualities are those determinable qualities that any body whatsoever must have. Thus, although having a particular shape is not essential to any body, having some shape is; in contrast, a body can exist without having any color at all. I do not see any trace of this way of drawing the distinction in Gassendi, perhaps because he does not hold the Lockean resemblance thesis often associated with it. For more on this, see section 7.

Density, unlike size, shape, and spatial location, is not a property individual atoms can possess. But someone who knew the size, shape, and spatial location of all the atomic components of a thing could immediately calculate its density. In contrast, knowing the color of a thing also requires knowing something about how the component atoms interact with each other.

(3) "[Q]ualities that pertain to interior faculties and less sensible operations, such as sympathy, antipathy, magnetism, electricity, and in a word all those said to be occult" (1.375a).

Two questions immediately arise when confronted with this taxonomy. First—since the Lockean account of primary and secondary qualities is the paradigm on which our understanding of the distinction relies—how does this taxonomy relate to the Lockean taxonomy of primary qualities, immediately perceived secondary qualities and mediately perceived secondary qualities? Second, what is the precise ontological status of these various types of qualities? Are they appearances, powers or textures—or should we assign different ontological statuses to the different types of qualities?

To the extent the text makes any clear suggestion, it suggests understanding all three types of qualities as textures.[19] No powers are mentioned, and although sensations are mentioned, there is no suggestion that the quality *is* the sensation.[20] Consider passages like the following:

Sound is nothing distinct from corpuscles configured in a certain way and continuously translated very quickly from the resounding thing, moving the organ [of hearing] and causing the sensation called Hearing (1.414b).

Or, in case the point is clearer in the case of a quality known via a contact sense rather than via corpuscular emissions:

It seems that taste, in those things that are called tasty, is nothing other than corpuscles configured in such a way that they enter into the tongue and palate . . . affecting them in such a way that the sensation which is called "taste" occurs (1.409b).

Qualities are corpuscles, configured in a certain way: that is, qualities are *textures*.[21]

[19] Of course, they are not all textures of the same things. In the case of "occult" qualities like electricity, gravity, and magnetism, what's relevant is the texture of the interior of the body and the texture of the corpuscles emitted. The various smells are also a matter of corpuscular emissions, although in this case it's the texture of the *surface* of the body that's relevant. In the case of qualities known via touch and taste, what's relevant is the texture of the body's surface. And in the case of qualities known by vision—which occurs through modifications of light rather than through corpuscular emissions—the relevant textures are the texture of the body's surface and the texture of the light corpuscles modified by it.

[20] However, Gassendi does sometimes (e.g. 1.410b) suggest that the quality, properly speaking, is primarily in the sense *organ* and only secondarily in the body sensed.

[21] I read Gassendi here as meaning that the quality is the configuration and not the corpuscle, in keeping with his insistence that qualities are modes.

I will argue that, given Gassendi's various philosophical assumptions and the constraints he is operating under, the texture answer makes the most philosophical sense for him. However, I shall also argue that the texture answer turns the primary–secondary quality distinction into a purely epistemic distinction. And since it is a crucial component of the primary–secondary quality distinction as commonly understood that it is a *metaphysical* distinction, the texture answer in effect erases the primary–secondary quality distinction. Because of this, and because it is so natural for mechanical atomists to embrace the primary–secondary quality distinction in either its Galilean or Lockean forms, it will be worth our while to work our way through the other two alternatives and see *why* Gassendi embraces the texture view.

Explaining the ontology of qualities and how Gassendi's taxonomy relates to Locke's will occupy the rest of the paper. First, however, it is worth saying a little about type 3 qualities: electricity, magnetism and the rest of the Aristotelian "occult qualities." On an Aristotelian picture, sensible qualities are not occult because the quality itself is grasped in sensation. What's exhibited to the mind is like what's really in the body. In contrast, qualities like magnetism are "hidden" in the sense that experience does not tell us about the quality itself, only its effects. Gassendi distinguishes type 2 and type 3 qualities mainly for the benefit of readers with an Aristotelian education.[22] He does not draw the Aristotelian distinction because he does not think that sensible qualities like color resemble our ideas of them any more than the occult quality of magnetism resembles the attraction of metal. Both derive from causes that are typically unknown but that are, in principle, knowable.[23]

In some passages, Gassendi contrasts occult qualities with sensible qualities. In others he has a trivision: occult qualities, sensible qualities, and "manifest" qualities, that is, insensible qualities whose causes are known (1.449b). From the perspective of the Aristotelian tradition, it seems easy and natural to equate sensible qualities with manifest qualities. But it does not make sense to do so on Gassendi's view. For by arguing that heat, color, and the like are textures, Gassendi in effect argues that the nature of these qualities extends far beyond what we perceive when we perceive hot or colored bodies. Gassendi typically talks about "those qualities commonly called occult," and Charleton has a chapter entitled "Occult Qualities Made Manifest." But it would be more accurate to say that Gassendi and Charleton turn almost *all* qualities into occult qualities: almost all of them have a nature that is not immediately apparent in sense perception.[24] I shall argue that this also applies to the shape, size, solidity, and motive power of macroscopic bodies.

[22] I say "mainly" because from the point of view of physics there is one important difference: type 3 qualities are a matter of the interior texture of the body while type 2 qualities have to do with surface textures.

[23] At 1.452a–1.457b, Gassendi explains occult qualities including magnetism, electricity and the healing power of the weapon salve in terms of corpuscular emissions. These are only partial explanations—he does not claim to know precisely what the relevant texture is in each case—but they are sufficient to show that he thinks such occult qualities are in principle knowable.

[24] I suspect that Charleton has in mind the view that occult qualities are unintelligible: by making them manifest, he is making them intelligible.

For, even in that case, there is a sharp distinction between the real nature of the quality in bodies and the appearance produced in our mind.

4. Appearances

The view that qualities are appearances in the mind would have been familiar to Gassendi. Galileo—one of his biggest philosophical influences—asserted that "tastes, odors, colors and so on . . . reside only in the consciousness".[25] One argument for this claim is the following:

> [P]eople . . . believe that heat is a real phenomenon, or property, or quality, which actually resides in the material by which we feel ourselves warmed. Now I say that whenever I conceive any material or corporeal substance, I immediately feel the need to think of it as bounded, and as having this or that shape; as being large or small [etc] . . . But that it must be white or red, bitter or sweet, noisy or silent, and of sweet or foul odor, my mind does not feel compelled to bring in as necessary accompaniments. Without the senses as our guides, reason or imagination unaided would probably never arrive at qualities like these. Hence I think that tastes, odors, colors, and so on are no more than mere names so far as the object in which we place them is concerned.[26]

I find the argument puzzling. Let us grant Galileo that bodies cannot be conceived without size and shape, but can be conceived without color or heat. How does it follow that color and heat are not actually in the body but in the perceiver? How, that is, does it follow that secondary qualities are purely mental? Matter can be conceived without magnetism, but no one is tempted to say that magnetism is really in the mind, not the world. We continue to think there is a distinction between magnetism and the idea of magnetism even after we realize that nothing resembling our idea of magnetism exists in bodies. This question is particularly salient since Locke agrees that the primary qualities are the ones that are "wholly inseparable from body" (2.8.10), but unlike Galileo locates the secondary qualities in bodies.

However, we can safely put this aside. Our main concern is why Gassendi rejects the Galilean position. As we have seen, his initial discussion of qualities suggests that atomism implies that qualities are modes of bodies. While this is neutral between the power view and the texture view, it is incompatible with the appearance view. But why is Gassendi so willing to assume that qualities are modes? Why does he discard Galileo's appearance view out of hand?

The basic form of Gassendi's argument is this:

(1) No individual atoms have the qualities of color and heat.
(2) Some macroscopic bodies *do* have the qualities of color and heat.
(3) Macroscopic bodies are just collections of atoms arranged in a certain texture.
(4) Therefore qualities are (or emerge from) textures.

[25] Galilei 1957, 274 (selection from "The Assayer").
[26] Ibid.

Gassendi's (2) is just the denial of Galileo's claim that color and heat are in the mind. Hence, it is implausible that Gassendi simply thought (2) is so uncontroversial as to need no defense. Why then does he believe (2)? We can find an answer, I think, by looking at what Gassendi is willing to count as evidence that a body has a certain quality. Although he never articulates a general view here, one can be elicited from his account of cold.

After discussing heat, Gassendi asks, "whether cold is a genuine and positive quality or a mere privation" (1.401b), and answers that cold should be considered a positive quality for the same reason that heat is considered a positive quality. We gain evidence that heat is a positive quality from observations like the following: "if you set a glass bottle next to a [burning] coal the water contained in that bottle is changed so that it becomes hotter and bubbles". But we have exactly parallel evidence concerning cold: "if you surround a glass bottle with snow or ice, the water is changed so that in a moderate amount of time it becomes colder and freezes." Thus cold should be considered a genuine and positive quality, too, on the principle that a privation is incapable of action (1.401b). In other words, cold must be a genuine, positive quality *because it has genuine effects.* And so we should reserve the term "cold" for something in bodies—not for a feeling in perceivers—else we have no term for the cause of that feeling (and of various other effects).

Thus, a quality is whatever causes a certain effect. For a body to have a certain quality is for it to have certain effects. So far, this is compatible with either the texture view or the power view. Let us go on to consider these two views and determine why Gassendi opted for the texture view.

5. Textures and powers

One implication of Gassendi's quick rejection of the appearance view is that it makes it easy for him to group qualities like color and heat together with qualities like flexibility, as metaphysical equals. His type 2 qualities include both what Locke would later call the immediately perceivable secondary qualities and the mediately perceivable ones. But are these qualities textures or powers? We need to answer this question to figure out whether there is a significant ontological distinction between type 1 and type 2 qualities for Gassendi—to see, that is, whether color and size are ontologically different in the way they are within the Cartesian or Lockean framework.[27]

[27] However, it can be argued that Locke reduces powers to primary qualities and hence holds that powers *are* textures in the sense I use the term. For instance, Locke says that "*Powers* are Relations, not Agents" (II. xxi.19: 243) and that "the different Bulk, Figure, Number, Texture, and Motion of [a body's] insensible Parts" (II.xxi.73: 287) is the *only* cause we can imagine for the ideas bodies produce in us and for the changes they bring about among one another. Thanks to Walter Ott for this point.

I said above that the text favors the texture reading. But what could be Gassendi's motivation for identifying qualities with textures? Since he does not explicitly consider the power view, we shall need to speculate a bit.

Gassendi's fundamental way of conceiving of a body as qualified is conceiving of it as having certain effects. So whatever it is in virtue of which the body has effects must be the quality. But what is it in virtue of which bodies have effects? Like many other seventeenth-century philosophers, Gassendi is hostile to the notion of ungrounded powers. We must identify a categorical cause, not just a bare disposition, to avoid slipping back into unsatisfactory Aristotelian metaphysics. What causes the magnet to attract iron is that it emits hooked corpuscles that attach onto pieces of iron—not that it has a magnetic power. Similarly, what causes the body to look red is its texture, not the power it has in virtue of having that texture. (And in any case, it is uncontroversial that the powers bodies have to cause certain sensations are grounded in their texture. Even Locke thinks that.) To put the point in somewhat anachronistic terms, Gassendi is committed to the texture view rather than the power view by identifying qualities with what realizes a certain functional role. And his reason for doing so is that in any actual causal situation, it's what realizes the functional role that does the causing.

This shows that we need to be a little bit careful in how we characterize the texture view. When we say that for a body to be red is for it to have the texture that causes red-sensations, we could mean one of two things:

(a) *x* is red just in case *x* has some texture that causes red-sensations (whatever that texture may actually be); *or*

(b) *x* is red just in case *x* has texture *t* and texture *t* is the texture that actually causes red-sensations.[28]

On (a), the texture view and the power view are much the same in spirit, if not in letter. For (a) makes bearing a certain relation to perceivers essential to being red. What I have in mind is (b). And in contrast, the reference to a perceiver in (b) is not essential. To figure out what texture *t* is, we must figure out what texture actually causes red-sensations. But a body can have texture *t* and hence be red without being such as to cause red-sensations. If the human perceptual apparatus were different, so that some other texture caused red-sensations, possessing texture *t* would still constitute redness.

The point can be put another way. On (a), being red is a relational property—a property something bears in virtue of standing in a certain relation to another thing, in this case the human perceptual apparatus. On (b), redness is not a relational property. It is an intrinsic property.

I am not aware of any text that favors (b) over (a). But thinking of the quality as what endows the body with certain causal powers fits better with (b). To say that a body is red because it has some texture that causes red-sensations—whatever that texture may actually

[28] Both (a) and (b) should be understood to include "in normal perceivers, under normal circumstances", etc.

be—is not to offer much of an explanation. Unless we actually specify what texture causes red-sensations, we are merely pointing at some unexplained power. We are not explaining what grounds that power, and hence have not advanced much past dormitive-virtue type explanations. So from now on, (b) is what I mean by the texture view.

If secondary qualities are powers or relational properties, there is a sharp metaphysical distinction between primary and secondary qualities. For primary qualities, on the typical view, are intrinsic and categorical. However, if secondary qualities are textures, in sense (b), then there is no real metaphysical difference between primary and secondary qualities. The difference lies simply in our different modes of epistemic access to them. We can characterize a quality like size or shape without making any reference to ourselves or our sensory apparatus. The same is not the case, Gassendi suggests, for qualities like heat and color. Given the present state of scientific knowledge, we can only refer to these qualities by identifying them as whatever textures cause certain sensations—or certain effects on other bodies. Our descriptions of secondary qualities must involve a relation, although they are not relational properties.

It is relatively easy to confuse the epistemic claim that we must characterize secondary qualities in relational terms with the metaphysical claim that secondary qualities are not relational properties. But we should be careful not to do this. Let us return to the example of heat to help clarify the picture.

Gassendi begins his discussion of heat by saying that "heat is often conceived from the relation it has to sensation" (1.394b), but that this common conception is misleading. For in fact, heat "cannot be explained except by the size, shape, and mobility of atoms" (1.394b). More specifically, we feel the sensation of heat when heat enters into the pores of the body and penetrates and loosens its various parts. Gassendi clarifies the point by admonishing the reader as follows. When he says that heat

> enters in, penetrates, loosens, etc, do not understand a certain nude and solitary quality but rather certain atoms insofar as they are furnished with such a size, such a shape, such a motion. (1.394b).

The other effects of heat occur when such corpuscles penetrate insensate bodies. Corpuscles possessed of such a size, shape, and motion are hence referred to as heat corpuscles. In other words, something is a heat corpuscle just in case it has a certain texture—that texture which in fact causes a certain sensation in perceivers (as well as certain other effects in other bodies).

6. The case of heat

If we read on, however, we will see that Gassendi's discussion of heat almost immediately complicates things. For he adds:

> Indeed these atoms do not have heat *ex se* or, what is the same thing, they are not hot, but can nevertheless be judged and called atoms of heat, or calorific atoms, insofar as they create heat, that is, have this effect (1.394b).

This is puzzling, on two counts. First, it seems that Gassendi should not be talking about *atoms* of heat at all, but rather about corpuscles or molecules—little atomic composites. Second, it is hard to know what to make of Gassendi's claim that heat atoms "are not hot". Let us consider these two puzzles in turn.

Olivier Bloch argues that heat and cold function as exceptional cases in Gassendi's account of qualities.[29] For, on his view, they are the two cases in which Gassendi uses the Democritean technique of reducing qualities to individual atoms rather than his more usual, and more complex, technique of reducing them to small atomic composites or molecules.[30] There is substantial textual evidence for this, since Gassendi very frequently uses the term "heat atom" as well as the more neutral term "heat corpuscle."[31] And clearly the Democritean view retained substantial influence on Gassendi. However, on balance I think we are best off understanding him as meaning heat *corpuscles*. While calling a compound an atom sounds terrible to modern ears, some of the chemical writers Gassendi could have been familiar with do so.[32] And there are some significant cases where Gassendi calls things "atoms" that he *clearly* thinks of as composite.[33]

This makes it possible to read Gassendi as thinking of heat in terms of molecules rather than atoms. Once this possibility is on the table, positive reason to go for it is not hard to find. As we saw, in his initial classification of qualities, Gassendi classifies heat among the qualities that depend on the properties of many atoms joined together (1.394b). He reiterates the point in the chapter "On heat, and cold" which begins, "Next follows those Qualities which depend on the properties of many Atoms joined together simultaneously" (1.394b). Elsewhere, he remarks that "heat, cold and other qualities are not congenital to Atoms but are proper to concretions and arise from . . . the qualities of atoms" (1.366a). And so on. A lone indivisible atom, then, cannot have the quality of heat: only corpuscles or molecules can have that quality.

Now for the second difficulty. Why does Gassendi say that heat corpuscles are not hot, that is, do not have heat *ex se*? This is puzzling: if being hot is just having the texture that causes certain effects, then heat corpuscles *are* hot. The passage is easily read

[29] Bloch 1971, 253.

[30] When atoms first combine, they form themselves into "certain very subtle composite corpuscles or very fine molecules . . . that are, as it were, the seeds of things" (1.472a; cf. 1.282b, 1.337a). Molecules do a great deal of explanatory work for Gassendi: for instance, by reinterpreting the chemical elements as molecules, he can capture what he sees as the successes of chemistry without its metaphysics.

[31] He refers to heat corpuscles at e.g. 1.396a and 1.397b. The term "corpuscle" is more neutral because a corpuscle—literally, a small body—can be either an atom (e.g. 1.256a) or a molecule (e.g. 1.357a).

[32] See e.g. Sennert 1636, 95 and 107, who speaks of "the second genus of atoms"—salt, sulphur and mercury, which are made up of the fundamental atoms earth, air, fire and water—and then a third genus of atoms such as gold.

[33] One example comes from Gassendi's explanation of the solubility of silver in *aqua fortis* and gold in *aqua regia*, which is that gold atoms fit the pores of *aqua regia* and silver atoms fit the pores of *aqua fortis* (2.33a ff.). Gassendi clearly does not think that there are indivisible atoms of silver and gold. Gold is a molecule or corpuscle, not an atom, as is shown by the discussion of the transmutation of lead into gold by implanting gold seeds which will re-texture the lead into gold (3.259a).

as suggesting that heat is a sensation in the mind, and that heat corpuscles should not be called hot because there is nothing in those corpuscles resembling the sensation. However, this is not the point Gassendi intends to make. He goes on to explain that such corpuscles can be called heat corpuscles because "they can excite heat by the emission of this sort of atoms [i.e. heat corpuscles]" (1.394b). The heat that he is talking about being excited here is not the *sensation* of heat, but rather the heat that is excited in a log or a piece of wax or fat when they burst into flame. Gassendi assumes that the same texture causes a person who puts their hand in front of the fire to feel warmth, and causes the log to blacken and smoke, so he might add that heat corpuscles excite heat in the skin of the perceiver. Then what is hot, properly speaking, would be the skin—not whatever corpuscular emission affected it. In this passage, Gassendi is concerned about the possible lack of resemblance between the qualities taken on by the corporeal effect and the qualities of its cause, not the possible lack of resemblance between states of sense organs and sensations in the mind.

Locke's claim that there is nothing in bodies that resembles our ideas of secondary qualities lies near the surface in any discussion of primary and secondary qualities, and it is easy to read it into Gassendi's discussion. However, this is a mistake. There is no talk of resemblance between sensations or ideas and qualities in the text; in fact, there is almost no talk of ideas in this section of the *Syntagma* at all. Perhaps more importantly, given Gassendi's other philosophical commitments, he cannot hold that ideas of shape and solidity resemble some real feature of bodies in a way that ideas of heat and color do not. There is a gap between appearance and reality for *all* sensible qualities, not just qualities like heat and color. Let us see how that gap arises.

7. Appearance and reality

The distinction between reality and appearance is central to Gassendi's way of thinking. It is a mainstay of his early *Exercitationes*, which uses conflicts among the appearances to argue that we have no knowledge of reality, and continues to recur in later philosophical works. But although Gassendi was at first tempted by skepticism, in his mature work he is committed to avoiding the Pyrrhonian problematic. His version of the Epicurean doctrine that the appearances are always true was developed to make Pyrrhonian worries impossible.

Consider two Pyrrhonian examples: the tower that looks round from a distance and square from close up, and the wine that tastes sweet to a healthy man and bitter to a sick man.[34] How can both ways the tower looks and both ways the wine tastes be "true"? Only—to put the point as briefly as possible—if the information conveyed by the appearances is understood as information about what is received in sensation rather than information about what the wine is really like. The appearance of the tower as

[34] For such examples, see Sextus Empiricus 2000.

round does not, properly speaking, inform us that the tower *is* round: it informs us that the tower *looks* round under conditions such as the current ones, "for causes having to be investigated by physics" (3.388b).

There may well be some tension between the way Gassendi handles the truth of the appearances and the way he handles qualities. He often seems to identify the quality with the appearance in the mind when he is outlining his theory of perception, although this is flatly inconsistent with his "official" account of qualities. However, this is not a sign of any deep philosophical confusion. The picture of what happens in perception is clear: the only thing unclear is whether we use the term "red" for what is in the body or what is in the mind.[35]

In any case, a tension here would not count against my interpretation. For Pyrrhonism is full of examples of perceptual error and relativity that pertain to the Lockean primary qualities as well as ones that pertain to qualities like heat and color. Thus if we took the doctrine of the truth of the appearances to motivate a view of qualities as appearances, we would have to think it motivates thinking of *all* qualities as appearances. But whether or not we understand tastes, colors, etc. as modes of body, we must understand macro-level size, shape, solidity, and motion as modes of body. These qualities cannot be simply appearances in the mind. Someone who reads Gassendi as thinking that heat and color are powers, or even mental entities, must still square his view of the Lockean primary qualities with the truth of the appearances.

So far, we have been discussing how perceptual error and relativity open up an appearance–reality gap for perception of qualities like shape and solidity. But in fact, on Gassendi's view, macroscopic shape and solidity differ in appearance and reality even in *ideal* cases. The appearance of roundness or solidity that a body produces in the mind does not resemble that body's texture, any more than its appearance of redness does.

Consider what bodies are like, on Gassendi's view. The material world is composed of atoms moving through the void. Thus, even apparently solid bodies are in fact composed mainly of void space. And even bodies with apparently smooth surfaces and regular shapes are in fact highly irregular and porous. Moreover, on Gassendi's view atoms are constantly in motion, even when the macroscopic bodies they compose are at rest.

Thus, just as Gassendi denies that anything like color as it appears to us in the world is really in bodies, he also denies that bodies have anything like the qualities of shape, solidity, and motion that we experience them as having. An orange appears to us as orange—but also as round, solid, and (let us suppose) stationary. But in reality, it is porous and irregularly shaped, it is composed mainly of void space, and its parts are in continuous motions. The appearances produced by the Lockean primary qualities do not inform us about what bodies in themselves are really like any more than our experiences of secondary–quality appearances do.[36]

[35] There is a parallel—and equally unserious—confusion in Locke (see *Essay* 2.8.8).

[36] Size is an exception here.

8. An epistemic difference

We have seen two main reasons to deny that Gassendi's distinction between type 1 and type 2 qualities is the distinction between primary and secondary qualities—and, more generally, to deny that he draws any significant distinction between primary and secondary qualities. First, both type 1 and type 2 qualities are categorical features of bodies that depend on their micro-level constituents. While it is true that we pick out type 2 qualities by means of the relation they bear to the human perceptual apparatus, this is merely an epistemic difference. Second, there is an appearance–reality distinction for both type 1 and type 2 qualities. Qualities of neither sort resemble the appearances they produce.

By not drawing any clear distinction between primary and secondary qualities, Gassendi may appear to side with the Aristotelians against new philosophers like Galileo and Descartes. But in a deeper sense, his view is the exact opposite of the standard Aristotelian view. Aristotelianism sees properties like color and taste as really in bodies, just as we perceive them, in exactly the same way size and shape are. For Gassendi, on the other hand, *no* sensible qualities are in bodies exactly as we perceive them. Thus while the standard Aristotelian view is that all sensible qualities resemble our ideas of them, Gassendi's view is that none of them do. Atomism emphasizes the gap between our manifest image of the world and the way the world really is. In doing so, it need not—and in fact should not—draw any strong distinction between primary and secondary qualities. The fact that we can specify the texture responsible for shape perception more easily than the texture responsible for color perception is no reason to think the two sorts of qualities are *metaphysically* different. And since the distinction between primary and secondary qualities is traditionally thought of as a metaphysical distinction, we are best off reading Gassendi as drawing no real distinction between primary and secondary qualities at all.

9. Conclusion

I have argued that Gassendi understands both primary and secondary qualities non-relationally, as textures of atoms.[37] In the case of qualities like color and taste, we must specify the relevant texture in terms of some relation to the human perceptual apparatus. For instance, given the current state of scientific knowledge, we can only refer to the texture that constitutes redness by describing it as the textures that causes red-sensations. In contrast, we can characterize the primary qualities without appealing to any relation. However, this is merely an epistemic difference between primary and secondary qualities. It does not imply that secondary qualities are relational properties. And this, I think, implies that there is no real distinction between primary and secondary qualities in Gassendi's version of mechanical atomism.

[37] Although I have not argued for this in any detail here, the same applies to Locke's mediately perceivable secondary qualities. For in Gassendi's taxonomy, these are type 2 qualities just like the secondary qualities.

This conclusion may well strike readers as surprising. Shouldn't any atomist—or indeed any mechanical philosopher—draw some sort of distinction between primary and secondary qualities? Why *didn't* the distinction between primary and secondary qualities strike Gassendi as important?

One clue as to why not is provided by the fact that Gassendi, unlike most other mechanical philosophers, was not involved in the project of quantifying nature. The main goal of Gassendi's physics is to show how it is possible for a world such as our own to be composed of nothing but atoms moving through void. His explanations are almost entirely qualitative. He explains the behavior of the magnet, for instance, by positing that it emits hook-shaped corpuscles—and explains the effects of gravity on falling bodies in roughly the same terms. Gassendi has very little interest in quantitative explanations of any kind.[38] Instead, he is interested in explaining how macro-level qualities, powers, and the like emerge from the interaction of atoms.

An implication of this approach to natural philosophy is that it leaves Gassendi no real reason to quantify the properties of macroscopic bodies. Thus, the fact that some properties of macroscopic bodies are far more easily quantified than others is not particularly salient in Gassendi's physics. And this is significant because the easily quantified properties of macroscopic bodies are the traditional primary qualities: size, shape, and motion. For Gassendi, the traditional primary qualities of macroscopic bodies are not used for explanatory purposes in physics. They are mere *explananda*, just like color and taste. And this leaves him with little reason to insist on a metaphysical difference between the two sorts of qualities.[39]

Bibliography

Bloch, O. 1971. *La Philosophie de Gassendi*, La Haye: Martinus Nijhoff.

Boyle, R. 1979 (ed.). M. A. Stewart. *Selected Philosophical Papers of Robert Boyle*, Manchester UK: Manchester University press.

Charleton, W. 1654. *Physiologia Epicuro-Gassendo-Charletoniana*, London: Printed by Tho. Newcomb for Thomas Heath.

Diogenes Laertius. 2000. *Lives of Eminent Philosophers*, trans. R. D. Hicks, Cambridge MA: Cambridge University Press.

Galilei, G. 1957. *Discoveries and Opinions of Galileo*, ed. Stillman Drake, Garden City, NJ: Anchor Books.

Gassendi, P. 1658. *Opera Omnia in sex tomos divisa*, Lyon: Laurent Anisson and Jean Baptiste Devenet.

[38] The one exception is his *De motu*, which makes use of the quantitative, Galilean science of motion. However, even in this work, his main interest is in explaining how micro-level atomic phenomena can account for the motion of macroscopic bodies and not in providing quantitative descriptions of that motion.

[39] I would like to thank Paul Lodge, Larry Nolan, Walter Ott, and an anonymous referee from this Press for helpful comments on previous versions of this essay.

—— 1959. *Dissertations en forme de paradoxes contre les Aristotéliciens (Exercitationes paradoxicae adversus Aristoteleos) Livres I et II*, edited and translated by Bernard Rochot, Paris: J. Vrin.

Goclenius, R. 1980. *Lexicon Philosophicum*, New York: G. Olms.

Helmont, J-B. van. 1648. *Ortus medicinae*, Amsterdam: Ludovic Elzevier.

Jackson, Frank. 1996. "The Primary Quality View of Color," *Noûs* 30 (Supplement: *Philosophical Perspectives* 10), 199–219.

Locke, John. *Essay Concerning Human Understanding*, ed. P. H. Nidditch, Oxford: Clarendon Press, 1975.

LoLordo, A. 2007. *Pierre Gassendi and the Birth of Early Modern Philosophy*, New York: Cambridge University Press.

—— 2008a. "Epicurus and Galileo in Gassendi's Physics," *Philosophy Compass* 3.2: 301–314.

—— 2008b. "Locke's Problem Concerning Perception," *Philosophy and Phenomenological Research* LXXVII.3 (November 2008), 705–724.

Sennert, D. 1636. *Hypomnemata Physica*, Frankfurt: Clement Schleich.

Sextus Empiricus. 2000. *Outlines of Scepticism*, trans. Julia Annas and Jonathan Barnes, Cambridge, UK: Cambridge University Press.

4

Descartes on "What We Call Color"

Lawrence Nolan

1. Introduction

It is well known that Descartes rejects what might be called the Scholastic "Resemblance Thesis," according to which 1) colors, sounds, odors, tastes, etc. are real qualities of bodies and 2) our perceptions of those qualities resemble them. This Thesis is sometimes stated loosely as "colors, etc. are in bodies in the way that we perceive them." While it is agreed that Descartes rejects this Thesis, it is generally assumed that he is, as much as the Scholastics, a realist about so-called "secondary qualities."[1] In other words, it is taken for granted that Descartes treats "colors" as real entities that must be located somewhere in the true ontology. But there is widespread disagreement among commentators about where exactly he locates them.

Legend has it that after banishing secondary qualities from the material universe in order to accommodate his austere, mechanistic conception of matter in terms of extension alone, Descartes sweeps colors into the "dustbin of the mind," treating them as mere sensations.[2] But over the past twenty years, English-speaking commentators have been reluctant to attribute this "subjectivist"[3] account to him, for a variety of reasons. John Cottingham, for example, thinks that it makes nonsense of our ordinary judgments concerning the properties of objects. If colors are in the mind, then Descartes is committed to such paradoxical-sounding statements as "snow is not white nor fire red."[4] In contrast to the subjectivist interpretation, Cottingham holds

[1] Descartes never uses the terms "primary quality" or "secondary quality," but it is generally agreed that he distinguishes between these two types of quality even if he did not use the terms that Boyle and Locke would later popularize.

[2] For an extended critique of this standard reading of Descartes, see Nolan and John Whipple (2006).

[3] I am using this term in the traditional sense to mean that secondary qualities just are sensations or mind-dependent entities. Contemporary color theorists often prefer to call this view "eliminativism" (or an "error theory").

[4] 1990. Although he does not address Cottingham directly, Michael Ayers challenges the assertion that such statements are paradoxical. See chapter 6 in this volume.

that Cartesian colors are in bodies, but just not in the way that we perceive them. Based on an important passage in the *Principles*, he and two other leading commentators have argued that Descartes affirms a dispositionalist account of color that anticipates Locke's famous theory of secondary qualities as mere powers in objects to produce ideas in us.[5] Other commentators have found yet a third view in Descartes writings, according to which colors are not dispositions but microphysical structures that might be said to underlie them (i.e. color physicalism).[6]

In light of these various interpretations and the texts upon which they are based, one might be inclined to suppose that Descartes affirms several accounts of the ontological status of color. Indeed, Margaret Wilson concludes just that. In a prominent essay, she argues that in various passages throughout the corpus Descartes vacillates between three views just mentioned—subjectivism, dispositionalism, and physicalism.[7] One problem with this conclusion is that, if true, it would mean that Descartes also contradicts himself, for many of these alleged vacillations occur in single works. But this seems implausible.

A final group of commentators have developed a more charitable line of interpretation that attempts to reconcile Descartes' various remarks about color, or at least to reconcile the putative "objectivist" strand that grants colors an existence in bodies independent from the perceiver and the putative "subjectivist" strand that treats them as sensations, and thus makes them utterly dependent on the perceiver. Margaret Atherton, most notably, has argued that Descartes holds a dualistic account of "color" that bifurcates its nature: there is one kind of color in minds and another kind of color in bodies.[8] Atherton concedes that as a philosophical position the dualistic view is inherently unsatisfying, inasmuch as it tries to have it both ways. But she argues that it befits Descartes' commitment to mind–body dualism and mind–body interactionism.

In this chapter, I intend to challenge the shared "realist" assumption of all these interpretations. Descartes does not take "colors" to be real entities with distinctive natures: his rejection of the Scholastic view is deeper than it has traditionally been understood. I shall argue that Descartes is a color nominalist: his positive claims are restricted to how we use color *terms* and do not purport to assert any metaphysical theses about the status of secondary qualities. Like the dualist view, the nominalist

[5] See Nicholas Jolley (1990, 83f) and Stephen Gaukroger (1995,159–64 and 345–46). Some contemporary color theorists also attribute this view to Descartes. See, e.g., Evan Thompson (1995b, 20).

[6] See, e.g. Margaret Wilson (1992) and Celia-Wolf Devine (1993, 46).

[7] 1992, 228 and 234. Focusing just on the scientific writings, Wolf-Devine draws the same conclusion (1993, 48). Unlike Wilson, however, she rightly dismisses the dispositional interpretation of Descartes on color on the ground that it conflicts with his strict mechanism. See my further discussion of this point in section 2. Wilson holds that Descartes is not unique: most of the early modern mechanical philosophers vacillated in the same way (1992, 228). Incidentally, Wilson's general position is not unprecedented; many philosophers have attributed such vacillations to Boyle and Locke, including J. L. Mackie 1976, 15.

[8] 2004. For a similar view, see Tad Schmaltz (1996, 49–50 and 1995, 391). He argues that, for Descartes, colors can be regarded either as properties in external objects or as sensations in us, and thus that the terms for sensible qualities generally are equivocal. This account is also implicit at times in Cottingham's essay.

interpretation is motivated in part by considerations of charity. It also seeks to explain *all* of the Cartesian texts on this topic rather than favoring one set of texts over another, as for example the dispositionalist and subjectivist readings have tended to do.

In arguing that Descartes is a color nominalist, one of the things that will frame my discussion is a much-neglected expression. In almost every one of the passages in which he is purported by commentators to be asserting a positive metaphysical claim about color, Descartes speaks of "what we call color" (or "what we call red", etc.). This locution is crucial for understanding his aims in these passages. Typically, when using it, he is referring to the properties of bodies that we ordinarily refer to as "colors." He is not speaking in his own voice or claiming, in light of philosophical reflection, that we *ought* to call such and such properties "colors." In short, he is best read as making a semantic point, rather than a metaphysical one, about how the term "color" is used in ordinary discourse. As he sees it, this general term and particular color terms (such as "red," "blue," "green," etc.) serve as placeholders in everyday parlance for whatever it is in bodies that causes our visual sensations.

Once one appreciates the significance and ubiquity of this expression, it becomes clear that passages that have traditionally been read as making metaphysical claims about the nature of color were written with very different purposes. Two such purposes loom large. First, in many of these passages, especially those contained in his scientific writings, Descartes is concerned to defeat the Resemblance Thesis, as characterized above. As a mechanist who aims to show that our sensations can be caused by something entirely different in nature from them, Descartes rejects the Resemblance Thesis and devotes much of his scientific work on perception to arguing against it. Second, Descartes maintains that our sensations can be clearly and distinctly perceived only when we regard them as modes of the mind. Such perceptions become confused and result in error when we judge, as the Scholastic does, that they resemble properties of bodies. In most of the other (non-scientific) passages devoted to "color," Descartes is concerned to diagnose this error and to explain how to guard against it.

In order to avoid being misunderstood, a defender of nominalism must issue a caveat about how he is going to use language. In the case at hand, one must avoid using color terms in a way that implies any form of realism of the sort that I have claimed Descartes rejects. Descartes has been misinterpreted in part, I believe, because he himself is not always so careful, using color terms in different ways without always indicating explicitly how he is employing them. Allow me to stipulate then that, except in contexts where I expressly say otherwise, I shall use the general term "color" (and particular color terms such as "blue," "red," "green," etc.) to refer to the product of one way of abstracting from our visual sensations. It will be part of my argument that, according to Descartes, such abstractions are confused and involve acts of false judgment, though my defense and elaboration of this point must wait till section 3. I will also sometimes use the term "color" to refer to the views of the color realist; this second use will be indicated by quote marks. Besides color terms, one must also be wary of the expressions "sensation" and "sense perception." In contemporary discussions, these terms are often used to refer to qualia, and thus presuppose a subjectivist account of secondary qualities. I do not think Descartes ever intended to use these terms in this sense, for reasons that will become clear in section 3. I shall use these expressions, as I believe Descartes typically does, to mean the perception *of an object.* In a well-known passage from the Third Meditation, Descartes states that all ideas—sensory or otherwise—are *as if* the images of things.[9] I take this to mean that all cognition, even non-veridical perception, is intentional.

This paper consists of two main parts and is divided according to Descartes' two purposes in the passages on color, as described above. In the next section, I examine those places in Descartes' scientific works where he develops a mechanical theory of vision and mounts a direct attack on the Resemblance Thesis. In keeping with my thesis, I argue that that is all he takes himself to be doing in these passages. We shall find him using the locution "what we call color" repeatedly to indicate the nominalist position that, with respect to bodies, "color" is just a name that we ordinarily use to refer to the physical causes of our sensations in the absence of a scientific account of the nature of these causes.[10] Contrary to the dispositionalist and physicalist interpretations, Descartes does not intend to be offering a realist account of color that locates such putative entities in bodies. In section 3, I take up those passages where Descartes diagnoses the source of the Scholastic Resemblance Thesis and explains how to guard against it, so that our visual sensations can be perceived clearly and distinctly. Some of these passages are ones in which Descartes is purported by commentators to affirm a subjectivist account of color. But I argue that in these cases too he uses the term "color" merely as a name, either for the external causes of our visual sensations or, more typically, for the sensations themselves. In this third section, I also analyze Descartes' account of how much is "given" in sense experience or, in his terminology, "taught by nature." Many contemporary philosophers take it for granted that "color qualia" are given in sense experience as discrete entities. It is traditionally assumed that Descartes shares this view, indeed, that his philosophy constitutes the *locus classicus* of qualia. But, on the interpretation developed here, Descartes would say that what philosophers call "color qualia" are merely the products of false judgment. This result will uncover the underlying philosophical motivation for his color nominalism.

[9] AT 7:37, CSM 2:25. References to Descartes' work are abbreviated as follows: AT: *Oeuvres de Descartes*, 11 vols., revised edition, Charles Adam and Paul Tannery, eds. (Paris: J. Vrin/C.N.R.S. 1964–1976). Passages are cited by volume and page numbers, respectively, separated by a colon. All English translations are based on *The Philosophical Writings of Descartes*, trans. John Cottingham, Robert Stoothoff, Dugald Murdoch, and (for vol. 3) Anthony Kenny (abbreviated as CSM(K)) (Cambridge: Cambridge University Press, 1984), and *Discourse on Method, Optics, Geometry, and Meteorology, trans.* and *ed.* Olscamp, P. J. (abbreviated as O) (Indianapolis: Bobbs-Merrill, 1965.). Any divergences from these translations are my own.

[10] These may only be occasional causes. I remain neutral in this paper on the debate whether Descartes was an occasionalist concerning body–body or body–mind causation.

2. Descartes' mechanical theory of vision and his polemic against the Resemblance Thesis

I begin with a brief discussion of Descartes' mechanical theory of vision, as he presents it in the *Optics* and the *Meteorology*. Some commentators have argued that in the course of laying out this theory, Descartes makes various metaphysical claims about the nature of "color" itself. But I shall argue that he is exclusively concerned with explaining vision. What have looked to commentators like metaphysical assertions are in fact claims about the external causes of visual perception.

Descartes' account of color vision is closely related to, and even depends on, his account of the perception of light. The following passage from the *Optics* gives one a sense of this relation.

> Regarding light and colour . . . we must suppose our soul to be of such a nature that what makes it have the sensation of light is the force of the movements taking place in the regions of the brain where the optic nerve-fibres originate, and what makes it have the sensations of colour is the manner of these movements. (AT 6:130–31, CSM 1:167)

This passage provides a rough sketch of Descartes' theory of color vision and its relation to his theory of light perception, but the full story is more complicated. What he envisages is a complex causal process in which extremely small particles emitted from a light source are deflected from the surface of an object and impinge on our retina. The motions of these particles are then transmitted to the fibres in our optic nerve, which, in turn, terminate at our pineal gland, where mind–body interaction purportedly occurs. As is well known, Descartes holds that cognition occurs solely in the mind, though he often stresses this point since it deviates from the Scholastic view.

This is Descartes' general account of color and light perception, but he offers more specific details about color vision by focusing on the motions of the particles involved. These particles undergo two different kinds of motion—rectilinear and rotational. The colors we perceive objects as having depend on the relation between these kinds of motion. We see red when the particles' spin (or rotation) greatly exceeds that of their rectilinear motion, yellow when their spin only slightly exceeds the other motion, green when they spin a bit more slowly, and blue when they spin more slowly still (*Meteorology*, AT 6:333, O 337–8).

Part of the goal of Descartes' general theory of optics was to showcase the power of the new mechanistic science to explain natural phenomena and to champion its superiority over Scholastic-Aristotelian accounts.[11] The latter assume that perception requires the transmission of intentional forms or species from the external object being perceived to the sense organs of the perceiver, through a medium such as air. Perception takes place because the sense organs of the perceiver receive something

[11] See Atherton (1990, 22f) and Wolf-Devine (1993, 1–9).

that is formally identical to what is in the object. In the case of color perception, this means that the "color" we perceive resembles, or even has the same nature as, the "color" in the object itself.[12]

In all of his writings on light and color, Descartes mounts a direct assault on the Resemblance Thesis and takes every opportunity to emphasize the important contrast between the Scholastic view and the mechanical theory of perception that he favors. For example, just after adumbrating the relation between color and light perception in the passage from the *Optics* cited above, Descartes adds: "But in all this there need be no resemblance between the ideas which the soul conceives and the movements which cause these ideas" (AT 6:130–1, CSM 1:167). He then tries to convince us of the falsity of the Resemblance Thesis by citing some of the many examples that eventually became standard among the mechanists. He notes that people struck in the eye seem to see sparks and flashes even if they shut their eyes or if they are in a dark place. Similarly, looking at a bright light can produce after-images with slowly fading colors. These phenomena can be intelligibly explained, he believes, only in mechanical terms. In the first case, the force of the blow sets the optic nerve-fibres in motion just as a bright light would do. In the second case, the optic nerve-fibres have been set in motion with such extraordinary force that it takes longer than usual for them to come to rest (AT 6:131, CSM 1:168). Earlier in the *Optics* he introduces the more famous blind-man analogy: merely by using a stick, a blind man can discern several differences between trees, rocks, water, etc. The implication is that by a similar set of processes involving only motion and resistance, and without any resemblance between the cause in the world and the sensory effects in us, one is able to perceive objects as being red, yellow, green, etc. By considering this analogy, "your mind will be delivered from all those little images flitting through the air, called 'intentional forms', which so exercise the imagination of the philosophers" (AT 6:85, CSM 1:153).

In the course of developing his polemic against the Resemblance Thesis, Descartes enlists the locution "what we call" that I mentioned in the Introduction. In the opening paragraphs of both the *Treatise on Light* and the *Optics*, he speaks of what we *call* color and/or of what we *call* light. In the first paragraph of the former, for example, he writes:

> The subject I propose to deal with in this treatise is light, and the first point I want to draw to your attention is that there may be a difference between the sensation we have of light (i.e. the idea of light which is formed in our imagination by the mediation of our eyes) and what it is in the objects that produces this sensation within us (i.e. what it is in a flame or the sun that *we call by the name "light")*. For although everyone is commonly convinced that the ideas we have in our mind are wholly similar to the objects from which they proceed, nevertheless I cannot see any reason which assures us that this is so. (AT 11:3, CSM 1:81; emphasis added)

[12] The Scholastics actually held something stronger than resemblance or qualitative similarity. They maintained that there is a formal identity between what is in the object and what is in the mind. See note 17 in Edwin McCann's chapter in this volume for an excellent discussion of how Descartes and Locke reinterpret the Scholastic notion of formal identity in terms of resemblance.

Descartes draws an important distinction here between our sensations (of light) and what it is in the material world that causes these sensations so as to undermine the Scholastic assumption that there is some resemblance or similarity between cause and effect. He uses the phrase "what . . . we call by the name 'light' " to refer to this cause, so that we are not misled by language into supposing that there is such a resemblance, or that the light that we perceive (in effect, the light that can be abstracted from our sensation) is actually in objects. The problem is that we ordinarily use the very same term for our sensations as we do to denominate the cause of these sensations in bodies. In later writings, Descartes explains why this is so.

> Corresponding to the different ways in which the nerves are moved, or have their normal motion checked, various different sensations are produced in the mind; and this is how the various tactile qualities get their names. <We *call* these qualities hardness, heaviness, heat, humidity and so on, but all that is meant by these terms is that the external bodies possess what is required to bring it about that our nerves excite in the soul the sensations of hardness, heaviness, heat etc.> (AT 8A:318, CSM 1:282; emphasis added)[13]

Descartes is concerned exclusively with tactile qualities in this particular passage, but his main point can be generalized. The mechanical properties of bodies that we call light, color, heat, or hardness, etc. receive their names from the sensations that they causally produce in our mind. Although Descartes does not say this here, the obvious reason why we pick out the external causes of our sensations in this way is that the real nature of these causes is unavailable to us in sense experience. The latter familiarizes us only with the effects of these causes.

This semantic point is crucial for understanding those passages in Descartes' scientific writings in which he is purported by commentators to endorse a realist account of color. One leading example of this occurs in the opening section of the *Optics*. As noted above, Descartes begins both the *Treatise on Light* and the *Optics* by invoking the "what is called . . . " locution. In the latter, he uses this locution twice, once in the case of light and once in the case of color, in the course of a single paragraph.

> I would have you consider the light in bodies we *call* "luminous" [*nomme lumineux*] to be nothing other than a certain movement, or very rapid and lively action, which passes to our eyes through the medium of the air and other transparent bodies, just as the movement or resistance of the bodies encountered by a blind man passes to his hand by means of his stick. . . . Nor will you find it strange that by means of this action we can see all sorts of colours. *You may perhaps even be prepared to believe that in the bodies we call "coloured"* [*nomme colorés*] *the colours are nothing other than the various ways in which the bodies receive light and reflect it against our eyes.*
> (AT 6:84, CSM 1:153; emphasis added)

[13] CSM use brackets here and elsewhere to indicate material added in the French translation of Descartes' original Latin text. Abbé Claude Picot produced the translation, which Descartes enthusiastically endorsed (see AT 9B:1, CSM 1:179).

Some commentators have read the last sentence of this citation as an endorsement of color physicalism, as defined above.[14] But given our previous discussion, we can see why such a reading is misguided. Descartes does not identify "colors" with the mechanical properties of bodies. On the contrary, he identifies what "we call 'colored'" with those properties. Standard readings of this passage consistently overlook this locution, which is essential for understanding the central point. Descartes is relying, as he had in the *Treatise on Light*, on a distinction between our sensations and the mechanical properties of bodies that cause those sensations so as to combat the Scholastic prejudice that our sensations resemble their causes. Far from making any positive ontological claims about the status of color, he employs the "what-we-call" locution to pick out the external causes of our color sensations in a metaphysically neutral way, for our ordinary way of referring to these causes encourages the Resemblance Thesis.

Descartes refers to "what we call color" several other times in the *Optics* and *Meteorology*. A couple of notable instances of this occur in the former, in a context where we are told how the minute particles that are responsible for light and color perception behave when they interact with different types of surface. Bodies with surfaces that break up the particles that meet them and remove their force "we call black"; other bodies, with highly polished surfaces that cause the particles to be reflected without changing their spin, "we call white." Descartes notes that there are still other bodies whose surfaces are such that they increase or diminish the spin of the particles that graze them, just as a racquet might do to a tennis ball. Those bodies we call red, yellow, blue, etc. (AT 6:90–2, O 71–3).[15] Once again, he is not making any metaphysical claims about the status of color. In particular, he is not identifying "color" with a reflectance or other micro-structural property of the surface of bodies, as a cursory reading might lead one to suppose. His use of the phrase "what we call" demonstrates that he is merely attempting to identify the mechanical causes of our sensations, in keeping with his scientific program.

To further confirm this interpretation, it is important to note that Descartes uses the "what-we-call" locution in the same way in other contexts. Most notably, in the *Treatise on Light*, he attempts to explain the various observable effects of fire by appealing to motion alone. Whereas Scholastic philosophers imagine a different property for every observable effect of fire, Descartes envisages only one. The violent motion of the fine particles of fire explain how it is able to consume wood and, similarly, how it "produces us with heat and light . . . [I]t is this motion alone which *is called* [*s'appelle*] now 'heat' and now 'light,' according to the different effects it

[14] See e.g. Atherton (2004, 28) and Cottingham (1990, 231–32). Also see Stephen Menn (1995), who draws the same conclusion on the basis of several other passages.

[15] Descartes does not explicitly use the "what-we-call" locution in this final statement but it is implicit given what he says before. This statement anticipates the passage from the *Meteorology*, discussed above, where we are told that the subtle particles produce different color sensations depending on the relation between their rectilinear and rotational motions.

produces" (AT 11:9, CSM 1:84; emphasis added). Here, again, Descartes is making a semantic point about how we pick out the properties of bodies on the basis of the sensations they occasion in us. But what is especially noteworthy is his further claim that in some cases we use different terms to denominate the very same property. The "what-we-call" locution demonstrates that Descartes intends only to be developing a scientific explanation of the observable effects of fire in a way that does not require resemblance (there is nothing in bodies "which is similar to the idea we conceive of heat").[16] It would strain credulity to suppose that he is offering a reductive metaphysical analysis of the nature of heat and light in terms of the very same mechanical property. The similarity with the passages on color from the *Optics* is obvious.

So far, we have been focusing on Descartes' early scientific writings. Some commentators claim that he continues to identify colors with properties of bodies in his later writings, especially the *Principles of Philosophy*. Indeed, there is one passage in this work that Cottingham and others cite as definitive evidence that he subscribed to a form of dispositionalism. As we shall see, this reading is mistaken. In the passage in question, Descartes continues to speak of "what we call color" as a way of referring to the mechanical properties of bodies that cause our sensations, without making any positive metaphysical claims about the nature of "color" in the realist's sense.

The passage in question appears at the very end of the *Principles* 4, within a series of twelve articles (188–199) in which Descartes once again develops a mechanical theory of sense perception, but in a much more compressed manner than he had in his earlier works. In the first of these articles, he reveals that he had originally intended to extend the *Principles*, with a fifth part on living things and a sixth part on man. But he confesses to being unclear about some of this other material. So to avoid delaying the publication of the first four parts, he appends to part 4 this short series of articles, which he intends to fill in the gaps of what he would have written, had he more time. In the first of these articles, he acknowledges that he owes the reader an explanation of (the sensations of) colors, smells, sounds, and the like. The explanation that follows is not an ontological account of sensible qualities, but a scientific account of how external objects produce sensations in our mind by transmitting motions to the various nerve endings in our body. Several sections are devoted to the internal senses and to each of the five external senses, with an emphasis on the different nerves involved in each case. There are references along the way, especially in the case of vision, to the much fuller treatment of these issues in the *Optics* and *Meteorology*. Descartes also sounds a familiar theme by arguing that sense perception does not require resemblance between sensations and their mechanical causes. It is simply in the nature of the mind to perceive various sensations as a result of the motions in our nerves (AT 8A:315–20, CSM 1:279–84). To convince us that causation does not require resemblance, he even cites some of the very same examples as he had in his earlier works—his famous sign analogy, first discussed in

[16] AT 11:10, CSM 1:84.

the *Treatise on Light*; the example of after-images that was discussed in the *Optics*—as well as a new analogy: when a sword strikes our body the ensuing pain resembles neither the motions of the sword nor the motions of the body that is cut (AT 8A:322, CSM 284). As before, Descartes champions the intelligibility of mechanical explanations of sensory phenomena and their superiority over Scholastic explanations in terms of substantial forms and occult qualities. We can understand how the mechanical properties (or the size, shape, and motion) of the corpuscles of one body can produce motion in another body, such as our own. But it is unintelligible how these same properties could produce something different in kind such as forms and real qualities, or how these qualities and forms could produce motions in other bodies, which would be required in order to affect our sense organs (AT 8A:322, CSM 285).

On the heels of this last remark, he concludes

> it must certainly be concluded that those things which, in external objects, *we call by the names* [*nominibus indigitamus*] of light, colour, odour, taste, sound, heat, cold—as well as the other tactile qualities and even what are called "substantial forms"—are, so far as we can see, simply various arrangements [*dispositiones*] in those objects which make them able to set up various kinds of motions in our nerves <which are required to produce all the various sensations in our soul>.
>
> (AT 8A:322–3, emphasis added)

This is the main passage that Cottingham, Stephen Gaukroger, Nicholas Jolley, and others cite as the proof text that Descartes endorses a proto-Lockean view of colors as dispositions or powers to produce sensations in us.[17] The main motivation for this reading is that the Latin term *dispositiones* is transliterated in the authoritative English edition of Descartes' works (CSM) as "dispositions." But as Celia Wolf-Devine notes, this rendering is misleading, for it suggests our contemporary understanding of dispositions as inherent powers. However, *dispositiones* literally means "arrangement," as in the spatial arrangement of the parts of bodies, along with their mechanical properties. This is why I have translated it as such here.[18] The larger context of this passage strongly supports this translation as well. Descartes has been arguing for the intelligibility of mechanical explanations of causal interactions between bodies over and against Scholastic explanations. "We can very well understand how the different size, shape and motion of the particles of one body can produce various local motions in another body," but not how substantial forms and real qualities could produce such changes. Later, in the passage in question, Descartes is best read as referring once again to these particles and their mechanical properties or *dispositiones*.

[17] See references in note 5.

[18] This is also how Rodger Miller and Reese Miller translate it (1991, 282) in their edition of the *Principles*. The term *disposition* in the French edition requires the same reading. Descartes explicitly uses the term *disposition* in this sense in the *Treatise on Light* (AT 11:9, CSM 1:84). Incidentally, Robert Boyle often uses the English word "disposition" to mean arrangement, speaking frequently for example of the "disposition of the parts" of matter. See, e.g. 1979, 20, 30, and 72. As Robert Anstey observes, however, this is not Boyle's only use of the term (2000, 108, notes 4–6).

Given these semantic and contextual considerations, the dispositionalist interpretation of Descartes on color is a non-starter, but one might still be tempted to suppose that he is making an ontological claim in this passage: if colors are not dispositions then they are the arrangements of the size, shape, and motion of the parts of bodies (what Boyle and Locke refer to as "textures"). Here again the suggestion is that he is endorsing color physicalism.[19] But there are features of this passage that indicate decisively that he did not see himself as making any sort of ontological claim about colors, etc. He simply does not intend to be staking out a position on the status of so-called secondary qualities. For one thing, as I argued above, Descartes' central aim in the larger series of articles in which this passage appears is to offer a mechanical theory of sense perception, in lieu of the complete theory of man that he would have provided had he written Part 6 of the *Principles*. He does not have any metaphysical pretensions concerning the ontological status of secondary qualities in any of the other articles in this series. On the contrary, he is merely concerned with identifying and explaining the causes of our sensations in external objects and in the motions those objects produce in our nerves. Moreover, this particular passage appears in one of two consecutive articles (197–198) in which Descartes attempts to defeat the Scholastic view that our sensations resemble their external causes, as he had in the *Treatise on Light*, the *Optics,* and the *Meteorology*. As before, he speaks in the passage in question of what "we call by the names of light, color, odor, taste, sound, heat, cold" so that we are not misled by language into supposing that there is such a resemblance. Recall that these are the terms that we ordinarily use to pick out the properties of bodies that cause our sensations. Since we are not acquainted with the nature of these properties in experience we use our sensations to denominate them. But now that we have completed the Cartesian scientific program we are in a position to understand that what we have been unwittingly referring to all along are the size, shape, and motion of bodies. So Descartes is best read as providing a proper referent for our ordinary ways of speaking when we refer to colors, sounds, tastes, etc. in bodies. The phrase "what we call" indicates that he is speaking with the vulgar and the Scholastic, and not offering a positive ontological account of so-called secondary qualities. In particular, he is not saying that we *should* call the mechanical properties of bodies by these names. If one needed any further confirmation of this reading, notice that he says "even what are called 'substantial forms' . . . are simply various arrangements." If Descartes were intending to identify secondary qualities with the mechanical properties of bodies then he would be doing the same with substantial forms. But surely he does not think that substantial forms are in bodies in any philosophically interesting sense. On the contrary, he is simply making a semantic point. As with the terms for qualities, the Scholastics use the term "substantial forms" to refer to whatever it is in bodies that enables them to affect other bodies.

[19] Without affirming this reading herself (given her dualist interpretation), Atherton (2004, 29) asserts that the text seems to support it.

But the only things in bodies that could intelligibly serve that role are the size, shape, and motion of their parts. So the Scholastics must (unwittingly) be referring to them.[20]

The primary aim of this section has been to show that Descartes uses the term "color" in his scientific writings merely as a name for whatever properties in bodies cause our visual sensations, without intending to make any positive metaphysical claims about the nature of "color" as such. This goes a long way toward establishing that he is a color nominalist, and undermining the physical and dispositionalist interpretations. However, in some of the passages that we have considered, especially from the *Optics* and *Meteorology*, Descartes speaks of color as an appearance or as the sensory effect of mechanical causes. This has led some commentators to suppose that he endorses, or at least flirts with, a subjectivist account of color.[21] In the next section, I confront this interpretation directly and show why Descartes does not accord any status to such putative entities, not even as sensations. I also uncover the motivations for his color nominalism.

3. "Colors" as the products of false judgment

My claim that Descartes is a color nominalist recalls Galileo's oft-cited remark about the status of sensible qualities from the *Assayer*:

> [*T*]*astes, odors, colors, and so on are no more than mere names so far as the object in which we place them is concerned*, and . . . reside only in the consciousness. Hence if the living creature were removed, all these qualities would be wiped away and annihilated.
>
> (Stillman Drake 1957, 274; emphasis added)

Galileo is clearly a nominalist about secondary qualities with respect to objects in the physical world. As he says here, insofar as we ascribe them to bodies, tastes, odors, colors, etc. are merely names. But he ultimately appears to be a subjectivist about secondary qualities, inasmuch as he locates them in the consciousness of perceivers. Given the seductive force of the subjectivist reading, one might be tempted to ascribe this limited form of nominalism to Descartes. But I shall argue in this section that he is a more thoroughgoing color nominalist than Galileo. For Descartes, colors, sounds, odors, etc. are merely names, whether ascribed to bodies or to the mind.

To illustrate the view I wish to attribute to Descartes, I would like to begin by considering one way of characterizing some of the phenomenological facts about our sensory experience. What these facts are exactly is controversial, but I take the following description to be one compelling account of them. Suppose one is sitting on

[20] The following remark to Regius admits of a similar treatment. "When you discuss colours, I cannot see why you exclude blackness, since the other colours too are only modes. I would simply say: 'Blackness is commonly counted as a colour, yet is its nothing but a certain arrangement'" (AT 3:372–73, CSMK 3:182–83). Although he does not explicitly use the locution here, Descartes is best read as saying "what are called" colors or blackness . . .

[21] See e.g. Wolf-Devine (1993, 47).

a beach, feeling the heat of the sun on one's skin, smelling the salty brine of the air, listening to the sound of the waves crashing, hearing the occasional cry of a seagull as it flies overhead, and watching two people toss a red beach ball back and forth, etc. Part of what the example brings out is the complexity of one's experience, which involves multiple sensory modalities (vision, audition, taste, touch, etc.) and complexity within each of those modalities (William James speaks aptly here of a "blooming, buzzing confusion"). One can, of course, draw distinctions within a complex sense perception by abstracting or selectively focusing. Since we are interested in the case of color, suppose one focuses exclusively on the visual elements in this perception. What is it that one sees? (Again, I am interested only in the phenomenological content of the experience.) Even that is highly complex: two sunbathers tossing a beach ball against a background of sea, sand, and sky. Suppose one attends to a single object within this visual scene, such as the red beach ball. Notice that one does not see colors as such. Rather, what one typically sees is a colored *object*—for example, a red beach ball, a yellow umbrella, etc.—with extension and shape. One can of course discriminate the redness of the beach ball from its round shape. One can also discriminate the redness of the beach ball from the blueness of the sky. But the important point is that the ability to make these discriminations does not require one to perceive or imagine redness apart from a shaped object, and fortunately so, for one cannot do that. One might object that one does not always see something shaped. Suppose, for example, one is looking through an opthamologist's apparatus and sees only blue. But even in that case one is seeing something extended—a blue color expanse.[22] Berkeley recognized that one cannot see or imagine extension apart from color, but the reverse is also true.

With this description of the phenomenology of our color experiences in hand, let us attempt to analyze what it is that the subjectivist means when she says that "colors" are properties of the mind or that "colors" are merely sensations. Using Descartes' favorite locution in this context, one can ask what should be an easy question to answer, but on the description above turns out to be an embarrassing one: what is the subjectivist calling a "color"? As noted above, what one experiences is not color as such, divorced from all geometric properties, but a colored thing with a determinate size and shape (or at least extension). As we have seen, one can abstract from the other sense modalities and attend only to vision. One can abstract further by attending to one object within this field, noticing in the case at hand that it is a red, round ball. Such abstract ways of attending to one's sensory experience are all legitimate. But this last way of abstracting marks the limits of our abilities. There is no sensuous perception of "color" apart from extension and, typically, shape. So what is the subjectivist calling a "color," the complex "redness-roundness"? Presumably not, for one might just as well call that confused complex "shape" or "beach ball." It would seem that what the subjectivist is reaching for with the

[22] Even this example might be idealized. Wouldn't one see the eyepiece, one's eyelashes, etc.? Might the brain also generate black spots or something to contrast with the red field?

term "color" is something that cannot be perceived or imagined, something that could only be the product of an illegitimate abstraction—that is, something non-sensuous! The conclusion to be drawn here is that the subjectivist position is unintelligible. The subjectivist could, of course, retreat to the position that all it means to say that "colors are in the mind" is that the sense perception of a colored object is in the mind. That position *is* intelligible, but also trivial and largely uncontroversial in the early modern period.[23] As such, it hardly constitutes an account of the status of so-called secondary qualities.

It might be thought that Berkeley was the first to appreciate that we do not see colors as such, only colored *things*; but in fact, there is at least one place in Descartes' writings in which he affirms this too. The passage in question (from the *Regulae*) has not received the attention it deserves because it appears in a complex context. As in the scientific writings on vision that we have already examined, Descartes is concerned to defeat the Resemblance Thesis. Contrary to this Thesis, he wants to establish that the external shape of bodies plays a causal role in all sense perception, whether it be of tactile sensations of the shape of a body, tactile sensations of heat and cold, visual sensations of color, etc. All sense perception occurs literally in the same way in which wax takes on an impression from a seal (AT 10:412, CSM 1:40). In this context he writes: "the concept of shape is so simple and common that it is involved in everything perceivable by the senses. For example, whatever you may suppose color to be, you will not deny that it is extended and consequently has shape" (AT 10:413, CSM 1:40–41). The latter sentence might seem to be gesturing at a realist account of the nature of "color," or at least suggesting that some such account is in the offing. But the context indicates otherwise. As in his scientific writings, what he means by "color" here is "what we call color"—in other words, whatever it is in bodies that causes our sensations. So one should read this sentence as: "whatever you may suppose the corporeal cause of our perception of a colored object to be, you will not deny that it is extended and consequently has shape." In the citation as a whole he intends to be drawing an analogy: just as the perception of a colored object depends *phenomenologically* on the perception of extension and shape, so likewise the sensation of a colored object depends *causally* on the actual extension and shape of bodies. He is using the phenomenological point that we have been discussing to motivate his mechanistic, anti-Scholastic causal thesis.

Descartes would agree then with the criticism of the subjectivist view developed above. I shall adduce further evidence for this conclusion in this section. Moreover, I shall argue that he would say—and in fact does say in one instance—that treating "redness" (or, in his example, "whiteness") as a quality involves not only an illegitimate abstraction but also a false judgment. Any attempt to reify so-called secondary qualities in this way meets with the same Cartesian objection. This is ironic because, as noted in

[23] With the exception of Malebranche, who holds that sense perception has both a mental and an ideational component, the latter of which is in God.

the Introduction, legend has it that after banishing secondary qualities from the physical world, and finding no other place to locate them, Descartes sweeps them into the dustbin of the mind. But his criticism of the Scholastic theory of real qualities is deeper than legend would have us believe. He objects not merely to locating "colors" in bodies, but to reifying them in the first place. One only perpetuates the latter mistake by relegating such putative entities to the mind.

I have been characterizing the negative side of Descartes' nominalism, but as a positive thesis, nominalism is primarily a claim about the meaning of words and how we use language. As we saw in the previous section, Descartes often uses the locution "what we call color" to refer in a metaphysically neutral manner to the properties of bodies that cause our sensations. But in passages where he sees himself as diagnosing the Scholastic mistake of attributing colors to bodies, he sometimes applies this expression to the sensations themselves. He speaks of "what we call the sensation of color" and of "sensations we call color, etc." The fact that he uses the "what-we-call" locution in this context shows once again that he sees himself as speaking with the vulgar and that we should thus be wary of how we understand these expressions. In particular, the genitive character of the expression "the sensation of color" might tempt us to suppose that colors are objects of perception. But what we call the "sensation of color" is in fact the perception of a colored object, regarded in an abstract manner. We might ordinarily refer to such a perception in this way precisely because we are regarding it abstractly. But we should beware of reifying this abstraction.

In arguing that Descartes is a color nominalist, who refuses to reify colors in any way, part of what I am denying is that he is committed to phenomenal qualia.[24] This result is surprising, for in contemporary debates in the philosophy of mind, Descartes' work is often cited as the *locus classicus* of qualia. But I think this is misguided. It is of course true that all Cartesian thought, sensory or otherwise, has a "phenomenological character," if we understand this term in the broad sense. Indeed, one might think that phenomenological character is the mark of the mental. But here one must keep in mind that Descartes takes sense perception to be highly confused. The confusion is important because it means that, although our sense experience has a phenomenological character or feel, it does not resolve neatly into discrete qualitative elements that can, in his terms, be clearly and distinctly perceived. Advocates of qualia take them to be "given" in sense experience, but I intend to show in what follows that, on Descartes' view, most of what we take to be given is in fact the product of false judgments, including what contemporary philosophers call "color qualia."

In the Sixth Meditation, and at greater detail in the *Principles*, Descartes takes up the issue of how much is given in sense experience. The specific question he focuses on there is not whether color qualia are given, but whether it is given that colors and other

[24] De Rosa (2007) denies this too, but for reasons very different from the ones marshaled here.

so-called sensible qualities are properties of bodies. As we shall see, seeing why the latter is not given will shed light on why Descartes thought that color qualia are not given either.

Now, Descartes does not speak of the "given" as such. Instead, he uses the phrase "taught by nature," where by "nature" he means one's nature as a mind–body union. This includes "the totality of things bestowed on me by God"—that is, all of my faculties, including my senses (AT 7:82, 80; CSM 2:56). So the question, as he frames it, is whether my nature teaches me that so-called sensible qualities such as color are in bodies. Since not only the Scholastic but also the philosophically benighted person is inclined to attribute such qualities to bodies, one might expect the answer to be yes. One might think that the reason the ordinary person ascribes colors to bodies is precisely because her senses "teach her" that this is so. Is this suggestion correct?

Several commentators have been inclined to think so on the ground that sensations confusedly represent bodies as colored.[25] But, in the *Principles*, Descartes states unequivocally: "sensations of tastes, smells, sounds, heat, cold, light, colors, and so on . . . do not represent anything located outside our thought" (AT 8A:35, CSM 1:219). I take this statement to constitute strong evidence that Cartesian sensations do not represent anything non-extensive in bodies.[26] Some commentators, however, maintain that Descartes may be saying only that our sensations do not *successfully* represent the properties of bodies.[27] On this reading, the passage is consistent with the view that sensations purport to represent bodies as colored, but succeed only in *mis*representing them. I submit that if Descartes were committed to this more qualified position, he would have indicated it. But, in fact, what he says in the remainder of this passage, and in the passage from the Sixth Meditation that we have been discussing, rules strongly against this reading. He maintains in both contexts that most of what we ascribe to our senses is the result of false judgments that we formed in early childhood and that now have become so habituated that we forget that we are making them. The judgment that the senses represent bodies as colored is included among these. So the senses do not even purport to represent objects as having colors, sounds, odors, etc.; they are only *judged* to represent in this way.[28] I develop this point in what follows by examining both texts at length.

Let us return to the passage from the Sixth Meditation with which we began. Descartes draws an important distinction between things taught by nature, in the sense already described, and things that only *seem* to have been taught by nature.

[25] See, e.g. Paul Hoffman (1996), Alison Simmons (1999), and Wilson (1999).

[26] I say "non-extensive" here because, as noted in the Introduction, I take Cartesian sensations always to be of an extended object, even if they only confusedly represent extension.

[27] Simmons expressed this view to me in conversation. Also see Lisa Downing's essay in this volume. Downing expresses sympathy for a view like Simmons', but at one point wonders whether Descartes is committed to the even stronger claim in this passage that sensations are not even as if of objects, something I deny in the my previous note.

[28] Here, and in the further discussion that follows, I owe much to Alan Nelson's work on Descartes' theory of sensory error (1996).

Among the former class he includes the fact that he has a body and that it is ill when he senses pain and that it needs food or drink when he experiences hunger or thirst. Nature also teaches him that his mind is intimately joined to his body—famously, not as a sailor is present in a ship, but in such a way that they compose one thing. Finally, nature teaches him that there are other bodies in the vicinity of his own, some of which are to be pursued and others avoided. Indeed, when these other bodies produce different sensations in him of colors, sounds, odors, tastes and the like, he is correct to conclude that these bodies possess variations corresponding to—though perhaps not resembling—the sensations themselves (AT 7:80–1, CSM 2:56).

Descartes' remarks here must be understood in light of his teleological account of the senses. The purpose of senses is not to deliver metaphysical truth about the nature of physical objects but to preserve the mind–body union by informing the mind of what is beneficial or harmful (*commoda . . . vel incommoda*) to the body to which it is united (AT 7:83, CSM 2:57). Thus, the only things that are taught by nature are those that serve this function. Descartes wants us to recognize that the teachings of nature are quite modest. Indeed, the list of things just given appears to be exhaustive.[29] By contrast, the class of things that only seems to have been taught by nature, but in fact results from "a custom of judging inconsiderately," is much larger. This class includes the judgment that a space in which there is nothing stimulating one's senses is empty; that stars, towers and other distant objects have the same size and shape that they exhibit to the senses; *and*, apropos our topic, that the very same heat, colors, and tastes that one senses are in bodies (AT 7:82, CSM 2:57).[30] Descartes of course takes all of these judgments to be false. He concludes:

> My nature, then, teaches me indeed to flee those things that induce a sensation of pain and to pursue those things that induce a sensation of pleasure . . . But it does not appear that this nature teaches us, in addition, that from these sensory perceptions we should conclude anything about the things posited outside us without the prior examination of the intellect, for knowing the truth about these things seems to belong to the mind alone, and not to the composite.
>
> (AT 7:82–3, my translation)

Here Descartes rehearses a theme familiar from earlier meditations, namely that the intellect, not the senses, is the primary source of knowledge. What is importantly new, and almost universally neglected by commentators, is the claim that our senses do not even purport to teach us about the nature of bodies.

Why then do these other things *seem* to be taught by nature, if in fact they are not? Descartes' explanation here, which we shall see further developed in the *Principles*, is

[29] Simmons (1999) takes the teachings of nature (or, on her view, the intrinsic representational contents of our sensory ideas) to be much more robust, but I do not think that the texts bear this out.

[30] As noted in the Introduction and in the opening paragraphs of this section, one should understand each of the terms "heat," "colors," and "tastes" here as referring to the sense perception of an object, where the perception is being regarded abstractly. Descartes should be read as expressing concern that we do not reify these abstractions by supposing, as the Scholastic does, that they reside in bodies.

that we have formed these judgments from our early childhood (*ineunte aestate*) without reason and without any "real or positive propensity." Once formed, these judgments become so habituated that we no longer realize that we are making them. It is important for him to show that such judgments are voluntary and thus that we are responsible for holding them, for if the senses or the teachings of nature were to blame, then God would be a deceiver. Indeed, this discussion immediately precedes his attempts to develop a theodicy of sensory error analogous to the theodicy of intellectual errors that he had produced in the Fourth Meditation. Descartes concludes the present discussion by noting that we have a tendency to "pervert the order of nature" by using our sense perceptions, which again were given to us for the sole purpose of preserving the mind–body union, as "absolute rules" for discovering the essence of bodies. The senses may teach us that a given body, such as fire, causes heat and pain, but they do not give us any reason to suppose that heat is in the fire, any more than they persuade us that there is something in the fire resembling the pain. "There is simply reason to suppose that there is something in the fire, whatever it may eventually turn out to be, which produces in us the sensations of heat or pain" (AT 7:83).[31]

This last set of points echoes our discussion in the previous section and uncovers the relation between the issues treated there and the present ones. As in his scientific writings, Descartes is concerned to combat the Resemblance Thesis. He does so in this instance by stressing that our senses do not teach us that there is any resemblance between our sensations and the properties of bodies; the implication is that this too is a result of ill-considered judgments. The only thing that nature teaches us in this regard is that there is something in bodies that causes our sensations.[32] As we have seen, Descartes uses the locution "what we call colour, etc." in his scientific writings to refer to this unknown cause in a metaphysically neutral manner. Although he does not invoke it in the Sixth Meditation, the phrase reappears several times in the corresponding section of the *Principles*. This section occurs just before the passage cited above, in which Descartes denies that sensations of color, etc. represent bodies.

It is clear, then, that *when we say* [*cum dicimus*] that we perceive colours in objects, this is really just the same as saying that we perceive something in the objects whose nature we do not know, but which produces in us a certain very clear and vivid sensation which *we call the sensation of colour*. But the way in which we make our judgement can vary very widely. As long as we merely judge that there is in the objects (that is, in the things, whatever they may turn out to be, which are the source of our sensations) something whose nature we do not know, then we avoid error; indeed, we are actually guarding against error, since the recognition that we are ignorant of something

[31] Cf. Descartes' claim in his proof of the external world that we have a great (God-given) propensity to believe that bodies cause our sensations (Sixth Meditation, AT 7:79–80, CSM 2:55).

[32] It seems unlikely that Descartes is claiming that it is part of the "representational content" of our sensory ideas that they are caused by properties of bodies. In his proof of the existence of body, which appears earlier in the Sixth Meditation, he says that our sensory ideas occur against our will (AT 7:79, CSM 2:55). It is natural to suppose that he is relying again on this claim, which seems to count as one of the teachings of nature.

> makes us less liable to make any rash judgement about it. But it is quite different when we suppose that we perceive colours in objects. Of course, we do not really know what it is that *we are calling by the name "colour"* [*nomine coloris appellamus*]; and we cannot find any intelligible resemblance between the colour which we suppose to be in objects and that which we experience in our sensation. But this is something we do not take account of; and, what is more, there are many other features, such as size, shape and number which we clearly perceive to be actually or at least possibly present in objects in a way exactly corresponding to our sensory perception or understanding. And so we easily fall into the error of judging that *what is called colour* [*quod in objectis vocamus colorem*] in objects is something exactly like the colour that we sense; and we make the mistake of believing that we clearly perceive what we do not perceive at all.
>
> (I, 70; AT 8A:34-5; CSM 218; emphasis added)[33]

Descartes begins by noting that we sometimes *say* that we perceive colors in bodies. In the language of the Sixth Meditation, we sometimes speak as if this is something taught to us by nature. Taken literally, this is false. But there is another way of understanding this statement depending on the type of judgment that underlies it. For Descartes, truth attaches to judgments in the first instance and to things we say only secondarily. So, before determining the truth of any claim, we must first understand the judgment that grounds it. He aptly titles this section, "There are two ways of making judgments concerning the things that can be perceived by the senses: the first enables us to avoid error, while the second allows us to fall into error." We err, obviously, when we judge that colors are in objects, but we judge soundly if we suppose merely that there is something in bodies that causes our sensations. We judge correctly in the latter case because, as we just learned in the Sixth Meditation, this *is* one of the teachings of nature. The claim that we perceive colors in bodies is unproblematic so long as we understand it in terms of this second form of judgment. This might seem like a peculiar way of speaking, given the meaning Descartes wishes to attach to it: saying that we perceive colors in bodies does not seem to be a claim about the cause of our sensations. But Descartes' rendering seems less unnatural if we recall that the properties of bodies that we term "red," "green," "blue," etc. receive their names from the sensations they causally produce in us. This is why he speaks once again of "what is called colour": the term "colour" serves as a placeholder for these properties of which, prior to doing science, "we are ignorant."

I mentioned earlier that Descartes sometimes applies the "what-we-call" locution not to the causes of our sensations, but to the sensations themselves. The passage above is the main example of this: he speaks in the first sentence of "a clear and vivid sensation which *we call the sensation of colour.*" Why does he use this expression in this way? We just noted that the properties of bodies that we term "red," "green," "blue," etc. receive their names from the sensations they causally produce in us. But as I have been stressing throughout this section, we do not have sensations of color as such. Focusing just on the phenomenal character of our experience, we always sense a colored object with extension and—typically—shape. But we may abstract from the spatial properties

[33] I have slightly modified the CSM translation to make it more literal.

presented in such an experience; if we do, we might call this abstraction the "sensation of red," etc. The expression "sensation of colour" could have another meaning within ordinary language, which again is the idiom in which Descartes is speaking. If we think of "sensing" as a Rylean success verb, then "sensation of colour" means the sensation of a property of bodies that causes that perception. This second way of rendering the locution marks a return to what I said in the previous paragraph. The important point is that, on either rendering of this expression, Descartes is not reifying colors or, in particular, affirming a subjectivist account of secondary qualities.

The first way of understanding the phrase "sensation of colour" provides a resource for parsing two other lines in this passage that are potentially misleading and that might seem to suggest a subjectivist interpretation. Descartes speaks of the "the colour... which we experience in our sensation" and "the colour that we sense." Both of these remarks appear in a context in which Descartes is trying to explain why we ascribe colors to bodies. His explanation presupposes that we are already regarding the sense perception of a colored object abstractly. So what is being called "colour" in these two lines is, again, just this abstraction.

So what is Descartes' explanation for why we ascribe colors—or what we now understand to be mental abstractions from our sensations—to bodies? In the Sixth Meditation, we learned that we form these and other such judgments in childhood without any rational basis, but at the end of the passage above we are informed for the first time why we are tempted to make them. Descartes' explanation reinforces the point that they do not derive from the teachings of nature: we clearly and distinctly perceive that various mechanical properties are possible attributes of bodies and mistakenly suppose that there is a similar correspondence between our sensations of color and the properties of bodies that produce them.

In *Principles* I, 71, previously adumbrated, Descartes expands on this account of why we attribute colors to bodies, as part of a more general account of the causes of human error. As before, voluntary judgments formed in childhood, before we were in possession of our reason, are identified as the main culprit. Indeed, the title of this section states that the chief cause of error stems from the "prejudices" of childhood, where the Latin term *praejudicia* literally means to "pre-judge." But, for the first time, Descartes distinguishes various stages in our childhood development. An appreciation of these stages shows that what we attribute to bodies is more complicated than it would first appear, and that we must distinguish what the vulgar ascribe to bodies (or their surfaces) at various stages and what the Scholastic philosopher ascribes to them. Descartes is not very careful or explicit about the latter, for he is mainly concerned in this section with analyzing how the vulgar go wrong. But such a distinction is implicit in what he says. The Scholastic philosopher's mistake is rooted in the prejudices or "pre-judgments" of the vulgar, but also goes beyond them.[34]

[34] I am indebted to Alan Nelson for conversations about how to interpret this passage. All misinterpretations are of course my own.

Descartes states that in our very earliest years we distinguished neither our mind from our body, nor this mind-body union from external bodies—that is, me (qua union) from not me. These facts are important, especially the latter, because they show that in this first stage, the mind did not "refer" any of its sensations, including sensations of color, to things outside the union, "but merely felt pain when something harmful was happening to the body and felt pleasure when something beneficial occurred" (AT 8A:35, CSM 1:218). Descartes says that only later in our development, when we learned that we could control our body to pursue agreeable things and flee disagreeable ones, did we distinguish the mind–body union from the external objects that we were pursuing or avoiding. It is during this second stage that we judged that sizes, shapes, motions, etc., as well as tastes, odors, colors, and so on, are in bodies. It is important to appreciate, however, that there is only one set of judgments here, not two. In our childhood, we did not have a clear and distinct idea of body as pure extension and thus did not distinguish size, shape, and extension from other so-called qualities. So what we attributed to objects at this second stage is not "color" as such (as the Scholastic does), but a confused sensory idea that includes extension (e.g. we might attribute red-round-extension to the beach ball).

In the continuation of this passage, Descartes says that, unlike colors, light, tastes, smells, and so on, sizes, shapes, motions, etc. are "presented" (*exhibebantur*) to us in sense experience as things or modes of things. This statement is in keeping with my claim, first enunciated in the Introduction, that our sensations are always as if of extended objects. But here we must be careful. We should not read Descartes as saying that our sensations *distinctly* represent bodies as having mechanical properties for, as was just noted, what we sense is always highly confused. With respect to the representational content of my perceptions, I see things that are shaped and hear things that have locations, etc., but, by its very nature, sense perception does not present us with a pure idea of extension or its modes. However, a confused sensory grasp of extension can sometimes induce a clear and distinct intellectual awareness. On this point, it is helpful to compare the present passage with what Descartes says in the proof of the existence of body just a few sections later, in *Principles* II, 1. There he writes that "we sense, *or rather as a result of being impelled by the senses*, we clearly and distinctly perceive a certain matter which is extended in length, breadth, and depth; the diverse parts of which are endowed with various shapes and subject to diverse movements" (AT 8A:40, CSM 1:223; emphasis added). Descartes is claiming that a confused sense perception of body can (to use the Platonic language of innate ideas) "trigger" or "awaken" a clear and distinct perception of it. But it is only in the latter case that sizes, shapes, motions, and so on are *clearly and distinctly* presented as its modes.

Returning to article 71, Descartes concludes by stressing once again the most important lesson of our broader discussion—namely, that we, not our senses, are to blame for the erroneous metaphysical claims that we make about bodies. The source of these errors are false judgments that we form in childhood. Once formed, they become entrenched and so automatic that we do not realize that we are making them, but instead conclude (as a second-order judgment) that they are taught by nature or "presented" to us in sense experience.[35]

> [O]ur mind has been filled from earliest childhood with a thousand . . . prejudices; which it subsequently, in youth, did not remember having adopted without sufficient examination but accepted as most true and evident; as if known by perception or imparted to it by nature.
> (AT 8A; MM 33)

I have attended carefully to Descartes' account of what it is that we ordinarily ascribe to bodies because I think it helps to illustrate how he would respond to the claim that colors are mind-dependent properties, apropos the subjectivist interpretation. Colors are not presented to us in sense experience as properties of the mind, any more than they are presented as properties of bodies. Rather, what we call "colors" are merely the products of false judgment. Support for this argument from analogy can be found in a passage from Descartes' conversation with Burman, the student who interviewed him toward the end of his life. Burman was curious about a remark from the Third Meditation in which Descartes makes a point similar to the one discussed above from *Principles* I, 70, namely that the chief and most common mistake that we make is supposing that our sensory ideas resemble things outside us. So long as we consider these ideas simply as modes of thought and do not refer them to bodies, we avoid error.[36] Burman took this to mean that we cannot err about the ideas themselves. But, in his reply, Descartes corrects him:

> Even if I do not refer my ideas to anything outside myself, there is still subject-matter for error, since I can make a mistake with regard to the actual nature of the ideas. For example, I may consider the idea of colour, and say that it is a thing or a quality; or I may say that the colour itself, which is represented by this idea, is something of the kind. For example, I may say whiteness is a quality; and even if I do not refer this idea to anything outside myself—even if I do not say or suppose that there is any white thing—I may still make a mistake in the abstract, with regard to whiteness itself and its nature or the idea I have of it. (AT 5:152, CSMK 3:337)

According to this passage, I can err with respect to (what I call) the sensory idea of a color even if I do not refer this idea to anything outside myself, that is, even if I do not judge that it represents anything in the world. I do this, he suggests, when I judge that whiteness, for example, is a thing or quality. Now, it might be pointed out that although Descartes invites us to consider our sensory ideas without referring them to bodies, he does not specifically say that I err when I judge whiteness to be a quality of the *mind*. But for the purposes of showing that Descartes would reject a subjective account of colors as mind-dependent properties, this is not necessary, for he is best read in this passage as making a general point. If I regard whiteness as a quality or thing of any type, even "in the abstract," as he says, then I err. In other words, I err if I reify

[35] For a further statement of this view, see Descartes' discussion of the "three grades of sensation" in the Sixth Replies (AT 7:437–38, CSM 2:294–95).

[36] AT 7:37, CSM 2:26.

colors in any way, which would include treating them as modes of mind.[37, 38] Note the important contrast between Descartes' approach to these issues and contemporary discussions of qualia in the philosophy of mind. Friends of qualia take them to be given in experience, whereas for Descartes even the claim that there is a white quale is not something taught by nature, but the product of judgment. As I mentioned at the beginning of this section, however, I do not think that Descartes is denying that sensations (like all thought) have a phenomenological character. What he is denying is that this character can be specified or analyzed into discrete qualitative elements, each having distinctive natures.

We have just seen why Descartes would be opposed, for philosophical reasons, to treating colors as properties of the mind and thus would reject the subjectivist view. But what are we to say about those texts in which he is purported by commentators to endorse such a view? As it turns out, the texts in question raise many of the same issues as we have discussed above. So it will be easy to reinterpret them in light of previous considerations. Given space constraints, we will not be able to discuss them all, but nor will we need to, for they all admit of a similar treatment. I will focus on those that have seemed to commentators to provide the strongest case for subjectivism.

The passage most often cited in favor of this interpretation is *Principles* I, 68, which is part of the same context as articles 70–71, discussed above. In particular, the theme of avoiding error by suspending judgment about whether our sensory ideas resemble anything in the world is at work here too.

> In order to distinguish what is clear in this connection from what is obscure, we must be very careful to note that pain and colour and so on are clearly and distinctly perceived when they are regarded merely as sensations or thoughts. But when they are judged to be certain things existing outside our mind, there is no way of understanding what sort of things they are.
>
> (AT 8A:33; CSM 1:217)

It is easy to see how a superficial reading of this passage, taken out of context, seems to support the view that Descartes reduces putative things such as "colors" to sensations or thoughts. But if we read the passage *in* context, a very different interpretation emerges—one that squares with his color nominalism. Article 68 appears at the end of a series of articles devoted largely to Descartes' epistemology of created substances and their properties. This series begins in article 48, where Descartes the dualist claims to recognize "only two ultimate classes of things: first, intellectual or thinking things . . . ; and secondly, material things" (AT 8A:22–3, CSM 1:208–9). Many of the

[37] Andrew Pessin has independently developed a similar reading of this passage in an unpublished manuscript. For alternative readings, see Calvin Normore (1986, 226) and Raffaella De Rosa (2007, 197).

[38] Some commentators question the reliability of the *Conversation with Burman* since it is a second-hand report of what Descartes actually said. In his illuminating introduction to the translation of this work, Cottingham handily deflects such concerns (1976, xvi). Moreover, in this instance, Descartes' reply to Burman is of a piece with his remarks about the role that judgment plays in sensory error and confusion from the Sixth Meditation and *Principles*, as discussed above.

articles between 48 and 68 are devoted to explaining how the modes and attributes of these two types of thing (i.e. minds and bodies) can be known or perceived clearly and distinctly. At the end of article 48, he had promised that an account of how appetites, emotions, and sensations can be known was forthcoming; at long last, the title of article 66 announces a return to this topic: "How sensations, emotions and appetites may be clearly known, despite the fact that we are frequently wrong in our judgments concerning them" (AT 8A:32, CSM 1:216). In the previous article, Descartes had explained how, in general, "the modes of thought and extension are to be known" and gave as examples of the former acts of understanding, imagination, memory, and volition (ibid.). Sensations, emotions, and passions are further examples of modes of thought. It would appear from article 66 and following that Descartes postponed discussing these modes of thought—especially sensations—because of the confusion that results from our false judgments concerning them. It is more difficult to perceive distinctly that sensations are modes of mind than, say, volitions or memories, because of our tendency (mentioned in both 66 and 68) to judge that there is something in bodies that "resembles" our sensations. The main lesson of these articles then is that one can clearly and distinctly perceive sensations only if one regards them as modes of mind and refrains from judging that there is anything corresponding to them outside thought. To repeat, Descartes is trying to give an account of how our *sensations* are known, not how "colors" qua sensible qualities are known. He is saying that the only way to perceive our sensations clearly and distinctly is by regarding them as modes of mind and withholding judgment about whether they resemble anything outside our mind.[39]

One has a tendency to lose sight of this point when reading article 68 in isolation, for in the excerpt cited, Descartes speaks not of regarding sensations as modes of mind, but of regarding pain and color as sensations. But as we have seen, the terms for sensible qualities are systematically ambiguous. We typically use the terms "color," "smell," "taste," "sound," etc. to refer to the properties in bodies that occasion our sensations. But we also sometimes (albeit rarely) use these terms to refer to sensations themselves. This is especially true in the case of pain, which is one of the main examples at issue in both articles 67 and 68. So I submit that the terms "pain" and "colour" are being used here merely to refer to different sensations, for Descartes is making an epistemic claim about how our sensations can be clearly and distinctly perceived.

This reading of article 68 is further confirmed by the French translation of the passage, which removes part of the ambiguity in the Latin original:

> But, in order that we may distinguish here what there is of clarity in our sensations (*sentiments*) from that which is obscure, we observe, in the first place, that we clearly and distinctly know pain, colour, and the other sensations (*sentiments*) when we consider them simply as thoughts.
>
> (AT 9B:56)

[39] Note how well this reading chimes with *Principles* I, 70, as discussed above.

Descartes is clearly concerned here with how we come to know our sensations distinctly, and the terms "pain" and "colour" are used to refer to different examples of sensations, not to assert that "pain" and "colour," qua sensible qualities, are reducible to sensations. We perceive our sensations clearly and distinctly by regarding them merely as thoughts or modes of the mind and, again, by refraining from judging that there is anything in bodies "resembling" them (ibid.).

Despite his admonition to Burman not to reify colors (qua mental abstractions), Descartes sometimes seems to make this mistake himself. Most notably, referring to the *Principles*, he writes to Chanut:

> it must be remembered, while reading this book, that although I consider nothing in bodies except the sizes, shapes and motions of their parts, I claim none the less to explain the nature of light and heat and all other qualities that are perceivable by the senses; for I presuppose that these *qualities are only in our senses*, like pleasure and pain, and not in the objects which we perceive by the senses, in which there are only certain shapes and motions which cause *the sensations we call light, heat, etc.* This I did not explain and prove until the end of Part Four; nevertheless it is useful to know and observe it from the beginning of the book, so as to understand it better.
>
> (AT 5:291–2, CSMK 3:369; emphasis added)

The claim that qualities such as light and heat are "only in our senses" might seem to suggest that they are real entities that enjoy a status in the perceiver. That is how defenders of the subjectivist interpretation have tended to interpret such passages.[40] But we need not suppose that Descartes is contradicting what he tells Burman, for there is a sense in which sensible qualities are "in the senses" even on the nominalist reading that I favor, namely, we can abstract them from sensations. As noted in the beginning of this section, we cannot form an idea of, say, a particular shade of red apart from extension and shape, but we can selectively attend to one without attending to the other. Recall that we encountered a similar phrase in *Principles* I, 70, where Descartes refers to "the colour that we sense." We explained this expression in the same way. Support for this reading may be found, first, in the fact that he also speaks here to Chanut of "the sensations *we call* light, heat, etc." As in the passage from *Principles* I, 68, this remark indicates that Descartes sees himself as using terms for sensible qualities as mere names for our sensations, abstractly considered, and is not advancing a view about the nature of such qualities as such.

Secondly, Descartes refers in this letter to Chanut to the series of articles that conclude Part 4 of the *Principles*. As we discussed in section 2, the aim of those articles is to identify the mechanical causes of our sensations in external objects in an effort to

[40] Cf. a similar passage from the Sixth Replies: "[C]olours, smells, tastes and so on, are, I observed, merely certain sensations which exist in my thought, and are as different from bodies as pain is different from the shape and motion of the weapon that produces it" (AT 7:440, CSM 2:297). As in the *Principles* I, 68, Descartes is best read as using the terms for sensible qualities to refer to our sensations. Again, we would refer to sensations in these ways only after having abstracted from them. Descartes' aim in this passage, as in others that we have seen, is to combat the Resemblance Thesis, not to defend an account of the status of sensible qualities as such.

defeat the Scholastic Resemblance Thesis. General questions about the nature of sensible qualities are never broached, let alone the specific issue about whether such putative entities are reducible to sensations. If this is right, then it seems highly unlikely that Descartes sees himself as making a metaphysical claim about sensible qualities in this letter to Chanut, since it is written in the service of the passage from the *Principles*.[41]

4. Conclusion

The aim of this chapter has been to establish that Descartes is a color nominalist. Color and other so-called secondary qualities are merely names for either 1) the mechanical causes of our sensations in external objects or 2) the sensations themselves, considered abstractly. Thus, if one wants to say that there is a distinction between primary and secondary qualities within Descartes' philosophy, it is a distinction between the mechanical properties of bodies that figure into scientific explanations and, the merely nominal properties that play a useful role in our ordinary, pre-scientific conception of the world, but are ultimately dispensable within science.

In the course of defending these claims, I have developed systematic reinterpretations of those passages in which he is purported by commentators to be endorsing this or that account of the ontological status of color. Rather than doing that, he almost always engaged in one of two other projects that are closely related: 1) devising a scientific theory of color vision, according to which the mechanical properties of bodies cause our sensations without resembling them or 2) explaining how our sensations can be clearly and distinctly perceived, and how we can avoid error with respect to them, by withholding judgment about whether they resemble anything outside us. Both projects converge in the effort to defeat the Scholastic Resemblance Thesis. As part of this effort, Descartes uses the locution "what we call colour" in almost every one of his discussions of this topic. The point of this locution, I have argued, is to refer to the causes of our sensations in a metaphysically neutral manner. Descartes thinks that we ordinarily pick out the properties of bodies that cause our sensations on the basis of the sensations themselves. The danger of doing so is that it encourages us to suppose that our sensations do resemble their external causes. Thus, by invoking the locution "what we call," Descartes is explicitly warning us not to be misled by ordinary usage. This is ironic because commentators have almost universally ignored this expression, mistakenly drawing ontological conclusions from passages that were written with the opposite intention.

We discovered the underlying motivation for Descartes' color nominalism within his general account of how much is given in sensory experience or, in his terms, "taught by nature." Descartes thinks that the sole purpose of the senses is to preserve the mind–body union. Thus, the things taught by nature are highly limited and

41 Downing makes a similar point in her essay in this volume, but in a different context.

restricted to serving this purpose. Most of what we take to be given in experience is in fact the product of false judgments formed in our early childhood and exacerbated by Scholastic philosophical training. These false judgments include not only the Scholastic view that "colors" are qualities in objects, but also the more fundamental position that "colors" are qualities at all. Surprisingly, Descartes is not a friend of qualia, contrary to a myth too long associated with his philosophy.[42]

Bibliography

Anstey, Peter. 2000. *The Philosophy of Robert Boyle*, London: Routledge.

Atherton, Margaret. 1990. *Berkeley's Revolution in Vision*, Ithaca: Cornell University Press.

—— 2004. "'Green is like Bread': The Nature of Descartes' Account of Color Perception," in *Perception and Reality*, ed. Ralph Schumacher, Paderborn: Mentis.

Boyle, Robert. 1666. *The Origin of Forms and Qualities* in Selected Philosophical Papers of Robert Boyle, ed. M. A. Stewart, Indianapolis: Hackett Publishing Co., 1991.

Cottingham, John. 1976. *Descartes' Conversation with Burman*, Oxford: Clarendon Press.

—— 1990. "Descartes on Color," *Proceedings of the Aristotelian Society*, New Series 90, 231–46.

De Rosa, Raffaella. 2007. "The Myth of Cartesian Qualia," *Pacific Philosophical Quarterly* 88, 181–207.

Descartes, Rene. 1965 [First published 1637]. *Discourse on Method, Optics, Geometry, and Meteorology*, trans. Paul J. Olscamp, New York: Bobbs-Merrill Co., Inc.

Drake, Stillman. 1957. *Discoveries and Opinions of Galileo, New York*: Doubleday & Company.

Gaukroger, Stephen. 1995. *Descartes: An Intellectual Biography*, Oxford: Oxford University Press.

Hoffman, Paul. 1996. "Descartes on Misrepresentation," *Journal of the History of Philosophy* 34, 357–81.

Jolley, Nicholas. 1990. *The Light of the Soul: Theories of Ideas in Leibniz, Malebranche, and Descartes*, Oxford: Clarendon Press.

Mackie, J. L. 1976. *Problems from Locke*, Oxford: Clarendon Press.

Menn, Stephen. 1995. "The Greatest Stumbling Block: Descartes' Denial of Real Qualities," *Descartes and His Contemporaries: Meditations, Objections, and Replies*, eds. Roger Ariew and Marjorie Grene, Chicago: The University of Chicago Press.

Miller, Valentine Rodger and Reese P. Miller. 1991. *Principles of Philosophy*, Dordrecht, the Netherlands: Kluwer Academic Publishers.

Nelson, Alan. 1996. "The Falsity in Sensory Ideas: Descartes and Arnauld," *Interpreting Arnauld*, ed. Elmar Kremer, Toronto: University of Toronto Press, 13–32.

Nolan, Lawrence and John Whipple. 2006. "The Dustbin Theory of Mind: A Cartesian Legacy?," *Oxford Studies in Early Modern Philosophy*, vol. 3, eds. Daniel Garber and Steven Nadler.

[42] This paper is an offshoot of an essay (2006) that I co-authored with John Whipple. He was involved in the early stages of researching the present paper, and I am deeply grateful for his contributions. I would also like to thank Margaret Atherton, Nicholas Jolley, Lex Newman, Tad Schmaltz, Al Spangler, Thomas Vinci, and especially Alan Nelson for comments on previous drafts. I am also indebted to audiences at the University of New Mexico, Albuquerque (February 2006); Emory University (November 2008); and University of North Carolina, Chapel Hill (March 2009), where various incarnations of this essay were presented.

Normore, Calvin. 1986. "Meaning and Objective Being: Descartes and His Sources," in *Essays on Descartes'* Meditations, ed. Amélie Oksenberg Rorty, Berkeley: University of California Press.

Olscamp, Paul J. (trans.). 1965. *Discourse on Method, Optics, Geometry and Meterology*. Indianapolis: Bobbs-Merrill.

Schmaltz, Tad. 1996. *Malebranche's Theory of the Soul: A Cartesian Interpretation*, New York: Oxford University Press, 49–50.

——— 1995. "Malebranche's Cartesianism and Lockean Colors," *History of Philosophy Quarterly* 12, 387–403.

Simmons, Alison. 1999. "Are Cartesian Sensations Representational?," *Noûs* 33(3), 347–369.

Thompson, Evan. 1995b. *Colour Vision: A Study in Cognitive Science and the Philosophy of Perception*, New York: Routledge.

Wilson, Margaret. 1992. "History of Philosophy in Philosophy Today; and the Case of the Sensible Qualities," *The Philosophical Review* 101, 191–243.

——— 1999. "Descartes on the Representationality of Sensation," *Ideas and Mechanism: Essays on Early Modern Philosophy*, Princeton: Princeton University Press, 69–83.

Wolf-Devine, Celia. 1993. *Descartes on Seeing: Epistemology and Visual Perception*, Carbondale: Southern Illinois University Press.

5

Sensible Qualities and Material Bodies in Descartes and Boyle

Lisa Downing

1. Introduction

Descartes and Boyle were the most influential proponents of strict mechanist accounts of the physical world, accounts which carried with them a distinction between primary and secondary (or sensible) qualities. For both, the distinction is a piece of natural philosophy. Nevertheless the distinction is quite differently articulated, and, especially, differently grounded in the two thinkers. For Descartes, reasoned reflection reveals to us that bodies must consist in mere extension and its modifications, and that sensible qualities as we conceive of them based on sense perception can pertain only to the mind. Just how we are supposed to arrive at this realization is, this essay will argue, a deep puzzle that brings us to the basic assumptions of Descartes' metaphysics. For Boyle, by contrast, while reflection can reveal the unique explanatory status of mechanism and, thus, the primary/secondary quality distinction, only experience can confirm its truth.

Our central focus will be on Descartes and on the question: How does he intend to remove the sensible qualities from the physical world; how does he strip them from bodies? I will try to show that Descartes has an argument that he takes to show a priori that sensible qualities cannot be attributed to the material world (as foundational qualities, or, as we conceive of them based on sense experience). The argument fails, however, leaving him with at best a partly empirical case for removing the sensible qualities, based on the purported explanatory success of his physics.

Boyle's aims, by contrast, are considerably more modest. He consistently holds that mechanism, including the distinction between primary affections and sensible qualities that is central to it, is an hypothesis whose truth could only be established as probable on the basis of experimental success. However, there are important conceptual elements to his case for the unique explanatory status of mechanism.

It will be convenient to have a label for the view that both Descartes and Boyle are committed to denying. Both deny the existence of *real corporeal sensible qualities.*[1] This is shorthand for the more careful characterization that both deny (1) that sensible qualities (such as color, taste, odor, heat and cold) are in bodies in any way that resembles our sensory experience of such qualities *and* (2) that they are in bodies as irreducible qualities, on a par with qualities such as size, shape, motion/rest.[2]

2. Descartes: demoting the sensible qualities

Descartes holds that bodies straightforwardly possess size, shape, motion, duration, position, number, and so on, but that color, smell, taste, sound, and so on cannot be attributed to bodies in this same straightforward sense (Pr I 69).[3] In what follows, I will refer to qualities on this first list as geometrical qualities, and qualities on the second list as sensible qualities.[4] This description of Descartes' doctrine is, of course, deliberately vague, for considerable controversy surrounds the question of the status of the sensible qualities for Descartes. What is uncontroversial is that the sensible qualities have a second-class status for Descartes: they are not intrinsic qualities distinct from, and on a par with, the geometrical ones; there are no real corporeal sensible qualities. What justification does Descartes have for demoting the sensible qualities from first-class status?

This question is of obvious interest, since it is central to the philosophical grounding that Descartes provides for his geometrical, mechanistic physics. Descartes' physics describes a material world that is *uniform*, differentiated into shapes and sizes only by motion. He cannot allow that sensible qualities are intrinsic, causally efficacious qualities distinct from the geometrical ones.[5] He thus needs to unseat the sensible qualities, and he needs to provide some argument for doing so.

The question of how Descartes demotes the sensible qualities is certainly an obvious one, yet it is not one to which there is a well-established answer. Indeed, Descartes' justification for this move is nearly invisible—although relevant texts are easily located,

[1] To be more accurate, Boyle denies this when he is speaking as a corpuscularian.

[2] This leaves open, of course, the possibility that sensible qualities are in bodies as textures or arrangements of particles, which is a view that both Descartes and Boyle at least take seriously.

[3] References to Descartes' *Principia Philosophiae* are abbreviated as Pr and given by part and article number; these are reproduced in all editions. References to other texts of Descartes' are to the standard Adam and Tannery (AT) edition and to the standard English translation (CSM or CSMK). The few instances where I have departed from the CSM translation are marked with footnotes.

[4] Although Descartes has a version of the primary/secondary quality distinction, he does not use any version of the labels "primary quality" and "secondary quality". (Those labels are, of course, Lockean, though Boyle's terminology, as we will note below, comes close.) Descartes tends to refer to the two groups of qualities by example, e.g. "weight, colour, and all other such qualities that are perceived by the senses as being in corporeal matter" (Pr II 4). Of course, the geometrical qualities can be sensed, for Descartes: my stipulated terminology is not meant to suggest otherwise.

[5] Or, more simply and generally, he cannot allow that the sensible qualities are on an ontological par with the geometrical ones.

it is exceedingly difficult to determine where exactly the arguments are taking place.[6] In what follows, I will show that Part I of the *Principles* contains a serious argument for demoting the sensible qualities. I will argue for the unique importance of this argument as the only argument that Descartes gives for demoting the sensible qualities that does not, in one way or another, rely on Ockham's razor. I show that locating and identifying that argument allows for a new understanding of the argumentative structure of Principles I and II vis-à-vis the nature of bodies. On my interpretation, however, Descartes' argument relies on a highly controversial premise whose justification is left obscure by the texts. In the paper's penultimate section (section 6), I develop several Cartesian strategies for justifying this premise, evaluating their relative strengths and weaknesses. In the end, I am forced to the conclusion that none of these strategies is promising. In the process, however, we will identify one way in which Descartes' physics leans (precariously) on his metaphysics. In addition, we will gain a better appreciation of what a difficult task it is, even for Descartes, to banish sensible qualities from the physical world.

3. Locating the argument: other arguments and Ockham's razor

First, we need to locate the relevant arguments. It might seem that one should look to the *Meditations* for Descartes' justification of his conception of body, since he regarded that work as his official metaphysics (AT V 291: CSMK III 369) and he famously told Mersenne (in confidence) that it formed the foundation for all his physics (AT III 297–8: CSMK III 173). However, it is a noteworthy fact about the *Meditations* that it contains no argument that bodies possess no non-geometrical qualities. In the wax argument of the Second Meditation, Descartes foreshadows the geometrical conception of body, but does not attempt to establish it. In the Fifth Meditation, he shows that we have a clear and distinct conception of bodies as merely geometrical objects. From this, in the Sixth Meditation, he concludes that bodies which are extended could exist, and then, via a problematic argument from God's veracity, that such bodies do exist. Descartes warns us repeatedly that we have no reason to conclude that bodies have all the qualities that we ordinarily attribute to them on the basis of sense perception. Of course, this is not to show that they in fact lack such qualities. And, although Descartes repeatedly *insinuates* that we are mistaken in attributing sensible qualities such as color to bodies, he does not actually claim to have established that bodies have only geometrical qualities.[7] Rather, he states his conclusion quite precisely as follows:

[6] Monte Cook (1996, 17, note 3) notes that Descartes' argument for the claim that bodies don't have color is surprisingly difficult to reconstruct. Jill Vance Buroker (1991) is driven to combing the *Rules* for an implicit justification for the move.

[7] Thus I am somewhat puzzled by Daniel Garber's strategy (1992, 77, 85) of tracing all of Descartes' arguments for his minimal conception of body back to the *Meditations*. Of course, elements of whatever arguments Descartes can make in this regard are to be found in the *Meditations*, but the conclusion is not.

> It follows that corporeal things exist. They may not all exist in a way that exactly corresponds with my sensory grasp of them, for in many cases the grasp of the senses is very obscure and confused. But at least they possess all the properties which I clearly and distinctly understand, that is, all those which, viewed in general terms, are comprised within the subject-matter of pure mathematics. (AT VII 80: CSM II 55)

At the end of the *Meditations*, then, an epistemic difference between geometrical qualities and sensible qualities has been established: we know that bodies have geometrical qualities corresponding to our clear and distinct geometrical ideas, while the status of sensible qualities is unclear. However, Descartes does not there actually reach the conclusion that bodies *lack* sensible qualities.

One might argue, however, that the epistemic point suffices for Descartes' purposes. Marleen Rozemond (1998, 66–75) defends Descartes' demotion of the sensible qualities in this fashion, seeing Descartes as pursuing a skeptical strategy which shifts the burden of proof to the defender of corporeal sensible qualities. I agree that there are grounds for attributing this sort of strategy to Descartes. In the rest of this section, I argue that all of Descartes' attempts to depose the sensible qualities, *save one*, in the end are of this same kind: they give some sort of reason to privilege geometrical qualities over sensible ones, and then rely (explicitly or implicitly) on an application of Ockham's razor, or a shifting of the burden of proof, to license the conclusion that we *ought not* to attribute the sensible qualities to bodies. Sections 4 and 6 of the paper will be devoted to Descartes' single attempt to justify a stronger conclusion.

Turning to the *Principles*, the most obvious place to look for a principled demotion of the sensible qualities is Part II, Article 4, where Descartes purports to establish that "the nature of body consists not in weight, hardness, colour, or the like, but simply in extension." Here Descartes appears to give an argument from eliminability[8] for his minimal conception of body:

> For as regards hardness, our sensation tells us no more than that the parts of a hard body resist the motion of our hands when they come into contact with them. If, whenever our hands moved in a given direction, all the bodies in that area were to move away at the same speed as that of our approaching hands, we should never have any sensation of hardness. And since it is quite unintelligible to suppose that, if bodies did move away in this fashion, they would thereby lose their bodily nature, it follows that this nature cannot consist in hardness. By the same reasoning it can be shown that weight, colour, and all other such qualities that are perceived by the senses as being in corporeal matter, can be removed from it, while the matter itself remains intact; it thus follows that its nature does not depend on any of these qualities. (Pr II 4)

An obvious, if arguably just, complaint is that Descartes' thought-experiment does not amount to conceiving of a body that is not hard.[9] We can set this concern aside,

[8] My initial exposition of this argument here derives from Garber's (1992, 77–80). In section 5 below, I offer a revised account of the role of this argument.

[9] Rather, it amounts to conceiving of a body whose hardness we cannot experience.

however, for Descartes' argument does not depend on the construction of this particular thought experiment. He argues both here and in Pr II 11 that we can conceive of bodies as lacking the sensible qualities and that we have *experienced* bodies as lacking sensible qualities such as color:[10]

Suppose we attend to the idea we have of some body, for example a stone, and leave out everything we know to be non-essential to the nature of body: we will first of all exclude hardness, since if the stone is melted or pulverized it will lose its hardness without thereby ceasing to be a body; next we will exclude colour, since we have often seen stones so transparent as to lack colour . . . After all this, we will see that nothing remains in the idea of the stone except that it is something extended in length, breadth, and depth. (Pr II 11)

This, he contends, reveals that the nature of body consists simply in extension, and that there is no real difference between space and corporeal substance. We may (with Berkeley) wish to resist Descartes' contention that we can in fact conceive of body as lacking both color and hardness; certainly we do not experience any bodies that possess only geometrical qualities.[11] Supposing, however, that we grant him this, we will grant that all bodies are extended and that all it takes to be a body is to be extended. But this is not to deny that bodies may have more qualities than the merely geometrical, and may be genuinely colored and hard. Thus, if Descartes' arguments of Pr II 4 and Pr II 11 are interpreted as attempts to strip bodies of their sensible qualities, they fall short. I will suggest a somewhat different understanding of the role of these passages in Section 5.

Descartes could, of course, appeal to Ockham's razor to supplement the argument, admonishing us not to attribute corporeal qualities without necessity. Why not try to get by with attributing to bodies only the qualities we must—the essential ones?[12] Indeed, something like this justification for his purely geometrical conception of body is suggested by Pr IV 203, where Descartes justifies his entire system as being (1) based on the simplest and clearest principles and (2) explanatorily adequate to the phenomena. One such phenomenon is sensory experience itself, which Descartes believes he can explain mechanistically. Supposing that Descartes can accomplish all this while attributing only geometrical qualities to bodies, it is otiose to posit any additional ones. In the end, I think we must conclude that this is the most persuasive and clearest argument that Descartes has for stripping the sensible qualities from bodies, though it is ultimately subject to a fatal objection: Descartes does not, in fact, develop a consistent and adequate physics, and his prospects would surely have been better with a less minimal starting

[10] Related considerations are raised in the wax argument.

[11] Thus, one way to resist the argument would be to contend that being colored or hard is essential to bodies. One of many metaphysical assumptions made by Descartes is that there could be no such basically disjunctive essential properties.

[12] One might worry here that this would not allow us to attribute motion to bodies. But Descartes sees being in-motion-or-at-rest as following from what it is to be an extended substance.

point. It is also an argument that licenses only a weak conclusion: We ought not to posit sensible qualities in bodies so long as we can get by (explanatorily) without it. Such an argument does not definitively strip bodies to their extended essence. As we will see below, Descartes does try to support a stronger conclusion elsewhere.

It may seem that Descartes himself tells us where to look for an argument in his letter to Chanut of February 26, 1649:

> it must be remembered, while reading this book [the *Principles*] that although I consider nothing in bodies except the sizes, shapes and motions of their parts, I claim none the less to explain the nature of light and heat and all other qualities that are perceivable by the senses; for I presuppose that these qualities are only in our senses, like pleasure and pain, and not in the objects which we perceive by the senses, in which there are only certain shapes and motions which cause the sensations we call light, heat, etc. This I did not explain and prove until the end of Part Four; nevertheless it is useful to know and observe it from the beginning of the book, so as to understand it better...
>
> (AT V 291–2: CSMK III 369)

This passage is somewhat misleading, however. In keeping with the above interpretation of the end of Part IV, what Descartes finally attempts to prove there is that his system has the resources to *explain* our perceptions of light, heat, etc. without positing any such qualities in objects as distinct from the geometrical qualities. This proof thus *complements* any prior argument that the sensible qualities are not in bodies, and in that sense it *completes* any such proof. It is also a necessary *component* of the argument from parsimony/ Ockham's razor. It is simply not true, however, that Descartes makes no earlier attempts to demote the sensible qualities, as I will show in the next section.

A stronger claim than one based merely on Ockham's razor may seem to be indicated by Pr IV 198, where Descartes argues that neurophysiology suggests that only local motion reaches the brain, that we do not understand how Scholastic substantial forms or real qualities could produce local motions, and that therefore "we have every reason to conclude that the properties in external objects to which we apply the terms light, colour, smell, taste, sound, heat and cold—as well as the other tactile qualities and even what are called 'substantial forms'—are, so far as we can see, simply various dispositions in those objects which make them able to set up various kinds of motions in our nerves". However, to the extent that this argument goes beyond an application of Ockham's razor (neurophysiology seems to require only shapes, sizes, and motions—posit no other qualities), it falls into circularity.[13] For Descartes' neurophysiological views look uncontroversial only in a mechanist context—something like the mechanist principle that all corporeal interaction is by impact at contact must be presupposed. But that principle is never specifically defended by

[13] Keating (2004) offers a sympathetic reading of this argument, but she does not (in effect) see it as going beyond an application of Ockham's razor. She sees Descartes as merely aiming to establish that the Cartesian mechanist explanation of sense perception is more intelligible than one that posits real corporeal sensible qualities, thus, we have reason to posit only geometrical qualities.

Descartes in the *Principles*. Rather, it simply falls out of his minimal notion of body as mere extension.[14, 15, 16]

4. The argument for stripping the sensible qualities from bodies: Pr I 66–71

For a definitive demotion of the sensible qualities, then, we must look elsewhere. The place to look, I suggest, is Part I of the *Principles*, to a set of passages that have sometimes been dismissed for their obscurity.[17] To identify the argument we must examine several sections in some detail, beginning with Pr I 68:

> In order to distinguish what is clear in this connection from what is obscure, we must be very careful to note that pain and color and so on are clearly and distinctly perceived when they are regarded merely as sensations or thoughts. But when they are judged to be real things existing outside our mind, there is plainly no way of understanding just what things they are. When someone says he sees color in some body or feels pain in some limb, it is the same thing as saying that he sees or feels something there such that he is completely ignorant of what it is, that is, that he does not know what he is seeing or feeling. Admittedly, if he is insufficiently attentive, he may easily convince himself that he has some knowledge of what he sees or feels, because he may suppose that it is something similar to the sensation of color or pain which he experiences within himself. But if he examines what it is that this sensation of color or pain represents [repræsentet] as being in the colored body or the painful part, he will realize that he is wholly ignorant of it.[18]

We may begin by distinguishing what is clear in section 68 from what is obscure. What is clear is that the sensible qualities and pain are clearly and distinctly understood when regarded as sensations or thoughts and, further, that some sort of error is involved in projecting them externally. The exact nature of this error, however, is less clear.

[14] That is, Descartes could be arguing from Ockham's razor in this fashion: My neurophysiology is the simplest and most intelligible, so we should employ it, and it implies that sensible qualities in objects are simply "various dispositions." If, on the other hand, Descartes is trying to claim that it is definitely established that only local motion reaches the brain, he is begging the question, since he has no defense of this in the *Principles* that is independent of the minimal notion of body as mere extension. In his discussion of fire in the *World*, Descartes suggests a more direct approach to a contact action principle, claiming that "it does not seem possible to conceive how one body could move another except through its own movement", and also suggesting that the only kind of change we can imagine here is motion (AT XI 7–8: CSM I 83), but he does not employ this strategy in the more rigorous context of the *Principles*.

[15] Interestingly, Descartes defends his denial of the reality of accidents in the *Sixth Replies* using the principle that "all sense-perception occurs through contact" (AT VII: 434: CSM II 293). In the *Fourth Replies*, he claims that this principle is uncontroversial and is accepted by Aristotle (AT VII 249: CSM II 173–4). But of course this principle cannot rule out the perceivability of real accidents unless it is understood in a controversially mechanist way.

[16] In section 7 below we will examine a more general argument that may be found in this passage, an argument also gestured at by Boyle.

[17] Rozemond (1998, 77) calls them "unilluminating," and does not see them as containing a serious argument.

[18] My translation.

It involves a false supposition of similitude between the object and the sensation. Descartes indicates in the last sentence what is supposed to reveal to us that this supposition is false: if we consider what is represented by the sensation of color as existing in the colored body, we realize that we are wholly ignorant of it. But this point too requires further elucidation. Is Descartes' claim merely that we do not know whether bodies actually have color, and thus do not know what, if anything, our sensations manage to latch onto in the physical world?

Descartes' point is illuminated by section 70, which, like 68, I quote in its entirety for future reference:

> It is clear, then, that when we say that we perceive colors in objects, this is really just the same as saying that we perceive something in objects such that we do not know what it is, but which produces in us a certain very manifest and vivid sensation which is called the sensation of color. But the way in which we make our judgement can vary very widely. For as long as we merely judge that there is something in objects (that is, in the things, of whatever kind exactly they may be, from which our sensations come to us) such that we do not know what it is, then we avoid error; indeed, we are actually guarding against error, since the recognition that we are ignorant of something makes us less liable to make any rash judgement about it. But it is quite different when we suppose that we perceive colors in objects. Of course, we do not really know what it is that we are thus calling by this name "color," and we cannot understand [*intellegere*] any resemblance [*similitudinem*] between the color that we suppose to be in objects and that which we experience in sensation. But because we do not notice this very fact, and because there are many other things, such as size, shape, number, etc., that we clearly perceive to be sensed or understood by us in a way that is not different from the way they are or at least could be in objects, we easily fall into the error of judging that what we call color in objects is entirely similar to the color which we sense, and thus of supposing that we clearly perceive what we in no way perceive.[19]

Descartes states that we cannot find any intelligible resemblance between the color which we suppose to be in objects and that which we experience in our sensation, although there is such an intelligible resemblance in the case of the geometrical qualities. Thus, what we are supposed to be able to observe, on reflection, is that our ideas of sensible qualities do not succeed in presenting or depicting even *possible* qualities of external objects.

This interpretation is further confirmed by the fact that Descartes feels obliged to explain (in Pr I 70–71) why we project our ideas of sensible qualities externally and experience no tension in doing so. We do so because (1) both sensible ideas[20] and geometrical ideas are evidently produced by external bodies[21] and (2) our geometrical

[19] My translation.

[20] Here and throughout the paper I use "sensible idea" as shorthand for "(sensed) idea of a sensible quality," i.e. a sensory idea of color, taste, or smell, etc. Of course, we can have geometrical ideas, ideas of shape, etc. through sense perception.

[21] I set aside here the important and difficult issue of whether Descartes is fully committed to body–mind causation. His language here is certainly causal, but an occasionalist gloss on these passages would generate no obvious difficulties.

ideas obviously *do* present possible features of external objects. This leads us to generalize unreflectively, attributing the same sort of correspondence between idea and object to sensible ideas. This supposition, however, is not merely false, in Descartes' view: it is *unintelligible*.

Descartes concludes in section 71 that "what we call the sensations of tastes, smells, sounds, heat, cold, light, colours and so on . . . do not represent anything located outside our thought," while "sizes, shapes, motions, and so on" are presented to the mind, by the geometrical ideas, "as things, or modes of things, existing (or at least capable of existing) outside thought." Thus, Descartes reaches the desired conclusion that body is mere extension, for the hypothesis that bodies have color or hardness in the way that they have shape turns out to be simply unintelligible, that is, no hypothesis at all. It is true that one might still resist by noting that Descartes has not proven that bodies have no qualities other than geometrical ones. However, since our sensations provide us with no genuine notion of other possible qualities of bodies, we cannot give any content to the proposal that bodies have color, taste, hardness, etc. as further qualities. It is thus an empty supposition. To put the point another way, while the arguments from Ockham's razor at best license the conclusion that we *ought not* to attribute the sensible qualities to bodies, this argument, if successful, entails that we *cannot*.

I take it that we have located, at this point, Descartes' only argument for the definitive demotion of the sensible qualities. The analysis of the argument, however, leaves us with a glaring question: Why did Descartes suppose that we can't coherently conceive of bodies as green, hard, or sour? What grounds could he supply for that obviously controversial claim? This question will fuel section 6 of the paper. First, however, we should consider how this analysis of Pr I 66–71 allows us to understand the overall structure of Pr I–II.

5. Consequences: a revised view of the argumentative structure of Principles I–II

Having identified Descartes' *Principles I* argument for demoting the sensible qualities, we are in a position to re-evaluate the overall structure of the relevant argumentation in *Principles I–II*, including the formerly quite unconvincing Pr II 4. In Pr I 66–71, Descartes argues that we cannot attribute sensible qualities (as basic or unreduced qualities) to bodies. The bodies under discussion here, however, are bodies conceived according to the idea of extension, geometrical bodies. That is, in Part I of the *Principles*, Descartes is discussing our ideas, and making a conceptual point about how some of these ideas (e.g. color and our geometrical idea of body) fail to fit together. Pr II 1 then rehearses the *Meditation 6* argument that geometrical bodies exist. What is then argued in Pr II 4 is that *our* bodies, the natural bodies of ordinary experience, have extension as their essence. Thus, they are the geometrical bodies and, further, it then purportedly follows from Pr I 66–71 that we cannot suppose that they have sensible qualities resembling our sensible ideas. Pr II 4 thus does *not* do the work of stripping sensible qualities from bodies. What it does, rather, is to make the connection between the abstract conception of geometrical bodies and the physical bodies of ordinary experience. Now this connection is not completely new in II 4, for it is implicated in II 1. In arguing for the existence of bodies, Descartes claims not just that we have a clear and distinct perception of geometrical body/matter, but that "we appear to see clearly that the idea of it comes to us from things located outside ourselves, which it wholly resembles" (Pr II 1). This does forge (though somewhat tentatively) the connection between these geometrical conceptions and the bodies around us. Pr II 1 thus initiates, as one would expect given its position, the transition from an examination of ideas/geometrical natures to an examination of the found natural world. Pr II 4 then reinforces this connection from the other direction: If we begin with our experience and ordinary understanding of the bodies around us, we will conclude that those bodies are essentially extended, essentially geometrical. Thus, they are the geometrical bodies. Furthermore, the conclusion that purportedly follows from I 66–71, that they do not possess sensible qualities as basic qualities, is unproblematic, for we find that those qualities are optional: we experience bodies without them, and we do not need them in order to conceive of body.

6. Three Cartesian answers to the question: Why can't I conceive of red bodies?

Having considered some of the consequences of this interpretation of Descartes' argument for the argumentative structure of Pr I–II, I want to turn to an extended consideration of the obvious and serious problem that faces that argument. According to the interpretation that I have argued for so far, Descartes holds that sensible ideas do not present possible qualities of external objects. Our sensible ideas provide us with no way of conceiving of something external as being green, cold, sour: we just don't know what it would be for something mind-independent to be like our experience in these cases, although it is obvious what it would be for something mind-independent to be like our experience of roundness, etc. I take myself to have shown that this is Descartes' position in the *Principles*, that it represents a central argument for demoting the sensible qualities, and that it allows him to reach his desired conclusion: that the sensible qualities, as we experience them, are not in bodies.[22] It may seem, however, that Descartes has bought this success at a high price. For surely it is counterintuitive to claim that our sensible ideas do not represent possible qualities of objects, that we do not even know what it would *be* for an apple to really be red. We want to say, "Of

[22] Or, more strictly, that we cannot make sense of the claim that they are in bodies, and so cannot attribute them to bodies.

course we know what it would be; it would be just like *that!*" Thus, without further elucidation, Descartes' claims seem excessively bold, even ridiculous. Why exactly would Descartes suppose that we couldn't conceive of red bodies? What is the source of the incoherence involved in projecting sensible qualities onto bodies, and how do we become aware of that incoherence? I do not think that there is a single, clear, developed answer to this question to be found in Descartes' texts. This is not to say, however, that he would have had nothing to say in response to this question. In this section, I develop and evaluate three Cartesian answers to this question. I think each of these options represents a prima facie plausible hypothesis as to how Descartes himself would have answered this question, though I will conclude that the last of them is most likely to reflect Descartes' own background views about the source of the unintelligibility in question. Unfortunately, we will find that each of these strategies for justifying Descartes' charge of unintelligibility threatens to sink under the weight of its attendant difficulties.

The structure of this discussion is complex, so let me begin with a roadmap. The organizing question is: Why does Descartes hold in the *Principles* that we cannot conceive of red bodies? I first consider the hypothesis that it has to do with the idea of red itself, which lands us in (I) the qualia interpretation. The alternative is that the problem Descartes sees has to do with projecting redness (and other sensible qualities) onto extended bodies. But what then is that problem? One answer is that the projection is supposed to be problematic for broadly mechanist reasons. This lands us in (II) the integrationist interpretation. Another possibility is that the problem with the projection is metaphysical. Here I contrast two different metaphysical accounts of the relation between mode and attribute. Essentialism (III) explains what's wrong with attributing redness to bodies, and so provides a basis for excluding the sensible qualities, but Descartes seems to have no good reason to assert it over the weaker unificationist account, which provides no such basis. As just indicated, I will argue that interpretation III seems to have the best Cartesian credentials, but that all three interpretations face significant philosophical problems.

The first possibility is to suppose that Descartes holds that attention to our sensible ideas reveals that they are purely qualitative, that is, mere qualia, which as such can only be attributed to a mind. For ease of reference, I will call this the qualia interpretation (I).[23] On this interpretation, Descartes is claiming that once we have distanced ourselves, insofar as we can, from the unreflective habit of projection, so that we can consider the experience itself, we will see that it is a mere *feeling*, something locatable solely in a thinking thing. Thus, the incoherence of projecting our sensations onto bodies derives from the mere fact that bodies are non-thinking things, together with the character of our sensible ideas.

[23] Conversation with Daniel Sutherland led me to take the qualia interpretation more seriously than I initially had. This interpretation is also related to Garber's complete concept argument (1992, 85–89).

This interpretation fits with the way in which sections 66–71 follow Descartes' outline of substance/mode ontology and his recommendations as to "how the modes of thought and extension are to be known" (Pr I 65). That is, one might think that these earlier sections prepare the reader to correctly divide the qualities into modes of extension and modes of thought, based simply on attention to their intrinsic content/character. It fits also with Descartes' claim that color, etc. are clearly conceived when conceived of as modes of mind. It is not, however, dictated by the texts; we will see below that other options are available.

The difficulty with this option is that, as it stands, this purported contention of Descartes' is unsupported and implausible. How does introspection into "what is strictly contained in our perception . . . that of which we have inner awareness" (Pr I 66) reveal color, as we experience it, to be merely mental? I do not see how to construct a particularly convincing case, here, although perhaps the most promising line available would be to argue, as Berkeley did, for internal, necessary connections between the sensible qualities and pleasure and pain. But aside from sometimes drawing an analogy between pain and the sensible qualities (Pr I 67), Descartes argues for no such connections in the *Principles*.[24]

If, however, this question (of how the purely mental character of the sensible qualities is established) is left unanswered, then we have made no progress, for the challenge can still be raised: Why isn't color like shape? The *idea* of shape must be attributed to mind, but *shape* is attributed to external objects. Color *seems* eligible for the same treatment. Descartes must say that this seeming is simply illusory, but on this interpretation he has provided very little to back up this contention. Furthermore, the claim that color is merely qualitative in this sense implies that color ideas are strongly non-representative, that is, not as if of objects, not externally directed. While I have argued above that Descartes is committed to the claim that sensible ideas do not succeed in representing any actual or possible sensible qualities of geometrical objects, he does not obviously need to make the stronger claim, which seems to conflict with the phenomenological facts of our experience, that they do not even *purport* to represent, are not even as if of objects. Moreover, Descartes' actual statements about the representationality of sensation are much more varied[25] than they ought to be on the qualia interpretation, which entails a single firm negative answer to the question: Do sensible ideas represent? If, on the other hand, Descartes were to retreat to the claim that sensible ideas are partly, but not entirely qualitative, then this would not secure the result, for the question would then again arise—why can't these ideas, like geometrical ideas, represent something non-mental?

[24] It is interesting to note that in the *World* Descartes does suggest this sort of line about heat: that the sensation of heat may be a kind of pain or a kind of tickling (AT XI 9–10, CSM I 84). Descartes' point is to dissuade us from supposing that there is something in bodies which is similar to our idea of heat. Thanks to an anonymous referee for this point.

[25] See Simmons 1999, Wilson 1999. For an extended defense of the claim that Cartesian sensations are at least as if of objects, see De Rosa 2007.

What alternative answers, then, are available to the question of why Descartes would suppose that we can't conceive of red bodies? In claiming that sensible ideas do not present possible qualities of external objects, we might see Descartes as claiming more specifically that we cannot project sensible qualities onto *extended* objects, that is, our sensible ideas do not present possible qualities of such objects. So interpreted, Descartes is challenging us to conceive of the manner in which the sensible qualities are to be attached to *geometrical* bodies. This is not circular because, as we have seen, Descartes has an independent argument that bodies are geometrical, the *Meditation 6* argument from God's veracity, rehearsed in Pr II 1. The question that needs to be settled is whether they may have *more* qualities. Because the problem derives from a lack of *fit* between sensible ideas and geometrical bodies, rather than from the purported fact that the sensible ideas themselves are not externally directed, such an interpretation would be able to accommodate the evident phenomenological fact that color and shape *seem* alike and in the same way external. Further, Descartes would not be assuming that it should be obvious from a consideration of the sensory experience alone that sensible ideas are mere (unprojectable) sensations. Rather, a certain kind of reflection reveals the incoherence of the projection.

On this interpretation thus far, then, Descartes contends that the sensible qualities cannot intelligibly be attached to geometrical objects. But why not? My first suggestion here is that Descartes may be objecting to the projection of sensible qualities from a *mechanist* perspective.

We can get some intuitive purchase on this line of thought (the second interpretation, II), by considering the example of sound. What do we mean by attributing sound to an object? Do we really suppose that clanging is an intrinsic property of the bell, on a par with its shape? How should we conceive of such a quality? *Where* exactly should we locate it? It seems that any answer we might propose here is objectionably arbitrary: Is it in the clapper of the bell, every part of the bell, the surrounding air, and, if the latter, how far out does it extend?[26] Descartes could argue that we should reach a similar state of perplexity for each of the sensible qualities. And indeed, one can work up such a state of perplexity about color: What do we mean in ascribing the greenness of our experience to the leaf? Is it a quality somehow spread out uniformly over the surface? Or does it penetrate the whole three-dimensional volume? If it does not permeate the

[26] Hume makes the point very strongly for taste:

> But whatever confus'd notions we may form of an union in place betwixt an extended body, as a fig, and its particular taste, 'tis certain that upon reflection we must observe in this union something altogether unintelligible and contradictory. For shou'd we ask ourselves one obvious question, *viz.* if the taste, which we conceive to be contain'd in the circumference of the body, is in every part of it or in one only, we must quickly find ourselves at a loss, and perceive the impossibility of ever giving a satisfactory answer. We cannot reply, that 'tis only in one part: For experience convinces us, that every part has the same relish. We can as little reply, that it exists in every part: For then we must suppose it figur'd and extended; which is absurd and incomprehensible. (Hume 2000, 1.4.5.13 (156); Hume 1978, 238)

Hume holds that the same problem applies to sound and odor (but *not* color), that these impressions (unlike visual and tangible impressions) are not properly spatial.

whole volume, how deep does it go? Is it present equally at every point? The parts of the leaf are (for Descartes) infinitely divisible: Are they green "all the way down"? Our sensible ideas give us insufficient guidance as to how to map sensible qualities onto extension, and thus, how to conceive of them as spatial.[27]

On this interpretation, what Descartes is demanding is that purported corporeal qualities be fully spatial, that is, systematically relatable (in a non-arbitrary fashion) to extension. In this sense, any purported qualities of bodies must be integrable with the geometrical ones.[28] I will label this position *integrationism*. Thus, on this interpretation, the reason for demoting the sensible qualities is that they (purportedly) cannot be integrated with the geometrical ones, and thus cannot intelligibly be projected onto bodies.

In some respects I think this interpretation is the most attractive of the three that I offer here, in that the position attributed to Descartes stems from his mechanism, rather than an under-motivated phenomenological or metaphysical thesis. There are two problems with it, however. (1) As an interpretation, it is the most speculative of the three—there are no direct indications that Descartes sees this problem of integration as the source of the unintelligibility he proclaims. (2) The reconstructed argument from integrationism does not seem effective enough to successfully eliminate real corporeal sensible qualities. One might ask: Isn't color spatial? Why is it not systematically relatable to space? I take myself to have illustrated above that it is reasonable to have doubts about the prospects for such integration. The main difficulty for this version of Descartes' argument is that the barrier to integration of the sensible qualities is not obviously the sort of *in principle* barrier provided by the other two interpretations. On the contrary, the barrier seems at best merely temporary: hard thought or further empirical research might show us how the sensible qualities can be properly integrated into the geometrical conception of the world.

The last possibility that I will consider is that the problem Descartes sees with attaching sensible qualities to extended bodies is metaphysical, and that the unintelligibility that Descartes is pointing to is one he associates with Scholastic metaphysics. One of Descartes' deepest disagreements with Scholasticism lies in his rejection of real qualities; he rejects what he sees as the Scholastic picture of sensible (and other) qualities as "tacked on" to substances, as *res* capable of independent existence.[29] Descartes

[27] Arguably, these sorts of considerations, if one takes them seriously, count not just against understanding sensible qualities as intrinsic, non-geometrical qualities of bodies, but *also* against identifying the sensible qualities with mechanical constitutions (arrangements of parts). This wouldn't disturb Descartes in the least, however. His interest is in maintaining that our red sensations have as their source a mechanical disposition which could be called red, though it does not resemble our sensory idea of red. The above considerations just point out further aspects of that nonresemblance.

[28] This fits rather nicely with the implications of Descartes' modal distinction (discussed below in connection with unificationism vs. essentialism). Descartes clearly holds that a mode of extension must be spatial, must presuppose space. Integrationism then adds that such a mode must be systematically and coherently spatial.

[29] See especially Menn 1995, and also Rosemond 1998, 102–138, Simmons 1994, 156–200, Garber 1992, 68–70.

opposes this by requiring that all of a body's qualities be modes of its central attribute or essence. Perhaps what Descartes is doing in these sections of the *Principles* is supporting this requirement, which thus far seems a mere stipulation, by highlighting the unintelligibility of the alternative. Descartes' claim would then be something like this: If we try to attribute, for example, color to bodies, simply on the basis of our sensory experience of color, we are stuck with a tacked on or free-floating quality, with no intelligible relation to the body itself, thus not genuinely a quality of the body at all.

But what sort of relation is Descartes then requiring between the qualities of bodies and extension? What is necessary in order to be a *mode* of bodies? The problem is that there are two possibilities here—a weaker requirement and a stronger requirement for being a mode of a substance. The difficulty for Descartes, as we will see, is that only the weak requirement is well motivated, but only the strong requirement succeeds in stripping the sensible qualities from bodies.

We see the weak requirement in Descartes' explication of "modal distinction," which indicates that one-way separability is characteristic of modes: "we can clearly perceive a substance apart from the mode which we say differs from it, whereas we cannot, conversely, understand the mode apart from the substance." (Pr I 61) And the somewhat more vague language that he uses in describing the relation between mode and attribute—modes are referred to the attribute, presuppose the attribute, are not intelligible apart from the attribute (Pr I 53)—coheres perfectly with the idea of one-way separability. Two-way separability, on the other hand, entails a real distinction and is characteristic of the relation between two substances, while two-way inseparability entails that at most a rational distinction is available. Descartes gives a conceptual test for separability, but he maintains that separability in clear and distinct understanding tracks separability in fact, since ". . . when we come to know God, we are certain that he can bring about anything of which we have a distinct understanding" (Pr I 60). I will label this understanding of modes—according to which all of a thing's qualities must be inseparable from, and inconceivable without, its attribute/essence—"unificationism," since what it requires is that all of a thing's qualities have some intrinsic connection to its essence. The essence thus is the core of the thing, unifying all of its qualities.

Sphericity thus qualifies as a mode of extension because it is inconceivable without extension, but extension is conceivable without it, that is, the extension might have some other shape instead. (Descartes has no need to claim that we can conceive of extended substance absolutely unmodified.) Descartes' geometrical qualities will qualify as modes on this understanding, since shape, position, and motion do seem conceptually dependent on extension.

The positive implications of unificationism thus fit with Descartes' commitments, but what about the negative ones? What isn't a quality of body on this view? The unificationist requirement that modes of a body must presuppose extension might eliminate some candidate qualities of bodies—for example, the Cartesian Louis de la Forge (1666, 251–2) argued that because the concept of force does not include the concept of extension, force cannot belong to matter. However, it is not at all clear that this criterion can discredit the sensible qualities as qualities of bodies. Color and hardness, in particular, do seem to presuppose extension and thus apparently meet the unificationist criterion for being a mode of body.[30]

I suggest that Descartes is implicitly relying on a stronger requirement for being a mode, according to which all qualities of bodies must be mere limitations of extension.[31] On this view, all qualities of bodies *follow from* extension in that any particular extended thing must have some size, shape, and motion-or-rest.[32] Another way to put this is that on this understanding of modes, only qualities that pertain to geometry are genuine qualities of bodies. In this very strong sense, the qualities of body must be "intelligible through" body's extended essence. I will call this general metaphysical view "essentialism," since it effectively requires that all of a thing's quality-types follow from its essence.[33] This then is interpretation III of Descartes' answer to the question, "Why can't I conceive of red bodies?"[34]

Essentialism has some Cartesian credentials: Malebranche seems to invoke such an assumption in arguing that all qualities of bodies must be relations of distance.[35] And essentialism does successfully strip the sensible qualities from bodies. Color, hardness, etc. are extraneous to geometry; they do not follow from or reduce to extension. Intuitively, we may say that they add something to extension, rather than merely

[30] As Berkeley famously argued in the case of color. The case of hardness may be trickier than that of color. If we conceive of hardness as a sort of repulsive force, arguably it can be attributed to a geometrical point. Is this to conceive of it as unextended? Not if "extended" really means "spatial".

[31] Another way to try to capture Descartes' view is to say that he requires that all modes of body be something like determinates of the determinable—extension. Jorge Secada (2000) holds that for Descartes, all the real properties of substances are determinates of the essence, which is a determinable. I don't think it is helpful in interpreting Descartes, however, to lean very heavily on twentieth-century notions of determinate and determinable, which are themselves open to debate. Secada holds that mass cannot be a determinate of extension, while hope, fear, etc. are determinates of the determinable thought, but the justification for this position is not fully clear. He refers (190) to Johnson and Searle for elaboration on "determinate" and "determinable", but the technical difficulties involved in their characterizations are amply demonstrated by Sanford 2002. He suggests (14) that doubt is a determinate of thought because "to understand doubt is to understand thought or consciousness" and "if someone knows that a doubting substance exists, he thereby knows that a thinking substance exists". This allows doubt to count as a mode of thought, but it would also, arguably, allow color and hardness to count as modes of extension. Alison Simmons (1994, 162) also uses the language of determinate/determinable.

[32] I am very close to agreement here with Simmons, who writes (1994, 190) that "The modes of extension are . . . *the result of* or *derivable from* body's having been divided into parts", and that divisibility into contiguous parts is the *ratio* of extension, for Descartes (189).

[33] A version of the distinction between unificationism and essentialism is acknowledged by Rozemond (1998, 85–88). Dennis Des Chene (1996, 366) seems to regard Descartes as an essentialist who could rule out color being a mode of body by observing that the possibility of color (unlike figure) is not implied in the very idea of extension. However, he does not explain why Descartes would be entitled to assume that all the modes of extension must be implied in the very idea of extension. Similarly, Simmons (1994, 192–197) nicely diagnoses Descartes essentialism, but does not directly address the question of why he is entitled to a stronger metaphysical assumption than unificationism. Dan Kaufman argues that Descartes holds that there is a mutual entailment between modes and the principle attribute (2008, 62), but doesn't attempt to justify Descartes' position, nor does he consider the problems it entails that are raised below.

[34] The answer is: "because redness is not intelligible through extension."

[35] Malebranche 1958–67, I 122–3; Malebranche 1980, 49.

limiting it in some way. However, essentialism poses a number of problems: First, it looks as though it may be too restrictive to fit Descartes' own views. I allowed above that motion is a mode of body on the essentialist view, but that claim can be challenged. Motion requires change over time, and time or duration is surely something over and above mere extension. Descartes can reply to this challenge, however. Extension as a nature or essence, he maintains, is nothing different from extended substance (Pr I 63), and substance is necessarily connected to duration: 'since a substance cannot cease to endure without also ceasing to be, the distinction between the substance and its duration is merely a conceptual one' (Pr I 62). In effect, it seems that Descartes' position is that all of the quality-types belonging to an extended substance must be consequences of being merely *an extended substance*,[36] and this position legitimates duration and motion-or-rest as qualities of bodies.

A second, less tractable worry concerns the application of essentialism to the realm of the mental: while hoping, fearing, and willing do presuppose thought (à la unificationism), they do not seem to follow from thought or to be mere limitations of thought.[37, 38] It is not obvious that there is any clear notion of mode available which excludes color as a mode of extension but includes volition (or the sensation of color!) as a mode of thought. Essentialism excludes color from bodies because color adds something not implicit in the mere notion of extension. But is this not true of fear, desire, or the sensation of color, in relation to thought?

One might wonder here about the implications of Descartes' celebrated reply to Elizabeth, which sets up a third primitive notion, in apparent tension with the *Principles* doctrine of two attributes:

> First I consider that there are in us certain primitive notions which are as it were the patterns on the basis of which we form all our other conceptions. There are very few such notions. First, there are the most general—those of being, number, duration, etc.—which apply to everything we can conceive. Then, as regards body in particular, we have only the notion of extension, from which follows the notions of shape and motion, and as regards the soul on its own, we have only the notion of thought, in which are included the perceptions of the intellect and the inclinations of the will. Lastly, as regards the soul and the body together, we have only the notion of their union, on which depends our notion of the soul's power to move the body, and the body's power to act on the soul and cause its sensations and passions. (AT III 665: CSMK III 218)[39]

One might try to defend Descartes against the preceding objection by suggesting that, e.g., fear and the sensation of color do not need to follow from mere thought, because they should be referred to the third primitive notion, that of mind–body union.

[36] See Garber 1992 66–68.

[37] In this context it is very revealing to note that Meditation 6 (AT VII, 79: CSM II, 55) specifically employs a unificationist criterion for being a mode of mind—any such mode must presuppose an act of understanding.

[38] Arguably, hoping and fearing, like being spherical, are too specific to follow from the attribute. Part of the difficulty here is that it isn't obvious what to count as a type. However, the objection works just as well if 'feeling an emotion' is substituted for 'fearing'.

[39] Translation slightly amended from CSMK.

Against this suggestion, there are two important points to be made: (1) What Descartes refers here to the mind–body union is very little—the soul's power to move the body and the body's power to act on the soul. These (unintelligible) powers are, appropriately enough, referred to the (unintelligible) notion of union, under the pressure of Elizabeth's repeated questioning. But Descartes tells us emphatically in the *Principles* that sensible qualities can be clearly understood as modes of mind, and he says nothing to contradict that here. (2) When describing the relation between extension and its modes, Descartes here uses language that suggests entailment: shape and motion follow from extension. Further, he says that the perceptions of the intellect and inclinations of the will are included (*comprises*) in thought. This statement is interestingly ambiguous. One way to read it is as claiming that perceptions of the intellect and inclinations of the will are built into the very notion of thought, analogously to the relation between extension and its modes. But this claim is problematic, and even more so for the less intellectualized modes of thought not mentioned here by Descartes. Another way to read it is as claiming that thought is a general notion which comprehends the two more specific ones: perceptions of the intellect and inclinations of the will are both kinds of thoughts. But that claim, if transposed to the realm of extension, will not do any work for him: it would be begging the question to presuppose that being red is not one way of being extended, so that red things are not a kind of extended thing. Thus, this passage provides more evidence that Descartes was an essentialist, while further illustrating the difficulty of applying essentialism to the mental realm.

The *most* serious worry about essentialism, however, is that it is unmotivated. Unificationism, by contrast, is very well motivated, in the context of a metaphysics built around notions of substance and essence. If modes didn't presuppose extension, they could exist independently of it, and thus would be free-floating entities, not genuinely part of the substance, little substances rather than qualities of a substance.[40] Versions of this complaint are put forward by Descartes in a number of places:

> I do not suppose that there are in nature any *real qualities*, which are attached to substances, like so many little souls to their bodies, and which are separable from them by divine power. [. . .] My principle reason for rejecting these real qualities is that I do not see that the human mind has any notion, or particular idea, to conceive them by; so that when we talk about them and assert their existence, we are asserting something we do not conceive and do not ourselves understand.
> (AT III 468–9: CSMK III 216)[41]

Of course they deny that heaviness is a substance, but that makes no difference, because they conceive it in fact as a substance since they think that it is real and that it is possible

[40] This may not seem completely fair to scholastics such as Suarez, since separable here means separable by God's absolute power, which is compatible with natural inseparability. Note that Descartes is aware of this nicety, however, as is shown by the quotations below.

[41] Simmons (1994, 193–194) cites this passage as though it made the same point as Pr I 69–70. I argue in this section that although Descartes himself very likely makes this connection, it is mistaken. The unintelligibility of real qualities does not suffice to show that attributing sensible qualities to bodies is unintelligible.

by some power (namely divine power) for it to exist without the stone (AT V 223: CSMK III 358). Descartes' objections to real qualities thus amount to a persuasive argument for unificationism: the alternative is unintelligible. But why is the denial of essentialism unintelligible?

I see no obvious answer to this question in Descartes. Nevertheless, I think this interpretation is most likely to reflect his own grounds for the unintelligibility he asserts in Pr I 68 and 70. We know that Descartes rejected real qualities as unintelligible; we know that he connected the question of the status of sensible qualities to the issue of real qualities (e.g. Pr IV 198), and his language suggests the essentialist position in more than one place. Moreover, this interpretation nicely explains the *obscurity* of Pr I 68 and 70: In his published works, Descartes was habitually cautious in challenging the Scholastic establishment, so it is no surprise that an unintelligibility that purportedly characterizes Scholastic metaphysics should be indicated in an oblique fashion.[42]

If Descartes did suppose, however, that the only alternative to real qualities was essentialism, he was mistaken. As we have seen, unificationism suffices to rule out real qualities, but unificationism cannot eliminate the possibility that sensible qualities like color and hardness are qualities of bodies. The essentialism which can appears unmotivated (except by its utility in stripping the sensible qualities from bodies). Thus, on this interpretation Descartes either fails to distinguish unificationism and essentialism,[43] or simply presupposes essentialism, despite the fact that he only has arguments for the weaker unificationist position, and despite the challenge that essentialism poses to the consistency of his metaphysics.

If this interpretation is correct, then, in effect Descartes founds his physics on an essentialist metaphysical intuition. Although, as I have argued above, Descartes has no argument to support this intuition, it is not difficult to see its appeal. All we need is one clear and distinct concept—extension (or thought)-and everything else pertaining to extended (or thinking) things is simply contained in some way in that very concept. Partisans of the mechanical philosophy of the seventeenth century praised mechanist physics for its intelligibility, but it is not always easy to say what virtue is being claimed for the theory under the rubric of "intelligibility". One accomplishment of this analysis is that it illuminates a specific sort of strong intelligibility enjoyed by Descartes' system. It is less clear, of course, why we should suppose that the world conforms to this very strong ideal of intelligibility. If we demand this sort of intelligibility from our science of

[42] See Garber 2001, 261. Admittedly, though, Descartes straightforwardly denounces real qualities and substantial forms at Pr IV 198. It is easy to imagine that he could not resist this bit of triumphalism as he reached the end of his magnum opus, which he hoped would replace Scholastic textbooks.

[43] This suggestion may gain some support from the Scholastic context: Stephen Menn (1995, 193) has argued that "Suarez seems to grant a presumption in favor of reality: for God can always create an accident without its subject unless this would involve a logical contradiction, and even if we cannot clearly conceive how the accident could exist without a subject, we should assume that God can bring this about unless we clearly perceive that he cannot." Thus, if a quality adds something not implicit in what it modifies, it may look like a candidate for *res*-hood. Thinking along these lines, Descartes may have supposed that the only alternative to treating sensible qualities as real qualities was essentialism.

bodies, and we agree that bodies are essentially extended, then Descartes' physics is the only physics, and bodies possess only geometrical qualities. Even if we are unwilling to assume essentialism, we might wish to pursue Descartes' program in order to determine whether his ideal of intelligibility can be vindicated. This, however, is again to retreat to a weaker defense of Descartes' stripping of the sensible qualities: Let's see whether the phenomena can be explained while attributing to bodies only qualities implied in the concept of extended existence.

In sum, then, I have argued that Descartes' single argument for the strong conclusion that sensible qualities (as we conceive of them based on sensory experience) cannot be attributed to bodies founders unless, with Descartes, we are willing to simply assume that all the genuine qualities of extended things must be implicit in the concept of extended existence. If we abandon this argument, we are left with several arguments for the weaker conclusion that, if possible, we ought to attribute to bodies only the clearly and distinctly conceived geometrical qualities. Sadly, the antecedent is not satisfied.

We will see in the next section that Robert Boyle, as befits his empiricist credentials, never asserts the strong conclusion, but makes his own careful case for his version of the weaker, a case grounded in a somewhat more modest ideal of intelligibility. We will also locate in both Boyle and Descartes an attempt to ground a conclusion of intermediate strength.

7. Robert Boyle

In some respects, Robert Boyle's treatment of the primary/secondary quality distinction is more focused and explicit than Descartes'. While Descartes' central aim in the *Principles* is to show how a fully developed physics flows from an understanding of the principal attribute of body, one of the main focuses of Boyle's canonical presentation of his corpuscularian physics, *The Origin of Forms and Qualities According to the Corpuscular Philosophy,* is the relative nature of sensible qualities. Further, Boyle provides categories that map well onto our post-Locke understanding of primary and secondary qualities. On the one hand, Boyle labels size, shape, and motion or rest the "primary affections" of bodies, which qualify and distinguish all the parts of bodies.[44] On the other hand, there are the sensible qualities, whose origin Boyle explains with uncharacteristic brevity in this passage:

That yet, there being Men in the World, whose Organs of Sense are contriv'd in such differing wayes, that one Sensory is fitted to receive Impressions from some, and another from other sorts of External Objects, or Bodies without them . . . , the Perceptions of these Impressions are by men call'd by several Names, as *Heat, Colour, Sound, Odour,* and are commonly imagin'd to

[44] From a Lockean perspective, it is noticeable that impenetrability is not on this list. The official reason for this is that because it belongs to all matter qua matter it does not serve to diversify bodies.

proceed from certain distinct and peculiar Qualities in the External Object, which have some resemblance to the Ideas, their action upon the Senses excites in the Mind; though indeed all these Sensible Qualities, and the rest that are to be met with in the Bodies without us, are but the Effects or Consequents of the above mentioned *primary Affections* of Matter, whose Operations are diversify'd according to the nature of the Sensories, or other Bodies they work upon.

(*Works* V 334: S 51–52)[45]

The passage gives the impression that "red" names a perception/idea, but it is far from clear that this is Boyle's considered view.[46] Boyle's main interest in discussing the status of the sensible qualities lies in dissuading us from the "commonly imagined" view outlined above.[47] Where exactly we should say that redness itself lies is of less interest to him, though he is very clear in *Origin of Forms and Qualities* that redness, along with the other sensible qualities, arises from a relation between bodies and perceivers.[48]

As with Descartes, we should focus on the question: What exactly is the basis for rejecting the commonly imagined view that redness, as we imagine it based on sense perception, is actually in bodies? The most obvious answer to be found to this question in Boyle is attractively straightforward: It is simply part of the corpuscularian doctrine that sensible qualities are not basic qualities, distinct from, but on a par with, size, shape, motion/rest. And the corpuscularian doctrine is put forward as an hypothesis, to be vindicated by its application to experience:

[Corpuscularianism] is to be Collated *with*, and to be either Confirmed, or Disproved by, the Historicall Truths, that will be deliver'd concerning Particular Qualities. (*Works* V 305: S 18)

Thus Boyle officially refrains from asserting the truth of corpuscularianism, on the grounds that the verdict of experience is not yet in.

So far, then, we have located only a purely hypothetical endorsement of the primary/secondary quality distinction: If the corpuscularian hypothesis is correct, there are no real corporeal sensible qualities. Despite his habitual diffidence, however, Boyle makes claims about corpuscularianism and sensible qualities that go beyond this mild hypotheticalism. Even in *Origin of Forms and Qualities*, where the overall stance is

[45] References to Boyle are to the standard edition of Boyle's works, Boyle 1999–2000, and are given by volume and page number and abbreviated as *Works*. Where the cited passage also occurs in the readily available Boyle 1991, I give that page reference as well, abbreviated as S.

[46] As Anstey notes (2000, 92–94), when Boyle treats color on its own (as opposed to discussing all the sensible qualities as such), he seems inclined to regard it as a modification of light.

[47] Whence the "commonly imagined" view? As Anstey emphasizes (2000, 95), given the anti-Aristotelian context of the *Origin of Forms and Qualities*, Boyle surely has in mind here Scholastic doctrines of real qualities. Nevertheless, I think that Boyle, like Descartes, is also countering the naïve view that bodies are really red as they appear to be, and their redness is on a par with their shape.

[48] Boyle specifically endorses the thesis that in a world without perceivers, bodies would not actually be colored, though he allows that we might say that that bodies in such a world would be "dispositively" endowed with color (*Works* V 319: S 34). For attempts to pin Boyle down to a more specific metaphysics of sensible qualities, see Anstey 2000, Kaufman 2006. I agree with Anstey that in the end Boyle's metaphysical commitments here are not as precise as we might like.

hypothetical, Boyle wants to defend the claim that we *needn't* adopt the commonly imagined view, for corpuscularian doctrine shows us how our experience can be explained without doing so. Further, although Boyle sincerely held that the hypothesis required further confirmation, he also maintained that it had received considerable confirmation already, and was explanatorily superior to its main competitors: Aristotelian physics and Paracelsian chemistry.

In *About the Excellency and Grounds of the Mechanical Hypothesis*, Boyle explicitly develops a case for the explanatory virtues of corpuscularianism, and thus for the claim that we ought, if possible, to attribute to bodies only primary affections. Boyle lauds corpuscularianism for the (purported) fact that its principles are few, clear (familiar from sense perception),[49] primary and simple (basic, irreducible), and comprehensive (able to explain all sorts of phenomena). Most interesting are Boyle's claims for the uniqueness of corpuscularianism, which can be condensed into the slogan, "by what ever Principles Natural things be *constituted*, 'tis by the Mechanical Principles that their Phænomena must be clearly *explicated*" (Works VIII 113: S 150). Boyle's most extended defense of this slogan comes at the end of the work:

> These Principles, *Matter, Motion* (to which *Rest* is related) *Bigness, Shape, Posture, Order, Texture* being so simple, clear, and *comprehensive*, are applicable to all the real Phaenomena of Nature, which seem not to be explicable by any other not consistent with ours. For, if recourse be had to an Immaterial Principle or Agent, it may be such an one, as is not intelligible; and however it will not enable us to *explain* the *Phænomena*, because its *way* of working upon things Material would probably be more difficult to be Physically made out, than a Mechanical account of the *Phænomena*. And, notwithstanding the Immateriality of a *created* Agent, we cannot conceive, how it should produce changes in a Body, without the help of Mechanical Principles, especially *Local Motion* . . .
>
> And if the Agents or active Principles resorted to, be not Immaterial, but of a Corporeal Nature, they must *either* in effect be the same with the Corporeal Principles above-nam'd; *or*, because of the great Universality & Simplicity of ours, the new ones propos'd must be less general than *they*, and consequently capable of being subordinated or reduc'd to *ours* . . . So that the fear, that so much of a *New* Physical Hypothesis, as is *true*, will overthrow or make useless the Mechanical Principles, is as if one should fear, that there will be a Language propos'd, that is discordant from, or not reducible to, the Letters of the Alphabet. (Works VIII 116: S 153–4)

An immaterial agent will "probably" leave its manner of working on material bodies unexplained. While this is not indisputable, the legacy of Cartesian dualism surely renders it compelling. But why can't nonmechanical material/corporeal principles do explanatory work? A first question here is: what all does Boyle include under the heading of mechanical principles? If we collapse "mechanical" into "matter and motion," as Boyle often does in *Excellency and Grounds*, then it could turn out to be

[49] Thus, although Boyle agrees with Descartes in holding that clarity distinguishes the corpuscularian primary affections from other purported qualities of bodies, the notion of clarity to which he appeals is distinctively empiricist, and contrasts with Descartes' appeal to the clarity and distinctness of geometry.

trivially true that any material principle must be a mechanical principle. It is clear, though, that Boyle's understanding of matter, though less explicitly spelled out here, remains the specific and spare one of *Origin of Forms and Qualities*, a substance extended and impenetrable. He is claiming, then, that any proposed corporeal principles are ultimately resolvable into extension, impenetrability, size, shape, motion, rest, texture. What Boyle has in mind here are chemical principles, such as salt or mercury, which he holds may be genuine agents, but agents that work in virtue of their specific corpuscularian microstructures.

How might his argument apply to sensible qualities such as redness? Boyle asserts that if colors are corporeal, they must be identical with, or reducible to, mechanical qualities, because of the simplicity and universality of mechanical principles. In claiming that the mechanical principles are simple, he claims that they are basic, foundational, and not complex. The reason for this is that we cannot conceive of them being reduced to other, more basic qualities. This conceptual point is challengeable (might we imagine size being reduced to location plus repulsive force?), but certainly intuitive. The mechanical principles are universal because they are present in all of matter, a point supported well enough by simple induction. But what grounds are offered here for excluding the sensible qualities from bodies? Why not suppose that redness (or saltiness, for that matter) is also a basic quality, irreducible to mechanical primary affections? It is not at all obvious that Boyle has any further argument here. He has offered no grounds for claiming that the mechanical affections *exhaust* the simple qualities. He might hold that neither color[50] nor flavor are universal, and that this is a reason to exclude them from bodies. But this works only via the question-begging mechanist assumption that matter is catholic, that is, that material stuff is everywhere the same, differentiated only by motion, size, shape, arrangement. If we bar this, as we should, all Boyle has to appeal to is comprehensiveness as spelled out in the alphabet analogy—mechanism has plenty of resources at its disposal, and offers prospects for explaining saltiness and redness without the need to posit additional qualities.

It seems, then, that we have located little beyond Ockham's razor to anchor the stripping of sensible qualities from bodies. When we ask, why ought we to deny that sensible qualities are really in bodies as we might naively take them to be, the best response we get is that we have an attractive hypothesis in corpuscularianism which promises to explain them away in terms of merely mechanical affections.

There is one more point in Boyle, however, which we have so far passed over, and which deserves to be explored. When Boyle discusses corpuscularianism's purportedly unique ability to explain how change is effected, he frequently alludes to motion:

[50] As with Descartes' apparent argument from elimination in Pr II 4 and 11, this argument is a nonstarter if one holds, with Berkeley, that there are no uncolored bodies, and that "pellucidness" is a color. (See entry 453 of Berkeley's notebooks, Berkeley 1948–57, I 56.) Further, if motion-or-rest (or mobility) is to count as a universal quality, why not count colored-or-uncolored?

. . . the *Mechanical* Philosopher being satisfied, that one part of Matter can act upon another but by vertue of Local Motion, or the effects and consequences of Local Motion, he considers, that *as*, if the propos'd *Agent* be not Intelligible and Physical, it can never Physically *explain* the *Phænomena* . . .

(*Works* VIII 109: S 145)

To be short, if we fancy any two of the Bodies about us, as a Stone, a Mettal, &c., to have nothing at all to do with any other Body in the Universe, 'tis not easy to conceive, either how one can act upon the other, but by Local Motion (of the whole Body, or its Corporeal Effuvia;) or how by Motion it can do any more, then put the Parts of the other Body into Motion too, and thereby produce in them a Change of Scituation and Texture, or of some other of its Mechanical Affections: though this (Passive) Body being plac'd among other Bodies in a World constituted as ours now is, and being brought to act upon the most curiously contriv'd Sensories of Animals, may upon both these accounts exhibit many different sensible *Phænomena*; which however we look upon them as distinct Qualities, are consequently but the Effects of the often mention'd Catholick affections of Matter, and deducible from the Size, Shape, Motion (or Rest,) Posture, Order, and the resulting Texture, of the Insensible parts of Bodies. (Works V 321: S 36)

In both of these passages, Boyle is engaging in understatement. He doesn't simply hold that the mechanical philosopher is satisfied that matter can act only by local motion, he thinks that we all ought to be so satisfied. He doesn't simply think that it isn't easy to conceive of how one body can act upon another but by local motion, but that no other manner of action is in fact conceivable by us. Locke put the same thought more boldly in the first edition of the *Essay*, 2.8.11:[51]

The next thing to be consider'd, is how *Bodies operate* one upon another, and that is manifestly *by impulse*, and nothing else. It being impossible to conceive, that Body should operate on what it does not touch, (which is all one has to imagine it can operate where it is not) or when it does touch, operate any other way than by Motion. (Locke 1975, 135)

If we cannot conceive of bodies as acting except by motion, then it looks as though corporeal sensible qualities must be otiose, for we cannot explain how redness as a basic, non-mechanical quality could be transmitted from object to perceiver. The upshot is not that bodies could not be really red, nor that it is (as Descartes had it) unintelligible to suppose that they are really red, but that the posit that they are really red can do no explanatory work, since any explanation of sense perception would have to trace back to mechanically produced motion. Thus this conclusion is stronger than the mere claim that we ought not to posit real corporeal sensible qualities because we have a superior theory (simpler, clearer, more reductive, etc.) without them. The purported conclusion is that we cannot posit sensible qualities if we want to formulate a legitimate hypothesis in natural philosophy, one that can do explanatory work.

[51] He was famously forced to modify this claim by the example of Newton, as he acknowledges to Stillingfleet (Locke 1823, IV 467–8).

This ought to remind us of an argument of Descartes' that was dismissed as question-begging at the end of section 3. Descartes' emphasis there, in Part IV of the Principles, was on the implications of neurophysiology for the sensible qualities. And this strategy I accused of circularity *if* the goal is to argue that bodies don't have real sensible qualities, rather than merely that we may be able to explain sensory experience without positing any such qualities. The circularity arises because Descartes' neurophysiological views look uncontroversial only in a mechanist context; thus his neurophysiology can't be used to support the foundations of his mechanism. The second half of the passage, however, floats free of the details of neurophysiology and looks very much like Boyle's attempts to make a conceptual point about motion and the sensible qualities:

> Finally, let us consider heat and other qualities perceived by the senses, in so far as those qualities are in objects, as well as the forms of purely material things, for example the form of fire: we often see these arising from the local motion of certain bodies and producing in turn other local motions in other bodies. Now we understand very well how the different size, shape and motion of the particles of one body can produce various local motions in another body. But there is no way of understanding how these same attributes (size, shape and motion) can produce something else whose nature is quite different from their own—like the substantial forms and real qualities which many <philosophers> suppose to inhere in things; and we cannot understand how these qualities or forms could have the power subsequently to produce local motions in other bodies. Not only is all this unintelligible, but we know that the nature of our soul is such that different local motions are quite sufficient to produce all the sensations in the soul. What is more, we actually experience the various sensations as they are produced in the soul, and we do not find that anything reaches the brain from the external sense organs except for motions of this kind. In view of all this we have every reason to conclude that the properties in external objects to which we apply the terms light, colour, smell, taste, sound, heat and cold . . . are, so far as we can see, simply various dispositions in those objects which make them able to set up various kinds of motions in our nerves <which are required to produce all the various sensations in our soul>.
> (Pr IV 198)

Descartes writes here about what we can and cannot understand, but the point is quite different from his Pr I 66–71 argument. The claim here is not that it is unintelligible to suppose that bodies have real corporeal sensible qualities, but rather that, if we make that posit, we cannot use it to explain sensory experience.

Having located a common argument here, what should we think of it? Surely what Boyle and Descartes succeed in doing here is simply issuing an explanatory challenge: If sensible qualities such as redness are real corporeal qualities, it must be explained how such further qualities engage with motion, and it is quite unobvious what such an explanation would look like.[52] Both Boyle and Descartes overreach by claiming that

[52] It is worth remembering that the Scholastics thought they had given such an explanation, by way of intentional species, though their modern detractors typically regarded it as unworthy of serious attention. Malebranche (1980, 220–221) does devote a few pages of his extensive treatment of vision in the *Search After Truth* to refuting it. Boyle treats the theory contemptuously in *Things Above Reason*. It is presented as a possible *reductio* of the category of things above reason—if we must admit things above reason, will we end up

no such explanation can be given.[53] Boyle, characteristically, refrains from a further sort of (Cartesian) overreaching on this point, claiming only to have revealed what we can and cannot understand, not what must be the case. For Boyle, the physical world may well transcend mechanism (and thus transcend the corpuscularian list of primary affections), but to the extent that it does, we will never be able to fully comprehend it:

> ... I see no necessity, That Intelligibility to a *humane Understanding*, should be necessary to the Truth or Existence of a thing; any more then that Visibility to a *Humane* Eye, should be necessary to the Existence of an Atome, or of a Corpuscle of Air... (Works IX 398–9)[54, 55]

Bibliography

Anstey, P. (2000). *The Philosophy of Robert Boyle*, London: Routledge.

Berkeley, G. (1948–1957). 9 vols, ed. A. A. Luce and T. E. Jessop. *The Works of George Berkeley, Bishop of Cloyne*, London: Thomas Nelson and Sons.

Boyle, Robert. (1991). *Selected Philosophical Papers of Robert Boyle*, Indianapolis: Hackett.

—— (1999–2000). *The Works of Robert Boyle*, London: Pickering and Chatto.

Buroker, J. V. (1991). "Descartes on Sensible Qualities," *Journal of the History of Philosophy* 29(4): 585–611.

Clarke, D. (1989). *Occult Powers and Hypotheses*, Oxford: Oxford University Press.

Cook, M. (1996). "Descartes and the Dustbin of the Mind," *History of Philosophy Quarterly* 13: 17–33.

Cottingham, J. (1989–1990). "Descartes on Colour," *Proceedings of the Aristotelian Society* 90: 231–246.

De Rosa, R. (2007). "The Myth of Cartesian Qualia," *Pacific Philosophical Quarterly* 88: 181–207.

Des Chene, D. (1996). *Physiologia*, Ithaca: Cornell University Press.

Descartes, R. (1984–1991). *The Philosophical Writings of Descartes*. 3 vols, ed. and trans. J. Cottingham, R. Stoothoff, D. Murdoch, A. Kenny, Cambridge: Cambridge University Press.

—— (1996). *Œuvres de Descartes*. 11 vols, ed. C. Adam and P. Tannery. Paris, J. Vrin.

Garber, D. (1992). *Descartes' Metaphysical Physics*, Chicago: University of Chicago Press.

believing in intentional species (*Works* IX 407)? The answer, I take it, is that we won't because no good positive arguments have been presented in favor of intentional species and it is therefore a "precarious *Tenet*" (Works IX 408). One charitable contemporary commentator, Alison Simmons (1994, 153), ultimately concludes: "Unfortunately, species nevertheless turn out to be physical and metaphysical anomalies within the Aristotelian framework."

[53] Cottingham (1989–90) justifies Descartes' move here as an application of a "Causal Similarity Principle," but I am reluctant to attribute CSP to Descartes.

[54] Of course, this is too forthright to be in Boyle's own voice. He is speaking through the dialog character Eugenius. The topic is things above reason, but Boyle holds that this category is not exhausted by the divine, but also includes aspects of the corporeal world.

[55] I am grateful to Abe Roth and Daniel Sutherland for helpful comments at an early stage of this paper's existence. I have also benefited from comments (on sections 2–6) from audiences at USC (especially Mathias Frisch), NIU, Notre Dame, U. of Cincinnati, and the New England Colloquium in Early Modern Philosophy, as well as from students in Descartes seminars at UIC and OSU. Thanks also to two anonymous referees for Oxford University Press whose comments improved the paper.

—— (2001). "Forms and Qualities in the *Sixth Replies*," in *Descartes Embodied*. Cambridge: Cambridge University Press: 257–273.

Hume, D. (1978). *A Treatise of Human Nature*, ed. P. H. Nidditch and L. A. Selby-Bigge, Oxford: Clarendon Press.

—— (2000). *A Treatise of Human Nature*, ed. D. F. Norton and M. J. Norton, Oxford: Oxford University Press.

Kaufman, D. (2006). "Locks, Schlocks, and Poisoned Peas: Boyle on Actual and Dispositive Qualities," *Oxford Studies in Early Modern Philosophy* (3): 153–198.

—— (2008). "Descartes on Composites, Incomplete Substances, and Kinds of Unity," *Archiv für Geschichte der Philosophie* 90: 39–73.

Keating, L. (2004). "The Role of the Concept of Sense in Principles IV, 189–98," *British Journal for the History of Philosophy* 12(2): 199–222.

La Forge, L. de (1666). *Traité de l'esprit de l'homme*, Amsterdam: Abraham Wolfgang. (Reprint edition: Hildesheim: Georg Olms Verlag, 1984).

Locke, J. (1823). *The Works of John Locke*, 10 vols, London: Thomas Davison, Whitefriars.

—— (1975). *An Essay Concerning Human Understanding*, ed. P. H. Nidditch, Oxford: Clarendon Press.

Malebranche, N. (1958–1967). *Oeuvres Complètes de Malebranche*, 20 vols, ed. André Robinet, Paris: J. Vrin.

—— (1980). *The Search After Truth*, trans. T. Lennon and P. Olscamp, Columbus: The Ohio State University Press.

Menn, S. (1995). "The Greatest Stumbling Block: Descartes' Denial of Real Qualities," *Descartes and his Contemporaries: Meditations, Objections, and Replies*, R. Ariew and M. Grene, Chicago: University of Chicago Press: 182–207.

Rozemond, M. (1998). *Descartes's Dualism*, Cambridge: Harvard University Press.

Sanford, D. H. (2002). "Determinates vs. Determinables," *The Stanford Encyclopedia of Philosophy*, E. Zalta. http://plato.stanford.edu/archives/sum2002/entries/determinate-determinables/

Secada, J. (2000). *Cartesian Metaphysics: The Late Scholastic Origins of Modern Philosophy*, Cambridge: Cambridge University Press.

Simmons, A. (1999). "Are Cartesian Sensations Representational?", *Noûs* 33(3): 347–369.

—— (1994). "Making Sense: The Philosophical Treatment of Phenomenal Qualities from the Late Aristotelians to Descartes," *Philosophy*, Philadelphia: University of Pennsylvania.

Wilson, M. (1999). "Descartes on the Representationality of Sensation," *Ideas and Mechanism: Essays on Early Modern Philosophy*, Princeton: Princeton University Press: 69–83.

6

Primary and Secondary Qualities in Locke's *Essay*

Michael Ayers

1. Two readings of Locke's argument

The chapter of *An Essay concerning Human Understanding* in which Locke draws the distinction between primary and secondary qualities is one of the classic passages of early modern philosophy, the one that established the continuing use of those terms. Many students of philosophy still cut their teeth on it, although (or, perhaps, because) Locke's position is ambivalent in more ways than one, and the text at least gives excuses for a variety of interpretations. Locke's general conclusion, however, is still widely accepted, somehow surviving a supporting argument that seems to appeal to outdated speculative physical theory and to some oddly unconvincing intuitions.[1] Some of the problems are terminological, remediable by sympathetic or, perhaps, just contextually sensitive interpretation. Locke's argument is also significantly affected by a wider unclarity running through the *Essay* with respect to the status of 'ideas', an unclarity due to there being two different models in play for the relation between ideas and their objects, and accordingly for what an idea is. I will offer a somewhat qualified defence of Locke on that front in section 4, but important as the topic of intentionality is, both in itself and in the context of the distinction between primary and secondary qualities, the main topic of the present article is another ambivalence in Locke's position that is at least as philosophically important, and is perhaps even more immediately relevant to present debates.

It is possible to read the chapter, as many do, simply as the argued exposition of the mechanistic model of the material world that became dominant in European thought during the latter half of the seventeenth century—a process that had been under way for decades by the time Locke started to write the *Essay*. His version of this physical

[1] e.g., II.vii.19: ''tis plain [*Porphyre*] *has no colour in the dark*'; II.viii.20: 'What real Alteration can the beating of the Pestle make in any Body, but an Alteration of the *Texture* of it?' The first passage is part of an argument to the effect that the role of light in the perception of colour shows that the coloured object's contribution consists simply in a reflective 'Configuration of Particles'. The second perhaps works more as an invitation to grasp a simplifying explanatory ('intelligible') hypothesis than as an appeal to untutored intuition.

theory or proto-theory took *roughly* the form in which it had been advanced by his associate Robert Boyle in a series of works in the 1660s. Locke would certainly have been aware of its origins in ancient atomism.[2] The primary qualities are listed as solidity, extension, figure, mobility (or motion and rest), and sometimes 'texture' and number. Secondary qualities mentioned at various points in the argument, but nowhere comprehensively listed, include colours, sounds, tastes, heat and cold, and smells. In salient passages, including the sections 9–10 in which the terms 'primary' and 'secondary' are first introduced, Locke seems quite clearly to be telling us that primary qualities are primary just because they are the qualities that must be ascribed to bodies generally, including the 'insensible parts' of bodies, and secondary qualities are secondary because the physical causality involved in our perception of them (and in perception generally—sections 11–13) can, or even must, be explained entirely in terms of the primary qualities of those insensible parts—that is, mechanistically. Secondary qualities are therefore simply powers the bodies possess to cause certain ideas or sensations in us—powers they possess in virtue of their structure or 'texture', including the motion of their constituent particles, with consequential effects on the sense organs, brains and consciousness of perceivers. Primary qualities are thus ways bodies are in themselves, secondary qualities are a matter of ways bodies appear to the senses, in their ontological status no different from any powers bodies possess to affect other things in virtue of their primary qualities.

On this account, like many philosophical physicists and philosophers of physics today—indeed, like many practitioners of currently fashionable 'analytic metaphysics' who write with a layman's eye on physical theory—Locke is simply drawing the conclusion from contemporary physics that the world is not as it seems to the senses to be, and that many of our everyday beliefs are systematically false or misleading. If that is right—if the distinction between primary and secondary qualities is simply part and parcel of an exposition of seventeenth-century 'corpuscularian' mechanistic physics and its supposed epistemological and ontological implications—then the distinction has presumably been consigned to history by more recent science. It may still deserve the interest of philosophers as a classic, early case of a scientific ontology coming apart from the ontology of everyday life or 'common sense'. Locke's discussion may be admired by some as an early step towards an appreciation of how radically modern physics should change our considered view of the world and what is in it, even if it does not correspondingly change everyday ways of talking about it. Such admiration may come more easily, perhaps, in so far as present-day physics has evolved, with whatever mutations, from corpuscularian speculation. On the other hand, the distinction, or the terms in which it is drawn, may be criticized by some present-day philosophers who reject the idea that fundamental physics characteristically undermines the everyday

[2] Presumably directly—he possessed the extant works of both Epicurus and Lucretius. Another ancestral line, more apparent in Descartes than in Boyle, goes back to Platonic and Neoplatonic conceptions of the relation between mathematics and the world.

view of the world, and who believe that, as Wittgenstein put it, 'ordinary language is all right', at least when it comes to such basic, structural features of our world view as that there are material objects that have colours and smells. For such philosophers, no scientific explanation can show that everyday beliefs are *systematically* false or misleading. In their not unreasonable view, the belief that there are coloured things is not at all like the false belief in witches, or that the world is flat. But whichever line is taken, the issue over the distinction as Locke drew it will have been left far behind. Physicists no longer think of fundamental particles as Boyle or Locke thought of the 'insensible parts' of things. If a primary–secondary distinction is taken to track physical theory, it should presumably be drawn at some quite different place, if it makes sense to draw it at all. Some philosophers even think that the progress of science has revealed that (strictly speaking) there are no material objects, large or small, since there is no such stuff as 'matter'. In that case, presumably, there is nothing to possess Lockean qualities, whether primary or secondary—or, for that matter, to possess 'bare powers'.

Much of Locke's argument is open to a rather different reading, however, as proposing or, at least, marking or responding to a distinction between two different kinds of attribute that are both observable, a distinction available to philosophical reflection and independent of specific scientific theory. Primary and secondary qualities, after all, are both, as Locke uses the term, 'sensible qualities', even if the former are supposed instantiated by things too small to be perceived, as well as by perceptible objects. A relevant question to ask here is whether Locke is arguing *for* the distinction *from* corpuscularian theory, or *from* distinguishing features of the two types of qualities *for* the corpuscularian view. Insofar as there is any reason to favour the latter reading of Locke's argument, there is reason to conclude that the distinction itself, as Locke conceived of it, is independent of corpuscularian assumptions. The question whether the distinction is properly and reasonably drawn is in that case similarly independent of physical theory—and here I mean the full ontological distinction that Locke drew by describing primary qualities as '*real*... *Qualities* [that] are in the things themselves, whether they are perceived or no', whereas secondary qualities are only 'Powers to produce several *Ideas* in us by our senses'.

That reasons for such a distinction might be offered independently of any physical theory or mechanistic model can be seen very simply in the possibility of drawing out ontological consequences from the point that a secondary quality such as redness or sweetness, unlike sensible squareness, is *essentially* a way its possessor appears to one sense in particular. It was a claim commonly brought against Scholastic Aristotelian 'real qualities' (and alluded to at *Essay* II.ii.1 without reference to corpuscular theory) that the variety of types of secondary qualities we assign to the material world—colours, tastes, smells, sounds—reflects the variety of sense modalities, not a correspondent variety in things themselves. Although the point does not appear in the argument of *Essay* II.viii, it is, on this interpretation, highly relevant to Locke's thesis that spatial properties are available to more senses than one—to sight and touch, as he recognizes,[3]

[3] *Essay* II.v.

but also to proprioception, not to speak of bats' or whales' echo-location or the like. Things are different with Locke's 'secondary qualities'. It is true that we can, in a sense, see the heat of a red-hot poker, as well as feel it. But the look of a hot poker can be reduced to a characteristic colour and luminosity—that is, it can be fully described, at least in principle, without reference to heat—whereas the feeling of warmth or the way red looks cannot be similarly reduced. This point is associated with the natural thought that heat is 'directly' felt, but only 'indirectly' visible.

The list of sense modalities by which primary qualities might be perceived, on the other hand, is in principle open-ended. Such broad accessibility is what is to be expected, if the spatial properties of material things, and relations between those things, constitute a feature of the world as it objectively is—arguably a feature apprehension of which is a condition of knowledge of any 'things' at all, not to say a condition of objective knowledge in general. Some spatial relations, for example directions and, perhaps, distance, can be heard and smelt, as well as seen and felt, and even taste has its location in what is in the mouth. These last are phenomena having more to do with the integration of different senses, perhaps, than with what is available to more than one sense (if such a distinction is ultimately tenable). Yet that perceptual integration around things in space speaks even more clearly of our being in sensory contact with the very structure of an objective reality of which we ourselves are part. I say 'around' things in space, since it is through the immediate, uninferred inter-sensory or trans-sensory identification of material structure that our senses are integrated with one another and with our physical self-awareness and capacity to act. This is not, as Kantians are still inclined to argue or assume, a conceptual matter, but a basic and, I think, evident fact about the way the senses work together in human and, surely, other higher animals. That is not to say that in perceiving secondary qualities, seeing colours, tasting sweetness or the like, we are not in immediate sensory contact with reality. Rather, these are *ways* of perceiving a spatial, material world or, perhaps better, aspects of our perception of such a world. More graphically, the perception of the material structure of our environment, involving perception of things' 'primary qualities', supplies the structure on which perceived 'secondary qualities' are hung—the structure that makes objective knowledge of the latter possible, underwriting their objectivity.

Nevertheless, in distinguishing, among the observable qualities of things, those that are 'primary' from those that are 'secondary', Locke could not simply argue for, or from, the very plausible general principle that qualities that are the proper objects of a single sense owe their existence and identity to that relationship—in his terms, are simply powers to operate on the sense in question. Solidity is a key primary quality, playing a vital role in Locke's account of body, not least in his anti-Cartesian argument for a distinction between body and space (II.xiii.11–26). And the idea of solidity, he tells us, 'we receive by our Touch' (II.iv.1; cf. II.iii.1). To have embraced the principle that proper objects of a single sense are sense-relative he would at least have had to qualify his conception of the idea of solidity as an idea of one sense. As we shall see, he effectively did just that, but without clearly recognizing it. At any rate, he did not construct his argument on that basis.[4] Rather, he pursued the reasonable thought characteristic of philosophical mechanism that primary qualities figure prominently and naturally in explanations of how perceptible material objects behave and interact. Corpuscularianism was not a theory plucked from the air, but was founded on intelligible observable processes. Round things normally and understandably roll as square things do not; cogs turn other interlocking cogs, and we immediately 'see why' they do. Of course, we can be surprised. Magnetized balls will not easily roll down smooth iron slopes, clockwork requires rigid and coherent cogs.[5] Nevertheless, as Locke plausibly supposed, such mechanical processes are not only at least relatively 'intelligible', they are the only observable processes that possess any such intelligibility.[6] It is extremely plausible and, I think, right to suppose that the observation of such dependable and intelligible interactions, interactions that somehow make sense to us, speaks of our being in cognitive contact with ways the real world works—with Locke's 'manners of operation'. It takes a further step, however, to be enticed into the mechanist view that it is the *only* way the material world works.

It is, at any rate, in the context of this kind of thought that we can understand the place of solidity in the list of primary qualities. It is assigned by Locke to one sense, touch, but feeling a body's solidity is not like seeing its colour or feeling its warmth, since to feel its solidity (as, perhaps, also its shape) it is necessary to feel its resistance: that is, it is necessary to be sensorily aware of its bodily, mechanical interaction with ourselves. Hume, in criticizing 'the modern philosophy',[7] takes Locke's 'idea of solidity' to be a kind of purely qualitative sensation, but if that thought is present in the *Essay* at all, it is merged with a different account of it as taken from our awareness of resistance:

> Whether we move, or rest . . . we always feel something under us, that supports us . . . ; and the Bodies we daily handle, make us perceive, that whilst they remain between them, they do by an insurmountable Force, hinder the approach of the parts of our Hands that press them.
>
> (*Essay* II.iv.1)

He distinguishes solidity from impenetrability, but the line is fine.[8] The example of a football, at II.iv.6, is presumably chosen to demonstrate that even air, being a body, possesses just such impenetrability as is not only felt but manifested in the otherwise perceptible way the football interacts with us. Indeed, the feeling itself is a feeling of resistance. We are tactually aware of resistance—that is, in Locke's terms, of a body

[4] Locke does, however, explicitly recognize the significance of the tight relation between colour and sight in another passage: 'I shall not enter any farther into that disquisition [about the causes of ideas of sensible qualities], it sufficing to my purpose to observe, that gold or saffron has a power to produce in us the idea of yellow, and snow or milk the idea of white, which we can only have by our sight' (*Essay* II.xxi.73).

[5] As Locke in effect points out, at *Essay* II.xxiii.23–26.

[6] Cf. *Essay* IV.iii.13, and the (as often noted) very qualified approval of 'the corpuscularian Hypothesis' at IV.iii.16.

[7] *Treatise* I.4.4.

[8] II.iv.1: 'the common Notion of Solidity will allow, if not justifie, this use of [the Term *Solidity*]; but if any one think it better to call it *Impenetrability*, he has my consent.' Locke suggests that impenetrability is a negative consequence of the 'positive' quality solidity, perhaps seeing the latter as actual, the former as a power; but the resistance that we are said to feel is both positive and actual.

operating. Solidity is no ordinary 'idea of one sense', and it is arguably correct to include it in an account of what makes a body a body, and so in the list of primary qualities.[9]

Turning to Locke's list of secondary qualities, however, not every item on the list is as easily represented as being sense-relative as are colours and smells, a point that raises questions about the unity of the list. Heat, for example, is like solidity, at least in having indefinitely many dependable physical effects through which it is identifiable and measurable, other than its direct effect on our sensibility. Someone both lacking sensitivity to heat and innocent of physical theory could know what heat is from experience, without linking it to any particular feeling. The broad causal role of heat manifest to ordinary pretheoretical experience ensures that 'warm' is not as tightly linked to the characteristic feeling of warmth as 'yellow' is tied to a characteristic way things look. A person blind from birth, as Locke famously insists, will not know what redness is. Indeed, in a more technical idiom, 'heat' functions as a rigid designator of a physical condition as 'yellow' does not.[10] Light, another of Locke's 'secondary qualities' and traditionally thought a proper object of sight, is clearly more like heat than like colour. The same seems true of sound, given the obvious point, reflected in natural and pre-theoretical ways of talking, that heat, light and sound are all typically 'produced' by objects, and may be, respectively, felt, seen, and heard away from unperceived objects that produce them. On the other hand, Locke's claim at II.xxxi.2 that there would be no more heat or light than pain in the world if there were no sentient creatures (the sun and Mount Aetna notwithstanding) is arguably more paradoxical than a similar claim about sounds. Such a general term as 'quality', then, covers a variety not easily encapsulated in a simple dichotomy. Locke's primary–secondary distinction can appear to be something of a Procrustean bed.

Nevertheless, it is significant that heat, as a sensible quality of warm bodies, does not satisfy Locke's account of the primary qualities of a body (whether a body actually perceived or one merely conceived of as a constituent particle of perceivable bodies) as 'such as are utterly inseparable from the Body, in what state soever it be'. The implied underlying principle, reminiscent of, but subtly different from, stronger corpuscularian claims to have identified the fundamental essence of matter, is that we cannot conceive (or 'distinctly' conceive) of a body both as the material body it is and as lacking primary qualities, whereas we can so conceive of it as lacking secondary qualities.[11] If all

[9] It is interesting to compare Locke's account of 'body' with accounts of what a material object is (the 'concept' of a material object) that are currently supplied and debated by philosophers and psychologists of perception.

[10] For the distinction, see Saul Kripke 1980, although I differ from him in its application. Kripke himself understands 'yellow' and even 'pain' to be rigid designators, but in different ways, holding that 'yellow' rigidly designates a kind of physical state, but 'pain' rigidly designates a kind of state of consciousness, a point he takes to have dualist implications. For critical discussion of his argument directly relevant to the present topic, see Ayers 1991, vol. I, ch. 23.

[11] See section 3, below, for further discussion of this passage. We can, of course, *think of* a particular material object otherwise than as having primary qualities. Indeed, we can do so without knowing that it is a

material things possess some degree of heat, that is something to be learnt, and indeed given meaning, through physical theory. And although we can, for example, experience the transfer of heat from one body to another, the direct perception of heat by feeling does not make its manifest causal role in observable change perspicuous as the direct perception of the shape and solidity of a cog can make its manifest role in an observable mechanical process perspicuous. Some generalizations about heat and sound, like some generalizations about tastes, colours and smells, or, indeed, pain, may appear 'natural' or 'intelligible', but in quite a different way. That is either because we are ourselves affected, or in virtue of evolutionary advantage—or both, as in the case of the principle that animals avoid what is painful, or, less universally, that the smell of rotting meat tends to disgust mammals. If there is something common to all Locke's secondary qualities, apart from their being directly sensible, it is something negative—the *absence* of the two defining features of primary qualities: first, their possession by all bodies, and their inclusion in all thought of a body qua body; second, their role in 'intelligible' observable causal processes.

2. A second tension: Locke as sceptic and Locke as corpuscularian

There is, then, a tension between reading Locke on the distinction between primary and secondary qualities as essentially putting over a mechanist and corpuscularian view of the world, and reading him as drawing out the ontological and epistemological implications of a point available to reflective common sense about two sorts of sensible qualities or ways we observe things to be.

It may be helpful at this point to set this tension beside another apparent tension between themes of the *Essay*. The mechanistic 'corpuscular' model is employed in very many other passages than II.viii. For example, Locke ascribes unknowable 'real essences' to species of substances and rather frequently suggests that they are unknowable precisely *because* they consist in the structure and activity of the 'minute parts' of individuals of the species.[12] Again, the life of a plant is said to lie in 'such a disposition of [particles of matter] as constitutes the parts of' the plant, together with the 'organization' of those parts. Animals are not relevantly different, and both plants and animals are compared to machines. Watches and clocks are favourite examples.[13] It may therefore seem unquestionable that, for Locke, as for Epicurus, matter is simply solid, extended substance and

material object, as I can think of John's birthday present without knowing that it was a sweater rather than a trip in a balloon–which is *not* what Locke would have counted as having a distinct idea of it.

[12] Cf. *Essay* III.vi.6, 9, 39–40, IV.iii.25, etc. Even II.xxiii has what appears as an optimistically corpuscularian passage (II.xxiii.11–13), although it is evidently designed to lead into the more sceptical argument discussed below.

[13] *Essay* II.xxvii.4–5. Cf. III.vi.39–41. Many other salient passages are listed by Edwin McCann in the present volume.

nothing else: the material world consists exclusively of tiny particles of homogeneous solid stuff, generally in motion, pushing and knocking one another about.[14]

The problem for the conscientious expositor of Locke's thought is to reconcile this apparently confident account of, it seems, the nature or essence of matter with another line of argument that dominates much of the *Essay*, one that is clearly directed against dogmatic claims to have knowledge of the fundamental nature or essence of anything at all. It is not as if Locke can easily be taken to be laying claim to a knowledge of the fundamental nature of matter while confessing ignorance only of the precise form of the mechanical process involved in any particular causal relation, or the precise structure or 'texture' of particles that constitutes the 'real essence' of any particular chemical or biological species. He is quite explicit that the essence of matter is itself unknown. As he puts it somewhat paradoxically in the chapter on the idea of substance, '*We have as clear a Notion of the Nature, or Substance of Spirit, as we have of Body*',[15] a point explicated by an extended argument to persuade us that we have no clear ideas of either. Such ideas as we have of matter and spirit do not, and cannot, go beyond those ideas of superficial or observable qualities, operations and powers that we get from experience. More directly on the present point, the argument includes extended, detailed, and cogent criticism of the explanatory pretensions of corpuscularian theory, with the striking claim that, because we do not understand the *coherence* of the postulated particles, even their *extension*, and the extension of bodies in general, is beyond our understanding.[16] That is the point of Locke's assertion early in the chapter on the idea of substance that, if the question is raised of what the solidity and extension of material particles inhere in, the only available answer is that it is 'something, we know not what'.[17] We don't know the fundamental nature of that which is extended and solid.

[14] Cf. *Essay* IV.x.10: 'you may as rationally expect to produce Sense, Thought, and Knowledge, by putting together in a certain Figure and Motion, gross Particles of Matter, as by those that are the very minutest, that do anywhere exist. They knock, impel, and resist one another . . . and that is all they can do.' This is not, however, as it might at first seem, part of an argument for mind–body dualism, but for the conclusion that thought could only have been brought into existence by an eternal *essentially* thinking (and therefore immaterial) thing, i.e. God. Locke's view, I take it, was that if it were known that some bodies are so constituted as to have the power of thought and/or sensation (and he almost certainly had such a view of non-human animals, at least), that would be yet another reason to conclude that current mechanist theories don't give us the essence of body.

[15] *Essay* II.xxiii.5, eds 1–3 (Locke's emphasis). In the parallel passage in Draft A, the phrase is 'the essence of body', in editions 4–5, simply 'the substance of body'. Some may see this change as evidence that Locke came to make a general ontological distinction between substance and essence or nature, rather than just a distinction between the general substance, matter or 'body', and determinate 'real essences' of species of bodies. 'Substance', on this view, is some kind of purely logical entity, a naked bearer of properties. But even if such an interpretation were more tenable than it is, it would not affect the present point that Locke explicitly rejects corpuscularian claims to knowledge of the essence of matter.

[16] *Essay* II.xxiii. A target, presumably, is the Cartesian and Malebranchean assumption that the extension of matter is paradigmatically perspicuous and actual.

[17] *Essay* II.xxiii.2.

The apparent tension is underlined by consideration of the so-called 'Draft A' of the *Essay*, written in 1671. Some commentators have been so impressed by Locke's employment of a mechanist model like Boyle's in the completed work that they have seen it as his basic commitment, as if his epistemology was constructed to conform to it. Recent work on his early career and writings, however, points to the conclusion that, while he knew Boyle and studied some of his writings closely, his chief mentor as he developed his philosophical ideas was probably Thomas Sydenham, a physician in the ancient tradition of medical 'empirics'. The choice of remedies, Sydenham argued (and Locke reiterated in medical papers), should be guided by experience rather than theories that could only be, at that time, wildly speculative. Knowledge of the structure and workings of the body was at too coarse a level for such theories to be verifiable.[18] Draft A is revealing because virtually all the main epistemological themes of the *Essay*, including the onslaught on dogmatic accounts of substances and their essences, are set out, sometimes in passages repeated almost word for word in the published work, with only occasional and passing allusion to corpuscularian speculation. In one passage, melting, magnetic attraction, and freezing are said to be mysterious to us because 'these alterations are made by particles soe small and minute that they come not within the observation of [the] senses'.[19] It is tentatively suggested that 'white and sweet & many other sensations in us be perhaps causd in us constantly by particles of certain figures'.[20] Neither allusion to particles has a significant role in the argument beyond reinforcing a sense of the opacity of the natural processes in question. Matter or body is identified as the substance of physical things, but it is explicitly argued that neither Descartes' nor any rival corpuscularian definition of body supplies a basis for demonstrative science, or is anything but arbitrary and purely verbal.[21] The seemingly stronger (if still qualified) approval of corpuscularian theory manifested in the argument of *Essay* II.viii not only came later[22] to Locke than the scepticism with respect to essences that motivated his main epistemological themes, but even at its height was at least more nuanced than wholehearted or wholesale acceptance.

For even at his moments of greatest enthusiasm for corpuscularian mechanism Locke is not committed to the claim that *all* powers observably possessed by bodies, or all

[18] Cf. Jonathan Walmsley 2004, 15–37.

[19] Draft A, sec.15. See P. H. Nidditch and G. A. J. Rogers 1990, vol. I, p. 31. Walmsley 2004, 18, points out that neither reference to particles nor a view that observable effects flow from processes at a microscopic level was peculiar to purely mechanistic explanations. Locke himself had, in his earlier medical writings, employed the notion of 'small and insensible' 'ferments' such as figured in the theories of van Helmont, Thomas Willis and others, a notion which was open to mechanical interpretation, but did not demand it. See also Walmsley 2003, 417–49.

[20] Draft A, sec. 17 (p. 32).

[21] Draft A, sec. 27 (p. 45–6). Compare the dismissive allusion to the corpuscularian explanation of 'Colour or Weight' at II.xxiii.2.

[22] Draft B, also of 1671, contains very brief, tentative anticipations of *Essay* II.viii. Sec.58 (*Drafts* vol. I, p. 161) mentions particles in a discussion of possibly privative causes of some simple ideas. Sec. 94, in a late interpolation (p. 209), suggests that many sensible qualities and their ideas 'are probably but the results and modifications of [Extension and Cohaesion of parts]'.

observable causal processes, can be explained mechanistically.[23] That it is equally mysterious on either dualist or materialist assumptions how matter (i.e. motions in the brain) should give rise to sensations is taken by Locke to be an indication that we do not know the essence of matter simply in knowing that it is extended and solid (and so mobile) substance: 'what Substance exists that has not something in it, which manifestly baffles our Understandings'.[24] Gravity, or attraction between bodies, was taken, at least in Locke's later defence of the sceptical message of the *Essay*,[25] to be another sign that there is more to matter than is contained in our idea of it. Bodies behave and have effects in ways we cannot understand, and can at best simply record, even if they also behave in ways that we can to an extent understand. None of this should be taken as evidence that Locke believed in two sorts of causal process, those that are in principle intelligible, and those that are simply brute regularities. He assumed that all causality is in principle fully rationally intelligible, although for us, with our limited stock of ideas, it divides into three types: observed (mechanical) causality, such as clockwork, that is, as observed, partially intelligible to us; observed or experienced causality (e.g. friction making a rod hot, or water seeming hot to one hand and cold to another),[26] not in itself even partially intelligible to us, but for which we can postulate, by analogy, a speculative, partially intelligible explanation or part-explanation (i.e. a mechanical hypothesis); and observed or experienced causality that is obstinately unintelligible to us, and which in our ignorance we are left to assign to 'the arbitrary Determination of that All-wise Agent, who has made them to be, and to operate as they do, in a way wholly above our weak Understandings to conceive'.[27] An example of this last, not seriously considered by Locke until after the publication of the *Essay*, would be the phenomenon of attraction or gravitation, which in *Elements of Natural Philosophy* is in effect contrasted with the quasi-axiomatic law of inertia, and is said only to appear 'as far as human observation reaches, to be a settled law of nature ... inexplicable by us, though made evident to us by experience, and so to be taken as a principle of natural philosophy.'[28]

[23] Cf. IV.iii.25: 'These insensible Corpuscles, being the active parts of matter ... on which depend not only *all* the Secondary Qualities, but also *most* of their natural Operations' (my emphases). The passage continues, knowledge of the primary qualities of the minute constituent parts of bodies would allow prediction 'without Trial' of 'several' of their operations (which perhaps means a variety of them, rather than a few).

[24] *Essay* IV.iii.6 (p. 543).

[25] *The Works of John Locke* (London 1823), vol. IV, pp. 467–8.

[26] *Essay* IV.xvi.12, p. 665–6; II.viii.21.

[27] IV.iii.28. Here I disagree with McCann and others who think that Locke believes that some or all laws are contingent regularities set up by God arbitrarily, in the sense that just the same causes could have been assigned quite different effects. Broadly speaking, if we are left to assign what experience teaches us is a dependable causal connection to God's arbitrary appointment ('good pleasure' or the like), that exigency is, for Locke (as implied in the passage quoted), a manifestation of our ignorance of the 'manner of operation' of the substances God has chosen to create. The issue has been much debated in the last thirty years.

[28] *The Works of John Locke* (London, 1823) IV 33–7.

Briefly, then, mechanistic corpuscularianism was for Locke the best available inadequate theory, and was employed in argument as such.[29] Sometimes its virtues, sometimes its inadequacies come to the fore. It is a question whether the same is true of the distinction between primary and secondary qualities—that is, whether Locke perceived his express doubts about corpuscularian theory as *ipso facto* doubts about the distinction. We have seen reasons why that might not be so, despite the fact that he may appear to be advancing a single argument for both at the same time.

3. A thought experiment, and intelligible causation: an argument for the corpuscular hypothesis

Let us, then, return to the question whether Locke is arguing in *Essay* II.viii *from* corpuscularian mechanism *for* a distinction between primary and secondary qualities, or the reverse.

The first sections of the chapter, which is vaguely and unpretentiously entitled 'Other Considerations concerning simple Ideas', deal with the consideration that certain ideas or perceptions 'in the mind', commonly suspected of having privative causes 'in the subject', are in themselves positive.[30] The *ideas* of cold, darkness, black, and rest, for example, are as positive as those of heat, light, white, and motion. Locke suggests that the question whether any simple ideas have privative causes hangs on the 'hard' question '*Whether Rest be any more of a privation than Motion*', a thought that seems already to imply that the causes are in some general sense mechanical.[31] The point of the discussion, however, is to emphasize the distinction between the ideas we get in sense perception and whatever is going on (or not) in the object (the 'modifications of matter', as he puts it in section 7) that causes those ideas. How we perceive the object to be, and how it is in itself, are not necessarily the same—or, as Locke puts it, ideas of

[29] Cf. *Essay* IV.iii.16 for a well-known expression of this attitude: 'I have here instanced in the corpuscularian Hypothesis, as that which is thought to go furthest in an intelligible Explication of the Qualities of Bodies; and I fear the Weakness of humane Understanding is scarce able to substitute another, which will afford us a fuller and clearer discovery of the necessary Connexion, and *Co-existence* of the Powers, which are observed united in several sorts of them.' This frank passage is nevertheless surrounded by otherwise unqualified appeals to the 'corpuscularian hypothesis', as at IV.iii.26: 'having no *Ideas* of the particular primary Qualities of the minute parts of [Sage and Hemlock], . . . we cannot tell what effects they will produce. . . . Thus having no *Ideas* of the particular mechanical Affections of the minute parts of Bodies . . . , we are ignorant of their Constitutions, Powers, and Operations.' But the context also famously contains examples of causal relations taken to be impossible to explain mechanically, such as the relations between brain events and sensations.

[30] Locke presumably saw himself as resolving or avoiding what was a problem for the Scholastic conception of 'real qualities'. He probably also had in mind Descartes' treatment of the issue in the Second Meditation.

[31] Michael Jacovides 2007c, in his thoughtful essay, takes the question supposedly underlying these cases to be whether motion is absolute or relative (128). That is unlikely, since that issue is irrelevant to such judgements as that coldness in an object is the absence of movement of its particles. Locke more probably had in mind the question of the status of rest as one determination of 'mobility'.

sensible qualities are not necessarily 'exactly the Images and *Resemblances* of something inherent in the Object' (II.viii.7).

After some terminological preliminaries (to which I will return) comes the most fully argued case for corpuscularian doctrine in the *Essay*. First comes an appeal to experience, coupled with a thought experiment (section 9). Whatever observable changes a body undergoes, if it remains perceptible it is perceived as possessing solidity, some size and shape, and 'mobility' (some 'motion or rest'), and if it is divided (for example, ground) into individually imperceptible parts, we have to conceive each of those parts as possessing those qualities. In effect, it is impossible even to conceive of a body as a body without such attributes. Locke therefore calls these properties '*original* or *primary* Qualities of Body'.[32] It is implied that we *can* conceive of solid, shaped particles without colour, smell, taste, heat, or the like, and section 10, in effect, tells us how. For we can understand how sensations of colour, etc. may be caused (as, allegedly, is 'in truth' the case) by the primary qualities of the 'insensible parts' of the sensible bodies to which we attribute those 'secondary qualities'—a point summed up by Locke's characterization of secondary qualities as 'Powers to produce various Sensations in us by their *primary Qualities*'.[33] Indeed, the 'only way we can conceive Bodies operate in' is '*by impulse*' (section 11), so that bodies perceived at a distance must therefore cause ideas in us by the medium of 'singly imperceptible Bodies' coming from them, a model applicable to the perception of both primary and secondary qualities (sections 12–13). As applied to the latter, we can understand how differences in the primary qualities of extremely small 'Particles, affecting the several Organs of our Senses, produce in us those different Sensations, that we have from the Colours and Smells of Bodies.' The sensations need not resemble their causes, any more than pain resembles the cutting of flesh that causes it. (s.13–14). Ideas of primary qualities, on the other hand, have 'patterns' in the perceived bodies, which they resemble (s.15).

Before considering what could be meant by 'resemblance', we may note again the role of Locke's notion of intelligible causality or action. As I have suggested, a main driving force behind corpuscularian theory was the intuitive conviction that mechanical processes such as clockwork are somehow rationally 'intelligible' as qualitative change is not. To observe such a process is not only to observe a succession of causally related

[32] At least, this is taken to be sufficient explanation of their primacy at this point in the argument, for the sake of the argument. Locke would no doubt have allowed that a *full* account of what it is for sensible qualities to be 'primary' would involve more than that. Accordingly, at *Essay* II.xxi.73, he suggests that in order to 'reduce' all our ideas of the qualities of bodies 'to these very few primary, and original ones' he would need to 'consider, as a Philosopher, and examine on what Causes they depend, and of what they are made'.

[33] McCann, in the present volume, rightly points out that section 10 is a late (Third Edition) interpolation which tends both to obscure the link in argument between abstracting out the primary qualities of all bodies and identifying intelligible (mechanical) causation, and clumsily to anticipate the conclusion of the whole argument as to the status of secondary qualities. (Cf. James Hill 2009 93–4.) Nevertheless its presence serves a purpose in the argument beyond introducing the idea or claim that secondary qualities are mere powers, since to accept the corpuscular explanation of perception (whether rightly or wrongly) is to conceive of bodies as existing without secondary qualities.

happenings, it is to be in a position, at least, to see *why* they happen as they do. Such intelligibility was standardly interpreted in a strong sense. When we know the physical structure of a mill at rest, so the Port Royal *Logic* tells us, we can predict 'infallibly' which millstone will turn when it is put in motion. Locke himself often expresses similar thoughts. A contrast between simply observing the movement of the hands of a clock and understanding their movement from sight of the works serves repeatedly as a close analogy for the difference between our actual need to learn from experience how natural substances behave, and the ideal, certain knowledge we would have of how they must behave, if we could observe their mechanical structure. Another analogy, much discussed by commentators, is between the deduction of properties from the essences of species of substances (impossible for us) and the demonstration of geometrical theorems.[34] The only difference, for Locke, is that we would have to have perceptual knowledge of the essences or fundamental constitutions of the bodies involved, whereas geometrical demonstration takes off from arbitrarily formed complex ideas of 'simple modes'. That difference is one reason why Locke believed that, unlike geometry, 'natural Philosophy is not capable of being made a Science'.[35]

There are strong echoes, doubtless fully intentional, of earlier corpuscularian arguments in the argument of II.viii.9–15. The thought-experiment follows a standard model for identifying essence by stripping away accidents in thought, comparable to Descartes' identification of the essence of matter,[36] and even more so to Hobbes' similar claim that an abstract consideration of just those properties of bodies that are common to all bodies—that constitute what it is to be a body—supplies us with all that is necessary for the laws of physics to become evident to us.[37] Spinoza offers a further version of the same thought.[38] But these philosophers are dogmatic mechanists, whereas, as I have argued and is in any case obvious enough, on the evidence of most of the *Essay* Locke is certainly not that. It is attractive, therefore, despite the apparent confidence of his espousal of corpuscularianism in II.viii, to look for a way of reading the thought-experiment as having in his hands a less dogmatic function. The corpuscularian hypothesis is not knowledge or 'science' for Locke, not only because it is the merely general supposition that imperceptible structures and processes are of the same kind as perceived mechanical structures and processes, but also, as we have seen,

[34] Cf. *Essay* IV.iii.25: 'I doubt not but if we could discover the Figure, Size, Texture, and Motion of the minute Constituent parts of any two Bodies, we should know without Trial several of their Operations one upon another, as we do now the Properties of a Square, or a Triangle. Did we know the Mechanical affections of the Particles of *Rhubarb, Hemlock, Opium,* and a *Man,* as a Watchmaker does those of a Watch... we should be able to tell before Hand, that *Rhubarb* will purge, *Hemlock* kill, and *Opium* make a Man sleep.' Cf. III.vi.3 and 9. Locke always uses the term 'property' in the standard sense of the 'predicables' of Scholastic logic: genus, difference, species, properties, and accidents. *Properties* of a genus or species (unlike accidents) are deducible from the definition of the genus or species by (higher) genus and difference.

[35] *Essay* IV.xii.10.

[36] *Principles of Philosophy* II.4.

[37] *De corpore* I.vi.1–6.

[38] *Ethics* II, Props 38–9.

because material structures and mechanical processes are not themselves comprehensively intelligible. Most fundamentally, the coherence (and therefore, Locke argues, the extension itself) of the postulated particles remains unexplained. Even the full intelligibility of action by impulse is itself impugned on the somewhat metaphysical ground that we cannot understand the transfer or communication of motion from one body to another, or even whether impulse is really an 'action' (II.xxiii.28). As I have suggested, such sceptical pronouncements feed on just that strong conception of rational intelligibility accepted by dogmatic mechanists: that is to say, Locke accepts that the world is, in a strong sense, intelligible in itself, but only very partially intelligible to us.

Such partial intelligibility, however, is evidently crucial to the argument of II.viii. Primary qualities are 'primary' because they belong to all bodies as perceived, and because it is impossible to conceive of a body, or matter in general, as existing without them. But it is because they, and they alone, are involved in the only kind of observable processes of which we have any understanding, that it is compelling to suppose that such processes at a microscopic level constitute the physical link between sensations or 'perceptions' of light, colour, heat, smell, etc. and their objects. Our understanding of mechanical process, that is to say, gives us the means to understand how it is or might be[39] that our ideas of other sensible qualities are due to powers bodies possess in virtue of the primary qualities of their minute parts—and more generally, how it is that bodies differ from one another in possessing a variety of powers to affect other bodies in observable ways.

To summarize the nub of the argument, Locke starts by considering what it is to be a body, and from that draws up a list of primary qualities that is independent of universal mechanism, or any physical theory. From the claim that the only way we can conceive bodies to operate is mechanically, he moves on to a mechanistic explanation of perception. From this he arrives at the conclusion that secondary qualities are not, as perceived, really in objects, but are merely powers to affect the senses in regular ways. So the class of primary qualities is identified independently and employed in an argument for corpuscularianism, which is then in turn employed to establish the ontological status of secondary qualities.

Nevertheless, some other considerations that Locke brings in support of the thesis that secondary qualities are not really in things otherwise than as powers are not so clearly dependent on the corpuscularian hypothesis. The assimilation of sensations of sweetness and whiteness with pain in sections 16–18 (for what it is worth) and the argument in section 19 that the role of light as a condition of vision shows that colours are merely powers to affect us, both come embellished with vague, speculative mechanistic explanations, but these physical explanations are not so much premises as illustrative, exemplary alternatives to the Scholastic model for perception. Moreover,

[39] Even in II.viii there are phrases to indicate speculation: 'we may conceive...', 'Let us suppose at present...' (sec. 13).

these paragraphs follow what comes closest in Locke's argument to a direct appeal to the intuition that at least some qualities that are perceivable by one sense only—colours, odours, tastes, sounds—are defined by their relationship to that sense: that is, are simply ways things appear to sight, smell, taste and hearing.

Take away the Sensation of them: let not the Eyes see Light, or Colours, not the Ears hear Sounds; let the Palate not Taste, nor Nose Smell, and all Colours, Tastes, Odors, and Sounds, as they such particular *Ideas*, vanish and cease, and are reduced to their Causes, *i.e.* Bulk, Figure, and Motion of Parts. (II.viii.17).

Although this passage is serving up a contrast with the '*real Qualities*' 'of the parts of Fire, or Snow', and ends with a mechanistic account of the causes of the ideas of the qualities mentioned, the intuitive force of the argument does not depend on the correctness of the corpuscularian hypothesis, but on the special relationship between quality and sense in each case.

So does the running appeal to the corpuscularian model and argument throughout *Essay* II.viii commit Locke to holding that his distinction between primary and secondary qualities stands or falls with the truth of his mechanist speculations? I have offered argument that such a distinction is available to reflective common sense. A version of the 'common sense' argument might run as follows:

Whatever the ultimate nature of matter, to perceive or conceive of a material object, a body, as such, is to perceive or conceive of it as possessing certain properties in virtue of which it has a presence in space. For a perceptible body has extension and shape, bound up with a certain causal presence, so to speak: it is coherent, resistant, solid, and mobile. These observable properties (call them primary qualities), without which a body would not be a body, are just those that are involved in those causal interactions between bodies that are peculiarly intelligible or open to us (and also, perhaps not accidentally, most intimately involved in human action)—, that is to say, mechanical interactions, as when a moving body pushes or knocks another body into motion. Whatever sensory equipment we may suppose non-human animals to have, if they perceive and discriminate material objects, they must perceive them as possessing these properties. Other sensible qualities that we ascribe to bodies (call them secondary qualities), such as colours and smells, so far from being necessary to the very perception or conception of the bodies, are evidently bound up with particular modes of perceiving things that may be peculiar to particular classes of animals. We can understand that much from common experience, without knowing anything more about the physics and physiology of perception. A certain speculation, however, may illustrate the physical possibilities and so help us to grasp the implications of the sense-relativity of secondary qualities. Let us suppose that objects appear differently coloured in daylight because daylight is composed of particles of various shapes and sizes, moving in straight lines, some of which are reflected from a seen object into the eye, while others are absorbed by the object, in each case depending on the surface texture of the object seen (cf. II.viii.13). Or perhaps heat is the violent motion of particles, which we feel as heat when some of the motion is transferred from an object to the particles of our body touching it. That would explain, incidentally, how the same water can feel warm to one hand and cold to the other, depending on the pre-existing motion in each hand (cf. II.viii.21).

This argument is clearly not far from Locke's argument in the *Essay*, and would perhaps have been even closer if his finished version had been less contaminated, so to speak, by his increased enthusiasm for mechanism.[40] I believe that it is a good argument, with a largely true conclusion. It is independent, not only of any particular physics and physiology of perception,[41] but of any particular philosophical view about the implications of fundamental scientific theory for a 'common sense' or pre-theoretical account of the world directly respondent to ordinary experience. The conclusion of the argument, indeed, is the product of reflective 'common sense'—of reflection on the explicanda accessible to us all, rather than being the implicate of a scientific theory. So to accept that there is a distinction more or less as drawn by Locke is not in itself to set foot on the slippery slope that ends with a declaration that, strictly speaking, there are no such things as material objects, plants, animals, people, or consciousness, just primary particles (or forces, or whatever). At the same time, there is room in the argument for a physiological story, whether well founded or consciously speculative, that may serve to fill out or illustrate (and so make more perspicuous) the proposal that secondary qualities, although correspondent to ways their possessors are,[42] are also somehow determined by modes of perception, as perceived primary qualities are not. There is relevance, too, for the consideration that there is something 'intelligible' about mechanical processes, although that (if Humeans will permit) valid point falls well short of full-blown corpuscularian mechanism, or even the limited version espoused by Locke.

4. Ideas, qualities, powers, and resemblance

My aim in the previous sections has been to disentangle two strands combined in Locke's argument, one of which essentially involves his (qualified) approval of corpuscularian mechanical physics, the other of which springs from insights about the perception of bodies and their interactions that are independent of any particular physical theory. I have not yet considered certain traditional criticisms (still, I think, very much alive) specifically aimed at his allegedly illegitimate and confused employment of the notions of resemblance and power. It has to be said that such criticisms have some excuse.

Much of the problem arises from an at least potential incoherence in his notion of an idea. 'Idea', Locke famously tells us, is the best available term for 'whatsoever is the Object of the Understanding when a Man thinks', an account that locates Lockean

[40] Or, less pejoratively, if in the *Essay* he had not employed the appeal to reflective common sense as a way of advancing corpuscularian mechanism, a simple and universal model for fundamental physics that was undoubtedly the most fertile available at the time, the seed-bed of modern science.

[41] That is not to say that increasing knowledge of the actual mechanisms of perception is philosophically irrelevant. It may complicate the issue in surprising ways.

[42] Not necessarily on a one-to-one basis, given, for example, the existence of 'metamers'—different distributions of wavelengths of light that give rise to perceptions of the same colour.

ideas close to Scholastic 'objective concepts' and Cartesian 'ideas taken objectively', otherwise identified as 'things as they are conceived of' or are 'in the mind'. Ideas taken 'formally', on the other hand, are acts of thinking, mental happenings which *have* intentional objects. This systematic ambiguity of 'idea' was compared by Descartes to the ambiguity of 'picture'. To describe a picture 'taken objectively' is to describe its content, the represented objects, as they are depicted. To describe it 'taken formally' is to describe its material structure. Both descriptions, in their different ways, characterize the same thing.[43] At any rate, given this provenance, and the ambiguity that, as Descartes rightly noted, runs through the ordinary language of representation or intentionality, it is hardly surprising if 'idea' is an ambiguous term in the *Essay*. But the situation is more complicated than that.

As Locke's definition of 'idea' would suggest, much of the *Essay* is indeed concerned with ideas taken objectively. Knowledge (or universal knowledge) is defined as the perception of a relation between ideas, for example between the idea of the angles of a triangle and the idea of two right angles, and the perceived relation is evidently taken to be between objects of thought, rather than between acts of thought. Geometry is not a branch of psychology. Ideas are the 'materials' of thought and knowledge, ultimately acquired in sensation and reflection: that is, we are dependent on experience for what we can think and what we can know.

In the context of the distinction between primary and secondary qualities, Locke's central conclusion that ideas of primary qualities *resemble* the qualities in the object, as ideas of secondary qualities do not, is easy to understand by analogy with the claim that a portrait—that is, the subject as depicted—resembles or fails to resemble the real subject. In perceiving the size, shape, and solidity of a material object, how we perceive it to be is the way it is. As Locke puts it, 'A Circle or Square are the same, whether in Idea or Existence; in the Mind, or in the Manna' ('the Manna' being a 'piece of *Manna* of a sensible Bulk'). 'In idea' and 'in the mind' are operators like 'in the story' and 'in the picture'. There is no need to cook up a special sense of 'resemble' or 'same', as some commentators on Locke have been inclined to do. Moreover, the notion of a relationship between how things are 'in the mind' and how things are 'in reality', whether resemblance or difference, corresponds to another traditional use of the formal-objective dichotomy, also taken over and explained by Descartes. The sun as it exists objectively in the minds of naïve observers is very different from the sun as it exists formally in reality. The former Descartes identifies with an idea of the sun.

That understanding of it does not meet all possible objections to Lockean talk of resemblance. What does it mean to say that our idea of green does not resemble a real quality in the object? Surely (a stickler for 'ordinary language' might ask) grass is green 'in reality'? It is not blue, as it might be 'in' some fauvist painting, or 'in the mind' of

[43] Strictly speaking, no doubt, depicted objects and the physical picture are logically distinct entities, having different principles of individuation—although, interestingly, what these are is open to fundamental dispute in both cases. But that is another story.

someone suffering from an unusual visual problem. An answer to that objection is that contrasts with what is 'really' so can slide, or be reiterative, in a way perhaps best explained by examples. The assertion that the sea that is purple in a doctored photograph was in reality blue is not in conflict with an assertion that the sea is only ever blue 'in appearance', since 'in reality' a 'blue' sea is simply reflecting the blue sky. And that is compatible with a contrast between the sky's being blue only 'in appearance' (there is nothing coloured up there at all) and grass's being green 'in reality'. And the assertion that the grass is 'in reality' green is not in conflict with the reflective or second-order assertion that in general things are coloured only 'in appearance', being 'in reality' simply so physically constituted as regularly to affect our sense of sight in certain ways in the presence of daylight (a theory about light can help to explain how). That such an assertion counts as 'philosophical' is hardly enough to disqualify it. No doubt there is a default or basic understanding of 'The lawn is not green' (since it has gone brown, or is composed of yellow grass) or 'The urine is colourless' (so the kidneys are all right). But ordinary language and ways of thought are flexible enough to allow it to be said with point, and truly, that colours 'as we perceive them' are just ways things systematically appear to sight, not 'real' physical features of things. And to repeat, the point is not necessarily the consequence of a general prejudice that all that are really out there (not to say, in here, in us) are the entities that get a mention in fundamental physics (if philosophers of physics can work out what those are). Rather, it is a result of reflection on the peculiar link that exists between colour and sight.[44]

Unfortunately for this liberal and favourable understanding of Locke's argument, he sometimes seems theoretically committed to giving a general account of the representative relation between ideas ('sensations, or perceptions') and their objects that is purely causal. Simply through 'the actual receiving of ideas from without' we come to know that something exists such as normally (Locke says 'always') causes the idea in question. We don't need to know or consider how it does so in order to think about this cause *through* the idea, simply as whatever causes it (IV.xi.2). This account of 'sensitive knowledge of existence' is consonant with a recurrent argument that all simple ideas are 'real', 'adequate', and 'true' just because they are the regular effects of powers in things, and so serve as 'Marks of distinction in Things'[45]. The latter argument focuses exclusively on ideas of secondary qualities, and seems designed to supplement the account in II.viii of how these ideas, despite their difference from ideas of primary qualities, can nevertheless represent ways external objects are. Locke's prime example of sensitive knowledge is also knowledge of the existence of a secondary quality, *white*. But both arguments are presented as if intended to have a more general application,

[44] J. L. Austin 1962, 62–77 gives a similar account of ordinary uses of 'real' and 'really'. But, while just mentioning distinctions between dreams, illusions, etc. and reality, Austin has his reasons for not focusing on the use of such expressions to draw the contrast with an intentional content (with what is so 'in the picture' or 'in her mind'), and would very possibly have disapproved of their use to make a philosophical distinction between whole classes of qualities.

[45] *Essay* II.xxxii.14. Cf. II.xxxi.2, etc.

extending to all 'simple ideas' and sensations, and they combine to stress that someone totally innocent of either knowledge or theory about the causality of perception can nevertheless know that the things they perceive *exist*, and can think about them systematically, at least to the extent of distinguishing and classifying them. Explicitly, it is simply irrelevant to such basic thought and knowledge of external objects whether 'the Mind (as in most Men I believe it does) judges these *Ideas* to be in the Things themselves.' A target here is surely Descartes, for whom *knowledge* of the existence of material objects requires reasoning about the cause of sensations employing an innate idea of matter as extended substance, not to mention the principle that God is not a deceiver. Such rational knowledge, for Descartes, could not possibly be combined with the belief that colours are real qualities of bodies.

Whatever their point, however, both of these arguments or theses of Locke's suggest that simple ideas or sensations are blank sensory effects that have objects and can be employed in thought only in so far as they are experienced as effects of something external to the perceiver. Such a conception of ideas is significantly different from the traditional conception of concepts or ideas as the essentially representational or intentional elements of experience and thought, capable (like 'thoughts' themselves) of being taken either 'formally' or 'objectively'. On this understanding of Locke's account, the intentionality of ideas is something added to them by the mind solely in virtue of its consciousness of their provenance in sense perception. They are less like Descartes' 'ideas taken formally' than like his 'sensations', with Hume's 'impressions' ancestors of twentieth-century 'sense-data'.

Acceptance of the notion that all sensory ideas or sensations are, in themselves, blank data makes the thought that ideas of primary qualities 'resemble' their objects problematic, if not absurd. To modify only slightly a famous objection of Berkeley's, how can a blank sensation be like anything but another blank sensation?[46] And, in any case, why should an effect be assumed to be like its cause, when the cause is known only through that effect? But even if the model is restricted to secondary qualities, there are problems for Locke's famous distinction at II.viii.8 between 'ideas' and 'qualities': 'Whatsoever the Mind perceives in it self, or is the immediate object of Perception . . . that I call *Idea*; and the Power to produce any *Idea* in our Mind, I call *Quality* of the Subject wherein that power is.' If the quality *blue* is explained as, simply, the power to cause a certain blank effect, namely 'the simple idea of blue', and is known only as the cause of that effect, then that effect, it seems, must be capable of being understood and identified independently of the quality—just as we understand what brittleness, or solubility, is through understanding what breaking, or dissolving, is. It is natural to conclude that the primary use of 'blue' is for ideas, and that its use for objects is secondary, equivalent to 'liable to cause blue ideas'. Locke makes just that move: '*Flame* is denominated *Hot* and *Light*; *Snow White* and *Cold*; and *Manna White* and

[46] Or to bring the question into the twentieth (even, I fear greatly, the twenty-first) century, how could a *quale* be like anything but another *quale*?

Sweet, from the *Ideas* they produce in us' (II.viii.16). An analogy with pain makes the model clear: 'Why is Whiteness and Coldness in Snow, and Pain not, when it produces the one and the other *Idea* in us; and can do neither, but by the Bulk, Number and Motion of its solid Parts?' Locke concludes that ordinary language is misleading:

> For though Fire be call'd painful to the Touch, whereby is signified the power of producing in us the *Idea* of Pain; yet it is denominated also Light and Hot; as if Light and Heat, were really something in the Fire, more than a power to excite these *Ideas* in us; and therefore are called *Qualities* in, or of the Fire. (*Essay* II.xxxi.2)

Even if we ignore the appeal to corpuscularian theory, there is something deeply mistaken about all this. The primary use of 'blue' is for objects, not in such expressions as 'a sensation of blue' or 'appearance of blue'. So if the quality of blueness in objects is a power, it is the power that some objects (surfaces, forms of light, etc.) have to appear a certain way to sight, namely blue. Does this circularity make nonsense of the explanation of secondary qualities as powers? Perhaps not.

One way in which to salvage an insight from that explanation or analysis may be to revert to the traditional understanding of 'ideas', either as essentially or intrinsically intentional mental states or happenings, or as intentional objects. The 'idea' or 'sensation' of blue is intentional because it is the apprehension of just one aspect of how something—characteristically, a material object—appears or looks. In the other sense of 'idea', it simply *is* that aspect of objects as they present to sight. Like any 'aspect' of objects as they appear, it can be considered abstractly, marked by a predicate. That possibility is implicit in the notion of a particular 'aspect', in this metaphorical use of the term. But that does not mean that observers of blue objects or surfaces in space are presented with their blueness as a separate entity, a blank effect 'in the mind'. Here, it is important to note, there is a danger of drawing too quick a contrast between colour and pain, in objection to Locke's analogy, by accepting his assumption that the pain caused by touching a hot poker is just such a distinct mental event or *quale*, separable from perception of the poker, as the idea of the poker's colour is not. That objection and contrast would be too quick, just because pain *is* a form of awareness of something, namely the body, an awareness integrated with proprioception. Platitudinously, physical pain is felt to have a location in the body. The answer to Locke's rhetorical question, quoted in the last paragraph, is not that the sensation of whiteness is intentional, whereas pain is not. It is that the whiteness is 'in' the snow, but the pain caused by the snow is not in it, because the whiteness in question, unlike the pain, is an aspect of the appearance or look of the snow. Physical pain, on the other hand, regarded as a mental state or occurrence, is a mode of awareness of some (or perhaps, in some bad cases, every) part of the body. Regarded as 'in' an object (and we do so speak of pain, of course) it is 'in', for example, the frozen fingers, although there are reasons why it is not therefore thought of as a *quality* of the fingers.[47]

[47] There is of course more to be said about pain, and the analogy with secondary qualities. Cold is different from both pain and colour, in that, in the case considered, both the snow and the fingers are likely to feel cold: i.e. coldness is 'in' both snow and fingers. For more discussion, see Ayers 1991, vol. I, 214–16.

Locke's 'blank effect' model, as we have seen, places true whiteness firmly in observers, with no more connection to the supposedly white (better, he thinks, called 'whiteful') object than sensations of sickness have to the indigestible food that causes them in virtue of its physical structure (II.viii.18). At other times he puts his point more subtly: 'Thus whiteness coldnesse roundnesse as they are sensations or perceptions in the understanding I call Ideas as they are in a snowball which has that power to produce these Ideas in the understanding I call them Qualitys.'[48] The whiteness, like Descartes' sun, is here taken in two ways, rather than being placed solely in the mind. This formulation does not avoid the circularity problem, but perhaps opens a way to understanding why the circularity is not vicious. First, the gist of the argument following is that, although both shapes and colours are seen in virtue of the light that things reflect and the effect of that light on the organs of sight, round things appear round because they are round, whereas white things appear white solely in virtue of the light they reflect, and its effect on perceivers.[49] I have proposed that the plausibility of this conclusion depends, not on Locke's vague and speculative mechanistic explanation, now outdated, but on something we are all at some level aware of: namely, that to possess the quality whiteness is essentially to look a certain way. However, it is to look that way simply, objectively, and irreducibly.

Things only have looks in relation to vision, but the look of a white thing that constitutes its whiteness is 'objective', because it is unconditional and unqualified, not set about with conditions involving particular or specific circumstances or observers (even 'normal conditions' and 'normal observers', phrases that simply invite further circularity). It is 'irreducible', because it cannot be reduced to the possession of other properties. If someone looks ill, their ill look can be reduced to their being observably pale, shivering, gasping or whatever, conditions that may vary from individual to individual, from illness to illness, even with the time of day. But if something *simply* and objectively looks white, there is nothing more to be said on those lines about *how* it looks white.[50] Hence the apparent circularity of the claim that whiteness consists in a certain look some things have. What things, and how do they look? White things, and they look white. But that may not matter in such a second-order claim, which is an attempt to come to terms with the intimate relation between colours and sight. It is not

[48] I quote from the English 'Epitome', since, as pointed out by John Milton and James Hill 2003, this sentence, despite the absence of punctuation, is clearer and simpler than the curiously complex version at II.viii.8, which raises other questions (not least, the question of why Locke made the change).

[49] Locke's point is probably a bit more complex than this. He presumably chose porphyry because the role of reflected light seemed more evident in its case (cf. *Essay* IV.iii.15), but he probably also took the need for light as analogous to the role of the Earth in determining weight, or the role of air in maintaining life or the power of flight (as spectacularly demonstrated in Locke's time by the vacuum pump). Cf. *Essay* IV.vi.11.

[50] This paragraph owes something that he is unlikely to recognize to Michael Martin's thoughts about 'looks', as delivered to a seminar in Berkeley in 2007. There may be cases in which looking white *is* reducible. To adapt an example of Descartes', if someone is seen from above wearing a tropical suit and solar topee in a film that is set in rural Africa in the late nineteenth century, then that person looks white. If something white 'looks red' in a red light, then in 'looking red', it looks white.

a first-order claim to the effect that all the things we take to be white only *look* white, and happen not to be *really* white. The second-order claim is a reflection on what it is to be really white in the latter, default use of 'really white'.

It should not be forgotten, moreover, that there are two terms to the contrast between primary and secondary qualities. What Locke says about primary qualities is at least as important as what he says about secondary qualities, since it involves a kind of recognition that the perception of bodies—or 'body'—in space is fundamental to the way in which (at least, higher) sentient creatures hook onto their environment. It is in perceiving the mechanical interaction of bodies, including our own body, that we are primarily in touch with the nitty-gritty of reality, achieve a pretheoretical grasp of how it works, and acquire some power to deal with it. It is that basic apprehension of the world, indeed, that provides the framework for the assignment of secondary qualities, and for predication generally—for all our thought about the world. It is certainly a shortcoming of Locke's general epistemology that he fails to build that point firmly and fundamentally into his explanation of 'sensitive knowledge'. It is also a certain shortcoming of his treatment of the distinction between primary and secondary qualities that that point is conflated with corpuscularian speculation. But 'Other Considerations concerning Simple *Ideas*' is not the only famous philosophical text made complex, and perhaps more interesting, by its author's inclination to ride several horses at once.

Bibliography

Austin, J. L. 1962. *Sense and Sensibilia*, Oxford: Clarendon Press.

Ayers, Michael. 1991. *Locke: Epistemology and Ontology*, 2 vols, London: Routledge.

Hill, James. 2009. 'Locke's Impulse Principle', *British Journal for the History of Philosophy* vol. 17, no. 1, 85–98.

Jacovides, Michael. 2007. 'Locke Distinctions between Primary and Secondary Qualities', in Lex Newman, ed., *The Cambridge Companion to Locke's 'Essay Concerning Human Understanding'*, Cambridge: Cambridge University Press, 101–129.

Kripke, Saul. 1980. *Naming and Necessity*, Cambridge: Cambridge University Press.

Locke, John. 1975. *An Essay Concerning Human Understanding*, ed. P. H. Nidditch, Oxford: Oxford University Press.

Milton, John and James Hill. 2003. 'The Epitome (*Abrégé*) of Locke's *Essay*', in *The Philosophy of John Locke: New perspectives*, ed. Peter R Anstey, Routledge, London and New York, 3–25.

Nidditch, P. H. and G. A. J. Rogers (eds.). 1990. *Drafts for the* Essay Concerning Human Understanding *and Other Philosophical Writings*, Vol. 1, Oxford: Oxford University Press.

Walmsley, Jonathan. 2004. 'Locke's Natural Philosophy in Draft A of the *Essay*', *Journal of the History of Ideas* 64, 15–37.

—— 2003. 'The Development of Locke's Mechanism in the Drafts of the *Essay*', *British Journal of the History of Philosophy* 11, 417–49.

7

Locke's Distinction between Primary Primary Qualities and Secondary Primary Qualities

Edwin McCann

I. Introduction

Locke did not explicitly mark this distinction, in these terms anyway, in the *Essay's* chapter on primary and secondary qualities (Book two, chapter 8, "Some further considerations concerning our simple ideas") or anywhere else. Nevertheless, as I hope to establish, the distinction is clearly implicit in some of Locke's key formulations of the distinction between primary qualities and secondary qualities, and it is a direct consequence of the main line of argument for that distinction.

My main goal in this chapter is not to establish that the distinction is to be found in Locke—although I do want to do that—but to explore some of the important interpretive results which come from attending to the distinction as it figures in the *Essay*. Close attention to Locke's distinction between primary primary qualities and secondary primary qualities will have multiple payoffs. First, it will help us to reconcile a number of seemingly conflicting statements Locke makes, in the chapter on primary and secondary qualities and other chapters, about primary qualities; some of these statements have to do with primary primary qualities, others with secondary primary qualities, and a number of them will be false if we take them to generalize over both kinds of primary quality. Second, it will help us to make better sense of two key claims that are made in *Essay* II.viii, namely, that ideas of primary qualities of bodies are resemblances of them, whereas ideas of secondary qualities of bodies are not resemblances of them (the resemblance claim), and the closely connected claim that primary qualities of bodies are really in those bodies, whereas secondary qualities are not really in them, so that primary qualities are "real qualities" and secondary qualities are not real qualities (the real qualities claim). Third, tracking this distinction through the text of Essay II.viii will enable us to better appreciate the structure of the overall argument for the primary-secondary quality distinction itself, and this in turn will put us in a better position to appreciate the limits on the justificatory force and the ontological bite that Locke can claim this argument to have.

First, what is the distinction between primary primary qualities and secondary primary qualities? The primary primary qualities are those mechanical affections of bodies (bulk, figure, extension, motion or rest, number, and solidity—which, taken together, constitute the "texture" of a body) which qualify the insensibly small parts of matter which compose the ordinary bodies with which our sensory experience of the world is conversant; the secondary primary qualities are those which appear to us directly to qualify those ordinary, middle-sized, observable bodies themselves. The difference, at least in the first instance, is one of magnitude, and not a qualitative difference, although as we'll note below, this difference in magnitude is connected with differences in causal primacy and in relative dependence on sensation. Locke emphasizes the qualitative similarity at II.viii.18:

> A piece of *Manna* of a sensible Bulk, is able to produce in us the *Idea* of a round or square Figure; and, by being removed from one place to another, the *Idea* of Motion. This *Idea* of Motion represents it, as it really is in the *Manna* moving: A Circle or Square are the same, whether in *Idea* or Existence; in the Mind, or in the *Manna*: And this, both *Motion and Figure are really in the Manna*, whether we take notice of them or no: This every Body is ready to agree to.[1]

We shouldn't take this passage, by the way, to be claiming that our sensible ideas of motion or shape, say those caused by a piece of manna, are always accurate or veridical, but instead only as making the point that the shape or motion we attribute to a body when we think of it as shaped or moved is exactly the same in qualitative character as the shape or motion we perceive in an observed object (whether or not that object is accurately perceived, or misperceived). This will be so whether the shape or motion in question is thought to qualify an observably large body (in which case there is the possibility of a disparity between the shape or motion such a body appears to us to have and the shape or motion which, after correction, we say it really has) or whether we attribute shape or motion to insensibly small bodies (in which case the possibility of disparity doesn't arise).

That's what the primary-primary/secondary-primary quality distinction is: is it to be found in Locke? There is a strong basis in the text; in the great majority of passages in which reference is made to primary qualities, and in almost all of the relevant passages in II.viii, he expressly restricts his claims about primary qualities to the primary qualities of the parts of bodies, that is, of the insensible parts, or the solid parts, or the solid insensible parts, or the like, of bodies (larger, composite, observable bodies), that are large enough singly to be perceived.[2] It would take far too much space to give the

[1] All citations from Locke's *An Essay Concerning Human Understanding*, ed. P. H. Nidditch (Oxford: Oxford University Press, 1975), are to book, chapter, and section.

[2] By the phrase "insensible parts," which he frequently uses, Locke means the parts of a body that are too small to be sensed by us, and not merely remarking that the parts don't themselves have sensations (although of course, in Locke's view, they don't).

whole context of each of these occurrences, so I'll just list the relevant phrases and the place they occur, giving the wider context in the case of a few especially important passages:

- At II.viii.10 (fourth and fifth edition version), where Locke contrasts secondary qualities with primary qualities, he does it in the following way (this is the passage in its entirety):

2ndly, such *Qualities*, which in truth are nothing in the Objects themselves, but Powers to produce various Sensations in us by their *primary Qualities, i.e.* by the Bulk, Figure, Texture, and Motion of their insensible parts, as Colours, Sounds, Tasts, *etc.* These I call *secondary Qualities.* To these might be added a third sort which are allowed to be barely Powers though they are as much real Qualities in the Subject, as those which I to comply with the common way of speaking call Qualities, but for distinction, *secondary Qualities.* For the power in Fire to produce a new Colour, or consistency, in Wax or Clay by its primary Qualities, is as much a quality in Fire, as the power it has to produce in me a new *Idea* or Sensation of warmth or burning, which I felt not before, by the same primary Qualities, *viz.* The Bulk, Texture, and Motion of its insensible parts.

- At II.viii.14, Locke says that colors, smells, tastes, sounds, and "*other the like sensible Qualities*" are "in truth nothing in the Objects themselves, but Powers to produce various Sensations in us, and *depend on those primary Qualities, viz.* Bulk, Figure, Texture, and Motion of Parts; as I have said."
- At II.viii.15, the passage containing the resemblance claim, quoted in its entirety:

From whence I think it easie to draw this Observation, that the *Ideas of primary Qualities* of Bodies *are Resemblances* of them, and their Patterns do really exist in the Bodies themselves; but the *Ideas, produced* in us *by* these *Secondary Qualities, have no resemblance* of them at all. There is nothing like our *Ideas*, existing in the Bodies themselves. They are in the Bodies, we denominate from them, only a Power to produce those Sensations in us: And what is Sweet, Blue, or Warm in *Idea*, is but the certain Bulk, Figure, and Motion of the insensible Parts in the Bodies themselves, which we call so.

- At II.viii.16 Locke gives the stock example of the idea of warmth becoming an idea of pain as the heat intensifies, and again following tradition (that of Lucretius and Epicurus), points to the arbitrariness of assigning different statuses to heat in a flame or whiteness and coldness in snow from that of pain "when it [the fire? the snowball? the fire or the snowball, indifferently?] produces the one and the other *Idea* in us; and can do neither, but by the Bulk, Figure, Number, and Motion of its solid Parts?"
- At II.viii.17 Locke makes the critical distinction between the "particular *Bulk, Number, Figure, and Motion of the Parts of Fire, or Snow*," which are "*really in them* [this can only be referring to the parts], whether any ones senses perceive them or no: And therefore they may be called *real Qualities,* because they really exist in those Bodies [the parts? the bodies the parts compose? either or both of these, indifferently?]." By contrast light, heat, whiteness or coldness "*are no more really in*

them, than Sickness or Pain is in Manna," and if we suppose that the bodies are not sensed "all Colours, Tastes, Odors and Sounds, as they are such particular *Ideas*, vanish and cease, and are reduced to their Causes, *i.e.* Bulk, Figure, and Motion of Parts."

- At II.viii.18 we get one of the surprisingly few explicit references to macro primary qualities (i.e. primary qualities of bodies large enough to be singly sensed), juxtaposed with mention of micro primary qualities (the primary qualities of insensibly small bodies, which are sometimes of course constituent parts of bodies large enough to be singly sensed); it's an important passage, so I'll quote it in its entirety:

A piece of *Manna* of a sensible Bulk is able to produce in us the *Idea* of a round or square Figure, and, by being removed from one place to another, the *Idea* of Motion. This *Idea* of Motion represents it, as it really is in the Manna moving: A Circle or Square are the same, whether in *Idea* or Existence; in the Mind, or in the *Manna*; And this, both *Motion and Figure are really in the Manna*, whether we take notice of them or no: This every Body is ready to agree to. Besides, *Manna* by the Bulk, Figure, Texture, and Motion of its Parts, has a Power to produce the Sensations of Sickness, and sometimes of acute Pains, or Gripings in us. That these *Ideas* of *Sickness and Pain are not in the* Manna, but Effects of its Operations on us, and are nowhere when we feel them not: This also every one readily agrees to. And yet Men are hardly to be brought to think, that *Sweetness and Whiteness are not really in Manna;* which are but the effects of the operations of *Manna*, by the motion, size, and figure of its Particles on the Eyes and Palate; as the Pain and Sickness caused by *Manna*, are confessedly nothing but the effects of its operations on the Stomach and Guts, by the size, motion, and figure of its insensible parts (for by nothing else can a Body operate, as has been proved:) As if it could not operate on the Eyes and Palate, and thereby produce in the Mind particular distinct *Ideas*, which in it self it has not, as well as we allow it can operate on the Guts and Stomach, and thereby produce distinct *Ideas*, which in itself it has not. These *Ideas*, being all effects of the operations of *Manna*, on several parts of our Bodies, by the size, figure, number, and motion of its parts, why those produced by the Eyes and Palate, should rather be thought to be really in the *Manna*, than those produced by the Stomach and Guts; or why the Pain and Sickness, *Ideas* that are the effect of *Manna*, should be thought to be no-where when they are not felt; and yet the Sweetness and Whiteness, effects of the same *Manna* on other parts of the body, by ways equally as unknown, should be thought to exist in the *Manna*, when they are not seen or tasted, would need some Reason to explain.

- At II.viii.19, in the porphyry example, Locke seeks to resolve both the question of how porphyry can come to lack any color when no light shines upon it (this being presumed not to cause any physical change in the stone itself) and the question why it should appear red to viewers from one angle and white to viewers from another angle by saying:

It has, indeed, such a Configuration of Particles, both Night and Day, as are apt by the Rays of Light rebounding from some parts of that hard Stone, to produce in us the *Idea* of redness, and from others the *Idea* of whiteness: But whiteness or redness are not in it at any time, but such a texture, that hath the power to produce such a sensation in us.

Similarly, in the II.viii.20 almond example and the II.viii.21 hands in hot and cold water example, he explains variation in color, taste, and consistency of the almond, and variation in perceived hotness or coldness of the water, by adverting to "the *Texture*" of the almond, and the motion of the "Corpuscles" and "*minute Particles*" in the water and the hands.

- At II.viii.23, in giving a summary of the distinction among qualities that his discussion has turned up, he writes (quoting in its entirety):

23. The *Qualities* then that are in bodies rightly considered, are of *Three sorts*.

First, The *Bulk*, *Figure*, *Number*, *Situation*, and *Motion, or Rest* of their solid Parts; those are in them, whether we perceive them or no; and when they are of that size, that we can discover them, we have by these an *Idea* of the thing as it is in it self, as is plain in artificial things. These I call *primary Qualities*.

Secondly, The *Power* that is in any Body, *by* Reason of *its* insensible *primary Qualities*, to operate after a peculiar manner on any of our Senses, and thereby *produce in us* the *different Ideas* of several Colours, Sounds, Smells, Tasts, *etc.* These are usually called sensible Qualities.

Thirdly, The *Power* that is in any Body, *by* Reason of the particular Constitution of its *primary Qualities*, to make such a *change* in the *Bulk*, *Figure*, *Texture*, and *Motion of another body*, as to make it operate on our Senses, differently from what it did before. Thus the Sun has a Power to make Wax white, and Fire to make Lead fluid. These are usually called Powers.

The First of these, as has been said, I think, may be properly called *real Original*, or *primary Qualities*, because they are in the things themselves, whether they are perceived or no: and upon their different modifications it is, that the secondary Qualities depend.

The other two, are only Powers to act differently upon other things, which Powers result from the different Modifications of those primary Qualities.

- At II.viii.25 and 26, the concluding sections of the chapter, Locke makes the point that we are apt to take colors, sounds, etc. as real qualities rather than bare powers in part because "Sensation discovers nothing of Bulk, Figure, or Motion of parts in their Production" (25) and then says (II.viii.26, entire):

To conclude, beside those before mentioned *primary Qualities* in bodies, *viz.* Bulk, Figure, Extension, Number, and Motion of their solid Parts; all the rest whereby we take notice of Bodies, and distinguish them one from another, are nothing else but several Powers in them depending on those primary Qualities; whereby they are fitted, either by immediately operating on our Bodies, to produce several different *Ideas* in us; or else by operating on other Bodies, so to change their primary Qualities, as to render them capable of producing *Ideas* in us, different from what before they did. The former of these, I think, may be called *secondary Qualities, immediately perceivable*: The latter, *secondary Qualities, mediately perceivable*.

- At II.xxi.3, noting that our idea of power contains some kind of relation, he asks:

For, our *Ideas* of Extension, Duration, and Number, do they not all contain in them a secret relation of the Parts? Figure and Motion have something relative in them much more visibly: And sensible Qualities, as Colours and Smells, *etc.* what are they but the *Powers* of different Bodies, in relation to our Perception? *etc.* And if considered in the things themselves, do they not depend on the Bulk, Figure, Texture, and Motion of the Parts? All which include some kind of relation in them.

- At II.xxi.73, the concluding section of the chapter "Of Power," Locke gives an overview of our "primary" and "original" ideas of body and of spirit or minds (quoting the entire section):

And thus I have, in a short draught, given a view of our *original Ideas*, from whence all the rest are derived, and of which they are made up; which if I would consider, as a Philosopher, and examine on what Causes they depend, and of what they are made, I believe they all might be reduced to these very few primary, and original ones, *viz. Extension*, *Solidity*, *Mobility*, or the Power of being moved; which by our *Senses* we receive from Body; *Perceptivity*, or the Power of perception, or thinking; *Motivity*, or the Power of moving; which by reflection we receive from our Minds. I crave leave to make use of these two new Words, to avoid the danger of being mistaken in the use of those which are equivocal. To which if we add *Existence*, *Duration*, *Number*, which belong both to the one, and the other: we have, perhaps, all the Original *Ideas* on which the rest depend. For by these, I imagine, might be explained the nature of Colours, Sounds, Tastes, Smells, and all other *Ideas* we have, if we had but Faculties acute enough to perceive the severally modified Extensions, and Motions, of these minute Bodies, which produce those several Sensations in us. But my present purpose being only to enquire into the Knowledge the Mind has of Things, by those *Ideas*, and Appearances, which *God* has fitted it to receive from them, and how the Mind comes by that Knowledge; rather than into their Causes, or manner of Production, I shall not, contrary to the Design of this Essay, set myself to enquire philosophically into the peculiar Constitution of Bodies, and the Configuration of Parts, whereby they have the Power to produce in us the *Ideas* of their sensible Qualities: I shall not enter any farther into that Disquisition; it sufficing to my purpose to observe, That Gold, or Saffron, has a Power to produce in us the *Idea* of Yellow; and Snow, or Milk, the *Idea* of White; which we can only have by our Sight, without examining the Texture of the Parts of those Bodies, or the particular Figures, or Motion of the Particles, which rebound from them, to cause in us that particular Sensation: though when we go beyond the bare *Ideas* in our Minds, and would enquire into their Causes, we cannot conceive any thing else, to be in any sensible Object, whereby it produces different *Ideas* in us, but the different Bulk, Figure, Number, Texture, and Motion of its insensible Parts.

- At a number of points in crucial passages in the *Essay's* chapter "Of the Names of Substances" (II.xxiii) Locke makes reference to what I'm calling primary primary qualities, as at II.xxiii.8 where he talks of "our Senses failing us, in the discovery of the Bulk, Texture and Figure of the minute parts of Bodies, on which their real Constitutions . . . depend" and, at II.xxiii.9, gives as an instance the way a loadstone acts on "the minute Particles of Iron"; at II.xxiii.10 he assigns the heat in the sun that a man perceives and the whiteness it produces as it blanches wax to "Powers in the Sun, operating, by the Motion and Figure of its insensible Parts"; the famous microscopical eyes passage at II.xxiii.11, where Locke notes that if our senses were acute enough to discern "the minute particles of Bodies" the yellow colour of gold "would then disappear, and instead of it we should see an admirable Texture of parts of a certain Size and Figure"; at II.xxiii.26, where the general theme is the difficulty, indeed perhaps impossibility, of accounting for the cohesion of bodies, he talks of "The little Bodies that compose that Fluid, we call *Water*" that are so small that no one has "pretended to perceive their distinct Bulk, Figure or Motion" and concludes that someone who could *per impossibile* discover what makes "these little Atoms" bind together so tightly when the water freezes would nevertheless "be far enough from making the extension of Body (which is the cohesion of its solid parts) intelligible, till he could shew, wherein consisted the union, or consolidation of the parts of those Bonds, or of that Cement, or the least Particle of Matter that exists"; at II.xxiii.30 he rounds off this discussion, listing the "Two primary Qualities or Properties of Body, *viz.* solid coherent parts and impulse" and noting that we have the ideas of "several Qualities inherent in Bodies, . . . which Qualities, are but the various modifications of the Extension of cohering solid Parts, and their motion;" at II.xxiii.37, the concluding section of the chapter, Locke again sounds the theme that most of the ideas of the sensible qualities of bodies "are only Powers, . . . all which *Ideas*, are nothing else, but so many relations to other Substances; and are not really in the Gold, considered barely in itself, though they depend on those real, and primary Qualities of its internal constitution, whereby it has a fitness, differently to operate, and be operated upon by several other Substances;" and perhaps most important, the first delineation in the chapter of the basic elements of our idea of body, II.xxiii.17 in its entirety:

The primary Ideas *we have peculiar to Body*, as contradistinguished to Spirit, *are the cohesion of solid*, and consequently separable, *parts, and a power of communicating Motion by impulse*. These, I think, are the original *Ideas* proper and peculiar to Body: for Figure is but the consequence of finite extension.

- In another very important chapter, IV.iii, "*Of the Extent of Humane Knowledge*," all of the references are to primary primary qualities: in IV.iii.11, stressing our ignorance of the microphysical constitutions of observable bodies, he allows for the possibility that we might be wrong in our view that these constitutions are the causal basis in the object of its secondary qualities. To quote IV.iii.11 in full:

The *Ideas*, that our complex ones of Substances are made up of, and about which our Knowledge, concerning Substances, is most employ'd, are those of their *secondary Qualities*; which depending all (as has been shewn) upon the primary Qualities of their minute and insensible parts; or if not upon them, upon something yet more remote from our Comprehension, 'tis impossible we should know, which have a necessary union or inconsistency one with another: For not knowing the Root they spring from, not knowing what size, figure, and texture of Parts they are, on which depend and from which result those Qualities which make our complex *Idea* of Gold,'tis impossible we should know what other Qualities result from, or are incompatible with the same Constitution of the insensible parts of *Gold*; and so consequently must always *co-exist* with that complex *Idea* we have of it, or else are *inconsistent* with it.

In the next section, IV.iii.12, Locke notes that beyond "this Ignorance of the primary Qualities of the insensible Parts of Bodies" there is "another and more incurable part of Ignorance" barring us from certain knowledge of the necessary connections between the sensible qualities and powers of bodies, namely "that there is no discoverable connection between any *secondary Quality, and those primary Qualities* that it depends on." The following section, IV.iii.13, quoted in full, rounds out the discussion:

That the size, figure, and motion of one Body should cause a change in the size, figure, and motion of another Body, is not beyond our Conception; the separation of the Parts of one Body, upon the intrusion of another; and the change from rest to motion, upon impulse; these, and the like, seem to us to have some *connexion* one with another. And if we knew these primary Qualities of Bodies, we might have reason to hope, we might be able to know a great deal more of these Operations of them one upon another: But our Minds not being able to discover any *connexion* betwixt these primary Qualities of Bodies, and the sensations that are produced in us by them, we can never be able to establish certain and undoubted Rules, of the Consequence or *Co-existence* of any secondary Qualities, though we could discover the size, figure, or motion of those invisible Parts, which immediately produce them. We are so far from knowing what figure, size, or motion of parts produce a yellow Colour, a sweet Taste, or a sharp Sound, that we can by no means conceive how any *size, figure, or motion* of any Particles, can possibly produce in us the *Idea* of any *Colour, Taste*, or *Sound* whatsoever; there is no conceivable *connexion* betwixt the one and the other.

- IV.iii.15 gives an example very similar to that of the porphyry example at II.viii.19 (this time using the opal, or infusion of lignium nephriticum, with a slightly fuller mechanical resolution of the phenomena.)
- IV.iii.25 is one of the key passages setting out Locke's conception of mechanistic explanation; because of its central importance I quote it in full:

If a great, nay far the greatest part of the several ranks of *Bodies* in the Universe, scape our notice by their remoteness, there are others that are no less concealed from us by their *Minuteness*. These insensible Corpuscles, being the active parts of Matter, and the great Instruments of Nature, on which depend not only all their secondary Qualities, but also most of their natural Operations, our want of precise distinct *Ideas* of their primary Qualities, keeps us in an uncurable Ignorance of what we desire to know about them. I doubt not but if we could discover the Figure, Size, Texture, and Motion of the minute Constituent parts of any two Bodies, we should know without Trial several of their Operations one upon another, as we do now the Properties of a Square, or a Triangle. Did we know the Mechanical affections of the Particles of *Rhubarb, Hemlock, Opium*, and a *Man*, as a Watchmaker does those of a Watch, whereby it performs its Operations, and of a File which by rubbing on them will alter the Figure of any of the Wheels, we should be able to tell before Hand, that *Rhubarb* will purge, *Hemlock* kill, and *Opium* make a Man sleep; as well as a Watch-maker can, that a little piece of Paper laid on the Balance, will keep the Watch from going, till it be removed; or that some small part of it, being rubb'd by a File, the Machin would quite lose its Motion, and the Watch go no more. The dissolving of Silver in *aqua fortis*, and Gold in *aqua Regia*, and not *vice versa*, would be then, perhaps, no more difficult to know, than it is to a Smith to understand, why the turning of one Key will open a Lock, and not the turning of another. But whilst we are destitute of Senses acute enough, to discover the minute Particles of Bodies, and to give us *Ideas* of their mechanical Affections, we must be content to be ignorant of their properties and ways of Operation; nor can we be assured about them any farther, than some few Trials we make, are able to reach. But whether they will succeed again another time, we cannot be certain. This hinders our certain Knowledge of universal Truths concerning natural Bodies: and our Reason carries us herein very little beyond particular matter of Fact.

The limits to our knowledge that this implies are brought out in the next section, IV.iii.26, which reads in part:

But having no *Ideas* of the particular primary Qualities of the minute parts of either of these Plants [sage or hemlock], nor of other Bodies which we would apply them to, we cannot tell what effects they will produce; Nor when we see those Effects, can we so much as guess, much less know, their manner of production. Thus having no *Ideas* of the particular mechanical Affections of the minute parts of Bodies, that are within our view and reach, we are ignorant of their Constitutions, Powers, and Operations.

After noting in section 27 that we are equally in the dark about the "different Natures, Conditions, States, Powers, and several Constitutions" of angelic intelligences and other spirits, without giving a specific cause of our ignorance as he has just done in the case of our ignorance of the constitutions of bodies, where the minuteness of the constituent particles is cited as the culprit (and also without hazarding a guess about what these differing "Constitutions" of spirits might be like), he goes on in IV.iii.28 and 29 to discuss more fully the "more incurable part of our Ignorance" of the necessary connections of the powers and qualities of bodies mentioned in IV.iii.12 and 13. We will be looking at these passages later on.

- Finally, in another very important chapter regarding the limits of our knowledge, IV.vi, "*Of Universal Propositions, their Truth and Certainty*," where the focus is on the contrast between the abstract ideas of substances that we actually have, made up of ideas of sensible qualities and powers, and the ideas of the constitutions of bodies and of the connections of these constitutions with the ideas of the sensible qualities that they produce; in addition to the segment of IV.vi.14 quoted below, see IV.vi and IV.vi.10:

Before we can have any tolerable knowledge of this kind [certainty in universal propositions concerning substances], we must first know what Changes the *primary Qualities* of one Body, do regularly produce in the *primary Qualities* of another, and how. Secondly, we must know what *primary Qualities* of any Body, produce certain Sensations or *Ideas* in us. This is in truth, no less than to know all the Effects of Matter, under its divers modifications of Bulk, Figure, Cohesion of Parts, Motion, and Rest. Which, I think, every body will allow, is utterly impossible to be known by us, without revelation. Nor if it were revealed to us, what sort of Figure, Bulk, and Motion of Corpuscles, would produce in us the Sensation of a *yellow* Colour, and what sort of Figure, Bulk, and Texture of Parts in the superficies of any Body, were fit to give such Corpuscles their due motion to produce that Colour, Would that be enough to make *universal* Propositions with certainty, concerning the several sorts of them, unless we had Faculties acute enough to perceive the precise Bulk, Figure, Texture, and Motion of Bodies in those minute Parts, by which they operate on our Senses, that so we might by those frame our abstract *Ideas* of them.

The implication of the discussion in IV.vi, taken together with that of IV.iii, is that if we were to be able to frame abstract ideas capturing the detailed microphysical constitutions of bodies, and if additionally we had knowledge of the laws connecting microphysical constitutions with the production of particular ideas of sensible qualities (something we can't have short of revelation), then we would be able to have demonstrative knowledge of the necessary connections amongst the observable powers and qualities of bodies.

In providing this overview of the relevant texts concerning primary primary qualities, I hope to have accomplished two main things: first, to show how pervasive in the text, not just in Book II, chapter 8 but in many other key passages in the *Essay*, are explicit references to the primary qualities of "the parts of bodies," "the insensible parts of bodies," "the particular primary qualities of the minute parts" or "the mechanical affections of the minute parts," and many similar expressions denoting primary primary qualities; and second, from the close attention to context we can see that many, if not most, of these references concern primary primary qualities (and the insensibly small bodies they qualify) as the causal basis in the object for the sensible qualities and powers that are observed in the large-scale bodies they compose.

2. The argument for the primary-secondary quality distinction

As we'll see in this section, there is a single three-stage basic line of argument in II.viii for the distinction between primary and secondary qualities, stretching from II.viii.9 to II.viii.13. Unfortunately, the overall shape of the argument is a bit harder to discern in the fourth and fifth editions of the *Essay*, given Locke's revisions to II.viii.9 and 10. Since the fourth edition was the copy-text for Nidditch's critical edition of the *Essay*, and since this is the edition most scholars and casual readers (relatively speaking) of the *Essay* use, the basic line of argument has not been immediately apparent to scholars.[3] Let's look at sections 9 and 10 as they appear in the first three editions of the *Essay*:

9. Concerning these *Qualities*, we may, I think, observe these *primary* ones in Bodies, that produce simple *Ideas* in us, *viz*. Solidity, Extension, Motion or Rest, Number and Figure.

[3] Nidditch does, of course, note these changes in the critical apparatus of his edition, but in a rather complicated manner, and only a reader already alert to the significance of these changes could be expected to pick them up.

10. These, which I call *original* or *primary Qualities* of Body, are wholly inseparable from it; and such as in all the alterations and changes it suffers, all the force can be used upon it, it constantly keeps; and such as Sense constantly finds in every particle of Matter, which has Bulk enough to be perceived, and the Mind finds inseparable from every particle of Matter, though less than to make it self singly be perceived by our Senses. v.g. Take a grain of Wheat, divide it into two parts, each part has still *Solidity*, *Extension*, *Figure*, and *Mobility*; divide it again, and it retains still the same qualities; and so divide it on, till the parts become insensible, they must retain still each of them all those qualities. For division (which is all that a Mill, or Pestle, or any other Body, does upon another, in reducing it to insensible parts) can never take away either Solidity, Extension, Figure, or Mobility from any Body, but only makes two distinct Bodies, or more, or one, which altogether after division have their certain number.

If we now contrast these two sections with their revised states in the fourth and fifth editions, we find two major changes: first, section 9 has been deleted, and what was section 10 in the first three editions has, with a few small additions (the most significant of these being the adding of the phrase "in what estate soever it be" after the words "are wholly inseparable from it") been made section 9; and second, an entirely new section 10 (quoted above), concerning secondary qualities, has been added.

No doubt Locke sought to aid the reader by introducing the other, secondary quality, side of the distinction earlier and in more explicit contrast to primary qualities than in the first three editions. However well-intentioned, these textual revisions had three untoward consequences. First, the excision of the section 9 reference to the ideas of primary qualities that observable bodies cause in us obscured an important strand of exposition that proceeded from section 9 into section 10, with section 9 making the claim, crucial for Locke's project of showing that all our ideas derive from simple ideas given in sensation and reflection, that we receive the ideas of primary qualities from bodies we perceive, that is, from bodies large enough to be observed. (As we'll soon see, the resemblance claim of II.viii.15 reflects the mind's transition from the primary qualities of observable bodies to those of their insensibly small parts.) Then in section 10 of the first three editions, which became section 9 of the fourth and fifth editions, Locke gives the division thought-experiment, which takes us from observing that the mechanical division of bodies that are large enough to be perceived into smaller but still observable bodies always leaves the resulting bodies with bulk, figure, mobility, number, extension, and solidity through any number of iterations of division until the point at which the resulting bodies are too small to be perceived, at which point "Sense" leaves off and "the Mind" "finds inseparable" from every particle of matter too small to make itself singly perceived by our senses the bulk, figure, mobility, number, extension, and solidity of each of these insensibly small parts. We'll return to this strand of argument presently.

Second, the changes to sections 9 and 10 in the fourth and fifth editions breaks up the line of reasoning running from section 9 through to 12 (in editions 1–3) concerning the primary qualities of bodies. There is a single connected argument in the first three editions that is based on (a) the ordinary conception of body as extended solid substance and (b) the ordinary conception of the causality of body working only through impulse or contact action. With the section 10 discussion concerning secondary qualities inserted in the middle of this line of thought, its structure is harder to make out.

Third, the inserted section 10, in which Locke simply announces without any prior argument that secondary qualities are nothing in the bodies themselves but powers to produce sensations in us by the primary qualities "of their insensible parts," leaves the misleading impression that the sole basis for this claim is an implied invidious comparison with primary qualities on point of inseparability from body, the main consideration set out in the fourth and fifth edition version of section 9. Reading through the editions 1–3 version of sections 9–14, we see that these sections form a single connected argument yielding, *inter alia*, the conclusion drawn in section 14 that secondary qualities, that is, sensible qualities such as colors, smells, tastes and sounds, are "in truth nothing in the Objects themselves, but Powers to produce various Sensations in us, and *depend on those primary Qualities, viz.* Bulk, Figure, Texture, and Motion of parts." These two claims, based on the argument of sections 9–13 (editions 1–3), were copied forward to the new section 10 in the fourth and fifth editions, with the resultant possible confusion about the basis on which they rest. This is a prime example of good authorial intentions gone awry.

Now let's turn to the line of argument in sections 9–14 (editions 1–3 version), although we'll later see that calling this an argument, rather than just a description of a line of thought we find it natural to engage in, might be somewhat misleading. As I've already noted, section 9 makes the point that we first obtain the ideas of primary qualities from sensory observation, from our experience, that is, of bodies large enough to be perceived. In the terminology I've suggested, that would be to say that secondary primary qualities are the source of our ideas of primary qualities, and would accordingly be, to use a good old Scholastic phrase, first in the order of knowledge, whereas primary primary qualities would be, as we'll see, first in the order of being. In any event, section 9 provides the empiricist credentials for ideas of primary qualities, and thus advances Locke's project of showing how all our ideas derive from sensation and reflection. Entirely cutting out this point about the origin of our ideas of primary qualities in our observation of bodies was a decided loss in Locke's revisions for the fourth and fifth editions.

Section 10 (editions 1–3) is often segmented by commentators[4] into four elements; at the outset, Locke notes of the primary qualities just mentioned in section 9 that they are (1) "wholly inseparable from it [body]"; (2) "such as in all alterations and changes it [body] suffers, all the force can be used on it, it constantly keeps"; (3) "such as Sense constantly finds in every particle of Matter which has bulk enough to be perceived";

[4] See, e.g. Robert A. Wilson 2002.

and (4) which "the Mind finds inseparable from every particle of Matter, though less than to make itself singly be perceived." It is the transition from (3) to (4) that is illustrated by the thought-experiment of dividing a grain of wheat, with which the section concludes. In the terms I've been using, this transition takes us from secondary primary qualities to primary primary qualities, and so it is important for my purposes to establish exactly how the transition goes.

First, though, let's examine the inseparability claim. Some have taken it to be offered as a criterion for being a primary quality, perhaps in conjunction with other criteria.[5] Others have taken it to be a consequence of something like a meaning-analysis of the term "body," or as in some other way being analytically contained in the concept of body. Finally, still others[6] take it to be the conclusion of an inference from the restricted universality of the claim that the primary qualities qualify all observed bodies to the unrestrictedly universal claim that they qualify all bodies whatsoever.

I don't have space to argue in detail against each of these suggestions, so for now I'll just float the suggestion that the inseparability claim ((1), as glossed by (2)), is itself put forward as the conclusion of the division thought-experiment and the progression from what is given in the senses (3) to what the imagination conjures (4). Less schematically, we can take section 10 as based on two closely connected claims: first, that our commonsense understanding of the notion of body as extended solid substance yields the list of primary qualities given in section 10 as qualities anything possessing the defining qualities of body must possess, simply by virtue of being body; and second, that this is confirmed by the naturalness of the imagined progression of division, considered as a mechanical process, all the way down to insensibly small products of division.

It will help at this point to consider an important passage from Boyle's exposition of the corpuscularian hypothesis near the beginning of the *Origine of formes and Qualities*; point III in this exposition runs as follows:

These two grand and most Catholick Principles of Bodies, Matter, and Motion, being thus establish'd, it will follow both, that Matter must be actually divided into Parts, that being the genuine Effect of variously determin'd Motion, and that each of the primitive Fragments, or other distinct and entire Masses of Matter must have two Attributes, its own Magnitude, or rather *Size*, and its own *Figure* or *Shape*. And since Experience shews us (especially that which is afforded us by Chymical Operations, in many of which Matter is divided into Parts, too small to be singly sensible,) that this division of Matter is frequently made into insensible Corpuscles or Particles, we may conclude, that the minutest fragments, as well as the biggest Masses of the Universal Matter are likewise endowed each with its peculiar Bulk and [p. 9] Shape. For being a finite Body, its Dimensions must be terminated and measurable: and though it may change its Figure, yet for the same reason it must necessarily have *some Figure* or other. So that now we have found out, and must admit three Essential Properties of each entire or undivided, though

[5] See Peter Alexander 1981, Jonathan Bennett 1971, Edwin Curley 1972, and Michael Jacovides 2007c.
[6] Robert A. Wilson 2002.

insensible part of Matter, namely, *Magnitude*, (by which I mean not quantity in general, but a determin'd quantity, which we in English oftentimes call the *Size* of a bodie,) *Shape*, and either *Motion* or *Rest*, (for betwixt them two there is no mean:) the two first of which may be called *inseparable Accidents* of each distinct part of Matter: *inseparable*, because being extended, and yet finite, it is Physically impossible, that it should be devoid of some Bulk or other, and som determinate Shape or other; and yet *Accidents*, because that whether or no the Shape can by Physical Agents be alter'd or the Body subdi- [p. 10] vided, yet mentally both the one and other may be done, the whole essence of matter remaining undestroy'd.[7]

There is an echo in Locke's text of several points in this passage, and not only in the use of the word "inseparable" and in the instancing of division, and in the conformity of Boyle's list of primary qualities (comprising what are for him the essential features of body, extension and solidity, together with, given the additional stipulation of finiteness, the implied inseparable accidents of shape and size). More significant, we can discern a hint at least of the pattern of argument found here that seeks to derive the necessity of a body's having determinate instances of the inseparable accidents from its being a finite extended solid thing in Locke's *Essay*, where at II.xxiii.17 Locke notes that "Figure is but the consequence of finite Extension," a passage in which "the *primary Ideas*" or "the original *Ideas* proper and peculiar to body," are listed as "*cohesion of solid*, and consequently separable *parts, and a power of communicating Motion by impulse*." This is one of a number of passages in *Essay* II.xxiii and in the Stillingfleet correspondence in which the "essence of body" is given as solidity and extension (often glossed as cohesion of solid parts, to distinguish the extension of body from the extension of space), as well as the power of communicating motion by impulse. Although it may be tempting to understand this line of argument in terms of analyzing the meaning of the term "body," as a number of recent commentators have done, we should not take this to be a piece of a priori conceptual analysis, in which the meaning of the term "body" is somehow fixed in advance of our experience, and can then be unpacked in an illuminating way. We need instead to recognize that, for Locke, the essence of body, for us, is simply what we've collected together into the general idea of body, following the same sort of process of abstraction from everyday sensory experience that yields the general ideas of the specific kinds of substances, for example, of horses, gold, water, etc., the difference being that body or matter are much more general kinds than those.[8] This idea can then serve as the basis for the kind of reasoning about physical possibility and impossibility that Boyle and Locke engage in, Boyle drawing the necessity of any

[7] Robert Boyle, *The Origine of Formes and Qualities*, (*According to the* Corpuscular Philosophy, *Illustrated by* Considerations *and Experiments*) (Oxford: Printed by H. Hall, Printer to the University, for Ric: Davis, 1666), 8–10. I've quoted from the 1666 (first) edition; in the 1667 (second) edition this text is to be found on pp. 5–7. See the reprint in M. A. Stewart, ed. *Selected Philosophical Papers of Robert Boyle* (Indianapolis and Cambridge, Mass.: Hackett Publishing Company, 1991), 20.

[8] I take this to be in line with Robert A. Wilson's criticism of the "conceptual point" approach, and with Atherton's (1992) emphasis on the crucial role of sensory experience in forming our conception of primary qualities.

body's having a determinate shape and size from its being a finite extended substance, and Locke drawing similar consequences from an imagined mechanical process of iterated division. In either case it is the standard acceptation of the essence of body as extended solid substance from which the reasoning, or exercise of the imagination, proceeds.

On this interpretation of Locke's argument in sections 9 and 10, there are at least three things it's not. It's not any sort of analogical or transdictive inference, or an inference of any kind, supposing that inference would be taken to provide justification in the belief in unobserved constituent parts of bodies, or that such parts would be qualified by the primary qualities;[9] there is nothing in it about primary qualities being in some way explanatorily basic, or about the role of primary qualities in causal explanation (that will come in the second stage of the argument);[10] nor, and this may well be more contentious, is inseparability offered as a criterion for distinguishing primary qualities from secondary qualities, rather than as a feature of those qualities which, because of their relation to the defining qualities of body, bodies must have in order to qualify as bodies. Inseparability of the primary qualities is thus a consequence of the way primary qualities relate to the definition of body, instead of being itself constitutive or partially constitutive of the notion of being a primary quality.[11] Close attention to the first through third edition versions of sections 9 and 10 thus yields the results that, first, it is our general conception of body as extended solid substance that is the basis for distinguishing and specifying the primary qualities of body, although as I've emphasized, our general conception of body is not some antecedently fixed or given concept, but is instead the result of selection and abstraction from everyday, common-sense experience of the world (like all our complex general ideas of substances, according to Locke), and second, the ideas of primary qualities we obtain in sensory experience of observably large bodies in our environment can be determined in imagination to represent to us the qualities of bodies too small to be sensed, which can then be thought to compose the larger scale bodies we observe. I've stressed that Locke shouldn't be taken to be striving at this point to *justify* the claim either that observable bodies are composed of insensibly small constituent bodies or that the insensibly small bodies are qualified only by primary qualities, but is instead showing how the ideas of primary qualities are derived from sensation and how they can be wielded by the imagination to afford the conception of insensibly small bodies as the constituent parts of observable bodies, a conception obviously required by the corpuscularian philosophy.

[9] *Pace* Robert A. Wilson 2002 and Mandelbaum 1964.

[10] *Pace* Alexander 1981, Curley 1972, and Mackie 1976.

[11] It's another one of the unfortunate consequences of the fourth and fifth edition insertion of the section 10 characterization of secondary qualities and deletion of the section 9 emphasis on the origin in sensory observation of the ideas of primary qualities that inseparability appears to be urged as a criterion of primaryness.

Now let's turn to the other strut of the argument concerning the primary-secondary quality distinction, which starts from our commonsense conception of the causality of body. There is a single connected stretch of argument from II.viii.11–14 that develops from the claim, stated in II.viii.11, that the only way we conceive bodies to act is by impulse.[12] In section 12, Locke simply put together this basic apprehension about the way bodies cause change with the plain fact, again part of the commonsense view of the world, that bodies act on us (that is, on our sensory systems) to produce ideas of "the Extension, Figure, Number, and Motion of Bodies, of an observable bigness" (the secondary primary qualities mentioned in the 1–3 editions version of section 9). Locke reasons in this section that since bodies act only by impulse, or at least that's the only way we can conceive that they act, and since the observable bodies with their observable primary qualities (their secondary primary qualities) are at a distance from us and so cannot themselves directly produce changes in motion via contact, we have to imagine that imperceptibly small bodies travel from the observable bodies, and by colliding with the particles making up our sensory system cause changes in their disposition and motion (in other words, in the texture of the bodies making up the sensory system) which in turn cause motions in the animal spirits to the brain, and by this mechanical chain of causation ultimately produce ideas of the observable primary qualities (secondary qualities) of the observable bodies. The proximate causes of our sensations, therefore, are not the observable bodies and/or their observable primary qualities, but the primary qualities of the insensibly small bodies (their primary primary qualities) that act as causal intermediaries.

We should pause and note here that it is probably misleading to call this, as some commentators do, a theory of perception. That title would seem to dignify the amalgam of our vague notions about the causation of body (we'll see in the next section of the paper how badly off they are) with a fanciful just-so story about how bodies at a distance act causally to produce, ultimately, sensory ideas in us, quite beyond what it deserves. Probably the most we can say of it is that it is the best we can do by way of a story about how bodies produce sensory ideas in us, given our rough-and-ready notions about what bodies are, and how they cause changes of any kind.

[12] This is the passage in which one of the better-known changes from editions 1–3 to editions 4 and 5 took effect. The 1-3 edition claim that bodies can only act by impulse is softened in editions 4 and 5 to the claim that that is the only way we can conceive them to act. In making this change Locke is keeping a promise he made to Stillingfleet: "You ask, 'how can my way of liberty agree with the idea that bodies can operate only by motion and impulse?' Answ. By the omnipotency of God, who can make all things agree, that involve not a contradiction. It is true, I say, 'that bodies operate by impulse, and nothing else.' And so I thought when I writ it, and can yet conceive no other way of their operation. But I am since convinced by the judicious Mr. Newton's incomparable book, that it is too bold a presumption to limit God's power, in this point, by my narrow conceptions. The gravitation of matter towards matter, by ways inconceivable to me, is not only a demonstration that God can, if he pleases, put into bodies powers and ways of operation above what can be derived from our idea of body, or can be explained by what we know of matter, but also an unquestionable and every where visible instance, that he has done so. And therefore in the next edition of my book I shall take care to have that passage rectified." (3rd Letter to Stillingfleet, *Works of John Locke* [1823 ed.] vol. IV, p. 467).

We should note, too, that given the at best quite indirect and causally mediated way in which observably large bodies work upon our sensory systems to produce ideas of the primary qualities of those bodies, there is no special reason to suppose that those ideas (ideas of secondary primary qualities) accurately represent those qualities of the large-scale bodies, or that they are especially impervious to illusion, distortion, and variation depending on the state of the observer, the features of the medium, or other confounding factors. Locke's implicit recognition of this fact thus neutralizes one of Berkeley's main strategies of argument against Locke's primary-secondary quality distinction, or at least one many commentators attribute to him.[13]

The same causal story developed in section 12 as regards the production in us of ideas of primary qualities of observable bodies (secondary primary qualities) is then extended to the production of ideas of secondary qualities, such as colors and smells. In editions 1–3, this is the first mention in the chapter of secondary qualities, and unlike the inserted section 10 in editions 4–5 there is no mention in this section of secondary qualities being powers; instead what happens is that the story about imperceptibly small bodies acting by impulse on our sensory systems to produce ideas of the primary qualities of perceptible bodies, sketched out in section 12, is simply extended to the production of the ideas of secondary qualities. The implicit line of argument begun in section 11, that this is the only causal story we can tell ourselves about how bodies, which as far as we can conceive act only by impulse transmitted by contact action, act upon us at a distance to produce sensory ideas, is thus simply applied to the case of secondary qualities. The big difference Locke notes is that the ideas of secondary qualities "have no similitude" with the motions that "we may conceive" cause them, but we can nevertheless conceive them to be linked (in a lawlike way, presumably) by God's having annexed these fundamentally incommensurable things.[14] This sets up the conclusion of the argument in section 14, in which the account given in section 13 of the causal ancestry of colors and odors is extended to tastes and sounds and "*other the like sensible Qualities*," and in which all of these sensible qualities are said to be "nothing in the Objects themselves, but Powers to produce various Sensations in us, and *depend on these primary Qualities*, *viz*. Bulk, Figure, Texture, and Motion of parts." This is the first appearance in the first three editions of the paired claims that the causal basis in the object of the production of sensations, and hence of the ideas of sensible qualities in us, is the primary qualities or mechanical affections of the insensibly small parts of objects, and that the secondary qualities as they exist in the objects themselves exist only as powers, based on these primary qualities of the parts of bodies. These paired claims were the ones transposed forward to section 10 in the fourth and fifth editions, where in that context they appear to be asserted without argument.

As they appear in section 14, as the conclusion of the consecutive argument begun in section 11, the paired claims come in an order of precedence. The claim that the causes

[13] See, *inter alia*, Margaret Wilson's classic paper (1982).

[14] There is thus an important link between this passage and IV.iii.28–9.

in the object of the secondary qualities are the primary qualities of the insensibly small constituent parts of the object is the direct conclusion of the line of argument begun in section 11. Let's note, in passing, that in this instance as well as in the case of the argument from what's included in or follows from our commonsense idea of body (sections 9–10), Locke is not trying to provide a justificatory argument for this claim, but is instead tracing out the consequences of our commonsense notions about what body is and about how bodies can cause things. Accordingly, the result that it is the primary qualities of the parts of bodies that are the ultimate causes in the body of its producing sensations, from which we take the ideas of secondary qualities, is not an inductive argument, or analogical argument, or argument from the best explanation, or any sort of pretended justification of the truth of the claim, but is simply an account of how we, plain folk, have to think about the causal ancestry of ideas of secondary qualities given our ideas, bad as they may be, about how bodies could cause sensations. A consequence of this, in turn, is that we have to think of secondary qualities as they are in the bodies as nothing but powers, which as Locke conceives of these entails that (a) secondary qualities are defined only relatively to our sensory experience, and/or our sensory systems,[15] and (b) they are not the ultimate causes of the sensations they produce, but are instead based on the ultimate causes, namely the primary qualities of the insensible parts of the body.

Locke draws a further important consequence from this line of argument for the primary-secondary quality distinction in section 15, the very much discussed resemblance claim. The claim is that ideas of primary qualities of bodies are resemblances of them (the syntax allows the interpretation of "them" to be either the bodies, or their primary qualities; either is plausible, but the latter interpretation fits better with the line of argument in sections 11–14 and in sections 15–22, as we'll shortly see), and that "their Patterns" really exist in the bodies themselves. In contrast, the ideas of secondary qualities have no resemblance of anything actually in the bodies themselves, as the secondary qualities are powers to produce sensations, which powers the bodies have by virtue of the bulk, figure, and motion of the insensible parts, that is, the primary primary qualities of the parts. Locke evidently takes the resemblance claim to need some elaboration; if we attend to the marginal summaries Locke added to the second edition, which generally are good guides to the argumentative structure of the text, we find "§§ 15–22. Ideas *of primary Qualities are resemblances*; *of secondary, not*" at the relevant location. If we go through the examples Locke provides in sections 16–21, we find that they are all variations on the two key themes mentioned above: first, the relativity to our senses, as shown by variation with no physical change in the object, that is characteristic of secondary qualities and that marks them as "not really in" the bodies or as not in "the bodies as they are in themselves," and second, that the causal agents in the production of sensations in us, which are the manifestations of the powers

[15] See particularly A. D. Smith 1990.

with which secondary qualities are identified, are, at least as far as they reside in the body, the primary qualities of the extended solid parts of the body.

The notion of resemblance deployed here is not mysterious. As the beginning of II. viii.18, quoted above, makes plain, the primary primary qualities which are really in the extended solid parts of the bodies we sense are exactly the same in kind as the secondary primary qualities that we sense directly. When we in imagination construct a picture of the microphysical mechanical composition of a body, we simply assign, as we saw above, different magnitudes to the pictured sizes, shapes, motions, etc. of the parts than those which characterize the qualities of bodies large enough to be perceived. We might say that the truth of the resemblance claim is an artifact of the way our conception of the primary primary qualities was constructed, together with our commitment, such as it is, to the impulse conception of the causality of body, which was the main strut of the claim that the only way we can conceive sensations to be caused in us by bodies acting at a distance was by the primary primary qualities of insensibly small particles in a mechanical chain of causation.

The resemblance claim has been interpreted in a great variety of ways, and the present interpretation departs in various ways from some previous suggestions. First, the notion of resemblance used here is a natural and straightforward one, in spite of the fact that it was put to use as a somewhat technical notion in the Scholastic theories of perception from which it most immediately derived. Bennett famously complained that "ideas cannot resemble either bodies or qualities of bodies," and offered as an acceptable transform of the resemblance claim the point that the causes of ideas of primary qualities can be described using the same vocabulary as is used in describing the ideas (e.g. shape-ideas are caused by shapes, etc.) whereas the causes of ideas of secondary qualities are not described in the same vocabulary (e.g. color-ideas are caused by shapes, etc.).[16] We might begin by noting that it's the fact of resemblance that makes it appropriate to use the same vocabulary in the case of primary quality ideas and primary qualities in bodies, and lack of resemblance that demands the different vocabularies in the case of secondary qualities. In other words, the order of explanation runs from resemblance or lack thereof to sameness or difference of vocabulary, and not the other way around. More important, Bennett's implicit shift from talk of the ideas as ideas to talk of their representative content, as he moves from stating the problem to giving his solution, reflects the right approach; in the first case, the talk of resemblance between ideas and qualities is indeed problematic, whereas the second case presents no problem at all.

We should remember that the immediate context which gives the significance to drawing a primary-secondary quality distinction is the Aristotelian-Scholastic theory of sense perception. According to that theory, the causal basis in the object for the production of any ideas of sensible qualities is a real quality which is a subordinate

[16] Jonathan Bennett 1971, 106.

form or species existing in the object. The form is propagated through the medium, and becomes the form of the act of mind in which the sensory perception of the relevant sensory quality consists. It is indeed the same form (numerically) existing first in the object, then taken on by the medium, and finally existing in the mind as the form of the act of perception, only in the latter case not existing as in matter. The act of mind thus has a formal similitude, a resemblance, to the quality in the object that it represents.[17] Just as Descartes had done, Locke argues against the claim that all ideas of sensible qualities are resemblances of something existing in the object, and by this argument rejects the Scholastic doctrine of real qualities. And also as Descartes had done, he finds that this doctrine originates in the commonsense prejudice that the ideas of sensible qualities are, all of them, resemblances of something really existing in the object itself, the technical Scholastic theory of perception being a sort of metaphysical overlay on this commonsense attitude. This is one of the main motivations for drawing the primary-secondary quality distinction, namely, to undermine, or at least challenge, the commonsense view that ideas of sensible qualities are, in general, resemblances of qualities actually in the object, and thus undermine the Scholastic theory built out of this prejudice. The key point to keep in mind is that it is common sense that provides the tools for the undoing of the prejudice, namely the commonsense understanding of the notion of body and of the causality of body. Hence one piece of common sense has to give way to another, and presumably one reason that Locke takes us through the number and variety of thought-experiments he provides in sections 15–22 (manna, almonds, porphyry, hot and cold water, etc.) is to drive home the conflict between the uniform resemblance claim and our commonsense view about the causality of body, and to help us see that the latter view trumps the former in our overall commonsense view of the world. Although these thought-experiments serve to do more than simply illustrate the differential resemblance claim they are brought in to support, in that they confirm to us the naturalness of the view of the causality of bodies that grounds the distinction by showing its application in a variety of circumstances, and provide us with the satisfaction of believing that the phenomena now have a certain intelligibility for us

[17] It's worth noting that Locke's and Descartes' reinterpretation of the Scholastic language of resemblance involves something of an equivocation; where the Scholastics imputed formal identity, the mechanical philosophers' resemblance claims hold only as a qualitative similarity, with the added proviso that the primary qualities as they are in the body 'look' or 'appear' to the mind as it represents them as they are in the body (in Locke, in imagination; in Descartes, in intellect) just as they do in the ideas themselves. Locke's characterization in II.viii.16 of heat and light in a flame, white and cold in snow, and white and sweet in manna ("Which Qualities are commonly thought to be the same in those Bodies, that those *Ideas* are in us, the one the perfect resemblance of the other, as they are in a Mirror") is making a negative point regarding the ideas of heat, light, etc., namely, that they don't resemble in that way. But it would seem to imply that the ideas of primary qualities do resemble in that way. I should note too that my account of resemblance has it that the ideas, as ideas (or in Cartesian language, the ideas in their formal reality), don't literally have the primary qualities of shape, size etc., but rather it is their representational content, or intentional objects, that have them. Ayers 1991, Jacovides 1999, and Winkler 1992 have argued that we should take Locke to hold that ideas literally have sizes, shapes, etc.; I don't have space here to counter their arguments, but I believe a case can be made against their interpretation of Locke.

(more on this in section 3 of the paper), they should not be mistaken for independent arguments brought to justify the claimed difference as regards resemblance of the qualities of bodies between primary and secondary qualities; for this task they would be manifestly inadequate, as Bennett and other commentators have shown.

The second important point about the resemblance claim, as we have interpreted it here, is that it does not assert that our ideas of primary qualities accurately represent, in full detail, either the primary qualities of the minute parts of bodies (the primary primary qualities) or the primary qualities of observable bodies (the secondary primary qualities). As regards the latter, there are two points to be made. First, Locke is not committed to denying that there are a host of perceptual illusions concerning the perceived shapes, sizes, motions, etc. of observably large bodies. The oblate shape turned at an angle to the eye, the misjudgments of the relative sizes of objects based on a misestimation of their relative distances from us, the train tracks that appear to converge at a distance, the appearance that the train next to ours is moving backward when it is our train moving forward, etc., are all phenomena Locke can readily admit without damage to his resemblance claim.[18] Even in the cases where there's no pronounced illusion, we can recognize, as in looking at the edge of a table and seeing it is straight and true (in the woodworker's sense), we can imagine that, given the limits of resolution of our visual system, what we see as straight and true may at the microlevel be quite jagged, gappy, and bumpy. As for the natural thought that the "real" (as opposed to apparent) observed length (e.g.) of a macro-sized object is a direct function of the lengths of the bodies which lie side by side to constitute the observed length, this is no doubt correct, but as we imagine the causal basis of this (the texture of the observable body that gives the small bodies their position, the motions which preserve the overall observable length by allowing the right sort of shifts of position of appropriately sized and shaped particles, the basis of the cohesion of the parts over time, etc.), there is much more involved than simply summing the lengths of the composing particles at the surface.[19] The resemblance claim asserts accuracy only down to the level

[18] This point has been made by Margaret Wilson and any number of other commentators who note that this seems to insulate Locke's differential resemblance claim from a key line of attack deployed by Berkeley. There is one place, II.viii.21, in the example of the hot and cold water, where Locke says something that has been taken as suggesting that the perception of primary qualities of observable bodies might not be subject to the same variability as is found in the perception of hot and cold: "For if we imagine *Warmth*, as it is *in our Hands*, to be *nothing but a certain sort and degree of Motion in the minute Particles of our Nerves, or animal Spirits*, we may understand, how it is possible, that the same Water may at the same time produce the Sensation of Heat in one Hand, and Cold in the other; which yet Figure never does, that never producing the *Idea* of a square by one Hand, which has produced the *Idea* of a Globe by another." When we consider the first clause of the sentence closely, as setting the context for understanding the difference claimed here, we see that the details of our picture of how to explain the variation in the hot and cold appearances—different degrees of motion in the particles of the different hands—would not suffice to produce a difference in felt shape. There is no reason to generalize the difference beyond this.

[19] These considerations also apply to the thought-experiments by which Bennett seeks to establish by argument his version of the primary-secondary quality distinction (Bennett 1971, 96–100).

of the broadly construed kinds of quality that have instances in the bodies, and no more detail than that.

Finally, attention to the primary primary quality-secondary primary quality distinction enables us to parse correctly claims about the causal efficacy of primary qualities. In general, the secondary primary qualities are not the ultimate causes of effects that are often attributed to them. The explanation of why it is that one can't fit a square peg in a round hole, for example, obviously refers at first blush to the (macro) shapes of the peg and the hole, and for most purposes that goes far enough. If the peg, with its square shape, were to be made of butter or silly putty rather than wood, say, then it would fit into the hole in the wooden board, as would happen if the peg were made of wood and the board of butter or silly putty. We would ultimately need to advert to facts about the microstructural constitution of the peg and the board to give the full explanation, and it is this characterization of the object, together with facts about our visual systems, that would provide the full explanation of the object's causing the relevant ideas of (macro) shape and size in us. So it is the primary primary qualities, rather than the secondary primary qualities, that are the causes of the secondary qualities and powers (and of the secondary primary qualities).

3. The primary-secondary quality distinction

The account I've given of the argument for the primary-secondary quality distinction has important consequences for our view of the status of the distinction itself, and the implications of drawing the distinction just as Locke did. I will sketch three interpretive consequences of the account given here.

First, on this account the corpuscularian hypothesis, as championed by such previous thinkers as Gassendi, Charleton, and most importantly Boyle, is not presupposed as an argumentative premiss for drawing the primary-secondary quality distinction. More exactly, Locke's argument for the distinction does not assume or rest on either a claim that corpuscularian mechanism is the true natural philosophy (as opposed to its Aristotelian, Spagyritic, or Cartesian competitors), or that it is the one best supported by evidence, or that it is on that and/or other grounds the best explanation of the nature and operation of bodies, and particularly of their qualities and powers, or any other variant of the claim that corpuscularianism is on scientific grounds superior to any alternative hypothesis. Mandelbaum, Curley, Alexander, Bennett, and other commentators have put forward one or another version of the view that Locke argues from the truth or explanatory superiority of corpuscularianism, while Lisa Downing has strongly resisted this view of the matter, as have I. Downing's view and mine can draw additional support from the interpretation given here, whereon the sole basis for drawing the primary-secondary quality distinction is the commonsense idea of what body is, together with the commonsense view about the causality of bodies, with nothing concerning the alleged truth or scientific superiority of corpuscularianism entering into the argument.

As with the other partisans of the Mechanical Philosophy who preceded him (Descartes, Gassendi, Charleton, Boyle, and others) Locke notes the special perspicacity which an account of the structure of simple machines (and not so simple ones, clocks being a favorite example) brings to our understanding of their function and capabilities. As far as it goes, the clock metaphor figures prominently in the PR for the mechanical philosophy, and funds in large part the invidious comparisons which champions of mechanism liked to make with Aristotelianism and spagyritic chemistry (the two major competitors to mechanism for the general theory of matter), and I think that Locke falls in with this general line of support for mechanism and attack on Aristotelianism. Locke is the first in the mechanist tradition, however, to express significant doubt about the ultimate intelligibility of corpuscularian mechanism, so that by contrast even such a modest and diffident (at least as regards rhetoric) proponent as Boyle can seem overweeningly boosterish, let alone such dogmatists as Descartes and Hobbes.

At one point or another in the *Essay* Locke expresses doubts about the key basic elements of the mechanistic hypothesis. Most of these passages are prominent and much discussed, at least recently, but one relatively less often remarked passage notes that the limits of our imaginative capacities puts severe constraints on the conceivability of corpuscularianism, at least as regards its claim that bodies can be seen as conglomerations of insensibly small parts. This passage is to be found at *Essay* II.xxix.16; the chapter concerns "*Clear and Obscure, Distinct and Confused* Ideas," and the immediate context is a doubt about the clearness of the question whether matter can be divided to infinity. Of course, atomistic versions of mechanism such as Gassendi's and Boyle's deny that matter is actually divisible to infinity, although they allow that matter may be conceptually so divisible, even if at some point physically indivisible. Locke's strictures would seem to apply to both kinds of infinite divisibility, but in making his point he expresses his doubts about our ability to conceive body divided very far beyond the limits of our visual resolution. Here's the beginning of that passage:

In Matter, we have no clear *Ideas* of the smalness of Parts, much beyond the smallest, that occur to any of our Senses: and therefore when we talk of the divisibility of Matter *in infinitum*, though we have clear *Ideas* of Division and Divisibility, and have also clear *Ideas* of Parts, made out of a whole, by Division; yet we have but very obscure, and confused *Ideas* of Corpuscles, or minute Bodies, so to be divided, when by former Divisions, they are reduced to a smallness, much exceeding the perception of any of our Senses; and so all that we have clear, and distinct *Ideas* of, is of what Division in general, or abstractly is, and the Relation of *Totum* and *Pars*: But of the bulk of the Body, to be thus infinitely divided after certain Progressions, I think, we have no clear, nor distinct *Idea* at all. For I ask any one, Whether taking the smallest Atom of Dust he ever saw, he has any distinct *Idea*, (bating still the Number which concerns not Extension,) betwixt the 100 000, and the 1000 000 part of it. Or if he think he can refine his *Ideas* to that Degree, without losing sight of them, let him add ten Cyphers to each of those Numbers. Such a degree of smalness is not unreasonable to be supposed, since a Division carried on so far brings it no nearer the end of infinite Division, than the first Division into two halfs does. I must confess for my part, I have no clear, distinct *Ideas* of the different Bulk, or Extension of those Bodies, having but a very obscure one of either of them. So that, I think, when we talk of Division of Bodies *in infinitum*, our *Idea* of their distinct Bulks, which is the Subject and Foundation of Division, comes after a little progression, to be confounded, and almost lost in Obscurity. For that *Idea*, which is to represent only Bigness, must be very obscure and confused, which we cannot distinguish from one ten times as big, but only by Number: so that we have clear, distinct *Ideas*, we may say of Ten and One, but no distinct *Ideas* of two such Extensions. 'Tis plain from hence, that when we talk of infinite Divisibility of Body, or Extension, our distinct and clear *Ideas* are only of Numbers: but the clear, distinct *Ideas* of Extension, after some Progress of Division, is quite lost; and of such minute Parts, we have no distinct *Ideas* at all; but it returns, as all our *Ideas* of Infinite do, at last to that of Number always to be added; but thereby never amounts to any distinct *Idea* of actual, infinite Parts.

We're encountering here one of the implications of Locke's rejection of Descartes' sharp distinction between intellect and imagination; on Descartes' view there could not be a divorce between "number" and extension in our intellectual conception of body of the sort that Locke alleges here, although Descartes would agree that such a divorce is possible for the imagination, as shown by the discussion of the chiliagon example in the Sixth Meditation.[20]

Far more troubling for a would-be booster of mechanism are the deep problems that Locke sees lying in the way of achieving a complete understanding of two of the most basic conceptual underpinnings of mechanism, the extension of body and the transmission of motion by impulse.[21] These problems are discussed mainly in the *Essay's* chapter "*Of our Complex* Ideas *of Substances*," in the context of an argument designed to show that, *pace* Descartes, the idea of mind or spirit is no more clear and distinct than the idea of body, and *pace* Malebranche, the idea of body is no more clear or distinct than the idea of mind or spirit; both of these general ideas are equally afflicted with conceptual unclarities. At *Essay* II.xxiii.23–27 Locke scouts most of the extant proposals for accounting for the cohesion of the parts of body, and subjects each to withering criticism; he states the general outcome in II.xxiii.26:

He that could find the Bonds, that tie these heaps of loose little Bodies together so firmly; he that could make known the Cement, that makes them stick so fast one to another, would discover a great, and yet unknown Secret: And yet when that was done, would he be far enough from making the extension of Body (which is the cohesion of its solid parts) intelligible, till he could shew wherein consisted the union, or consolidation of the parts of those Bonds, or of that Cement, or of the least Particle of Matter that exists. Whereby it appears that this primary and supposed obvious Quality of Body, will be found, when examined, to be as incomprehensible, as

[20] Compare Locke's discussion of the chilihedron example two sections earlier, at II.xxix.14.

[21] Locke seems not to think that that other basic conception of the mechanistic view of the world, solidity, is subject to the same conceptual worries. He takes it that the problem of conceiving the basis (or bases) of the cohesion of the parts of a body calls into question only our notion of the extension of body, and not of its solidity.

any thing belonging to our Minds, and *a solid extended Substance, as hard to be conceived, as a thinking immaterial one*, whatever difficulties some would raise against it.[22]

Shortly following this very negative estimate of the intelligibility of the extension of body, Locke takes up the topic of the transmission of motion by impulse in II.xxiii.28:

Another *Idea* we have of Body, is the power of *communication of Motion by impulse;* and of our Souls, the power of *exciting of Motion by Thought*. These *Ideas,* the one of Body, the other of our Minds, every days experience clearly furnishes us with: But if here again we enquire how this is done, we *are equally in the dark*. For in the communication of Motion by impulse, wherein as much Motion is lost to one Body, as is got to the other, which is the ordinariest case, we can have no other conception, but of the passing of Motion out of one Body into another; which, I think, is as obscure and unconceivable, as how our Minds move or stop our Bodies by Thought; which we every moment find they do.[23]

Both of these large holes in our comprehension of body—the cohesion of solid parts and the transmission of motion through impulse—are not, it should be noted, difficulties which originally arise only in the context of scientific or philosophical theorizing around the corpuscularian hypothesis, or mechanism generally, but are instead already to be found in the commonsense, prescientific notions of body and its causality which we saw to be the basis of the primary-secondary quality distinction. This very much reduces the prospects for according any very significant justificatory force for Locke's basic argument for the primary-secondary quality distinction, resting as it does on foundations as shaky as these.

Locke's distinction between primary and secondary qualities also encounters difficulties in the face of another, and more celebrated, conceptual gap: that between (primary) primary quality constitutions of bodies and the sensations they produce in us. As we've seen, the claim is that primary primary qualities are the ultimate causal basis, in the body affecting our senses, of the body's producing sensations in us, and so of the powers bodies have to produce these sensations, these powers finally being identified with secondary qualities. In IV.iii.28, after having noted that our lack of detailed ideas of the microphysical constitutions of bodies hinders us from forming any universal and certain knowledge of the necessary connections of the powers and qualities in bodies, he speaks of what he earlier (IV.iii.12) called "another and more incurable part of our

[22] Two points to note: first, in this passage and a number of others in which the extension of body is discussed, Locke is making a strong distinction between extension simpliciter (the extension of space, which space and body share) and the extension of body, which consists in the cohesion of solid parts, and which of course space cannot share; and second, the problem of cohesion is here explicitly said to pertain to atoms or corpuscles as well as to conglomerations of these particles, and it is clear that the problem does go, as it were, all the way down (with perhaps different accounts of cohesion at the different levels). Of course, the larger context of this issue is the well-known problem that corpuscularian mechanism has with accounting for the unity of substance in the case of bodies, the focus of Aristotelian and Aristotelian-inspired (including, notably, Leibnizean) objections to mechanism.

[23] See also II.xxi.4, and II.xxiii.29–30. IV.x.19 has an interesting discussion of the difficulty of conceiving how thought can produce motion in a body.

Ignorance," namely that "there is no discoverable connection between any *secondary Quality, and those primary Qualities* which it depends on." IV.iii.28 runs thus, in part:

In the next place, another cause of Ignorance, of no less moment, is a want of *a discoverable Connection* between those *Ideas* which we have. For wherever we want that, we are utterly uncapable of universal and certain Knowledge; and are, as in the former case, left only to Observation and Experiment: which how narrow and confined it is, how far from general Knowledge, we need not be told. I shall give some few instances of this cause of our Ignorance and so leave it. 'Tis evident that the bulk, figure, and motion of several Bodies about us, produce in us several Sensations, as of Colours, Sounds, Tastes, Smells, Pleasure and Pain, *etc.* These mechanical Affections of Bodies, having no affinity at all with those *Ideas*, they produce in us, (there being no conceivable connexion between any impulse of any sort of Body, and any perception of a Colour, or Smell, which we find in our Minds) we can have no distinct knowledge of such Operations beyond our Experience; and can reason no otherwise about them, than as effects produced by the appointment of an infinitely Wise Agent, which perfectly surpass our Comprehensions. As the *Ideas* of sensible secondary Qualities, which we have in our Minds, can, by us, be no way deduced from bodily Causes, nor any correspondence or connexion be found between them and those primary Qualities which (Experience shews us) produce them in us; so on the other side, the Operation of our Minds upon our Bodies is as unconceivable. How any thought should produce a motion in Body is as remote from the nature of our *Ideas*, as how any Body should produce any Thought in the Mind. That it is so, if Experience did not convince us, the Consideration of the Things themselves would never be able, in the least, to discover to us. These, and the like, though they have a constant and regular connexion, in the ordinary course of Things: yet that connexion being not discoverable in the *Ideas* themselves, which appearing to have no necessary dependance one on another, we can attribute their connexion to nothing else, but the arbitrary Determination of that All-wise Agent, who has made them to be, and to operate as they do, in a way wholly above our weak Understandings to conceive.

The conceptual gap noted here is a consequence of our general inability to put our ideas of matter and of thinking into any sort of explanatory connection each with the other, and this is the basis of Locke's famous (or notorious) doctrine of the possibility of thinking matter, set out in IV.iii.6. Partway through that section Locke declares:

We have the *Ideas* of *Matter* and *Thinking*, but possibly shall never be able to know, whether any mere material Being thinks, or no; it being impossible for us, by the contemplation of our own *Ideas*, without revelation, to discover, whether Omnipotency has not given to some Systems of Matter fitly disposed, a power to perceive and think, or else joined and fixed to Matter so disposed, a thinking immaterial Substance.

He continues:

What certainty of Knowledge can any one have that some perceptions, such as *v.g.* pleasure and pain, should not be in some bodies themselves, after a certain manner modified and moved, as well as that they should be in an immaterial Substance, upon the Motion of the parts of Body: Body as far as we can conceive being able only to strike and affect body; and Motion, according to the utmost reach of our *Ideas*, being able to produce nothing but Motion, so that when we allow it to produce pleasure or pain, or the *Idea* of a Colour, or Sound, we are fain to quit our Reason, go beyond our *Ideas*, and attribute it wholly to the good Pleasure of our Maker. For since we must allow he has annexed Effects to Motion, which we can no way conceive Motion able to produce, what reason have we to conclude, that he could not order them as well to be produced in a Subject we cannot conceive capable of them, as well as in a Subject we cannot conceive the motion of Matter can any way operate upon?

This gap is a serious challenge to the ultimate intelligibility of the primary-secondary distinction. As we have seen, a crucial part of that distinction is the claim that secondary qualities are powers only, and their causal basis in the object is the (primary) primary qualities of the body; in the passages above Locke is claiming that we cannot see, even in the broadest terms, how it could be that primary qualities should cause sensations in perceivers, and it is of course in terms of the production of particular sensations in us that secondary qualities are defined.

Locke's highlighting of these, according to him, irremediable conceptual gaps concerning the cohesion of the parts of body, the causality of body via impulse, and the causal connections between primary and secondary qualities, very much stands in the way of any interpretation on which Locke is supposed to be resting his case for corpuscularian mechanism or for any of its corollary theses, notably the primary-secondary quality distinction, on a claimed special or superior intelligibility. The conceptual gaps lie at the very heart of the corpuscularian hypothesis, so that only the most superficial intelligibility, or appearance of intelligibility, can be claimed for the hypothesis and its corollaries. These latter do not stand (up) to reason.

The unclarities and conceptual gaps to be found at the basis of the corpuscularian hypothesis not only disqualify it from serving as an epistemological or metaphysical foundation for a mechanistic picture of the world, but they preclude even the more modest philosophical role that Downing has claimed for it, namely that of serving to illustrate the philosophical notions of quality and real essence. She writes:

I have developed an interpretation of Locke's discussion of real essences and the primary-secondary quality distinction consistent with this, according to which these are in the first instance metaphysical distinctions, with corpuscularianism serving as an illustration or "instance" of what the primary qualities of bodies might be and what the real essences of bodies might be like.[24]

Downing's interpretation has, as we can now see, several problems. First, while the primary-secondary quality distinction is, in the context of Scholastic philosophy anyway, a relatively new, or at least recently revived notion, the notion of real essence, as Locke's comments in introducing the distinction between real and nominal essences in III.iii.15 and 17 reflect, a good old notion, common property of the Scholastics and the new mechanist philosophers, bating the confusion that the former threw that

[24] Downing 1998.

notion into when they muddled it together with "the artificial Constitution of *Genus* and *Species*." But what that means is that the notion of a real essence, at least in its "proper original signification," was not in any particular need of clarification or illustration, while the primary-secondary quality distinction is not a mere clarification or illustration of the abstract metaphysical notion of a quality of body, but is instead a central element in a direct frontal assault on the Scholastic doctrine of real qualities, and hence one the Scholastics would reject as an interpretation of the metaphysical notion of a quality. In the paragraph following the one I quoted, Downing avers that Locke's intent in employing corpuscularianism to illustrate these abstract metaphysical notions is somewhat less modest than might be inferred from the above formulation:

> As it stands, however, this underplays somewhat the extent of Locke's allegiance to mechanism. Corpuscularianism is not, for Locke, a mere illustration—it is not simply one theory among many to which he might have appealed. Corpuscularianism has a special status for Locke in that it is uniquely natural, and it is so because the theoretical account of body it gives is the one that we distill from ordinary sense experience; corpuscularianism posits that the real essence of body corresponds to the nominal essence we assign to "body." This naturalness, along with the theory's clarity and explanatory potential, make it uniquely qualified to illustrate, not just these metaphysical notions, but also Locke's conception of scientia.[25]

We can't rest too much on the clarity and explanatory potential of the corpuscularian hypothesis, given that it has very little of either of these, thanks to the deep conceptual problems afflicting it. As for its "naturalness," I agree with Downing that the corpuscularian hypothesis coheres with our ordinary commonsense idea of body, and that this idea is gathered from everyday sensory experience, but the process of acquisition is shot through with the same ultimately arbitrary selectivity that characterizes nominal essences generally (making them apt to be called "the workmanship of the understanding,"[26] and the resultant idea is so limited (as the conceptual gaps show) that it's hard to see that it can illuminate or illustrate very much. So it may not be up to playing even the modest role that Downing claims for it.

Conclusion

We've seen that Locke's distinction between primary and secondary qualities rests directly on the commonsense idea of body as extended solid substance, and the commonsense notion that bodies cause their effects through the transmission of motion by impulse and consequent alterations in the mechanical constitutions of the bodies they act upon, which in turn produce alterations in the sensible qualities those bodies exhibit. We've also seen that Locke regards both these notions as somewhat shaky, in that while they are derived from sensory experience, there is a strong component of selectivity and arbitrariness in the process, not to mention that they are subject to deep

[25] Loc. cit. [26] III.iii.13.

conceptual problems if we try to spell them out very fully. The idea of body has the deep unclarities about the cohesion of solid parts (extension of body) at its core; the idea of causation by impulse has its attendant unclarities, and is perhaps in worse shape than the idea of body, since with respect to that idea, the idea of body, it's only that we can't know that it actually hits off the deepest truth about body (see again IV.iii.11 and 16), whereas with respect to the idea of causation by impulse we positively know (because of gravitational attraction) that it is inadequate to the task. Putting both of these ideas together, we find we cannot begin to conceive how it could be that changes of motion in bodies should produce sensations in our minds.

This is hardly the basis on which to build a robust justificatory story, either about the status of mechanism as a would-be explanatory theory or illustration of metaphysical notions, or about the ontology of qualities and powers, as has already been suggested. What, then, might be Locke's best hopes for the primary-secondary quality distinction, as he's drawn it? There are three possibilities. The first, and probably the one most widely attributed to Locke, is that he is seeking to draw a distinction concerning the ontological status of qualities (or qualities and powers), with the primary qualities held to be real in a sense in which the secondary qualities, given their dependence on, or essential relation to, our sensations, are not. Now it may be that this view of Locke's aims can be suitably qualified or hedged so as to remain consonant with the extreme limitations on any kind of justificatory claim which Locke would be in a position, given his argument for the distinction, to assert. One obvious way to go here would be to say that Locke means, in drawing the primary-secondary quality distinction, not to convince us about how things are, but instead, in something like the style of a transcendental argument, to delineate for us how we think (or *must* think) things are. But Locke doesn't give any such arguments, and he's not got the materials for one, at least if we consider the defining feature of that type of argument to be that it rests its claims on "the necessary conditions of the possibility of experience," not to mention that it would be quite a stretch to attribute to him the transcendental idealist metaphysics on which the results yielded by transcendental arguments can claim justificatory force. So we should reject the prevailing view that Locke should be taken to be trying to establish a straightforward ontological claim about the difference in status between primary and secondary qualities.

The limitations on the results Locke can claim from his argument are also a problem for a somewhat more modest aim he's commonly interpreted to have, namely that of using his account of primary and secondary qualities to refute or undermine the Aristotelian theory of real qualities. Now the way he summarizes the conclusions of the chapter in II.viii.24–6 makes it clear that he thinks he has exposed a common mistake people make in taking secondary qualities for real qualities, and he rehearses the line of argument that is supposed to convince them that secondary qualities are much more like what they hold to be "bare powers" than they are like the primary primary qualities that are the causes in the object of the relevant sensations in us. And although Locke does not give any extended critical discussion of the deep obscurities in the Aristotelian theory of real qualities, including the nature and ontological status of sensible and intelligible species, their relation to the substance of the body which is qualified by the real qualities, the propagation of species through the medium, the relation of all of these to the sensory organs which receive them and then to the phantasms they produce, etc., his basic claim that we cannot make sense of the causal story this theory has to tell, on which bodies act not by impulse or contact action but in entirely nonmechanical ways, and the claim that we can, at least in broad terms, understand the causality of bodies mechanistically, does succeed in casting a good bit of doubt on the Scholastic theory. But this does not amount to a decisive refutation of the theory. Even though we can't make sense of it, Locke hasn't established that it, or something like it, couldn't be the truth of the matter, that is, that something functionally similar to species could be transmitted to our sensories via some non-mechanical causal mechanism and be the cause of sensation. Even though, as I think Locke has established, the corpuscularian theory, with its distinction between primary and secondary qualities, fits better with our pre-theoretic conceptions of body and its ways of causing things to happen, and even if, as he's also established, it provides a generally intelligible account of sense perception, there remain all the deep obscurities and conceptual puzzles at the heart of mechanism. So while this edge that the corpuscularian theory has over the Scholastic theory may give us some reason to prefer the former to the latter, we have not been given reason to decisively reject the latter, nor any very strong justification for accepting the former.

If Locke can't claim to have justified any weighty ontological assertions about qualities, and if he can't claim to have definitively refuted the rival Aristotelian theory of real qualities, what work does he mean his distinction between primary and secondary qualities to do? The answer is suggested by the title of the chapter on primary and secondary qualities, and that chapter's placement in Book II of the *Essay*. The title of II.viii is "*Some farther Considerations concerning our simple* Ideas," and it closes off the discussion of simple ideas as such given in the first seven chapters of Book II. It is followed by three chapters on the faculties of mind concerned in one way or another with processing the simple ideas discussed in Book II, chapters 1–8 (specifically, perception (chapter 9), memory (chapter 10), and discerning and other operations of the mind (chapter 11)), which in turn lead into the discussion of complex ideas beginning at II.xxii. So the basic topic of II.viii is simple ideas, and it is under this rubric that the primary-secondary quality distinction is introduced. The discussion in II.viii (and cognate passages in II.xxiii) thus sets up, and chimes very well with the claims Locke makes near the end of Book II about simple ideas of sensation, which are always real (as opposed to fantastical), that is, always agree with the truth of things (II.xxx.2), always adequate (II.xxxi.2), and always true in regard to the real existence of things (II.xxxii.14–16), and in all these ways contrast sharply with the complex ideas of substances. Once we recognize the primary-secondary quality distinction, and can parse claims that actually concern the different ways in which we take our sensible ideas to relate to, representatively, the qualities and powers in the object which we take them to present to us, and in particular once we recognize the deep difference in the way we take powers to be in objects and the way we take real qualities (the primary primary qualities) to be in them, we will see the baselessness, and ill conformity with common sense, of the Scholastic theory of real qualities, and will see how the relatively esoteric corpuscularian hypothesis, fashioned as it is by the virtuosi, nevertheless hits off common sense very well.[27] This doesn't carry much, if any, justificatory force in favor of corpuscularianism and/or against Aristotelianism, but that's not important in the context of the project of giving a natural history of the human understanding, which is, after all, what Locke is mainly about.

Bibliography

Alexander, Peter. 1985. *Ideas, Qualities and Corpuscles: Locke and Boyle on the External World*, Cambridge: Cambridge University Press.

Atherton, Margaret. 1992. "'Ideas in the Mind, Qualities in Bodies': Some Distinctive Features of Locke's Account of Primary and Secondary Qualities," in *Minds, Ideas, and Concepts: Essays on the Theory of Representation in Modern Philosophy*, eds. Phillip D. Cummins and Guenter Zoeller, 111–24, Atascadero, California: Ridgeview.

Ayers, Michael. 1991. *Locke: Epistemology and Ontology*, 2 vols, London: Routledge.

Bennett, Jonathan. 1971. *Locke, Berkeley, Hume: Central Themes*, Oxford: Clarendon Press.

Curley, Edwin. 1972. "Locke, Boyle, and the Distinction between Primary and Secondary Qualities," *The Philosophical Review* 81: 438–64.

Downing, Lisa. 1998. "The Status of Mechanism in Locke's Essay," *The Philosophical Review* 107: 381–414.

—— 1999. "Locke's Resemblance Theses," *Philosophical Review 108*: 461–96.

Jacovides, Michael. 2007. "Locke's Distinctions between Primary and Secondary Qualities," in *The Cambridge Companion to Locke's Essay*, ed. Lex Newman, Cambridge: Cambridge University Press.

Locke, John. 1975. *An Essay Concerning Human Understanding*, ed. P. H. Nidditch, Oxford: Oxford University Press.

Mackie, J. L. 1976. *Problems from Locke*, Oxford: Clarendon Press.

[27] I take this view to be very close to the one Margaret Atherton puts forward (1992, especially 119-20). I take it that she is not saying, in claiming that Locke is primarily interested in the distinction between ideas in minds and qualities of things, that Locke is trying in this chapter to establish that there is such a distinction, or that the three-way distinction between ideas in minds, powers in objects to cause these ideas, and the real quality constitutions of bodies which are the causal basis in the object of these causal powers is not in fact the most basic one. I certainly want to deny these claims, and I believe her discussion is consonant with their denial. I'll also point out that her brief suggestion of the importance of taking seriously the chapter's opening discussion of positive ideas and privative causes (II.viii.1–6) (see 1992, 120f, and in particular the contrast between Locke and Descartes) is something that very much supports the interpretation given here. I should also note that I think it would be wrong to suppose that Atherton is claiming that Locke is giving a theory of mental representation here; instead I think she and I agree in thinking that Locke is simply giving an account of the ways in which we, ordinary people, given our commonsense commitments, take our simple ideas of sensation to relate to the objects.

Mandelbaum, Maurice. 1964. *Philosophy, Science and Sense Perception: Historical and Critical Studies*, Baltimore: The John Hopkins University Press.

Nidditch, P. H. and G. A. J. Rogers (eds.). 1990. *Drafts for the* Essay Concerning Human Understanding *and Other Philosophical Writings*, Vol. 1, Oxford: Oxford University Press.

Smith, A. D. 1990. "Of Primary and Secondary Qualities," *Philosophical Review* 99, 221–54.

Wilson, Margaret D. 1982. "Did Berkeley Completely Misunderstand the Basis of the Primary–Secondary Quality Distinction in Locke?", in Colin Turbayne (ed.), *Berkeley: Critical and Interpretive Essays*, 108–23, Minneapolis: University of Minnesota Press.

Wilson, Robert A. 2002. "Locke's Primary Qualities," *Journal of the History of Philosophy* 40, 201–28.

Winkler, Kenneth P. 1992. "Ideas, Sentiments, and Qualities," in *Minds, Ideas, and Concepts: Essays on the Theory of Representation in Modern Philosophy*, eds. Phillip D. Cummins and Guenter Zoeller, Atascadero, CA: Ridgeview, 151–65.

8

Primary and Secondary Qualities in the Phenomenalist Theory of Leibniz

Martha Brandt Bolton

Leibniz sides broadly with the mechanists on issues concerning explanation in the natural sciences. This is not to say he is in total agreement with the natural philosophical theories of any of his near contemporaries. Two points of divergence are especially prominent. Whereas his contemporaries pay little, if any, attention to forces, or the causes of motion, Leibniz contends that dynamics is an indispensable part of physical theory. He assigns physical forces a further metaphysical role as the sole source of individual and qualitative diversity in corporeal things. Motion presupposes different bodies, different places, and different times. In a world without atoms, which are "philosophers' abstractions" in Leibniz's dismissive phrase, nothing but differently directed, active, effective tendencies toward motion can diversify bodies, and thus spatial and temporal positions. Without acting forces, there is no motion; without motion, no figure nor magnitude, nor any of the sensible qualities the latter are supposed to explain.[1] On two counts, then, forces are more basic than the canonical primary qualities, extension, figure, motion, and size.[2] Moreover, the German philosopher strenuously argues that the *reality* of bodies cannot be understood apart from immaterial substantial forms. A metaphysical throwback to Aristotelian thought, the theory of forms was badly discredited in the eyes of other early moderns; mechanism was, indeed, partly intended to correct the doctrine's perceived inadequacies—for purposes of both metaphysics and natural science. In explaining natural phenomena, they are useless, Leibniz agrees.[3] He could be as disdainful of supposed Scholastic modes of explanation as

[1] See "On Nature Itself" (1695), 13, Leibniz (1989), 163–4.

[2] "... there is something over and above extension, in fact, something prior to extension, namely, force of nature implanted everywhere by the Creator," *Specimen Dynamicum* (1695), Leibniz (1989), 118.

[3] When I speak of "natural science" in this paper, I am referring to what seventeenth-century mechanists generally conceived of it; this hardly includes the study of minds or souls. By contrast, Leibniz urges that psychology and pneumatology are legitimate explanatory sciences, and advocated theoretical explanations of various cognitive operations. As we will see, the differences between primary and secondary qualities he recognizes can only be explicated in the framework of such a theory.

anyone: "It is as if we were content to say that a clock has a quality of clockness derived from its form without considering in what all of this consists; that would be sufficient for the person who buys the clock, provided that he turns over its care to another."[4] Nevertheless, in metaphysics he argues, forms, or souls, provide the substantial unity required to give reality to merely extended material mass. Leibniz is a mechanist, but with a difference.

This prompts a question about his attitude to the seventeenth-century doctrine of primary and secondary qualities. It was drawn from Boyle's corpuscular hypothesis, designed to encompass all versions of contemporary mechanism to the exclusion of the several competing theories abroad at the time.[5] Since Leibniz identifies himself as a mechanist, we may presume he endorses the division of qualities articulated by Locke. Still, his divergence from the typical mechanists' views in physics and metaphysics might make one suspect that he cannot consistently accept the prevailing doctrine of qualities—at least not without significant modification. For one thing, Leibnizian physical forces don't fit neatly into the doctrine because they are prior to the canonical primary qualities: that is, forces are required for an adequate natural scientific explanation of extension and its modifications. With regard to secondary qualities, Leibniz clearly does maintain that the qualities on this list are importantly different from other sensible qualities, but the interesting question is what he takes to be distinctive of them. This involves issues in theory of perception and knowledge on which Leibniz and other seventeenth-century mechanists are by no means in accord. This paper develops the distinctive features of Leibniz's account of the distinction of qualities in several stages. Section 1 addresses respects in which Leibniz's views differ from the established doctrine, especially with regard to the mind-dependence of both sorts of quality. Section 2 uses A.D. Smith's penetrating analysis of seventeenth-century mechanism as a platform from which to identify respects in which Leibniz's program of explanation in the natural sciences agrees with the standard distinction of qualities.[6] The remaining sections of the paper develop more subtle ways in which Leibniz departs from the standard model as Smith understands it. Section 3 concerns the unbridgeable gap between any physical theory and the concrete facts it can be used to explain, according to Leibniz. Section 4 argues that Leibniz certainly does not share the account of secondary qualities Smith ascribes to mechanists in general, but rather links the distinctive features of secondary qualities to the endemic confusion of sense perception. Section 5 draws some overall conclusions about the difference between primary, as opposed to secondary, qualities according to Leibniz.

4 "Discourse on Metaphysics" (1686), sec. 10; Leibniz (1989), 42.

5 "Some Specimens of an Attempt to make *Chymical* Experiments useful, etc.," Boyle (1661), 355.

6 Smith (1990).

1. Leibniz's departures from the established doctrine of qualities

One important reason for thinking he does not adhere to the doctrine of primary and secondary qualities abroad in the late seventeenth century is his phenomenalist theory of the material world. Caution is in order here. Leibniz's commitment to phenomenalism is controversial. Many scholars contend either that he adopts phenomenalism only in his later years, or that he constantly waivers between realist and phenomenalist views, or that he never fully worked out a phenomenalist metaphysics. These are complicated issues. But however they should be resolved, there is a great deal of evidence that a phenomenalist strain appears in theorizing throughout his career. In this paper, I consider only the phenomenalist strain. It is plain that Leibniz is attracted to it and it brings out his unique way of thinking about sensible qualities.

In 1704, Leibniz declares "there is nothing in the world except simple substances and, in them, perception and appetite."[7] Simple substances are not material. Material things fit into this spare ontology as nothing more than the intentional contents of the perceptual modifications of substances: "Matter and motion . . . are . . . phenomena of percipient beings, whose reality is located in the harmony of the percipient with himself (at different times) and with other percipient beings."[8] As phenomena, matter and its modifications are nothing apart from what they are perceived to be. Any philosopher with such a view must take care to account for the difference between real and imaginary phenomena, between dreams, and the like, and what exists in nature. As Leibniz explains in a short essay on real and imaginary phenomena, the things a substance purports to perceive can be regarded as real by this subject, if they are governed by laws of nature, or conform to a single hypothesis, or are predictable on the basis of previous perceptions. A further condition is inter-subjective, namely, that the law-governed phenomena of each substance cohere with those of every other substance allowing for their different perspectives.[9] In a few texts, the ultimate standard for reality and truth of perceptual phenomena is identified with God's intuitive knowledge (*scientia visionis*).[10] In many other texts, however, intra-substantial predictability and inter-substantial agreement suffice.

Each simple substance perceives, or "expresses", its own body and, through it, perceives other bodies, as well. The body that belongs to a substance, in turn, expresses this substance. That is, the body reflects the perceptions, appetites, thoughts, feelings, and purposes of the substance; indeed, the body and the substance exactly "mirror" each other. For Leibniz, every body in the universe either expresses a simple substance in this direct way or it is composed of bodies that do so; lumps of mud do not expresses

[7] To De Volder (1704), Leibniz (1970), 537.

[8] To De Volder (1704), Leibniz (1970), 537.

[9] "On the Method of Distinguishing Real from Imaginary Phenomena" (1683–6), Leibniz (1970), 364.

[10] To Des Bossess (1712), Leibniz (2007), 232; see Adams (1994), 255–61.

perceiving substances, but at some level, they are composed of bodies that do. In virtue of this pervasive expression relation, bodies in general are said to be "well founded phenomena", that is founded on non-material simple perceiving substances. "Express" is Leibniz's word for all sorts of representation, and he distinguishes perceptual representation, which is roughly imagistic, and intellectual representation, which is conceptual.[11] Immaterial entities are strictly outside the range of perception, so they are not among the perceptual phenomena; humans grasp that many of the bodies they perceive contain minds, souls, or soul-like entities, but only because humans have an intellectual faculty.[12] With regard to the reality of phenomena, the role of a simple substance is two-fold: from its point of view, the substance perceives its body and through it all contiguous bodies, and from the point of view of other substances, each simple substance gives a reflected unity to the perceptual phenomena that constitute its body. In this scheme, immaterial metaphysical foundations of phenomena are not pertinent to natural scientific inquiry; substantial forms, for instance, are beside the point.[13] Indeed, the facts to be explained by physics and other natural sciences would not be affected if our phenomena were not well-founded:

> If bodies were mere phenomena, they would not deceive the senses on account of that. For the senses do not make known anything about metaphysical matters. The veracity of the senses consists in the fact that the phenomena agree among themselves, and we shall not be deceived by events, if we follow reasons properly built on experience.
>
> (To Des Bosses [1716]; Leibniz [2007], 369)[14]

Accordingly, immaterial sub-structure is not relevant to the explanation of sensible qualities.

The phenomenalism we are discussing is akin to Berkeley's idealism, but some notable differences need to be mentioned here.[15] Unlike Berkeley, the earlier philosopher recognizes non-conscious perceptions, and along with them, the actual infinite division of perceptual phenomena; he also posits physical forces, or natural causes of motion.[16] Moreover, Leibniz recognizes not just spirits, but non-rational souls and, more important, non-sentient perceivers. The Irishman, of course, inveighs against the

[11] E.g. Leibniz (1967), 144.

[12] See Bolton (2007).

[13] It is, however, unclear that Leibniz has, or wants, a basis for individuating bodies other than by reference to the different immaterial substances they express; absent that, there is no basis on which to say that a body is one and the same thing but only flimsy considerations such as juxtaposition, sensory appearance, or human convenience (To Arnuald [1686–87], Leibniz [1967], 88–9, 120–2, 126–8). This affects the topic of this paper, because as far as I can see, he has no way of individuating perceptions except by reference to the bodies they express, so to the extent the individuation of inanimate bodies (e.g. lumps of mud, stones, watches) is conventional, so must the individuation of perceptions be conventional.

[14] Also Leibniz (1967), 122–3.

[15] Some scholars maintain that Berkeley identifies sensible things with perceptions construed as mental acts or states, but I would urge that, like Leibniz, he identifies sensible things with the intentional objects of such acts or states.

[16] See Margaret Wilson (1999b); Adams (1994), 224–8; Daniels (2007).

doctrine of primary and secondary qualities, as he construes it; above all, he condemns the opinion that primary qualities have "an absolute existence without the mind", or without being perceived or conceived by some mind or other. Leibniz could hardly disagree with this. As a phenomenalist about bodies, he cannot subscribe to the tenets of mechanism inasmuch as they imply that matter and its modifications exist independently of substances and their perceptual states.

Leibniz, too, assimilates the metaphysical status of the primary qualities of bodies and that of colors, odors, tastes, and the like. Shape and motion "involve something of the imaginary, no less than heat and color and other sensible qualities."[17] This is, at least in part, the result of arguments he devised purporting to show that composition of the continuum is impossible. From this, he concludes that nothing in the natural world has continuous extension; instead, every extended thing is actually divided into different extended parts.[18] To be sure, bodies appear to our *senses* to have smooth unbroken figures, but the boundaries are actually formed from parts of the boundaries of their parts, each moving, or tending to move, differently from the rest, and there is no end to this division and diversity. There is "no fixed, precise shape" in bodies. The seemingly continuous and describable boundaries of sensible objects are to some extent imaginary.[19] Some texts propound a more sweeping argument to the effect that forces are real by contrast with extension and its canonical modifications, precisely because the latter depend on imagination:

> the notion of extension is not as clear as is commonly believed. For from the fact that no body is so small that it is not actually divided into parts which are excited by various motions, it follows that no determinate shape can be assigned to any body. . . . And so shape involves something imaginary. . . . The same is to be said of motion; for motion, just as much as place, consists in relation alone . . . But motive power, i.e. the power of acting, is something real and can be discerned in bodies. And so the essence of a body is not to be located in extension and its modifications . . . for these involve something imaginary, no less than heat and colour and other sensible qualities. It is to be located in the power of acting and resisting alone, which we perceive with the intellect and not with the imagination.
>
> ("A Specimen of Discoveries, etc." [1688]; Morris and Parkinson [1973], 81–2)

The canonical primary qualities are relative and dependent on imagination, just as secondary qualities are.[20] Physical forces, or causes of motion, are "more real" than motions if judged by a cognitive standard, namely, that things known by intellect are more real than those known through imagination. Leibniz apparently thinks physical

[17] "A Specimen of Discoveries, etc." (1688?), Leibniz (1973), 82.

[18] See Levey (2005). Levey argues that this result does not imply that the indeterminate shapes of bodies are perceiver-dependent, in Leibniz's view; Crockett (2009) challenges this interpretation.

[19] Also Leibniz (1967), 96, 122, 123–4, 152; Leibniz (1989), 44.

[20] Again, ". . . shape, far from being constitutive of bodies, is not even a wholly real and specific quality outside of thought, . . . [a]nd I can say the same about magnitude and motion, namely that these qualities . . . partake of the phenomenal as do colours and sounds . . ." To Arnauld (1687), (Leibniz (1967), 119; also "Discourse on Metaphysics" (1686), sec. 12.

forces are conceived by intellect and also perceived by sense, for a later text unambiguously assigns them to the phenomena.[21]

In his fine exposition of Leibniz's phenomenalist theory, Robert Adams observes that the doctrine of qualities articulated by Locke and Boyle is not Leibniz's own. He takes it up in *New Essays*, but it is not entirely at home in the Leibnizian philosophy:

> [Leibniz] thought that the only fundamental difference between the two sorts of sensible qualities is in the degree of confusion with which they express a deeper reality. He regarded the degree of that difference as large . . . but placed it within a spectrum in which no sensible quality occupies a sufficiently distinguished position to merit the designation "primary quality". He thought there were qualities (namely, forces) that belong to bodies in a more primary way than any strictly sensible quality does. (Adams [1994], 228)

For Leibniz, the canonical primary and secondary qualities differ only in our manner of knowing them: the former, distinctly; the latter, confusedly. The "deeper reality" to which Adams alludes pertains to physical forces. As above, forces are more real than motion and figure, and are presupposed by all qualitative differences among bodies. Leibniz cannot agree with other mechanists who hold that the canonical primary qualities are fundamental in either metaphysics or scientific explanation.

Nevertheless, mechanism envisages a program for natural science that can, up to a point, be considered in abstraction from Leibniz's metaphysical doctrines in their entirety. He evidently believes his distinctive views do not preclude endorsing the program supplemented with physical forces. On the strength of this, we might think he largely accepts the doctrine of qualities spawned by the mechanist scheme. An interesting article by A. D. Smith, which aims to explicate the seventeenth-century doctrine of qualities, ascribes this position to Leibniz.[22] There is, then, something to be said on the positive side of the question before us.

2. Extent of Leibniz's adherence to the central doctrine of qualities

Locke's discussion of primary and secondary qualities receives the following response in *New Essays* (1704–6): "I think it could be said that when a power is intelligible and admits of being distinctly explained, it should be included among the primary qualities, but when it is merely sensible and yields only a confused idea it should be put among the secondary qualities."[23] Smith cites this as an "admirable" expression of the core

[21] To De Volder (1703), Leibniz (1970), 530; also *Specimen Dynamicum* (1695), Leibniz (1989), 118. The mode in which we cognize physical forces needs more discussion than it gets in this paper.

[22] Smith (1990). According to Smith, Descartes is more explicit: "[E]ven bodies are not properly known by the sense or by the faculty of imagination, but by the understanding only . . ." (Descartes [1979], 159; Smith [1990], 222).

[23] Leibniz (1990, 1981), 130.

mechanist rationale for the division of qualities. Although the distinction is shared by seventeenth-century mechanists generally, Smith claims that the rationalists among them articulate it best.

There are several themes in Smith's account of the historical doctrine.[24] One is that mechanists envisage a highly unified, systematic model for explaining the many different powers and operations exhibited by things in the corporeal world. It is meant to oppose the pattern adopted by common Scholastics as the moderns construe it. The traditionalists allegedly posited a different form to explain every different sort of observed natural occurrence, a form individuated by reference to the sort of events it is meant to explain, and intrinsically characterized by nothing but the power to produce events of this sort. In place of this vacuous and piecemeal approach, Descartes and the others propose to explain all observed qualities and operations of bodies on the basis of the relatively few attributes or powers that are possessed by all material things, as such.[25] Being extended, figured, in motion or at rest, and spatially positioned are obvious examples of properties universal in material things; at the very least, they are strong candidates to be basic in explanation. On Smith's account, it is for this reason that they are called "primary". By contrast, qualities that are not universal among bodies are to be explained as specific sets of determinations of universal qualities, that is, as such-such determinate figures, sizes, motions, and mutual arrangements of assembled particles.[26] Thus some mechanist philosophers offer the following simple empirical argument to prove the secondary status of colors, odors, and the like. We observe that some bodies are colorless, others are odorless, tasteless, soundless, and so on; these qualities are not shared by bodies, as such; so they are "secondary" in the sense of being explicable.[27] Leibniz's remark in *New Essays* may not seem to endorse the explanatory program, as Smith claims, but properly understood, the comment can be seen to endorse tenets of this program.

The remark is based on logical and methodological doctrines explained elsewhere in *New Essays*, but elaborated at more length in earlier writings.[28] By "logical" I mean concerned with the classification of concepts. To begin there: Leibniz constructs a three-level scheme of classification. A concept is "clear", as opposed to "obscure", provided, that it enables a person who has it to identify its instances reliably; we readily recognize them in experience or discourse. A clear concept is either "distinct", as opposed to "confused", just in case either (i) it is indefinable or (ii) a person who has it

[24] The sketch of Smith's account in the present paper does not do justice to the complex and subtle exposition to be found in the article.

[25] See also Ayers (1991), 135–41.

[26] This is similar to Locke's notion in that secondary qualities are defined as powers to produce certain effects by means of the primary qualities of insensible particles. It differs in that Locke defines secondary qualities as powers to produce sensations, and distinguishes them from a third sort of quality, defined as powers to produce changes in the qualities of bodies; see e.g. *Essay* 2.8.10, 23.

[27] Smith (1990), 235.

[28] Especially "Meditations on Knowledge, Truth, and Ideas" (1684), Leibniz (1998), 23–8; also "Discourse on Metaphysics" (1686), 24, Leibniz (1989), 56–7; *New Essays* (1704–6), Leibniz (1981, 1990), 254–5.

can state a definition of it (or its intentional object).[29] For this purpose, a definition is any necessary and sufficient condition of the object of the concept; it need not be a priori, and certainly need not be an analysis of the concept into its ultimately simple constituents. Our concepts of colors are standard examples of *confused* concepts, for although we easily identify colors, we cannot define them, but they are susceptible of definition for reasons we will mention shortly. Standard examples of *distinct* concepts include those of gold and fusibility: assayers have marks by which to identify gold; a fusible body is one that "ceases to be firm when heated". Finally, some distinct concepts, for example, our concepts of extension, figure, motion, angle, and the like, enable a person who has them to define them on the basis of concepts drawn exclusively from the intellect, as opposed to those based at least in part on experience. This logical typology has implications for the method of natural scientific inquiry. Concepts of the primary qualities are plainly of the third type, but more important: they are required by the laws of mathematics and mechanics.

In early essays on natural science, sensible qualities are ranked into three kinds in accord with their concepts: "attributes which are sensible can be divided into confused and distinct by intellectual principles. Confused attributes are those which are indeed composite in themselves or by intellectual principles but are simple to the senses and whose definition therefore cannot be explained."[30] Warmth is paradigmatic, for "the senses do not show us by what mechanism the state of a body is produced which brings about the sensation of warmth in us". In effect, this compresses the following mechanist line of thought: when we sense warmth, we are perceiving a complex mechanical bodily state, namely, warmth;[31] in view of its complexity, the state is susceptible to explanation; but the state is "simple" in sensory awareness, a simplicity reflected in our sense-based concept of warmth, so warmth can be defined, but not on the basis of our sense-based concept of warmth, which is "confused" in the logical sense. A second class of sensible qualities includes those with distinct concepts, such as fusibility.[32] The fact that they can be defined in terms of other sensible attributes has methodological significance, because they can be reduced to their *definiens*, thereby minimizing the phenomena to be explained.[33] Finally

The third class of attributes contains qualities definable in purely intellectual terms:

attributes common to several senses are to be regarded as distinct ... for they are resolvable ... into concepts attained by intellect. Such attributes are magnitude, position, duration, and

[29] Few if any of the concepts of which we are aware are ultimately simple, e.g. Leibniz (1998), 24.

[30] "On the Elements of Natural Science" (1678–9?), Leibniz (1970), 285.

[31] A deeper expression of Leibnizian mechanism comes later in the essay: "But the way in which a body operates cannot be explained distinctly unless we explain what its parts contribute. This cannot be understood, however, unless we understand their relation to each other and to the whole in a mechanical sense, that is, their figure and position, the change of this position or motion, their magnitude, their pores, and other things of this mechanical kind, for these always vary the operation." "On the Elements, etc." (1678–9?), Leibniz (1970), 288.

[32] Other examples are firmness, friability, solvent, coagulant, precipitant; e.g. Leibniz (1966b), 38–9. These attributes correspond to Locke's third sort of qualities, *Essay* 2.8.24; Locke (1975), 141.

[33] Leibniz (1970), 287.

motion. We need not wonder at this, for since they are common to several senses, they do not depend upon the particular constitution of a sense organ ... or upon its insensible movements, the subtlety and number of which lead to our confused perception.

("On the Elements, etc." [1678–9?], Leibniz [1970], 286)

Such attributes are most desirable for purposes of natural science. In virtue of their definitions, they can be subsumed under mathematical and mechanical laws, in accord with the basic mechanist scheme:

But the distinct attributes are to be preferred, namely duration, magnitude, motion, figure, and other circumstances, for we can reason only to the extent that we consider distinct attributes. The application of mathematics to physical science consists in such considerations of the distinct attributes which accompany confused ones.... Since everything confused is by its nature resolvable into the distinct, even though it may not always be in our power to do this, it follows that all qualities and mutations of bodies can, according to their nature, at length be reduced to certain distinct qualities. ("On the Elements, etc." [1678–9?], Leibniz [1970], 287–8)[34]

The "confused" qualities, those simple to sense, pose an especially difficult problem because of the opacity of our concepts of them.

Texts just cited imply that confused qualities of bodies are their complex microstructures; they can, in principle, be reduced to distinct attributes. Other texts develop several lines of argument in support of this contingent claim about the physical world.[35] All of this supports the mechanist mode of explanation: "Unless principles are advanced from geometry and mechanics, which can be applied with equal ease to sensible and insensible things alike, nature in its subtlety will escape us."[36] To Leibniz's mind, a main problem of method is finding ways to construct definitions, or at least find necessary and sufficient conditions, for confused qualities which will bring them under mechanical principles. Empirical methods must be used in an effort to discover attributes that always accompany a given confused quality, preferably attributes that have intellectual definitions. Different texts suggest somewhat different strategies for achieving this result.[37] An instructive early note reasons as follows:

these simple qualities cannot be the subject of discursive knowledge except in so far as they are customarily joined together with ... composite qualities or, better, the common qualities magnitude, local position, and motion. Thus simple qualities are to be brought along by history, that is one ought to enumerate how such qualities, themselves, are accustomed to be conjoined and

[34] Near the end of the same treatise: "For even though the confused attributes of bodies can be referred back to distinct ones, we must recognize that there are two kinds of distinct attributes, only one of which must be sought in mathematics, the other in metaphysics. Mathematical science provides magnitude, figure, situation, and their variations, but metaphysics provides existence, duration, action and passion, force of acting, and end of action, or the perception of the agent." "On the Elements, etc." (1678-9?), Leibniz (1970), 289.

[35] For a review of the main ones, see Wilson (1998a), 326.

[36] Leibniz (1970), 282–3, translation slightly altered.

[37] See Bolton (2001).

how joined with qualities that are studied under geometry and mechanics; thus theorems can be brought to light about the causes and effects of purely sensible qualities.

(*Consilium de Encyclopaedia nova*, etc. [1679], Leibniz [1999], 679; Leibniz [1966b], 38–9)

Read in context of these doctrines, the *New Essays* remark admired by Smith expresses the mechanist idea that basic explanatory laws of nature mention primary qualities (Leibniz's distinct intelligible attributes), but not secondary qualities (confused attributes simple to sense).

A second main theme in Smith's exposition of the seventeenth-century doctrine ascribes a distinctive nature to secondary qualities. The author contends that early mechanists discovered a reason, in addition to that mentioned above, for assigning secondary status to colors, and the rest. The aforementioned argument is premised on the empirical fact that some bodies have no color, or odor, etc. and thus stand to be explained by attributes common to all bodies, as such. In addition, Smith maintains, there is an a priori reason for the secondary status of colors, and the rest.

It is significant, in his view, that the list of secondary qualities is co-extensive with the list of Aristotelian proper sensibles, objects proper, or proprietary, to a single faculty of sense. Further, he claims, it is necessary that a secondary quality should be perceived exclusively by the sense modality by which it is perceived: necessarily, colors are perceived, *as* colors, only by sight; sounds, only by hearing; heat and cold, only by touch, and so on. This is not to deny that we ascribe extension, figures, and motions to things on the basis of experience. The difference is that the relevant sensory appearances are not limited to a single sensory mode. Figure, motion, size are perceived by both sight and touch; this, too, is necessary, according to Smith. It reflects the spatial character of extension and its modifications, and experience is essentially structured by spatial and temporal relations, he contends. Accordingly, it is no accident that we have intellectual, or non-sense based, concepts of extension, figure, magnitude, and motion, for without them we could not integrate our experiences of sight, touch, and the other modes of sense. Here again, Leibniz is in tune inasmuch as he assigns perception of figure, motion, etc. to the "common sense", which deploys nothing but concepts drawn from intellect, alone, as he has it.[38]

Although secondary qualities are sense mode specific, Smith urges, the physical qualities to which we respond, say, by sight could, for all we know, be detected tactually by other subjects. Such subjects would feel the physical attributes that are seen as colors, by us. "*What* appears to such a subject would be the same as what appears to us: but *how* it appears would be quite different."[39] Smith infers from this that the intrinsic difference between visual and tactual modes of presentation is the sole basis on which visual experiences are differentiated from tactual ones; similarly, for the distinctions among experiences proper to each of the sense modalities. In particular, the

[38] Leibniz (1981, 1990), 128, quoted in Smith (1990).

[39] Smith (1990), 240.

classification of experiences as visual, auditory, tactual, and so on is not based on physical organs of sight, hearing, touch. Nor do the physical qualities we perceive, say, by sight or touch determine what is distinctive of visual and tactual modes of presentation; instead their phenomenal character is determined by "the intrinsic nature of sense experiences". Or, as Smith puts it:

> Secondary qualities are those physical features of objects that appear to a sentient subject by the realization in its experience of sensory qualia. So how a secondary quality appears, and what intuitively it is taken to be, are determined by the intrinsic features of experiential states. Such qualia cannot themselves be qualities of insentient physical objects since *the realization of sensory qualia constitutes the occurrence of sensory experience.* (Smith [1990], 240)

These features of experience are "not in physical reality at all."[40]

Finally, because experiences of secondary qualities are intentionally directed to qualities that are physically real, although the experiences comprise physically unrealizable qualia, such experiences *misrepresent* the qualities to which they respond. This trait is passed on to our concepts of colors, etc.; because our concepts of these qualities are grounded on our experiences of them, the concepts, too, misrepresent their intentional objects. So, as Smith urges, when we critically reflect on the question whether our sense-based conception of the world represents things as they are, some naïve concepts are found wanting: "those concepts that we discard as failing faithfully to represent the world as it really is are regarded as being responses to secondary qualities." Again, "Only where we have a concept that is in some way seen as misrepresenting the quality to which it corresponds can we make sense of denominating that quality secondary."[41] Let me roughly summarize this account of secondary qualities, for our purposes, by the following interconnected claims. (1) Necessarily colors, as colors, are perceived by sight; *mutatis mutandis* for the other secondary qualities. (2) The phenomenal characters of colors, etc. are determined by nothing but the inner nature of visual experience, and so on; in particular, they are not determined, even in part, by the physical properties to which experiences of color, etc. respond. (3) The phenomenal character of visual, auditory, etc. experience is constituted by qualia. (4) Our concepts of colors, sounds, etc. misrepresent the physical qualities to which they respond.

In support of his claim that (1) through (4) capture the pervasive seventeenth-century notion of a secondary quality, Smith notes that the latter was intended to correct a common mistake. Something like this is true of Descartes and Locke,[42] and here Leibniz is quoted again:

[40] Smith (1990), 238.

[41] Ibid. 230.

[42] According to Descartes, sensory ideas of cold are suspected of being 'false', or 'representing nothing as if it were something,' and they do in fact prompt false beliefs about the nature of cold; but they do not *mis*represent their intentional object, cold, or so I would urge. (Bolton (1986)). Locke maintains that all simple ideas of sensation are true with reference to the real existence of things (Locke (1975), 388–9); still he supposes we wrongly think our ideas of secondary qualities resemble their bodily causes (Locke [1975], 134, 388–9).

Descartes, following the ancients, rendered a useful service in eradicating the prejudice that makes heat, colors, and other phenomena seem to be things outside us . . . [I]t seems that no such thing exists outside us, the phantasm of which appears in our imagination.

("Critical Thoughts on . . . the Principles of Descartes" [1692], Leibniz [1970], 390–1; as quoted in Smith [1990], 236)

In fact, Leibniz is not very much of a mind with Descartes. As we saw, extension, figure, and motion are hardly less dependent on imagination than heat and colors are, according to the later philosopher. More below on Leibniz's reasoning in this comment.

Still, there is considerable evidence that, with some qualifications, Leibniz agrees with the doctrine of qualities Smith ascribes to mechanists. Neither main theme of Smith's account is an entirely accurate expression of Leibniz's position, and claims (1) through (4), above, turn out to be inconsistent with his theory of perception. Still the picture is a good platform from which to bring out what is peculiarly his own in Leibniz's thinking about the qualities called "primary" and "secondary". Two strains in his thinking are especially relevant: his understanding of the gulf between theory and reality, and his reason for ascribing a special degree of confusion to sense perception of colors, warmth, and so on. Leibniz thought more carefully about the gulf between mathematical and mechanical principles and the diversity and complexity of physical reality than his contemporaries seem to have done. To Leibniz, this presented itself as both a metaphysical and methodological problem akin to the opposition between the manifest and scientific images of the world, as we say nowadays. It may be helpful at this point to review the organization of topics in the remainder of this paper. In the next section, Leibniz's approach to the methodological problem is sketched. Section 4 addresses his theory of perception and the peculiar confusion of sense perceptions of colors, and the like. In the final section, Leibniz's theory of intellectual, as opposed to perceptual, cognition is brought into play in some final remarks about what is distinctive of qualities of each sort in his view.

3. The gap between physical reality and explanatory theory

Secondary qualities, unlike primary ones, cannot be defined; they "can be imparted not by description but only by pointing them out to the senses".[43] To show how deeply they resist intelligible description, Leibniz asks us to imagine a land where men have cold blood and there is no heat:

surely they cannot be made to understand what heat is merely by describing it, for even if someone were to explain to them the innermost secrets of nature and even interpret perfectly the cause of heat, they would still not recognize heat from this description if it were presented to

[43] "On the Elements, etc." (1678–9?), Leibniz (1970), 285.

them, for they could not know that this peculiar sensation which they perceived in their minds is produced by this particular motion, since we cannot notice distinctly what arises in our mind and what in our organs. . . . Similarly a man born blind could learn the whole of optics yet not acquire the idea of light. ("On the Elements, etc." [1678–9?], Leibniz [1970], 285)

Despite having complete theoretical knowledge of heat, a person would be unable to recognize heat upon first sensing warmth.[44] Now Smith's account explains this passage in a way familiar nowadays, namely, the claim that tactual experiences of warmth comprise qualia essentially outside the scope of physical theory. The passage may not preclude Smith's explanation, but it suggests one that is physical as well as psychological. The complexity of relevant physical circumstances is one factor; limitation on human powers of discrimination is another. In particular, warmth is, in effect, identified with a bodily state consisting of many moving particles, which cause motions in the tactual organs of those who sense them. We do not recognize these micro-events in sensations of warmth, because the physical process offers no basis on which we can distinguish motions in bodies we touch from their effects in our own sensory organs. Even so, to some readers it may seem obvious that the sensation is opaque in this respect because it is essentially non-physical.

Acknowledging the difficulty of interpreting such texts, Margaret Wilson concludes their author is torn between two opposing notions of the nature of sensible qualities. The texts strongly suggest that heat, cold, etc. are mechanistic micro-structures and, thus, that even the inhabitants of a frigid land could understand the physical theory of heat. At the same time, the thought-experiment shows the residents lack the concept of heat, since they cannot recognize heat when they sense it. But a person who acquires theoretical knowledge of what heat is thereby acquires the concept of heat, she plausibly claims. So Leibniz seems torn between mutually inconsistent intuitions with regard to the nature of warmth, and the like.[45] In supposing that physics may aspire to explain such qualities, and thus provide distinct concepts of heat, cold, and so on, he thinks of them as "properties in physical objects that happen to be detected by our senses". In supposing that even a scientist who understands what heat is cannot acquire the concept of heat without experiencing it, he tends to assume the nature of heat "is completely bound up with the nature of sensory experience". This ambivalence "seems to be an unrationalized, pervasive feature of Leibniz's thinking."[46]

[44] It is true that heat-deprived subjects who first sense heat would be able to recognize it indirectly, if they knew that some other sensible quality is constantly conjoined with heat and detected that other quality. I take this to be beside the point of the thought experiment, which is to show how very difficult it is to bring the physical quality in range of mechanist reasoning.

[45] Wilson charges Leibniz with a related inconsistency. In some contexts, Leibniz carefully separates percepts and concepts and the different senses of "distinctness" and "confusion" that apply to them. In the text in view, however, the feeling of warmth is said to be confused, but the theoretical concept of heat would, of course, be distinct. By saying that warmth is confused, thereby implying that the concept of warmth is confused, Leibniz conflates the percept of heat and the concept of heat, which is an error on his own showing, Wilson argues.

[46] Wilson (1999a), 329–30.

There is a great deal of plausibility to this crisp analysis. But it is correct only if Leibniz does, indeed, believe that the natures of heat, colors, and the like can be fully explicated by a theory which humans might master. Certainly he encourages empirical investigation of these qualities with the aim of bringing them into reach of mechanist reasoning. But the essays on the method of natural science are pragmatic in orientation;[47] they mainly advocate strategies that can improve our knowledge of nature but do not yet attain the intellectual ideal.[48] As we said, the method for investigating confused qualities is empirical discovery of those qualities that regularly concur with them in the same subject. In this way, observations might support generalizations, for instance that yellow is generally attended by refracted, as opposed to reflected, light rays. The latter attribute is intellectually distinct, but assuming the constant conjunction does not put us in a position to demonstrate—to make clear—the nature of yellowness. Leibniz's interests are practical: "it is enough for us to show what exists objectively in bodies from which yellowness arises, and that is sufficient for the needs of life. Thus we shall have a means of producing confused qualities."[49] As another example of the pragmatic approach, consider this general strategy Leibniz promotes if we have competing hypotheses, each of which satisfies a few phenomena; in such cases, those hypotheses "are to be chosen which are the simpler; these are to be presented, in the interim, in place of true causes."[50]

The point I want to bring out is that Leibniz seeks explanations that are provisional or non-demonstrative, or in other ways not optimally perspicuous. While they fall short of ideal theoretical knowledge, their practical value is immense. It is, then, important to look carefully at the sort of mechanist account of confused attributes deemed insufficient for possession of their concepts. Unless it is a complete and thoroughly distinct definition of warmth, for instance, a person's "understanding" of warmth would not allow her to acquire the concept of heat without experiencing it. Close attention suggests relevant texts make either vague or qualified claims about the sort of understanding of confused attributes humans might have. According to the essay that records the thought experiment, "warmth . . . will only then be adequately understood when we explain of what it consists or distinctly describe its proximate cause—perhaps the expansion of air."[51] It remains to say what standard of adequacy is in view, and what counts as an explanation: certainly knowing the cause of heat is different from knowing its nature or having its concept. With regard to color, we are said to have an "empirical resolution" of green if we are correct in thinking it is the nature of green to

[47] On Leibniz's pragmatism in science, see Beeley (2001), 86–92.

[48] "Every science is to be sought after, not for the sake of curiosity or ostentation, but for the sake of action. . . . the knowledge of bodies is therefore most important on two grounds—first, it perfects our mind through an understanding of the purposes and causes of things; second, to conserve and nurture our bodies." ("On the Elements, etc." [1678–9?], Leibniz [1970], L 280).

[49] *Revoactio qualitatium confusarum ad distinctum* (1677?), Leibniz (1999), 1962; Parkinson (1982), 20.

[50] Although the hypothesis may be false, it is "sufficient for everyday use" ("On the Elements, etc." [1678–9?], Leibniz [1970], 283).

[51] "On the Elements, etc." (1678–9?), Leibniz (1970), 285.

be a mixture of blue and yellow. But as the passage goes on to say, "What is resolved in this way does not cease being confused. We do not grasp how the third color is given us through the confused appearance of these two colors."[52] To be sure, "a man born blind could learn the whole of optics yet not acquire the idea of light." Does this imply that the blind man has an intellectual understanding of the nature of light, or a distinct concept of light? Optical theory makes some assumptions about the nature of light; what it purports to explain is the process of vision.[53, 54] Admittedly, this would be tiresome nit-picking were it not for the practical aims of the methodological texts, which recommend notions of understanding, explanation, and resolution inferior to the intellectually distinct ideal. With this in view, it can be doubted that when Leibniz speaks of a person privy to the "innermost secrets of nature", he means someone with complete ideal knowledge of nature. Short of that, he may consistently deny that the initiate is assured of possessing the concept of heat, or the like. There is further reason to think the reductive explanations assumed in Wilson's criticism are not abroad in the texts.

For Leibniz, the sheer multitude of physical circumstances recorded by a sensation of heat, for instance, is a factor relevant to our means of acquiring the concept of heat. One early essay describes an indirect method for discovering what is "real and distinct" in confused qualities, such as yellowness—that is, discovering the distinctly known qualities that generally concur in the same subject with yellowness. The text continues:

> For that remainder which we do not know how to explain (e.g. in what way that very appearance which we call yellowness arises from that in which we discovered yellowness to consist) must be known to depend, not on the thing itself, but on the disposition of our organs and on the most minute structure [*constitutionibus*] of things."
>
> (*Revoactio qualitatum confusarum ad distinctum* [1677?], Leibniz [1999], 1962; Parkinson [1982], 20, n. 26)

Unknown physical arrangements are invoked to account for the unexplained residue; the minutest details are relevant. The suggestion is that the "real and distinct" attributes known to be present in yellow bodies, in general, specify a physical structure insufficiently complex and too local to the body to which color is ascribed to explain the appearance of yellowness.

[52] "On the Elements, etc." (1678–9?), Leibniz (1970), 287.

[53] "Once we have learned that the angles of incidence and reflection of a ray of light are equal and that these angles are taken with respect to the perpendicular striking a plane tangent to the surface at the point of incidence, then we can easily establish the science of catoptrics. Similarly few experiments about refraction are needed to set up the foundations of dioptrics." ("On the Elements, etc." [1678–9?], Leibniz [1970], 287).

[54] Wilson cites the passage, considered above, to the effect that the *cause* of heat might *perhaps* be the expansion of air (Leibniz (1970), 285, emphasis added) in support of the claim that Leibniz envisages mechanist reductions of confused sensible qualities. Other passages mention theories without endorsing them: "if red is the rotation of certain small globes as some propose light to be; if heat is a whirlwind of a very fine powder; if sound is in the air as circles in the water where a stone has been tossed, as some philosophers claim, this is something we do not see, and we do not understand how this rotation, these whirls, and these circles, if they should be true, make just those perceptions we have of red, heat, and sound," (Leibniz [1879–90], VI.490). Also see "On What is Independent of Sense and Matter" (1702) Leibniz (1970), 546.

Leibniz's sense of the daunting complexity of nature has not, so far, been fully exhibited. It is a principle of his version of mechanism that the qualities of every composite body are to be explained on the basis of the qualities of its parts: "But the way in which a body operates cannot be explained distinctly unless we explain what its parts contribute."; another passage refers to "... the parts of a thing, or all the entities by means of which the thing can be understood."[55] Some mechanists are atomists, but as mentioned above, Leibniz holds that every body is endlessly composed of smaller bodies. Moreover, according to a distinctively Leibnizian metaphysical principle, no two individuals in nature are exactly alike, but rather each differs, in some intrinsic, or qualitative, respect, from every other.[56] Accordingly, a given body's qualities are affected by each of the endlessly many and endlessly diverse bodies of which it is composed.[57] Adams makes the crucial point:

> Even when we perceive a body of limited extension, such as the body of a human being, Leibniz believes that the reality represented by our perception is infinitely complex, and that all of that infinite complexity is relevant to the explanation of some of the salient features of the body's behavior.[58]

No human intellect is capable of understanding such explanations in full detail. We reason and explain only by ignoring the heterogeneous details:

> abstraction is not an error as long as one knows that what one is pretending not to notice, is *there*. This is what mathematicians are doing when they ask us to consider perfect lines and uniform motions and other regular effects, although matter (i.e. the jumble of effects of the surrounding infinity) always provides some exception. (*New Essays* [1704–6], Leibniz [1990, 1981], 57)

The plain consequence is that an explanatory theory must omit some details of nature, which are nonetheless explanatorily relevant, because it is the nature of such theories to rank individuals under kinds which abstract from individual differences. A theory has explanatory force, at all, only because it assimilates open-ended classes of heterogeneous particulars to a small number of homogenous kinds, which are the subjects of general principles; "Abstractions are needed for the scientific explanation of things."[59] In principle, the gulf between ever-diverse physical reality and principle-based mechanist explanations cannot be entirely closed.

Leibniz's pragmatism about explanation is one manifestation of the gap. As he often contends, it follows from the principle that nature is nowhere homogenous that there is

[55] "On the Elements, etc." (1678–9?), Leibniz (1970), 288, 277.

[56] E.g. "in consequence of imperceptible variations no two individual things could be perfectly alike . . . they must always differ more than numerically." *New Essays* (1704–6), Leibniz (1990, 1981), 57; also "Discourse in Metaphysics" (1684), 9, Leibniz (1989), 41–2; "On Nature Itself" (1695), Leibniz (1989), 164.

[57] The circumstances affecting the qualities of a body are even more complex than this suggests: "everything is a plenum [*sc.* full], which makes all matter interconnected. In a plenum, every motion has some effect on distant bodies, in proportion to their distance. . . . As a result, every body is affected by everything that happens in the universe . . ." ("Monadology" [1714], 61, Leibniz [1989], 221).

[58] Adams (1994), 228.

[59] To De Volder (1703), Leibniz (1970), 531.

no line perfectly straight over the least interval, no regularity in curves, no perfectly equal quantities; but because nature is created in accord with mathematical principles, the deviation can often be overlooked: for example, the inequality among angles at which individual light rays are refracted is negligible.[60] No theory can be both intelligible and responsive to the infinite division of bodies although it may get close enough for the purpose at hand: "But just as architects need to press the analysis of materials only up to a certain point, physicists also can arrive at a certain analysis of sensible things, which serves in practice."[61] No matter how fine-grained the parts to which reference is made in explanatory principles, nature contains smaller parts that affect the phenomena to be explained; theory cannot reach all the explanatorily relevant details. This points to the conclusion that an unexplained, and yet explicable, residue escapes the reach of any theoretical natural science. For this reason, if no other, secondary qualities elude theoretical reduction to determinate mechanical affections. The inexplicable aspects of our sensory experience of secondary qualities is accountable to the unintelligible complexity of the physical circumstances that affect it. This suffices to explain Leibniz's remarks to the effect that we must appeal to experience to acquire concepts of warmth, colors, and the like, no matter how much scientific theory we may know.

The first theme of Smith's characterization of mechanism, which concerns its distinctive program of explanation, describes Leibniz's mechanism only up to a point. For practical purposes, colors, warmth, and so on can be given a sort of explanation on the basis of mechanist principles. For all that, there can be no complete theoretical reduction of secondary qualities to determinate primary qualities of insensible particles.[62] Nor does the second theme seem to be entirely true of Leibniz's views. He plainly identifies secondary qualities with different sorts of physical structures, which strongly suggests he would not accept the gist of claims (1) through (4). That states that the distinctive characters of colors, and the rest are determined by essentially mental qualia, whereas Leibniz does not need to invoke essentially non-physical constituents of experience to account for the *je ne sais quoi* of yellowness, and so on. Still Smith finds evidence that Leibniz endorses (1) through (4) in his comment on Descartes quoted above. On closer look, this is less than decisive.

Although Leibniz commends his predecessor, he reaches the Cartesian conclusion by a route not taken in *Principles*. This is the comment in its entirety:

Descartes, following the ancients, rendered a useful service in eradicating the prejudice that makes heat, colors, and other phenomena seem to be things outside us, since it is evident that the same hand in which water seemed very hot soon finds it tepid; and a man who observes a green color in a powdered mixture no longer sees it as green when his eye is aided by an instrument,

[60] Beeley (2001), 89.

[61] Quoted by Beeley (2001), 87; also 88, note 5.

[62] It may be that Smith does not mean to imply that complete reduction is part of the mechanist program; but he clearly does mean that mechanists have an entirely different sort of reason for thinking that secondary qualities cannot be explained by physical theory.

but as a mixture of yellow and blue and can grasp the causes of these two colors with the use of better instruments and other observations or reasons. From these considerations it seems that there is, placed outside us, no thing of such a kind as the phantasm found in our imagination.
("Critical Thoughts on . . . the Principles of Descartes" [1692]; Leibniz [1970), 390–1)

In fact, the argument is hard to pin down. It might seem to propound a "perceiver-relativity" argument for the conclusion that heat, colors, etc. exist only in the mind.[63] In any case, the text shows no trace of the reasoning contained in *Principles*, I.65–8. The argument there depends on a premise to the effect that perceptions of color, etc. contain "sensations".[64] A man "may suppose" that the nature of what he sees or feels "is something similar to the sensation of colour or pain which he experiences in himself"; but by attending to what is "represented by the sensation—what is represented as existing in the coloured body or the painful part—he will realize that he is wholly ignorant of it."[65] Descartes is committed to mind–body dualism. For him, sensations are mental modifications which cannot possibly modify material substance. Accordingly sensations intrinsically convey no information about the natures of the corporeal modifications to which they typically correspond. Leibniz's appreciative remark on this material says nothing of the metaphysical and semantic assumptions on which Descartes' conclusion rests. Claims (1) through (4) may fit Descartes, but once again, we have reason to doubt the ascription to Leibniz. We will see in the next section that Leibniz effectively repudiates them.

4. The veracity and confusion endemic to perceptions of secondary qualities

The feature that, for Leibniz, separates qualities "simple to the senses" from other sensible qualities is their *confusion*—both perceptual and conceptual.[66] Perceptual confusion is the more fundamental, it seems to me. The difference between confused and distinct concepts is already familiar to us. The following passage may serve to introduce the notion of confused perception:

. . . each substance expresses the whole universe according to its position and point of view, in so far as the others are related to it. Hence it is necessary that certain of our perceptions, although clear, are confused, since they involve an infinite number of things—e.g. colour, heat, and the like.
("A Specimen of Discoveries" [1688?], Leibniz [1973], 77)[67]

It is well known that, according to Leibniz, each substance perceives every thing and event in the corporeal universe from its unique point of view. Evidently it is not as

[63] But Leibniz notes the fallacy in *New Essays* (1704–6), Leibniz (1990, 1981), 132.
[64] See *Principles* I.66, 68, Descartes (1984), I.216–7.
[65] *Principles*, I.68; Descartes (1984), I.216. Also see the texts on "materially false ideas", *Meditation* III and "Fourth Replies", Descartes (1984), II.30, 164.
[66] See Wilson (1999a), Parkinson (1982).
[67] On expression, see Leibniz (1967), 144.

widely recognized that "our perceptions are always true, it is our judgments, which come from ourselves, that deceive us."[68] The confusion of perceptions distances the scope and fidelity of creaturely cognition from divine omniscience.[69] This is a matter of degree: the more confused perceptions are, the less distinct; confusedness is a measure of inferiority qua cognition of the world. In effect, it is Leibniz's device for a seemingly impossible task, enabling creatures with limited cognitive capacities to have complete and utterly faithful cognition of the entire universe. As we will see, far from thinking that our experiences of secondary qualities misrepresent the physical arrangements to which they respond, as in claim (4), Leibniz invokes the peculiar confusion of such experiences to account for their veracity.

In general, a substance accomplishes the task because it models the universe.[70] It is an empirical fact that the corporeal universe consists of a spatially and temporally ordered array of parts and wholes. An immaterial substance has no parts, but it has many modifications, many simultaneous modifications as well as successive ones. The substance models the universe by virtue of having modifications with a structure *analogous*, in a rule-governed way, to the part-whole structure of the universe.[71] A perception is, then, a complex modification of a substance formally analogous to the composite structure of the corporal things that are the intentional objects of the perception. There are no referential devices similar to pointing, the use of proper names, or reliance on causal connections to designate things perceived; nor does perception involve concepts. A substance perceives all that it models, in accord with the pertinent principle, and nothing more. The operative analogy is based on a suitable fixed rule, which perceivers naturally follow but seldom, if ever, apprehend as a general principle.[72] It would seem to follow from this that perception cannot fail to represent its intentional object just as it is; otherwise, it would not represent at all, for the analogy would fail.[73]

[68] "Discourse on Metaphysics" (1686), 14 (Leibniz (1989), 47. Judgments come under the faculty of intellect, rather than perception.

[69] A substance "expresses confusedly, everything that happens in the universe, whether past, present, or future—this has some resemblance to an infinite perception and knowledge." "Discourse on Metaphysics" (1686), 9, Leibniz (1989), 42.

[70] In context of a phenomenalist theory, a substance "models" the world in a sense that does not imply that the world is ontologically distinct from the model, or corresponds to it. It has a non-relational intentional object. Nevertheless, the model's intentional content is true in virtue of the intra-substantial coherence and inter-substantial agreement mentioned above; further, perceptual phenomena are "founded" on immaterial substances. We might say a substance models the corporeal world in the sense in which an architect's mock-up models a building even if no such building is ever in fact constructed, or, a painting depicts an imaginary scene.

[71] "... that which is composition of parts outside is represented only by the composition of modifications in the monad." To Masson (1716), Leibniz (1989), 229. On the analogy of structure between perceptions and their intentional objects, see Swoyer (1995).

[72] "The representation has a natural relation to that which is to be represented." *Theodicy* (1710), Leibniz (1951), 356; also Leibniz (1875–90), V.372.

[73] This and the following claim assume that a perceptual modification "expresses" its intentional object in virtue of a mapping of the modification *onto* the portion of the world it represents that preserves an analogue of structure; see Swoyer (1995); Kulstad (1977) argues that some instances of expression are mappings *into* a range. Although this may well be correct, it is not the case with perceptual expression, or so I would urge.

For a similar reason, I would urge, a substance cannot perceive any part of the universe unless it perceives the entire universe, nor can it perceive any whole without perceiving its parts. For it cannot faithfully model a part (or whole) without modeling the whole that contains it (or the parts it contains). The doctrine of perceptual truth and universal scope are thus deeply grounded in Leibniz's theory of perception.

But although all perceptions are alike in modeling their intentional objects, the perceptions of any given substance differ with respect to their comparative confusion (distinctness). More confused perceptions, it would seem, tend to blend many objects together, whereas distinct perceptions tend to highlight several different objects, so, perhaps, a tree viewed at a distance is typically seen more distinctly than its individual leaves.[74] The difference is often illustrated on the basis of what we can, and cannot, notice in things we consciously perceive:

> When we hear the sound of water flowing at a distance, we hear many crashing swells, for there is no reason why we should hear one rather than another; and if we hear none, certainly we hear nothing. Thus this perception is confused. (*De distincta perceptione* [1678] Leibniz [1999], 58)

Because the parts of any given body are endlessly composed of other parts and each is affected by all contiguous bodies, "... each distinct [perception] contains an infinity [of confused] perceptions because of its relation to everything external."[75] In Leibniz's view it is contingent, but true, that individually different bodies have different spatial-temporal positions;[76] given this, we can see that a more distinct perception of a body is a more distinct perception of its position in the spatial-temporal ordering.[77] As a rule, we perceive the spatial, or primary, qualities of whole bodies more distinctly than we perceive their parts (and their primary qualities). A distinct perception, inasmuch as it is distinct, skims a mechanist arrangement from its mechanist underpinnings. Because each relatively distinct perception is composed of relatively confused ones, the burden of perceiving, or expressing, the entire universe falls on the side of confusedness.[78] Since the series of perceptions contained in a given perception is endless, and each perception expresses a (whole) bodily part, the task of expressing the entire infinitely complex universe gets done. The confusion endemic to our perceptions of colors, etc.

[74] My example; see e.g. Leibniz (1989), 208, 216; Leibniz (1973), 25. The relevant notion of degrees of distinctness (confusion) requires much more discussion; in fact, commentators have had difficulty understanding how Leibniz intends to explicate it; Wilson (1999c); Bennett (2001), 307–11.

[75] "A Specimen, etc." (1688?), Leibniz (1973), 77; quoted above.

[76] E.g. *New Essays* (1704–6), Leibniz (1990, 1981), 124, 126.

[77] "Distinct cognition gives order to a thing... For order is simply a distinctive relation of several things; confusion is when several things are present, but there is no way of distinguishing one from another" ("A Résumé of Metaphysics", Leibniz [1973], 146 [translation altered]).

[78] "Each soul knows the infinite—knows all—but confusedly.... confused perceptions are the result of impressions that the whole universe makes upon us..." ("Principles of Nature and Grace" [1714], 12, Leibniz [1989], 211).

is a consequence of Leibniz's mechanist thesis that sensible qualities are mechanical configurations of endlessly divided and diversified material parts.[79]

The point I want to stress is that the peculiar confusion of our perceptions of secondary qualities has an essential role in this overall theory of perception. It preserves the utter truthfulness of a substance's perceptions while it limits the accessibility of most of this information; in effect, it dampens its effects on the substance's functioning, or its actions.[80] As Leibniz describes confused perception:

> The representation often suppresses something in the objects when it is imperfect; but it can add nothing: that would render it, not more than perfect, but false. Moreover, the suppression is never complete in our perceptions, and there is in the representation, confused as it is, more than we see there. Thus there is reason for supposing that the ideas [*sc.* sensory impressions] of heat, cold, colours, etc., also only represent the small movements carried out in the organs, when one is conscious of these qualities, although the multiplicity and the diminutive character of these movements prevents their distinct representation. (*Theodicy* [1710], Leibniz [1951], 339)

Conscious perceptions of color, for instance, suppress intentional content but are truthful nonetheless, because there is more "than we see there", more than we can attend to. Falsity is avoided because our conscious perceptions are perceptions of a multiplicity of motions—when feeling the sensation of warmth we are, in fact, perceiving many moving particles. But to perceive them is not, so far, to be capable of discriminating them; we can't notice them individually because of their number, size, and mutual similarity.[81]

New Essays elaborates with the example of a spinning cogwheel which one may see in a clock maker's shop: "The wheel's rotation makes the teeth disappear and an imaginary continual transparency appears in their place; it is made up of successive appearances of teeth and of gaps between them, but . . . our imagination cannot distinguish them."[82] We understand that it expresses what happens in the wheel by "blurring successive things together into an apparent simultaneity". As Margaret Wilson suggests, the argument is that "there is no good reason to deny that the individual cogs contribute any less to our perceptions when they are moving fast than when they are moving slowly."[83]

[79] "These minute perceptions, then, are more effective in their results than has been recognized. They constitute that *je ne sais quoi*, those flavours, those images of sensible qualities, vivid in the aggregate but confused as to the parts; those impressions which are made on us by the bodies around us and which involve the infinite; that connection that each being has with all the rest of the universe." *New Essays* (1704–6), Leibniz (1990, 1981), 54–5.

[80] I argue for this in an unpublished paper, "The Psychological Foundations of Distinct and Confused Perceptions".

[81] ". . . at every moment there is in us an infinity of perceptions, unaccompanied by awareness or reflection; that is, of alterations in the soul itself, of which we are unaware because these impressions are either too minute and too numerous, or else too unvarying, so that they are not sufficiently distinctive on their own." *New Essays* (1704–6), Leibniz (1990, 1981), 53.

[82] Leibniz (1990, 1981), 403.

[83] Wilson (1999a), 326; also 338.

Another argument, endlessly repeated, is found in a passage quoted above: the principle that we could not perceive qualities if we did not at the same time perceive their parts. The principle holds for primary qualities, too, but the usual examples are secondary qualities.[84] To hear the roar of the sea, we must "hear the parts which make up this whole, that is the noise of each wave"; for if we did not perceive each wave, we would perceive nothing "since a hundred thousand nothings cannot make something."[85] The homogeneity of the sound is merely apparent, and we are, in fact, perceiving a multitude of noises.[86]

On the basis of this very doctrine, Leibniz opposes Locke's account of the difference between sensory ideas of primary and secondary qualities. According to the *Essay*, sensations of warmth are no more like a quality of fire than a pain is like the motion of the pin that causes it: neither intrinsically carries information about its intentional object. The claim is extended to sense impressions of all the secondary qualities. There is no resemblance between the sensation produced by a secondary quality and that physical quality.[87] Leibniz contends otherwise: "I would say, rather, that there is a resemblance of a kind—not a perfect one which holds all the way through, but a resemblance in which one thing expresses another through some orderly relationship between them."[88] Leibniz does not mean that there is a systematic correlation between sorts of sensations and sorts of physical qualities, with which Locke agrees. Leibniz claims there is a structural analogy between each perceptual sensation and the physical quality thereby perceived; the sensation carries information about the quality, as we might say. Behind this semantic disagreement is a more fundamental epistemic one. Locke holds, and Leibniz denies, that sensory presentations are just what they appear to us to be. For this reason, according to Locke, reflective attention guarantees the truth of judgments with regard to the intrinsic properties of one's occurent sense impressions;[89] sensations of color, and the like appear simple so they are simple. But as Leibniz sees it, "these sensible ideas appear simple because they are confused".[90] Confused ideas, as such, are not at all as they appear to be; they only appear to be homogeneous, whereas they actually have structures analogous to those of the physical attributes color, warmth, and so on.[91] Although (1) through (4) may capture a view held by other early mechanists, Leibniz explicitly rejects it.

[84] Primary qualities "appear simple", or homogeneous, just as colors, etc. do: "distant things ... appear rounded because one cannot discern their angles, even though one is receiving some confused impression of them" (*New Essays* [1704–6], Leibniz (1990, 1981), 120).

[85] *New Essays* (1704–6), Leibniz (1990, 1981), 54.

[86] See Parkinson (1982).

[87] *Essay* 2.8.15-18; on the uninformative nature of sensations of color, etc., see especially 2.23.14, Locke (1975), 137–8, 388–9.

[88] *New Essays* (1704–6), Leibniz (1990, 1981), 131; also 132–3, 404.

[89] *Essay*, 4.1.4, Locke (1975), 525–6.

[90] Leibniz (1990, 1981), 120.

[91] *New Essays*, (1704–6), Leibniz (1990, 1981), 131.

5. Conclusion

With regard to primary qualities, Smith's second theme is closer to Leibniz. The theme includes a claim to the effect that necessarily the intentional objects of experience have spatial properties, including the primary qualities. Although Leibniz does not, as far as I can tell, commit himself to this thesis, it might be argued that his theory of perceptual representation does, at least, require that the intentional objects of perception be arrayed as parts and wholes. Moreover, our concepts of extension, figure, and other geometrical entities are innate, according to Leibniz; they contain intelligible concepts, none of them drawn from the senses. It is by using such concepts that our faculty of common sense ensures that the proper objects of our sight and touch are mutually located in a single geometrical order. So a man who lacks sight and a man with no tactual faculty share the same sense of space: "These two geometries, the blind man's and the paralytic's, must come together, and agree, and indeed ultimately rest on the same ideas [concepts], even though they have no [sensory] images in common."[92] But there is no suggestion that it is necessary that we have a geometry common to our several sensory modalities.

Still, the fact is that our intelligible concepts of extension and its modifications do apply to the material (phenomenal) world, with reasonable accuracy. Two explanations are offered in the early essays on scientific method. One appeals to the metaphysical principle of sufficient reason. Or, to be more exact, everything in the universe can be intelligibly explained: in body, regarded as merely material or spatially extended, "nothing can be conceived distinctly beyond magnitude and figure which are themselves contained in intelligible space, and motion which is a variation of space." Our concepts of magnitude, figure, and motion must apply to the material world, if there are to be intelligible explanations of the phenomena.[93] Perhaps more interesting:

> The attributes common to several senses are to be regarded as distinct in comparison with others, for they are resolvable not into confused ones and then again into those dependent upon the sense, but into concepts attained by the intellect. Such attributes are magnitude, position, duration, and motion. We need not wonder at this, for since they are common to several senses, they do not depend upon the particular constitution of a sense organ or upon its insensible movements, the subtlety and number of which lead to our confused perceptions. They depend rather upon a nature common to diverse organs, that is the nature of body itself, and so they are freed from the confusion of particular perceptions.
>
> ("On the Elements, etc." [1678–9?], Leibniz [1970], 286 [partly quoted above])

This second explanation is drawn from the *physical* world, the spatial nature of material things and the physical structure of the organs of sense perception.

The gist of Smith's second theme is to ground the distinction between primary and secondary qualities on an analysis of the internal structure essential to sense experience,

[92] *New Essays,* (1704–6*)*, Leibniz (1990, 1981), 137.
[93] "On the Elements, etc." (1678–9?), Leibniz (1970), 287, 288.

an approach reminiscent of Kant. Leibniz's tendency, we have seen, is rather to account for the characteristics of perception in general on the basis of a pair of considerations, facts about the corporeal universe conjoined with facts about our cognitive capacities. On one hand, the material universe is spatially extended, endlessly composed of extended parts, everywhere diverse, and infinitely interconnected. On the other hand, we perceive the entire universe, and do so truthfully, but our discriminative powers are severely limited. These two factors account for the confusion of all our perceptions, and above all, perceptions of secondary qualities (aggregated parts of bodily wholes). Moreover, we have innate intelligible concepts of extension and its modifications, available for purposes of physical theory; opportunity to apply them to the intentional content of perception is afforded by relatively distinct conscious perceptions, which highlight an ordered array of bodies at the expense of their endless parts. As for why the nature of the material world and the concepts innate in us should fit each other in this way, Leibniz seems inclined to ascribe it to the demands of the principle of sufficient reason.

Among the many contrasts that might be drawn between his take on the doctrine of qualities and those of his near-contemporaries, we might end with these. To those unfamiliar with his views, they might have a paradoxical air. Leibniz can hardly suppose that mechanist science is capable of reducing colors, flavors, etc. to determinate primary qualities of assembled particles, unlike Descartes and, perhaps, Locke; yet he holds that such qualities *are* mechanical structures. He agrees with rationalist mechanists who say that natural science should seek to explain natural phenomena on the basis of concepts and principles which are not drawn from sense, but rather innate in rational minds. Sense-based concepts are unsuited for theory because the senses are inherently subjective and unintelligible. Yet Leibniz resists Descartes' claim that sense perceptions of colors, and the like, contain sensations which cannot exist in the material world.[94] Moreover, he resists Locke's related claim that sense impressions of secondary qualities are intrinsically non-intentional, but represent bodily qualities solely in virtue of regular causal connections. Finally, like Berkeley, and unlike typical mechanists, Leibniz assigns the same ontological status to primary and secondary qualities, as far as the corporal world, or the intentional content of perception, is concerned. Yet Leibniz gives some credit to the distinction on the basis of considerations of intelligibility unrecognized by Berkeley.

Bibliography

Adams, Robert. 1994. *Leibniz: Determinist, Theist, Idealist*, Oxford: Oxford University Press.

Ayers, Michael. 1991. *Locke: II. Ontology*, London: Routledge.

Beeley, Philip. 2002. "Pragmatism and Perspectivism in Leibniz," in *Nihil Sine Ratione*, VII, Internationaler Leibniz Kongress, ed. Hans Poser, Hannover: Gottfried-Wilhelm-Leibniz-Gesellschaft.

[94] See above, p. 22, note lxiv.

Bennett, Jonathan. 2001. *Learning from Six Philosophers* I, Cambridge: Cambridge University Press.

Bolton, Martha Brandt 1986. "Confused and Obscure Ideas of Sense," in *Essays On Descartes' Meditations*, ed. Amélie Oksenberg Rorty, Berkeley: University of California Press, 389–404.

—— 2002. "Sensible Qualities and Sufficient Reason: Can Qualities Like Heat, Cold, Colors, Odors be Explained?" in *Nihil Sine Ratione*, VII, Internationaler Leibniz Kongress, ed. Hans Poser, Hannover: Gottfried-Wilhelm-Leibniz-Gesellschaft.

——. 2007. "Leibniz and the Limits of Perception," in *Einheit in der Vielheit*, VIII, Internationaler Leibniz Kongress, ed. Hans Poser, Hannover: Gottfried-Wilhelm-Leibniz-Gesellschaft.

Boyle, Robert. 1661. "Some Specimens of an Attempt to make *Chymical* Experiments useful to illustrate the Notions of the *Corpuscular* Philosophy," in *Works of the Honourable Robert Boyle*, I. ed. Thomas Birch. London: 1772, 354–58.

—— 1666. "The Origin of Forms and Qualities, etc.," in *Works of the Honourable Robert Boyle*, III, ed. Thomas Birch. London: 1772, 7–137.

Crockett, Timothy. 2009. "The Fluid Plenum: Leibniz on Surfaces and the Individuation of Body," *British Journal for the History of Philosophy* 17, 735–67.

Daniels, Stephen. 2007. "The Harmony of the Leibniz-Berkeley Juxtaposition," in *Leibniz and the English-Speaking World*, ed. Stuart Brown and Pauline Phemister, Dordrecht: Springer.

Descartes, René. 1979. *The Philosophical Writings of Descartes*, I, tr. Elizabeth S. Haldane and G. R. T. Ross, Cambridge: Cambridge University Press.

—— 1984. *Philosophical Writings of Descartes*, 3 vols, tr. John Cottingham, Robert Stoothoff, and Dugald Murdoch, Cambridge: Cambridge University Press.

Kulstad, Mark. 1977. "Leibniz's Conception of Expression," *Studia Leibnitiana* 9, 55–76.

Leibniz, Gottfried Wilhelm. 1875–90. *Die Philosophischen Schriften von Gottfried Wilhelm Leibniz*, 7, vols, ed. C. I. Gerhardt, Berlin: Weidmann. Reprint Hildesheim: Georg Olms, 1965.

—— 1951. *Theodicy*, tr. E. M. Huggard, London: Routledge & Kegan Paul Ltd.

—— 1966a. *Logical Papers*, tr. G. H. R. Parkinson, Oxford: Clarendon Press.

—— 1966b. *Opuscules et Fragments Inédits de Leibniz*, ed. Louis Couturat, Hildesheim: Georg Olms Verlag.

—— 1967. *The Leibniz-Arnauld Correspondence*, ed. and trans. H. T. Mason, Manchester: Manchester University Press.

—— 1969. *Philosophical Papers and Letters*, ed. and trans. Leroy Loemker, second edn., Dordrecht: Reidel Publishing Company.

—— 1973. *Philosophical Writings*, tr. Mary Morris and G. H. R. Parkinson, London: Dent.

—— 1980. *Philosophischen Schriften*, VI, iii, Berlin: Akademie-Verlag.

—— 1981. *New Essays on Human Understanding*, trans. Peter Remnant and Jonathan Bennett, Cambridge: Cambridge University Press.

—— 1989. *Philosophical Essays*, ed. and tr. Roger Ariew and Daniel Garber, Indianapolis: Hackett Publishing Company.

—— 1990. *Philosophischen Schriften,* VI.vi, *Nouveaux essais sur l'entendement humain*, Berlin: Akademie-Verlag.

—— 1999. *Philosophischen Schriften*, VI.iv, Berlin: Akademie Verlag.

—— 2007. *The Leibniz-Des Bosses Corespondence*, ed. and tr. Brandon C. Look and Donald Rutherford, New Haven: Yale University Press.

Levey, Samuel. 2005. "Leibniz on Precise Shapes and the Corporeal World," in *Leibniz: Nature and Freedom*, ed. J. Cover and D. Rutherford, Oxford: Oxford University Press, 69–94.

Locke, John. 1975. *Essay Concerning Human Understanding*, ed. Peter H. Nidditch, Oxford: Clarendon Press.

Parkinson, G. H. R. 1982. "The 'Intellectualization of Appearances': Aspects of Leibniz's Theory of Sense and Thought," in *Leibniz: Critical and Interpretive Essays*, ed. Michael Hooker, Minneapolis: University of Minnesota Press.

Rutherford, Donald. 1995. *Leibniz and the Rational Order of Nature*, Cambridge: Cambridge University Press.

Smith, A. D. 1990. "Of Primary and Secondary Qualities," *Philosophical Review* 99, 221–54.

Swoyer, Chris. 1995. "Leibnizian Expression," *Journal of the History of Philosophy* 33, 65–99.

Wilson, Margaret Dauler. 1999a. "Confused Ideas," in *Ideas and Mechanism: Essays on Early Modern Philosophy*, Princeton: Princeton University Press.

—— 1999b. "The Phenomenalisms of Leibniz and Berkeley," in *Ideas and Mechanism: Essays on Early Modern Philosophy*, Princeton: Princeton University Press.

—— 1999c. "Confused vs. Distinct Perception in Leibniz: Consciousness, Representation, and God's Mind," in *Ideas and Mechanism: Essays on Early Modern Philosophy*, Princeton: Princeton University Press.

9

Qualities and Simple Ideas: Hume and his Debt to Berkeley

Alan Nelson and David Landy

1. Introduction

This chapter examines the nature of qualities and simple ideas in some early modern empiricist theories of ideas. We will concentrate on interpreting the theory found in Hume's *Treatise*. Nevertheless, the core issues are much the same in Locke and Berkeley and even in schemes more removed from Hume's own. Our principal thesis about this theoretical framework is that simple ideas, especially simple ideas understood to be minimum sensibles, are ultimately at the crux of the most interesting and important matters concerning *qualities*. In Berkeley's and Hume's theories of ideas, we maintain that simple ideas *are* simple qualities. Moreover, in Hume's theory (at least) simple ideas (or qualities) are not straightforwardly perceived, but are instead explanatory posits within the philosophical theory. Perception always involves complex ideas and is, therefore, inherently complex. The interpretation we advance has the further consequence that the distinction between primary and secondary qualities is not metaphysical, but has only pragmatic import.[1]

Section 2 is concerned with the connection between qualities and simple ideas in Locke's and Berkeley's versions of the theory. Berkeley's emphasis on *minima sensibilia* is presented as stemming from difficulties in Locke's scheme. The refinement of this device turns out to be an important feature of Hume's theory. Section 3 introduces our interpretation of Hume's version of the theory by drawing a distinction between the sense in which every experience is of nothing but simple ideas, and a sense in which simple ideas are never experienced "as such." Section 4 then develops this part of the interpretive thesis by responding to some potential objections. Doing so requires us to analyze anew Hume's treatment of the *minimum sensibile*. Section 5 extends the interpretation by arguing that Hume's simple ideas are unobservable, theoretical posits.

[1] This last claim is not original at least as it concerns Berkeley. Winkler (1992), for example, finds it to be a consequence of Berkeley's theory of ideas and credits John Dewey for recognizing it.

Section 6 then explores the difficult task of explaining the meaning of the term "simple idea" in Hume's theory. The main difficulty here is that his theory of ideas includes a semantics according to which the meaning of a term directly involves an idea. This obliges us to tackle the daunting problem of accounting for the meaning of "simple idea" by analyzing the idea *of* a simple idea.[2] Section 7 is an investigation of the nature of Hume's commitment to the existence of simple ideas. He is not a realist about them in any philosophically familiar sense, but they fall on the realist side of his own theoretical divide between what is real and what is arbitrarily constructed. We conclude with some observations about the connection between the theory of ideas and the phenomena it is intended to explain.

2. Locke and Berkeley on simple ideas and qualities

Locke proposed a tight connection between the qualities of things and our simple ideas.

> Though the Qualities that affect our Senses, are, in the things themselves, so united and blended, that there is no separation, no distance between them; yet 'tis plain, the *Ideas* they produce in the Mind, enter by the Senses simple and unmixed.... The coldness and hardness which a Man feels in a piece of *Ice*, being as distinct *Ideas* in the Mind, as the Smell and Whiteness of a Lily; or as the taste of Sugar, and the smell of a Rose: And there is nothing can be plainer to a Man, than the clear and distinct Perception he has of these simple Ideas; which, being each in itself uncompounded, contains in it nothing but *one uniform Appearance*, or Conception in the mind, and is not distinguishable into different *Ideas*. (2.2.1; 119).[3]

For Locke, it follows that our cognition of the qualities that affect our senses must be traceable to simple ideas, because the mind's perceptions include only simple ideas and the ideas resulting from the mind's operations on these simples.[4] The connection is further established in 2.8 of the *Essay* in which Locke famously characterizes the distinction between primary and secondary qualities of bodies. It is tellingly entitled, "*Some farther Considerations concerning our simple* Ideas." The point is again that qualities, whether primary or secondary, positive or privative, are such as to produce simple ideas in the understanding.

[2] Some commentators on Hume have argued that the various challenges are insurmountable, and that the distinction between simple and complex ideas is either too vague to be useful or, worse, incoherent. See Laird (1932), Stroud (1977), Baillie (2000), and Bennett (2001). For a comprehensive recent discussion of the issues as they arise in Locke, see Brown (2006).

[3] We refer to Locke's *Essay* by Book, Chapter, Section and page number in Locke (1690/1975). Berkeley's works are cited by section number and the following abbreviations: *Principles* = *A Treatise Concerning the Principles of Human Knowledge*, *NTV* = *An Essay towards a New Theory of Vision*, *TVV* = *The Theory of Vision Vindicated and Explained*, *PC* = *Philosophical Commentaries*, all from Luce and Jessop (1948–57). Hume's *Treatise of Human Nature* is cited with the abbreviation T followed by Book, Part, Section, and paragraph numbers from Hume (1739–40/[2007]).

[4] 2.2.2; 119–20.

What Locke means in the quoted passage by "*one uniform Appearance,* or conception in the mind" is not at all obvious. Here is an attempt to unpack it. Suppose one catches sight of an apple that appears in one, uniform red shade. Locke does not think that the simple idea, *red,*[5] that is produced by the apple is an apple-shaped red patch. The apple-shaped red patch idea includes a "compounding" or "uniting" of (at least) the simple *red* and the apple-shape idea. The experience somehow includes the simple *red*: it is not a green apple or a transparent apple in view. It is not, however, possible to experience the simple *red* unless it is compounded with, at least, a shape. Perhaps Locke was thinking that the "Smell and Whiteness of a Lily" must be separate simple ideas because he thought they were obviously produced by different *qualities* of a lily. Moreover, if the wind changes direction then the *smell* might be absent while the *white* remains. So, just as the idea of the white, fragrant lily is a compound of (at least) the *smell* and the *white,* so the idea of the red, apple-shaped object is a compound of (at least) *red* and *apple-shaped,* even though those ideas co-occur in perceptions of the apple more reliably than the *smell* and the *white* do in the lily. The interpretation of Locke is greatly vexed on this point and others closely related to it.[6]

In any event, Locke distinguishes primary qualities like shape from secondary qualities like red. Primary qualities of bodies produce ideas that are inseparable from ideas of bodies and resemble bodies; secondary qualities differ from primary qualities in both respects.[7] The main part of Berkeley's attack on Locke's version of the theory of ideas addresses just these points. First, Berkeley's own version of the empiricist theory of ideas is shaped by his finding "plain" exactly the opposite of what Locke finds plain about the connection between qualities and ideas. Locke insisted that *red* enters the mind simple and unmixed, albeit co-occurring with *apple*-shaped when viewing an apple. Berkeley objected that our inability actually to experience red apart from visible shape, for example, indicated generally that color ideas are not distinct from visible shape ideas[8]. Berkeley thought that to suppose that they are distinct is to suppose erroneously that an abstracted color idea can be derived from a color-patch idea. In other words, he thought that Locke was committed to our being able to experience red with no shape whatsoever or triangles that are neither equilateral, isosceles, nor scalene.[9] The upshot for Berkeley is that qualities cannot be intelligibly connected with Locke's wrongly constructed list of simple ideas.

[5] The italics indicate that the word signifies an idea.

[6] *White* necessarily co-occurs with some shape or other (barring purely abstract ideas) while it might seem possible to perceive a smell with no shapes or colors at all. It is not obvious that smells are not always "accompanied" by a visual field, but the phenomenology of this accompaniment bears an unclear relation to Locke's co-occurrence.

[7] 2.8.9, 2.8.15. These aspects of the distinction are our current concern. For a recent attempt to taxonomize Locke's distinction more fully, see Jacovides (2007c).

[8] Berkeley, again unlike Locke, does not think that there is an idea of extension that is separate from visible and tangible ideas. Berkeley thought that erroneously supposing that uniform extension can be abstracted from visible and tangible ideas was a source of faulty distinctions between primary and secondary qualities (*TVV* 15).

[9] *Principles 10.* Controversy still rages over whether Berkeley correctly assessed Locke's commitments regarding abstract ideas.

Berkeley's account of qualities also differs from Locke's insofar as he is an immaterialist for whom *esse est percipi*. Because of this, he obviously must reject Locke's characterization of qualities in terms of material bodies. In the first section of his *Principles,* material bodies are, in effect, replaced with "sensible things" that are ". . . marked by one name and so to be reputed as one thing." It is in terms of these sensible things or "sensible objects" that Berkleyan qualities must be described. It is important that a sensible object be "marked by one name," because each of them is a composite of ideas. "Thus, for example, a certain colour, taste, smell, figure and consistence having been observed to go together, are accounted one distinct thing, signified by the name *apple"* (*Principles* 1). In other words, the qualities of sensible objects just are the ideas of color, taste, etc. that are together "marked by one name" and regarded as a single thing. An apple's having the quality *red* is nothing more than a certain idea being part of the composite marked by the word, "apple."[10] For Berkeley, it follows that there can be no metaphysical distinction between primary and secondary qualities. General terms such as "shape" and "motion" that are used to mark ideas will be distinguished from general terms such as "red" and "pain" to the extent that the former play a distinctive role in mechanical explanations of the behavior of sensible objects.[11] That fits well with the historical fact that advances in scientific explanation played an important role in the development of the familiar distinction.

There is a complicated difficulty in Berkeley's expression of his own view that needs to be brought out. When he lists an apple's color as among the ideas composing the apple as a sensible object, it would be natural to suppose that he means *red* or *green* as the case may be. But as we have noted, Berkeley maintains against Locke that red and green are not separable from a visible shape. So the collection of ideas constituting the apple does not contain any ideas that could be identified with Locke's simple ideas *red* or *green*. But it would seem odd for most philosophers to take what they would consider a "color-patch-idea" to be a quality of an apple. For one thing, a color patch is not simple; unless it appears very tiny, various parts can be distinguished—top and bottom, left and right, etc. Recognizing this, Berkeley does have his own version of the simple idea; it is the *minimum sensibile*—an idea that cannot be in any way divided, diminished, or attenuated (*NTV* 54).

These ideas are not to be understood as those which, as a matter of empirical fact, have no parts distinguishable by human beings. They are instead metaphysically minimal.

It will perhaps be objected that the *minimum visibile* of a man doth really and in itself contain parts whereby it surpasses that of a mite, though they are not perceivable by a man. To which I answer, the *minimum visibile* having (in like manner as all other the proper and immediate objects of sight)

[10] Berkeley also holds that ideas of different sense modalities are not strongly unified by their composition. It is more accurate to say that a certain olfactory idea can *suggest* a visible shape (e.g. *TVV* 28, 39, 42).

[11] Below we shall revisit Berkeley's theory of general terms in the context of Hume's more fully developed treatment.

been shewn not to have any existence without the mind of him who sees it, it follows there cannot be any part of it that is not actually perceived, and therefore visible. (*NTV* 81)

A mite, therefore, would experience a "new world" (*NTV* 85) of ideas, just as we do through a microscope. But neither human vision aided by that optical instrument, nor the mite's eye, can further resolve the *minimum visibile*.

This leaves Berkeley with three options for handling qualities. He could maintain that sensible minima just are qualities—simple qualities that might appear, for example, in aggregated color patches. This suggestion parallels Locke's connection between qualities and simple ideas, but there is no textual evidence that Berkeley was attracted to it. There is, in contrast, considerable textual support for taking qualities to be inseparable "aspects" of ideas that can be brought into focus by mental acts of attention. On this second interpretation, the composition of our apple's red visible shape by sensible minima is ignored. The apple and a rose could then be found to resemble each other in virtue of each intrinsically having a red aspect. This second option has been strongly supported by Kenneth Winkler.[12] The third reading of Berkeley on qualities, like the second reading, emphasizes the connection between qualities and relations of resemblance. The main difference is that qualities are not taken to be intrinsic aspects of sensible objects or their component ideas. On the third reading it is mind's activity of grouping objects together under a general term that *constitutes* the resemblance then found among the sensible objects. In other words, objects do not resemble each other *because* they have intrinsic, trope-like qualities in common. This differentiates the third interpretation from the second. Instead, it is *because* the mind groups them together under a term that they are said to share a quality. The third interpretation thus nominalizes qualities—we have names for the groupings of objects. Only then does it become convenient to regard members of the groups as sharing "aspects." In the next section, we begin to argue that Hume is best interpreted as holding a sophisticated version of this reductive, nominalizing theory of qualities. Some texts that strongly suggest that Berkeley was also committed to this position will be noted, but we are not convinced that Berkeley had a settled view on the matter.

3. The experience of simple ideas

We begin our investigation of simple ideas in Hume's theory of ideas with an observation about human experience. This is to be set against the observations that

[12] Winkler (1989, Chapter 3) prefers to describe this by saying that Berkeley rejects simple ideas altogether. If by "simple idea" one means items on Locke's list (e.g. *red*), then Berkeley certainly does reject these as impossible abstract ideas. On this interpretation, even the *minimum sensibile* is not simple, but has a complex structure of intrinsic aspects. Winkler notes that Berkeley does not use the term "simple idea" in the works he published, but we think it apt for preserving an important continuity from Berkeley's theory to Hume's that will be developed in what follows.

Locke and Berkeley make; for example, Locke's claim that *red* and *ovoid* as they co-occur in the perception of an apple are nevertheless simple and unmixed, and Berkeley's contradiction of that claim. In what follows we'll use the term "experience" to refer to the phenomenology of perception. The observation we make is that experience is always complex. Complexity enters spatially and temporally, and experience is further made complex by the various modalities of sense. At any time, considering any *one* sense modality, our experience consists of a multitude of distinguishable parts, be they parts of our visual field, parts of our aural field, parts of our tactile field, etc. Furthermore, each of these complex modal fields itself constitutes only one part of experience at any given time, and all of these fields taken collectively at a time, constitute only part of our diachronic experience. Throw in copies of all of the Humean impressions of both sense and reflection, ideas that copy these, etc., and the complexity is multidimensionally rich. We never at a time experience only perfect simplicity, and a fortiori never do so across times. Doing so would require an absolutely "clear and distinct perception" in Descartes' sense—and not even Descartes is always interpreted as holding out for such perfectly simple perceptions.

It is, in other words, phenomenologically obvious that we never have any experience that is completely and perfectly simple. So suppose that we do experience a simple idea embedded in the rest of our experience. Insofar as we discriminate this idea from the rest of our experience, we perform a mental act: we discriminate, make a distinction, or to use Locke's terminology, we perform the operation of discernment. This, however, leaves us with an air of paradox. Here is why. To experience a simple idea as an individual, we must note its individuality by discriminating it from the rest of our experience. But discriminating *a* from *b* is a complex experience. Consider a carefully selected, unusually simple, visual example. Suppose one sees a uniform red circle of light against a green background while looking into a psychologist's apparatus. And suppose that the red light is so small that it is barely perceptible. Here we might be initially inclined to say that the subject is aware of something that Locke and Berkeley could agree is a simple idea. But if asked to describe the visual experience, the accurate answer would be that what is seen is a red light *against a green background*. If the psychologist instructs the subject to ignore the background, then compliance requires *discerning* the red circle from the background.

Having what might naïvely be called an "isolated" experience of the red circle, therefore, requires the experience of a *relation* between the circle and the background. That is an experience of a complex, relational idea. The seeming paradox, then, is that whatever we might call the experience of a simple idea is, in fact, the experience of a complex idea. We put this point by saying that there is no experience of simple ideas "as such." A simple idea is never experienced perfectly *as simple*: it is never experienced except as a component of the experience of a complex idea.

This is not to deny that there is another sense in which we experience nothing but simple ideas. That is because complex ideas are composed of simple ideas; experiencing complexes just is experiencing their related, component simples. But this is not what one would carelessly describe as "having a simple idea", or "thinking about a simple idea." Those expressions suggest a mental focus on a simple idea, but the very act of focusing involves a complex relational idea that includes the simple in question.[13] Before proceeding, something must be done to clear the air of paradox as much as possible and to respond to some natural objections to the thesis that simple ideas are not experienced as such.

4. Minima sensibilia

Because simple ideas constitute complex ideas, it can be said that all experience is of simple ideas. This sense in which we do experience simples should be brought into sharper contrast with the sense in which we never experience simple ideas as such. The contrast can be clarified with ordinary examples from science. Suppose, for example, that a pure sample of mercury in a beaker consists of nothing but mercury atoms. Now when we look at this mercury or plunge in a finger and feel it, we certainly do not have visual or tactile experience of individual mercury atoms. This is so despite the fact that, by assumption, we are seeing or feeling nothing but the mercury atoms insofar as we see or feel the sample of mercury. In much the same way, it is a consequence of the theory of ideas that all of our experience is constituted by simple ideas that are never perfectly experienced *as* simple. It is helpful to note here that *given* the machinery of Hume's theory of ideas the point is a logical one—it follows from what the theory says about the nature of ideas. The whole theoretical enterprise is nevertheless empirical because it is ultimately answerable to the phenomena of human nature that are to be explained.

A potential objection to this development might be raised by appealing to the power of selective attention. One might think that, by dint of sheer will power, one's attention can be focused on a simple idea (even as a component of a complex) with no involvement of complex ideas whatsoever. Or perhaps the will need not be involved at all: might one's attention not happen to fall upon a simple idea by accident? Consider again the red circle, call it x, against the green background, call that y. How could these two experiences differ: 1) attending to x, and 2) attending to the composite of x and y?

Since one does not simply expunge y from experience, the answer must be that 1) requires one to take note of the distinction between x and y, to compare them, and to increase attention to what is not-y and, is likely to decrease attention to y. In short, even in this extremely impoverished case, the temporal series of perceptions that we call "focusing attention on x" terminates in a complex consideration of both x and y. In more realistic cases where we have more ideas in different sensory modalities, the

[13] In developing this interpretation of Hume's theory, we are agreeing with commentators who argue that mental acts are nothing over and above perceptions (i.e. impressions and ideas) or complexes of perceptions. See, for example, Ainslie (2008), Allison (2008), Garrett (1981, 344), and Stroud (1977, 130–131). For an opposing treatment of Humean mental acts as something over and above perceptions, see Waxman (1994).

complexity will be much greater. And if we try to understand what might be involved in "the operation of the will" in the process of selective attention, there will be still more complexity.

Another apparent difficulty with the thesis that simple ideas are not experienced as such is textual. Berkeley and Hume both put much weight on the perception of simple ideas as *minima sensibilia*. Hume even gives us an experimental procedure for getting at them.

> Put a spot of ink upon paper, fix your eye upon that spot, and retire to such a distance, that at last you lose sight of it; 'tis plain, that the moment before it vanish'd the image or impression was perfectly indivisible.... Nothing can be more minute, than some ideas, which we form in the fancy; and images, which appear to the senses; since these are ideas and images perfectly simple and indivisible. (T 1.2.1.4–5)

Hume plainly thinks that this experiment yields an idea that is indivisible. The main thrust of this section of the *Treatise* is to reject the rationalist doctrine that space and time are infinitely divisible. So Hume argues from the indivisibility of ideas of minute objects to the indivisibility of the objects. This experiment seem adequate to Hume's purpose. It establishes that some ideas are phenomenally indivisible; we cannot experience a separation of the barely visible spot into parts. If we produce an enlarged image with a microscope, we no longer have a *barely visible spot*. Nor do we have identically the *same* spot because we could discriminate a number of component spots in the microscopic image of the enlarged spot (as Berkeley argued in *NTV* 85–6). And one sense that can be given to the term 'simple idea' would capture just this kind of indivisibility. But there are two senses of 'simple idea' at work in Hume because ideas that are 'simple' in this one technical sense are nevertheless composite. Notice that Hume's instruction is to "fix your eye upon that spot." This fixation requires, as argued above, that the spot be discriminated from the paper, but the paper cannot be expunged from the experience of the spot. Moreover, Hume's experiment is in some important respects quite untidy, as he notes a little later:

> Put a spot of ink upon paper, and retire to such a distance, that the spot becomes altogether invisible; you will find, that upon your return and nearer approach the spot first becomes visible by short intervals; and afterwards becomes always visible; and afterwards acquires only a new force in its colouring without augmenting its bulk; and afterwards, when it has encreas'd to such a degree as to be really extended, 'tis still difficult for the imagination to break it into its component parts, because of the uneasiness it finds in the conception of such a minute object as a single point. *This infirmity affects most of our reasoning on the present subject, and makes it almost impossible to answer in an intelligible matter, and in proper expressions, many questions which may arise concerning it.* (T 1.2.4.7, emphasis added)

In this more circumspect description of the experiment, the "uneasiness" Hume refers to is the impossibility of maintaining precise visual focus on the spot. Near the limits of visual acuity, changes in ambient lighting and the orientation of the paper, normal visual disturbances like floaters and subtle changes in focus, etc. make it very difficult to track the image appropriately. These "infirmities" make it impossible to give good answers to many questions that Hume does not mention here; we shall mention some important ones that he does come to later. It has already been noted that the process of uneasily fixing upon the spot requires some complex discriminations. We have, however, not yet considered diachronic complexities, and in Hume's experiment these are absolutely unavoidable.

When the spot recedes until invisible and then reappears, what justifies the conclusion that it is the identical spot? For it is a *conclusion* of "our reasoning on the present subject." One might cite the facts that we continually see the spot-marked paper, and the hand or easel holding the paper, the ground, etc. So from these considerations of "coherence and constancy" (T 1.4.2.20) we infer the continued existence of the spot. But in the subject at hand, namely *minima sensibilia,* the "uneasiness" of the images makes our already questionable reasonings especially "infirm." We are not now importing considerations from T 1.4.2 which is entitled "Of scepticism with regard to the senses" to raise sceptical concerns about simple ideas. The point is instead that the diachronic issues raised by Hume himself in the spot experiment reinforce the fact that the experience of the spot involves massive complexity. So this *minimum sensibile* is indivisible because we cannot make any further discriminations with respect to the spot. It should be added here that we are able to make other discriminations in the experience of the spot. We might notice, for instance, that we are better able to fix on the spot visually if we stop up our ears. But we would not ordinarily say that separating off the aural component of the experience in this way amounted to a division. So we can conclude that Hume's ink spot experiment is meant to establish one kind of indivisibility. But this indivisibility does not yield *simplicity* of the kind we are examining. It does not enable us to experience simple ideas as such—we never experience uncompounded, non-complex ideas.

5. Simple ideas as theoretical posits

These developments face us with a new philosophical and interpretive difficulty. Before presenting the solution, the difficulty itself must be set up with some care. Hume begins the *Treatise* by distinguishing impressions and ideas according to their degrees of force and liveliness (T 1.1.1.1). He immediately proceeds to divide both kinds of perceptions (his general term for ideas and impressions) into simple and complex (T 1.1.1.2).[14] The simple/complex distinction is first introduced with the example of an apple. in which the color, taste, and smell are distinguishable. This shows that the perception of the apple is complex. It is useful here to make explicit a point left implicit by Hume. Since he here defines a simple perception as one such as to "admit of

[14] This is a respect in which the *Enquiry's* treatment is almost exactly the same; see Hume (2006, section 2.6).

no distinction nor separation" (T 1.1.1.2), the qualities corresponding to the perceptions of color, taste, and smell ideas are not simple. This is so even though they are, in one sense, *simpler* than the perception of the apple. As we argued above, an experience of the colored shape (for example) as distinguished from the apple is more complex than the experience of the apple because it involves a comparison of the two. Here, however, we are interested in the easier point that the colored shape itself can be distinguished by left and right, and there might be some brown spots, so it does not satisfy Hume's definition of a simple perception. At this point in Hume's exposition, one might suspect that he has no use for perceptions, either impressions or ideas, that are simple in the defined sense, and that he wants only relative simplicity.[15] It might seem so far that all perceptions are complex, but some are more complex than others. That might warrant calling an idea which is a component of another idea 'simple', that is, simple relative to the more complex idea. Hume's theory does however, as we shall see, often rely on ideas and impressions that are simple in an absolute and not merely relative sense.

Now our difficulty can be clearly stated. How can Hume rely on absolutely simple ideas to explain experience when we experience only complex ideas? The answer we propose is that simple ideas are theoretical posits. Hume's "science of man" (T Intro.4) is meant to explain various phenomena. And like the natural sciences, Hume's science of human nature will employ in its explanations theoretical objects that are themselves not phenomena and not directly experienced. They are, in a later parlance, *unobservables*. Hume posits such entities on the grounds that they *explain* certain phenomena—in this case mental phenomena—in need of explaining. In particular, Hume posits simple ideas on the grounds that they explain how it is that experience alone can account for the complex ideas that we do have. This strategy can be seen as being introduced in the opening passages of *Treatise* that we have already begun to discuss.

In these opening paragraphs, Hume is aiming at the first, crucial theoretical proposition, the Copy Principle: *that all our simple ideas in their first appearance are deriv'd from simple impressions, which are correspondent to them, and which they exactly represent* (T 1.1.1.7, emphasis in the original). He first motivates the Copy Principle by affecting to notice that all of his ideas exactly resemble some impression he has experienced.

> The first circumstance, that strikes my eye, is the great resemblance betwixt our impressions and ideas in every other particular, except their degree of force and vivacity. The one seem to be in a manner the reflection of the other; so that all the perceptions of the mind are double, and appear both as impressions and ideas. (T 1.1.1.3)

Upon further reflection he sees that he has many ideas of which this appears to be untrue, offering as examples the imagined New Jerusalem and inaccurately remembered Paris.

[15] One might, indeed, reach an analogous conclusion while trying to interpret Locke or Berkeley.

> Upon a more accurate survey I find that I have been carried away too far by the first appearance [...] I observe, that many of our complex ideas never had impressions, that correspond to them, and that many of our complex impressions are never exactly copy'd in ideas. (T 1.1.1.4)

The resemblance between ideas and impressions struck him as a plausible, naive beginning to an account of the origin of these ideas. In fact, once these apparent counterexamples are dealt with, Hume will go on to use the exact resemblance of simple ideas to simple impressions to do an enormous amount of work in the remainder of the *Treatise.* So, already treating the Copy Principle as true, he suggests that our mental architecture must be more nuanced than one might suppose pre-theoretically. In particular, he now puts to work the distinction between simple and complex ideas that he introduced a few paragraphs previously.[16]

> I perceive, therefore, that tho' there is in general a great resemblance betwixt our *complex* impressions and ideas, yet the rule is not universally true, that they are exact copies of each other. We may next consider how the case stands with our *simple* perceptions. After the most accurate examination, of which I am capable, I venture to affirm, that the rule here holds without an exception, and that every simple idea has a simple impression, which resembles it; and every simple impression a correspondent idea. (T 1.1.1.5)[17]

In line with the interpretation of Hume as realizing that simple ideas are not experienced as such, this passage should not be read as saying that he confirms the Copy Principle by an "accurate examination" of simple ideas as such along with copied impressions that are simple as such. Hume is instead noticing that it will be virtually impossible to find a counterexample to this thesis: the imagination can construct complex ideas from postulated simple ideas that are themselves always copied from correspondingly postulated simple impressions.

Of course, just as an ad hoc positing of mercury atoms does no explanatory work for mercury until we say something about their nature, so positing simple ideas does no explanatory work until we say something about *their* nature. In fact, Hume introduces simple ideas in much the same way that other scientists introduce their own theoretical posits. He introduces a *model* for simple ideas, and then describes how the posit both

[16] We mustn't be misled into thinking that because the simple/complex distinction was drawn shortly *before* this point in the *Treatise*, that it is not drawn in response to exactly these concerns. The expository structure of the *Treatise* does not necessarily represent exactly the structure of Hume's thought on these issues. For instance, it is plausible to suppose that Hume would find it more rhetorically forceful a) to present all the distinctions he will subsequently employ at the outset, rather than piecemeal as he proceeds, and b) that these distinctions be first presented as hypotheses drawn from common sense.

[17] At this point, it is relevant to note that there are texts suggesting that Berkeley had already explored this path. In his early notebooks we find, "Ideas of Sense are the Real things or Archetypes. Ideas of Imagination, Dreams etc. are copies, images of these." *PC* 833, p. 98. And in *Principles* 1, he wrote, "It is evident to anyone who takes a survey of the objects of human knowledge, that they are either ideas actually imprinted on the senses, or else such as are perceived by attending to the passions and operations of the mind, or lastly *ideas formed by help of memory and imagination, either compounding, dividing, or barely representing those originally perceived in the aforesaid ways.*" (emphasis added).

resembles and differs from the model.[18] In Hume's case, the model is *a complex idea* that is experienced in the normal way.

> Simple perceptions or impressions and ideas are such as admit no distinction nor separation. The complex are contrary to these, and may be distinguish'd into parts. Tho' a particular colour, taste, and smell are qualities all united together in this apple, 'tis easy to perceive they are not the same, but are at least distinguishable from each other. (T 1.1.1.2)

Simple ideas are much like complex ideas; most importantly, they are copies. The main difference is that the complexes, but not the simples, can be distinguished into parts. As we see later on in the *Treatise*, this model is enough to do heavy lifting for Hume. It specifies how simple impressions are copied by simple ideas. Furthermore, as copies, simple ideas can be both caused by impressions and exactly resemble them. It also explains how complex ideas can come to have the structure they do. Because they are composed of simple ideas, their content derives from the simple ideas. And, as already noted, we have an explanation of how complex ideas often, but not always, resemble complex impressions. Simple ideas resemble simple impressions, but can be recombined to form novel complex ideas.

What all of this amounts to is a *theoretical scientific account* of experience. Our experience, the phenomena that a science of human nature must explain, is of only complex ideas. The nature of experience is explained in terms of posited simple perceptions that are governed by general laws and principles such as the Copy Principle. This scientific theory of ideas should be contrasted with a descriptive phenomenology. If we restricted ourselves to experiential items that can be introspectively isolated, we would not appeal to simple ideas. To repeat, simple ideas are *posits*, or *theoretical entities*, because we have no direct experience of them as simple. It does, however, seem in line with an important strand in Hume's philosophy that simple ideas come to be known through a sophisticated scientific analogy with complex ideas. Hume's commitment to simple ideas is grounded, not in direct experience of them, but in their explanatory utility.[19]

6. The idea of a simple idea

We seem to have in hand a solution to the interpretive and philosophical difficulty with which the last section began. More work nevertheless needs to be done because the solution of the last difficulty brings in its wake a subtle, new problem that threatens the entire enterprise of an empiricist theory of ideas. The problem emerges from the

[18] Further following good scientific practice, he leaves open for further examination the question of how many respects in which the posit resembles the model. For instance, it only comes out later, in T 1.2 , "Of The ideas of space and time," that simple ideas, unlike complex ideas, cannot individually represent extended objects.

[19] In the philosophy of science, there are important debates about how to understand the commitment to unobservable theoretical posits in our best theories. Below, we briefly consider versions of scientific realism and instrumentalism about the ontological status of simple ideas that might be in play in the theory of ideas.

empiricist theory of meaning. Language is meaningful only insofar as it is clearly and reliably associated with ideas. We have interpreted Hume as relying heavily on simple ideas in his comprehensive theory of ideas. So if Hume's theory is expressed using the term "simple idea", internal consistency seems to demand that meaningful use of the expression "simple idea" itself requires a clear and reliable association with ideas. When making such theoretical assertions as, "simple ideas are like complex ideas except that complex ideas can be distinguished into parts," the term "simple idea" does not get a semantic free ride. Hume is explicitly in the business of tracing up *all* of our ideas to their origins. Hume is therefore committed to there being an idea *of* simple ideas to serve as the meaning for "simple idea." And of course there must a story about how we come to have that idea. We need to tell this story. This task promises to be a delicate business. We will need to navigate some rocky issues connected with the separability and distinguishability of ideas.[20] And finally, a central role is played by the notorious Berkleyan analysis of ideas that represent in a way that is general or abstract.

A tempting, but faulty story would make an idea *of* a simple idea be a copy or resembling representation of a simple idea that is simple as such. Within the theory of ideas, ideas can represent or be *of* other perceptions only by resembling or copying them.[21] This does not work because there are no simple ideas as such, so there cannot be ideas that *as such* represent simple ideas as such. Simple ideas occur in experience only in complexes, so an idea that represented them as they are in experience would itself have to be complex. That point can also be put the other way around. A complex idea cannot represent a simple idea because a complex idea cannot resemble the simplicity of a simple idea. It does not improve matters to say that a complex idea *C* can represent a simple idea *S*, because a simple idea resembling *S*, call it *S'*, is a component of *C*. That would leave us without any account of how it is that we *think* about *S*. It identifies thinking of a simple idea with thinking of a complex idea, and that cannot be right.

The right approach emerges once we realize that what is needed is a meaning for "simple idea" as a *general* term. Just as scientific propositions about mercury atoms almost never require reference to specific individual atoms, the theory of ideas needs to refer to the class of simple ideas. Simplicity is a way in which ideas resemble each other. *Simplicity is itself a quality.*[22]

Hume follows Berkeley in having a semantics for general terms picking out classes of particulars that eschews ideas that are general or abstract *as such*. We now examine this

[20] See Russow (1980), Westphal (1984), Baxter (1997) and Garrett (1997: 58–75) for more detail than we can provide here.

[21] Landy (2006) argues that on a strict reading of Hume's Theory of ideas, ideas can represent only other perceptions. Representation requires likeness and, as Berkeley noted, ideas can resemble only other ideas. But the point need not immediately concern us.

[22] "And of this we may be certain, even from the very abstract terms *simple idea*. They comprehend all simple ideas under them. These resemble each other in their simplicity. (T 1.1.7.7, footnote 5app).

reductive account of how we come to *think* of simple ideas in general, and this will in turn shed light on how we think of particular simple ideas. It must be admitted that this procedure looks, on its face, entirely backwards. It is well known that Hume's account of general ideas piggybacks on his account of singular ideas, and that it is the latter which determines the content of the former. How, then, can it be the case that to have a singular idea of a simple idea requires having a *general* idea of it first? On the face of it, beginning with ideas that are general is not compatible with empiricism.

The answer to the question draws first and foremost on the peculiar nature of our idea of simple ideas. Remember that we have been reading Hume so as to construe simple ideas as unobservable, *theoretical* entities. It follows that we can have no direct experience of simple ideas and, in turn, that we can have no singular ideas of them prior to their theoretical introduction. The way out of the difficulty must respect the fact that Hume requires general ideas to piggyback on *some* singular ideas. The crucial step concerns what is special about the case of ideas of theoretical entities. Hume does *not* require that a general idea piggyback on singular ideas of something like *the object* of the general idea. To begin, let's recall Hume's account of general representation.

> When we have found a resemblance among several objects, that often occur to us, we apply the same name to all of them, whatever differences we may observe in the degrees of their quantity and quality, and whatever other differences may appear among them. After we have acquir'd a custom of this kind, the hearing of that name revives the idea of one of these objects, and makes the imagination conceive it with all its particular circumstances and proportions. But as the same word is suppos'd to have been frequently apply'd to other individuals, that are different in many respects from that idea, which is immediately present to the mind; the word not being able to revive the idea of all these individuals, only touches the soul, if I may be allow'd so to speak, and revives that custom, which we have acquir'd by surveying them. They are not really and in fact present to the mind, but only in power, nor do we draw them all out distinctly in the imagination, but keep ourselves in a readiness to survey any of them, as we may be prompted by a present design or necessity. (T 1.1.7.7)

We find certain objects to resemble one another, and so apply a single word to all of them. Upon later hearing this word, we call to mind one or more of these objects. At the same time, we are disposed to recall the rest of the resembling ideas when appropriately prompted. A particular idea thus made general represents the set of all of the ideas that we are disposed to recall upon hearing a certain word. We call this set the Revival Set (following Garrett 1997: 24). And the meaning of the word, therefore, also extends to the entire set.

We need to show how to distinguish individual sensible minima from kinds of sensible minima. Let's illustrate by reusing Hume's example of the apple. When bringing the apple to our mouth to bite into it, we initially have the ideas of the taste, smell, sound, feel, and color of an apple all roughly concurrently. It is easy to notice that this complex idea has the ideas of the particular *qualities* of taste, smell, etc. as components. But these are not yet simple. Even if the apple is experienced as uniformly red, this quality is a complex because we can distinguish top and bottom, left and right, and so on. The tactile idea also has easily distinguishable tactile parts. It seems the best we could do would be to perform analogs of Hume's famous receding-spot experiment that would here similarly result in *minima sensibilia.* The phenomenology of sound, taste, and smell is more elusive. Hume would probably agree with Berkeley that in humans these ideas could do no more than suggest other, spatially related ideas. It is hard to know what to do with echolocation in bats, olfactory location in dogs, and the sensitivity of sharks to spatial gradients of nutrient concentration, etc. But the general point is unaffected by these cases. Spatiality aside, it would not be hard to design an experiment showing that sounds, smells, and tastes are temporally divisible. thereby finding temporal *minima sensibilia.*[23] Minima can also be realized on intensive scales. A sound might be at the threshold of audibility, for instance. We hasten to add that we still do not achieve experiences of simples as such when these procedures focus attention on the *minima*; these minima are experienced as components of complexes just as in the receding spot experiment. Now that we have sensible minima, we need to proceed to kinds of sensible minima.

Let us continue this investigation by supposing that we begin, not with the apple, but with seeing a fire hydrant of the same shade of red. If we again manage to get divisions of the red shape down to a *minimum sensibile* we will (by assumption) have the same simple idea (of that shade of red). And if, instead of the fire hydrant, we begin with the smell of an apple-scented car freshener or the taste of some Calvados, we shall arrive at the same simple ideas of apple-smell and apple-taste that we distinguished in the apple. Now attention has been focused first on individual *minima* and then on *kinds* of *minima.* With that preparation, we are ready to propose Revival Sets for various kinds of ideas of simple ideas and for the most general of all these kinds—the idea of simple idea. This will also constitute a proposal for reducing the perception of the corresponding *qualities* to perceptions backed up by Revival Sets.

Start with the example of one's idea of the simple idea of a (particular shade of) red. That Revival Set will include some of the discriminating processes that one has used to distinguish the simple idea of red from, for example, apples, fire hydrants, etc. That is already an extremely complicated set. To become occurrently aware of a particular, minimal red sensible, it might suffice to remember the result of backing away from an apple until it is barely visible, but one might need to remember the whole experimental procedure or even to conduct the experiment again. If we were actually to enumerate all the ideas involved, the complexity would be daunting. Yet another order of complexity is required to get the Revival Set for "simple idea of red" (as opposed to "THIS simple idea of red"). We would need, for example, the result of backing away from a fire hydrant (and perhaps the whole procedure of backing away would be included), and then the result of similarly backing away from a red Rothko painting,

[23] So Garrett's argument that color patches are "type" simple, but not "token" simple (i.e. *minima sensibilia*) is good, but he is wrong to restrict the result to colors and feels (1997: 60–64). For an entirely different approach to *minima sensibilia* in Hume, see Waxman (1994).

etc. This is how one would get resembling distinguish*ings* of simple ideas to which the word "red" could be appropriately associated. To build the Revival Set for the most general idea of simple ideas, yet another level of complexity is required. One would need to incorporate the Revival Set for simple idea of red just described, but also the similarly describable Revival Sets for the simple idea of apple-smell, the simple idea of apple-taste, and some of the other kinds of simple ideas of which one has ideas (e.g. various shades of blue, various timbres of middle-C, etc.).

The result would be a set of sets that resemble each other in virtue of being the Revival Sets for ideas of kinds of simple ideas. After all this, if everything goes correctly, one would be prepared to meaningfully use the general term "simple idea" When one encountered the phrase "simple idea" one would recall an element of this Revival Set. It might be the element that is itself the Revival Set for "simple idea of red." Furthermore, recalling Hume and Berkeley on the function of general terms and ideas made general, one would be disposed to recall other members of the grand Revival set when appropriately prompted.

From one perspective, this all seems fantastically and monstrously complex. The complexity is, however, built from readily understood elements. And consider that giving the details of how to build a macroscopic sample of liquid mercury from individual atoms would also be unimaginably complex. But that complexity does not detract from the explanatory power of atomic theory because the theory's explanations do not require the explicit display of the complex construction.

There is another helpful consideration that the early moderns were not themselves always very clear about. The meaning of a term is given by the mental item with which it is regularly and appropriately associated. One does not know the meaning of a term unless one can have the appropriate perception. It is nevertheless possible in real life to use a term with good practical effect without at that time perceiving its meaning. This is like using a banknote to pay for a valuable commodity without thinking about, or even being able to think about, the complex circumstances that make the banknote valuable. Remembering this pragmatic consideration will forestall the objection that a theorist of ideas would have to explicitly make use of the Revival Set every time she effectively used the term 'simple idea' in everyday philosophical discourse. Again, one would need to perform this feat to know fully the meaning of the term, or to be theoretically *justified* in using it.

The theoretical device just described solves the final problem facing the use of particular simple ideas in the theory of ideas. It was necessary to provide genuine Empiricist bona fides for these theoretical simple ideas. That, in turn, made it necessary to show that there is an *idea of* a simple idea, and that this general *idea of* a simple idea is not innate in a bad sense, but is acquired through experience. We have now detailed how it is that the general idea of a simple idea is grounded in our experience of complex ideas. The result is not any particular simple idea that can be experienced as such. We hope it no longer sounds paradoxical to assert that the idea of a simple idea is not itself a simple idea. The important conclusion that can now be drawn is that the theorist of ideas has an internally consistent justification for appealing to simple ideas when explaining the phenomena of experience.

7. Primary and secondary qualities

Having given this account of the meaning of "simple idea" in terms of the Revival Set associated with the words "simple idea", there is still a pressing, unanswered question about the whole story. We might wonder what *quality* simple ideas have in common that makes them all simple. In respect of what do they resemble each other such that we group them under the kind, simple idea? We have argued that all it is to *be* a simple idea is to belong to the Revival Set of "simple idea". Belonging to this Revival Set requires only that some idea of a simple idea *resemble* the other ideas in that set. Hume is committed to denying the independent, extrinsic reality of relations between ideas, including that of resemblance.[24] So, what is it for some idea of a kind of simple idea to resemble the other ideas in the Revival Set of "simple ideas"? The answer is that it amounts to no more than *those* two ideas belonging to the even larger Revival Set of "resemblance". What all of this implies is that our earlier claim that Hume is committed to simple ideas comes to little more than the claim that he can get us to associate certain ideas with the words "simple ideas". *That* is not much of a substantial claim at all.

But are complex ideas *really* complexes of simple ideas? Does Hume believe in these non-experienced items? Do they really exist, or is that no more than a useful story we tell? The first thing to notice about this question is that the kind of worry behind it applies equally to many other doctrines of Hume's philosophy. The worry, in short, is that Hume's commitment to (for example) simple ideas is highly deflationary. Of course, almost every belief and assertion receives a deflationary analysis in his theory of ideas—that is part of the point of the theory. If it turns out *Hume's* distinction between theoretical entities to be believed in and those not to be believed is not an inflationary reading of the distinction, then that should come as no surprise.

Hume's deflationary strategy is supplemented by more explanatory details that help his case. In particular, two related topics immediately present themselves as worthy of consideration. First, to believe in a Humean way in the *existence* of a thing is to stop short of a philosophical eliminativism with respect to that thing. We attempt to exploit this by taking a detour to see what it would mean for Hume to believe in the existence of simple ideas. Secondly, there seems to be a certain parallel between Hume's commitment to the simple/complex distinction and his commitment to the impression/idea distinction. So, another brief detour to explore this analogy also seems worth making. We will begin with belief and existence. Here is Hume on the nature of belief in the existence of a thing:

[24] Russow (1980) brings out why Hume must take this position and the trouble that it causes him to do so.

'Tis also evident, that the idea of existence is nothing different from the idea of any object, and that when after the simple conception of any thing we wou'd conceive it as existent, we in reality make no addition to or alteration on our first idea. Thus when we affirm, that God is existent, we simply form the idea of such a being, as he is represented to us (T 1.3.7.2)

Since our idea of simple ideas is a general idea, this passage implies that to affirm the existence of simple ideas is just to *have* that general idea. Of course, there is another factor required for belief.

An opinion, therefore, or belief may be most accurately defin'd, a lively idea related to or associated with a present impressions (T 1.3.7.5)

To believe in simple ideas will be to have i) the general idea "simple ideas", ii) for this idea to be *lively*, and iii) for this liveliness to be the result of an association with a present impression (for instance, an impression which is particularly well suited to trigger our disposition to recall the Revival Set of "simple ideas"). Of course, most humans will never affirm the general idea of simple ideas, let alone have the idea with considerable liveliness. What could vivify it?

Perhaps the best way to answer this question is by contrasting the case at hand (one in which we have a properly enlivened idea) with its opposite (one in which we have an idea of a thing, but this idea is not properly enlivened). It is important to remember as usual we are not here trying to make the case that *Hume's* accounts of belief, or realism, etc., are things that everyone should find convincing today. We are merely trying to bring out the relevant contrasts that we can draw on Hume's behalf between believing in simple ideas, and not doing so. The worry, again, was that given what Hume has to say about general ideas, association, and resemblance, a belief in simple ideas amounts to little more than being trained to recall certain ideas (to wit, elements of the Revival Set of "simple ideas") upon, for example, hearing the words "simple ideas". The example we are about to describe should, if successful, show that simple ideas have more status than that.

Before we proceed, it will be helpful to distinguish two kinds of cases of belief that necessitate different treatments. The first is a case of a singular idea, the object of which is believed in. This is the kind of case with which Hume is most explicitly concerned in the *Treatise*, and involves a simple and straightforward application of his account of belief. To believe in such an object is just for the idea of that object to be properly enlivened. We will not be concerned with this kind of case because, as we have already seen, our idea of simple ideas is decidedly a *general, non-singular* idea, and so needs to be treated slightly differently. This case is more complicated because here it is unclear exactly *what* is to be believed. Since the *content* of a general idea is just the sum of the content of the ideas in the Revival Set, one possibility is that what is believed in is the existence of the objects of all of these ideas. But it seems psychologically impossible that a present impression vivify the whole Revival Set at once. Another possibility is that Hume never intended for his account of belief to be applied to general ideas. That is a genuine possibility, but there are good reasons to reject it.[25] What we suggest, therefore, is that when a general idea is believed, what is believed is that the Revival Set captures a real difference between the ideas in it and those that are not. Obviously, this suggestion seems to be directly contrary to the position of our interlocutor, who (correctly) maintains that Hume does not believe in the reality of relations. We will argue that, despite appearances, inappropriately reified relations are not involved. Now to turn to our example.

Consider the hypothetical general idea "glorp", for which the Revival Set is five arbitrarily chosen items from around the room Hume used as a study. Suppose, as an experiment, that we trained some subjects to have the idea of one of these objects, and to be disposed to recall the other four upon further prompting when hearing the word "glorp". This would be sufficient for the subjects' having the general idea "glorp". Now further suppose that the subjects understand that "glorp" is an arbitrarily constructed general idea with little use. Upon listening to the word "glorp", each subject would recall his idea of one of these objects, and be disposed to recall the others upon further prompting, but most would not be particularly moved by these mental processes. Most would be rather indifferent to them and be easily distracted, though it is easy to imagine that a few extremely zealous subjects would become obsessed with "glorp"—leave them aside.

Now suppose that the normal subjects also had command of such general ideas as "dog", "person", "water", etc. Again, presumably, these general ideas would function somewhat differently in their mental lives. They would occur more frequently, forcefully, and vivaciously, with more liveliness to them.[26] These general ideas could be considered ones in which the subjects strongly *believed*, in contrast to "glorp", in which they could be considered to have no strong belief. The example illustrates how some general ideas, or concepts, are found to be *better* than others. It is probably not possible to give more than a very broad characterization of how belief tracks what is "better." It has much to do with the frequency with which the particulars are encountered, the practical import of these encounters, the broadly construed utility of the general idea, how closely the particulars and the general idea are integrated into one's overall cognitive economy, etc. We can nevertheless conclude that it is not trivial to say that there is an important difference between "glorp" and "dog". Since Hume has *a* way of capturing this difference, even if it is not an ordinary way of doing so, he a fortiori has some way of capturing the difference between believing in the existence of certain general ideas and not others. Hume can describe a kind of realism about "dog"

[25] Here are two such reasons. First there is no prime facie reason for thinking that we *cannot* believe in general ideas, and all things being equal, it would be best if Hume had an explanation of what such beliefs amount to. Second, as we will see a bit farther on, there is good sense to be made of the impression/idea distinction that *only* works on the supposition that there is a sensible contrast to be made between good and bad distinctions, or between general ideas properly and improperly believed.

[26] It is a well-known challenge to Hume's Theory of ideas to find a precise explication of the various adjectives Hume uses for "manners" of perception: lively, vivacious, forceful, etc.

and a correlative anti-realism about "glorp". One interesting complication is that our subjects might believe in the existence of the objects of each of the singular ideas in the Revival Sets of "dog", "person", "water", and "glorp" equally. In fact, it seems reasonable to suppose that because they know that the objects in the Revival Set of "glorp" all exist, whereas *not* all of the objects in the Revival Set of "dog" exist (Cerebus, for instance), the particular singular ideas in the Revival Set of "glorp" might be *more* lively than some of those in the Revival Set of "dog". This suggests that the way in which singular and general belief work are subtly different. More technically, the general term "belief" must itself have at least two elements, themselves Revival Sets for the different kinds of belief, in *its* Revival Set. That is yet another illustration of how Hume's theory can handle by brute force problems arising from applying the theory to its own theoretical vocabulary.

Another, more substantial example might help here. Consider the distinction, so important in the *Treatise*, between impressions and ideas. Whether one takes this distinction to consist in a difference in degree of force and vivacity, a difference in relation to the external world, a difference in their status as copies, etc, it is clear that Hume thinks that there is *some* important difference between these two kinds of perceptions. If there were no difference, then Hume's claim that all simple ideas are copies of some simple impression would be worthless. So whatever else has been said in defense of our interpretation of the simple/complex distinction, if *that* distinction fails to amount to anything on the grounds that *no* such distinction can amount to anything, then the impression/idea distinction, along with everything in the theory of ideas that rests on that distinction, falls with it.

Now, we have seen that we cannot defend these distinctions in virtue of their reflecting real relations in which their objects stand to one another. They don't; Hume has no place in his philosophical theory for real relations. How then can Hume make a defensible case that distinctions such as impression/idea and simple/complex are importantly different from ones such as "glorp"/"non-glorp"? In order to answer these questions we would like to quickly walk through a certain interpretation of Hume's presentation of the impression/idea distinction to see exactly how he *does*, in fact, think of that distinction. According to that interpretation the difference between an impression and an idea is that the latter, but not the former, is a copy of some other mental entity. It is not the plausibility of this interpretation of that distinction that concerns us here, but rather one of the interesting moves that gets made in its defense.

According to this interpretation of the impression/idea distinction, what Hume does in the opening paragraph of the *Treatise* is not to present the criteria for distinguishing an impression from an idea. He instead merely makes various moves to call the reader's attention to a distinction with which his reader is supposed to be antecedently acquainted. He cites paradigm examples of both impressions and ideas: sensations, passions, emotions, memories, etc. He offers such phenomenological indicators as higher and lower degrees of force and vivacity. He presents the closely related common-sense distinction between feeling and thinking. Suppose that all of these moves are made simply in order to prepare the reader to acquire the proper Revival Sets for "impression" and "idea". The move we are interested in happens next, a couple of paragraphs along. This is where Hume offers evidence that the distinction between this pair of general ideas is *mere* association, plus something more (T 1.1.1.8). He presents evidence, that the distinction we now draw between impressions and ideas is in fact *grounded* in the distinction between perceptions that are copies of other perceptions, and those that are not. The question before us now is in what this grounding consists. Given that Hume is here engaged in a self-proclaimed scientific examination of human nature, one plausible suggestion is that a refined version of the pre-theoretical distinction is codified as a principle in the scientific theory. That is, what Hume discovers upon his examination of the pre-theoretical distinction is that, when properly construed as a distinction between copies and non-copies, the refined distinction is able to do important scientific explanatory work. In particular, it can do all the work that Hume subsequently has it do throughout the *Treatise*.

8. Conclusion

The suggestion we have defended is that the employment of an idea in a theory is legitimate if it serves some scientific-explanatory purpose. The impression/idea distinction is legitimate because it does important work in Hume's science of human nature. We have argued that the simple/complex distinction can be legitimated along exactly similar lines. Hume's science of human nature cannot proceed without the simple/complex distinction. It is indispensable. This distinction is therefore of a privileged kind and occupies a logical place of special importance. It ought to be counted among those distinctions, or general terms, that have scientific-explanatory value, and are thus not merely arbitrary. While it is nevertheless incorrect to say that the simple/complex distinction represents an (ontologically) *real* relation between mental entities, it is correct to say that Hume is a (scientific) real*ist* about the distinction.

The distinction between primary and secondary qualities can be handled in the same way. Purely from the perspective of Hume's Theory of ideas, the distinction is wholly arbitrary, which is to say that the distinction cannot be drawn metaphysically. But if an important practice, namely the practice of natural science, makes customary the appropriate Revival Sets, then Hume can explain how scientists are committed to a primary/secondary quality distinction in the same way that Hume's own theory is committed to the simple/complex distinction.

One interesting consequence of this essay's interpretation is that much is ultimately made to rest on the gap between what is pre-theoretical and what belongs to the technical apparatus of the Theory of ideas. The simple/complex and impression/idea divisions in the Theory are both refinements of what is available to common sense. But now, how are we to understand the distinction between the pre-theoretical and the theoretical themselves? Is this distinction itself something explained by the Theory? If we say it is, then we are ultimately responsible for characterizing the Revival Set for the term "Theory of ideas" or for the term "science of human nature", and well-known problems of self-reference might emerge[27]. If we say the distinction between the pre-theoretical and the theoretical is itself somehow extra-theoretical, then it seems that a proper foundation for the entire enterprise might be lacking. Theorists are trained to develop the appropriate Revival Sets for their theoretical apparatuses. But that is not enough; giving their technical ideas the necessary liveliness means that these ideas will play an important pragmatic role in the lives of the theorists. Hume was well aware of how hard it is to maintain those practices and attitudes and he expressed the difficulty vividly:

> I dine, I play a game of back-gammon, I converse, and am merry with my friends; and when after three or four hour's amusement, I wou'd return to these [theoretical] speculations, they appear so cold, and strain'd, and ridiculous, that I cannot find in my heart to enter into them any farther. (T 1.4.7.8)

The facts of human nature dictate that the theory of human nature has an intermittent grip and that the knowledge it delivers finds a rather modest place in the hurly-burly of life.[28]

Bibliography

Ainslie, Donald. 2008. "Hume on Personal Identity," in Radcliffe, E., ed. *A Companion to Hume*, Oxford: Blackwell.

Allison, Henry. 2008. *Custom and Reason in Hume*, Oxford: Oxford University Press.

Baillie, James. 2000. *Hume on Morality*, London: Routledge.

Baxter, Donald. 1997. "Abstraction, Inseparability, and Identity," *Philosophy and Phenomenological Research* 57: 307–30.

Bennett, Jonathan. 2001. *Learning from Six Philosophers*, Vol. 2, Oxford: Oxford University Press.

Brown, D. Kenneth. 2006. "The Strict Interpretation of Locke's Theory of Ideas," Ph.D dissertation, University of California, Irvine.

Chappell, Vere. 1994. "Locke's Theory of Ideas," in ed. Chappell, *The Cambridge Companion to Locke*, Cambridge: Cambridge University Press.

Garrett, Don. 1981. "Hume's Self-Doubts about Personal Identity," *The Philosophical Review* 90: 337–58.

—— 1997. *Cognition and Commitment in Hume's Philosophy*, New York: Oxford University Press.

Hume, David. 1739–40/2007. *A Treatise of Human Nature*, eds. David F. Norton and Mary J. Norton, Oxford: Oxford University Press.

—— 1755/2006. *An Enquiry Concerning Human Understanding*, ed. Tom L. Beauchamp, Oxford: Oxford University Press.

27 In a much later empiricist work, Bas van Fraassen (1980) argued that the divide between what is observable and unobservable is itself to be settled by the best available empirical theories. Our interpretation of Hume shows how some motivation for that doctrine is already present in his Theory of ideas.

28 Some of the ideas in this chapter were presented at the 2008 conference of the International Berkeley Society. We thank the participants there and also Ken Brown, Don Garrett, Emily Kelahan, Thomas Lennon, Larry Nolan, Matt Priselac, and OUP's anonymous readers for helpful suggestions.

Jacovides, Michael. 2007. "Locke's Distinctions between Primary and Secondary Qualities," in Lex Newman ed., *The Cambridge Companion to Locke's* Essay Concerning Human Understanding, Cambridge: Cambridge University Press.

Laird, John. 1932. *Hume's Philosophy of Human Nature*, London: Methuen.

Landy, David. 2006. "Hume's Impression-Idea Distinction," *Hume Studies* 32: 119–39.

—— 2007. "A (Sellarsian) Kantian Critique of Hume's Theory of Concepts," *Pacific Philosophical Quarterly* 88: 445–57.

—— (forthcoming). "The Premise That Even Hume Must Accept," *Self, Language, and World: Essays to celebrate the work of Jay F. Rosenberg*, eds. Jim O'Shea and Eric Rubenstein.

Locke, John. 1690/1975. *An Essay concerning Human Understanding*, ed. P. Nidditch, Oxford: Oxford University Press.

Luce A. A. and T. E. Jessop (eds.). 1948–57. *The Works of George Berkeley, Bishop of Cloyne*, 9 Vols, London: Nelson.

Russow, Lilly-Marlene. 1980. "Simple Ideas and Resemblance," *The Philosophical Quarterly* 30: 342–50.

Stroud, Barry. 1977. *Hume*. London: Routledge.

van Fraassen, Bas. 1980. *The Scientific Image*. Oxford: Oxford University Press.

Waxman, Wayne. 1994. *Hume's Theory of Consciousness*. Cambridge: Cambridge University Press.

Westphal, Jonathan. 1984. "The Complexity of Quality," *Philosophy*, 59: 457–71.

Winkler, Kenneth. 1989. *Berkeley: An Interpretation*, Oxford: Oxford University Press.

—— 1992. "Ideas, Sentiments, and Qualities," in *Minds, Ideas, and Objects*, eds. P. Cummins and G. Zoeller, Atascadero, CA: Ridgeview Publishing Company.

10

Hume and the Sensible Qualities

Kenneth P. Winkler

1. Introduction

In Hume's estimation, what makes "the modern philosophy" modern is, above all, its treatment of the sensible qualities.[1] Nature, as the modern philosophy represents it, is conveniently austere: a world of corpuscles in space, stripped of the forms and qualities of earlier philosophy and ready for brisk intellectual handling. "The new Philosophy," as even the skeptic Pierre Huet marveled, "is founded upon so small a Number of Principles, and those so pure and simple."[2] In the *Essay concerning Human Understanding*, Locke had described himself as clearing rubbish from the path of advancing master scientists.[3] When, half a century later, Hume published his *Treatise of Human Nature*, it seemed to him that the rubbish—the fictions of the ancient philosophers—was very nearly gone. Some of the rubbish had, Hume thought, been relatively easy to remove:[4]

> There is a very remarkable inclination in human nature, to bestow on external objects the same emotions, which it observes in itself; and to find every where those ideas, which are most present to it. This inclination, 'tis true, is suppress'd by a little reflection, and only takes place in children, poets, and the antient philosophers. It appears in children, by their desire of beating the stones, which hurt them: In poets, by their readiness to personify every thing: And in the ancient philosophers, by . . . fictions of sympathy and antipathy. We must pardon children, because of their age; poets, because they profess to follow implicitly the suggestions of their fancy: But what excuse shall we find to justify our philosophers in so signal a weakness?
>
> (T 1.4.3.11; SBN 224–5)

[1] An earlier version of this paper was presented to the Society for Early Modern Philosophy at Yale. I am grateful to Tim Clarke, Michael Della Rocca, Charles More, and Ian Proops for questions and advice, and to Jani Hakkarainen for written comments. I am also indebted to an anonymous referee for the Press, whose thoughtful comments led to several improvements.

[2] *A philosophical treatise concerning the weakness of human understanding* (London: Gysbert Dummer, 1725), 5.

[3] *An Essay concerning Human Understanding*, edited by Peter H. Nidditch (Oxford: Clarendon Press, 1975), The Epistle to the Reader, 9–10.

[4] I quote from David Hume, *A Treatise of Human Nature* ("T"), edited by David Fate Norton and Mary J. Norton (Oxford: Oxford University Press, 2000), citing passages, as the editors do, by book, part, section, and paragraph. I also provide page numbers to David Hume, *A Treatise of Human Nature*, second edition ("SBN"), edited by L. A. Selby-Bigge and P. H. Nidditch (Oxford: Clarendon Press, 1978).

Other fictions were, however, harder to clear away. When Ralph Cudworth, for example, described nature, "in its naked Hue," as "nothing but a Heap of Dust or Atoms, of several Figures and Magnitudes, variously agitated up and down," it was hard not to feel some disappointment.[5] What had become of its engaging colors, sounds, tastes, and odors, its soothing warmth and bitter cold? For Cudworth these were "not properly the Modifications of Bodies themselves, but several Modifications, Passions and Affections of our own Souls." Here Cudworth articulates what is, according to Hume, "the fundamental principle" of the modern philosophy, the opinion that "colors, sounds, tastes, smells, heat and cold" are "nothing but impressions in the mind" (T 1.4.4.3; SBN 226). When we think of these qualities unphilosophically, as qualities really existing in nature, Cudworth grants, "they do in a manner mock us." Yet, he adds, "it was not the Intention of God or Nature to abuse us herein, but a most wise Contrivance thus to beautify and adorn the visible and material World, to add Lustre or Imbellishment to it, that it might have Charms, Relishes, and Allurements in it, to gratify our Appetites." But can the world continue to charm and gratify us if, as followers of the modern philosophy, we suspend our tendency to project "our own Shadows, the vital passive Energies of our own Souls" onto things themselves? At least one poet, who may have been following Cudworth, thought it could. Were it not for the "pow'rful charm" of our senses, wrote Edward Young—the charm being, I assume, a spell our senses cast—"Earth were a rude, uncolour'd chaos still." "*Objects*," he continues, "are but th' occasion: ours th' *exploit*;/Ours is the cloth, the pencil, and the paint,/Which nature's admirable picture draws,/And beautifies creation's ample dome."[6] In Young's view even a poet can think clear-headedly about the natural world and be fully animated by its charms—charms the poet knows it to occasion, not to contain.

My aim in this paper is to better understand Hume's response to the modern philosophy and its "fundamental principle." Does he endorse it? Does he offer divergent assessments of it in the *Treatise* and the *Enquiry*? Can he rely on the modern philosophy in his account of moral judgment, as he does in the following passage from the *Treatise*?

> Vice and virtue... may be compar'd to sounds, colours, heat and cold, which, according to modern philosophy, are not qualities in objects, but perceptions in the mind: And this discovery in morals, like that other in physics, is to be regarded as a considerable advancement of the speculative sciences.... (T 3.1.1.26; SBN 469)

And can he accept the suggestion, made by Cudworth and Young, that passionate engagement in the world of our senses can survive intellectual entry into the world of

[5] From *A Treatise concerning Eternal and Immutable Morality*, in *British Moralists*, 2 volumes, edited by L. A. Selby-Bigge (Oxford: Clarendon Press, 1897), 2: 263.

[6] Edward Young, *Night thoughts on life, death, and immortality* (London: J. French and others, 1777), 2 volumes, 1: 203, lines 429–434.

the modern philosophers—that we can take the world's colors seriously even after outgrowing (or if outgrowing is too much to ask for, gaining perspective on) the projective tendencies of infancy?

The last of these interpretive questions it the only one that can be answered easily. In Hume's view the modern philosophy leaves common life pretty much as it was. The passage just quoted concludes with the observation that the mentioned discovery in morals, "like that [in physics]," has "little or no influence on practice," an observation echoed in the following passage from Hume's character study of "The Sceptic":[7]

> Were I not afraid of appearing too philosophical, I should remind my reader of that famous doctrine, supposed to be fully proved in modern times, "That tastes and colours, and all other sensible qualities, lie not in the bodies, but merely in the senses." The case is the same with beauty and deformity, virtue and vice. This doctrine, however, takes off no more from the reality of the latter qualities, than from that of the former; nor need it give any umbrage either to critics to moralists. Though colours were allowed to lie only in the eye, would dyers or painters even be less regarded or esteemed? There is a sufficient uniformity of the senses and feelings of mankind, to make all these qualities the objects of art and reasoning, and to have the greatest influence on life and manners. And as it is certain, that the discovery above-mentioned in natural philosophy, makes no alteration on actions and conduct; why should a like discovery in moral philosophy make any alteration?

Hume uses "sensible qualities" in two ways: as an all-purpose label for the qualities available to sense (for example at T 1.4.3.2 [SBN 219] and 1.4.3.7 [SBN222]), and as a way of designating the secondary qualities in particular (for example at *An Enquiry concerning Human Understanding* 12.16 [SBN 155]).[8] In the next section of the paper, I will try to clarify this apparent carelessness, present not only in Hume but in Berkeley. I will try as well to exhibit some of the other conceptual "potentials"—ambiguities and occasions for divergence of opinion—in early modern ways of speaking and thinking about sensible and secondary qualities. Hume discusses sensible qualities, or adverts to them, at many points in his philosophical writings, but his treatment of "the modern philosophy" in section 4 of the fourth and final part of Book I of the *Treatise* lies at the center of his thinking about them, and in subsequent sections I will examine it, along with the briefer treatment of the same topic in part 1 of section 12 of the *Enquiry*. Commentators have worked very closely through the fourth part of Book I, but "Of the modern philosophy" has received comparatively scant attention. Its significance for Hume's philosophy as a whole is, I think, much greater than most of its interpreters realize. I take up *Treatise* I i 4 and *Enquiry* 12 i in the third section of the paper, where

[7] I quote from David Hume, *Essays Moral, Political, and Literary*, revised edition, edited by Eugene F. Miller (Indianapolis: Liberty Fund, 1987), 166.

[8] I use David Hume, *An Enquiry concerning Human Understanding* (hereafter "EHU"), edited by Tom L. Beauchamp (Oxford: Clarendon Press, 2000), and follow Beauchamp in citing passages by section and paragraph. I also provide page numbers in David Hume, *Enquiries concerning Human Understanding and concerning the Principles of Morals*, third edition, edited by L. A. Selby-Bigge and P. H. Nidditch ("SBN") (Oxford: Clarendon Press, 1975).

I examine three ways in which Hume uses perceptual relativity. I will then discuss, in section 4 of the paper, a difficulty into which the third use leads him. Hume, I will suggest, is pulled in opposite directions by competing conceptions of belief in objectivity. I do not think Hume unambiguously indicates the direction in which he wants, all things considered, to move. In the fifth and final section I will consider how he *might* have moved. I conclude, rather bleakly, that Hume probably cannot be satisfied by any philosophy of the sensible qualities that he is in a position to provide.

2. The sensible and the secondary

In his valuable study *Hume's Scepticism and Realism: Two* Profound *Arguments against the Senses in* An Enquiry concerning Human Understanding, Jani Hakkarainen makes some pregnant observations about sensible and secondary qualities.[9] First, he notices that in some of Hume's predecessors, among them Locke, the expressions "sensible quality" and "secondary quality" do not function in the same way. Locke, he proposes, uses "secondary quality" to pick out a power in a body, while he uses "sensible quality" to pick out a qualitative property perceived by one of the five senses (p. 99). In general, when Locke, Descartes, and Malebranche say of sensible qualities that they exist not in things but in the mind, they are, in Hakkarainen's view, contemplating what we now call *qualia*, the qualities immediately present in sensation (p. 102). Hakkarainen then proposes that in the following passage from the *Enquiry*, Hume is likewise thinking about sensible qualities so understood, rather than about secondary qualities viewed (as according to Locke they should be) as powers in bodies:

> It is universally allowed by modern enquirers, that all the sensible qualities of objects, such as hard, soft, hot, cold, white, black *&c.* are merely secondary, and exist not in the objects themselves, but are perceptions of the mind, without any external archetype or model, which they represent. (EHU 12.15; SBN 154)

What is universally allowed, according to Hakkarainen's Hume, is not that Lockean secondary qualities exist in the mind, but that sensible qualities do (p. 103). Hume, as Hakkarainen reads him, is well aware that secondary qualities, as Locke understands them, are not in the mind but in objects (p. 104).[10]

Without examining Hakkarainen's specific observations about Locke and Hume's reading of Locke, which deserve more discussion than I can give them here, I want to build and enlarge on his incontestable insight into the conceptual separation of the sensible and the secondary by examining passages from a diverse collection of seventeenth- and early eighteenth-century writers. My aim is to exhibit both the conceptual

[9] Published in Tampere, Finland by the Tampere University Press (Acta Universitatis Tamperensis 1267), 2007.

[10] For a very different argument that Hume does not misread Locke, see P. J. E. Kail, *Projection and Realism in Hume's Philosophy* (Oxford: Oxford University Press, 2007), 151–8.

separation Hakkarainen has identified, as well as the various "potentials" to which it gives rise.[11]

I will begin with a passage from Robert Boyle. In *Certain physiological essays and other tracts* (1661), Boyle describes an experiment that "affords us an instance, by which we may discern that Motion, Figure, and Disposition of parts, and such like primary and mechanical Affections (if I may so call them) of Matter, may suffice to produce those more secondary Affections of Bodies which are wont to be called sensible qualities" (section xii, p. 137).[12] Here Boyle excuses himself for speaking of motion, figure, and the disposition of parts as primary and mechanical affections of matter, which suggests that this part of his vocabulary is innovative, but says that the more secondary affections of body are *wont* to be called sensible qualities, which suggests that here, he is taking advantage of already established usage. Other seventeenth-century texts seem to support these suggestions. The already established difference between a "primary" and "secondary" quality, which I will discuss first, was roughly this: a primary quality was viewed as fundamental, and a secondary quality was viewed as derivative. The contrast between primary and secondary was already established as a *topic-neutral* contrast in explanatory role.

Before Boyle, and for a wide variety of purposes, seventeenth-century writers distinguished between primary and secondary qualities. Henry Burton, for example, in *Truth's triumph over Trent: or, the great gulfe between Sion and Babylon* (1629), distinguished between "the prime property" of believing, which is faith, and the "secondary qualities" of it, which include "acts of hoping of louing" (chapter 7, p. 104).[13] In *Three books of occult philosophy* (1651), Henry Cornelius Agrippa distinguishes between the

[11] This conceptual separation has been discussed by many commentators, among them William Hamilton (in Note D to his edition of *The Works of Thomas Reid*, two volumes [Edinburgh: Maclachlan and Stewart, 1863], 825–45), to whom Hakkarainen refers. A distinction between sensible and secondary qualities figures prominently in some recent work on Locke and Boyle. See, for example, Peter Alexander, *Ideas, Qualities and Corpuscles: Locke and Boyle on the External World* (Cambridge: Cambridge University Press, 1985), 168–82, and especially Peter J. Anstey, *The Philosophy of Robert Boyle* (London: Routledge, 2000), whose richly documented account of "Distinctions among the qualities" (chapter 1 of his book, 17–38) ranges far beyond Boyle. The broad outlines of what I go on to say will therefore be familiar to many readers. What I offer is deliberately modeled on the methods of German historians of social and political concepts practicing what they call *Begriffgeschichte*. For general discussion of their methods, see Reinhart Koselleck, "*Begriffgeschichte* and Social History," in his *Futures Past: On the Semantics of Historical Time*, translated by Keith Tribe (New York: Columbia University Press, 2004), 75–92, and Melvin Richter, *The History of Political and Social Concepts: A Critical Introduction* (New York: Oxford University Press, 1995). For an extended example, see Koselleck, "The Historical-Political Semantics of Asymmetric Counterconcepts," 155–91 in *Futures Past*. For an example relevant to the present paper (but dealing with familiar philosophical texts, rather than with the less canonical materials—dictionaries, for example—that have drawn the attention of *Begriffgeschichte* historians of social and political concepts, and that I sometimes make use of here), see "Qualität," in *Historisches Wörterbuch der Philosophie*, ed. Joachim Ritter and Karlfried Gründer, 13 volumes (Basel and Stuttgart, 1971–2007), volume 7, panels 1748–80.

[12] The passage appears in "A Physico-Chemical Essay, containing and Experiment with Some Considerations touching... Salt-Petre." *Certain physiological essays* was published in London by Henry Herringman in 1661.

[13] Published in London by Mich. Sparke.

virtues of things that are "Elementary" or "first qualities" and the "secondary qualities" or virtues that "follow the nature, and proportion" of the "first vertues" (chapter 9, p. 22).[14] His list of first virtues includes "to heat, to cool, to moisten, [and] to dry"; the secondary qualities (to dip selectively into a very long list) include "digesting, . . . mollifying, hardening, . . . corroding, burning, . . . evaporating" and "many more."[15] The distinction between primary and secondary qualities is, for these authors, a distinction between causally (or perhaps constitutively) fundamental qualities and causally (or constitutively) derivative ones. It is an abstract, topic-neutral, or syncategorematic distinction with no particular connection to mechanism—or, I suspect, to any particular body of theory or doctrine. Boyle simply takes it over and therefore does not pause to explain or justify his use of it: his is a use of "primary" and "secondary" already vested in the words themselves, which his readers would very readily appreciate.

Confirmation of my suggestion comes from a source more familiar to philosophers: the first part of the *Elements of Philosophy* (1656), "*COMPUTATION or LOGIQUE*," by Thomas Hobbes.[16] There (p. 19) Hobbes divides not the qualities of things but the acts or operations of perceiving them into "primary" and "secondary." The primary operations of perception are seeing, hearing, smelling, tasting, and touching. The secondary are "Imagination" and pleasant or unpleasant "Affection." It seems clear that imagination and affection count as "secondary" modes of perception because they derive from sense.

The evidence I have assembled so far is selective and probably insufficient to support a final judgment, but it strongly suggests not only that "primary" and "secondary" were not, when Boyle used them and Locke repeated them, anything like the terms of art they are for philosophers today, but that neither Boyle nor Locke ever expected them to become terms of art. Their qualities were "primary" and "secondary" in perfectly familiar dictionary senses of those words. Primary qualities might also be (and were) called "elementary." They are basic in the order of explanation, or perhaps in the order of constitution. (Constitution can be viewed as a special case of explanation: the parts explain the whole, the elements entering into a composition explain the thing composed; the "principles" explain whatever it is that's derivative.) Thus we find Samuel Clarke, in his *Demonstration*, speaking of the secondary qualities as "compositions" of elements.[17]

[14] Henry Cornelius Agrippa von Nettesheim, *Three books of occult philosophy* (London: Gregory Moule, 1651).

[15] In his *Compound of alchymy* (London: Thomas Orwin, 1591), George Ripley describes a preparation that destroys "the first qualitie" and produces "secondary qualities more glorious" (on the third unnumbered page of the "Recapitulatio"), though I suppose these may be secondary simply in the sense of coming later in time.

[16] London: Andrew Crooke, 1656.

[17] See, for example, Samuel Clarke, *A Demonstration of the Being and Attributes of God*, edited by Ezio Vailati (Cambridge: Cambridge University Press, 1998), 39, 40, and 42.

The most compelling confirmation of my suggestion is the fact, widely acknowledged in the seventeenth century, that a distinction between first and second qualities was a long-standing element in the lexicon of Aristotelianism. According, for example, to Malebranche, the word "primary" is used by the Peripatetics for the qualities (heat and cold, wet and dry) that differentiate the four elements (p. 132 in the Lennon and Olscamp translation, as well as p. 473, 474, 477). In his longest discussion of this aspect of Aristotelianism, Malebranche distinguishes between the "elementary qualities" of Aristotle and the "secondary qualities" (*les qualitez secondes*) that are (tellingly, in view of Clarke's later use of the English-language equivalent) allegedly "composed" of them (p. 479). Elsewhere in the *Search after Truth*, Malebranche testifies to the prominent role of a distinction between "elementary" and "secondary" qualities in books, like the ones I have reviewed in recent paragraphs, dealing with "physics, medicine, chemistry, and all other specific areas of nature" (p. 242). The same Aristotelian vocabulary is discussed by Leibniz and examined in some detail, in the nineteenth century, by William Hamilton.[18]

Boyle's second suggestion is that "sensible quality" was a familiar label for qualities such as colors, tastes, and smells, and of course it was: "sensible quality" was the English-language equivalent of a long-established piece of Latin philosophical vocabulary (*qualitas sensibilis*). The expression "sensible qualities" is prominent not only in Boyle but in Cudworth's *True Intellectual System*, and its French counterpart (*les qualitez sensibles*) is equally prominent in Malebranche. Cudworth explicitly traces the term to the ancient philosophers. The *lists* of sensible qualities in seventeenth- and eighteenth-century writers were, however, extraordinarily varied. Kenelm Digby, in *Of bodies and of mans soul* (1669), writes that "the Sensible Qualities of Bodies are not any positive real thing," but are "merely the very body, as it affects our senses" (p. 305).[19] Light, he says, is the "principal" one among them (p. 48), a point later granted by Boyle: "I grant [light] to be the noblest of Sensible Qualities" (p. 116 in *A free inquiry into the vulgarly receiv'd notion of nature* [1686]).[20] Thomas Sprat, in his *History of the Royal-Society of London for the improving of natural knowledge* (1667), includes in his catalogue of experiments a "sort" that "are about those which are call'd *sensible Qualities*: as of freezing: of

[18] For Leibniz see, for example, "A New Method for Learning and Teaching Jurisprudence," 88–9 in Loemker, and "Letter to Jacob Thomasius," 100–1. For Hamilton see *The Works of Thomas Reid*, volume 2, 836 and the brief discussion of his views and those of Rudolf Eucken in "Qualität," *Historisches Wörterbuch* 7 (1989), panel 1759.

[19] London: John Williams, 1669.

[20] London: H. Clark for John Taylor, 1686. For remarks on light in more familiar sources, see Malebranche's *Search after Truth*, p. 48 in the translation by Thomas Lennon and Paul Olscamp (Columbus: Ohio State University Press, 1980); Locke at *Essay* III iv 10; and the opening section of Berkeley's *Principles*: "By sight I have the ideas of light and colours with their several degrees and variation" (in *The Works of George Berkeley, Bishop of Cloyne*, edited by A. A. Luce and T. E. Jessop, 9 volumes [London: Thomas Nelson, 1948–57], volume 2). Whether light is a sensible quality (*qualitas sensibilis*) is a question considered by St. Thomas in the *Summa Theologiae*, Ia 67 3. Wilkins, in his *Essay towards a real character* (London, 1668), classifies light as a "primary" visible quality and color as a "secondary visible quality" (pp. 214–15).

cold and heat: of freezing Water freed from Air: of the time, and manner of the contraction in freezing luke-warm Water: of the temperature of several places, by seal'd *Thermometer*, as of several Countries; of the bottom of deep Mines, Wells, Vaults, on the tops of Hills, and at the bottom of the Sea" (p. 224).[21] Light, sound, color, taste, and smell are, interestingly, the subjects of another sort of experiment, described on p. 225, which leads me to wonder whether "sensible," for Sprat, might have meant "tangible" or "sensible by touch." In the eighteenth century, Isaac Watts speaks of "*Body* or *Solid Extension*" as a "sufficient Subject or Support for any other *corporeal or Sensible Qualities*, whether it be Figure, Size, Colour, Motion, Rest, Resistance, Situation, *&c.* they all plainly subsist in *solid Extension* as in their Subject" (p. 52).[22] He contrasts them with "*intellectual* Qualities" such as consciousness, knowing, reasoning, doubting, fearing, hoping, wishing, and resolving.

Although the lists vary, the sensible qualities in question are all of course *sensed*. They are all *manifest*. And this, I think, is the contrast that gave "sensible quality" its primary early modern meaning. It was a way of designating our *mode of access* to a quality. It had nothing to do, at least not directly, with the quality's being (or not being) fundamental or derivative, but merely with the manner in which it was thought to be known.[23] To say a quality is known by sense is, of course, to say it is not unknown, but the more important contrasts are with other modes of cognitive access. For Watts, at least in the passage I have quoted, the governing "counter-concept" is what is known by purely intellectual means. But I believe that a more significant contrast was one between sensible or manifest qualities on the one hand and occult, hidden, or secret qualities on the other. This is the contrast emphasized by Ephraim Chambers in the article on "QUALITY" in his famous *Cyclopedia, or an universal dictionary of the arts and sciences.*[24] He explains that the Aristotelian philosophers "distinguished *Qualities* into *sensible* and *occult*":

> *Sensible*, or *manifest* Qualities, are those arising from certainly modifications of matter and which become immediately objects of our senses.
>
> *Occult* Qualities, are certain latent powers arising from the specific forms of things, whereof no rational solution can be given on any principles of physics.

In denying that occult qualities admit of "rational solution," Chambers plainly implies that they are not fundamental: that there is a pressing need to account for them (a need so far unmet, and perhaps doomed to remain so). His contrast, therefore, is not purely one of access. When Walter Charlton, in his *Physiologia* (1654), boasted of "occult qualities made manifest" (in the title of Book III, chapter xv, p. 341), he was hoping,

[21] London: J. Martyn, 1667.

[22] *Philosophical essays on various subjects*, third edition (London: James Brackstone, 1742).

[23] It is still used in this sense today, for example by Alex Byrne in "Sensory Qualities, Sensible Qualities, Sensational Qualities," in *The Oxford Handbook of Philosophy of Mind*, ed. Brian McLaughlin and Ansgar Beckermann (Oxford: Oxford University Press, 2009), 268–80.

[24] Second edition (London: D. Midwinter, 1738).

in effect, for a purer contrast, one that would render the word "occult" a less "unhappy and discouraging Epithite" (p. 341).[25] That occult qualities are in one way "*Immanifest*"—that is, insensible—need not mean that they are unintelligible (p. 341). "The *Insensibility* of a thing [need not] necessitate, nay, nor aggravate the *Unintelligibility* thereof," Charlton proclaims, there being "many things, which are above the sphere of the Senses" that "may yet be as much within the reach of our Reason, as the most sensible whatever" (p. 342). A pure contrast of access between the sensible and the occult is drawn by John Wilkins in his *Essay towards a real character, and a philosophical language* (1668): "BY SENSIBLE QUALITY is meant such kind of Quality as falls under our outward Senses, or the Affections of Bodies considered as they are Objects of Sense: To which may be opposed the Notion of OCCULT QUALITY" (p. 214). A similarly pure one is drawn by Johann Amos Comenius in *Natural philosophie reformed by divine light, or, A synopsis of physicks* (1651).[26] "*A manifest quality*," Comenius writes on p. 54, "*is, that which may be perceived by sense, and is therefore to be called sensible.*" "*An occult quality*," by contrast, "*is, that which is known only by experience, that is, by its effect,* (as the love of iron in the loadstone, &c.) *therefore it is called insensible*" (p. 55). His view seems to be that an occult quality is inferred from its effect as its postulated cause, on the basis of experience that accumulates over time.[27]

The root text for his entry, as Chambers indicates, is Aristotle's *De Anima*. In the post-Aristotelian tradition I have been tracing, the notion of a sensible quality is *epistemological*, while that of a secondary quality is ontological or *physical* (in the early modern sense of pertaining to the nature of things). This conceptual separation between the sensible and the secondary has a number of important consequences, but before discussing them I want to follow Chambers's remarks on an ambiguity I have already acknowledged in connection with Berkeley and Hume.

If, when we speak of sensible qualities, the regulating contrast is with qualities deemed hidden or occult, *all* of the Lockean primary and secondary qualities will have instances that qualify as "sensible."[28] When Berkeley and Hume speak of all such qualities as sensible, I believe this is the contrast they are activating. But if we want to distinguish between different modes of sensory access, we might find ourselves using the word "sensible" more narrowly. For example, we might want to use the word "sensible" to pick out those qualities we can access through one or another of the five senses and not by any other: those qualities *proper* to the various senses. If we attend to the fact that a quality can be accessed by the senses, taken collectively, we will think of the primary qualities as sensible qualities, as do many of the authors I have cited. But if we think in terms of qualities that can be accessed by one sense and not by others,

[25] London: Thomas Heath, 1654.

[26] London: Sa. Gellibrand, 1651.

[27] In "The Author's Epistle to the Reader" in his *Elements of Philosophy* (1656), Hobbes says that the fourth part of the book contains "the doctrine of Sensible Qualities" (first page, unnumbered). He seems to use "*Sensible Quality*" there for whatever qualities we find in "*Sensible Creatures*."

[28] Some instances, because they are qualities of insensible things, will not of course be sensible.

we will exclude the primary qualities, or some of them, because they are common sensibles. Chambers takes careful note of the relevant ambiguity. "In strictness," he says, "those only are said to be *sensible Qualities* which affect some one sense alone, as colour does the eye, sound the ear, *&c.*" (Here Chambers seems to be following Aristotle: "Of the objects which are perceived in themselves it is the special-objects which are the objects of perception properly" [*De Anima* 418a24, in D. W. Hamlyn's translation].) Francis Hutcheson likewise writes that the secondary qualities are "qualities which are sensible in the proper sense that we perceive each of them only by a single sense."[29] Later Chambers acknowledges the prevalence of a looser usage: "*Sensible Qualities*," he announces, "are usually subdivided into *primary* and *secondary*." In much the same way Hutcheson, after saying that only colors, sounds, smells, tastes, heat, and cold are qualities "in the proper sense," describes extension, figure, position, motion, and rest as the "primary and true qualities of bodies" (*Compend of Logic*, p. 12). The division, for both Chambers and Hutcheson, is explanatory, and has nothing (directly) to do with access—confirmation of the conceptual separation I have been emphasizing.

The first important consequence of the conceptual separation between the sensible and the secondary is that what might be called Boyle's thesis—that the sensible qualities (narrowly understood) are secondary—was not, in the seventeenth and early eighteenth centuries, the tautology it may now be to our ears, but a substantive thesis. To say that the sensible qualities are secondary is to say that a certain set of qualities, picked out by the way in which we come to know them, are causally or "physically" derivative. According to Boyle, those qualities derive from, and are explained by, the mechanical affections of matter. To call these affections "primary" is to assign them this explanatory role. We are now in a position to detect, in the passage from Hume's *Enquiry* brought forward so effectively by Hakkarainen, the meanings Hume himself is likely to have heard when he described "sensible qualities" as "secondary":

> It is universally allowed by modern enquirers, that all the sensible qualities of objects, such as hard, soft, hot, cold, white, black *&c.* are merely secondary, and exist not in the objects themselves, but are perceptions of the mind, without any external archetype or model, which they represent. (EHU 12.15; SBN 154)

That the sensible qualities (narrowly construed) are derivative, and derivable specifically from mechanical affections, is a boldly substantive claim. Note especially Hume's description of hard, soft, cold, and the others as *merely* secondary: the qualification would not be in place if "secondary" were simply a label attached to a list made by Locke. The qualities Hume identifies are *merely* secondary because they are *wholly* derivative: they have no archetype or model in things themselves.

[29] *A Compend of Logic*, p. 12 in Francis Hutcheson, *Logic, Metaphysics, and the Natural Sociability of Mankind*, edited by James Moore and Michael Silverthorne (Indianapolis: Liberty Fund, 2006).

A second consequence of the conceptual separation is the opening up of the following field of possibilities, created by the crosscutting of two opposed pairs of terms (see Table 10.1):

Table 10.1 The classification of qualities

	manifest or sensible	occult or hidden
primary or fundamental		
secondary or derivative		

Bulk and figure presumably fall in the upper left-hand corner, and color, taste, and odor in the space below. But what about gravity, which Hume sometimes includes among the primary qualities? If, as Hume conjectures, it is fundamental ("elasticity, gravity, cohesion of parts, communication of motion by impulse; these are probably the ultimate causes and principles which we shall ever discover in nature" [EHU 4.12; SBN 30])—that is, incapable of explanatory derivation—it belongs somewhere in the top line. But exactly where depends on how it is viewed. Samuel Clarke insisted (against Leibniz) that by "gravity," Newton had in mind a *phenomenon*, a pattern of behavior found in bodies. But many would balk at the classification of "phenomenal" gravity as manifest. It is certainly not manifest in the same way figure or color is. If, instead, gravity is viewed as the cause of a phenomenal pattern, it will be occult or hidden—a quality postulated by means of the kind of process outlined by Comenius. The word "occult" was, however, at least for many writers in the seventeenth and eighteenth centuries, a term of disapprobation, implying that anyone speaking of occult qualities was dealing irresponsibly in mysteries.[30] We might therefore want to introduce a new column for qualities that are *induced* or *hypothesized*. They resemble the more straightforwardly manifest qualities insofar as experiment or observation can verify their presence, but differ from them insofar as such verification is achievable only after an hypothesis defining them has been formulated. They resemble occult or hidden qualities insofar as their discovery depends on inference (an operation of reason or intellect rather than sense), but differ from them insofar as the inference is not from effect to cause. Newton's distinction between induction, of which he approves, and hypothesizing, which he claims to abjure—a distinction that I am deliberately blurring when I speak of primary qualities in this third class as *either* hypothesized or induced—is perhaps an attempt to create room for a quality that is neither straightforwardly manifest nor causally fundamental.

Texture, understood in Boyle's sense as the arrangement of particles within a body, is another interesting case. Boyle regards it as a primary quality. Locke's view is more equivocal: texture is listed among the primary qualities at *Essay* 2.8.10, but it is absent

[30] This disapprobation is present, in a muted form, in Chambers, and Charlton seems to be responding to it. For further discussion, see for example Anstey, *The Philosophy of Robert Boyle*, 22–4.

from the better-known list ("Solidity, Extension, Figure, Motion, or Rest, and Number") at *Essay* 2.8.9. Locke's vacillation may be due to uncertainty over the standards that a causally fundamental quality needs to meet. Because a body's texture is nothing over and above the arrangement of the body's parts, texture is arguably less than fundamental: specify the location of every part (or of every part down to a certain size), and the texture (to that degree of resolution) will have been described. But Locke does not actually include location among a body's primary qualities, and if we settle for a list omitting texture, we will be unable to account for the likely difference in causal power between two ways of arranging the same set of particles.

What the table above offers, I think, is a chance to free ourselves from the tendency to think that the list of primary qualities was somehow fixed by Boyle and Locke. If by "primary qualities" Hume means those qualities that are explanatorily basic (or those causally relevant qualities that are resistant to reduction or explanation—potentially a different matter), he may think he can enlarge the list passed on to him by Boyle or Locke without compromising its spirit.

A third and final consequence of the conceptual separation—or, rather, of the conceptual identities behind it—is the accommodation of another ambiguity. If the fundamental principle of the modern philosophy is that the sensible qualities (narrowly understood) are secondary and derivative (and derivative from the mechanical affections of matter in particular), the sensible qualities might be interpreted in either of two ways. They might be interpreted in the way Hobbes, Cudworth, Bayle, and Clarke all interpreted them, as qualities, ideas, or sensations existing in the mind, but they might also be interpreted in Locke's way, as powers existing in bodies. In either case they will be derivative: their presence will be accounted for by the mechanical affections of matter, and there will be nothing "like them"—no archetype or model for them—in things themselves.

3. Three uses of relativity

I return now to Hume. In his view, at least in the *Treatise*, considerations of perceptual relativity—of the ways in which human perceptions vary, while external objects remain the same—provide the modern philosophy with its only credible support. "Upon examination," he writes, he finds "only one of the reasons commonly produced" for the fundamental commitment of the modern philosophy "to be satisfactory, *viz.* that deriv'd from the variation of... impressions, even while the external object, to all appearance, continues the same" (T 1.4.4.3; SBN 226). This use of relativity considerations is, however, only one of three that Hume recognizes. Viewing it alongside the other, less daring uses will help to clarify Hume's complicated—and, in my view, less than fully definite—response to it.

The first use of relativity is one that Hume, in the *Enquiry*, traces to the ancient skeptics. It is one of several considerations that skeptics bring against the evidence of sense, considerations so familiar that they are almost beneath mention:

I need not insist upon the more trite topics, employed by the sceptics in all ages, against the evidence of *sense*; such as those which are derived from the imperfection and fallaciousness of our organs, on numberless occasions; the crooked appearance of an oar in water; the various aspects of objects, according to their different distances; the double images which arise from the pressing one eye; with many other appearances of a like nature. (EHU 12.6; SBN 151)

The "various aspects of objects, according to their different distances" are clear cases of relativity, but the oar in water and the pressed eye that sees double also satisfy the definition of relativity that Hume works with in the *Treatise*: as I row, I may see the oar as crooked when it catches the water and straight when it moves above it, even though it remains straight in the view of my friends onshore, who cannot see below the surface; when I press my eye I may see two pears, even though my friends at the table continue to see (and my second hand, reaching the fruit bowl, continues to feel) just one. These appeals to relativity do not, in Hume's view, carry much skeptical punch:

These sceptical topics . . . are only sufficient to prove, that the senses alone are not implicitly to be depended on; but that we must correct their evidence by reason, and by considerations, derived from the nature of the medium, the distance of the object, and the disposition of the organ, in order to render them, within their sphere, the proper *criteria* of truth and falsehood.
(EHU 12.6; SBN 151)

Hume's verdict on the limited force of relativity in its first use recalls a passage in which Berkeley observes that the appeal to perceptual relativity "doth not so much prove that there is no extension or colour in an outward object, as that we do not know by sense which is the true extension or colour of the object" (*Principles* 15, in *Works*, volume 2). Like Hume, Berkeley thinks that to fix the true extension or color of an object, we need to reason. The point had already been made by Lucretius, in an effort to protect the data of sense (suitably interpreted by reason) from skeptical assault.

The second use of relativity recognized by Hume is to establish that we immediately perceive only our own impressions (or as others would say, our own ideas). Here too Hume recalls Berkeley, who, having made it an unargued premiss of the *Principles* that we immediately perceive only our own ideas, defends that premiss at length, by means of relativity, in the first of the *Three Dialogues*. According to Hume, "the slightest philosophy . . . teaches us, that nothing can ever be present to the mind but an image or perception, and that the senses are only the inlets, through which these images are conveyed, without being able to produce any immediate intercourse between the mind and the object" (EHU 12.9; SBN 152). Here is the supposed proof:

The table, which we see, seems to diminish, as we remove farther from it: but the real table, which exists independent of us, suffers no alteration: it was, therefore, nothing but the image, which was present to the mind. These are the obvious dictates of reason; and no man, who reflects, every doubted, that the existences, which we consider, when we say, *this house* and *that tree*, are nothing but perceptions in the mind, and fleeting copies or representations of other existences, which remain uniform and independent. (EHU 12.9; SBN 152)

By this point, Hume has moved beyond the "trite topics" that constitute the first use of relativity; the second use of relativity is one he associates with "other[,] more profound" arguments against the senses (EHU 12.6; SBN 151). But he sees nothing characteristically modern about the second use. It is a use made of relativity by "the slightest philosophy," to secure a conclusion that "no man, who reflects" ever doubted. It is, I suspect, a use of relativity that was, in Hume's view, already familiar to the ancient philosophers—to Plato, for example, in the *Theaetetus*:[31]

> The most vulgar philosophy informs us, that no external object can make itself known to the mind immediately, and without the interposition of an image or perception. The table, which just now appears to me, is only a perception, and all its qualities are qualities of a perception.
> (T 1.4.5.15; SBN 239)

In the *Treatise* Hume doesn't explain why the table that is my immediate object is merely a perception, but it is a safe conjecture that the reason is the very one he gives at EHU 112.9 (SBN 152), in application to the same example. What the *Enquiry* calls the "slightest" philosophy is, here, the most "vulgar"—that is, common or usual—one, and since this use of relativity is prominent among the ancient philosophers, where it is *not* generally linked with a distinction between primary and secondary qualities, it seems fair to infer that the second use of relativity is not, as Hume sees it, distinctively modern. It teaches that our immediate objects are only perceptions, but makes no invidious distinction among those perceptions or the qualities or things that are their objects.[32]

It is the third use of relativity that is, in Hume's view, characteristically modern (though it too seems to be found in Lucretius, for example at *De rerum natura* 2 800–17). Here again Berkeley serves as a model, and perhaps as an influence: he speaks of "the... manner" in which "modern philosophers prove certain sensible qualities to have no existence in matter, or without the mind" (*Principles* 14). Hume's only full presentation of the third use comes in the *Treatise*, and I will quote it at length:

> The fundamental principle of [the modern philosophy] is the opinion concerning colours, sounds, tastes, smells, heat and cold; which it asserts to be nothing but impressions in the mind, deriv'd from the operation of external objects, and without any resemblance to the qualities of the objects. Upon examination, I find only one of the reasons commonly produc'd for this opinion to be satisfactory, *viz.* that deriv'd from the variations of those impressions, even while the external object, to all appearance, continues the same. These variations depend upon several circumstances. Upon the different situations of our health: A man in a malady feels a

[31] Reid observes that "all philosophers, from Plato to Mr. Hume, agree in this, That we do not perceive external objects immediately, and that the immediate object of perception must be some image present to the mind" (*Essays on the Intellectual Powers* II vii, 263 in volume 1 of *The Works of Thomas Reid*, ed. William Hamilton, sixth edition [Edinburgh: Maclachlan and Stewart, 1863]).

[32] At T 1.4.2.12 (SBN 192), Hume says that "the vulgar" take colors, tastes, smells, sounds, heat, and cold to be "on the same footing" as figure, bulk, motion, and solidity, and that "philosophers" do not. But here "philosophers" means "modern philosophers," as the following paragraph indicates.

disagreeable taste in meats, which before pleas'd him the most. Upon the different complexions and constitutions of men: That seems bitter to one, which is sweet to another. Upon the difference of their external situation and position: Colours reflected from the clouds change according to the distance of the clouds, and according to the angle they make with the eye and luminous body. Fire also communicates the sensation of pleasure at one distance, and that of pain at another. Instances of this kind are very numerous and frequent.

The conclusion drawn from them, is likewise as satisfactory as can possibly be imagin'd. 'Tis certain, that when different impressions of the same sense arise from any object, every one of these impressions has not a resembling quality existent in the object. For as the same object cannot, at the same time, be endow'd with different qualities of the same sense, and as the same quality cannot resemble impressions entirely different; it evidently follows, that many of our impressions have no external model or archetype. Now from like effects we presume like causes. Many of the impressions of colour, sounds, *&c.* are confest to be nothing but internal existences, and to arise from causes, which no ways resemble them. These impressions are in appearance nothing different from the other impressions of colour, sound, *&c.* We conclude, therefore, that they are, all of them, deriv'd from a like origin. (T 1.4.4.3–4; SBN 226–7)

No argument even remotely like this is presented in the *Enquiry*. There Hume simply reports (as he had in other parts of the *Treatise*) that "it is universally allowed by modern enquirers, that all the sensible qualities of objects, such as hard, soft, hot, cold, white, black &c. are merely secondary, and exist not in objects themselves, but are perceptions of the mind, without any external archetype or model, which they represent" (EHU 12.15; SBN 154). Hume uses this modern doctrine to generate what he describes as an objection to the evidence of the senses that is "derived from the *most* profound philosophy" (EHU 12.15; SBN 154; my emphasis). This objection represents the belief in external objects "as contrary to reason"—"at least," Hume adds, "if it be a principle of reason, that all sensible qualities are in the mind, not in the object." His reference to "a principle of reason" may indicate that he takes the modern doctrine to rest on argument, but if so, he does not say what that argument is. It could be the argument presented at length in the *Treatise*, and if it is, it is not hard to imagine that it is an argument Hume no longer wants to stand behind, because its reliance on the principle "like effects, like causes" is, as I will suggest below, very crude.

Whatever Hume, at the time of the *Enquiry*, may have taken the argument to be, it is clear that he wants to separate the third use of relativity from the second. The third goes beyond the second in carrying us towards the view that among the perceptions that are our only immediate objects, some have external archetypes and some do not. As Hume says, in the paragraph that follows the long passage from the *Treatise* quoted above,

this principle being once admitted, all the other doctrines of that philosophy seem to follow by an easy consequence. For upon the removal of sounds, colours, heat, cold, and other sensible qualities, from the rank of continu'd independent existences, we are reduc'd merely to what are called primary qualities, as the only *real* ones, of which we have any adequate notion. These primary qualities are extension and solidity, with their different mixtures and modifications; figure, motion, gravity, and cohesion. The generation, encrease, decay, and corruption of animals and vegetables, are nothing but changes of figure and motion; as also the operations of all bodies on each other; of fire, of light, water, air, earth, and of all the elements and powers of nature. One figure and motion produces another figure and motion; nor does there remain in the material universe any other principle, either active or passive, of which we can form the most distant idea. (T 1.4.4.5; SBN 227)

The third use differs from the second not only in its upshot, but in the explanatory interest that generates it. The lesson of the second use is that impressions or ideas are, in perception, our only immediate objects. The third use tells us that *all* of those impressions with *all* of their qualities—their color and taste as well as their figure and motion—are caused, and wholly accounted for, by objects with (models or archetypes of) only *some* of those qualities. Hume is keenly aware of the explanatory interest that inspires the third use of relativity. In the paragraph that concludes "Of the modern philosophy," he describes the lessons of the modern philosophy as "conclusions we form from cause and effect" (T 1.4.5.15; SBN 231). The relation of cause and effect plays no direct role in either the first use, by which the senses are condemned as unworthy of trust simply because of the ever-varying impressions they convey to us, or the second, in which our ever-changing impressions are held up for comparison against the unchanging objects we presume they represent.[33]

Our task now is to consider whether Hume approves or disapproves of these three uses of relativity. It is, I think, a question we can settle confidently only with respect to the first use. Relativity considerations do not, in Hume's view, directly overthrow the evidence of sense; all they show is that reason has to weigh that evidence carefully. With respect to uses two and three, the situation is much more complicated.[34]

The second use of relativity is, Hume says, an achievement of "the slightest philosophy" (EHU 12.9; SBN 152). We are "necessitated by reasoning" (EHU 12.10; SBN 152) to accept its conclusion, a conclusion of which "the most vulgar philosophy *informs* us" (T 1.4.5.15; SBN 239; emphasis mine). These remarks are,

[33] I have long been curious that Hume does not follow Berkeley in observing (to use Berkeley's words) that "after the same manner, as modern philosophers prove certain sensible qualities to have no existence in matter, or without the mind, the same thing may be likewise proved of all other sensible qualities whatsoever" (*Principles* 14, in volume 2 of the *Works*). (Pierre Bayle makes a broadly similar point in his article on "Pyrrho," but in my view he states it much less effectively.) If Hume had argued in this way, he could have avoided arguing that we cannot abstract the primary qualities from the secondary. He could have argued that just as our varying impressions of color prove that color does not exist in objects, our varying impressions of extension and figure prove that they do not exist in objects either. Hume applies relativity considerations directly to the primary qualities in both the first and second uses. Why does he not do so in the third? A close look at the third use reveals that it is explicitly restricted to variations in the "qualities *of the same sense*" (T 1.4.4.4; SBN 227, my emphasis). It is explicitly restricted, in other words, to proper sensibles. I suspect it is so restricted because Hume sees that the argument would lose its force once applied to common sensibles. The point of the argument is that no one impression of color can be privileged over others. But consider our visual impressions of figure. Although they vary no less than impressions of color do, for all Hume says some of them may "click" with tactile impressions of figure in a way that others do not. The principle of *like effects, like causes* will no longer be clearly applicable. A "clicking" visual impression of figure will differ from one that fails to click, and this may entitle us to privilege it as "true."

[34] Scholarly opinion is therefore very divided. For a helpful survey, see Hakkarainen, chapter 4.

perhaps, intended as compliments, but they are not high compliments, and they are not unambiguous. Thomas Reid read Hume as accepting the second use of relativity, but that may be because Reid, on other grounds, took Hume to believe that we immediately perceive nothing but our own impressions or ideas, and when he searched the *Treatise* and the *Enquiry* for a defense of this "common theory of ideas," the diminishing table of EHU 12.9 (SBN 152) was the only argument he could locate. If we were not already persuaded that Hume accepts the common theory of ideas, would we see EHU 12.9 (SBN 152) as the wholehearted endorsement of an argument in favor of it? And is Reid clearly correct in thinking that Hume accepts the common theory of ideas?

These two questions are too large to be definitively answered here, but let me indicate, at least in the case of the second, some of the evidence on the two sides. Favoring a positive answer are a number of passages, unambiguous in themselves, from the *Treatise*, for example at I i vi:

> We may observe, that 'tis universally allow'd be philosophers, and is besides pretty obvious of itself, that nothing is ever really present with the mind but its perceptions or impressions and ideas, and that external objects become known to us only by those perceptions they occasion.... Now since nothing is ever present to the mind but perceptions... (T 1.2.6.7; SBN 67)

Another such passage appears in I iv 2. "Properly speaking," Hume writes there, "'tis not our body we perceive, when we regard our limbs and members, but certain impressions, which enter by the senses; so that ascribing a real and corporeal existence to these impressions, or to their objects, is an act of the mind as difficult to explain, as that which we examine at present" (T 1.4.2.9; SBN 191). In general, in contexts concerning the justification of the belief in external existence, Hume tends to write, in both the *Treatise* and the *Enquiry*, as if what he here calls "real and corporeal existence" would have to be inferred if it is not directly sensed, and in those same contexts he standardly insists that neither inference nor direct sensation can supply the justification sought for. The senses "convey to us nothing but a single perception, and never give us the least intimation of any thing beyond" (T 1.4.2.4; SBN 189). As for inference by reason, "philosophy informs us, that every thing, which appears to the mind, is nothing but a perception, and is interrupted, and dependent on the mind; whereas the vulgar confound perceptions and objects, and attribute a distinct continu'd existence to the very things they feel and see" (T 1.4.2.14; SBN 193). "This sentiment," he then says, "is entirely unreasonable," and must therefore "proceed from some other faculty that the understanding." He takes the same view in the *Enquiry*:

> It is a question of fact, whether the perceptions of the senses be produced by external objects, resembling them: how shall this question be determined? By experience surely; as all other questions of a like nature. But here experience is, and must be entirely silent. The mind has never anything present to it but the perceptions, and cannot possibly reach any experience of their connexion with objects. The supposition of such a connexion is, therefore, without any foundation in reasoning. (EHU 12.12; SBN 153)

If we abandon the common-sense assumption that "the very perception or sensible image is the external object" in favor of the "more rational opinion, that the perceptions are only representations of something external," we are still unable to "satisfy" our reason, because in the end we are unable to "find any convincing argument from experience to prove, that the perceptions are connected with any external objects" (EHU 12.14; SBN 154).

So far, then, we have considerable evidence that Reid was right to find "the common theory of ideas" in Hume. But there is plenty of evidence on the other side. When justification is not at issue and the explanation of our deepest cognitive commitments is not in view—that is, most of the time, even in the *Treatise*—Hume speaks as a common-sense realist, for whom the immediate objects of perception are not ideas but enduring objects. It is true that in *Treatise* I iv 2, the direct realism of common sense is not psychologically ultimate, but the output of a process that takes fleeting and dependent perceptions as input. Yet Hume dispenses with this explanation in his later (and perhaps more measured) *Enquiry*, where direct realism is described as "the primary opinion of all men."[35]

It is difficult, then, to appraise Hume's response to the second use of relativity, and when it comes to the third, matters are, if anything, stickier. One reason is that the third use *may* presuppose the success of the second. As Hume understands it, the modern philosophy may amount to the opinion that *among the perceptions that are our only immediate objects*, some (those of the primary qualities) are copies of external archetypes and some (those of the secondary) are not. The interpretation of Hume's third use of relativity may therefore inherit all of the difficulties facing the interpretation of the second. A second reason is that the compliments Hume pays to the third use are, besides being less than ringing endorsements, offset by signs of hesitation, caution, or dissatisfaction. Hume does say, for example, that the third use of relativity is a "satisfactory" reason for the defining commitment of the modern philosophy (T 1.4.4.3; SBN 226). Indeed he says, more specifically, that relevant instances of relativity are "very numerous and frequent" (T 1.4.4.3; SBN T 226), and that "the conclusion drawn from them is likewise as satisfactory as can possibly be imagin'd" (T 1.4.4.4; SBN 227). The premiss is good, he seems to be saying, and the conclusion—the fundamental principle of the modern philosophy—justly derived. From this it would seem to follow that the conclusion itself is true. But he says in the *Treatise* that "many objections might be made" to the emerging system, and in the *Enquiry* he hints it may in the end not be a "principle of reason, that all sensible qualities are in the mind, not in the object," the word *principle* recalling the *Treatise*, where "the fundamental principle" of the modern philosophy was said to be the opinion that "colours, sounds, tastes, smells, heat and cold" are "nothing but impressions in the mind ... without any resemblance to

[35] The opinion can, of course, be primary without being psychologically ultimate. It may be that the processes of I iv 2 do their work early—and unseen.

the qualities of the objects." That he chooses in the *Enquiry* not to argue for the principle may itself be significant.

A third reason why it is difficult to assess Hume's attitude towards the third use of relativity is that he may want to distinguish between the fundamental principle of the modern philosophy and the larger system of consequences that emerge from it. It is true that the elements of the larger system materialize by what he calls "easy consequence" (T 1.4.4.5; SBN 227), but an "easy" consequence may be one it is easy to fall for, rather than one that rightly captures the assent of a judicious critic. Hume's discussion of the system of consequences is, in any case, very careless. Among the primary qualities he lists not only extension and solidity ("with their different mixtures and modifications"), figure, and motion, but also gravity and cohesion (T 1.4.4.5; SBN 227). Yet he then goes on to describe all natural changes and operations as functions of figure and motion, ignoring years of debate about the mechanical basis of cohesion and gravity—debates with which he was, certainly by the time of the *Enquiry*, very well acquainted.[36] *Of course* many objections might be made to a system according to which there is, "in the material universe," no principle other than figure or motion, "either active or passive, of which we can form the most distant idea." Such a scheme would be dogmatically mechanistic and therefore completely at odds with the sensibly open-minded viewpoint of the *Enquiry*, where Hume speculates that "elasticity, gravity, cohesion of parts, [and] communication of motion by impulse . . . are probably the ultimate causes and principles that we shall ever discover in nature" (EHU 4.12; SBN 30; see also the comment on Boyle in Hume's *History*). If the system of the modern philosophers goes far beyond their fundamental principle, the system might be open to many objections even if the principle is satisfactory. But Hume's apparent carelessness in laying out the system makes it hard to determine whether he wants to insist on the distinction.

4. Two conceptions of belief in objectivity

I said earlier that by the time he wrote the *Enquiry*, Hume may have lost confidence in an argument he rated, at the time of the *Treatise*, as the only satisfactory reason for accepting the modern philosophy. A loss of confidence would have been justified, because Hume's *Treatise* argument is uncharacteristically creaky. My hope is that a study of its defects, supplemented by discussion of its underlying motivation, will give us a tentative overall picture of what a Humean philosophy of the sensible qualities *could possibly be*, even if we cannot say it is the view that Hume himself settled on.

[36] See T 2.3.1.3 and 8 (SBN 399 and 401) for evidence that he was aware of these debates, even when he published the second and third books of the *Treatise*. The piece of marble he mentions in the latter passage was a standard example in debates about cohesion, and is among the mysteries contemplated in the *Dialogues concerning Natural Religion*, 1.13. Mentions of gravity elsewhere in Book I of the *Treatise* suggest that Hume inserted it very deliberately into the list of primary qualities.

Hume's argument at T 1.4.4.3–4 (SBN 226–7) can be summarized as follows: because they vary while their object remains uniform, many of our impressions must have their causes in objects that do not resemble them; but like effects have like causes, and our various impressions are phenomenologically alike; hence all of our impressions must have their causes in objects that do not resemble them. An argument very much like this is presented by Montaigne in his *Apology for Raymond Sebond*:[37]

> The attributes of illness, madness or sleep make things appear different from what they do to the healthy, the sane and the waking man: is it not likely therefore that our rightful state and our natural humours also have attributes which can endow an object with a mode of being corresponding to their own characteristics, making it conform to themselves, just as our disordered humors do? Why should a temperate complexion not endow objects with a form corresponding to itself just as our distempers can, stamping its own imprint upon them? On to his wine the queasy man loads [*charge*] tastelessness; the healthy man, a bouquet; the thirsty man, sheer delight.
>
> Now, since our state makes things correspond to itself and transforms them in conformity with itself, we can no longer claim to know what anything truly is: nothing reaches us except as altered and falsified by our senses.

Montaigne handles the argument more delicately, and more convincingly, than Hume does. (His talk of the mind's "loading" objects with its own sensations and feelings, incidentally, anticipates Hume's well-known image, probably derived from Malebranche, of the mind's "spreading" itself on objects.[38]) Hume's appeal to "like effects, like causes," the central plank in the platform for the logic of cause and effect that he outlines in *Treatise* I iii 15 ("Rules by which to judge of causes and effects"), is evidence that he takes what he is saying very seriously, but it makes his argument blunt and heavy-handed. Two things can be alike in many different ways. It is obvious that the causes of our varying impressions are complex, including not only objects but also our own bodies. If our various impressions are alike, then they must (according to Hume's logic) have like causes, but the *total* causes may be alike in *certain* ways (in involving some interaction between the object and my sense organs, for example) even if certain *constituents* of those totalities are not alike in *other* ways (in, say, failing to resemble the impressions caused). Hume might, of course, insist that where the effects are alike, their causes must be alike "all the way down," in every part or aspect. But this is an implausibly strong requirement, and even if we acquiesce in it, that the effects are not in all respects alike is the very starting point of Hume's argument. If the effects differ, is there any reason why the causes cannot differ too? (One of Hume's own rules for judging cause and effect is that where there is a difference in the effects, there must be a corresponding difference in the causes [T 1.3.15.8; SBN 174].) Against this last

[37] p. 184 in Michel de Montaigne, *An Apology for Raymond Sebond*, translated by M. A. Screech (London: Penguin, 1993).

[38] For Malebranche on the mind's "spreading" sensations over objects, see the Lennon and Olscamp translation of the *Search*, pp. 58 (I xii 5) and 201 (III [1] i 3).

point it might be objected that the difference between an object that resembles the impression it (partly) causes and one that does not is not the *kind* of difference that can account for felt differences among impressions. This is the point being urged, in effect, by Montaigne: he is demanding a uniform account of all impressions, one in which the impression we take to be accurate or "true" is caused in the same way as any other. But consider a *camera obscura* that is moving along a line parallel to the surface of a table, projecting images of the table on a screen. All of the images are caused in the same way, but the image projected when the camera confronts the table head on may resemble the surface of the table more closely than the images it projects when it stands to the right or left. From the fact that faithful impressions must be caused in the same way as false ones, it does not follow that they cannot be faithful.[39]

Rather than attempting detailed repairs of Hume's argument, I would like to shift our attention to its underlying motivation. Hume's guiding thought in the argument at T 1.4.4.3–4 (SBN 226–7) is that colors, sounds, tastes, and smells are not *causally relevant* features of objects. Relativity considerations show that they play no role in the production of impressions. This is the same thought guiding both Montaigne in *An Apology for Raymond Sebond* and Locke in chapter 8 of Book II of the *Essay*. Unlike Montaigne and Locke, Hume is armed with what he takes to be a theory of causal relevance: a "Logic" that it is "proper to employ in [our] reasoning" (T 1.3.15.11; SBN 175). The theory is formed by his formal definitions of *cause* (T 1.3.14.31, 35; SBN 169–70, and EHU 7.29; SBN 76–7) and by the rules for judging of cause and effect that he derives from them (T 1.3.15; SBN 173–4, and in a revised and very much abbreviated form at EHU 9.5 [SBN 107], where they are consigned to a footnote). Hume's appeal to the principle *like effects, like causes*, a crucial element in his theory (see rules 4, 5, and 6 at T 1.3.15.6–8; SBN 173–4), is evidence that he takes the argument of T 1.4.4.3–4 (SBN 226–7) to be an argument concerning causal relevance. Hume's theory of causal relevance is, however, highly unsatisfactory.[40] Given his conception of causation as constant conjunction, a satisfactory theory of causal relevance was probably beyond his reach. But whether or not the theory was doomed from the start, the argument of T 1.4.4.3–4 (SBN 226-7) is right to question the causal relevance of the secondary qualities, and right to suggest that their lack of causal relevance gives us reason to doubt that they have what Hume calls "continu'd and distinct existence" (and what I will call *objectivity*).

[39] For analysis and assessment of Hume's argument, see Don Garrett, *Cognition and Commitment in Hume's Philosophy* (New York: Oxford University Press, 1997), 215–20; Louis E. Loeb, *Stability and Justification in Hume's* Treatise (Oxford: Oxford University Press, 2002), 217–223; and Hakkarainen, *Hume's Scepticism and Realism*, chapters 3 and 4.

[40] Consider, for example, T 1.4.5.12 (SBN 237), where Hume writes that "the taste and smell of any fruit are inseparable from its other qualities of colour and tangibility; and which-ever of them be the cause of the other, 'tis certain they are always co-existent." A good theory of causal relevance will tell us how to make this determination, but it is far from clear, when events are strictly co-existent, how easy this will be for Hume.

As Hume notes at T 1.3.15.1 (SBN 173), it is a consequence of his two definitions of *cause* that "any thing may produce any thing." It is precisely because it is possible "for all objects to become causes or effects to each other" that he undertakes to state "some general rules, by which we may know when they really are so" (T 1.3.15.1; SBN 173). Many of these rules are ways of excluding pretended causes. Rule 1 stipulates that cause and effect must be contiguous in space and time; causes operating over an unmediated distance, spatial or temporal, are thereby excluded (T 1.3.15.3; SBN 173). Rule 2 requires that the cause be prior to the effect, and rule 3 requires that they be constantly conjoined. It is rule 4 that is most directly relevant to the argument of T 1.4.4.3–4 (SBN 226–7). The "philosophical reasonings" to which Hume refers are what we would call scientific reasonings:

> The same cause always produces the same effect, and the same effect never arises but from the same cause. This principle we derive from experience, and is the source of most of our philosophical reasonings. For when by any clear experiment we have discover'd the causes or effects of any phenomenon, we immediately extend our observation to every phenomenon of the same kind, without waiting for that constant repetition, from which the first idea of this relation is deriv'd. (T 1.3.15.6; SBN 173–4)

In the paragraph that brings *Treatise* I iv 4 to a close, Hume writes that "when we reason from cause and effect, we conclude, that neither colour, sound, taste, nor smell have a continu'd and independent existence" (T 1.4.4.15; SBN 231). The argument of T 1.4.4.3–4 (SBN 226–7) is an argument from cause and effect, conducted according to rule 4. In his statement of the argument, Hume uses rule 4 like a bludgeon. Used more delicately, as Montaigne and Locke use it, it tells us this: that if we are seeking a uniform account of the production of impressions, relativity considerations suggest that we should dispense with color, sound, taste, and smell as explanatory principles and look instead to bulk, figure, and motion.

I believe Hume is genuinely drawn to this way of defeating the causal relevance of color, sound, taste, and smell. This is because he is attracted by what I will call a *causal conception of belief in objectivity*. That conception, which I will go on to refine, is roughly this:

> we believe that a quality is objective if and only if we believe that it stands in a causal relation to some existing thing.

To be objective in the sense I have in mind is to exist in what Hume calls the "external world" (T 1.4.2.57; SBN 218). According to the analysis of such existence that Hume provides in *Treatise* I iv 2 (and to which he recurs in the *Enquiry* [12.7; SBN 151]) to exist in the external world (or what the *Enquiry* calls the "external universe") is to possess "continu'd and distinct existence" (T 1.4.2.2; SBN 188). An object enjoys continued existence when it exists unperceived; it enjoys distinct existence when, standing outside the mind in space, it exists and operates independently of our perceptions of it (T 1.4.2.2; SBN 188).[41] The causal conception of belief in objectivity can therefore be restated as follows:

we believe that a quality is objective—an inhabitant of the external world or universe—if and only if we believe that its continued and distinct existence stands in a causal relation to some existing thing.

Despite the official account of distinct existence that he lays down at T 1.4.2.2 (SBN 188), there seem to be times when Hume wants to sever its connection with external existence in space. "We may observe," he says at T 1.4.2.10 (SBN 191), "that when we talk of real distinct existences, we have commonly more in our eye their independency than external situation in place, and think an object has a sufficient reality, when its Being is uninterrupted, and independent of the incessant revolutions, which we are conscious of in ourselves." This fits in with his later argument, at *Treatise* I iv 5, that all perceptions, being "different from each other, and from every thing else in the universe," are "distinct and separable, and may be consider'd as separately existing, and may exist separately, and have no need of any thing else"—our perceiving minds, for example—"to support their existence" (T 1.4.5.5; SBN 233). This is true, he believes, even of those perceptions—the majority of perceptions, in his view (T 1.4.5.11; SBN 235)—that have no spatial existence (T 1.4.5.11; SBN 235–6). Since the modern philosophy is concerned, not with qualities that possess (or fail to possess) this attenuated sort of existence, but with qualities that exist (or fail to exist) in bodies in space, I am going to restate it yet again:

we believe that a quality is objective—an inhabitant of the external world or material universe—if and only if we believe that its continued and distinct existence in body stands in a causal relation to some existing thing.

As so far formulated, the causal conception gives us both a sufficient condition for the objectivity of a quality and a necessary one. But the latter condition may be too stringent, at least for Hume, because the continued and distinct existence of a quality may be (in his view) something of which we are immediately aware. This will be true if, as Cass Weller for example has suggested, Hume is a direct realist, rather than a sincere advocate of what Reid calls the "common theory of ideas."[42] I have already indicated my reluctance to come down, here, on one side or another of this interpretive debate. I will try to step around it by reframing the causal conception as follows:

we believe that a quality is objective—an inhabitant of the external world or material universe—if and (supposing its continued and distinct existence is not, or has not been, immediately perceived) only if we believe that its continued and distinct existence in body stands in a causal relation to some existing thing.

[41] Hume emphasizes that continued existence and distinct existence go hand in hand: that each implies the other. He finds the belief in continued existence easier to work with, so he generally proceeds by explaining the belief in continued existence directly, and then deriving the belief in distinct existence from it.

[42] See Weller, "Why Hume is a Direct Realist," *Archiv für Geschichte der Philosophie* 83 (2001), 258–85.

This allows that a quality might be objective even if it plays no causal role, so long as we immediately perceive its existence in body. It might therefore seem to block the inference (which I want to attribute to Hume) from the causal irrelevance of the secondary qualities to their fleeting and dependent (and therefore less-than-objective) existence. I am going to assume, however (subject to a qualification that will figure prominently in my later argument), that in Hume's view, the continued and distinct existence of the secondary qualities is *not* something that we (in general) immediately perceive: that if he is, as some contend, a direct realist, the enduring and independent qualities that we would then (in his view) immediately perceive would not include all of the secondary qualities. I am hoping, in other words, to make the debate over the character of Hume's realism irrelevant to my further argument.

The causal conception says that an objective quality must be causally related to an existing thing, *but the existing thing need not itself be objective*. The existing thing may be a fleeting perception, an item in what Hume calls the "internal world" (T 1.4.2.57; SBN 218), and at T 1.4.4.3–4 (SBN 226–7), where the second use of relativity is, in my view, being taken for granted, it is items in the internal world—our own perceptions or impressions—for which we are trying to account. Because all the features of these impressions are, in the view of the modern philosophy, caused (and therefore explained) by figure, motion, and other primary qualities alone, the modern philosophers deny that the so-called secondary qualities exist in the objective world. The modern philosophers (as Hume imagines them) adhere to the causal conception of objectivity, and I believe Hume does as well.

The causal conception of objectivity figures prominently in both the *Treatise* and the *Enquiry*. Its most memorable appearance comes, perhaps, in the following passage from *Treatise* I iii 9:

'Tis evident, that whatever is present to the memory, striking upon the mind with a vivacity, which resembles an immediate impression, must become of considerable moment in all the operations of the mind, and must easily distinguish itself above the mere fictions of the imagination. Of these impressions or ideas of the memory we form a kind of system, comprehending whatever we remember to have been present, either to our internal perception or sense; and every particular of that system, joined to the present impressions, we are pleas'd to call a *reality*. But the mind stops not here. For finding, that with this system of perceptions, there is another connected by custom, or if you will, by the relation of cause and effect, it proceeds to the consideration of their ideas; and as it feels that 'tis in a manner necessarily determin'd to view these particular ideas, and that the custom or relation, by which it is determin'd, admits not of the least change, it forms them into a new system, which it likewise dignifies with the title of *realities*. The first of these systems is the object of the memory and senses; the second of the judgment.

'Tis this latter principle, which peoples the world, and brings us acquainted with such existences, as by their revival in time and place, lie beyond the reach of the senses and memory.

(T 1.3.9.3–4; SBN 107–8)

In the *Enquiry*, the conception figures in familiar passages concerning "the nature of that evidence which assures us of any real existence and matter of fact, beyond the present testimony of our senses, or the records of our memory" (EHU 4.3; SBN 26). All such assurance, Hume contends there, seems to be "founded on the relation of *Cause and Effect*." "By means of that relation alone," he continues, "we can go beyond the evidence of our memory and senses" (EHU 4.4 [SBN 26]; see also EHU 4.14 [SBN 32]).[43]

The causal conception of objectivity brings us up against the "very decisive" objection that Hume raises against the system of the modern philosophers, because by removing all secondary qualities from objects, it seems to leave us with no way of conceiving the primary:

> I assert, that instead of explaining the operations of external objects by its means [another acknowledgment of the explanatory ambitions of the modern philosophy], we utterly annihilate all these objects, and reduce ourselves to the opinions of the most extravagant scepticism concerning them. If colours, sounds, tastes, and smells be merely perceptions, nothing we can conceive is possest of a real, continu'd, and independent existence; not even motion, extension and solidity, which are the primary qualities chiefly insisted on (T 1.4.4.6; SBN 227–8).

Hume condemns the modern philosophy in very similar terms in the *Enquiry*:

> It is universally allowed by modern enquirers, that all of the sensible qualities of objects, such as hard, soft, hot, cold, white, black, &c. are merely secondary, and exist not in the objects themselves, but are perceptions of the mind, without any external archetype or model, which they represent. If this be allowed, with regard to secondary qualities, it must also follow, with regard to the supposed primary qualities of extension and solidity. . . . Nothing can save us from this conclusion, but the asserting, that the ideas of those primary qualities are attained by *Abstraction*, an opinion, which, if we examine it accurately, we shall find to be unintelligible, and even absurd. An extension, that is neither tangible nor visible, cannot possibly be conceived: and a tangible or visible extension, which is neither hard not soft, black nor white, is equally beyond the reach of human conception. . . . Bereave matter of all its intelligible qualities, both primary and secondary, you in a manner annihilate it, and leave only a certain, unknown, inexplicable *something*, as the cause of our perceptions; a notion so imperfect, that no sceptic will think it worth while to contend against it. (E 12.15; SBN 154–5)

The reasoning on which Hume rests his apparent condemnation is not the same in the two works. In the *Enquiry*, correctly tracing the argument to Berkeley (EHU 12.16; SBN 155), he offers nothing of substance beyond what I've quoted. The reasoning in the *Treatise* is more complex: Hume devotes particular attention to solidity, arguing for

[43] Many other passages give voice to the same view. The only relation not depending merely on ideas "that can be trac'd beyond our senses, and informs us of existences and objects, which we do not see or feel," Hume writes in the *Treatise*, "is *causation*" (T 1.3.2.2; SBN 74). According to the "Abstract" it is "evident" that "all reasonings concerning *matter of fact* are founded on the relation of cause and effect, and that we can never infer the existence of one object from another, unless they be connected together, either mediately or immediately" (Abstract, paragraph 8; SBN 649).

example that to conceive of one body's resisting the entry of another into the space it occupies, we must invest each body with a quality that the modern philosophy has cast out of the world (T 1.4.4.9–10; SBN 228–9). The upshot of that reasoning is that "there is," as Hume says in the final paragraph of I iv 4, "a direct and total opposition betwixt our reason and our senses; or more properly speaking, betwixt those conclusions we form from cause and effect, and those that persuade us of the continu'd existence of body. When we reason from cause and effect, we conclude, that neither colour, sound, taste, nor smell have a continu'd and independent existence. When we exclude these sensible qualities there remains nothing in the universe, which has such an existence" (T 1.4.4.15; SBN 231).[44] In *Treatise* I iv 7 Hume says, referring back to I iv 4, that these two operations—reasoning from cause and effect, and convincing ourselves of the continued existence of external objects—are "equally natural and necessary in the human mind," but "in some circumstances they are directly contrary, nor is it possible for us to reason justly and regularly from causes and effects, and at the same time believe the continu'd existence of objects" (T 1.4.7.4; SBN 266). If we "successively assent to both, as is usual among philosophers, with what confidence can we afterwards usurp that glorious title, when we thus knowingly embrace a manifest contradiction?" (T 1.4.7.4; SBN 266).[45] This manifest contradiction undermines the distinction, credited to the modern philosophy as I iv 4 began, between the principles of imagination that are "permanent, irresistable, and universal"—and, Hume adds at T 1.4.4.2 (SBN 226) (though it is entailed by the features already listed), mutually consistent—and those that are "changeable, weak, and irregular" (T 1.4.4.1; SBN 225). It seems to me that in the *Enquiry* the opposition between reason and sense has not been left behind, despite Hume's insinuation that it may not be a principle of reason that all secondary qualities are in the mind and not in objects (EHU 12.16; SBN155). It is impossible, Hume says later in section 12, that anything but natural instinct can free us from Pyrrhonian doubt (EHU 12.25; SBN 162), and the metaphorical "annihilation" of

[44] The conflict between reason and the senses is even more direct than Hume realizes, because the mechanisms outlined in I iv 2 can be applied directly to "disembodied" sensible qualities. Our impressions of colors, sounds, tastes, and odors exhibit the same constancy and coherence as our impressions of things. Consider a drone, for example, or a waning siren: each is, in view of its constancy or coherence, an ideal trigger for the processes Hume describes in I iv 2. Other such triggers include the changing colors of a fall leaf, the flashing and dimming colors of a sky at sunset, the gradual warming of a rock in mid-day, the souring of fermenting liquor, and the changing smells of earth in spring. Here it might be helpful to recall T 1.4.2.13 (SBN 192), where the vulgar are said to believe that colors, sounds, and heat and cold enjoy continued and distinct existence, though there Hume is probably not imagining that they vulgar take them to exist independently of things. "So strong is the prejudice for the distinct continu'd existence of [these] qualities," Hume writes, "that when the contrary opinion is advanc'd by modern philosophers, people imagine they can almost refute it from their feeling and experience, and that their very senses contradict this philosophy."

[45] Don Garrett writes of this passage that in "raising . . . questions . . . resulting from what he takes to be a real difficulty of modern philosophers, Hume is expressing feelings of skeptical discomfort. But in raising them he does not make or defend any epistemic evaluation of those feelings, nor does he make or defend any recommendation concerning our response to them" (*Cognition and Commitment*, 220). It seems to me that what Garrett describes as "feelings of skeptical discomfort" are, for Hume, epistemic evaluations.

matter is one prominent instance of such doubt. Reason speaks in its favor (the annihilation of matter "*admit*[s] *of no answer*"), even though human nature speaks against it (it "*produce*[s] *no conviction*," EHU 12.15; SBN 155).

Contributing to the opposition between sense and reason is a second conception of the conditions for belief in objectivity. According to this conception, if a quality is conceptually compulsory—if we cannot conceive of the continued and distinct existence of body without it—then we believe that quality is objective, even if it is without causal relevance. Instead of earning its objectivity by causal relevance, the quality can piggyback on the objectivity of the body it modifies:

> we believe that a quality is objective if we believe in the continued and distinct existence of a body that cannot be conceived to exist without it.

Our belief in the continued and distinct existence of body is not, in Hume's view, a reasoned belief. But if we hold the belief (as according to Hume we all do, most of the time), then relative to that belief, we have reason to believe in the objective existence of any quality without which the body cannot be conceived. The point of the principle as I have stated it, though, is not that we have reason to believe in the objectivity of a quality if it is conceptually compulsory, but that we *actually do* believe in it. Hence the second conception of belief in objectivity stands in straightforward conflict with the first: according to the second, compulsoriness is sufficient for belief in objectivity; according to the first, causal relevance, which a compulsory quality may lack, is necessary.[46]

It is clearly Hume's view, at least in the *Treatise*, that we cannot conceive of body without some "space-filling" attribute: "I . . . have shewn," he writes at T 1.4.4.8 (SBN 228), thinking of *Treatise* I ii, "that 'tis impossible to conceive extension, but as compos'd of parts, endow'd with colour or solidity." If solidity could do the job, the modern philosophy would be saved, because solidity is a primary quality. But in paragraphs 9–14 of *Treatise* I iv 4, Hume brings a series of arguments against our having a "just [or] satisfactory" idea of solidity, at least one of which, in his judgment, "appear[s] entirely conclusive" (T 1.4.4.9, 10; SBN 229). No arguments are brought against color, which is excluded from consideration only because the modern philosophy denies its real existence (T 1.4.4.8; SBN 228).[47]

[46] The second conception of belief in objectivity could be framed as a normative principle, according to which we *should* believe that a quality is objective when it meets the specified condition. There would still be a conflict with the second conception but it would be less straightforward. For the sake of simplicity I propose to work with the formulation I have given, without claiming that it is more faithful than the other to Hume's intentions.

[47] It may seem that the argument of T 1.4.4.14 (SBN 230–1) applies to color, because it turns on the simplicity of our unextended impressions of touch. It is true that unextended impressions of color are also simple, but the argument Hume presents has no convincing analogue in the case of color. He asks us to compare a man pressing a solid stone with two solid stones pressing upon each other. The two cases are clearly different, insofar as the first includes an impression of touch missing from the second, and we can make them alike only by removing the impression—something that must be done wholesale, since the impression is

Does Hume believe, then, that color is conceptually compulsory? I wish I could say yes, but there is another candidate for the role of filling space that Hume silently sets aside (I do not know why) in I iv 4: impressions of touch or feeling, which are, according to *Treatise* I iv 5, conceived to exist in space and to generate figures and quantities (T 1.4.5.10; SBN 235–6), even if (as I iv 4 argues) they do not resemble solidity. These impressions are, however, secondary qualities, so in my view we can say this: Hume believes that it is compulsory for us, whenever we conceive of size, figure, or motion, to conceive of some secondary quality or other, even thought he does not say (and, perhaps, cannot say) which. I therefore think that the conflict between the two conceptions of objectivity is, for Hume, a genuine one: the first conception draws him to the conclusion that no secondary qualities are objective, while the second draws him to the conclusion that some secondary qualities are. I turn now to ways of eliminating or alleviating the conflict, but I should say in advance that I so far have been unable to find one that Hume would—or should—find altogether satisfying.

5. Three ways of resolving the conflict

An ideal strategy for easing the conflict between the two conceptions would allow Hume to preserve the analogy between virtue and vice and the secondary qualities. I believe there are three strategies that deserve consideration.

One possibility is to say that, even if matter bereft of secondary qualities cannot in the strict sense be *conceived*, its existence can be *supposed*. There need not be a conflict, then, between the two conceptions, even if we are compelled to conceive of matter as possessing some secondary quality or other, so long as we can count something as a cause without (in the strict sense) conceiving of it. Objects (or more exactly, traits of mind and character) can in the strict sense be *conceived* as bereft of moral qualities, but the analogy between moral qualities and secondary qualities is nonetheless preserved, because it requires only that we have, in each case, *some* way of latching on to the thought that the qualities in question do not exist in things themselves. This is a response to the conflict that will appeal to many who read Hume as a "skeptical realist," but in my view it resolves the conflict far too easily to be described as Humean. John P. Wright says that "when we remind ourselves that all the fundamental beliefs which Hume seeks to found in the *Treatise* are based upon . . . inconceivable suppositions, then his objections to the modern theory of matter seem negligible."[48] The problem is that Hume treats those objections, in both the *Treatise* and the *Enquiry*, as anything but negligible. Victory over the conflict must, I think, be harder-won.

simple. Hume's point is that the impression of touch cannot resemble solidity if it is precisely the impression that must be removed in order to make the first case like the second. No corresponding point can be made about color, because no foothold has been provided for a distinction between the impressions of sight on the one hand and objective colors on the other.

[48] *The Sceptical Realism of Hume* (Minneapolis: University of Minnesota Press, 1983), 111.

A second possible response is simply to relax the first conception, either by eliminating causal relevance as a necessary condition of belief in objectivity or by reckoning a quality as causally relevant if some quality deemed causally relevant on other grounds cannot be conceived apart from it. I will comment separately on each of these alternatives.

On the first alternative, causal relevance remains a sufficient condition of belief in objectivity. But it is no longer a necessary condition, so the conflict with conceptual inescapability, also a sufficient condition, is removed. I am sympathetic to this response, insofar as it grants a certain priority to the second conception, and expects the first conception to give way. As Hume says, after presenting his decisive objection, "*instead of explaining the operations of external objects by . . . means* [of the modern philosophy], we utterly annihilate all these objects, and reduce ourselves to the opinions of the most extravagant scepticism concerning them" (T 1.4.4.6; SBN 227–8, my emphasis). Any cause we enlist in explanation must, in Hume's view, be something of which we can *conceive*. If body cannot be conceived without some secondary quality or other, the modern philosophy cannot make good on its promise to explain how bodies operate upon us. For Hume, then, the work of conceiving is prior to (and unavoidably implicated in) the work of explanation. Another advantage of this response is its economy. If color turns out to be conceptually compulsory, the modern philosophers cannot deny its objectivity. But this does not oblige them to make use of it in explanation. They remain free to distinguish between objective qualities that are predictively powerful and those that are not. It may be that a body's bulk and figure cannot be conceived apart from color, but if color variations have, directly, no predictive or explanatory relevance, color is not something our explanations need to mention, however necessary it may be to our ideas. But I am unhappy with this response for two reasons. First, because it admits some secondary qualities into the objective world (even if it does not grant them causal relevance), it fails fully to preserve the analogy between the secondary qualities and the moral qualities of virtue and vice. Second, it seems to me to underestimate Hume's attachment to causal relevance as a necessary condition of belief in objectivity.

The second alternative does not suggest that Hume be released from that attachment: it retains causal relevance as a necessary condition, but reconstrues it. Now it is fair, perhaps, for a compulsory quality to piggyback on an otherwise causally relevant quality that cannot be conceived without it. But this alternative likewise fails to preserve the analogy between secondary qualities and moral qualities, and here the failure is more extreme, for the very reason that seemed to lend the alternative promise: some of the qualities Hume would have us compare to virtue and vice turn out to be not merely objective, but causally relevant. The alternative also faces a second difficulty, one that seems to me to be no less serious though it will take me some time to explain it.

My remarks on causal relevance have so far been one-sided. I have said a great deal about objects, whose causally relevant qualities are, in the view of the modern philosophy, a privileged selection from among the many qualities that common-sense, consciousness, and earlier philosophy ascribe to them. I have said little or nothing about the other party in perception, the living subject. In Hume's version of the modern philosophy, the range of causally relevant properties on the side of the subject is not diminished but enlarged. This is because the Humean subject is not, as we might say, "simply open" to the world. It is the possessor of what Francis Hutcheson calls a *sense*, a "*Determination of our Minds to receive Ideas independently on our Will*"[49]—a subject with a special susceptibility. This susceptibility is a matter of its make-up, as Hume often emphasizes. In the *Treatise*, for example, he introduces his comparison between virtue and vice and the secondary qualities with the observation that "when you pronounce any action or character to be vicious, you mean nothing, but that *from the constitution of your nature* you have a feeling or sentiment of blame from the contemplation of it" (T 3.1.1.26; SBN 469, my emphasis). In "The Sceptic," the comparison is in a footnote attached to his remark that without "delicacy of temper," or a constitution that equips him to feel the required sentiment, a man "possessed of the science and understanding of an angel" would be altogether ignorant of poetic beauty (p. 166 in Miller's edition of the *Essays*). Our constitution plays what Hume elsewhere describes as a productive role:[50]

> The distinct boundaries of *reason* and *taste* are easily ascertained. The former conveys the knowledge of truth and falsehood: The latter gives the sentiment of beauty and deformity, vice and virtue. The one discovers objects, as they really stand in nature, without addition or diminution: The other has a productive faculty, and gilding or staining all natural objects with the colours, borrowed from internal sentiment, raises, in a manner, a new creation.

We have, then, two causally relevant participants in perception: the primary qualities of objects on one side and the determinations of our own constitution on the other. That constitution plays, in Hume's view, a quasi-creative role, much as it did for the poet Edward Young. According to the second use of relativity, we immediately perceive ideas or images. According to the third, the qualities of those ideas or images are not in things themselves. If we put the third use together with Hume's portrayal of the human constitution as productive or quasi-creative, it suggests that our senses, stimulated by the primary qualities of objects, give rise to whole qualitative dimensions, of which the various secondary qualities are specifications. This is, I think, what brings Hume to make a fourth appeal to relativity—not a perceptual relativity that figures as a premiss in his arguments, but a metaphysical relativity that serves as a conclusion. In the first two editions of the *Enquiry concerning Human Understanding*, Hume praises Hutcheson for teaching, "by the most convincing Arguments, that Morality is nothing in the abstract nature of Things, but is entirely relative to the Sentiment or mental Taste of each particular Being; in the same Manner as the Distinctions of sweet and bitter, hot and

[49] *An Essay on the Nature and Conduct of the Passions and Affections, with Illustrations on the Moral Sense*, edited by Aaron Garrett (Indianapolis: Liberty Fund, 2002), 17.

[50] David Hume, *An Enquiry concerning the Principles of Morals*, eds by Tom L. Beauchamp (Oxford: Clarendon Press, 1998), Appendix 1, paragraph 21, p. 294 in *Enquiries*, eds by Selby-Bigge and Nidditch.

cold, arise from the particular Feeling of each Sense or Organ."[51] From this he concludes that "Mental Perceptions . . . ought not to be class'd with the Operations of the Understanding, but with the Tastes or Sentiments."[52] To acknowledge the causal relevance of the human constitution is, then, precisely to *deny* the causal relevance of the secondary qualities, conceived as residing in objects. This completely undermines what I have been calling the second alternative, at least as a reading of Hume. Hume's way of assigning causal relevance, instead of relieving the tension between the two conceptions of belief in objectivity, presents us with a particularly compelling reminder of it. If we acknowledge the causal relevance of the human constitution, we will have to deny the causal relevance of the secondary qualities at the very moment we affirm the causal relevance of the primary. Yet if Hume is right, we cannot conceive of objects with size, shape, and motion unless we take them to possess, no less objectively, some secondary quality—a quality that is, in fact, entirely relative to us, a quality that belongs only to ideas and images, and not to things themselves.[53]

[51] See p. 232 in Beauchamp's edition of the *Enquiry*. In "Hutcheson and Hume on the Color of Virtue," *Hume Studies* 22 (1996), 3–22, I explore one way of explaining why, beginning with the third edition, Hume forfeited this footnote. One further possibility is that Hume came to believe that the analogy misleadingly suggests that the sentiments of vice and virtue are (like sensations of color and taste) immediate effects of our "primary constitution." In section 6 of *A Dissertation on the Passions*, Hume gives a disjunctive characterization of what he calls "the most probable system, which has been advanced to explain the difference between vice and virtue": it is, he writes, the view "that *either* from a primary constitution of nature, *or* from a sense of public or private interest, certain characters, upon the very view and contemplation, produce uneasiness; and others, in like manner, excite pleasure" (my emphasis). In arguing that the virtues are either immediately agreeable or useful, the *Enquiry concerning Morals* laid stress on both alternatives. The analogy disappeared from the *Enquiry concerning Human Understanding* when it was brought together with the *Enquiry concerning Morals*, first published in 1751 (and the *Dissertation*, first published in 1757), in Hume's 1758 collection, *Essays and Treatises on Several Subjects*.

[52] Hume makes a similar claim of relativity in a letter to Hutcheson, asking for advice on the writing of the passage from T 3.1.1.26 (SBN 469) discussed above. For discussion of the letter see "Hutcheson and Hume on the Color of Virtue."

[53] There is a second reason to question the causal relevance of color even when it is assumed to be compulsory. It may seem that, on a constant conjunction view of causation, a compulsory quality can easily piggy-back its way to causal relevance: if *F* is causally relevant and inconceivable apart from G, won't G be causally relevant too—constantly conjoined, that is, with whatever it is with which *F* is constantly conjoined? I am uncertain whether Hume's theory of causation will enable him to deny the causal relevance of a piggybacking G. But I think he should deny it, and that his stated rules suggest a way of doing so. "When any object encreases or diminishes with the encrease of diminution of its cause," he writes in rule 7, "'tis to be regarded as a compounded effect, deriv'd from the union of the several different effects, which arise from the several difference parts of the cause" (T 1.3.15.9; SBN 174). Hume is concerned here with the effects of an increase (or diminution) in the quantity or "extensive magnitude" of a cause: if it is followed by an increase (or diminution) in the effect, that increase (or diminution) should be regarded as the compound effect of the action of the parts of the cause, which are more numerous when the quantity of the cause is greater and less numerous when its quantity is less. But causes (or alleged causes) can also vary in quality or "intensive magnitude," as color does. Hume maintains that we cannot conceive of a body without (say) some color or other. But the color's particular shade may have no bearing on the causal powers of the colored body: its quality or intensive magnitude may vary while the body's powers remain the same. Another possibility is that, although we must conceive of a body's parts as having some color or other, the actual colors of the parts have no bearing on the body's powers. (Note that we must conceive of the body as having some color or other, but no particular color is necessary. As far as the demands of conception are concerned, the body's color may be in constant flux, and if its particular shade is, as things turns out, a wheel that turns nothing in the

This brings me to a third and final response to the conflict between the two conceptions: that Hume admit the conflict but work around it. In the section of the *Treatise* that follows "Of the modern philosophy," Hume argues that tastes, sounds, and smells have no existence in space. We tend, he thinks, to "incorporate and conjoin" such qualities with body, supposing for example that sweet taste exists in a fig and bitter taste in an olive (T 1.4.5.11; SBN 236). This is a tendency Hume thinks he can explain (T 1.4.5.12; SBN 237), but however explicable it may be psychologically, he condemns the emerging opinion as "altogether unintelligible," "contradictory," and "absurd" (T 1.4.5.13; 238). For where, he asks, does the taste reside: in every part of the body or just one? We cannot reasonably say it is lodged in only one, because "experience convinces us, that every part has the same relish." But if it is lodged in every part, then the taste as a whole must be extended and figured, its size and shape a function of the tastes (which Hume is perhaps conceiving as "points" of taste lacking size and shape) that enter into it. This is, he declares, is "absurd and incomprehensible" (T 1.4.5.13; SBN 238). Tastes and smells cannot possibly have size and shape, and the same is true for the majority of our perceptions (T 1.4.5.10; SBN 235): for "all our perceptions and objects, except those of sight and feeling [that is, touch]" (T 1.4.5.10; SBN 236).[54]

For our purposes, the crucial point is that tastes, smells, and sounds are not, in Hume's view, conceptually compulsory: we can conceive of body perfectly well without them.[55] From this it follows that in the case of taste, smell, and sound, there is nothing

mechanism, the causal powers of the body will be unaffected. On the kind of view I take to lie behind the third use of relativity, we assume that bodies have durable shapes and sizes because that assumption makes the best sense of our experience. We may have no comparable motive when it comes to color.)

[54] What is the status of heat and cold? Are they spatial or non-spatial? And would Hume count a "neutral" perception of temperature (what Berkeley in the *Three Dialogues* calls an "indolence") as an impression positioned somewhere along the heat-and-cold axis or simply as an impression of texture or resistance? Sound is another puzzling case. Hume says that only the impressions of sight and touch are spatial, but sounds certainly *seem* to be spatially located. They might even seem to be extended. At *Treatise* I iii 14, Hume says "it is a common observation, that the mind has a great propensity to spread itself on external objects, and to conjoin with them any internal impressions which they occasion, and which always make their appearance at the same time that these objects discover themselves to the senses. Thus, as certain sounds and smells are always found to attend certain visible objects, we naturally imagine a conjunction, even in place, betwixt the objects and qualities, though the qualities be of such a nature as to admit of no such conjunction, and really exist no where." He promises "more" on this "hereafter," and appends a footnote directing readers to I iv 5 (T 1.3.14.25; SBN 167). So it seems to be his firm opinion that sounds are, with tastes, and smells, non-spatial secondary qualities. *Treatise* I iv 2 says the same: "Sounds, and tastes, and smells, though commonly regarded by the mind as continued independent qualities, appear not to have any existence in extension, and consequently cannot appear to the senses as situated externally to the body. The reason why we ascribe a place to them shall be considered afterwards" (T 1.4.2.9; SBN 191). *Treatise* I iv 5 itself makes it clear enough that Hume takes sounds to be no less non-spatial than tastes and smells (T 1.4.5.9, 10, and 14, SBN 235, 236, 239). Perhaps what makes sound seem unlike smell and (especially) taste is that experience teaches us to associate sounds with variations in the distance and direction of bodies (see T 1.4.5.9; SBN 235, where Hume discusses the influence of "custom and reflection").

[55] Here I assume that we can refrain from "incorporating" taste and smell into body. I see no evidence that Hume regards incorporation as inevitable. I assume that if Hume is a direct realist, the non-spatial secondary qualities will not be among the qualities whose continued and distinct existence we immediately perceive.

to threaten the conclusion for which the modern philosophy is reaching: that in view of the third use of relativity, they are not in things themselves. This means that with respect to non-spatial secondary qualities like taste, smell, and sound, the modern philosophy is something we can wholeheartedly embrace. We can accept relativity arguments, so long as they pose no threat to qualities that are conceptually compulsory. The analogy between virtue and vice and the secondary qualities can therefore be preserved, *in part*. We just have to take care to compare virtue and vice to non-spatial secondary qualities, following an example Hume himself sets when he compares beauty to taste:

> Though it be certain, that beauty and deformity, more than sweet and bitter, are not qualities in objects, but belong entirely to the sentiment, internal or external; it must be allowed, that there are certain qualities in objects, which are fitted by nature to produce those particular feelings.
> ("Of the Standard of Taste," p. 235 in Miller's edition of the *Essays*)

Unfortunately, this partial, and to that extent uneasy, acceptance of the analogy between virtue and the secondary qualities does not give Hume all that he requires.[56] It does not preserve the analogy as stated, which is an analogy between vice and virtue and *all* of the secondary qualities, and it seems unacceptably ad hoc, or at least undesirably superficial. If the relativity arguments of the third sort succeed in showing that taste, smell, and sound are not in things themselves, why do they not show the same of color, or whatever other quality turns out to be conceptually compulsory? We could, of course, simply decree that conceptual demands take priority over what any argument from relativity might show, but as yet we have no explanation of why such a demand would be appropriate.

I am brought reluctantly to the conclusion that, with the materials Hume has provided, it is probably impossible to construct a philosophy of the sensible qualities that he can find altogether satisfying.[57]

Bibliography

Agrippa von Nettesheim, Henry Cornelius. 1651. *Three books of occult philosophy,* London: Gregory Moule.

Alexander, Peter. 1985. *Ideas, Qualities and Corpuscles: Locke and Boyle on the External World,* Cambridge: Cambridge University Press.

Anstey, Peter J. 2000. *The Philosophy of Robert Boyle,* London: Routledge.

Aquinas, St. Thomas. *Summa theologiae.*

Aristotle. *De anima.*

Berkeley, George. 1948–57. *The Works of George Berkeley, Bishop of Cloyne,* Nine volumes, edited by A. A. Luce and T. E. Jessop, London: Thomas Nelson.

[56] If color is compulsory, it is not projected—not, at any rate, onto our (visual) experiences of body.

[57] In "Hutcheson and Hume on the Color of Virtue" I was more optimistic. My present view is close to that of Simon Blackburn, the conclusions of whose paper "Hume on the Mezzanine Level" (*Hume Studies* 19 (1993), 273–88) I was then trying to resist.

Blackburn, Simon. 1993. "Hume on the Mezzanine Level," *Hume Studies* 19: 273–8.

Boyle, Robert. 1661. *Certain physiological essays*, London: Henry Herringman.

—— 1686. *A free inquiry into the vulgarly receiv'd notion of nature,* London: H. Clark for John Taylor.

Burton, Henry. 1629. *Truth's triumph over Trent: Or, the great gulfe between Sion and Babylon*, London: Mich. Sparke.

Byrne, Alex. 2009a. "Sensory Qualities, Sensible Qualities, Sensational Qualities," in *The Oxford Handbook of Philosophy of Mind*, edited by Brian McLaughlin and Ansgar Beckermann, 268–80, Oxford: Oxford University Press.

Chambers, Ephraim. 1738. *Cyclopedia, or an universal dictionary of the arts and sciences,* second edition, London: D. Midwinter.

Charlton, Walter. 1654. *Physiologia*, London: Thomas Heath.

Clarke, Samuel. 1998. *A Demonstration of the Being and Attributes of God*, edited by Ezio Vailati, Cambridge: Cambridge University Press.

Comenius, John Amos. 1651. *Natural philosophie reformed by divine light, or, A synopsis of physicks*, London: Sa[muel] Gellibrand.

Cudworth, Ralph. 1678. *The true intellectual system of the universe,* London: Richard Royston.

Digby, Kenelm. 1669. *Of bodies and mans soul,* London: John Williams.

Garrett, Don. 1997. *Cognition and Commitment in Hume's Philosophy,* New York: Oxford University Press.

Hakkarainen, Jani. 2007. *Hume's Scepticism and Realism: Two* Profound *Arguments against the Senses in* An Enquiry concerning Human Understanding, Acta Universitatis Tamperensis 1267. Tampere, Finland: Tampere University Press.

Hamilton, William. See under Reid, Thomas.

Hobbes, Thomas. 1656. *Elements of philosophy*, London: Andrew Crooke.

Huet, Pierre. 1725. *A philosophical treatise concerning the weakness of human understanding*, London: Gysbert Dummer.

Hume, David. 1777. "A dissertation on the passions," in *Essays and Treatises on Several Subjects*, volume 2, 175–212. London: T. Cadell.

—— 1975. *Enquiries concerning Human Understanding and concerning the Principles of Morals*, third edition, edited by L. A. Selby-Bigge and P. H. Nidditch, Oxford: Clarendon Press.

—— 1978. *A Treatise of Human Nature*, second edition, edited by L. A. Selby-Bigge and P. H. Nidditch, Oxford: Clarendon Press.

—— 1987. *Essays Moral, Political, and Literary*, revised edition, edited by Eugene F. Miller, Indianapolis: Liberty Fund.

—— 1993. "Dialogues concerning Natural Religion," in *Principal Writings on Religion*, edited by J. C. A. Gaskin, Oxford: Oxford University Press.

—— 1998. *An Enquiry concerning the Principles of Morals*, edited by Tom L. Beauchamp, Oxford: Clarendon Press.

—— 2000a. *An Enquiry concerning Human Understanding*, edited by Tom L. Beauchamp, Oxford: Clarendon Press.

—— 2000b. *A Treatise of Human Nature*,. edited by David Fate Norton and Mary J. Norton, Oxford: Oxford University Press.

Hutcheson, Francis. 2002. *An Essay on the Nature and Conduct of the Passions and Affections, with Illustrations on the Moral Sense*, edited by Aaron Garrett, Indianapolis: Liberty Fund.

—— 2006. *Logic, Metaphysics, and the Natural Sociability of Mankind*, edited by James Moore and Michael Silverthorne, Indianapolis: Liberty Fund.

Kail, P. J. E. 2007. *Projection and Realism in Hume's Philosophy*, Oxford: Oxford University Press.

Koselleck, Reinhart. 2004. *Futures Past*, translated by Keith Tribe, New York: Columbia University Press.

Leibniz, G. W. 1970. *Philosophical Papers and Letters*, second edition, edited by Leroy E. Loemker, Dordrecht: D. Reidel.

Locke, John. 1975. *An Essay concerning Human Understanding*, edited by Peter H. Nidditch. Oxford: Clarendon Press.

Loeb, Louis E. 2002. *Stability and Justification in Hume's* Treatise, Oxford: Oxford University Press.

Lucretius. *De rerum natura.*

Malebranche, Nicolas. 1980. *The Search after Truth*, translated by Thomas Lennon and Paul Olscamp, Columbus: Ohio State University Press.

Montaigne, Michel de. 1993. *An Apology for Raymond Sebond*, translated by M. A. Screech, London: Penguin.

Reid, Thomas. 1863. *The Works of Thomas Reid*, sixth edition, two volumes, edited by William Hamilton, Edinburgh: Maclachlan and Stewart.

Richter, Melvin. 1995. *The History of Social and Political Concepts: A Critical Introduction,* New York: Oxford University Press.

Ripley, George, 1591. *Compound of alchymy,* London: Thomas Orwin.

Ritter, Joachim, and Karlfried Gründer. 1971–2007. *Historisches Wörterbuch der Philosophie,* thirteen volumes, Basel and Stuttgart: Schwabe.

Selby-Bigge, L. A. (ed.). 1897. *British Moralists*, two volumes, Oxford: Clarendon Press.

Sprat, Thomas. 1667. *History of the Royal-Society of London for the improving of natural knowledge,* London: J. Martyn.

Watts, Isaac. 1742. *Philosophical essays on various subjects,* third edition, London: James Brackstone.

Weller, Cass. 2001. "Why Hume is a Direct Realist," *Archiv für Geschichte der Philosophie* 83: 258–85.

Wilkins, John. 1668. *An essay towards a real character: And a philosophical language,* London: Sa[muel] Gellibrand.

Winkler, Kenneth P. 1996. "Hutcheson and Hume on the Color of Virtue." *Hume Studies* 22: 3–22.

Wright, John P. 1983. *The Sceptical Realism of David Hume.* Minneapolis: University of Minnesota Press.

Young, Edward. 1777. *Night thoughts on life, death, and immortality.* Two volumes. London: J. French and others.

11

Reid on the Real Foundation of the Primary–Secondary Quality Distinction

James Van Cleve

The distinction betwixt primary and secondary qualities hath had several revolutions. Democritus and Epicurus, and their followers, maintained it. Aristotle and the Peripatetics abolished it. Des Cartes, Malebranche, and Locke, revived it, and were thought to have put it in a very clear light. But Bishop Berkeley again discarded this distinction, by such proofs as must be convincing to those that hold the received doctrine of ideas. Yet, after all, there appears to be a real foundation for it in the principles of our nature.

Thomas Reid[1]

1. Reid's relation to Locke and Berkeley

Every student of philosophy knows how to draw up the lists of primary and secondary qualities. On the left go extension, size, shape or figure, solidity, motion or rest, and number; on the right go color, sound, scent, taste, heat and cold. But what is the principle of the distinction? Does it have to do with objective versus subjective? Categorical versus dispositional? Intrinsic versus extrinsic? Or something else? And does the distinction stand up to the criticisms that various philosophers have made of it? In this chapter, I expound the answers to these questions given or made possible by Thomas Reid.

[1] Thomas Reid, *An Inquiry into the Human Mind on the Principles of Common Sense*, edited by Derek R. Brookes (Edinburgh: Edinburgh University Press, 1997; first published in 1764), chapter 5, Section 4, 62. Subsequent references to this work will be in this style: IHM 5.4, 62. A similar passage occurs in Reid's *Essays on the Intellectual Powers of Man*, edited by Derek R. Brookes (University Park, PA: Pennsylvania State University Press, 2002; first published in 1785) in Essay II, Chapter 17, 201. Subsequent references to this work will be in this style: EIP 2.17, 201.

Though the term 'secondary quality' was introduced by Boyle, the distinction between primary and secondary qualities comes down to us mainly through Locke and Berkeley. Here is how Locke defines secondary qualities:

[Secondary qualities are] Such *Qualities*, which in truth are nothing in the Objects themselves, but Powers to produce various Sensations in us by their *primary Qualities*, i.e. by the Bulk, Figure, Texture, and Motion of their insensible parts.[2]

It is clear from this passage that what Locke understands by a secondary quality is something quite definitely in the object. Locke scholars may disagree about whether this something is a dispositional property or its categorical basis—an interpretive issue we shall shortly encounter in connection with Reid as well—but in either case, secondary qualities reside in external objects.[3]

When Berkeley came to present Locke's teaching on primary and secondary qualities, he did not adhere to Locke's own understanding of what a secondary quality is. Here is how Berkeley has Hylas present the distinction in the *Three Dialogues*:

You must know sensible qualities are by philosophers divided into *primary* and *secondary*. The former are extension, figure, solidity, gravity, motion, and rest. And these they hold exist really in bodies. The latter are those above enumerated [colors, sounds, tastes, etc.]; or briefly, all sensible qualities beside the primary, which they assert are only so many sensations or ideas existing nowhere but in the mind.[4]

As Hylas uses the term, a secondary quality is a quality that exists nowhere but in the mind. This divergence in usage—secondary qualities as properties (if only dispositional ones) in external objects versus secondary qualities as properties existing only in the mind—persists down to the present day. Unfortunately, there is not only divergence from one writer to another, but also sometimes even divergence from one passage to another in the same writer.[5] Students do well not to be confused by this.

[2] John Locke, *An Essay Concerning Human Understanding*, 2.8.10.

[3] Students sometimes stumble on Locke's comma, taking him to say that secondary qualities are "nothing in objects themselves." But that reading conflicts with the rest of the sentence, which says that secondary qualities are powers, which can hardly be anywhere but in the object. On this point, see Mackie, *Problems from Locke*, 12, or Edwin McCann, "Locke's Philosophy of Body," in *The Cambridge Companion to Locke*, 56–88, at p. 63.

[4] George Berkeley, *Three Dialogues Between Hylas and Philonous*.

[5] Hume and Putnam may be mentioned as classical and contemporary cases in point. Hume compares his account of moral virtues and vices to the account of secondary qualities given by the modern philosophy. He says his philosophy "defines virtue to be *whatever mental action or quality gives to a spectator the pleasing sentiment of approbation*; and vice the contrary" (*An Enquiry Concerning the Principles of Morals*, 289). That definition puts virtue and vice in the action contemplated, not in the spectator. But he also says this: "When you pronounce any action or character to be vicious, you mean nothing, but that from the constitution of your nature you have a feeling or sentiment of blame from the contemplation of it. Vice and virtue, therefore, may be compar'd to sounds, colours, heat and cold, which, according to modern philosophy, are not qualities in objects, but perceptions in the mind" (*A Treatise of Human Nature,* 3.1.1, 469). That comparison puts virtues and secondary qualities in the mind. The same double usage occurs in Hilary Putnam, *The Many Faces of Realism* (La Salle, Ill.: Open Court, 1987). Putnam characterizes secondary qualities both as "dispositions to

Despite their divergence in terminology, we can identify an important thesis on which Locke and Berkeley agree. If by 'red' we mean the occurrent, sensuous, aesthetically significant quality that most of us initially mean by the term (as opposed, say, to the power of objects to reflect light of certain wavelengths and absorb the rest), then redness is not in external objects, but only in minds. It is a feature of sensations or ideas only, as Hylas says. This is the thesis that Locke states in terms of resemblance:

> The ideas of primary qualities of bodies are resemblances of them, and their patterns do really exist in the bodies themselves; but the ideas produced in us by these secondary qualities have no resemblance of them at all.[6]

Locke is saying that colors, tastes, and so on—"the ideas produced in us by these secondary qualities"—do not resemble any properties in the objects that cause them.

We can also identify significant points on which Locke and Berkeley disagree. For Locke, there certainly are primary qualities in objects, and they do resemble the ideas "of" them in our minds. For Berkeley, by contrast, all qualities reside in the mind alone, and nothing in the mind resembles anything outside it.

How now does Reid relate to Locke and Berkeley? He agrees and disagrees with each of them on important points. In agreement with Locke and in opposition to Berkeley, he maintains that there are indeed objects outside the mind, and that they are invested with the primary qualities. In agreement with Berkeley and in opposition to Locke, he maintains that ideas or sensations do not resemble external things in respect of primary qualities any more than they do in respect of secondary qualities.

Reid's resistance to Locke's positive resemblance thesis comes out most strongly in his *experimentum crucis*—the thought experiment by which he seeks to show that we have clear conceptions of certain qualities (notably, extension and hardness) that we could never have derived from our sensations.[7] In the thought experiment, we are to imagine a person stripped of his notion of extension and thus of the primary qualities generally (since size, shape, and motion all presuppose extension). We are to consider whether such a person could recover the notion of extension just from tactile sensations and the power of reasoning. Reid describes a sequence of progressively richer sensations—the prick of a pin, the pressure of a blunt instrument, the drawing of a finger across the subject's back, the feelings of moving his arm with and without resistance—and contends that at no step of the way would any of these sensations afford the subject any conception of extension. Reid concludes that the notion of extension must be innate in those who have it, constituting an exception to Hume's principle that

affect us in certain ways" (p. 8), which puts them in objects, and as properties that are "merely 'appearance', or merely something we 'project' onto the object" (p. 9), which puts them in minds.

[6] Locke, *Essay*, 2.8.15. Ideas "of" primary qualities are not necessarily intentional states; they may simply be ideas produced in us by primary qualities, in parallel with Locke's language in the second half of the sentence.

[7] For this thought experiment, see IHM 5.6, pp. 65–67. Reid refers back to it as his '*experimentum crucis*' on p. 70.

all our ideas are copies of impressions. The interesting implication for present purposes is that there is *no resemblance* between our sensations and extended objects. If there were, the subject of the experiment *could* get the conception of extension by reflection on his sensations.[8]

To summarize this section, the basis of the primary/secondary quality distinction for Reid cannot be that primary qualities reside in objects and secondary qualities do not (as Berkeley's Hylas has it), since *both* sets of qualities reside in objects. Nor can it be that primary qualities resemble their associated ideas or sensations and secondary qualities do not (as Locke has it), since in *neither* case is there any resemblance. So what, if anything, is the basis for the distinction?

2. The real foundation: epistemological or metaphysical?

Reid gives his own account of the primary/secondary quality distinction in the following passage from the chapter in the *Intellectual Powers* devoted to the distinction:

> Is there a just foundation for this distinction? Is there anything common to the primary which belongs not to the secondary? And what is it?
>
> I answer, That there appears to me to be a real foundation for the distinction; and it is this: That our senses give us a direct and a distinct notion of the primary qualities, and inform us what they are in themselves: But of the secondary qualities, our senses give us only a relative and obscure notion. They inform us only, that they are qualities that affect us in a certain manner, that is, produce in us a certain sensation; but as to what they are in themselves, our senses leave us in the dark. (EIP 2.17, 201)

A few paragraphs later, he gives a reprise:

> Thus I think it appears, that there is a real foundation for the distinction of primary from secondary qualities; and that they are distinguished by this, that of the primary we have by our senses a direct and distinct notion; but of the secondary only a relative notion, which must, because it is only relative, be obscure; they are conceived only as the unknown causes or occasion of certain sensations with which we are well acquainted. (EIP 2.17, 202)

So there we have it: our notions of primary qualities are *direct* and *distinct*, whereas our notions of secondary qualities are *relative* and *obscure*.

'Direct' is the opposite of 'relative'. Reid explains what he means by 'relative' as follows:

> A relative notion of a thing, is, strictly speaking, no notion of the thing at all, but only of some relation which it bears to something else. (EIP 2.17, 201)

[8] I have always thought there is an odd disparity in the reasons Reid gives for his doctrine of "no resemblance" between sensations and external things. Sometimes he presents it as though it were the result of careful introspection: attend to your sensations carefully enough, and you will see that they resemble nothing in the external world (IHM 6.6, p. 92; EIP 2.17 209 lines 10–18). At other times he presents it as though it were a matter of a priori ontology: sensations are mind-dependent, traits of external objects are not, and no resemblance can span such fundamentally different types of being (IHM 6.6, p. 94; EIP 2.17, 209 lines 31–38). At EIP 2.17, p. 203, he presents both considerations seamlessly in the same paragraph.

> This [the notion of gravity as whatever causes one body to be drawn toward another] is a relative notion, and it must be obscure, because it gives no conception of what the thing is, but of what relation it bears to something else. (EIP 2.17, 202)

An example of a relative notion would be the notion conveyed by the description 'the object that was in Descartes' pocket on the day he died'; clearly, such a description leaves us in the dark about what the object was or what it was like. Reid cites medicine as a source of further examples: terms such as 'astringent' and 'narcotic', which signify qualities known only by their effects on animal bodies (IHM 6.5, p. 88).

Examples of direct notions are our notions of the various shapes and the notion of hardness, which Reid defines as the firm adhesion of the parts of a body so as to make it resistant to change of shape (IHM 5.4, 61–62). When we know a thing to be hard or square, we know what it is like in itself, not merely how it is related to something else.

'Distinct' is the opposite of 'obscure'. It appears to have been Reid's view when he wrote the EIP chapter on secondary qualities that relative notions are *ipso facto* obscure: when we know only what relation a thing bears to something else, we have no distinct notion of it, but "only a relative notion, *which must, because it is only relative*, be obscure" (emphasis added).[9]

According to Reid's official account of the difference between primary and secondary qualities, then, our notions of the former are direct and distinct while our notions of the latter are relative and obscure. This account may well prompt in the reader the following thought: Reid's distinction between primary and secondary qualities is merely epistemological, not metaphysical. The two types of quality differ not in their own natures, but in the types of access we have to them. This is the understanding of Reid advocated by Lehrer and McKitrick, and there is undeniably support for it in Reid's text.[10] But I believe it is also possible to interpret Reid in such a way that his distinction between primary and secondary qualities is rooted in the nature of the qualities themselves after all: primary qualities are *intrinsic* and secondary qualities are *extrinsic*. In the next two subsections, I explore what can be said for and against these two interpretations.

[9] By the time he wrote the *Essays on the Active Powers of the Human Mind*, however, he had come around to the position that some relative notions are distinct, not obscure. For example, he says that the relative notion we form of a chiliagon by considering its relations to polygons of a greater or lesser number of sides is distinct—indeed, more distinct than the direct conception of a chiliagon we obtain when we see or imagine one. This change of mind was no doubt meant to accommodate his view that notion of *active power* is relative to its effects, yet distinct for all that. See *Essays on the Active Powers of the Human Mind*, edited by Baruch Brody (Cambridge, Mass.: MIT Press, 1969), 7–9.

[10] Jennifer McKitrick, "Reid's Foundation for the Primary/Secondary Quality Distinction," *The Philosophical Quarterly*, 52 (2002), 478–94; reprinted in *The Philosophy of Thomas Reid*, edited by John Haldane and Stephen Read (Oxford: Blackwell, 2003), 65–81; Keith Lehrer, "Reid on Primary and Secondary Qualities," *The Monist*, 61 (1978), 184–91, at p. 186.

A. Dispositions or bases?

The question whether Reid's foundation for the distinction is epistemological or metaphysical is closely aligned with another question: does Reid think of secondary qualities as mere *dispositions* in objects, or does he think of them as the *causal bases* of dispositions? As explained below, the 'disposition' answer suggests a metaphysical foundation for the distinction, whereas the 'base' answer suggests a merely epistemological one.

Where contemporary philosophers use the term 'disposition', Reid more often uses the terms 'power' and (with no pejorative intent) 'occult quality'.[11] I shall generally use the contemporary term in what follows.

Dispositions are often defined by subjunctive conditionals. To say that the glass is fragile is to say that if it were struck, it would break; to say that sugar is soluble is to say that if it were placed in water, it would dissolve; and so on. Schematically, x has a certain disposition (to exhibit manifestation M in circumstances C) IFF if x were placed in C, it would exhibit M. A definition of the color red fitting this schema might look like this:

x is red IFF if x were placed in view of a normal human observer in daylight, the observer would receive red* sensations.

By 'red* sensations', I refer to the type of sensations you get when something looks red to you—a type I could define ostensively by putting you in the right circumstances and letting you see what happens.[12] I use 'red*' rather than 'red' in the definiens for two reasons: (i) I do not want to give the appearance of a circular definition, and (ii) in Reid's view, sensations and external things are certainly not red in the same sense (else we would have an instance of the resemblance thesis he so strenuously opposes).

The *causal base* of a disposition is the categorical property (if any) in virtue of which the disposition is possessed—in other words, it is some non-dispositional property of the object such that it is a causal law that objects with that property exhibit M in C. The basis of the fragility of glass is presumably some aspect of its molecular structure, its pattern of bonding or whatnot; the basis of an object's looking red (i.e. producing red* sensations in observers) might be whatever properties of its surface make it reflect light of certain wavelengths while absorbing light of other wavelengths. Philosophers debate the question whether all dispositions must have categorical bases; I shall simply assume here that the answer is yes.[13]

[11] See, for example, IHM 6.5 88 and EIP 2.18, p. 216. We do have 'disposition' at EIP 2.17, p. 204.

[12] My device of starring does much the same work as Peacocke's device of priming predicates; I prefer it only for typographical reasons. See Christopher Peacocke, *Sense and Content* (Oxford: Oxford University Press, 1983), ch. 2.

[13] Elsewhere I have argued for a yes answer with one qualification: although *universal* dispositions (those possessed by everything) need not have categorical bases, dispositions possessed by some things but not others must have them. See my "Putnam, Kant, and Secondary Qualities," *Philosophical Papers*, 24 (1995), 83–109. Also see the Appendix to this chapter.

Now we may pose the issue of this subsection: are Reidian secondary qualities dispositions to produce sensations, or are they the bases of such dispositions?[14] Bases, say McKitrick and Wolterstorff; dispositions, say Yaffe and I.[15] This question is related to the epistemological versus metaphysical issue in a clear-cut way. If secondary qualities are bases, they may simply be (as in Locke's view they explicitly are) combinations of primary qualities, in which case, of course, they would be the same in nature as primary qualities. Secondary qualities would differ from primary qualities only in our mode of access to them (via their effects). But if secondary qualities are dispositions, they will differ metaphysically from primary qualities—they will be relational or extrinsic properties, in a sense to be explicated further below, whereas primary qualities are intrinsic.

The textual evidence on the disposition versus base issue pulls in both directions. Reid sometimes says that a secondary quality is a "certain power or virtue in bodies" (IHM 6.5, 87, lines 9–12; see also IHM 2.9, 43, line 3), suggesting a dispositional account. However, his more frequent formula is that secondary qualities are *unknown causes of known effects*. Here is a sampling of passages:

> [T]he qualities in bodies which we call *heat* and *cold*, are unknown. They are only conceived by us, as unknown causes or occasions of the sensations to which we give the same names. (IHM 5.1, 54)

> [T]hat idea [a term Reid uses here interchangeably with 'sensation'] which we have called *the appearance of colour*, suggests the conception and belief of some unknown quality in the body, which occasions the idea; and it is to this quality, and not to the idea, that we give the name of *colour*. (IHM 6.4, 86)

> But of the secondary qualities, our senses . . . inform us only, that they are qualities that affect us in a certain manner, that is, produce in us a certain sensation. (EIP, 2.17; 201)

> [S]mell in the rose is an unknown quality or modification, which is the cause or occasion of a sensation which I know well. . . . The same reasoning will apply to every secondary quality. (EIP 2.17, 202)

[14] The question "disposition or base?" is short-circuited by those philosophers who *identify* dispositions with their bases, as D. M. Armstrong professes to do. There are objections to such an identity view, however. To mention just one, the same disposition may have different bases in different objects and cannot be identical with them all. (For this objection along with two others, see Elizabeth W. Prior, Robert Pargetter, and Frank Jackson, "Three Theses about Dispositions," *American Philosophical Quarterly*, 19 (1982), 251–57.) Moreover, in some of Armstrong's own elucidations of his so-called identity view, it appears that he really holds something else. In "Dispositions as Categorical States," his contribution to *Dispositions: A Debate*, edited by Tim Crane (London: Routledge, 1996), he spells out his view thus: what it is for glass to be brittle is for it to have a categorical property that, together with its being struck and the laws of nature, entails that it shatters. That makes dispositions supervenient on categorical properties without being identical with them.

[15] For the view that Reidian secondary qualities are bases, see McKitrick; Nicholas Wolterstorff, *Thomas Reid and the Story of Epistemology* (Cambridge: Cambridge University Press, 2001), 112–13, where it is said that this is Reid's "dominant tendency"; and Barry Maund, "Color," *The Stanford Encyclopedia of Philosophy* (Fall 2008 Edition), Edward N. Zalta(ed.), forthcoming URL = <http://plato.stanford.edu/archives/fall2008/entries/color/>. For the view that Reidian secondary qualities are dispositional (and relational) properties, see Gideon Yaffe, "Thomas Reid", *The Stanford Encyclopedia of Philosophy* (Fall 2008 Edition), Edward N. Zalta(ed.), forthcoming URL = <http://plato.stanford.edu/archives/fall2008/entries/reid/>.

Characterizing secondary qualities as "unknown causes" suggests that secondary qualities are bases rather than dispositions for two reasons: it is bases, not dispositions, that do the causing,[16] and it is bases that are unknown.[17]

The second of these points has been pressed by Wolterstorff: "If green were a disposition in things to cause certain sensations under certain conditions and not the physical basis of that disposition, we would know what it was."[18] This argument is presumably to be spelled out as follows:

1. If green were a disposition in things to cause certain sensations in us, we would know what green is (for we know what that disposition is).[19]
2. According to Reid, we do *not* know what green is—it is an unknown quality, etc.
3. Therefore, Reid's view implies that green is not a disposition, but its base—for it is the base of which we are ignorant.

Call this the argument from ignorance.

It seems to me that this argument cannot be decisive, since it may be countered by an equally good argument from knowledge. If we do not know *what* green is, then we do not know of anything *that* it is green. This is an instance of the general principle that you know x to be F only if you know what it is to be F. But it is clear that for Reid, we *do* often know of things that they are green. Hence, we must know what it is for them to be green, contrary to premise 2 in the argument from ignorance.[20]

I said above that the textual evidence on the disposition versus base issue pulls both ways. Here is a passage that makes trouble for the base view and favors the disposition view:

> [Sensations belonging to secondary qualities] are not only signs of the object perceived, but they bear a capital part in the notion we form of it. We conceive it only as that which occasions such a sensation, and therefore cannot reflect upon it without thinking of the sensation which it occasions. (EIP 2.17, 204; see also IHM 6.4, p. 86, lines 31–36)

[16] See Prior, Pargetter, and Jackson for an argument that dispositions are causally impotent.

[17] A related point is that if Reid were thinking of secondary qualities as dispositions, it would be more natural for him to speak of the property *of* causing such-and-such sensations rather than the property *that* causes them.

[18] Wolterstorff, 112.

[19] Compare what Reid says about gravity at EIP 2.17, pp. 201–202: when the word is used to signify the tendency of bodies toward the earth (as opposed to the cause of this tendency), we know perfectly what it is.

[20] Reid's own attitude to the argument I have just given is difficult to make out. At EIP 203–204, he seems to repudiate its general principle (that you know something is F only if you know what it is to be F): "Our feeling informs us that the fire is hot; but it does not inform us what that heat of the fire is." Yet before the paragraph is over, he acknowledges that "if we had not some notion of what is meant by the heat of fire, and by an inebriating quality, we could affirm nothing of either with understanding." He seeks to reconcile this remark with the preceding one by saying that our notion of heat is merely relative—what we know in knowing the fire to be hot is that it contains some cause of our heat sensations, but not what this cause is. I shall be arguing below that his reconciliation is best effected by taking the notion of heat to be dispositional.

Call this the "capital part" thesis. The thesis is clearly true if secondary qualities are dispositions, defined in the manner above. The definiens in each dispositional definition of a secondary quality makes reference to a type of sensation, and for that reason, we could not conceive of the property without conceiving of the sensation. But the thesis is not so clearly true, and indeed seems false, if secondary qualities are bases. The base might be a primary quality with which we are in fact acquainted (perhaps without knowing that it is the base), and in that case we would be able to conceive of it without conceiving of any sensation. People who do not know that motion is the base of the disposition to produce heat sensations (and even those who do) may conceive of motion without conceiving of heat sensations.

The argument I have just given may raise suspicions. An instance of it would be the following:

1. I cannot conceive of heat without conceiving of heat sensations. (The "capital part" thesis)
2. I can conceive of motion without conceiving of heat sensations.
3. Therefore, heat is not motion.

We know nowadays that heat is a form of motion, so must there not be something wrong with the argument?

The validity of the argument ought to be conceded by anyone who adopts an intensional criterion for the identity of properties, and premise 2 seems beyond question. The controversial part is premise 1. Contemporary readers who know their Kripke would say that if we characterize heat by the formula "Heat is the cause of heat sensations," we are not *giving the meaning* of "heat", but fixing its reference. We are not saying that "heat" is synonymous with "whatever causes heat sensations", but are saying instead something that amounts to this: there is a property P that causes heat sensations, and heat is *that property P*. If motion turns out to be the cause of heat sensations, it would then follow that heat is motion.[21] The first premise and the conclusion of the argument above would both be false.

The argument is therefore contentious. What matters for our interpretive purposes, however, is whether Reid would have accepted its first premise. I believe he would have. When he affirms his "capital part" thesis, I do not believe he is merely expressing a deficiency in human knowledge—that in our ignorance of the causes of certain types of sensations, we can only refer to them indirectly as whatever properties cause the sensations. I believe he is affirming an essential link between the concept of heat and heat sensations, the concept of color and color sensations, and so on. In Lehrer's terms, he is saying that sensations are "semantic constituents" of secondary-quality concepts;

[21] Galileo was one of the first to conjecture that molecular motions are the cause of heat sensations. It is of interest that he states his conjecture by saying that motion is the cause of *heat*. In other words, he identifies heat with the sensations and not with their cause. This shows just how much the semantics of "heat" has changed between Galileo's day and our own. See *Thus Spoke Galileo*, edited by A. Frova and M. Marenzana (Oxford: University Press, 1998), p. 409.

in McDowell's terms, he is saying that secondary qualities are "essentially phenomenal qualities," that is, "qualities that could not be adequately conceived except in terms of how their possessors would look."[22]

We have now reviewed two sets of passages in Reid that seem to pull in opposite directions on the present issue—the "unknown cause" passages, which suggest that secondary qualities are causal bases, and the "capital part" passages, which suggest that secondary qualities are dispositions essentially defined in terms of certain sorts of sensations. Is there any way to accommodate them all? Perhaps not, if we must remain true to their letter, but perhaps so, if we may hazard a certain guess as to their intent or spirit. In what follows, I take up an idea mentioned by McKitrick, though not attributed by her to Reid.

McKitrick points out that some philosophers analyze dispositions along the following lines:

X has disposition D to produce manifestation M in circumstances C IFF there is some property P such that (X has P & P would cause M in C).[23]

A disposition as defined by a definition in this style is a *second-order* property—the property of having some property that satisfies a certain condition.[24] If redness were a disposition in this sense, it would be the property of having some property P that causes red* sensations in humans (in the specified circumstances). It would not be whatever *specific* property causes red* sensations—perhaps there is more than one—but the property of having *some property or other* that causes red* sensations. Properties that are dispositional in this sense are also dispositional in the "bare" sense discussed earlier (defined in terms of subjunctive conditionals), but the converse is not necessarily true—the bare sense leaves it open whether there is a causal base, and the second-order sense does not.

McKitrick does not ascribe to Reid the view that secondary qualities are dispositions on the second-order property model—she thinks secondary qualities for Reid are bases.[25] But I think the second-order view may be just what we need to accommodate some of the things Reid says. Look again at this passage:

[22] Keith Lehrer, *Thomas Reid* (London: Routledge 1989), 27; John McDowell, "Values and Secondary Qualities," in *Morality and Objectivity: A Tribute to J. L. Mackie*, edited by Ted Honderich (London: Routledge and Kegan Paul, 1985); reprinted in *Moral Discourse and Practice: Some Philosophical Approaches*, edited by Stephen Darwall, Allan Gibbard, and Peter Railton (Oxford University Press, 1997), 201–13. The quoted words occur on p. 203 in the latter volume. McDowell goes on to say that if in light of improved microphysical knowledge of the causal base of redness, we began to ascribe the microphysical quality to objects that look red to us, we would no longer be ascribing redness to them.

[23] McKitrick, 67–68.

[24] This notion of a second-order property should not be confused with another that also goes by the name "second-order property", namely, a property had by first-order properties rather than individuals. Second-order properties in the current sense may be had by individuals: they are called second-order because in the specification of them we quantify over other properties.

[25] Her view is actually more complicated than this, as she ascribes to Reid the supposedly Armstrongian view that dispositions and bases are identical. In my view, this leaves her hard pressed to handle Wolterstorff's observation that dispositions are known and bases are not, as well as the objections mentioned in n. 13.

> [T]hat idea [sensation] which we have called *the appearance of colour*, suggests the conception and belief of some unknown quality in the body, which occasions the idea; and it is to this quality, and not to the idea, that we give the name of *colour*. (IHM 6.4, 86)

How should we characterize the "belief of some unknown quality in the body" that occasions the sensation? There are two possibilities. One is

(1) We believe there is a property P such that (P is in the object & P causes such-and-such sensations in us).

and the other is

(2) There is a property P such that we believe (P is in the object & P causes such-and-such sensations in us).

The second formula cannot be right, precisely because the quality that causes red* sensations is unknown to us; until we have discovered which quality it is, we do not really believe of any property that *it* is the cause of our sensations. What we believe is better captured by the first formula—we believe that some property or other is in the object and causes red* sensations. Now if that is what we *believe* when we believe an object is red, it would be natural to say as well that that is what it *is* for an object to be red: namely, to have some property P that causes red* sensations in us. That would make redness a disposition as dispositions are construed on the second-order property model.

To be sure, Reid says that we give the name of color to the property that does the causing. But that is because he is operating with just two alternatives: is redness the cause in the object, or is it the effect in us? His main concern is to reject the second alternative—he wants to locate secondary qualities in objects. Given just those two alternatives, he plainly prefers the former. But were he given three alternatives—the effect in us, the specific cause of this effect, or the property of containing some cause or other of this effect—I bet he would opt for the third. That would nicely accommodate the following passage, which is the *Inquiry*'s version of the "capital part" thesis:

> [The notion of color] is really in some sort compounded. It involves an unknown cause, and a known effect. . . . But as the cause is unknown, we can form no distinct conception of it, but by its relation to the known effect. (IHM 6.4, 86)

The second-order conception involves both elements Reid requires—the known sensory effect by direct reference to it and the unknown cause by existential quantification over it. But it does not identify secondary qualities with unknown causes.

So let us adopt the hypothesis that secondary qualities are dispositions to produce certain sorts of sensations in us and see if that gives us a metaphysical foundation for the primary/secondary quality distinction. I think it does. This will be so regardless of whether we think of dispositions as defined simply by conditionals or as defined in terms of second-order properties.

B. *Intrinsic versus extrinsic*

If secondary qualities are dispositions to produce sensations rather than their bases, then there is at least one important metaphysical difference between primary and secondary qualities: primary qualities are *intrinsic* properties of their bearers, while secondary qualities are not.

To establish this point, it is necessary first to take some care with the notion of an intrinsic property. Intrinsic properties are often contrasted with relational properties, and relational properties are sometimes explicated as properties whose exemplification requires the existence of something else beyond the thing having it.[26] Kant gave a famous test for whether a property P is intrinsic in this sense:

Kant's test: A property P is intrinsic iff it would be possible for an object that was all alone in the universe to have P.[27]

Although dispositional properties are often regarded as being relational or extrinsic, a little thought shows they are intrinsic by Kant's test. Take a typical disposition, for example, the water-solubility of sugar—its being such that if it were placed in water it would dissolve. Is water-solubility a relation to water? No, for a given sugar cube would presumably still be water-soluble even if all water were removed from the universe.

There is another sense, however, in which dispositional properties *are* correctly thought of as extrinsic rather than intrinsic. This sense is brought out by another test:

Moore's test: A kind of [property] is intrinsic if and only if, when anything possesses it, that same thing or anything exactly like it would *necessarily* or *must* always, under all circumstances, possess it in exactly the same degree.[28]

I maintain that being such as to dissolve in water and being such as to give human beings who view it red* sensations are not intrinsic properties by Moore's test. An object that is *just like* one of the red objects in our world (having the same surface structure, reflectancy, etc.) could be situated in another possible world where it is no longer red. This could happen if the neural constitution of humans in that world were such that they did not get red* sensations upon viewing it; it could also happen if human beings were the same, but the laws of nature connecting causes with effects were different.

[26] By 'beyond x' I mean not merely *distinct* from x, but *discrete* from x, i.e. having no part in common with x. Otherwise, any property that implied having proper parts, such as being square, would count as relational, which is not what is intended.

[27] Kant invokes this test in "On the First Ground of the Distinction of Directions in Space" to show that the property of being a right hand is not a relational property involving other material things. For discussion, see James Van Cleve, "Right, Left, and the Fourth Dimension," *The Philosophical Review*, 96 (1987), 33–68.

[28] G. E. Moore, "The Conception of Intrinsic Value," in *Philosophical Studies* (Totowa, New Jersey: Littlefield, Adams, & Co., 1968; first published in London by Routledge and Kegan Paul in 1922), 253–75, at p. 265. Moore actually stated this just as a criterion for when *values* are intrinsic, but the criterion may be extended to properties in general. That, in effect, is what David Lewis has done with his suggestion that an intrinsic property is one that can never differ between two duplicates; see *On the Plurality of Worlds* (Oxford: Blackwell, 1986), 59–63.

I am obviously presupposing here that the laws of nature are contingent—that they could have been different from what they are.[29] This is an assumption with which Reid agrees—he notes in many places that for laws of nature, no other reason can be given but that they are the will of our Maker. It is also the view of Hume, who holds that there are no necessary connections between distinct existences, and of Locke, who says that God must "superadd" the power to produce certain sensations in us to its physical basis in bodies.[30]

Let us now return to what Reid says about the real foundation of the distinction between primary and secondary qualities—that as regards the former, our senses inform us what they are in themselves, but as regards the latter, our senses leave us in the dark, telling us only how they affect us. I would put his point thus: in knowing that an object is square, we know something about how it is intrinsically, or as Reid puts it, how it is in itself. We do not merely know something about how it would interact with our sensory apparatus. By contrast, in knowing that an object is red, we do not know anything about how it is in itself. We only know that it is such as to produce a certain kind of sensation in us, but that is something an object could do even if it were intrinsically quite different. An object's being red does not tell us how the object is in itself. This is not an epistemic point, but a point about the natures of the properties known; it concerns the informational contents of *x is square* and *x is red*. Reid's thesis about the difference between primary and secondary qualities is a metaphysical thesis about the nature of what is known, not a thesis about our manner of knowing it.

C. *Fixed or variable?*

I turn now to an interesting issue raised by McKitrick: whether Reid's way of drawing the primary/secondary quality distinction makes it relative to individuals and times. Might the same quality be secondary for one individual and primary for another, or secondary at one time and primary at another?

On McKitrick's understanding of Reid, it may seem initially that the answer is yes. According to her,

> Both [primary and secondary] qualities are causal bases of dispositions to cause sensations.... Reid's account of the foundation of the distinction is that the sensations caused by primary qualities suggest or signify [for us] something about the intrinsic nature of those qualities, while the sensations caused by secondary qualities signify only some unknown cause of that sensation.... On this picture, the only difference between primary and secondary qualities is 'in the head,' not in the properties. There is no metaphysical difference in the properties, only a difference in our epistemic access to them.[31]

[29] For a defense of this position against some contemporary views that oppose it, see Jonathan Schaffer, "Quiddistic Knowledge," in *Lewisian Themes*, edited by Frank Jackson and Graham Priest (Oxford: Clarendon Press, 2004), 210–30. In Schaffer's terms, I am a *quiddistic contingentist*.

[30] For a good discussion of Locke's views on this issue, see Rae Langton, "Locke's Relations and God's Good Pleasure," *Proceedings of the Aristotelian Society*, 100 (2000), 75–91.

[31] McKitrick, 77–78.

This account suggests that if our heads change in the right way, the status of a given quality as primary or secondary would also change. Suppose that heat sensations prompt us to believe that some quality of an external object is causing our sensations, but we have no idea of what this cause is—we conceive of it *only* as the cause of our sensations. Suppose further that as science progresses, we come to know exactly what property of hot objects causes heat sensations in us,[32] and that we teach ourselves and our offspring to respond to the sensations by attributing that property. Would heat not then have become a primary quality for us?

Before we answer this question, let us note that if the primary/secondary quality distinction must be relativized to individuals and times, it must also be relativized in a further way not noted by McKitrick—to types of sensations. The fully relativized notion would be something like this:

Q is a {primary, secondary} quality relative to S, t, and K iff (i) Q causes K sensations or impressions in S at t, and (ii) S is disposed at t to respond to K sensations by deploying a {direct, relative} conception of Q.

To see why we need the reference to K as well as to S and t, suppose that molecular motions at certain energy levels are the cause of heat sensations in us, and suppose (as in a figure of Locke's) that we are endowed with microscopical eyes, enabling us to see those very motions. If the relationship between motion and heat sensations is subtle enough, we may not realize that the motions we see (and form direct conceptions of as prompted by our visual impressions) are the cause of our heat sensations we will respond to our heat sensations by conceiving of the state of motion that causes them merely as "whatever causes heat sensations," and we will respond to our visual impressions by forming a direct conception of this very state of motion. In this circumstance, motion would be a primary quality relative to visual impressions and a secondary quality relative to heat sensations.

Now let us return to McKitrick's question. In the situation envisioned two paragraphs back, would heat have become a primary quality for us (relative to heat sensations) owing to the advance in our knowledge? Her answer is no. She points out that on Reid's understanding of primary qualities, they are qualities of which our senses *naturally* or *by our original constitution* give us a direct notion.[33] So if we discover what quality in objects causes our heat sensations and teach ourselves to respond to our

[32] Reid certainly envisioned this possibility. McKitrick cites EIP 2.17, p. 204: "The nature of secondary qualities is a proper subject of philosophical disquisition; and in this, philosophy has made some progress. It has been discovered, that the sensation of smell is occasioned by the effluvia of bodies; that of sound by their vibration. The disposition of bodies to reflect a particular kind of light occasions the sensation of colour. Very curious discoveries have been made of the nature of heat, and an ample field of discovery in these subjects remains."

[33] At IHM 6.4, p. 61, Reid contrasts secondary qualities with primary by saying that of the secondary "we know no more *naturally*, than that they are adapted to raise certain sensations in us." On the next page, he says that our conceptions and beliefs in primary qualities "are invariably connected with the corresponding sensations, by an *original* principle of human nature." (Both emphases are mine.)

sensations by forming a direct conception of this quality, it will not yet be the case that heat has become for us a primary quality. For it to be a primary quality, heat sensations would have to prompt us to form a direct conception of their external cause as part of our native endowment.[34]

But let us take her scenario one step further. Suppose we do not merely *train* ourselves to respond to heat sensations with a direct conception of their cause, but somehow *evolve* into creatures who so respond as part of their native constitution. In that case, heat would indeed have become a primary quality for our descendants. McKitrick concludes that although Reid's primary/secondary distinction need not be relativized to individual perceivers and times, it must be relativized to species.[35]

That conclusion would be correct if the primary/secondary quality distinction were merely epistemological, as McKitrick believes. But what if primary qualities are intrinsic and secondary qualities are extrinsic, as I have proposed? In that case, there could be no such thing as a secondary quality becoming primary (or vice versa), because there is no such thing as an extrinsic property becoming intrinsic (or vice versa).[36]

3. Four views that conflict with Reid's

To bring the contours of Reid's views about primary and secondary qualities into sharper relief, I now discuss four significant views that are opposed to his (and therefore ruled out if he is right). The four oppositions hold up regardless of the outcome of the debate discussed in the previous section—that is, regardless of whether Reid's foundation for the primary/secondary quality distinction is epistemological or metaphysical.

[34] McKitrick connects this point with Reid's distinction between original and acquired perception. We have acquired perception of a feature F when we form perceptual beliefs about the presence of F only because we have learned a correlation between F and other features perceived originally. For example, we do not, in Reid's view, have original perception of three-dimensional shape by sight, but only by touch. Once we have learned correlations between two-dimensional visual cues (shading, etc.) and three-dimensional shape (as gauged by touch), we automatically respond to the cues by conceiving of, and believing in, the three-dimensional shape of the object. In the case of learning to respond to heat sensations by conceiving of molecular motion, McKitrick would say that this is only acquired perception, not original perception. I would add: whether it would even count as acquired perception depends on whether the microstate that causes heat sensations is directly accessible to us through some other sense modality or whether it is something we learn about only through the hypothetico-deductive method.

[35] McKitrick, 81.

[36] What *might* be possible on Reid's view, however, is that a property should pass from primary to *non-primary* or vice versa. I have not aligned the primary/secondary distinction completely with the intrinsic/extrinsic distinction. Powers to produce changes in other insentient things—what Locke scholars sometimes call tertiary qualities—are extrinsic properties without being secondary qualities. There is also room in Reid's scheme for the converse combination of intrinsic properties that are not primary qualities. To qualify as primary in what seems to be Reid's view, a quality must not only be intrinsic, but also such as to produce sensations that natively trigger in us a direct conception of the property. If so, a property could gain or lose its status as primary in consequence of a change in the native sensory or cognitive endowment of human beings. If hardness ceased to produce any sensations in us, or if the sensations it did produce ceased to elicit in us a direct conception of hardness, hardness would no longer count as a primary quality.

A. Naïve realism: sensuous color is in the object

Reid, the self-proclaimed champion of common sense, seldom admits to holding any views at odds with those of the plain man. He thinks that the central tenet of modern philosophers about the secondary qualities, with which he agrees, is not at variance with common sense, but appears to be so only because of the philosophers' misleading use of ambiguous terms. In particular, he thinks that secondary quality terms are systematically ambiguous, the same term, such as "heat", being used both as the name of a type of sensation and as the name of a power in objects to produce that sensation in us. When philosophers deny that there is heat in the fire, they are only denying that the fire has any sensations, which the vulgar would readily deny as well. When the vulgar affirm that there is heat in the fire, they are only affirming that there is some quality in the fire that causes heat sensations in us, which the philosophers admit as well. So it is with color and the other secondary qualities—the apparent dispute between philosophy and common sense is only verbal:

> [O]ne of the most remarkable paradoxes of modern philosophy . . . is, in reality, when examined to the bottom, nothing else but an abuse of words. . . . [W]hen philosophers affirm that colour is not in bodies, but in the mind; and the vulgar affirm, that colour is not in the mind, but is a quality of bodies; there is no difference between them about things, but only about the meaning of a word.
>
> (IHM 6.5, 88; the same point is made again in EIP 2.17 at pp. 205–06)[37]

It seems to me, however, that there is something the man in the street believes that Reid, along with the philosophers, denies.[38] It is this: there is *sensuous color* in external objects. Call this naïve realism about color.[39] A good emblem for naïve realism (as I once heard George Pappas say) is the "cover the earth" logo of the Sherwin-Williams paint company, in which red paint pours out of a tilted bucket and coats the globe. Despite the fact (as it seems to me) that naïve realism is what most of us believe most of the time, it is not an easy view to pin down for a philosophical audience. It is not enough to characterize the view simply by saying that objects really are red, for there are meanings of that formula under which Lockean dispositionalists and Australian materialists (and Reid, depending on which of these camps we assimilate him to) would all assent to it. Yes, says Locke, objects are red, for they have the power to give us red* sensations; yes, says the Australian materialist, objects are red, because their microstructure is such that they absorb light of most wavelengths while reflecting light of wavelengths in the 760-to-647 nanometer range. But I do not believe that either of those

[37] Interestingly, Reid holds in his published work that color terms are the one exception to the systematic ambiguity of secondary-quality terms. He says that color terms never refer to sensations, but only to the external qualities that cause them (IHM 6.4, 85–87).

[38] Reid admits as much in an unpublished manuscript of unknown date, but presumably earlier than the *Inquiry*: "Color is imagined to be in the body by the vulgar but not by philosophers . . ." (Aberdeen University Library MS 2131/8/VI/3).

[39] I distinguish naïve realism from direct realism, the view that external things are directly perceived. I take Reid to be a direct realist, but not a naïve realist.

things is what a child or a poet believes who believes that a rose is red. How shall we characterize the property that is attributed to objects by the naïve and the romantic? It is a property that has no dependence on sentient minds; it is categorical, not dispositional; it is intrinsic; its nature is manifest to those who know nothing of physics; its nature is not manifest to those who know a lot of physics but have never experienced it. The various sophisticated philosophers' versions of red do not have all these characteristics.[40]

I am not necessarily saying that Reid is *wrong* to exclude sensuous color from external objects. I am only saying that he is wrong to think that in so excluding it, his views are compatible with common sense. On this point, I agree with Lorne Falkenstein, who has observed that "Reid is really *denying* that visible figures are 'coloured' in the truly common sense of the term."[41]

B. Mill, Putnam, and Langton: all properties are secondary qualities

I turn now to a view at the other end of the spectrum from naïve common sense: the view that *all* properties of external things, or at least all properties we know of, are secondary qualities in Locke's sense—powers to produce sensations in us. Mill, Putnam, and Langton have all attributed versions of this thesis to Kant, as well as favorably entertaining it themselves.

Here is Putnam's version:

> I suggest that (as a first approximation) the way to read Kant is as saying that what Locke said about secondary qualities is true of *all* qualities.... If *all properties are secondary*, what follows? It follows that *everything* we say about an object is of the form: it is such as to affect *us* in such-and-such a way. *Nothing at all* we say about any object describes the object as it is 'in itself', independently of its effect on *us*.[42]
>
> 'All properties are secondary' (i.e. *all properties are Powers*).[43]

Putnam is apparently attributing to Kant the thesis that the only properties *there are* in external things are powers to affect us in certain ways. This raises two interesting issues that I cannot pursue here. If one thinks of powers to affect us as relations, the question arises whether all properties of things can be relational. If one thinks instead of powers to affect us as dispositions, the question arises whether all properties of a thing can be dispositions, or whether instead the dispositions must have some categorical basis. I have discussed both issues elsewhere.[44]

[40] Naïve realism is not the prerogative of the vulgar alone, but has been defended as well by able philosophers, including John Campbell, "A Simple View of Colour," in *Reality, Representation, and Projection*, edited by John Haldane and Crispin Wright (Oxford: Clarendon Press, 1994), 257–69, and Peter Unger, *All the Power in the World* (Oxford: Oxford University Press, 2006), especially chapter IV.

[41] Lorne Falkenstein, "Reid's Account of Localization," *Philosophy and Phenomenological Research*, 61 (2000), 305–28, at p. 322.

[42] Hilary Putnam, *Reason, Truth, and History* (Cambridge: Cambridge University Press, 1981), pp. 59 and 61.

[43] Ibid. 63.

[44] James Van Cleve, "Putnam, Kant, and Secondary Qualities," *Philosophical Papers*, 24 (1995), 83–109.

A somewhat less extreme view, making a claim not about *all* the properties of external things but just the ones we *know of*, is expounded by Mill under the label 'the relativity of knowledge':

[T]hat all the attributes which we ascribe to objects, consist in their having the power of exciting one or another variety of sensation in our minds; that to us the properties of an object have this and no other meaning.... This is the doctrine of the Relativity of Knowledge to the knowing mind....[45]

Mill attributes this doctrine to a number of philosophers, including Kant. We may distinguish two versions of it: one according to which the only properties we can *know objects to have* are powers to produce sensations in us, and another according to which the only properties of external things we can even *form any conception of* are powers to produce sensations in us. Mill's language somewhat more strongly suggests the second.[46]

Reid's views are clearly at odds with Putnam's thesis and both versions of Mill's. Squareness and hardness, according to him, are intrinsic properties of objects in the sense we have discussed above; they are not merely dispositions to give us sensations, even if they imply such dispositions. They are also properties that we can both conceive of, and know, objects to possess.[47]

Why would anyone hold that we couldn't have any knowledge of the intrinsic properties of things? Rae Langton has given one answer to this question in her book *Kantian Humility*.[48] She reconstructs what she takes to be one of the central arguments of the *Critique of Pure Reason* as follows:

Receptivity: Human knowledge depends on sensibility, and sensibility is receptive: we can have knowledge of an object only in so far as it affects us. We have knowledge only of those properties of things in virtue of which they enter into causal relations with us.

Irreducibility: The relations and relational properties of substances (which include their powers to affect us) are not reducible to the intrinsic properties of things. The causal relations between things are not necessitated by their intrinsic properties. *Therefore*,

Humility: We have no knowledge of the intrinsic properties of things.

[45] John Stuart Mill, *An Examination of Sir William Hamilton's Philosophy* (Boston: W.V. Spencer, 1865), Vol. 1, 16.

[46] For a contemporary incarnation of Mill's doctrine, see John Foster, *The Case for Idealism* (London: Routledge, 1982), 63.

[47] One qualification is called for. What I can know *immediately* through vision is that an object is visibly elliptical, i.e. that it looks elliptical from a certain angle or to a viewer situated at a certain place in relation to it. This is a relational property of the object, not an intrinsic property of it. It is founded on an intrinsic property, however: the object's being round, together with its lying obliquely to my line of sight. I can have *mediate* knowledge (which eventually becomes acquired perception) of the object's roundness by inference from what I know immediately through sight, and I can verify this knowledge by the immediate knowledge I have through touch. For Reid's discussions of these matters, see IHM 6.3 and 6.7 as well as his various discussions of acquired perception.

[48] Rae Langton, *Kantian Humility: Our Ignorance of Things in Themselves* (Oxford: Clarendon Press, 1998).

Langton explains that by an intrinsic property she means "a property something can have, no matter what else exists—and no matter what the laws are . . . ."[49] The first clause—"no matter what exists"—says in effect that intrinsic properties must pass Kant's test; the second—"no matter what the laws are"—implies they must pass Moore's. Langton takes the Irreducibility premise to be true because she thinks (as I do) that a thing with the same intrinsic properties as a given thing need not have the same powers as the original if placed in a setting with different laws.

I find it striking that Reid accepts both premises of Langton's Kantian argument, but rejects the conclusion. Human beings are so constituted, Reid tells us, that they achieve knowledge of the world around them only because objects affect their sense organs, giving rise to physical impressions, which in turn give rise to mental sensations, which are the occasions for perception.[50] This is Receptivity. Moreover, of the laws whereby this sequence of operations takes place, we can give no explanation except that they are the will of God: "Who knows but their connection may be arbitrary, and owing to the will of our Maker?"[51] This clearly implies that laws of nature are contingent, and thus implies as much of the Irreducibility premise as is needed in Langton's argument. Yet Reid is far from accepting Humility. When we know something is square—as we sometimes do—we know how it is in itself and not merely how it affects our sensibility. So Reid would have cited the primary qualities as exceptions to Kantian Humility.

If Reid is right—as I believe he is—Langton's argument must be unsound. So what in particular is wrong with it? Inspection reveals that the argument is invalid as it stands. It would be valid only if supplemented by the following unstated premise: a causal relation holds between two things in virtue of certain of their properties only if it is *necessary* that any two things with those properties are causally related. For short, there is causation only where there is necessitation. This is a premise that Reid (siding for once with Hume) would deny—as would I. We can be affected by things in virtue of their intrinsic properties, even if those properties do not necessarily have the effects they do.[52]

C. *Berkeley and Hume: no object could have the primary qualities exclusively*

An issue raised by Berkeley and Hume for "the modern philosophy" is this: *could* an object have the primary qualities exclusively, without having any properties from the list of secondary qualities?[53] Finding it inconceivable that an object should have the primary qualities without any secondary qualities, Berkeley and Hume both say no. Reid says yes.

49 p. 119. 50 IHM 6.21, p. 174. 51 *Ibid.*, p. 176.

52 I have discussed Langton's argument at greater length and considered further ways of making it valid in James Van Cleve, "Receptivity and our Knowledge of Intrinsic Properties," *Philosophy and Phenomenological Research*, 65 (2002), 218–36.

53 Ironically, two of the issues raised by the thesis that all properties are secondary—could all properties be relational, and could all properties be dispositional?—are thought by some writers to arise for the thesis that all properties are *primary*. In his *Philosophy and Scientific Realism* (London: Routledge and Kegan Paul, 1963), J. J. C. Smart notes, "All the properties which science ascribes to physical objects [mass, charge, spin, even shape insofar as it is defined in terms of length] seem to be purely relational" (p. 72), and he equates the question 'Can a thing have the primary qualities alone?' with the question "Can a thing have relational properties

Let us be clear about the issue Berkeley and Hume are raising. As we have seen above, some authors identify secondary qualities with dispositions in objects to produce sensations in us, and other authors with the bases of such dispositions. Berkeley and Hume are not asking whether an object could have primary qualities but no power to produce sensations in us. The answer to that question, if I am right about the contingency of laws, is obviously yes. Nor are they asking whether an object could have primary qualities without having those qualities that are in fact the bases of powers to produce sensations. Given that the causal bases of such powers *are* primary qualities—as Locke explicitly says—the answer to that question is obviously no. What Berkeley and Hume are asking is a question of which the following is a more concrete instance: could an object have a shape without having any *sensuous* color or texture to fill in its boundaries and differentiate it from its surroundings? To that question, their answer is no.

In the rest of this section, let it be understood that "color" without qualification means "sensuous color" in the sense of the term I have tried to indicate above,[54] and let it further be understood that we are talking of *seen* objects, for which tangible properties would not suffice as their sensuous "filling."

If there can neither be (nor be conceived) shape without color, as Berkeley and Hume maintain, what follows? Three interesting lines of argument open up. The first is an argument for naïve realism: there is no shape without color; there is shape in external things; therefore, there is color in external things. The second is Berkeley's argument for extending idealism to shapes: there is no shape without color; there is no color except in minds; therefore, there is no shape without minds.[55] The third is Hume's twist on Berkeley: we cannot conceive of an object with extension or figure but no color; color exists only in internal impressions; therefore (since we cannot conceive of external things if we do not conceive of them as extended), we cannot conceive of external things.[56]

only?" (pp. 73–74). Simon Blackburn, who like Smart is trying to clear the way for the view that objects have only the properties that science ascribes to them, sees his task as defending the possibility that all properties of objects are dispositional. See his "Filling in Space," *Analysis*, 50 (1990), 62–65.

[54] With this exception: sensuous color for Berkeley and Hume is not independent of minds.

[55] Here is how Berkeley states the argument in the *Principles of Human Knowledge*, section 10: "For my own part, I see evidently that it is not in my power to frame an idea of a body extended and moved, but I must withal give it some colour or other sensible quality which is acknowledged to exist only in the mind. In short, extension, figure, and motion, abstracted from all other qualities, are inconceivable. Where therefore the other sensible qualities are, there must these be also, to wit, in the mind and nowhere else."

[56] Hume's argument in the *Treatise of Human Nature* (1.4.4, pp. 228–29) is actually more complicated, running as follows: it is impossible to conceive of a body as extended without conceiving of it as either colored or solid; color is excluded from bodies by the modern philosophy; the idea of solidity is the idea of being impenetrable by other bodies and therefore presupposes an antecedent conception of what bodies are; therefore, the modern philosophy leaves us no just conception of bodies. Since we are concerned at present only with what sensuous properties *visible* extension must have, we can work with the simpler argument I use in the text.

Reid disputes the conclusions of all three arguments. He holds that we *do* have a conception of external things, that they *are* endowed with shape, and that they are *not* endowed with sensuous color. Since he accepts the minor premise in each argument, it is incumbent on him to deny the major—that there can neither be, nor be conceived, shape without color. That is exactly what he implicitly does in his discussion of visible figure in section 5.8 of the *Inquiry*. Curiously, however, he does not there connect the discussion with the issues I am raising now, nor mention Berkeley and Hume as his antagonists.[57]

In IHM 5.8, Reid argues that it would be possible to see shape without seeing any color. As we are presently constituted, he says, the stimulation of a point on one of our retinas (which Reid calls the "material impression" involved in vision) has two effects: it makes us see a point of the object at a certain location (along the straight line from the point of stimulation running through the center of the eye and out into the environment), and it gives us a sensation of color. The stimulation of many retinal points simultaneously makes us see an array of object points at various locations, and that is just what it is to see figure. (Visible figure is determined by the location of all the points in an object with respect to the eye.) Now if it had pleased our Maker, Reid says, our eyes might have been so framed that retinal stimulations had the first of these effects without having the second—the perception of figure without any sensation of color.[58] Contrary to Berkeley and Hume, then, it would be possible to see shape without seeing any color. This takes away their reason for saying there could not *be* an object with shape but no color.

On the question whether there could *be* objects with shape but no color, I side with Reid. There is nothing inconceivable in the idea of a hexagonal pane of perfectly clear glass. What seems more doubtful to me is his contention that one could *see* an object as shaped without seeing any color in it or its surroundings. That is what Reid says we would do if endowed with the eye he imagines; it is even arguably what we do on Reid's view as we are constituted now.

Reid allows that under our present constitution, color is always "joined with" figure in our perception of figure (p. 101, lines 10–13). But we must note what this being "joined with" amounts to. It certainly does not mean that sensuous color is spread out over objects or is co-located with any of the object's surface points. The closest things we can get to instantiators of sensuous color in Reid's philosophy are color sensations, but it would be a category mistake on his view to think that color sensations take up

[57] He does take explicit exception to Berkeley and Hume on the shape-color issue in a discourse delivered before the Aberdeen Philosophical Society, but never published: "I think both Berkly & Hume affirm that there can be no idea of visible space without colour. I am of a contrary opinion & think I have a distinct conception of visible extension without colour" (p. 277 in the Brookes edition of the *Inquiry*).

[58] Reid also argues for the converse possibility of an eye in which retinal stimulations have the second effect without the first, in which case one would see color without perceiving location, extension, or figure. He thinks this is actually or nearly what happens in those who suffer from severe cataracts—"such persons see things as one does through a glass of broken gelly." If he means to show that one could perceive color without extension, I demur. Does not the cataract sufferer perceive blurry extension?

any area or are located at any point. What can be spread over an area is at best some primary quality that causes the sensations in us. So that which Berkeley and Hume regard as impossible—seeing an object with figure but no sensuous color—is not only possible on Reid's view, but actual: it happens whenever we see at all.[59]

Without sensuous color, I do not see what satisfactory account Reid can give of seeing boundaries. What happens, on his account, when I see a wall painted green on the left side of a central line and red on the right? (i) Concerning the locations on the left side of the line, I have the perception-induced beliefs "there is something *there* and something *there* and something *there*," and similarly for locations on the right. (What are the *somethings*? That is going to be the nub of my problem.) (ii) The retinal stimulations that cause beliefs with respect to environmental locations also cause color sensations: points of the retina stimulated by light from the left side of the wall cause green* sensations, and points stimulated by light from the right side cause red* sensations. (iii) I believe that the sensations are caused by properties instantiated in my environment in various parts of the wall.

Conditions (i)–(iii) cannot be the whole story, however. They are not enough to distinguish seeing green on the left and red on the right from seeing things the other way around, for all three conditions are satisfied in both cases. What must we add?

On Reid's view, the following condition will also be satisfied: (iv) I believe, concerning the various locations on the left, "something *there* is causing green* sensations in me," and concerning the various locations on the right, "something *there* is causing red* sensations in me." I have qualms about whether Reid is entitled to say this.[60] Assuming that he is, however, I wish to raise the question whether (iv) would be sufficient for perceiving boundaries.

My question is whether a perceptible boundary can be created for me just by the fact that I believe objects on one side to cause aspatial F-sensations and objects on the other to cause aspatial G-sensations. Recall that color sensations are no more spatial for Reid than olfactory sensations. Suppose I were blindfolded and placed before a tangle of honeysuckle on the left and a heap of pine mulch on the right. If I believed that the sweet scent had its cause on the left and the pungent smell had its cause on the right, would that create a perceptible boundary for me? I doubt that it would, and the same doubt carries over to color sensations. While agreeing with Reid, then, that the world might be a locus of primary qualities without being a locus of sensuous colors, I cannot believe that we could ever *see* objects in a world like that.

[59] Some contemporary "error theories" of color have it that we mistakenly paint objects with colors or project colors onto them. The error itself (if we take the description of it literally) is an impossibility on Reid's view, as it is contrary to the nature of color sensations to be projected onto any surface.

[60] The qualms arise from a suspicion that Reid faces some sort of binding problem. What can enable the believer to place the causes of aspatial sensations in various locations? Perhaps Reid can solve the problem with material impressions, which (unlike sensations) carry spatial information, and which might be able to inject the sensations they cause into the contents of beliefs about locations.

D. Smart, Harman, and Armstrong: we do not know what sensations are like intrinsically

The last anti-Reidian view I shall consider is that we do not know what our sensations are like intrinsically. This might be held on the basis of any of the following successively stronger doctrines, sometimes advanced under the banner 'the transparency of sensations':

1) that we seldom, if ever, notice our sensations;
2) that even in attending to our sensations, we are aware only of their relational features, not their intrinsic features;
3) that sensations do not even *have* any intrinsic features.

Views along one or another of these lines have been put forward by many contemporary philosophers, including Smart, Armstrong, and Harman. The motive, in many cases, is to make the world safe for materialism—if we are not aware of any intrinsic features of our sensations, then we cannot claim that sensations have features that no brain state could have.[61]

Reid himself goes part way with the *first* transparency doctrine. It is a recurrent theme of his philosophy that for the sensations in a broad range, we seldom notice them and can do so only with a special effort. He compares sensations to "the words of a language, wherein we do not attend to the sound, but to the sense" (IHM 2.9, 43) And he often says things like this:

> We are so accustomed to use the sensation [of hardness] as a sign, and to pass immediately to the hardness signified, that, as far as appears, it was never made an object of thought, either by the vulgar or by philosophers. . . . There is no sensation more distinct, or more frequent; yet it is never attended to, but passes through the mind instantaneously, and serves only to introduce that quality in bodies, which, by a law of our constitution, it suggests. (IHM 5.2, 56)

But Reid would have opposed the extreme form of the first transparency doctrine, which says we are *never* aware of our sensations. His analogy with the words of a language tells us as much, for there is nothing to prevent our attending to the sounds that express the various senses. Moreover, in the case of sensations associated with secondary qualities, we are bound to be aware of them, as we know from the "capital part" thesis: we can conceive of the qualities only by reference to the sensations.[62] Finally, even in the case of sensations associated with primary qualities, which normally make our thoughts leap immediately to the qualities they signify, we can know what

[61] Such was the motive for Smart's thesis of "topic-neutrality," a version of transparency in the early days of identity-theory materialism. According to Smart, we can conceptualize our experiences only by descriptions along the lines of "it's like what goes on in me when I see ripe tomatoes." See J. J. C. Smart, "Sensations and Brain Processes," *The Philosophical Review*, 68 (1959), 141–156.

[62] We do not always attend to them, though. Reid was one of the first authors to emphasize the various perceptual constancies. He notes that a plain man who is not a painter will perceive an object that is moved from near to far or light to shade as remaining constant in color, though the various color appearances or sensations have certainly changed. See IHM 6.3, p. 83.

they are like by careful attention. We must be able to do this to carry out his *expermimentum crucis*, which teaches us that tactile sensations are nothing like the extension, hardness, and other primary qualities they signify.

Those who hold the *second* transparency doctrine listed above hold that the only features of our sensations or experiences we are aware of are their relational features—typically, their intentional features or their causal relations (the first of which some philosophers try to reduce to the second). Thus Harman:

> When Eloise sees a tree before her ... [she does not] experience any features of anything as intrinsic features of her experiences. ... She is aware only of the intentional or relational features of her experience, not of its intrinsic non-intentional features.[63]

And Armstrong:

> A perception of something green will involve a green-sensitive element, that is to say, something which, in a normal environment, is characteristically brought into existence by green things. A green-sensitive element within need not be green, nor is it introspected as something green, nor indeed is it introspected as having any quality at all. It is introspected simply as something having sophisticated causal relationships to green things.[64]

Reid would say that Armstrong has things precisely backwards. Rather than being able to characterize our sensations only by reference to their causes—say, green things—we can characterize green things only by reference to the sensations they cause in us. As for the sensations themselves, we do know what they are like intrinsically. If our notions of them were only relative—a matter of how they are related to something else—we would not have distinct notions of them, but we do: "Upon reflection I find, that I have a distinct notion of the sensation which [that quality in a rose I call its smell] produces in my mind" (EIP 2.17, 202). Reid even goes so far as to say we know our sensations *perfectly*: "The sensations of heat and cold are perfectly known; for they neither are, nor can be, any thing else than what we feel them to be" (IHM 5.1, 54).

The *third* transparency doctrine listed above was espoused by Moore, from whom contemporary writers have taken the term 'transparency', but often without realizing how radical his view really was. The sensation of blue, says Moore, "seems, if I may use a metaphor, to be transparent—we look through it and see nothing but the blue."[65] His point is not just that we are unaware of the intrinsic nature of the sensation, but that the sensation itself *has* no intrinsic nature: everything it is, it owes to its object. Sensory consciousness is like a clear pane of glass through which we view objects, the glass

[63] Gilbert Harman, "The Intrinsic Quality of Experience," in *Philosophical Perspectives*, edited by James Tomberlin, Vol. 4 (Atascadero, CA: Ridgeview Publishing Co., 1990), 52–79; reprinted in *The Nature of Consciousness*, edited by Ned Block, Owen Flanagan, and Guven Guzeldere (Cambridge, MA: MIT Press, 1997), 663–75. The quotation is from p. 667 of the latter.

[64] David M. Armstrong, "Qualities: an Excerpt from *Consciousness and Causality*, in *Metaphysics: The Big Questions*, edited by Peter van Inwagen and Dean W. Zimmerman (Oxford: Blackwell, 1998), 273 and 275.

[65] G. E. Moore, "The Refutation of Idealism," originally in *Mind* for 1903, but reprinted in *Philosophical Studies* (London: Kegan Paul, 1922), 1–30, at p. 20.

differing from one episode of consciousness to the next only in what lies on the other side.[66] Reid's view cannot be like this, for he holds that sensations do not *have* objects: they are simply modifications of the mind. Sensing bluely and sensing greenly differ intrinsically, rather than in their relation to anything beyond themselves.

An especially unsettling combination of un-Reidian views would arise if we combined the thesis of Mill, Putnam, and Langton with that of Smart, Armstrong, and Harman: we know nothing intrinsic about external things (but only that they are related to mental states in certain ways), nor anything intrinsic about mental states (but only that they are related to external things in certain ways). That would mean we have no knowledge of the intrinsic properties of *anything*—knowledge of the relational features of some things would always dissolve away into knowledge of the relational features of yet other things, with nothing to anchor the system.[67] Needless to say, Reid would oppose this combination even more strenuously than he opposes each element separately.

Appendix: having it both ways?

By the "capital part" thesis, I mean Reid's thesis that sensations play a capital part in the notions we form of secondary qualities, the qualities being conceivable only in terms of the sensations. As Lehrer puts it, sensations are "semantic constituents" of our secondary quality concepts.[68] This thesis would be true on a dispositional understanding of secondary qualities.

By the "physical supervenience" thesis, I mean the thesis that the color of an object supervenes on its intrinsic physical character in the following sense: anything just like a given red object in all intrinsic physical respects would itself be red.[69] This thesis would be espoused by any physicalist worth his salt; it would presumably also be attributed to Reid by anyone who thought he identified colors with the causal bases of dispositions rather than the dispositions themselves.

Is it possible to define secondary qualities in a way that makes *both* theses true? Three ways of defining or specifying secondary qualities have been discussed in this chapter. The first is the simple conditional definition of red as a disposition:

D1. x is red =df if x were placed in view of a normal human observer in normal circumstances, the observer would be caused to experience red* sensations.

The second is the second-order property definition of red as a disposition:

[66] I have developed this interpretation of Moore at greater length in "Troubles for Radical Transparency," forthcoming in a festschrift for Jaegwon Kim.

[67] If I am not mistaken, this is the real upshot of Langton's Kantian argument from Receptivity, for knowledge of our own mental states presumably depends, just as much as our knowledge of external things does, on our being affected by them.

[68] Lehrer 1989, 27.

[69] For one expression of this thesis, see Crispin Wright 1992, 113.

D2. x is red =df there is some property P such that x has P & P causes red* sensations in normal human observers in normal circumstances.

From now on, let's abbreviate 'causes red* sensations in normal human observers in normal circumstances' to 'causes red* sensations in humans'. The third definition identifies red with the causal base of the disposition defined by D1 or D2, using sensations only to fix the reference of 'red':

D3. There is a property P such that P causes red* sensations in humans; x is red =df x has that property P.

How do our two theses fare under these definitions? D1 makes the capital part thesis true, since sensations figure in its definiens. (I am relying on the old-fashioned idea that the definiendum in an apt definition must, in Spinoza's language, be "conceived through" the definiens.) But it makes the physical supervenience thesis false, since a thing in another world just like a red thing in our world might *not* be such that humans who looked at it would get red* sensations. Perhaps the neural structure of humans is different in that world, or perhaps the laws of nature are different there.

D2 also makes the capital part thesis true, since it again defines color in terms of sensations. And like D1, it makes the physical supervenience thesis false, because humans or the laws might be different in some world containing a physical duplicate of a red object. In such a world, the duplicate need not have any property making things that have it look red (= cause red* sensations).

D3 reverses the verdicts yielded by D1 and D2. It makes the capital part thesis false, since it mentions sensations only outside the definition proper, using them merely to fix the reference of 'red'. Redness under this definition is a certain microphysical property, and you can grasp that property without conceiving of red* sensations. By the same token, it makes the physical supervenience thesis true, because if redness just is a certain physical property, then anything physically just like a red thing would be red, regardless of whether it causes red* sensations in humans.

None of our definitions, then, makes both theses true. Is there any way of understanding secondary qualities that *does* make both theses true? The answer is yes, although it involves a tricky device of contemporary philosophical logic that was unknown to Reid.

Definitions imply necessarily true biconditionals, and such biconditionals hold in all possible worlds. The most natural way to understand D2 in terms of possible worlds would be this:

D2a. For all worlds w: x is red in w =df for some property P, x has P in w & in w P causes red* sensations in humans.

But we can also understand D2 in another way—and here comes the trick—by indexing the second conjunct in the definiens to the actual world, @:

D2b. For all worlds w: x is red in w =df for some property P, x has P in w & in @ P causes red* sensations in humans.

D2a and D2b both imply the same verdict on the capital part thesis, since as with D1 and D2, they define redness in terms of sensations. But they part ways on the supervenience thesis, D2a making it false (as D2 did) and D2b making it true. D2b makes it true because if an object x in @ has a property P making it look red, any physical duplicate of x in another world w will also have that property P; and since P makes things *in* @ look red, possession of P by the duplicate in w makes it red even if it does not *look* red in w.

Our results so far may be summed up in the following table:

Table 11.1 Four ways of defining secondary qualities

	D1	D2a	D2b	D3
Is the capital Part thesis true?	yes	yes	yes	no
Is the physical supervenience thesis true?	no	no	yes	yes

If one wanted both theses to be true, then, one should opt for definition D2b.

Yet there are a number of problems or puzzles that arise if we try to explicate Reid's views using definitions in the style of D2b. Ryan Nichols has suggested that a definition parallel to D2b would be equally true in the case of a primary quality like hardness:

D2b'. For all worlds w: x is hard in w =df for some property P, x has P in w & in @ P causes hard* sensations in humans.[70]

This might be thought problematic for two reasons. Does it not imply that hardness counts as a secondary quality? And does it not also imply that sensations of a certain sort are a capital part of our notion of hardness? Both implications would be un-Reidian.

In reply to these supposed difficulties, I would note two things. First, what makes something a primary quality is not that it cannot be defined in the D2b way, but that it *can* be defined in some other way. Reid defines hardness thus: a thing is hard when its parts "adhere so firmly, that it cannot easily be made to change its figure" (IHM 5.2, 55), and that is a definition that tells us how a hard thing is in itself, as befits the definition of a primary quality. Second, though the biconditional corresponding to D2b' is a necessary truth, that does not mean that D2b' is correct as a definition. The symbol '=df' is a hyperintensional connective, which is to say that a statement of the form 'P =df Q' is not automatically true simply because the corresponding biconditional 'P iff Q' is a necessary truth. So D2b' may not be true in the definitional way needed to sustain the capital part thesis in the case of hardness.

[70] Nichols 2007, 179. Nichols is addressing an earlier version of my proposal that was couched in terms of laws of nature rather than causation; I have adapted his point to apply to my proposal in its current wording.

But other drawbacks of using D2b to explicate Reid's thought remain. I have wanted to keep alive the interpretive possibility that Reidian secondary qualities are dispositions rather than their bases. Is the property defined by D2b a disposition? It is a second-order property like the property defined by D2a, which we agreed was a disposition; yet it is necessarily co-extensive with the property defined by D3, which I said was a base. By including the reference to @ in D2b, we may have constructed a definition that no longer defines a disposition.

The suspicion that D2b does not define a disposition may be reinforced if we use a diagnostic scheme offered by Wolterstorff.[71] Suppose that camellias in some world w have the same intrinsic physical characteristics as our camellias, but look green rather than red to inhabitants of w. Are camellias in that world red or green? If you say green, you are thinking of colors as dispositions; if you say red, you are thinking of them as bases. The property defined by D2b does not satisfy this test for being a disposition.

The bottom line is that we cannot have things all *three* of the following ways: colors are conceived in terms of the sensations they produce; they supervene on the intrinsic physical characteristics of things; and they are dispositions.[72]

Bibliography

Armstrong, David. 1996. "Dispositions as Categorical States," in *Dispositions: A Debate*, edited by Tim Crane, London: Routledge.

—— 1998. "Qualities: an Excerpt from *Consciousness and Causality*," in *Metaphysics: The Big Questions*, edited by Peter van Inwagen and Dean W. Zimmerman, 272–81, Oxford: Blackwell.

Berkeley, George. 1710. *Principles of Human Knowledge.*

—— 1713. *Three Dialogues Between Hylas and Philonous.*

Blackburn, Simon. 1990. "Filling in Space," *Analysis*, 50: 62–65.

Campbell, John. 1994. "A Simple View of Colour," in *Reality, Representation, and Projection*, edited by John Haldane and Crispin Wright, 257–69, Oxford: Clarendon Press.

Falkenstein, Lorne. 2000. "Reid's Account of Localization," *Philosophy and Phenomenological Research*, 61: 305–28.

Foster, John. 1982. *The Case for Idealism,* London: Routledge.

Galilei, Galileo. 1998. *Thus Spoke Galileo*, edited by A. Frova and M. Marenzana, Oxford: University Press.

[71] Wolterstorff 2001, 112.

[72] The complications that arise when definitions in the D2b style are introduced can be illustrated by noting that the following set of propositions is inconsistent: (1) properties defined as second-order properties (like redness as defined in D2a) are dispositions; (2) if the property defined in D2a is a disposition, so is the property defined in D2b; (3) the property defined in D2b is co-intensive with the property defined in D3; (4) if one of two co-intensive properties is a disposition, so is the other; (5) the property defined in D3 is not a disposition, but the base of one. I have suggested above that (2) is false. In correspondence, Maya Eddon and David Manley have both suggested to me that (4) is also false.

Harman, Gilbert. 1990. "The Intrinsic Quality of Experience," in *Philosophical Perspectives*, edited by James Tomberlin, Vol. 4, 52–79, Atascadero, CA: Ridgeview Publishing Co. Reprinted in *The Nature of Consciousness*, edited by Ned Block, Owen Flanagan, and Guven Guzeldere, 663–75, Cambridge, MA: MIT Press, 1997.

Hume, David. 1739. *A Treatise of Human Nature*, edited by L.A. Selby-Bigge; second edition by P.H. Nidditch, Oxford: Clarendon, 1978.

—— 1751. *An Enquiry Concerning the Principles of Morals.*

Kant, Immanuel. 1768. "On the First Ground of the Distinction of Directions in Space."

Langton, Rae. 1998. *Kantian Humility: Our Ignorance of Things in Themselves*, Oxford: Clarendon Press.

——. 2000. "Locke's Relations and God's Good Pleasure," *Proceedings of the Aristotelian Society*, 100: 75–91.

Lehrer, Keith. 1978. "Reid on Primary and Secondary Qualities," *The Monist*, 61: 184–91.

——. 1989. *Thomas Reid,* London: Routledge.

Lewis, David. 1986. *On the Plurality of Worlds.* Oxford: Blackwell.

Locke, John. 1690. *An Essay Concerning Human Understanding*, edited by Peter. Nidditch, Oxford: Clarendon Press, 1975.

Mackie, J. L. 1976. *Problems from Locke,* Oxford: Oxford University Press.

Maund, Barry. 2008. "Color," in *The Stanford Encyclopedia of Philosophy*, edited by Edward N. Zalta. URL = <http://plato.stanford.edu/archives/fall2008/entries/color/>.

McCann, Edwin. 1994. "Locke's Philosophy of Body," in *The Cambridge Companion to Locke*, edited by Vere Chappell, 56–88, Cambridge: Cambridge University Press.

McDowell, John. 1985. "Values and Secondary Qualities," in *Morality and Objectivity: A Tribute to J. L. Mackie*, edited by Ted Honderich,. London: Routledge and Kegan Paul. Reprinted in *Moral Discourse and Practice: Some Philosophical Approaches*, edited by Stephen Darwall, Allan Gibbard, and Peter Railton,. Oxford University Press, 1997, 201–13.

McKitrick, Jennifer. 2002. "Reid's Foundation for the Primary/Secondary Quality Distinction," *The Philosophical Quarterly*, 52: 478–94.

Mill, John Stuart. 1865. *An Examination of Sir William Hamilton's Philosophy*, Boston: W.V. Spencer.

Moore, G. E. 1903. "The Refutation of Idealism," *Mind*, 12: 433–53. Reprinted in *Philosophical Studies,* 1–30, London: Kegan Paul, 1922.

—— 1922. "The Conception of Intrinsic Value," in *Philosophical Studies*. Totowa, New Jersey: Littlefield, Adams, & Co., 1968; first published in London by Routledge and Kegan Paul in 1922.

Nichols, Ryan. 2007. *Thomas Reid's Theory of Perception*, Oxford: Clarendon Press.

Peacocke, Christopher. 1983. *Sense and Content,* Oxford: Oxford University Press.

Prior, Elizabeth, Robert Pargetter, and Frank Jackson. 1982. "Three Theses about Dispositions," *American Philosophical Quarterly*, 19: 251–57.

Putnam, Hilary. 1981. *Reason, Truth, and History*, Cambridge: Cambridge University Press.

—— 1987. *The Many Faces of Realism*, La Salle, Ill.: Open Court.

Reid, Thomas. 1764. *An Inquiry into the Human Mind on the Principles of Common Sense*, edited by Derek R. Brookes, Edinburgh: Edinburgh University Press, 1997.

—— 1785 *Essays on the Intellectual Powers of Man*, edited by Derek R. Brookes, University Park, PA: Pennsylvania State University Press, 2002.

—— 1788. *Essays on the Active Powers of the Human Mind,* edited by Baruch Brody, Cambridge, Mass.: MIT Press, 1969.

Schaffer, Jonathan. 2004. "Quiddistic Knowledge," in *Lewisian Themes*, edited by Frank Jackson and Graham Priest, 210–30, Oxford: Clarendon Press.

Smart, J. J. C. 1959. "Sensations and Brain Processes," *The Philosophical Review* 68: 141–56.

—— 1963. *Philosophy and Scientific Realism*, London: Routledge and Kegan Paul.

Unger, Peter. 2006. *All the Power in the World*, Oxford: Oxford University Press.

Van Cleve, James. 1987. "Right, Left, and the Fourth Dimension," *The Philosophical Review* 96: 33–68.

—— 1995. "Putnam, Kant, and Secondary Qualities," *Philosophical Papers* 24: 83–109.

—— 2001. "Receptivity and our Knowledge of Intrinsic Properties," *Philosophy and Phenomenological Research* 65: 218–36.

—— (forthcoming). "Troubles for Radical Transparency."

Wolterstorff, Nicholas. 2001. *Thomas Reid and the Story of Epistemology*, Cambridge: Cambridge University Press.

Wright, Crispin. 1992. *Truth and Objectivity*, Cambridge, Mass.: Harvard University Press.

Yaffe, Gideon. 2008. "Thomas Reid," in *The Stanford Encyclopedia of Philosophy,* edited by Edward N. Zalta. URL = <http://plato.stanford.edu/archives/fall2008/entries/reid/>.

12

Kant and Helmholtz on Primary and Secondary Qualities

Gary Hatfield

1. Primary and Secondary Qualities

During the seventeenth century, natural philosophers and metaphysicians advocated a new conception of the fundamental properties of matter. This new theory of matter stripped it of the forms and qualities of the previously dominant Aristotelian natural philosophy and offered a short list of basic properties, by which all other properties were to be explained. According to what historians of science have termed the "mechanical philosophy" of Galileo, Descartes, and Boyle, these properties included size, shape, position, and motion.[1] The properties and effects to be secondarily explained by these primary or fundamental properties included not only physical processes such as fire or magnetism, but also the perceived qualities of bodies, such as colors, sounds, tastes, odors, and tactual qualities. In the latter part of the seventeenth century, John Locke, adopting wording from Robert Boyle, distinguished fundamental properties from the sensory qualities just listed, calling the first "primary qualities" and the others "secondary qualities."[2] Previously, Galileo and Descartes had advocated their own versions of the distinction, without using Boyle and Locke's terminology. Various versions of the distinction found a place in the writings of Spinoza, Leibniz, Malebranche, and Berkeley.

In the latter part of the seventeenth century and into the eighteenth century, Newton changed the character of the mechanical philosophy by establishing a new mechanics that incorporated some aspects of his predecessors' views but that differed at base. While continuing to refer to sizes, shapes, motions, and positions of atoms of matter in some of his explanations, Newton offered mass and force as fundamental properties of matter. During the eighteenth century, Newtonian mechanics became

[1] For an overview of the literature on the "mechanical philosophy," see Henry (2008), ch. 5.

[2] Locke (1690), II.viii; Boyle (1666, 38–49/1979, 30–4). Boyle did not originate the terminology. In Aristotelian natural philosophy, the "primary qualities" were hot, cold, wet, and dry; these produced other, "secondary" qualities (Steneck 1976, chs. 3.2, 6.1).

the new core of philosophical reflections on natural philosophy, and it remained so for much of the nineteenth century.

Kant and Helmholtz were among those who reflected on the new mechanics and who discussed versions of the distinction between primary and secondary qualities—a distinction that Kant invoked by name and that he ascribed to Locke. In the *Prolegomena*, Kant famously compared the status of space in his transcendental idealism with that of color in Locke's distinction between primary and secondary qualities. By contrast with the unknown thing in itself, he labeled space as an appearance, in that way comparing spatial properties with secondary qualities as he understood them. Subsequently, various nineteenth-century metaphysicians and scientists, including Helmholtz, came to endorse the Kantian notion that the thing in itself is unknowable, thereby placing both color and spatial properties on the side of the appearances (or "phenomena"). Nonetheless, Kant did not treat the status of color and space as equivalent from his critical standpoint, and Helmholtz did not treat them as equivalent within the phenomena.

This chapter first considers more closely the distinction between primary and secondary qualities and its origin. It then examines Kant's and Helmholtz's positions on primary and secondary qualities. Kant always treated color as a mere sensation. In his early period, he was a metaphysical realist about space and spatial relations. When he subsequently adopted transcendental idealism, he considered space and spatialized forces from two perspectives: as appearances in relation to things considered as they are in themselves, and as physically fundamental properties in relation to color sensations and other sensory qualities. Helmholtz's position also changed over his career. He always treated color as a secondary quality and distinguished it from the spatial qualities. As regards the latter, he switched from realism about Newtonian primary qualities (spatially distributed masses and forces) to an epistemically modest form of empiricism in which the laws governing what we experience as the spatial distribution of forces remain fundamental, but realism about space itself cannot be established.

Although the distinction between primary and secondary qualities is commonly associated with Locke, there is less unanimity on what his distinction amounted to. Many presentations describe Locke's distinction, or portray the distinction itself, as essentially ascribing primary qualities to bodies as real properties and as locating secondary qualities "in the mind." Accordingly, the distinction would entail that bodies are not really colored and that color exists only in the mind. On some versions of this interpretation, to ascribe color to bodies is to fall prey to a projectivist illusion. This portrayal has been widely repeated in general discussions of the early modern origins of the distinction.[3]

[3] Stroud (2000, 8–10) assimilates Descartes, Boyle, and Locke to Galileo's position (described below), and says that for them "the natural or commonsense belief that objects have many qualities beyond the 'primary' qualities mentioned in a purely physical account is thereby exposed as a mistake, illusion, confusion, or expression of mere 'appearance'." (10). Mundle (1971, 40–1) interprets Locke in a similar fashion, while

Nonetheless, close study of Locke's text reveals that he assigned both primary and secondary qualities to bodies, and located only *ideas* of secondary qualities (as well as of primary qualities) in the mind. Accordingly, primary and secondary qualities in objects possess the causal power to produce ideas or sensations in the mind. The difference between the two types of qualities stems from the representational relation between idea and quality. Locke held that the ideas of primary qualities resemble the primary qualities of the bodies that cause the ideas. Bodies are experienced (by means of ideas) as possessing size, shape, and motion, and they really do possess those properties, independently of our perception of them. Even if, on occasion, we misperceive shape or size, the idea presents us with a property of a kind that is possessed by the object as the kind of property we experience (as a shape or a size). By contrast, the ideas of secondary qualities do not resemble the qualities in objects that cause them (Locke 1690, II. viii.15). Secondary qualities in objects are defined as powers to produce sensory ideas, or sensations, of secondary qualities in the mind. These powers are based in the primary qualities of things.

The key to this interpretation is the notion that, according to Locke, secondary qualities are "in truth nothing in the objects themselves, but powers to produce various sensations in us by their *primary qualities*" (1690, II.viii.10). The force of this "nothing but" is to exclude secondary qualities such as color from among the fundamental physical properties of things. A red body is red inasmuch as it standardly causes red-ideas in perceivers (II.viii.13–14), whereas bodies possess primary qualities independently of a relation to perceivers (II.viii.9). Secondary qualities are defined by their causal powers. Primary qualities are not so defined: they are non-relational, intrinsic properties of things. The metaphysics of powers and their realization by primary qualities (including size, shape, and motion) is complex and interpreters disagree on how to characterize Locke's position on these finer matters. But Locke scholars generally agree that Locke held that secondary qualities are powers of bodies, so that colors (such as red) really are properties of bodies.[4] As qualities of bodies, they are defined relationally in terms of the causal powers of bodies to affect perceivers (by affecting the light that is reflected into the eyes).[5] Color experiences are not illusory,

noting that Locke sometimes speaks as if secondary qualities were powers of objects—a position that Mundle marginalizes. Hacker (1987, 2, 39–40, 55–60) claims that scientists and philosophers such as Galileo, Descartes, Boyle, and Locke assert, in an ordinary-language context, that "what we see . . . is not (objectively, publicly) coloured" (56); Hacker (ch. 1) assimilates the positions of the latter three figures to Galileo's position, while noting that they sometimes exploited an "ambiguity" (10, 25) in speaking of secondary qualities as causes in or powers of objects, in this sense attributing color and other qualities to objects.

[4] Alexander (1974); Ayers (1991), vol. 1, ch. 23; Woolhouse (1983), ch. 4, sec. 16.

[5] Locke also defined a third type of quality, which we may call "tertiary qualities," as "the power that is in any body, by reason of the particular constitution of its primary qualities, to make such a change in the bulk, figure, texture, and motion of another body, as to make it operate on our senses, differently from what it did before" (II.viii.23). He offers as examples the power of the sun to make wax white and of the fire to melt lead. Thus, light and heat count as both secondary and tertiary qualities, and we may suppose that color might also be a tertiary quality (e.g. black paint has the power to heat metal placed in sunlight more quickly and hotter than does white paint).

even if they don't directly reveal the causal basis in bodies of color as a secondary quality.

Once colors have been rendered as relational properties, making sense of the relation in a noncircular manner requires that one distinguish between "color in objects" and "color as a type of qualitative experience." Arguably, the majority of the adherents of the new mechanical philosophy made just such a distinction, including Descartes and Boyle as well as Locke.[6] They held that it is proper to speak, in one sense, of what color is in objects, and also to describe a mind-dependent experience of color. In essence, they endorsed a double use of color terms: color-in-objects and color-in-experience.

Although they do not generally deny that color belongs to bodies, these authors nonetheless do, in a specific and limited sense, fit the common portrayal that removes color from bodies and places it "in the mind." By contrast with the Aristotelian natural philosophy, they denied that an instance of one and the same qualitative "form" is present in objects and in color experience. According to Aristotelian theory, color is a "real quality" in bodies: red is a quality inhering in the surface of objects, which transmits its form through the medium and into the eyes of the perceiver, becoming expressed in the sensitive soul as the experience of red (Hatfield 1998, 956–9). On this theory, what you see is pretty much what you get: the body's redness is of a kind with the qualitative experience of perceivers. Early modern philosophers often described this Aristotelian theory as ascribing a "resemblance" between color as experienced and color as a quality of bodies. Descartes (1644, I.68–70, IV.197–9) and Locke (II.viii.22, 24–5) denied this resemblance thesis. They denied that color is in bodies as a "real quality," and they located phenomenal color in the mind. This position does not deny that secondary qualities such as color are real or are in bodies (as the causes of, or the powers to produce, phenomenal experiences), but its analysis of what those qualities are in bodies differs from the Aristotelian conception.

Not all thinkers associated by historians of science with the mechanical philosophy drew the distinction between fundamental physical properties and sense-based qualities in this manner. Galileo, in particular, came much closer to the common portrayal mentioned above, that is, he effectively denied color to bodies and rendered color

[6] On Descartes, see Hatfield (2003), 291–3. Boyle (1666, 38–49/1979, 30–4); Locke (1690), II.viii.8. Thomas Reid also argued that "colour is a quality of bodies, not a sensation of the mind" (1785, 171); he concluded that "colour is not a sensation, but a secondary quality of bodies, in the sense we have already explained; that it is a certain power or virtue in bodies, that in fair day-light exhibits to the eye an appearance, which is very familiar, although it has no name" (176). He ascribed the origin of the term "secondary quality" to Locke (190). Nonetheless, Reid read Locke as affirming, in tension with Locke's own principles, that color is "only an idea in the mind" (177). He granted that Locke distinguished the power in bodies from the idea but believed that, in his zeal to reject the scholastic doctrine of resemblance, Locke denied color to bodies (189–91). Locke's expression of this zeal helps explain, on my reading, why some of his contemporaries misread Locke's position. Thus, when Locke says that "light, heat, whiteness, or coldness, are no more really in them [viz., bodies], than sickness or pain is in manna" (1690, II.viii.17), we should take him to be speaking of these qualities as found in ideas and to be denying the Aristotelian doctrine of real qualities. Hence, I see Reid as agreeing with and expressing Locke's actual doctrine, while mistakenly attributing a Galilean position to Locke.

experience as illusory. In a now oft-quoted passage from the *Assayer*, Galileo contended:

I say that upon conceiving of a material or corporeal substance I immediately feel the need to conceive simultaneously that it is bounded and has this or that shape; that it is in this place or that at any given time; that it moves or stands still; that it does or does not touch another body; and that it is one, few, or many. I cannot separate it from these conditions by any stretch of my imagination. But that it must be white or red, bitter or sweet, noisy or silent, of sweet or foul odor, my mind feels no compulsion to understand as necessary accompaniments. Indeed, without the senses to guide us, reason or imagination alone would perhaps never arrive at such qualities. For that reason I think that tastes, odors, colors, and so forth are no more than mere names so far as pertains to the subject wherein they reside, and that they have their habitation only in the sensorium. Thus, if the living creature were removed, all these qualities would be removed and annihilated. (Galileo 1960, 309)

In making the existence of color dependent upon the perceiver, in that limited sense this passage presents a position that is similar to the relationalist positions subsequently adopted by Descartes, Boyle, and Locke. But it does not offer a relationalist account of color; rather, it apparently makes color into a mind-dependent illusion: it restricts the place of color to the sensorium, that is, to the sensation or experience of color. As regards the object, colors are "mere names." As he says just subsequently, such qualities lack "solid existence" (310) and so are unlike the "real attributes" (309) of shape, time, motion, position, and number.[7] Galileo doesn't speak of "resemblance," but his point about "real attributes" is similar to that later made by Locke about primary qualities: we experience bodies as having shapes, and they really are shaped. But according to Galileo they do not possess color, which has its place only in the mind.

This Galilean position feeds into the now common view that secondary qualities exist only "in the mind" and not in bodies. By itself, his position cannot explain the widespread adoption of that conception of secondary qualities in the latter part of the twentieth century, for this Galilean passage, though long discussed by historians of science, has only recently regained the attention of philosophers. Moreover, Galileo's statement cannot explain why some theorists would ascribe to Locke the view that color exists only in the mind.

We can find misreadings of Locke on the status of secondary qualities in subsequent authors, beginning with Berkeley. Notoriously, Berkeley turns the doctrine of secondary qualities against any theorist who both draws a distinction between primary and secondary qualities and maintains that extended matter exists. He does so by characterizing his opponent as allowing that secondary qualities exist only in the mind:

[7] One can find passages in Locke that deny color or other secondary qualities to objects if perceivers are taken away. That is consistent with the definition of secondary qualities as relational qualities or as powers to cause a certain effect in perceivers. The difference is that Locke seems to suppose that relational qualities are real, whereas from the relational nature of color Galileo concludes that it is not a real property of objects.

They who assert that figure, motion, and the rest of the primary or original qualities do exist without the mind, in the unthinking substances, do at the same time acknowledge that colours, sounds, heat, cold, and such like secondary qualities, do not, which they tell us are sensations existing in the mind alone, that depend on and are occasioned by the different size, texture and motion of the minute particles of matter. (1710, I.10)

He correctly acknowledges what both Galileo and Locke believe: that color sensations are caused by objects in virtue of the primary qualities of those objects. But he attributes to Locke a position closer to that of Galileo: a position that equates secondary qualities with sensations, as opposed to treating them as powers of bodies (founded in primary qualities) to cause sensations. Accordingly, Berkeley misrepresents Locke as simply equating secondary qualities with sensations.[8] He goes on to argue that since the secondary qualities are in the mind, and since primary qualities are experienced along with secondary qualities (visible objects appear with both shape and color), primary qualities must be in the mind, too. He further attacks the Lockean notion that ideas of primary qualities resemble properties in the mind-independent objects.

Hume also cites the distinction as characteristic of modern philosophy, and as entailing that bodies are not colored. In the first *Enquiry*, he describes what he takes to be a standard view among modern philosophers:

It is universally allowed by modern enquirers, that all the sensible qualities of objects, such as hard, soft, hot, cold, white, black, etc. are merely secondary, and exist not in the objects themselves, but are perceptions of the mind, without any external archetype or model, which they represent. If this be allowed, with regard to secondary qualities, it must also follow with regard to the supposed primary qualities of extension and solidity; nor can the latter be any more entitled to that denomination than the former. The idea of extension is entirely acquired from the senses of sight and feeling; and if all the qualities, perceived by the senses, be in the mind, not in the object, the same conclusion must reach the idea of extension, which is wholly dependent on the sensible ideas or the ideas of secondary qualities. (Hume 1999, 202–3)

Like Berkeley, Hume uses the supposed status of secondary qualities as existing only in the mind to raise a doubt about the existence of primary qualities beyond the mind. Hume's argument yields the conclusion that neither primary nor secondary qualities have "archetypes" in external objects. In the *Treatise*, he argued that since secondary qualities as experienced are held not to "resemble" qualities in objects, by parity of reasoning, the perceptions of primary qualities cannot be known to resemble properties in objects (Hume 1739–40, 226–31).

[8] An earlier controversy arose about whether Berkeley misread Locke on the use of "relativity" arguments (Stroud 1980, 149; Wilson 1982, 109) to ground the distinction between primary and secondary qualities. Scholars no longer believe that Locke relied primarily on relativity arguments (a belief that may have reflected the heavy use of such arguments in early to mid twentieth-century discussions of sense data). They recognize that Berkeley used a variety of arguments to oppose the notion of matter as extended substance. I am here noting that one of Berkeley's arguments starts from the premise that Locke held that secondary qualities themselves (as opposed to ideas of secondary qualities) exist only "in the mind," and I suggest that this premise misrepresents Locke's position.

The divergence between Locke's views (or a plausible interpretation thereof) and the restatement of those views by Berkeley and Hume might partly be ascribed to the polemical aims of the latter two philosophers: by so construing Locke's position, they open the door to their arguments against his realism about bodies and their primary qualities. However, we need not attribute such self-serving motives to Berkeley and Hume. We can understand their interpretation as emphasizing two out of three factors that characterize Locke's position, and as interpreting a third factor in a way that renders Locke's position equivalent to Galileo's.

Galileo, Descartes, and Locke agree that sensory ideas of color do not resemble the properties in objects that cause the ideas. This is the *no resemblance* thesis regarding secondary qualities, which is tacitly or explicitly aligned with a *resemblance* thesis about primary qualities:

> *(No) Resemblance*: Ideas of primary qualities do, and ideas of secondary qualities do not, resemble the basic qualities of objects.

Galileo, Descartes, and Locke also agree that the primary qualities or attributes of objects are ontologically and explanatorily basic. They are the basic or fundamental properties of objects (or of the parts of objects), and they serve to explain the other properties and characteristics of objects, which leads us to a second thesis:

> *Basicality*: Primary qualities are ontologically and explanatorily basic.

The No Resemblance thesis amounts to the rejection of the Aristotelian doctrine that color is a real quality, or that the ideas of color resemble color in bodies. The Basicality thesis holds that size, shape, position, and motion are the basic properties of objects. Other properties are to be explained by appealing to the sizes, shapes, and motions of the particles that, according to the mechanical philosophy, make up objects. Together, these two points entail a rejection of forms and qualities as explanatorily basic, in favor of matter in motion.

As part of their position that objects possess the quality or property of being colored, Descartes and Locke adopted a third principle, which is that secondary qualities such as color are powers in objects for producing non-resembling sensory ideas in perceivers:

> *Powers*: Secondary qualities in objects are powers for producing non-resembling sensory ideas in perceivers.

This thesis allowed Descartes and Locke to continue to speak of objects as colored, because they attribute a color property (albeit a relational one) to objects.

By contrast, Galileo's position employs a different third factor, *bare causation*, to describe the status of the properties in objects that cause the experience, idea, or sensation of color and other such qualities:

> *Bare Causation*: The physically basic properties of bodies serve as bare causes for sensations of color, etc., and such colors exist only in the mind.

This factor agrees with Powers that properties in objects cause sensations of color, but it disagrees with Powers by denying that objects therefore possess color as a property or (secondary) quality. Accordingly, the causal features of bodies and other physical media do not provide a basis for analyzing what it is for bodies or light *to be* colored; rather, they are simply causes of certain sorts of subjective sensory experiences. On this view, it is correct to say that bodies are not really colored, and that color exists only in the mind.

In characterizing Locke's position, Berkeley and Hume substituted Bare Causation for his third factor, Powers. They used the thesis of No Resemblance between ideas of secondary qualities and properties in objects as the defining conception of secondary qualities. They then attacked Basicality by challenging the intelligibility or the 'knowability' of size, shape, and motion as the basic explanatory properties of mind-independent bodies. For Berkeley, this meant that color and spatial properties were ontologically on a par, existing only as qualities in ideas. He did not conclude from this that the two sets of qualities were equivalent in all respects; he touted the usefulness of mechanical explanations (appealing to size, shape, and motion) for guiding practical actions. For him, size, shape, and motion were simply aspects of experience that sustained useful generalizations (laws of nature). Hume was less generous toward the mechanical philosophy, but he did recognize the importance of relations of space and time, and he acknowledged the achievements of Newton, who formulated laws that privilege space and time. Since Hume also acknowledged that precise relations could hold among qualities, it is not clear that he privileged space and time over quality as explanatorily basic. Indeed, in his science of man, relations of resemblance or similarity among qualities underlie a principle of association, which serves as a basic law of nature.

Against this background, I examine the arguments and conclusions of Kant and Helmholtz. Section 2 scouts Kant's early views on primary qualities and Section 3 shows that Kant ascribed to Locke a version of the distinction according to which colors and other secondary qualities exist only as "appearances." Kant himself treated both space and color as "appearances" by contrast with the things in themselves (which cause such appearances), while also holding that the spatial properties are physically fundamental (within appearances).

2. Kant's Early Views on Primary Qualities

From his early writings in the 1740s and 1750s, Kant was interested in the theory of space and the basis of spatial properties in substances. Over the years, his position shifted from a relational theory of space, to a Newtonian container view in 1768, and in his critical period to a synthesis of Newton and Leibniz, which joined an a priori spatial framework (as the form of intuition) with a relational view of what fills it (the matter of sensation as synthesized into a spatial object).[9] In his early period, he was a realist about

[9] On the development of Kant's views on space and spatial perception, see Hatfield (2006); on his mature view of physical space, see Friedman (2001).

spatial relations and our knowledge of them, that is, he believed that spatial perception represents the real spatial relations of things. He regarded color as a mere sensation that is caused by the light-reflecting properties of bodies in space. He retained this view of color even as his conception of the metaphysical reality of spatial properties changed with the transcendental idealism of his critical period.

In the *Physical Monadology* of 1756, Kant laid out a relational view of space that combined elements of a Leibnizo-Wolffian relational view with a suggestion from the German metaphysician Christian August Crusius. Leibniz, Wolff, and Crusius all agreed in positing simple substances as the primary beings of the natural world. In his correspondence with Clark (1717/1720), Leibniz wrote as if these simple substances possess real relations to one another, which are the basis for the general representation of space (which is general in that it abstracts from the particular beings that are in the relations). His actual position (in his mature period) was that monads possess no external relations to one another. The German philosopher Wolff, whom Leibniz befriended, did not follow Leibniz's actual position but instead posited real causal and spatial relations among monadic simples (Wolff 1736, §§713–14, 880–2; 1737, §§184, 221–30).

On this Leibnizo-Wolffian view, it remained a puzzle how simple, unextended monads, even if standing in relations, could form the basis of an infinitely divisible space. The standard mathematical theories of the day excluded the possibility that the continuum might be "composed" from extensionless points (a possibility that came to be accepted during the nineteenth century, when lines came to be viewed as composed from the real numbers). Crusius (1745) sought to solve this puzzle by suggesting that simple, indivisible substances might "fill space" with a field of force or causal power. He posited God as such an indivisible but space-filling being, who "fills" Newtonian absolute space, which itself is populated with indivisible material elements that also "fill" the space around them and are conjoined by causal relations to form infinitely divisible matter (1745, §§48–53, 108–19, 252–3, 351–6, 440).

Kant's position in the *Physical Monadology* adapted the "space-filling" monads of Crusius (1745) to the relational view of Wolff. He dropped Crusius' notion that God sustains an absolute spatial framework. Like both Wolff and Crusius, he posited simple substances that are in relation through causal interactions that create an infinitely divisible physical space. Kant rendered the primary space-filling causal power as a force of repulsion (to which he joined a force of attraction, as well as motive force). The resulting physical space underlies the perceptual appearance of a continuous, infinitely divisible space. The space of perceptual experience reveals a metaphysically real, mind-independent physical space.

Kant was in this period a realist about spatial properties, and to this extent he may be seen as a realist about primary qualities. But his conception of what the fundamental or primary properties are was different from that of Galileo, Descartes, and Locke. These authors viewed matter as impenetrable extended stuff, whether formed into indivisible atoms or into divisible corpuscles. Kant explained extension through causation and force. The elemental monads are themselves simple and unextended substances. They gain spatial extension and spatial relations through their repulsive, attractive, and motive forces. The repulsive force accounts for the perceived impenetrability of matter. Extension is a product of repulsive force, and so is a derived property of matter. In addition to the forces of repulsion and attraction, elemental substances possess mass in the form of a "force of inertia" (1756, prop. 11). The primary or fundamental properties of elemental material substances are thus various kinds of forces, including the mass-giving force of inertia. Kant's conception of fundamental properties is conditioned by Newtonian mechanics, as altered to accommodate a conception that makes force the basis of material extension and mass. Forces thereby become the "primary qualities." They meet the conditions of Resemblance (as regards the spatial character of their operation) and Basicality.

The evidence for Kant's views on sensory qualities in the pre-critical period is scant, but what evidence there is[10] suggests that he had the same view as in his critical period: he viewed sensations as the subjective effects of the physical properties of bodies, in accordance with Galilean secondary qualities. We will consider this view as expressed in his critical writings.

3. Primary and secondary qualities in Kant's critical writings

During the 1770s, Kant conceived a radical project in philosophy through which he would reconsider the fundamental relations between substances and our mental apprehension of them. This new project was described in a letter to Marcus Herz in 1772, and its first public fruit was the *Critique of Pure Reason* (1781; 2nd edn., 1787), followed soon by the *Prolegomena to Any Future Metaphysics* (1783).[11] Some general features of this new philosophy are undisputed: Kant now claimed that we cannot know substances "as they are in themselves"; he treated space and time as "appearances" that arise from human "forms of intuition" and placed physical bodies with their spatial properties among the appearances; and he allowed that we know with certainty

[10] J. G. Herder's notes from Kant's course on metaphysics (dated to 1762–4) contain a cryptic remark that "all sensation of bodies outside us is merely *in* us," giving beauty, ugliness, and color as instances (Kant 1997, 5; 28: 42). In these notes, Kant attributes this view of sensation to Berkeley, and describes it as plausible; Kant (who did not read English, and Berkeley was as yet untranslated into Latin, French, or German) may have learned of Berkeley's philosophy from Carl Heinrich Rappolt, who taught at Königsberg and studied English-language philosophy, or from a friend such as J. G. Hamann, who read philosophy in English (Kuehn 2001, 76–7). Also, in the *Inaugural Dissertation*, on the cusp of the critical period, Kant invokes the matter/form distinction in which sensations are mere matter that awaken the intuition of space, the latter being an appearance but also the formal principle of the sensible world as a world governed by natural laws (1770, §15E).

[11] The first *Critique* is cited (as usual) using "A" and "B" to refer to the first and second editions; citations of the *Prolegomena* follow the Academy edition pagination (vol. 4). These paginations appear in the margins of Kant (1998) and (2004). My citation practice more generally is described at the beginning of the Bibliography.

many principles that apply within the domain of all possible human sensory experience, including the principles of Euclid's geometry, as well as principles of causation.

If spatial properties are on the side of the appearances, are they rendered as Lockean, or perhaps Galilean, secondary qualities? Kant answers this question one way in the *Critique* and another way in the *Prolegomena*. In both cases, he contrasts spatial properties (and spatially acting forces), as appearances, with things in themselves as causes of appearances. Any comparison of his position with Locke or Galileo depends on how we interpret Kantian "appearances" and related terms, including "sensation," "intuition," "form of intuition," and "matter" (as sensation), in relation to the terms he used to describe bodies, including "objects," "things," and "matter" (as the stuff bodies are made of). We must also consider the relation between bodies, as appearances, and things in themselves, as "causes" (so Kant frequently says) of the matter of sensation and so of the appearances themselves.

Kant's most extensive comparison of the distinction between primary and secondary qualities with his distinction between appearances and things in themselves occurs in the *Prolegomena* (First Part, Note II). In the First Part, which corresponds to the Transcendental Aesthetic in the *Critique*, Kant presents arguments for the ideality of space and for our having synthetic *a priori* knowledge of the geometrical (Euclidean) properties of space and of bodies in space. In Note II, he defends this position from the charge of Berkeleyan idealism, which had been leveled in the Garve–Feder review of 1782 (translated in Kant 2004).

Kant begins his defense by summarizing his conclusions in the First Part of the *Prolegomena*:

> Everything that is to be given to us as object must be given to us in intuition. But all our intuition happens only by means of the senses; the understanding intuits nothing, but only reflects. Now since, in accordance with what has just been proven, the senses never and in no single instance enable us to cognize things in themselves, but only their appearances, and as these are mere representations of sensibility, "consequently all bodies together with the space in which they are found must be taken for nothing but mere representations in us, and exist nowhere else than merely in our thoughts." Now is this not manifest idealism? (4:288)

This is a statement of transcendental idealism: we don't know things in themselves; space and spatial properties don't belong to things in themselves but exist only as our way of representing those things. Kant's statement that bodies and space "are nothing but mere representations in us" might be understood as committing him to actually spatial representations, that is, to circular or cubical or otherwise shaped entities in the mind, like mental sense data. More plausibly, in saying that bodies and space are representations, Kant is treating them as representational contents, and he is affirming that bodies and space, insofar as they appear as bodies and space, are contents by which we represent the otherwise unknown things in themselves.

He continues by distinguishing his position from idealism proper, by which he understands the immaterialist idealism of Berkeley:

Idealism consists in the claim that there are none other than thinking beings; the other things that we believe we perceive in intuition are only representations in thinking beings, to which in fact no object existing outside these beings corresponds. I say in opposition: There are things given to us as objects of our senses existing outside us, yet we know nothing of them as they may be in themselves, but are acquainted only with their appearances, that is, with the representations that they produce in us because they affect our senses. Accordingly, I by all means avow that there are bodies outside us, that is, things which, though completely unknown to us as to what they may be in themselves, we know through the representations which their influence on our sensibility provides for us, and to which we give the name of a body—which word therefore merely signifies the appearance of this object that is unknown to us but is nonetheless real. Can this be called idealism? It is the very opposite of it. (4:288–9)

Things in themselves exist and they "affect" and "influence" human sensibility. Although, as Kant explains in the Second Part of the *Prolegomena* (and had asserted in the *Critique*), all cognition and experience of causation falls within the domain of possible experience, he nonetheless treats things in themselves as responsible for the appearances. "Bodies" are a way in which things in themselves appear to us, and appearances are the only way in which we know these things in themselves. We do not know them as they are in themselves.[12]

Although there is discussion of whether Kant should actually be attributed the positions that he summarizes in the previous passage, I am taking him at his word. The question then becomes: How shall we understand the relation between things in themselves and the bodies (with their properties) that appear to us in sensory experience? Kant suggests an answer in the ensuing passage, in which he compares the appearances, including spatial properties within the appearances, to Lockean secondary qualities.

That one could, without detracting from the actual existence of outer things, say of a great many of their predicates: they belong not to these things in themselves, but only to their appearances and have no existence of their own outside our representation, is something that was generally accepted and acknowledged long before *Locke's* time, though more commonly thereafter. To these predicates belong warmth, color, taste, etc. That I, however, even beyond these, include (for weighty reasons) also among mere appearances the remaining qualities of bodies, which are called *primarias*: extension, place, and more generally space along with everything that depends on it (impenetrability or materiality, shape, etc.), is something against which not the least ground

[12] I here align myself with Prauss' (1974) interpretation of Kant's language of "things in themselves" as, in the first instance, concerning a distinction between things "considered as they are in themselves" and those same things "considered as they appear." Others (e.g. Collins 1999; Ameriks 2003, 17–41) build on this outlook to endorse a "one world" and "two aspects" view of Kant's philosophy: empirically given objects are not a distinct set of objects set apart from things in themselves, but they are things in themselves as experienced by human subjects. Findlay (1981) and Langton (1998) ascribe to Kant a similar realism about things in themselves in relation to appearances.

of uncertainty can be raised; and as little as someone can be called an idealist because he wants to admit colors as properties that attach not to the object in itself, but only to the sense of vision as modifications, just as little can my system be called idealist simply because I find that even more of, *nay, all of the properties that make up the intuition of a body* belong merely to its appearance: for the existence of the thing that appears is not thereby nullified, as with real idealism, but it is only shown that through the senses we cannot cognize it at all as it is in itself. I would very much like to know how then my claims must be framed so as not to contain any idealism. Without doubt I would have to say: that the representation of space not only is perfectly in accordance with the relation that our sensibility has to objects, for I have said that, but that it is even fully similar to the object; an assertion to which I can attach no sense, any more than to the assertion that the sensation of red is similar to the property of cinnabar that excites this sensation in me.

(4:289–90)

In comparing his position on spatial properties to Lockean secondary qualities, he affirms two of the factors regarding secondary qualities that I isolated in Section 1: No Resemblance and Bare Causation. He extends No Resemblance from color to spatial properties.

Kant's characterization of Lockean secondary qualities as "having no existence outside their representation" is more appropriate to the Galilean conception of color as a bare sensation that is caused in us by bodies. So we have here another source for subsequent Galilean (mis)understandings of Locke's distinction.[13] Central to Kant's own purpose is the conclusion that primary qualities also do not "resemble" properties of things in themselves. This point requires additional interpretive attention, because he also asserts that bodies, as objects of possible experience, can be known a priori to possess spatial properties and to conform to causal laws. Indeed, he spends the whole of Note III arguing that the ideality of space and time does not render the sensible world into a mere illusion and, as in Note I, contending that his view alone can explain the objective application of geometry to bodies in physical space.

In the first *Critique*, Kant also affirms the existence and causal powers of things in themselves. In the A edition, his tortured discussion of the "transcendental object" and its distinction from the *noumenon* leads him to assert that "the word 'appearance' must already indicate a relation to something the immediate representation of which is, to be sure, sensible, but which in itself, without this constitution of our sensibility (on which the form of our intuition is grounded), must be something, i.e., an object independent of sensibility" (A 252). In a corresponding passage in the B edition, he straightforwardly

[13] The Galilean reading of the status of color was familiar in German philosophy. Poley's translation of Locke's *Essay* (1757) was preceded by a translation of Gilbert's (1752) abstract, which described secondary qualities as ideas produced by external bodies: "The several Dispositions in Bodies to produce several Sensations in us; whence Colours, Sounds, Tastes, etc. which are indeed only Sensations produced in the Animal, by the Operation or Action of such Primary Qualities," the latter including motion, rest, figure, and texture (1752, 5–6; German translation in Locke 1757). Further, J. H. Lambert described the status of color (by contrast with extension, solidity, and mobility) as follows: "Wir können demnach den Begriff der Farben weder den Objecten noch dem Lichte zueignen, sondern er gehört in das Gedankenreich, und wird durch die Structur der Objecte und die daherrührenden Modificationen der Lichtstralen nur veranlasst" (1764, 2:255).

affirms that "beings of understanding must certainly correspond to the beings of sense" (B 308).[14] It was a theme of Kant's, emphasized more strongly in the B edition, that the concept of appearance implies a thing in itself that appears (A 42/B 59; B xxxvi–xxvii, 164). In both editions, he also speaks of something that "affects" the sensibility to produce appearances (A 19/B 33; B 129, 156, 207), which must be the thing in itself, and he directly affirms that things in themselves cause the representations that constitute appearances (A 494, 496, 538, 696/B 522, 524, 566, 724).

When Kant addresses the relation between appearances and things in themselves in the *Critique*, he resists comparing the status of spatial properties in his system to (Galilean) secondary qualities. By his lights, such a comparison would diminish spatial appearances to mere subjective sensations. He holds that spatial representations have a unique status: "there is no other subjective representation related to something external that could be called *a priori* objective" (A 28/B 44) in the way that space and time are. Without using the terminology of primary or secondary qualities, he again affirms his understanding that, on the standard view, colors are mere subjective sensations that exist only in subjective mental states. In the A edition he offers an elaborate discussion of the status of tastes and colors, saying that "colors are not objective qualities of the bodies to the intuition of which they are attached, but are also only modifications of the sense of sight, which is affected by light in a certain way" (A 28). In B he reduces the discussion but still affirms that "the sensations of colors, sounds, and warmth . . . are mere sensations and not intuitions" (B 44). The A version makes clear that he views colors in a Galilean mode, as mere subjective effects in the mind (see also A 45–6/B 62–3). He invokes Bare Causality and suggests No Resemblance.

In both editions, Kant continues the discussion by explaining why he does not want to compare the subjectivity of spatial representations to colors and the like.

> The aim of this remark is only to prevent one from thinking of illustrating the asserted ideality of space with completely inadequate examples, since things like colors, tastes, etc., are correctly considered not as qualities of things but as mere alterations of our subject, which can even be different in different people. For in this case that which is originally itself only appearance, e.g., a rose, counts in an empirical sense as a thing in itself, which yet can appear different to every eye in regard to color. The transcendental concept of appearances in space, on the contrary, is a critical reminder that absolutely nothing that is intuited in space is a thing in itself, and that space is not a form that is proper to anything in itself, but rather that objects in themselves are not known to us at all, and that what we call outer objects are nothing other than mere representations of our sensibility, whose form is space, but whose true correlate, i.e., the thing in itself, is not and cannot be cognized through them, but is also never asked after in experience. (A 29–30/B 45)

[14] Collins (1999), ch. 4, discusses the difference between *noumena*, which would be things in themselves as cognized by an intuitive intellect, and things considered as they are in themselves independently of such an intellectual intuition. Kant assumes the latter throughout the *Critique* and treats the concept of the former as "problematic" but needed.

He here warns against the very comparison that he uses in the *Prolegomena*. Nonetheless, he still affirms that both color and spatial representations are merely subjective. He stresses a difference between the two kinds of representations that he also highlights in Notes I and III in the *Prolegomena*: spatial representations support universally valid synthetic a priori knowledge (and color sensations do not). Within the domain of appearances, spatially characterized objects (and their related forces) are recognized as the causes of subjective sensations of color in human subjects. In this regard, a physical object, such as a rose, counts "in an empirical sense as a thing in itself." The rose as an appearance is reckoned as a cause of what is mere appearance, the color. In this sense, the rose is analogous, in the empirical realm, to the thing in itself considered transcendentally. But in relation to the thing in itself, "the true correlate" of the representations in experience, the rose, together with its causally fundamental spatial properties and forces, is itself an appearance. His point in also stressing that spatial representations are ideal and subjective is to contrast them with things as they are in themselves, which he here reminds us are not spatial.[15]

So Kant affirms No Resemblance for both space and color. But he distinguishes between spatial properties and color by invoking Basicality. Spatial properties and relations (together with temporal properties and relations) set the framework for objective knowledge of the physical world, including the laws of nature, which embody causal relations as expressed in space and time. Indeed, in filling out his picture of matter, Kant appeals to causal laws (ultimately expressed as laws of repulsion, attraction, and inertia) to explain the fundamental properties of matter, as portrayed most fully in the *Metaphysical Foundations of Natural Science* (1786).

Kant's physical "primary qualities" become, then, the spatiotemporal expression of the forces that underlie the properties of matter. In this way, his later philosophy echoes the earlier: force is primary in explaining the impenetrability and inertia of matter. There is, though, a large difference between his early and his critical views on the status of these primary qualities. Whereas the early Kant was a metaphysical realist about space and spatially expressed causal relations, the critical Kant is a transcendental idealist. The spatial primary qualities are physically fundamental, but they are no longer, in the metaphysical realist's sense, metaphysically fundamental. The traditional object of metaphysics, substantial being as it is in itself, is now placed beyond the pale of

[15] Passages such as the above are used to support a doctrine of double affection, according to which things in themselves cause spatially organized appearances, and those appearances then cause color sensations (Findlay 1981, ch. 8). I prefer to see the appearances as caused by things in themselves, and as displaying under the guise of space and time the causally fundamental aspects of things in themselves, which fundamental aspects then serve, within the appearances, in physical, causal explanations. Appearances do not cause appearances, but some appearances (interpreted according to Kant's critical principles) represent causally fundamental properties and forces. I also note that the spatially fundamental properties of things must be known through both the matter and form of intuition; that is, moving things are seen as moving *colored* things or felt as moving *cold* and *hard* things, etc. The "mere" sensations cannot drop out completely, although it is the relations among qualitatively experienced objects that are crucial (red thing here, now red thing there) and not the characteristics of the color or tactile qualities themselves.

human knowledge. Whereas for Descartes and, in his own empiricist way, Locke, primary qualities reveal what is both physically and metaphysically basic, for Kant human knowledge does not extend to substances as they are in themselves.

Nonetheless, to the embarrassment of some of his commentators, Kant speaks of things in themselves as causes of the appearances. So perhaps he has two concepts of primary qualities, or at least two ways of conceiving of basic things: through the spatiotemporal forces manifest in experience and as the things in themselves that cause the appearances. The first would be physically basic, the second would be metaphysically, or perhaps transcendentally, basic.

I endorse the view that Kant thought of things in themselves as basic entities whose properties as they are in themselves are not revealed to us, but whose fundamental causal powers (as regards nature) are manifested in our experience of forces and motions in space. In this respect, I agree with Langton's (1998) interpretation of Kant as holding that we know the relational properties of things in themselves through our spatialized experience (we know these relations as spatial, and not as they are in themselves). Langton further holds that Kant contended that only the relational properties of things in themselves are revealed in experience, because only they, and not the intrinsic properties of the (otherwise unknown) substances, have a direct causal relation to us. She argues that Kant denies that that these relational properties can be reduced to, and hence derived from, the intrinsic properties of substances. But as regards the relational properties, the things in themselves are that which appears in the appearances.

I agree with Langton and others (see n. 12) that the things in themselves are the objects of appearances. Indeed, I take at face value Kant's rare statements that, in some sense, the appearances *represent* things in themselves: "appearances are only representations of things that exist without cognition of what they might be in themselves" (B 164). But I disagree with Langton's conclusion that appearances represent only the relations among things in themselves and not the unitary substances with their intrinsic properties. On my view, the unknown substances with their relations stand as the "correlates" and the "causes" of representations and appearances. I thus differ with Langton over Kant's basis for transcendental idealism. She finds this basis in his alleged belief that relations are irreducible to intrinsic properties, which leaves it that only the relations affect us and that substances as things-in-themselves taken by themselves do not. I don't find Kant relying on this latter view. Rather, I find him concluding that neither the things in themselves nor their relations can be known to us as they are in themselves, because our cognition is limited to objects that are, or could be, given through sensory intuition. Things in themselves and their relations are both revealed to us only as appearances. I locate his basis for this conclusion in his answer to a question he posed in the letter to Herz (Kant 1999, 10:132): "What is the ground of the relation to the object of that in us which is called representation?"

With this question, Kant is asking how the understanding could come to represent objects "as they are," that is, the "things themselves" (10:131). He distinguishes three cases, none of which can explain or justify the relation. The first case is bare sensory representation, which does not reveal the objects but only our sensory response to being affected by them. The representation "comprises only the manner in which the subject is affected by the object," and it therefore conforms to the object "as an effect conforms to its cause," but without revealing things as they are (10:130). As a merely subjective effect, the representation does not reveal the properties of its cause. The second case is that of an archetypal intellect that creates the object according to the representation; God would work in this way, creating objects that conform to their representations through and through (presumably, resemblance would obtain). The third way would be if the intellect had insight into the things as they are in themselves, not by means of the senses, nor by means of active creation, but because intellectual representations are directly in harmony with the essences of things. Kant reviews and rejects various ways in which this intellectual harmony might be established (namely, pure concepts established either by Platonic intuition or by divine implantation). Kant's own answer to the above question, in his critical philosophy, develops aspects of the first and third answers. Things in themselves have a subjective effect on our sensibility; this effect contains merely subjective "matter" of sensation (e.g. color); this matter is conditioned by spatial and temporal forms of intuition that allow for synthetic a priori knowledge within the appearances; we represent and cognize objects within these spatial and temporal appearances only by bringing our own concepts (the categories) to bear on actual or possible sensory experiences. Our knowledge is thereby limited to appearances, by contrast with things in themselves.

Kant returns in the *Prolegomena* to the line of thinking in the letter to Herz. He is ultimately concerned with establishing how a priori spatial intuitions are possible, such as might explain the possibility of apodictic geometrical knowledge. In the course of this quest, he asks whether we might be able to intuit things as they are in themselves. He answers:

> If our intuition had to be of the kind that represented things *as they are in themselves*, then absolutely no intuition *a priori* would take place, but it would always be empirical. For I can only know what may be contained in the object in itself if the object is present and given to me. Of course, even then it is incomprehensible how the intuition of a thing that is present should allow me to cognize it the way it is in itself, since its properties cannot migrate over into my power of representation. (4:282)

As in the letter to Herz, he denies that mere empirical sensory contact could reveal things in themselves as they are. Sensory representations of objects do not reveal the objects as they are in themselves, because the properties of objects cannot migrate into our sensory powers (as they are supposed to do in the Aristotelian scheme—but even there, it is only accidents that so migrate). Empirical sensory contact provides only the effect of Bare Causation. If we are to have a priori knowledge of sensed properties, it can extend only to our manner of representing things, in this case, to our spatial manner of representing the relations among things. Accordingly, by means of the forms of intuition "we can cognize objects only as they appear to us (to our senses), not as they may be in themselves" (4:283). We know a priori the universal (and abstract) features of spatial structure because our own form of sensibility supplies those features.

In Part Two of the *Prolegomena*, which corresponds to the Transcendental Analytic of the *Critique*, Kant explains that we cognize objects through a combination of intuitions and concepts (the categories). The concepts involved include substance and causality. These concepts make possible our experience of objects. But by themselves the concepts do not give us objects of cognition. Human knowers are subject to the limitation that they are given objects of cognition only through a combination of concepts with sensory intuitions. The concepts and forms of intuition are furnishings of the mind given a priori which make possible certain bodies of synthetic a priori cognition in mathematics and natural science. At the same time, Kant allows that we can use the concepts to "think," rather than to cognize, intelligible objects. Such objects cannot be known, but they can be thought about abstractly (A 254/B 310, B xxvi, 4:316, 354–5). If we could cognize things in themselves, it would be as intelligible objects of this sort.

Kant clearly believes that we can talk about things in themselves abstractly, and that we should think of them as (unknown) causes that affect our faculty of sense. How then shall we conceive of these things in themselves, which are in causal interaction with us? I agree with those commentators who use Kant's earlier writings as a guide to his conception of the things in themselves.[16] Such things are conceived as simple substances that are in relation through causal interaction. Accordingly, both the substances themselves and their relations are implicated when they affect our sensibility. The individual simple substances are the "real" that corresponds to the matter of sensation. The relations among the substances are the grounds in the things in themselves for ordering the sensations into the forms of space and time. Those relations appear to us as space and time, which are merely subjective conditions of our sensibility and which, like Galilean secondary qualities, would vanish if we, as perceiving subjects, were removed:

> We have therefore wanted to say that all our intuition is nothing but the representation of appearance; that the things that we intuit are not in themselves what we intuit them to be, nor are their relations so constituted in themselves as they appear to us; and that if we remove our own subject or even only the subjective constitution of the senses in general, then all the constitution, all relations of objects in space and time, indeed space and time themselves would disappear, and as appearances they cannot exist in themselves, but only in us.
>
> (A 42/B 59)

[16] Findlay (1981); Ameriks (2003), 25. In his earlier views (see Hatfield 2006), Kant conceived of the natural world as composed of simple substances through whose relations in causal interaction spatial extension arises. In the first *Critique*, Kant affirms things in themselves and their interrelations: "For if we have abstracted from all conditions of intuition, then indeed there remains for us in the mere concept nothing other than the inner in general and the relation of the same reciprocally, through which alone the outer is possible" (A 284/B 341*); in the continuation, he makes clear that such relations would be causal (A 285/B 341–2).

We do not know how things in themselves are constituted, either intrinsically or through their relations. But the appearances present things in themselves through the matter of appearance (sensations) and the spatial relations in which that matter is experienced. Accordingly, along with Note II in the *Prolegomena*, both color and space are like Galilean secondary qualities in that they are merely subjective forms that do not reveal the way things in themselves actually are. With Notes I and III and the passages from the Aesthetic, space and time differ from color in that they are the basis for synthetic a priori principles, and provide a common framework among subjects for knowledge of the physical properties of bodies and the causal relations among bodies as expressed in spatiotemporal processes involving forces. Finally, in accordance with the letter to Herz, both the *Critique* (A 283–5/ B 339–41) and the *Prolegomena* (4:316, 354–5) teach that the understanding does not have direct access into the intrinsic nature of things in themselves and hence cannot provide us with knowledge of those things or of the character of the relations among them. But, in accordance with the notion that the things in themselves are what causes our appearances and what appears to us, the relations among things in themselves appear to us as spatial relations, even though the relations among such things are not spatial.

Accordingly, it is correct to say that both the primary qualities and the secondary qualities fall within the appearances for Kant, by contrast with things considered as they are in themselves. By contrast with Locke, Kant denies Resemblance for both primary and secondary qualities. But the two sorts of qualities do not have the same status. Primary qualities are spatialized forces that fill the Basicality function: they explain the other properties of matter as well as the empirically known effects of bodies on the senses. Secondary qualities are, in the Galilean mode, bare sensations that bodies cause in us. From the standpoint of the things in themselves, spatial representations are also bare effects on human sensibility. But Kant adds a wrinkle: spatial structure, which provides the form in which Basic forces are known, is the subject of a body of synthetic a priori knowledge that applies to all possible sensory experience. Perceived and intuited spatial structure therefore Resembles the empirically real, but transcendentally ideal (that is, ascribed to the domain of appearances) spatial structure of physical forces and physical bodies. In one sense, things in themselves are the basic causes of appearances. But this does us no good as regards the explanatory practices of natural science or everyday cognition. The Basicality role as an explanatory role falls to spatialized forces and bodies within the domain of appearances. The cognitively operative Kantian distinction between primary and secondary qualities thus falls within the appearances; the distinction is between scientifically basic properties (spatialized forces) and mere subjective effects (color).

4. Helmholtz on secondary qualities

In one way or another, Kant's transcendental idealism and his distinction between appearances and things in themselves dominated German intellectual life throughout the nineteenth century. His immediate reception by the German Idealists has received the most attention within the history of philosophy. His doctrines also provided a rallying point for other philosophical schools, whether they opposed him or instead sought to correct him and carry on in his spirit. Among the former are J. F. Herbart and his followers, and among the latter is J. F. Fries. Outside philosophy, Kant's thought on appearances and things in themselves spurred responses from sensory physiologists and psychologists, including Johann Georg Steinbuch, Caspar Theobald Tourtual, and Johannes Müller. These thinkers sought to resolve Kant's distinction between things in themselves and appearances in terms of a realistic interpretation of the spatial properties of bodies. They differed over how and even whether they justified this realism: Steinbuch sought to provide a psychological justification for spatial realism; Tourtual assumed spatial realism and offered an account of spatial perception aimed at sustaining Kant's explanation of geometrical knowledge; and Müller adopted a form of Herbartian metaphysical realism, in which real spatial relations are grounded in simple substances and their relations.

Hermann Helmholtz entered this scene as a student in physiology at Müller's Berlin institute. Even as a medical student, he was interested in physics, and he published his memoir "On the Conservation of Force" in 1847. Nonetheless, his first academic positions were in anatomy and physiology, and he engaged in sustained work on color and then spatial perception and auditory perception throughout his life, even after his appointment as professor of physics in 1871. He also published philosophical essays over his entire career: an inaugural address "On the Nature of Human Sensations" (1852); his famous Kant Memorial Lecture (1855), "On Human Vision"; his most accomplished work of epistemology, "The Facts in Perception" (1878); and a final essay in the year of his death, "On the Origin and Correct Interpretation of our Sensory Impressions" (1894). Further, his original draft of the conservation paper had an even more extensive philosophical preface than does the published version, and the introduction to the third part of his *Physiological Optics* (1867) addressed philosophical themes, as did his subsequent sequence of popular lectures, "Recent Progress in the Theory of Vision" (1868).

In the writings just listed, Helmholtz regularly invoked the name of Immanuel Kant. In the preface to the third edition of his *Vorträge und Reden* (1884, as in Helmholtz 1896), he paused to consider his relation to Kantian thought over the years:

> I was at the beginning of my career a more faithful Kantian than I am now; or rather, I believed then that what I wanted to see altered in Kant were unimportant minor points, which would not come into consideration in comparison to what I even now esteem highly as his principal achievement, until I later discovered that the strict Kantians of today chiefly fasten to and see as the highest development of the philosopher the places where in my opinion Kant had not completely overcome the unsatisfactory basic knowledge of his time and specifically its metaphysical prejudices and had not completely reached the goal that he had set for himself.
>
> (VR 1: viii–ix)

This passage says a lot, but perhaps it doesn't say all that it seems to say. At first Helmholtz says he is less Kantian now than he was before. But what he goes on to say is consistent with his still being, in his own mind, as much of a Kantian as he ever was, except that now he realizes that those who call themselves Kantians wouldn't accept that assessment, even though he considers it correct. For he now realizes that he values quite different things in Kant than do Kant's followers, especially those with whom he has been discussing Kant's position on geometry. In effect, he is saying that he believes that some points which are not essential in Kant remain valued by some of Kant's followers, who have missed the essential point of Kant's teaching.

In tracing Helmholtz's relation to Kant and its implications for his views of primary and secondary qualities, we can begin by considering how Helmholtz situated the results of sensory physiology in relation to Kant. He did so in two respects, each having to do with the subjective basis of human knowledge. First, in 1847 and 1855 he invoked the "law of cause" as something that Kant had considered to be "a law of our thought given before all experience" (1855, 116). We will consider the changing role of the law of cause as we consider Helmholtz's changing conceptions of the status of spatial properties. Second, in 1852, 1855, 1868, and 1878, he in various ways invoked the subjectivity of our sensory impressions: that their character depends on "the nature of our senses" (1855, 99). At first, Helmholtz limited this subjective aspect to sensory qualities, such as color, sound, etc.—effectively, the secondary qualities. But subsequently, he acknowledged that Kant extended his point about the subjectivity of representation to space and time, and Helmholtz then announced a psychological and physiological counterpart to Kant's notion of space as a "transcendental" form of intuition: in Helmholtz's view, spatial representation is transcendental or dependent on the subject because it arises from our physiological and psychological endowments, that is, from our "mental and corporeal capacity" for moving our limbs (1878, 124).

By Helmholtz's lights, then, the fundamental Kantian insight concerns the mind's or the subject's contribution to knowledge. Helmholtz himself described the task of philosophy in a manner he credited to Kant. First, he characterized the "problem of epistemology" as formulated by philosophers in Kant's time and just after:

> What is true in our intuition and thought? In what sense do our representations correspond to actuality? (1878, 117)

He then distinguished the approaches of philosophy and natural science to this fundamental question, which concerns them both:

> Philosophy . . . which considers the mental side, seeks to separate out from our knowledge and representation what originates from the influences of the corporeal world, in order to set forth unalloyed what belongs to the mind's own workings. (1878, 117–18)

Science, by contrast, "seeks to separate off that which is definition, symbolism, representational form, or hypothesis, in order to have unalloyed what belongs to the world of actuality, whose laws it seeks" (1878, 118*). Philosophy's task is to find what is intrinsic to the mind, or what the mind brings to knowledge, by contrast with science, which seeks the bare laws of "actuality."

We can characterize more closely Helmholtz's changing relations to Kant by noting some positions that he maintained verbally throughout his career, even as he changed his interpretation of the meaning of these verbal formulations. I have mentioned his commitment to a law of cause. His other epistemological commitments pertained to sensory perception as the basis for knowledge of the external world. Helmholtz maintained that our sensory perceptions start from sensations that vary only in quality and intensity: sensations of light and color with a brightness, sensations of tone at a pitch with a loudness, and so on. Sensations originally are not spatial. Spatiality is built up from sensation through psychological processes in response to repeated sensory experiences. From 1855 on, Helmholtz characterized these processes as unconscious inferences (though he did not use that exact phrase until a few years later). Such inferences make use of the law of cause, but in ways that changed from 1847 to 1878.

Here are three theses that Helmholtz endorsed throughout his career:

(1) Sensations are "symbols" or "signs" of their causes in objects. There is no *similarity* or *resemblance* between the character of the sensations and the properties in objects that cause the sensations. The *character* of the sensation is determined by the law of specific nerve energies, which says that each nerve fiber produces only its own characteristic type of sensation, no matter how the nerve is stimulated. Physical light, pressure, or electric spark will all cause a sensation of light to be produced by an optic nerve fiber.
(2) All sensory nerve fibers produce sensations varying only in quality and intensity. These sensations lack spatiality, which develops through psychological processes of inference.
(3) The law of cause guides these inferences.

From 1855 to the end of his life, Helmholtz held thesis (1) without significant change, except as regards the notion of cause. Color sensations are in regular correspondence with their causes, so that we can be sure that differing color sensations arise from different causes. Beyond that, the sensations themselves offer no information about the character of that cause (No Resemblance). He also retained the portion of (2) pertaining to the lack of original spatiality in sensations, but his understanding of the notion of inference changed. He held to some form of (3) as well, but he came to offer two interpretations of the law of cause: one fully acceptable within science, and one that went along with a realistic metaphysical outlook or hypothesis.

Helmholtz's view of the status of color sensations did not change fundamentally from 1852 to 1878 (and beyond). He regarded the character of all sensations as subjective, by which he meant that both the mode (visual, tactual, auditory, etc.) and the specific character of sensations (specific shade of red, etc.) are determined by the nervous system as subjective effects and do not provide a direct copy, image, or apprehension of their external causes. He described this finding as a consequence of

Müller's law of specific nerve energies, which in his 1855 lecture he stated as follows: "the quality of our sensations, whether they might be light, warmth, sound, or taste, and so forth, does not depend on the perceived external object but on the sensory nerve that mediates the sensation" (1855, 98). The same stimulus, say, a red light, yields a red sensation when it affects the eye but results in a feeling of warmth when it falls on the skin (1852, 603–4; 1855, 96–8). Further, sensations of light and color can be aroused by other stimuli, including pressure on the eye or electric spark applied to the eye (1852, 602; 1855, 96). The character of the sensation is not intrinsically tied to the physical stimulus. Rather, the eye is such that, in normal circumstances, only light affects the retina and optic nerves. Hence, we rightly take a visual sensation as a sign of light as its cause. All the same, even in normal circumstances we cannot infer the specific physical cause from the fact that a red sensation has occurred, since many different combinations of wavelengths can cause the same sensation. We can infer that the physical stimulus is different if, all else being the same, we experience a different sensation.

With these arguments, Helmholtz used recent advances in physics and physiology to further the sort of arguments that Descartes and Locke had previously given, in characterizing the causes of sensations in terms of the sizes, shapes, positions, and motions of particles. Helmholtz took into account the new conception that the sun's light and heat were aether vibrations of various wavelengths, some of which (e.g. the infrared) were not visible, and some of which (the visible spectrum) were. Further, he was aware of color metamerism: that the eye can react exactly in the same manner to physically distinct combinations of wavelengths (1868, 173). Because physically different stimuli (as with metamers) might cause identical sensations and physically identical stimuli different sensations (as with light causing color and heat sensations), he decoupled the precise physical stimulus from the quality of the sensation.

Helmholtz described color sensations as *signs* of their causes, rather than *images*. A sign has a regular correlation to its cause. In the case of vision: "Similar light produces under like conditions a like sensation of color. Light which under like conditions excites unlike sensation of color is dissimilar" (1868, 185). This sign relationship contrasts with a representational image:

> In an *image*, the representation must be of the same kind as that which is represented. Indeed, it is only an image to the extent that it is like in kind. A statue is an image of a man insofar as its form reproduces his; even if it is executed on a smaller scale, every dimension must be represented in proportion. (1868, 185–6*)

In effect, Helmholtz here invokes Resemblance as holding between an image and the thing imaged. A statue reproduces the form of the man, and is to that extent an image of his figure. By contrast, a sign can be in arbitrary relation to the thing it signifies, as exemplified by the relation between the words of a language and their referents (1852, 608).

In characterizing color sensations as signs, Helmholtz did not deny their usefulness or the regularity of their causation in normal conditions; nor did he deny that bodies are colored, or assert that color is an illusion. Rather, he laid out a dispositionalist account of what it is for bodies to be colored, an account that he took to be in accordance with "the most important principles on which the right interpretation of sensible qualities depends," principles that had been "correctly laid down" by Locke (1868, 186).

Helmholtz discussed the status of color sensations most fully in his 1868 lectures. There he sought to overcome certain "popular conceptions," according to which colors simply are as they seem. In order to explain the Lockean viewpoint, he drew a conceptual distinction between phenomenon (*Erscheinung*) and appearance (*Schein*):[17]

> We must not be led astray by confounding the notions of *phenomenon* and *appearance*. The different colors of objects are phenomena caused by certain real differences in their constitution. They are, according to the scientific as well as to the uninstructed view, no mere appearance, even though the way they appear depends chiefly upon the constitution of our nervous system. A deceptive appearance occurs when the normal phenomena of one object are confounded with those of another, but the sensation of color is by no means a deceptive appearance. There is no other way in which color can appear, so there is nothing which we could describe as the normal phenomenon in distinction from the impressions of color received by means of the eye. (1868, 187)

Helmholtz affirms, with "the uninstructed," that color is no mere appearance and hence that in perceiving objects as colored there is no illusion.[18] He differs from those unfamiliar with the science of vision in recognizing that colors as experienced are conditioned by the subject. Once this subjective factor is taken into account, the notion of color in an object, or of the object's color quality, must be viewed as dispositional and relational.

Helmholtz continued by explaining that the notion of quality is intrinsically relational. He in fact extended this principle to all qualities, in a way that ultimately had implications for his conception of primary qualities:

> Here the principal difficulty seems to me to lie in the notion of *quality*. All difficulty vanishes as soon as we clearly understand that each quality or property of a thing is, in reality, nothing but its capability of exercising certain effects upon other things. These actions either go on between adjacent parts of the same body and so produce alterations in its aggregate condition; or they proceed from one body to another, as in the case of chemical reactions; or they produce their effect on our sense organs and are there recognized as sensations, such as those of sight. Any of these actions is called a property when the object it acts on is understood without being expressly

[17] The German word *Erscheinung*, in the passages from Kant quoted above, was translated as "appearance." If that translation were adopted here, then *Schein* would be translated as "illusion." I have retained the translation of Helmholtz's word as "phenomenon" because it reflects a nineteenth-century distinction between phenomena and the metaphysical reality behind them. Nonetheless, Helmholtz's point in the following quotation could be made using the usual Kantian translation of "appearance" (*Erscheinung*), as opposed to mere semblance or "illusion" (*Schein*).

[18] I differ in my interpretation of this passage from Hacker (1987, 45), who reads the final sentence of the quotation as Helmholtz's assertion that there is no fact of the matter about whether color experience is illusory (an assertion that I take Helmholtz to deny in this passage). Hacker summarizes Helmholtz's legacy as the view bodies aren't colored and that color exists only as a sensation (a Galilean view), mistakenly portraying Helmholtz's description of Kant's position as his own (1987, 44, quotation with n. 6).

mentioned. Thus, when we speak of the solubility of a substance, we mean its behavior toward water; when we speak of its weight, we mean its attraction to the earth; and in the same way we may correctly call a substance blue, understanding as a tacit assumption that we are speaking of its action upon a normal eye. (1868, 187)

As regards the secondary qualities, Helmholtz here directly affirms that it is correct to call objects "blue." This denomination, when fully analyzed, carries with it a tacit understanding that things are blue in virtue of their effects on normal perceivers (in standard conditions). He has adopted an updated Lockean position.

In the lectures, Helmholtz contrasted the status of color sensations and spatial perceptions. By contrast with color sensations, which are signs but not images of their causes, he effectively affirmed that perceptions of spatial and temporal properties have the status of images:

Only the relations of time, space, and equality and those which are derived from them (number, size, and regularity of coexistence and sequence)—mathematical relations, in short—are common to the outer and inner worlds, and for these we can in fact aspire to a complete correspondence between representations and the things portrayed. (1868, 222*; VR 1:365)

In this passage, Helmholtz seems to assert full Resemblance as holding for spatiotemporal properties and relations. In fact, his views on the primary qualities are more subtle than that, and they changed and developed over his career.

5. Helmholtz on primary qualities

In his Kant memorial lecture, Helmholtz honored Kant by endorsing his teaching on causality. According to Helmholtz, Kant considered the proposition "no effect without a cause" to be "a law of our thought given before all experience" (1855, 116). We can forgive Helmholtz for stating the law in a form that Kant would consider to be a trivial analysis of the concept of an *effect* (that effects require causes): Helmholtz clearly meant to agree with Kant that nothing *arises* without a cause. We may also note, without pursuing it, that Helmholtz treats the Kantian a priori as a matter of being inborn or innate.

I wish to focus on Helmholtz's use of his Kantian affirmation to posit a world of objects in space. In his lecture, Helmholtz developed his view about the subjectivity of sensations, and he endorsed the principle that each type of nerve fiber produces only sensations of a particular kind. He also hinted that sensations originally lack spatiality, and that spatial organization arises through a process of learning (1855, 114–16). Near the end of the lecture, he considered how a world of objects in space might be inferred from non-spatial sensations. He recognized that:

If a connection is to arise between our sensations and the representation of a body of a certain appearance and in a specific location, then we must first possess the representation of such a body. As it is with the eye, so is it also with the other senses; we never perceive the objects of the external world immediately, rather we perceive only the effects of these objects on our nervous apparatus. (1855, 115)

How does the representation of bodies in space arise? It is here that Helmholtz invokes Kant. The representation arises by our positing objects as the causes of our sensations, and we make such posits in accordance with the proposition, "no effect without a cause." He explains that

we need this proposition before we have any knowledge whatsoever of the things of the external world; we need it, in order merely to come to the knowledge in general that there are objects in space around us, between which there can exist a relation of cause and effect. (1855, 116)

Helmholtz relies on the causal law as a "law of thought" to justify, or at least to enable, an inference from sensations to mind-independent causes.

In the second quotation, Helmholtz does not stop with the inference that there is some cause for our sensations. Rather, he uses the law to account for the properties that are attributed to such causes: that the causes are in space, that they are themselves spatial objects, and that causal relations exist among them. This picture of external objects as material things arrayed in space and acting on one another causally (through forces) is the one that he had presented at the beginning of his conservation paper (1847), there also citing Kant. Unfortunately, in the context of his 1855 paper, this invocation of causality will not sustain the work that he expects of it. He has set himself the task of explaining the representation of objects in space from the course of experienced sensations varying only in quality and intensity. The law of cause, if assumed at the outset, might sustain the result that the sensations must have *some* cause. But at this juncture, Helmholtz neither offers, nor can offer, any explanation for how it gets us causes arrayed in space, instead of causes having some other unknown relational structure.

It is not surprising that Helmholtz had no explanation in 1855 for how the representation of spatiality arises from the causal law. Up to that time, his work in sensory physiology and psychology had focused on color perception. Only subsequently did he take up spatial perception, in preparation for writing the third part of his *Physiological Optics*. In that part, he again invokes the law of cause. He now invokes it, not as an objective law of thought that reveals an independent law of nature as in 1847 and 1855, but as a subjective "urge" of the intellect to make natural phenomena intelligible by seeking regularities within the phenomena (1867, 3:31).

Helmholtz continued to treat secondary-quality sensations as "symbols" of their causes, and he analyzed them dispositionally, as before (1867, 3:17–20). But we also perceive the world *as in space and time*. Helmholtz remained a realist about time (in effect invoking Resemblance): "the only respect in which there can be a real agreement between our perceptions and reality is the time-sequence of the events" (1867

3:21). But he altered his opinion about the status of spatial perception. He now regarded the spatial representations merely as embodying information allowing one to infer subsequent sequences of sensations:

> The idea of a single individual table which I carry in my mind is correct and exact, provided I can deduce from it correctly the precise sensations I shall have when my eye and my hand are brought into this or that definite relation with respect to the table. I do not know how to conceive any other sort of similarity that can exist between such an idea and the body that it represents. One is the mental sign of the other. The kind of sign was not chosen by me arbitrarily, but was forced on me by the nature of my organ of sense and of my mind. (1867, 3:21–2*)

Gone is any suggestion of strict Resemblance between spatial representations and objects. Helmholtz now speaks of spatial representations as a series of signs. Has he completely assimilated his account of spatial perception to his sign conception of the secondary qualities?

No. In the ensuing discussion, Helmholtz reinterprets the notion of an image to include patterns of relations. Our spatial representations can be taken as images of relations among external things, even if we are uncertain that the relations among those things are in fact spatial.[19] They can represent truly the relations among things, even if they aren't Resembling images:

> we must be on our guard against saying that all our ideas of things are consequently *false*, because they are not *equal* to the things themselves, and that hence we are not able to know anything as to the *true nature* of things. That they cannot be equal to things, is in the nature of knowledge. Ideas are merely pictures of things. Every image is the image of a thing merely for him who knows how to read it, and who is enabled by the aid of the image to form an idea of the thing. Every image is similar to its object in one respect, and dissimilar in all others, whether it be a painting, a statue, the musical or dramatic representation of a mental mood, etc. Thus the ideas of the external world are images of the regular sequence of natural events, and if they are formed correctly according to the laws of our thinking, and we are able by our actions to translate them back into actuality again, the ideas we have are also the *only true* ones for our mental capacity.
> (1867, 3:22*)

Spatial representations capture actual relations among really existing external things, and to that extent allow us to operate successfully. In particular, the relations among sensations as ordered by us in space and time correspond to the relations among things, even if we don't know those things as they are in themselves (that is, even if the relations that we

[19] In effect, Helmholtz posits a "homomorphism" (Palmer 1999, 77–8) between perceived spatial relations and the otherwise unknown relations among external things. Accordingly, the perceiver has direct access to the spatial relations but does not know the form (beyond its abstract structure) of the corresponding relations among external things. This sort of relation has also been discussed as an "abstract first-order isomorphism" (on which, see Hatfield 2009, 157–8).

represent spatially aren't in fact spatial in the things).[20] Helmholtz has retained his realism about external causes, but is no longer a realist about spatial properties.

In his 1878 address, given as Rector in Berlin during celebrations of the founding of the University, Helmholtz entered more deeply into the epistemic standing of color sensations and spatial perceptions. At the beginning of the lecture, he characterized the "problem of epistemology" by posing two questions:

> What is true in our intuition and thought? In what sense do our representations correspond to actuality? (1878, 117)

He is not asking which of our *individual* thoughts are true or correspond to something beyond them; rather, he seeks an assessment of the truth or accuracy of the *kinds* of representations we have, and specifically of our sensory representations as they have been worked up into thoughts. He is asking what color sensations and spatial perceptions reveal to us about something beyond themselves. He again uses the language of *images* as opposed to *signs*: do our sensory representations provide an *image* of the external world as it is, or are they mere *signs* of it? In terms of our earlier analysis: do our perceptions serve as images that represent through Resemblance, or are they merely Bare Causal effects ("signs") of external objects?

On this topic, his position remained as in 1867 for color and space: he held that color sensations are "subjective" and act as mere signs, not as images of their causes, and that spatial representations are abstract images of causal relations whose true form is unknown to us:

> although our sensations, as regards their quality, are only signs whose particular character depends wholly upon our own makeup, they are not to be dismissed as empty appearance, but they are precisely signs of something, be it something existing or happening, and—what is most important—they can form for us an image of the law of this thing which is happening. (1878, 122*).

Regarding their "subjectivity," or dependence on the sensory apparatus and psychological processes of the perceiving subject, Helmholtz compared spatial representations to sensory qualities such as red, sweet, and cold (1878, 124). But he again distinguished spatial perception from sensations of secondary qualities: spatial representations provide an image of the causal relations or lawful interactions among things.

Helmholtz framed his further discussion as a comparison between his position and Kant's. In this discussion, he showed in some ways that he did not fully understand—or at least did not accurately portray—Kant's actual position. Thus, he described Kant as treating sensory qualities such as colors as a "form of intuition" (1878, 124), a position

[20] Helmholtz's discussion in the third part of the *Physiological Optics*, completed in 1866 and published as a unified volume in 1867, may seem to be in tension with his spatial realism at the end of the lectures of 1868 (as quoted at the end of Section 4, above). The tension is eased if we take the "complete correspondence" between spatial representations and external objects to be mediated by an abstract set of mathematical relations. This reading essentially reinterprets the conclusion of the 1868 popular lecture so as to bring it into conformity with the more studied conclusions of the *Physiological Optics*.

he had invoked earlier in comparing Müller's law of specific nerve energy to Kant's position on space. In so doing, Helmholtz meant to stress that in Kant's view both sensory qualities and spatial representations were subjectively conditioned. Kant, however, would have resisted the assimilation of sensory qualities to "forms of intuition." He adopted a Galilean attitude toward sensory qualities and did not treat them as exhibiting the regularity that Helmholtz ascribed to them. More importantly, Kant did not allow that sensory qualities such as color were the object of synthetic a priori principles of the sort that he grounded in what, in his terminology, are the only human "forms of intuition," space and time. Nonetheless, Helmholtz did recognize that Kant treated space differently from sensory qualities, in that he treated it as a necessary "transcendental" form.

Helmholtz presented a physiologized version of Kant's doctrine. He treated space as a necessary form of the outer world because the outer world is by definition intrinsically spatial. Space is a "given" form of intuition ("possessed prior to all experience") in the sense that our sensorimotor apparatus is so constituted that we naturally develop spatial representations in the course of sensory experience. He departed from the historical Kant in making the precise form of visual and physical space into an empirical matter. According to Helmholtz, the axioms of geometry, inasmuch as they apply to physical space, must be empirically determined.

For our purposes, the important point is that, although Helmholtz in 1878 continued to treat spatial perceptions as providing an image of the laws of nature and thus as moving beyond the mere sign-status of color sensations, he changed his position concerning the realistic basis for spatial relations. He presented two positions. First, he developed a realism similar to that of 1867: he posited otherwise-unknown properties and forces as active causes of sensations and as having relations that correspond in some way to the relations among sensations. But now he regarded this outlook as a mere hypothesis, of the sort that scientists may entertain but cannot confirm. In particular, he believed that the realist hypothesis could not be decisively established in preference to idealism: "I do not see how we could refute a system of even the most extreme subjective idealism, if it regarded life as a dream." Idealism might be regarded as "improbable" or "unsatisfying," but it cannot be ruled out (1878, 137). Helmholtz, the physicist, now treats matter and any transphenomenal notion of force or causal agency as merely hypothetical.

So what is left for the scientist who does not wish to be subjected to "idealist doubts" (1878, 143)? In the course of the paper, Helmholtz distinguishes between "the actual" and "the real" (1878, 140). "The real" is what the realist hypothesis posits: enduring independent substances possessing properties and forces.[21] "The actual" is the bare concept of activity as what is responsible for the phenomena. Strictly speaking, science can only chart relations among the effects of such activity, that is, it can seek the lawful among the phenomena: "what we can find unambiguously, and as a fact without

[21] We may assume that Helmholtz's realist hypothesis of 1878 corresponds to his realism of 1867, in which really existing external causes cannot be known to have spatial relations, but perceived spatial relations are a subjectively conditioned image of the real relations among external entities.

anything being insinuated hypothetically, is the lawlike in the phenomena" (1878, 138). Accordingly, the regularities among non-spatial sensations that yield spatial representations must be viewed as signs for future patterns of sensations, not as signs for mind-independent objects. Nerves, brains, and the relations between nerves and sensations all must be reconstructed as patterns of sensations. The law of cause has the status of a subjective and natural tendency for perceivers to associate patterns of sensations that are constantly conjoined. Constant conjunction is actual enough, but from the standpoint of science proper, it is not an indicator of properties and forces behind the phenomena. Within science proper, Helmholtz has retreated to a pure phenomenalism. That was not his preferred position overall: he preferred the realist hypothesis. But he has relegated that position to the status of a metaphysical hypothesis whose affirmation natural science cannot provide.

Helmholtz in effect restricts science to the domain of appearances or phenomena. Within those phenomena, laws are expressed as spatial forces. However, the scientist, by paying attention to the results of sensory physiology, can discount spatiality as a subjective aspect of human sensory experience. In this regard, space is similar to color. But Helmholtz did not treat space and color as epistemically equivalent. Rather, spatial relations are more fundamental because they are the manifestation of the lawlike. Lawful relations are basic, and these are what would meet the Basicality criterion for counting as primary qualities. If we stay within the phenomena, these lawful relations are expressed spatially. But if we follow the realist hypothesis, then we must treat these as lawful relations as holding among otherwise unknown things in themselves, considered in abstraction from their spatial clothing. Such laws might be expressed as bare relations of magnitude, without treating the magnitudes as spatial (they become magnitudes that are expressed as quantitative relations among factors X, Y, and Z).

Nonetheless, within human experience forces are expressed in space (as when forces vary with distance). Further, human actions, such as walking or reaching, are guided by a spatial framework. We thus treat spatial magnitudes as providing the framework for physics and for everyday activity. Color sensations are also useful, as picking out similar causes or the same cause being met again. But color perceptions do not provide a framework in which the lawfulness of the appearances is expressed. They are signs of their own causes, but they do not provide a general framework of external causal relations, as the spatialized laws do.

In effect, Helmholtz has allowed that, in abstract relations of lawfulness, we get as close as we can to the Kantian thing in itself. In this regard, he was close to Kant's own position, if we see Kant as maintaining that spatial perceptions are the appearance of underlying relations among things in themselves, relations that we are not able to further specify, and about which we know nothing as to how they may be in themselves. Color and space both fall on the side of the appearances, but spatial relations are physically more fundamental. Helmholtz differs from Kant on the extent to which color sensations are arbitrary: they are, in his view, regular signs of their causes. Further, Helmholtz, while affirming No Resemblance for color, nonetheless was willing to speak of bodies as colored inasmuch as they regularly cause color sensations of specific type in normal perceivers under standard conditions. Contrary to Kant, he adopts a Lockean notion of secondary qualities and of color as a secondary quality.

6. Conclusions

The distinction between primary and secondary qualities, as expressed by Galileo, Descartes, and Locke, had both metaphysical and epistemological aspects. Primary qualities are metaphysically and epistemically basic. They characterize the fundamental parts of matter as they are. The list of primary qualities (including size, shape, position, and motion) provides the explanatory categories that are used to account for the other properties and qualities of bodies, whether these be secondary or tertiary (in Lockean terms). There is a close relation between what is metaphysically Basic and what is epistemically Basic. This close relation is expressed in the thesis of Resemblance for primary qualities. By contrast, for Descartes and Locke secondary qualities are genuine qualities of bodies, but Resemblance does not hold between these qualities and our ideas of them, and secondary qualities are to be explained in terms of primary qualities. For Galileo, the ideas of secondary qualities are Bare Causal effects in perceivers, and secondary qualities have only subjective existence.

In the accounts of Kant and Helmholtz, distance is placed between things in themselves as metaphysically (ontologically) fundamental and primary qualities as explanatorily basic within physics. Kant and Helmholtz both accepted that within physics as applied to appearances or phenomena (as opposed to a futile attempt to develop a physics of things in themselves), spatialized forces are primary (by contrast with the hard particles of Galileo, Descartes, and Locke). These are Newtonian primary qualities (as Newtonian mechanics came to be interpreted, with force underlying extended matter). Because the forces are conceived spatially, they render the spatial properties as explanatorily basic. Size, shape, and motion remain basic in descriptions of interactions among forces and of the manifestation of such forces in physical phenomena.

Kant, as interpreted herein, held that spatial representations are the appearance of the relations among things in themselves, which relations remain unknown as to how they may be in themselves. Things in themselves affect sensibility and cause both the matter of sensation (including color sensations) and the appearance of bodies arrayed in space. In this regard, things in themselves are causally Basic. But they are epistemically remote. Both space and color are on the side of appearances and are to that extent subjective. But spatial properties as met with in experience remain explanatorily Basic. In Kant's view, color is merely subjective; he was Galilean about the secondary qualities, whether their cause is regarded as things in themselves or as spatialized forces. In either case, Kant considered the relation between color sensations and their cause to be idiosyncratically subjective. Color is merely a sensation in the mind.

Helmholtz began as a realist about spatialized forces as primary qualities and as a Lockean about secondary qualities. He retained his Lockeanism about secondary qualities, but he withdrew from his spatial realism. In his most extreme withdrawal, he allowed that only phenomenalism can be justified within science. But he preferred to be a realist about external causes. However, in his 1867 and 1878 works, he denied Resemblance between spatial perception and external causes. If realism is correct, then spatial representations are subjectively conditioned images of external relations that are known in themselves only by abstracting from spatial relations and positing a system of relations that are unknown as to their form, but are reflected in spatial experience. If one sticks to what is scientifically admissible, then spatial relations are the epistemically Basic description of physical forces. But they are not metaphysically Basic.

In either case, in Helmholtz's view, color remains a secondary quality that is attributed to bodies in a dispositionalist manner. Unlike Kant (and Galileo), Helmholtz did not deny color to bodies (*pace* Hacker 1987, 44). He used the recent findings of sensory physiology to support his dispositionalism in a more compelling manner than could Descartes or Locke, who had merely programmatic theories of the character of light and of the physical basis of color and other secondary qualities, such as heat. In this way, Helmholtz moved along the understanding of secondary-quality dispositionalism. The scientific understanding of what colors are in bodies on a dispositionalist account has advanced yet further since Helmholtz's time, with increased understanding of the physical basis for the selective absorption of visible light by the colored surfaces that reflect it and the effect of such light on the eyes. This new understanding allows the basis of such reflectances and physiological effects to be understood in terms of spatialized properties of atomic and molecular structure, achieving explanatory Basicality for spatialized forces as underlying dispositions.

That story would take us beyond Kant and Helmholtz into more recent physics, physiology, and sensory psychology, and into the ongoing philosophical disputes concerning the metaphysics of color. Scientific accounts of color perception have progressed since Helmholtz, and yet some philosophical discussions of secondary qualities and color metaphysics do not take into account even Newton and Helmholtz, let alone more recent science. That seems unwise, since, from its inception in the seventeenth century, the distinction has gained its motivation and plausibility through engagement with current theories of how vision works. In this area, one can't really do philosophy without knowing something about how things work. Which doesn't mean that now, any more than with Descartes, Locke, or Kant, science dictates answers to philosophy's questions and problems. But science can be crucial for understanding the questions and problems themselves.[22]

[22] Thanks to Rolf Horstmann, Dina Emundts, and Krisanna Scheiter for comments and discussion.

Bibliography

The works of Kant and Helmholtz are cited by the date of the original German or Latin editions; where a translation exists, page references are to the translation, except when the translation shows the pagination of the original, in which case the original pagination is used (the practice is noted in each bibliographic entry). I usually follow the cited translation; emendations are marked with an asterisk (*).

Alexander, Peter. 1974. "Boyle and Locke on Primary and Secondary Qualities," *Ratio* 16: 51–67.

Ameriks, Karl. 2003. *Interpreting Kant's Critiques*, Oxford: Clarendon Press.

Ayers, Michael. 1991. *Locke*, London: Routledge.

Berkeley, George. 1710. *Treatise Concerning the Principles of Human Knowledge*, Dublin: Pepyat. Introduction and Part I (the projected Part II was never published).

Boyle, Robert. 1666. *The Origine of Formes and Qualities, According to the Corpuscular Philosophy*, Oxford: Davis. Partially republished as *The Origin of Forms and Qualities According to the Corpuscular Philosophy* in Boyle (1979), 1–96.

——. 1979. *Selected Philosophical Papers of Robert Boyle*, ed. M. A. Stewart, Manchester: Manchester University Press.

Collins, Arthur. 1999. *Possible Experience: Understanding Kant's Critique of Pure Reason*, Berkeley: University of California Press.

Crusius, Christian August. 1745. *Entwurf der nothwendigen Vernunft-Wahrheiten*, Leipzig: Gleditsch.

Descartes, René. 1644. *Principia philosophiae*, Amsterdam: Elzevir.

Findlay, J. N. 1981. *Kant and the Transcendental Object*, Oxford: Clarendon Press.

Friedman, Michael. 2001. "Matter and Motion in the Metaphysical Foundations and the First Critique," in Eric Watkins (ed.), *Kant and the Sciences*, 53–69, Oxford: Oxford University Press.

Galilei, Galileo. 1960. *Controversy on the Comets of 1618*, Philadelphia: University of Pennsylvania Press.

Gilbert, Jeffrey. 1752. *An Abstract of Mr. Locke's Essay on Human Understanding*, London: Sandby.

Hacker, P. M. S. 1987. *Appearance and Reality*, Oxford: Blackwell.

Hatfield, Gary. 1998. "The Cognitive Faculties." In M. Ayers and D. Garber (eds.), *Cambridge History of Seventeenth-Century Philosophy*, 953–1002, Cambridge: Cambridge University Press.

——. 2003. *Descartes and the Meditations*, London: Routledge.

——. 2006. "Kant on the Perception of Space (and Time)," in Paul Guyer (ed.), *Cambridge Companion to Kant and Modern Philosophy*, 61–93, Cambridge: Cambridge University Press.

——. 2009. *Perception and Cognition: Essays in the Philosophy of Psychology*, Oxford: Clarendon Press.

Helmholtz, Hermann. 1847. *Ueber die Erhaltung der Kraft*. Berlin: Reimer, trans. "The Conservation of Force: A Physical Memoir," in Helmholtz (1971), 3–55.

——. 1852. "Ueber die Natur der menschlichen Sinnesempfindungen," *Königsberger naturwissenschaftliche Unterhaltungen* 3: 1–20. Cited as in Helmholtz (1882–95), 2: 591–609.

——. 1855. *Ueber das Sehen des Menschen*, Leipzig: Voss. Cited as in Helmholtz (1896), 1: 85–117.

——. 1867. *Handbuch der physiologischen Optik*, Leipzig: Voss. Republished in the third German edition, 3 vols., Leipzig: Voss, 1910, trans. Helmholtz (1924–5). Page citations are to the 3rd German edn., the pagination of which is also shown in the translation (at the top of each page).

——. 1868. "Die neueren Fortschritte in der Theorie des Sehens," *Preussischen Jahrbücher*. Republished in Helmholtz (1896), 1: 265–365. Page citations to trans., "Recent Progress in the Theory of Vision," in Helmholtz (1971), 144–222.

——. 1878. *Die Thatsachen in der Wahrnehmung*, Berlin: Hirschwald. Republished in Helmholtz (1896), 2: 213–47, 387–406. Page citations to trans., "The Facts in Perception," in Helmholtz (1977), 115–63.

——. 1882–95. *Wissenschaftliche Abhandlungen*, 3 vols, Leipzig: Barth.

——. 1894. "Über den Ursprung der richtigen Deutung unserer Sinneseindrücke," *Zeitschrift für Psychologie und Physiologie der Sinnesorgane* 7: 81–96. Trans. as "The Origin and Correct Interpretation of Our Sense Impressions," in Helmholtz (1971), 501–12.

——. 1896. *Vorträge und Reden*, 4th edn., 2 vols, Braunschweig: Vieweg. Cited as "VR," plus volume and page number.

——. 1924–5. *Helmholtz's Treatise on Physiological Optics*, ed. and trans. James P. C. Southall, 3 vols, Rochester: Optical Society of America, trans. from 3rd German edn.

——. 1971. *Selected Writings of Hermann von Helmholtz*, ed. Russell Kahl, Middletown, Conn.: Wesleyan University Press.

——. 1977. *Epistemological Writings*, trans. Malcolm F. Lowe, Dordrecht: Reidel.

Henry, John. 2008. *The Scientific Revolution and the Origins of Modern Science*, 3rd edn., Houndmills, Hampshire: Palgrave Macmillan.

Hume, David. 1739–40. *Treatise of Human Nature*, 3 vols, London: Noon and Longman.

——. 1999. *An Enquiry Concerning Human Understanding*, ed. Tom L. Beauchamp, Oxford: Oxford University Press. Originally published in 1748 as *Philosophical Essays Concerning Human Understanding*.

Kant, Immanuel. 1756. *Metaphysicae cum geometria junetae usus in philosophia naturali, cuius specimen I continet Monadologiam physicam*, Königsberg: Hartung. Trans. *The Employment in Natural Philosophy of Metaphysics Combined with Geometry, of which sample I contains the Physical Monadology*, in Kant (1992).

——. 1770. *De mundi sensibilis atque intelligibilis forma et principiis*, Königsberg: Kanter. Trans. *On the Form and Principles of the Sensible and the Intelligible World* [Inaugural Dissertation], in Kant (1992).

——. 1781. *Kritik der reinen Vernunft*, Riga: Hartnoch, trans. Kant (1998).

——. 1783. *Prolegomena zu einer jeden künftigen Metaphysik*. Riga: Hartnoch, trans. Kant (2004).

——. 1786. *Metaphysische Anfangsgründe der Naturwissenschaft*, Riga: Hartknoch. Trans. Michael Friedman as *Metaphysical Foundations of Natural Science*, in Kant (2002).

——. 1787. *Kritik der reinen Vernunft*, 2nd edn., Riga: Hartnoch, trans. as Kant (1998).

——. 1992. *Theoretical philosophy, 1755–1770*, ed. and trans. David Walford, with Ralf Meerbote, Cambridge: Cambridge University Press.

——. 1997. *Lectures on Metaphysics*, ed. and trans. Karl Ameriks and Steve Naragon, Cambridge: Cambridge University Press.

——. 1998. *Critique of Pure Reason*, ed. and trans. Paul Guyer and Allen Wood, Cambridge: Cambridge University Press.

Kant, Immanuel. 1999. *Correspondence*, ed. and trans. Arnulf Zweig, Cambridge: Cambridge University Press. Cited in the pagination of the Akademie Edition.

——. 2002. *Theoretical Philosophy after 1781*, ed. Henry Allison and Peter Heath, Cambridge: Cambridge University Press.

——. 2004. *Prolegomena to Any Future Metaphysics*, ed. and trans. Gary Hatfield, 2nd edn., Cambridge: Cambridge University Press. Page citations are to the Akademie Edition.

Kuehn, Manfred. 2001. *Kant: A Biography*, Cambridge: Cambridge University Press.

Lambert, Johann Heinrich. 1764. *Neues Organon*, 2 vols, Lepzig: Johann Wendler.

Langton, Rae. 1998. *Kantian Humility: Our Ignorance of Things in Themselves*, Oxford: Clarendon Press.

Leibniz, Gottfried Wilhelm, and Samuel Clarke. 1717. *A Collection of Papers, which Passed between the Late Learned Mr. Leibnitz, and Dr. Clarke, in the Years 1715 and 1716*, London: Knapton.

——. 1720. *Merckwürdige Schrifften zwischen dem Herrn Baron von Leibnitz, und dem Herrn D. Clarcke, über besondere Materien der natrlichen Religion, in Frantzös. und Englischer Sprache gewechselt, und nunmehro mit einer Vorrede Herrn Christian Wolffens*, ed. Heinrich Khlern, Frankfurt and Leipzig: Meyer.

Locke, John. 1690. *An Essay Concerning Human Understanding*, London: Bassett. Republished, with variations from later editions, ed. Peter H. Nidditch, Oxford: Clarendon Press, 1975. Cited by book, chapter, and section number.

——. 1757. *Herrn Johann Lockens Versuch vom menschlichen Verstande*, trans. Heinrich Engelhard Poley, Altenburg: Richter.

Mundle, C. W. K. 1971. *Perception: Facts and Theories*, Oxford: Oxford University Press.

Palmer, Stephen E. 1999. *Vision Science: Photons to Phenomenology*, Cambridge: MIT Press.

Prauss, Gerold. 1974. *Kant und das Problem der Dinge an Sich*, Bonn: Bouvier Verlag Herbert Grundmann.

Reid, Thomas. 1785. *An Inquiry into the Human Mind*, 4th edn., London: T. Cadell.

Steneck, Nicholas H. 1976. *Science and Creation in the Middle Ages*, Notre Dame: University of Notre Dame Press.

Stroud, Barry. 1980. "Berkeley v. Locke on Primary Qualities," *Philosophy* 55: 149–66.

——. 2000. *The Quest for Reality: Subjectivism and the Metaphysics of Color*, New York: Oxford University Press.

Wilson, Margaret D. 1982. "Did Berkeley Completely Misunderstand the Basis of the Primary–Secondary Quality Distinction in Locke?" in Colin Turbayne (ed.), *Berkeley: Critical and Interpretive Essays*, 108–23, Minneapolis: University of Minnesota Press.

Wolff, Christian. 1736. *Philosophia prima, sive ontologia*, new edn., Frankfurt: Renger.

——. 1737. *Cosmologia generalis*, new edn., Frankfurt am Main: Renger.

Woolhouse, R. S. 1983. *Locke*, Minneapolis: University of Minnesota Press.

13

Are Colors Secondary Qualities?*

Alex Byrne and David R. Hilbert

Color is an affair of the mind, while light is purely physical, but you cannot have one without the other.

The Dangerous Book for Boys

1. Introduction

Seventeenth- and eighteenth-century discussions of the senses are often thought to contain a profound truth: some perceptible properties are *secondary qualities*, dispositions to produce certain sorts of experiences in perceivers. Any apparent plausibility this has often derives, we argue, from an erroneous picture of perception. The colors are typically held to be one of the clearest examples of secondary qualities, and so we shall focus on these.

Since the terminology of "secondary qualities" is liable to produce misunderstanding, some extra clarification won't go amiss. First, for the purposes of this paper, secondary qualities are just stipulated to be dispositions to produce experiences—that is the way this terminology is (mostly) used by the contemporary philosophers we principally discuss. So, for example, Rae Langton's (1998) account of Kant's "primary/ secondary quality distinction" as a distinction between *intrinsic* and *relational* properties, and her partial defense of Kant's apparent claim that we can only know the secondary qualities of objects, is not relevant to present concerns. (A Kantian "secondary quality" on Langton's interpretation need not involve relations to *perceivers*.) Also not relevant are secondary qualities in either of Berkeley's two senses: a quality that exists "nowhere but in the mind" (see Van Cleve 1999: 167); or a quality that is either a color, or a sound, or a taste, or a smell, or . . . (see Armstrong 1968a: 270).

Second, although arguably Locke was an "eliminativist" about color, and hence did *not* hold that colors are secondary qualities (see note 24 below), sometimes contempor-

* A remote ancestor of this paper was given at the Central APA in 2002; thanks to the commentator, Justin Broackes. Mark Kalderon provided much help with an even earlier version, as did others whom we have now forgotten. Thanks to an anonymous referee for comments on the penultimate draft.

ary arguments for the secondary quality theory of color are said to derive from the *Essay*. We assume that all possible support from this source has trickled into the contemporary literature: accordingly the *Essay* will be set aside.

The basic schematic claim of the secondary quality theory of color, or *dispositionalism*, can be illustrated as follows:

(D) The property green = the disposition to cause in perceivers of kind *P* in conditions of kind *C*, visual experiences of kind *K*.

There are two importantly different ways of specifying the *manifestation* of the disposition, the "visual experiences of kind *K*" (cf. Boghossian and Velleman 1989: 84–5). The specification may be *non-reductive*: the visual experiences are as of a *green* object. Put more plainly, the experiences consist in the disposed object's *looking green* to perceivers of kind *P* (e.g. McGinn 1983).[1] The relevant interpretation of ***looks green*** (etc.) can be explained by example. First, a paradigmatically green object (say, a cucumber) looks green to someone with normal color vision who sees the cucumber in daylight from a few feet away. Second, a white patch illuminated by a small green spotlight, in an array of normally illuminated colored patches, looks green to someone with normal color vision who sees the patch. Third, we may imagine that a certain green car looks a distinctive shade of grey in the artificial light of an underground parking garage. Even though the car can be identified as green by sight in the garage (no car is that peculiar shade of grey), it does not look green to someone with normal color vision who sees it in the garage. (No doubt there is an understanding of ***looks green*** on which the green car *does* look green; this is the "epistemic use" of looks that can be made more explicit by saying that the car looks *as if* it is green; cf. Jackson 1977: ch. 2.)

On the alternative *reductive* specification of the "visual experiences of kind *K*", the visual experiences are *not* specified using ***green*** or any cognate expressions. Just how they *are* specified is a tricky issue, which we will discuss at length later (section 3).

The *reductive* dispositionalist's neck, then, is stuck out the furthest. Everyone can agree, with the non-reductive dispositionalist, that cucumbers *are* disposed to look green; the bone of contention is whether this disposition *is* the property green. In contrast, it is disputed whether cucumbers even have a disposition to cause "visual experiences of kind K", as the reductive dispositionalist conceives of them.[2, 3]

[1] On this specification of the manifestation, the otherwise problematic notion of a "visual experience" drops out; on the notion of an "experience" in the philosophy of perception, see Byrne 2009b.

[2] Notice that this constraint on the reductive dispositionalist is compatible with the intentionalist or representationalist view that the phenomenal character distinctive of a color experience is determined by its representational content, the way the experience represents the world as being. Shoemaker (1994) is an intentionalist who thinks that the phenomenal character of a color experience is *not* determined by its *color* content—the aspect of its representational content that concerns the colors of things.

[3] It might be claimed that there is a use of ***looks green*** on which to describe an object as looking green is not to comment in any way on its color, real or apparent, but rather to characterize the phenomenal character of one's visual experience (this would be similar to the alleged "qualitative sense" of ***looks the same***—see Shoemaker 1982: 365, Block 1990: 54). If so, a reductive dispositionalist could then express her thesis

Sometimes dispositionalism is not put in terms of property identity, but rather as a biconditional claim. For example: necessarily, something is pink iff it's disposed to look pink. (This biconditional formulation might be preferred on nominalist grounds.) We shall (mostly) take dispositionalism to be an identity claim, but this assumption is only for convenience. In any case, on the (defensible) view that necessary coextensiveness is sufficient for property identity, the biconditional and identity formulations are equivalent.[4]

One common objection to dispositionalism is that there are problems with specifying the dispositionalist's "perceivers" and "conditions" in a principled manner (see, e.g. Hardin 1993: 67–91). Although this is a serious problem, we shall ignore it, chiefly because we think the deeper difficulties lie elsewhere.[5]

2. Colors *might* be (non-reductive) dispositions

Having advertised this paper as an anti-dispositionalist manifesto, we now must confess that colors might, after all, be dispositions to affect perceivers in certain ways.[6] Maybe there could be some especially well-calibrated type of perceiver, and some particularly revealing conditions, such that necessarily something is blue iff it is disposed to look blue to this type of perceiver in these revealing conditions, and similarly for the other colors. Without making controversial assumptions about colors and color perception, it is hard definitively to rule this out. If such a biconditional is true, and granting that necessary coextensiveness is sufficient for property identity, then *non-reductive* dispositionalism is true.[7, 8]

using ***looks green*** (see Boghossian and Velleman 1989: 85). We do not think there is such a use, but in any case it does not occur here.

[4] McGinn has recently retracted his position in *The Subjective View* (1983) that colors *are* dispositions to look colored, and retreated to the claim that they are necessarily coextensive with such dispositions (1996). (So, of course, he is obliged to deny that necessary coextensiveness is sufficient for property identity.) Although the identity claim is the official target of this paper, the overall argument works equally well against either the identity or biconditional formulations of dispositionalism.

[5] For a response to Hardin, see Johnston 1992: 155–8.

[6] On some views, colors are certain kinds of dispositions to reflect light (Hilbert 1987, Matthen 1988, Tye 1995, Byrne and Hilbert 1997a, Tye 2000), not dispositions to affect perceivers.

[7] It might be objected that the truth of such a biconditional (granted that necessary coextensiveness is sufficient for property identity) would merely establish that any color could be (rigidly) designated by a dispositional locution, which is not sufficient for a property to be a disposition (cf. Jackson 1998: 94). Be that as it may, for the purposes of this paper we can be concessive to the dispositionalist: if the colors can be designated by dispositional locutions involving perceivers and conditions not too far removed from actual human beings and the actual conditions in which they see objects, then (given the assumption about property identity) dispositionalism is true. With this concession, the objection to dispositionalism based on the premise that "dispositions do not cause their manifestations, their causal bases do that" is to some degree finessed. The objection needs the principle that dispositions are *distinct* from their causal bases, and the main argument for this principle fails on the present catholic notion of a disposition. (For the principle and the argument, see Prior et al. 1982: 253–4. For the objection, see Jackson and Pargetter 1987, Jackson 1998: 91–3. For the reply that Jackson and Pargetter's "primary quality" theory of color suffers from a similar defect, see Johnston 1992: 148–9.)

[8] Admittedly, any dispositional account has to face some serious objections in the style of Kripke's "killer yellow" example (e.g. Broackes 1992: 203–4). Surely there could be a yellow object (Medusa's face, say) that would instantly kill anyone who looked at it. So if someone were to gaze at Medusa, her face would not look

Of course, if the above speculations turned out to be correct, this would only vindicate dispositionalism in letter, not in spirit. The dispositionalist typically takes her thesis to be justified on a priori grounds, or at least on the basis of ordinary color experience: recherché empirical investigation is not necessary. And that is what we dispute. Dispositionalism—at any rate of the non-reductive variety—is perfectly coherent, but cannot be established a priori, or by reflection on ordinary visual experience.

2.1 Circularity

There is, however, an aura of disreputability surrounding non-reductive dispositionalism, deriving from its circularity. Recall that according to the non-reductive dispositionalist:

(D_{NR}) The property green = the disposition to look green to perceivers of kind *P* in conditions of kind *C*.

The circularity of this thesis is evident on its face: ***green*** appears univocally on both sides of the identity predicate. The mere fact that a statement of property identity is circular is not itself a cause for concern: modulo the existence of properties, ***the property green = the property green*** can hardly be problematic! Neither does circularity imply that the thesis is trivial: ***the property square = the disposition to look square*** is not trivial; indeed, it is usually regarded as false. (Cf. Boghossian and Velleman 1989: 87–8.)

However, there is a legitimate worry about circularity if the non-reductive dispositionalist is not content merely to make a claim about property identity. The crucial distinction can be seen in Sellars's *Empiricism and the Philosophy of Mind.*[9] When Sellars first discusses non-reductive dispositionalism he takes it to be an attempt at "a definition of *physical redness* in terms of *looking red*" (1956, sec. 12) and claims without argument that it is objectionably circular. When he later (sec. 18) finds ostensibly the same thesis unproblematic it is because, although he takes it to be knowable a priori, he no longer understands it as offering a "definition", or an "analysis", of "*x is red*... in terms of *x looks red to y*".

Although it's not particularly clear what Sellars takes a definition to be, the circularity worry is clear enough. If (D_{NR}) is taken to provide a way of *explaining what redness is*, to someone who is entirely ignorant of it, or to provide a *synonym of the word* **red**, then the fact that ***red*** appears in the explanans, or in the allegedly synonymous phrase, is a glaring obstacle. If someone has absolutely no idea what redness is, we can hardly presume that he understands the word. And given a modest assumption about meanings or semantic values ***red*** cannot be synonymous with a phrase containing ***looks red***.

yellow to that person. If it follows that Medusa's face is not *disposed* to look yellow, then this is a counterexample to dispositionalism. But this sort of case is usually taken instead to be a counterexample to a simple counterfactual analysis of dispositions (see Johnston 1992: 145–7 and also Lewis 1997a: 144–5, 1997b: 334–5).

[9] Although he doesn't discuss Sellars, Watkins (1994) makes the distinction quite nicely.

The semantic value of the larger phrase is presumably composed of the semantic values of its constituents, which include ***looks*** and ***red***. If so, identifying the semantic value of ***red*** with the semantic value of the larger phrase is in effect to (incorrectly) identify a proper part with the whole.

Another example of this sort of concern is provided by Christopher Peacocke. After claiming that "visual experience seems to occupy a special position in an explanation of what it is for something to be red", he points out the difficulty:

> [This is] precisely what we should expect if looking red is conceptually more fundamental than being red. Yet on the other hand the expression "looks red" is not semantically unstructured. Its sense is determined by that of its constituents. If one does not understand those constituents, one does not fully understand the compound. (1984: 51–2)

Non-reductive dispositionalism, as we are understanding it, is simply a claim of property identity, and makes no claims about analysis, synonymy, or conceptual priority. One might have thought, then, that while circularity undermines some dispositionalist projects, it leaves non-reductive dispositionalism unscathed. However, Boghossian and Velleman have influentially argued that the circularity of (D_{NR}) is actually fatal. Their argument has persuaded some (e.g. Averill 1992: 556, McGinn 1996: 543–4, Levin 2000, Glüer 2007) but, we will now argue, it shouldn't have.[10]

2.2. Boghossian and Velleman's circularity argument

Boghossian and Velleman express non-reductive dispositionalism thus:

(*) "*Red* [i.e. the property that objects are seen as having when they look red] $=_{def}$ a disposition to appear red under standard conditions" (1989: 84)

This appears to be a simple statement of property identity (and so is a minor variant of (D_{NR})), and Boghossian and Velleman gloss it as such: "the property that objects are represented as having when they look red is just this: a disposition to look red under standard conditions" (84).[11]

They then argue as follows:

> Under the terms of [(*)], an experience can represent its object as red only by representing it as disposed to produce visual experiences that represent it as red. The problem here is that the experiences that the object is thus represented as disposed to produce must themselves be represented as experiences that represent the object as red, rather than some other colour—lest

[10] A similar—if not identical—objection to non-reductive dispositionalism is in Stroud 2000: 140–3. There is a complicated and rather distantly related objection in Johnston 1998: 13–5, and Johnston 2001b: 195–9; for discussion see Wedgwood 2001 and Johnston 2001a.

[11] Boghossian and Velleman actually describe (*) as a "biconditional"; taking it as an identity statement seems more faithful to their overall intent. The presence of *def* in (*) might suggest that it is a metalinguistic claim: ***red*** is synonymous with ***the disposition to appear red***, or something of the sort. But this would certainly be a misreading. Boghossian and Velleman presumably have in mind Aristotelian *real definitions*. In this sense, to give the real definition of a thing is to specify its nature.

the object be represented as disposed to appear something other than red. Yet these experiences can be represented as representing the object as red only if they are represented as representing it as disposed to produce experiences that represent it as red. And here the circle gets vicious. In order for an object to appear red rather than blue, it must appear disposed to appear red, rather than disposed to appear blue; and in order to appear disposed to appear red, rather than disposed to appear blue, it must appear disposed to appear disposed to appear red, rather than disposed to appear disposed to appear blue; and so on. Until this regress reaches an end, the object's appearance will not amount to the appearance of one colour rather than another. Unfortunately, the regress never reaches an end. (88–90)

The problem with the regress is summarized later:

[T]he subject of visual experience cannot see what colour an object has. For he cannot see that particular colour of an object except by seeing the particular way the object tends to appear; and he cannot see the way it tends to appear except by seeing the way it tends to appear as tending to appear; and so on, *ad infinitum*. (90)

The argument may be reconstructed as follows (suppressing the reference to standard conditions):

(A_1) The property red = the disposition to appear (look) to have the property red.

By (A_1), substituting the right hand side for ***the property red*** throughout:

(A_2) The disposition to appear to have the property red = the disposition to appear to have the disposition to appear to have the property red.

And so on. In an obvious notation:

(A_{n+1}) [The disposition to appear to have]^n the property red = [the disposition to appear to have]$^{n+1}$ the property red.

Now suppose:

(B_1) The fire truck appears (looks) to Griffin to have the property red.[12]

Then, by (A_1), substituting its right hand side for ***the property red***:

(B_2) The fire truck appears to Griffin to have the disposition to appear to have the property red.

And by (A_2), substituting its right hand side for ***the disposition to appear to have the property red***:

[12] Since the exposition will be simplified if the substituends are noun phrases rather than verb phrases, we have used ***the fire truck appears to Griffin to have* the property red** as opposed to the more natural ***the fire truck* appears red *to Griffin***. But this is just for convenience.

(B_3) The fire truck appears to Griffin to have the disposition to appear to have the disposition to appear to have the property red.

And so on. By (A_3), . . . , (A_n):

(B_{n+1}) The fire truck appears to Griffin to have [the disposition to appear to have]^n the property red.

(C) By the B-series, Griffin cannot see the particular color of the fire truck except by seeing the particular way the fire truck tends to appear; and he cannot see the way it tends to appear except by seeing the way it tends to appear as tending to appear; and so on, ad infinitum. Hence he cannot see it as having a color, which is absurd. And so, by *reductio*, (A_1) is false.

Let us look at the A-series of inferences first. On the (natural) non-transparent *de dicto* reading of ***appear to have . . .***, they are invalid. So—putting aside the question of Boghossian and Velleman's intentions—***appear to have . . .*** must be read transparently.[13] On this reading, ***The fire truck appears to have the disposition to appear to have the property red*** is true just in case there is a property P such that the fire truck appears to have it, and P is the disposition to appear to have the property red. So understood, the A-series is unobjectionable.

What about the inferences in the B-series? On the *de dicto* reading of ***The fire truck appears to Griffin to have . . .***, they are invalid. So—again putting aside the question of Boghossian and Velleman's intentions—***The fire truck appears to Griffin to have . . .*** must be read transparently. On this reading, ***The fire truck appears to Griffin to have the disposition to appear to have the property red*** is true just in case there is a property P such that Griffin sees that the fire truck appears to have it, and P is the disposition to appear to have the property red. So understood, the B-series is also unobjectionable.

That leaves (C), the final part of the argument. To rebut it, note that given the assumptions required to generate the B-series ((*) and the transparent readings), each member of the series demands *exactly the same* of Griffin: that, of the property red (i.e. the disposition to appear to have the property red, i.e. the disposition to appear to have the disposition . . .), the fire truck appears to Griffin to have *it*. Hence, although it is true (given the assumptions just mentioned) that Griffin cannot see the color of the fire truck *except by seeing* the particular way the fire truck tends to appear, this is a feat he can easily manage: he just needs to see the property that is the color of the fire truck, namely red. He is not required, as Boghossian and Velleman claim, "to run an endless gamut of visual appearances" (89).

[13] As McGinn observed in a related context (1983, 143). Subsequently, though, he characterized this observation as having been made "somewhat desperately . . . the maneuver does nothing to avert the fundamental intuitive point that [dispositionalism] is *phenomenologically* incorrect: we just do not *see* colors *as* dispositions to cause experiences" (1996, 538). Boghossian and Velleman make a similar claim (see the following note, and note 25 below).

To conclude: if the A- and B-series inferences are valid, (C) is invalid, and therefore so is the reconstructed argument against non-reductive dispositionalism.[14]

3. The natural sign theory and reductive dispositionalism

Thus far, we have distinguished two sorts of dispositionalism, and argued that the circularity of non-reductive dispositionalism is unproblematic. It is now time to consider the main question of this paper: is either sort of dispositionalism true?

Let us start with reductive dispositionalism, historically the favored variety; subsequent sections will focus on non-reductive dispositionalism. The main motivation for reductive dispositionalism is a picture of perception that we shall call—borrowing some terminology from Thomas Reid—***the natural sign theory***. According to it, color perception (for example) is a matter of figuring out the colors of objects in the environment from the distinctive mental effects they cause in us, the "natural signs" of colors.[15] As will be apparent, once the natural sign theory is assumed, (reductive) dispositionalism is not far behind.

[14] Two other points are worth noting. First, Boghossian and Velleman really do seem to insist on the *de dicto* reading of constructions like ***appears to have...***: before arguing that (*) is viciously circular they give another argument against it, starting from the premise that colors do not look like dispositions (86). This earlier argument would make little sense if they had transparent readings in mind. In any event, *even if* we temporarily concede that (*) does generate the B-series read *de dicto*, (C) still fails. True, each member of the B-series now does demand something different of Griffin, but this is only a concern if in order for the fire truck to appear to Griffin to have [the disposition to appear to have]^n the property red, the fire truck must to appear to Griffin to have [the disposition to appear to have]$^{n+1}$ the property red *first*, which generates a problematic infinite temporal regress. However, the argument gives no reason to suppose that there is such a temporal dependence between members of the B-series: Griffin might be able to comply with their demands simultaneously. Of course, if the dispositionalist *is* committed to these *de dicto* readings, she's in big trouble, because it's false (read *de dicto*) that, for all n, the fire truck appears to Griffin to have [the disposition to appear to have]^n the property red. This is *another* argument entirely, to which the right response is to deny the commitment to the *de dicto* readings. It does not seem to be an argument that Boghossian and Velleman have in mind, however. Second, immediately before the passages quoted above, there is the following gloss on the argument to come:

> [The dispositionalist] says that the content of the visual experience of red must contain, as a proper part, the content of the visual experience of red. To see something as red, according to [(*)], is to have an experience whose content is that the thing is disposed to produce visual experiences *with the content that it is red*. The experiential content that something is red is thus embedded within itself, and this is a reflexive relation that no determinate content can occupy. (88)

(This, by the way, is more confirmation that the *de dicto* reading of ***appears that...*** is intended.) This quotation suggests, not the bad regress argument, but a much better argument of the sort we mentioned when discussing non-reductive dispositionalism as supplying a synonym of ***red*** in the previous section. Here is how such an argument would go in the case of "the experiential content that something is red". Assume that propositions are structured entities of either a Fregean or Russellian sort; hence, the proposition that something is red has, inter alia, the sense of ***red***, or the property red, as a constituent. Then the proposition that something is red is not identical to the proposition that something is disposed to look red (the latter has *more stuff* in it than the former). However, this argument does not seem to fit at all well with the longer quotation given in the text, and is directed against a position that any sensible dispositionalist will not hold.

[15] Talk of a *property's* causing such-and-such is shorthand for something along the lines of: o*'s having the property at time* t causes such-and-such. For our purposes, further precision is unnecessary.

Not only are reductive dispositionalism and the natural sign theory often found in bed together, but also the natural sign theory itself can seem like the merest common sense. This is probably part of the explanation of why dispositionalism continues to retain its appeal.

Mark Johnston alluringly expresses the natural sign theory as follows:

Consider two familiar philosophical cartoons by which the traditional skeptical problem of the external world is typically presented—the case of the eternal movie buff and the case of the brain in the vat . . . In both cartoons sensory experience is clearly depicted as simply an effect of external causes whose natures are in no way revealed by the experiences they cause. Sensory experience in no way acquaints the brain or the buff with the nature of the external causes of that experience. In this respect, sensory experience is unsatisfyingly like Morse code transmission: both involve interpretable effects at the end of an information-bearing process or signal. But the intrinsic natures of the originators of the signal are not manifest in the signal. This is a very depressing comparison. (1992: 166)

This picture is also expressed—equally alluringly—by Descartes at the beginning of *The World or Treatise on Light*:

In proposing to treat here of light, the first thing I want to make clear to you is that there can be a difference between our sensation of light (i.e. the idea that is formed in our imagination through the intermediary of our eyes) and what is in the objects that produces that sensation in us (i.e. what is in the flame or in the sun that is called by the name of "light". For, even though everyone is commonly persuaded that the ideas that are the objects of our thought are wholly like the objects from which they proceed, nevertheless I can see no reasoning that assures us that this is the case. On the contrary, I note many experiences that should cause us to doubt it.

You well know that words bear no resemblance to the things they signify, and yet they do not cease for that reason to cause us to conceive of those things, indeed often without our paying attention to the sound of the words or to their syllables. Thus it can happen that, after having heard a discourse, the sense of which we have very well understood, we might not be able to say in what language it was uttered. Now, if words, which signify nothing except by human convention, suffice to cause us to conceive of things to which they bear no resemblance, why could not nature also have established a certain sign that would cause us to have the sensation of light, even though that sign in itself bore no similarity to that sensation? Is it not thus that she has established laughter and tears, to cause us to read joy and sorrow on the faces of men? (1664/1985: 81)[16, 17]

Perception, on this view, is the process of discerning the layout of one's environment on the basis of the mental effects caused by external things. What are those mental effects?

[16] Note that Descartes' "signs" are the *causes* of our sensations; the "natural signs" of the natural sign theory are the sensations themselves.

[17] For another notable expression of the natural sign theory, see Russell 1912: ch. 1.

3.1 Effects as sensations

Descartes gives one historically popular answer: "sensations". So, for example, when one perceives a blueberry, among the sensations one receives are some of a distinctive chromatic sort—blue* sensations, we can call them. These blue* sensations are all one has to go on as far as the blueberry's color is concerned. What properties might one reasonably take the blueberry to have, given that it is currently causing one to have blue* sensations? A little experimentation soon shows that the effect is quite robust—under many changes of the lighting or the viewing angle, blue* sensations still result. The blueberry, then, likely has a disposition to cause one to have blue* sensations in normal conditions. Further, since other perceivers are similar to oneself, it likely has a disposition to cause *normal perceivers* to have blue* sensations in normal conditions. And this second disposition is the obvious candidate to be the referent of the English word ***blue***: it is a disposition that is not specified in terms of particular individuals (e.g. oneself), but rather the general class of normal perceivers; blueberries may safely be taken to have it; and (like the color blue) it is a property that blueberries have when they are not being observed. Thus, reductive dispositionalism is established.

What is a "blue* sensation" supposed to be? Since this is a technical expression, some explanation is required. The usual implicit answer is that it is a chromatic counterpart of a sensation in the ordinary sense—a sensation of pain or heat, for example. And sensations in the ordinary sense are—at least on one traditional view—mere affectations of the mind; they are not *intentional* or *representational* states or events. "[I]n sensation", Reid writes, "there is no object distinct from the act of the mind by which it is felt—and this holds true with regard to all sensations" (Reid 1785/1941: II.16).

The inadequacy of reductive dispositionalism explained in terms of this Reidian conception of blue* sensations can be illustrated by challenging an example of Wittgenstein's:

> Let us imagine the following: the surfaces of the things around us (stones, plants, etc.) have patches and regions which produce pain in our skin when we touch them. (Perhaps through the chemical composition of these surfaces. But we need not know that.) In this case we should speak of pain-patches on the leaf of a particular plant just as at present we speak of red patches. I am supposing that it is useful to us to notice these patches and their shapes; that we can infer important properties of the objects from them. (Wittgenstein 1958: sec. 312)

In fact, Wittgenstein's hypothetical scenario is not so distant. The leaves of stinging nettles produce pain in our skin and can be described as painful; moreover, it is useful to us to notice this fact.[18] If the parallel with color is as close as Wittgenstein claims, then dispositionalism (about color) is true, because dispositionalism is clearly correct as an account of *painful leaves*: a leaf is painful just in case it is disposed to produce pain in the

[18] And not just for the obvious reason that it is useful to avoid walking through a patch of nettles: the irritants in the leaves have a variety of medicinal uses.

skin of normal subjects in normal conditions, or something along similar lines. To say this is just to recapitulate the easy slide to dispositionalism from the natural sign theory.

However—*pace* Wittgenstein—the parallel is not at all close, as indicated by the twin facts that (a) nettle leaves do not appear (or feel) painful as red patches appear (or look) red, and (b) we do not speak of visual sensations when looking at a red patch. (At any rate, the common man uncontaminated by philosophy does not speak of visual sensations.)

Concerning (a), imagine that you put your hand in your pocket and then feel a stinging sensation in your hand. You might conjecture that your hand brushed against something in your pocket that caused the sensation, perhaps the leaf of a stinging nettle. The stinging sensation itself gives you no external object to single out and think that *it* is disposed to cause stinging sensations. If you empty your pocket and only find a harmless piece of fluff, there is no temptation to think that the piece of fluff (misleadingly) appeared or felt painful. Similarly, if you discover that your pocket is empty, there is no temptation to think that you were hallucinating a painful object. Contrast peering into your pocket and seeming to see something red. You may wonder whether *that thing* really is how it looks or appears, namely red. If that thing is *not* red, then you are misperceiving it; if there is no object there at all, then you are having some kind of color hallucination.

Concerning (b), when you look into your pocket, you are aware of the red object there, if there is one; you can attend to that object, and wonder whether it is a red M&M, for instance. But there is no visual counterpart of the sensation of pain, no "red* sensation" in your eyes, or head, or mind. At least, if there is such an item, it is remarkably self-effacing, not at all like a stinging sensation.

3.2 Effects as sense-data

If the sensory effect of the blueberry is not a mere affectation of the mind, what else could it be? Another historically popular answer is that the blueberry produces an awareness of a distinctive sort of *sense-datum*, an entity that is (in some sense) "mind-dependent", and that has the properties that it appears to have. On this view, the effect of the blueberry is an *intentional* state—to be aware of a sense-datum is for the mind to be "directed on" an object, namely the sense-datum itself.

Suppose, then, that blueberries cause normal perceivers to become aware of sense-data of a distinctive kind—*blue*† sense-data, let us say. This proposal at least has the merit of describing visual experience somewhat more faithfully than the Reidian proposal we previously considered. That proposal located the sensuous chromatic character of vision in "sensations", entirely detached from any object. At least the present proposal locates it where it belongs, in the objects of vision.

On the sense-datum version of reductive dispositionalism, something is blue if and only if it is disposed to cause (awareness of) blue† sense-data in normal perceivers, or something along these lines. But what is the property blue†? Of course, if this account stands a chance of working, it cannot be the property blue. The problem is that, given the way sense-datum terminology is usually introduced, it is. Here, for example, is G. E. Moore's explanation:

> [I]n order to point out to the reader what sort of things I mean by sense-data, I need only ask him to look at his own right hand. If he does this he will be able to pick out something (and, unless he is seeing double, *only* one thing) with regard to which he will see that it is, at first sight, a natural view to take that that thing is identical, not, indeed, with his whole right hand, but with that part of its surface which he is actually seeing, but will also (on a little reflection) be able to see that it is doubtful whether it can be identical with the part of the surface of his hand in question. Things *of the sort* (in a certain respect) of which this thing is, which he sees in looking at his hand, and with regard to which he can understand how some philosophers should have supposed it to be the part of the surface of his hand which he is seeing, while others have supposed that it can't be, are what I mean by "sense-data". (1959: 54)

For the sake of the argument, let us agree that when looking at one's right hand, one sees an object *o* that one would offhand take to be part of the hand's surface, but doubt such an identification "on a little reflection". Further, let us grant (as Moore goes on to argue) that *o* is not, in fact, identical to any part of the surface of one's hand. What must *o* be like, in order to be easily mistaken by sight for a region of skin? Presumably *o* must be a *colored patch* of some sort, and of course that is precisely what Moore and every other sense-datum theorist thought. Here are some examples collected by Firth:

> [O]ur sense-datum when we look at a dog, according to Russell, is "a canoid patch of colour". And when we look at a penny stamp, according to Broad, our sensum is "a red patch of approximately square shape". And when we look at an apple, according to Lewis, what is given is a "round, ruddy . . . somewhat". And when we look at a tomato, according to Price, our sense-datum is "a red patch of a round and somewhat bulgy shape." (1949: 438)

The sense-datum version of reductive dispositionalism is therefore unworkable, even granting the existence of sense-data, because sense-data, if there are such things, are evidently colored. If the sense-datum theory is true, then eliminativism is the correct theory of color: public objects like tomatoes and penny stamps from the reign of George V are not colored.[19]

3.3. Peacocke's proposal

So far, we have looked at two candidates for the distinctive mental effect that according to the natural sign theory is produced by a colored object: a non-intentional sensation, and (an awareness of) a sense-datum. If the effects are non-intentional sensations, then non-reductive dispositionalism is hard to resist, but there do not appear to be any such

[19] It might be replied that color terms are ambiguous. In one sense they denote properties of sense-data; in another sense they denote different properties of objects like tomatoes and penny stamps. Although there is no evidence of any such ambiguity, Moore later held this view; for a recent defense see Brown 2006, and for further discussion see Byrne 2009a. Of course, there is no inconsistency in supposing that both sense-data and public objects are colored, just complete lack of motivation. See also the following section.

sensations. If, on the other hand, the effects are sense-data, then the supported theory of color is eliminativism rather than dispositionalism.

The chief problem with the sense-data option is that, if sense-data exist at all, they are obviously the color bearers. But that is only true on what we might call the "classical" conception of sense-data. And in fact Peacocke has defended an alternative conception of sense-data on which they are *not* colored. So let us turn to the details of his account.

Suppose one sees a red poker chip tilted at an angle. The chip looks red and circular. According to a classical sense-datum theorist, one sees a red elliptical sense-datum. According to Peacocke, one is, or can be, aware of an elliptical region of one's "visual field"—a curved plane in space that Peacocke locates (in the monocular case) at the retina (2008: 11). If this elliptical region were opaque, it would exactly occlude the circular chip, and the region has a property that Peacocke calls ***red′***; in additional Peacockean terminology, red′ is an example of a *sensational* property. The sensational property red′ is not, on Peacocke's view, the property red, hence the "prime" notation. Peacocke's "visual field", then has spatial properties, but it is not colored.

Given this conception, it is no surprise that Peacocke is a reductive dispositionalist: an object is red, he thinks, iff it is disposed "in normal circumstances to cause the region of the visual field in which it is presented to be red′ in normal humans" (1983: 39; see also 1984: 60).

In his early book *Sense and Content* (1983), in which the "prime" notation was introduced, Peacocke attached primes to spatial as well as color predicates. On this initial version of Peacocke's view, the poker chip case involves an *elliptical′* region of the visual field, which is (presumably) not an elliptical one. And since Peacocke clearly did not think it had some *other* shape, this implies that the "visual field" is not itself composed of spatial regions, any more than it is composed of colored regions. But now we have a serious puzzle, because insofar as Peacocke's talk of a visual field is intelligible at all, it apparently makes perfectly good sense to apply spatial vocabulary to both regions and external objects. For instance: "The region of the visual field in which the poker chip is presented, and this drawing, are both elliptical", and "This pencil points upwards in the visual field". As Peacocke has recently observed, remarks of this sort seem "impossible to make sense of... under the hypothesis that spatial talk in describing sensational properties is not to be taken literally" (2008: 12). For this and other reasons, Peacocke now holds that "the visual field is related to, indeed is located in, real space. Location, distance, size and shape in the visual field are spatial properties and relations in a genuinely spatial plane" (11).

Why do not similar considerations also show that regions of the visual field are colored? Imagine looking at the tilted poker chip. According to Peacocke, one may attend to the relevant elliptical region of one's visual field, and to the distinctive property, red′, that it has. Granted that there is such a property, what could it possibly be, if not the color red, or at least a color? Can't we literally speak of it as dark, or saturated, or similar to orange, for example?

Admittedly, if red′ = red, and so a region of space located at the retina is literally red when the subject is looking at a tomato in good light, then this is a very surprising discovery about color. Whether or not such a region is red will depend on the sort of experience the perceiver is currently having—according to Peacocke, red′ regions of one's visual field can be erased simply by turning down the lights, for example. But if physical objects like tomatoes are colored at all, their colors are not similarly sensitive to the perceptual experiences of perceivers—unseen tomatoes remain red, or so we suppose. That is one reason why it is hard to maintain that the visual field and physical objects like tomatoes are both colored. Another reason is simpler: if the visual field were colored, this would apparently prevent the subject from seeing the alleged colors of tomatoes; it might even prevent the subject from seeing *tomatoes*, which would really be a disaster. (The idea that the visual field is colored but translucent, like a sheet of cellophane, could hardly be more phenomenologically inapt.)

Peacocke agrees that if the visual field is colored, physical objects aren't; since he thinks it is clear that physical objects are colored, he concludes that the visual field isn't. He writes:

> Being red is a public property of a physical surface; or of a solid, for example a lump of red Murano glass; or of light, as with a neon sign, a ray of theatre light, or a red firework exploding in the sky. A region of the visual field is not of any of these sorts. If the visual field were literally red, one would be faced with absurd issues: why is it not itself perceived, why cannot many people perceive it? This is why sensational properties should be characterized as primed properties. (2008: 10)

If the Peacockean visual field has "primed properties", such as red′, and if physical objects like tomatoes are red, then there are compelling reasons to deny that red′ = red. But none of this shows that there are any primed properties in the first place. Indeed, the existence of such things is highly doubtful. Return to the example of the red poker chip. One may adopt the "pictorial attitude" (cf. Peacocke 1983: 23–4), and switch attention from the chip's circular shape and red color to the elliptical shape that it projects on a plane parallel to the line of sight. Such an attention switch does not change what *color* one is attending to, and still less introduces some new *non*-color property.

What is wanted is an actual case where a red′ region is unaccompanied by awareness of red; this would serve to illustrate just what non-color property Peacocke has in mind. One of Peacocke's examples might be thought to fit the bill. "[W]hen facing towards the noonday sun with eyes closed, there can be red′ regions of one's visual field without a surface, volume, external event or object looking red" (2008: 22). But, whether or not something *looks* red in such a situation, one is surely aware of a color, in particular yellowish-red. (And of course it is no mystery why it is that particular color, given that the sunlight is diffused through one's blood-filled eyelids.) So this example is not, after all, a case where red′ can be discerned without danger of confusing it with red.[20]

[20] It is not clear to us that Peacocke intends the example this way (see his earlier description of it on 8–9).

Peacocke gives another example, of looking at a scene through "rose-tinted spectacles" (22; cf. 1983: 38–9, 1984: 59). A white object in the scene looks white, but it is presented "in a pinkish′ region of one's visual field". Provided one is *not* aware of pink, then this is an example of the required sort. However, the natural way of describing the object is as white and illuminated by pink light. Hence one *is* aware of pink, for that is the apparent color of the illuminant.[21]

If regions of the visual field have primed properties such as red′, and physical objects are colored, then reductive dispositionalism is a natural view to hold. This is cold comfort, since the search for red′ has come up empty.

3.4 Natural signs and vision science

There are some superficial similarities between the natural sign theory and modern empirical approaches to the study of vision. Electrophysiology, measurement of the electrical activity of neurons, has been an important aspect of vision science for the last fifty years. One of the most important kinds of data comprises recordings from single cells used to characterize their receptive field properties. Single-cell recordings are commonly taken as evidence for what properties, proximal or distal, the activity of the cell encodes. Cells later in the visual pathway can then use this activity as a sign of whatever environmental information is encoded. Here we have something that might look very much like the natural sign theory in operation at the sub-personal level. Although it is later neurons, rather than people, that interpret earlier neuronal activity, the similarity in basic structure might suggest that "neural" reductive dispositionalism for perception in general should be lurking in the vicinity. In the case of color perception, it would be of this sort: the property green = the disposition to cause in perceivers of kind *P* in conditions of kind *C*, neural activity of kind *N*.[22]

However, nothing like reductive dispositionalism has figured in empirical discussions of color vision, and the reason is that the "neural signs" are taken to be signs of ecologically relevant environmental features like illumination and reflectance, which are not themselves dispositions to cause neural activity. The dominant approach is to assume that neurons encode such stimulus features, and to take these representational facts as basic.[23] The fundamental task of vision science on this view is to understand the mechanisms that establish the covariation between neural activity responses and these environmental features. If what one wants to understand is how the illumination-varying cone outputs drive the illumination-independent response of cells in some extrastriate cortical areas, then the observation that cone outputs encode the informa-

[21] Cf. Peacocke's apt but slightly less natural description: "the experience as of a white object seen through pink glass" (22). For further discussion of this kind of case, see Hilbert 2005.

[22] This is not a possibility that seems to have played much role in philosophical discussions of color. A view with some similarities, although at the personal level and complicated by intentionalist assumptions, is defended in Harman 1996.

[23] An early clear statement of this view can be found in opening chapters of Marr's influential textbook (1982).

tion that there is something in the environment disposed to cause cone outputs is not to the point.

These considerations do not show that neural reductive dispositionalism is false, but they do show that it receives no support from the practice of vision science.

4. Is non-reductive dispositionalism a "conceptual truth"?

Reductive dispositionalism looks unpromising, to say the least. In this section and the next we consider the case for non-reductive dispositionalism. Perhaps remarkably, that version has struck many philosophers as something close to self-evident. For example, David Wiggins writes: "Surely it is simply obvious that colour is something subjective", which in the context clearly refers to non-reductive dispositionalism (1987: 189). According to Colin McGinn, it is a "logical or conceptual" truth that *x* is red iff *x* (standardly) seems red (1983: 6 and n. 2); and "[i]t is a conceptual truth that red things *typically* look red" (11). McGinn does not supply any argument for this himself, saying that "others have argued convincingly for the key points" (2).

Is there anything to be said for these claims? The notion of a conceptual (or "analytic") truth is obscure. One way of clarifying it, following Quine (1951), is to say that *S* is a conceptual truth iff *S* can be turned into a logical truth by substituting synonyms for synonyms. Thus, if ***is disposed to look red*** is synonymous with ***is red***, then ***x is red iff x is disposed to look red*** is a conceptual truth. But, as we saw in section 2.1, there are compelling reasons to deny the synonymy.

Another idea is that *S* is a conceptual truth if and only if *S* is true and anyone who understands *S* is disposed to assent to it. Thus stable denial of the dispositionalist biconditional would manifest incomplete understanding of the terms involved. It is quite doubtful whether any truth, even the most elementary logical truth, counts as conceptual by this test (see Williamson 2007: ch. 4), but the dispositionalist biconditional certainly doesn't. The view that material objects are not colored, despite being disposed to look colored, has enjoyed a long and popular following, including (waiving scholarly qualifications) Descartes, Malebranche, Locke, Hume, and Kant, as well as many contemporary philosophers and color scientists.[24] It is not credible that this reflects a failure to understand color vocabulary.

Alternatively, talk of "conceptual truth" could be disregarded in place of Wiggins's more prosaic claim that the dispositionalist biconditional is "simply obvious". The mathematician G. H. Hardy is said to have emerged from a long intense period of

[24] See Descartes 1644/1985: I.lxx, Malebranche 1678/1997: 10, Replies to Second Objection, Locke 1689/1975: II.viii.17, Hume 1740/1978: I.iv.iv, Kant 1787/1933: A28–9. In support of the "eliminativist" interpretation of Locke, see Alexander 1976–77, Smith 1990, and Wilson 1992 for more general discussion. For some contemporary philosophical examples of eliminativism, see Mackie 1976, Jackson 1977, Boghossian and Velleman 1989, Landesman 1989, Boghossian and Velleman 1991, Averill 1992, Hardin 1993, Maund 1995, Clark 1996. For some professions of eliminativism from color scientists, see Maund 1995: 27–9.

contemplation with the announcement that a certain theorem was indeed obvious. As the above list of distinguished dissenters indicates, if the dispositionalist biconditional is obvious, it can only be in this Pickwickian sense.[25]

5. Johnston's argument for (non-reductive) dispositionalism

Johnston appears to endorse something like the Reidian version of the natural sign theory in his important paper "How to speak of the colors" (1992). Therefore the dispositionalism he defends ought to be the reductive sort. However, most of the time he writes in a non-reductive manner of dispositions "to look red", "experiences as of a canary yellow thing", and so forth.[26] Partly because of this, the *non-reductive* dispositionalist might well think he can co-opt Johnston's case for dispositionalism. For that reason, as well as for the argument's considerable intrinsic interest, we need to consider it here.[27]

According to Johnston, for broadly pragmatic considerations we ought to adopt a certain dispositional conception of the colors. The argument runs roughly as follows. No properties fit *all* our naive "core beliefs" about color (those beliefs such that their falsity would incline us towards eliminativism about color). But it would be a "characteristic fallacy" (142), familiar from debates about eliminativism in the philosophy of mind, to conclude that no physical objects are colored. That would be like saying, to borrow an example from David Lewis, that since the special theory of relativity shows us that simultaneity cannot be a frame-independent equivalence relation, no one ever whistled while he worked. For in fact there are relations that fit *enough* of our core beliefs about simultaneity to be rightly called ***simultaneity***—and *enough* need not mean *all*. Similarly, Johnston argues, in the case of color. According to Johnston, two candidates stand out as good enough to be the colors—the physical properties that typically cause our color experiences ("the Primary Quality View"), and "typically realized" dispositions to look colored. Which of these two candidates is the least imperfect deserver of the color names? Here Johnston makes an ingenious appeal to "something we very much value: acquaintance with the colors" (167). It is, Johnston

[25] One argument in the vicinity is that colors are dispositions because that it the way they look (Langsam 2000). We are setting this aside because the usual claim is the reverse, that colors *don't* look like dispositions (Boghossian and Velleman 1989, McGinn 1996; a qualified endorsement of this claim is in Johnston 1992). Langsam's argument is examined in Byrne 2001; for a related discussion, see Levin 2000.

[26] Although sometimes the terminology has a strong reductivist flavor: "if teal is essentially the disposition to manifest *a certain appearance Te* and turquoise is essentially the disposition to manifest *the appearance Tq*" (152, our italics).

[27] We should emphasize that Johnston now disowns dispositionalism, and holds a primitivist view similar to Campbell's (1993) and Yablo's (1995): objects generally have the colors they appear to have, and the colors cannot be identified with either psychological dispositions or physical properties. (See, in particular, Johnston 1997, 1998, and his in-progress manuscript *The Manifest*.) But the argument of "How to Speak of the Colors" deservedly remains influential. (For a critical discussion of primitivism, see Byrne and Hilbert 2007.)

says, "somewhat obscure" just what acquaintance with a property ("knowing the nature of a property") amounts to (164). But we have enough of a grasp of it, he argues, to see that dispositions to look colored are properties with which vision can acquaint us, and physical properties are not. Hence, "[t]he ultimate defect of the Primary Quality View is therefore a practical one. From the point of view of what we might call the ethics of perception, the Secondary Quality Account is to be preferred. It provides for acquaintance with the colors" (167).

We should look askance at the final step—that we should "refigure" our color concepts to favour dispositionalism because this will allow us "to secure an important cognitive value", acquaintance with the colors (167). What does "refiguring our color concepts" amount to? It seems to involve using our color vocabulary much as before, but now meaning something slightly different by it. So although the typically realized disposition to look crimson is not a perfect candidate for the referent of ***crimson***, Johnston is recommending that we henceforth use color terminology so that this property is a perfect candidate.

But such a revision will *not* satisfy the original desire to be acquainted with the colors. To be sure, assuming Johnston is right about acquaintance, after the revision we will speak truly when we utter ***We are acquainted with the colors***. But that doesn't help. Example: suppose I want to be loved by Lara (a goddess who, I subsequently discover, is merely a fictional character). I am in fact loved by Cara (a flesh-and-blood approximation to Lara). I now call Cara ***Lara***, and so can henceforth truly utter ***I am loved by Lara***. Were love so easily requited!

In fact, Johnston doesn't need this argument to break the tie between dispositionalism and the Primary Quality View. For by his own lights, dispositions do better than physical properties at satisfying our "core beliefs" about the colors (see especially 149–54).

Taking canary yellow as an example, the "core beliefs" may be summarized thus (see 138):

(1) Paradigms: "Some of what we take to be paradigms of canary yellow things (e.g. some canaries) are canary yellow".
(2) Explanation: The fact of something's being canary yellow "sometimes causally explains our visual experiences as of canary yellow things".
(3) Unity: canary yellow stands in certain similarity, difference, and exclusion relations to the other colors (e.g. "canary yellow is not as similar to the shades of blue as they are similar among themselves").
(4) Perceptual Availability: "Justified belief about the canary yellowness of external things is available simply on the basis of visual perception . . . and general background beliefs".
(5) Revelation: "The intrinsic nature of canary yellow is fully revealed by a standard visual experience as of a canary yellow thing".

According to Johnston, the disposition to look canary yellow satisfies (1)–(4).[28] (The fifth core belief is somewhat elusive, as Johnston admits; we do not need to discuss it further here.)[29] However, there are two serious objections to concluding from this that the disposition to look canary yellow is, at least loosely speaking, the property canary yellow.

The first is this. There are properties one can visually detect only by having appropriate background knowledge (of a relatively sophisticated sort). For example, take *being a cricket ball*. Given appropriate background knowledge (that cricket balls are red, round, leathery . . .), one can use one's eyes to acquire knowledge that an object is a cricket ball; on the other hand, someone who had no knowledge of cricket would be unable to recognize cricket balls as such. Let us say that these sorts of properties are *indirectly available*. Other properties are *directly* available: no specific relatively sophisticated background knowledge is required in order to acquire knowledge about the *shape* of a cricket ball. (This distinction is obviously vague; for our purposes this is harmless, since we will only appeal to clear cases.)

Now, could it turn out that a property is canary yellow, at least loosely speaking, even though it was *indirectly* available? Arguably not. A property that could only be visually detected with a suitable stock of relatively sophisticated background knowledge would be an extremely imperfect deserver of the name ***canary yellow***.[30] So, if we are to conclude that the disposition to look canary yellow is the property canary yellow, then we need to establish that this disposition is directly available. But it is quite unclear how this might be done. Notice that satisfying (1)–(4) does not suffice for direct availability. The first core belief gives a necessary condition, the second two are not relevant, and the fourth (ignoring the difference between knowledge and justified belief) merely imposes the constraint that the property in question is either indirectly available or directly available.

Once the first objection has been stated, a second, more conclusive, objection immediately suggests itself. For there *is* a directly available property—call it CY—that objects like canaries, some New York taxi cabs, and legal notepads visually appear to have.[31] (At least, CY is directly available if canaries and the like actually possess it.) Surely if any property is canary yellowness, CY is canary yellowness: imagine looking at a canary, a canary yellow taxi cab, and a legal notepad; attend to the distinctive way that they each appear; slowly say to yourself "Maybe this is *not* the best candidate for being the property canary yellow". It doesn't matter whether we can find a disposition

[28] It is clear what Johnston means by saying that a property P "satisfies" a core belief (n). In the sentence expressing (n), replace all occurrences of ***canary yellow[ness]*** with ***the property canary yellow***, making adjustments for grammar. So, e.g. ***canary yellow things*** becomes***things that have the property canary yellow***. However, leave ***visual experience as of a canary yellow thing*** and its plural untouched. Now replace every occurrence of ***the property canary yellow*** with a name of P. P satisfies (n) iff the result is true.

[29] For further discussion, see Byrne and Hilbert 2007.

[30] Here we are granting for the sake of the argument the neo-description theory of reference that Johnston is assuming, on which canary yellow is the property that best fits our "core beliefs" about it. We do not think this theory is correct, however.

[31] Cf. Johnston 1997: 174, on the "visual concept of canary yellow."

that is possessed by canaries, that stands in the right similarity relations, and so forth; if it isn't CY, then it's *not* the property canary yellow. But Johnston supplies no argument that this disposition is CY.[32]

So, to summarize, Johnston's pragmatic argument for dispositionalism and his more straightforward "best candidate" argument are both mistaken.

If we recall Johnston's apparent endorsement of the natural sign theory, then it becomes perfectly understandable why directly available properties like CY were overlooked. Color perception, on the natural sign theory, is a matter of figuring out the properties of external things from their "known effects", as one might try to reconstruct the murder from the pattern of blood drops. Relatively sophisticated background knowledge will thus be needed if color experience is to yield knowledge about the properties of external things. In other words, according to the natural sign theory no properties of external things are *directly* available in color experience, and in particular *there is no such property as CY.*

6. Summing up

Janet Levin has defended dispositionalism against the complaint that it fails to respect the phenomenology of color experience. Her starting point is clear: "In fairly recent work, both Colin McGinn and Mark Johnston have (in my view ably and effectively) defended a dispositional theory of color on the grounds that it best conforms to our common sense views about what sorts of properties colors are" (2000: 152); she then goes on ably and effectively to deflect the complaint. This paper has questioned Levin's starting point: the major contemporary arguments for dispositionalism have all been found wanting. Perhaps other arguments will do the job: the paper presents a challenge to dispositionalists, not a refutation.

What *is* completely misguided, or so we have argued, is the natural sign theory. Getting rid of that removes the central motivation for reductive dispositionalism. More importantly, it restores the thought that we have better than second-hand epistemic access to the properties of external things.

Non-reductive dispositionalism fares slightly better than its reductive counterpart. Although the frequent claim that it is a "conceptual truth" or some such is most improbable, there is no lurking incoherence in the view. Still, the influence of the pernicious natural sign theory is present even here, as we saw at the end of our discussion of Johnston's argument.

In any event, what needs emphasizing is that non-reductive dispositionalism is not of any great philosophical moment. The property that the non-reductive dispositionalist identifies with the color red is one that objects uncontroversially have—tomatoes and

[32] Cf. Yablo 1995: 485: "the claim here is that yellowness is itself something familiar and known; our ordinary, non-expert ways of conceiving it tell as good as story as any about what it is." The present objection appeals to the part before the semi-colon, not the part after.

the like *are* disposed to look red to certain humans in certain conditions. That tomatoes have such dispositions will not overturn any apple carts: in particular, it does not imply that tomatoes are partly constituted by us, or have "subjective properties", in some philosophically important sense of that phrase.[33]

Further, granted that tomatoes and the like actually are red, the color and the dispositional property are at the very least often coinstantiated. All that dispositionalism adds is that the disposition to look red is identical to (and so is necessarily coinstantiated with) a certain directly available property—redness. This addition simply identifies the disposition as a property that the human color vision system is in the business of detecting. Without the addition, the perceived world is not interestingly subjective; with the addition, the situation remains unchanged. Further, non-reductive dispositionalism does not constrain the nature of redness in any significant way—it is perfectly compatible with the view that colors are physical properties of a certain sort, for example. The chief problem with non-reductive dispositionalism is not falsity, but insipidity.

Bibliography

Alexander, P. 1976–77. "The Names of Secondary Qualities," *Proceedings of the Aristotelian Society* 77: 203–20.

Armstrong, D. M. 1968a. *A Materialist Theory of the Mind*, New York: Humanities Press.

Averill, E. W. 1992. "The Relational Nature of Color," *Philosophical Review* 101: 551–88.

Block, N. 1990. "Inverted Earth," *Philosophical Perspectives* 4: 53–79.

Boghossian, P. A., and J. D. Velleman. 1989. "Colour as a Secondary Quality." *Mind* 98: 81–103. Reference to the reprint in Byrne and Hilbert 1997b.

——. 1991. "Physicalist Theories of Color," *Philosophical Review* 100: 67–106.

Broackes, J. 1992. "The Autonomy of Colour," *Reduction, Explanation and Realism*. ed. D. Charles and K. Lennon, Oxford: Oxford University Press. Reference to the reprint in Byrne and Hilbert 1997b.

Brown, D. 2006. "On the Dual Referent Approach to Colour Theory," *Philosophical Quarterly* 56: 96–113.

Byrne, A. 2001. "Do Colours Look Like Dispositions? Reply to Langsam and Others," *Philosophical Quarterly*: 238–45.

——. 2009a. "Sensory Qualities, Sensible Qualities, Sensational Qualities," *The Oxford Handbook of Philosophy of Mind*. ed. B. McLaughlin, A. Beckermann, and S. Walter, Oxford: Oxford University Press.

——. 2009b. "Experience and Content," *Philosophical Quarterly* 59: 429–51.

Byrne, A. and D. R. Hilbert. 1997a. "Colors and Reflectances," *Readings on Color, Volume 1: The Philosophy of Color*. ed. A. Byrne and D. R. Hilbert, Cambridge, MA: MIT Press.

Byrne, A. and D. Hilbert. 2007. "Color Primitivism," *Erkenntnis* 66: 73–105.

——. (eds.). 1997b. *Readings on Color, Volume 1: The Philosophy of Color*, Cambridge, MA: MIT Press.

[33] For a potent antidote to the tendency to think otherwise, see Rosen 1994.

Campbell, J. 1993. "A Simple View of Colour," *Reality, Representation and Projection*, ed. J. Haldane and C. Wright, Oxford University Press.

Clark, A. 1996. "True Theories, False Colors," *Philosophy of Science* 63: S143–50.

Descartes, R. 1644/1985. *Principles of Philosophy. The Philosophical Writings of Descartes, Volume 1*, translated by J. Cottingham, R. Stootfhoff and D. Murdoch, Cambridge: Cambridge University Press.

——. 1664/1985. *The World or Treatise on Light: The Philosophical Writings of Descartes, Volume 1*, translated by J. Cottingham, R. Stootfhoff, and D. Murdoch, Cambridge: Cambridge University Press.

Firth, R. 1949. "Sense-Data and the Percept Theory," *Mind* 58: 434–65.

Glüer, K. 2007. "Colors Without Circles?" *Erkenntnis* 66: 107–31.

Hardin, C. L. 1993. *Color for Philosophers: Unweaving the Rainbow (expanded edition)*, Indianapolis: Hackett.

Harman, G. 1996. "Explaining Objective Color in Terms of Subjective Reactions," *Philosophical Issues* 7: 1–17. Reference to the reprint in Byrne and Hilbert 1997b.

Hilbert, D. R. 1987. *Color and Color Perception: A Study in Anthropocentric Realism*, Stanford: CSLI.

——. 2005. "Color Constancy and the Complexity of Color," *Philosophical Topics* 33: 141–58.

Hume, D. 1740/1978. *A Treatise of Human Nature*, edited by L. A. Selby-Bigge, Oxford: Oxford University Press.

Jackson, F. 1977. *Perception: A Representative Theory*, Cambridge: Cambridge University Press.

——. 1998. *From Metaphysics to Ethics: A Defence of Conceptual Analysis*, New York: Oxford University Press.

Jackson, F and R. Pargetter. 1987. "An Objectivist's Guide to Subjectivism about Colour," *Revue Internationale de Philosophie* 41: 127–41. Reference to the reprint in Byrne and Hilbert 1997b.

Johnston, M. 1992. "How to Speak of the Colors," *Philosophical Studies* 68: 221–63. Reference to the reprint in Byrne and Hilbert 1997b.

——. 1997. "Postscript: Visual Experience," *Readings on Color, Volume 1: The Philosophy of Color*, ed. A. Byrne and D. R. Hilbert, Cambridge, MA: MIT Press.

——. 1998. "Are Manifest Qualities Response-Dependent?" *The Monist* 81: 3–43.

——. 2001a. "Is Affect Always Mere Effect?" *Philosophy and Phenomenological Research* 63: 225–8.

——. 2001b. "The Authority of Affect," *Philosophy and Phenomenological Research* 63: 181–214.

Kant, I. 1787/1933. *Critique of Pure Reason*, translated by N. K. Smith, London: Macmillan.

Landesman, C. 1989. *Color and Consciousness: An Essay in Metaphysics*, Philadelphia: Temple University Press.

Langsam, H. 2000. "Why Colours Do Look Like Dispositions," *Philosophical Quarterly* 50: 68–75.

Langton, R. 1998. *Kantian Humility*, Oxford: Oxford University Press.

Levin, J. 2000. "Dispositional Theories of Color and the Claims of Common Sense," *Philosophical Studies* 100: 151–74.

Lewis, D. 1997a. "Finkish Dispositions," *Philosophical Quarterly* 47: 143–58.

——. 1997b. "Naming the Colors," *Australasian Journal of Philosophy* 75: 325–42.

Locke, J. 1689/1975. *An Essay Concerning Human Understanding*, Oxford: Oxford University Press.

McGinn, C. 1983. *The Subjective View: Secondary Qualities and Indexical Thoughts*, Oxford: Oxford University Press.

——. 1996. "Another Look at Color," *Journal of Philosophy* 93: 537–53.

Mackie, J. L. 1976. *Problems From Locke*, Oxford: Clarendon Press.

Malebranche, N. 1678/1997. *The Search After Truth: With Elucidations of The Search After Truth*, translated by T. M. Lennon and P. J. Oscamp, Cambridge: Cambridge University Press.

Marr, D. 1982. *Vision: A Computational Investigation into the Human Representation and Processing of Visual Information*, San Francisco: W. H. Freeman.

Matthen, M. 1988. "Biological Functions and Perceptual Content," *Journal of Philosophy* 85: 5–27.

Maund, J. B. 1995. *Colours: Their Nature and Representation*, Cambridge: Cambridge University Press.

Moore, G. E. 1959. "A Defence of Common Sense," *Philosophical Papers*, London: Allen & Unwin.

Peacocke, C. 1983. *Sense and Content: Experience, Thought, and their Relations*, Oxford: Oxford University Press.

——. 1984. "Colour Concepts and Colour Experience," *Synthese* 58: 365–82. Reference to the reprint in Byrne and Hilbert 1997b.

——. 2008. "Sensational Properties: Theses to Accept and Theses to Reject," *Revue Internationale de Philosophie* 62: 7–24.

Prior, E., R. Pargetter, and F. Jackson. 1982. "Three Theses About Dispositions," *American Philosophical Quarterly* 19: 251–7.

Quine, W. V. O. 1951. "Two Dogmas of Empiricism," *Philosophical Review* 60: 20–43.

Reid, T. 1785/1941. *Essays on the Intellectual Powers of Man*, edited by A. D. Woozley, London: Macmillan.

Rosen, G. 1994. "Objectivity and Modern Idealism: What is the Question? *Philosophy in Mind: The Place of Philosophy in the Study of Mind*, ed. M. Michael and J. O'Leary-Hawthorne.

Russell, B. 1912. *The Problems of Philosophy*, Oxford: Oxford University Press.

Sellars, W. 1956. "Empiricism and the Philosophy of Mind," *Minnesota Studies in the Philosophy of Science*, ed. H. Feigl and M. Scriven.

Shoemaker, S. 1982. "The Inverted Spectrum," *Journal of Philosophy* 79: 357–81.

——. 1994. "Phenomenal Character," *Nos* 28: 21–38. Reference to the reprint in Byrne and Hilbert 1997b.

Smith, A. D. 1990. "Of Primary and Secondary Qualities," *Philosophical Review* 99: 221–54.

Stroud, B. 2000. *The Quest for Reality: Subjectivism and the Metaphysics of Colour*, New York: Oxford University Press.

Tye, M. 1995. *Ten Problems of Consciousness: A Representational Theory of the Phenomenal Mind, Representation and mind*, Cambridge, MA: MIT Press.

——. 2000. *Consciousness, Color, and Content*, Cambridge, MA: MIT Press.

Van Cleve, J. 1999. *Problems from Kant*, Oxford: Oxford University Press.

Watkins, M. 1994. "Dispositionalism, Ostension, and Austerity," *Philosophical Studies* 73: 55–86.

Wedgwood, R. 2001. "Sensing Values?" *Philosophy and Phenomenological Research* 63: 215–23.

Wiggins, D. 1987. "A Sensible Subjectivism?" *Needs, Values, Truth*, Oxford: Basil Blackwell.

Williamson, T. 2007. *The Philosophy of Philosophy*, Oxford: Blackwell.

Wilson, M. D. 1992. "History of Philosophy in Philosophy Today; and the Case of the Sensible Qualities," *Philosophical Review* 101: 191–243.

Wittgenstein, L. 1958. *Philosophical Investigations*, 2nd ed. Oxford: Basil Blackwell.

Yablo, S. 1995. "Singling out Properties," *Philosophical Perspectives*. ed. J. Tomberlin, Atascadero, CA: Ridgeview.

14

Colour Eliminativism

Barry Maund

1. Introduction

I think that, with qualification, the right theory of colour is a form of eliminativism. By 'eliminativism', I mean the thesis that, even though the colour of physical objects, such as peaches and foxes and trees and lips and glasses of wine, and skies, etc., would seem to be their most visually conspicuous of features, these objects do not have the colours they appear to have.

There are, however, two qualifications. The first is that the subject of colour is complex, and an adequate theory of the subject, likewise, will be complex, containing both metaphysical and semantic theses. Eliminativism, rightly understood, comprises only part of the story. The second qualification is that it has to be the right kind of eliminativism, for there are several varieties. We can distinguish, for example, between an ontological form and a conceptual one. I hold that we can be ontological eliminativists, holding that there are no colours, as ordinarily understood, without being conceptual eliminativists. For, I argue, there are important reasons for retaining the ordinary concept, even though it is not instantiated. With respect to colour, I think that the right attitude, for an eliminativist to adopt, is a fictionalist attitude: to 'make-believe' that the ordinary colour sentences are true—at least for very many contexts.[1]

Finally, there is an added complication. Once we make the distinction between ontological and conceptual forms of eliminativism, a further possibility opens up. Besides endorsing let us say, 'conceptual conservationism', with respect to colour, it is possible, as well, to have a place in our thinking for new concepts of colour. That is to say, it is possible to consistently hold that there are, in the world, certain qualities that deserve to be called 'colours', though, of course, they are not colours as understood in the traditional sense. The reason why we can adopt both theses is that there may be different purposes served by having different concepts. Given that this is so, there may be reason for maintaining an existing concept, for one set of purposes, while revising the concepts for another set of purposes.

[1] I wish to acknowledge Dimitria Gatzia (2007) for convincing me of the full merits of Fictionalism.

In this paper, I defend eliminativism, but do so in the context of bringing out the complexities that attach themselves to such a thesis.

2. Fixing the subject matter for Colour Eliminativism

Any form of eliminativism, that is, eliminativism about X, requires that we spell out what the X is that is supposed (or not) to be eliminated. We need to specify what sort of entity or kind or property X is, or would be, if it did exist. The Eliminativist needs then to marshal arguments to show that there is no such entity, or kind, or property.

I gave a brief characterization of the colour to be eliminated in the Introduction, where I referred to colour as 'seeming to be the most visually conspicuous of features possessed by physical objects such as peaches, foxes, skies...' This characterization was incomplete: it only worked because I knew that the reader would know very well what the colours are that I was referring to. I knew she would be very familiar with colours, would have an extensive colour vocabulary, for example, *pink, yellow, cyan, purple, light blue,* etc., and could roll off the tongue a whole set of colour paradigms: for 'red': apples, tomatoes, etc.; for 'blue': skies, Frank Sinatra's eyes; for 'yellow': bananas, Britney Spears' hair, and so on. And I took it that the reader would take it that it was these kinds of colours that I was denying when I said that I endorsed Colour Eliminativism. Colour Eliminativism is the denial that physical objects have the colours that we attribute to them, in our everyday thought and talk: the visually conspicuous features that we naïvely and pre-reflectively attribute to physical objects. And Colour Realism (at least, in one form) is the natural opponent for eliminativism, is the denial of this denial.[2]

This being so, the first step for a Colour Eliminativist (and for the opposing Colour Realist) is to spell out, in more precise detail, what our ordinary understanding consists in, and what are the properties our ordinary colour names name. Our enquiry thus begins with addressing some conceptual and semantic questions. This point is important since it seems at odds with what some leading Colour Realists have said. For example, Byrne and Hilbert hold that the problem of colour realism 'concerns various especially salient properties that objects visually appear to have' (Byrne and Hilbert 2003:4). It is said to be primarily a problem in 'the theory of perception, not a problem in the theory of thought or language' (Byrne and Hilbert 2003, 4). By way of explanation, they say:

> Consider an analogy. From the point of view of the biologist, the word "food" is applied by ordinary people in a somewhat arbitrary way.... An investigation of how ordinary people use the word "food" is not particularly relevant to biology....
>
> The problem of colour realism is like the investigation of what humans can digest, not the investigation of the folk category of food. The enquiry concerns certain properties that objects visually appear to have, not how ordinary people use colour words, or how they conceptualize colour categories. (Byrne and Hilbert 2003, 4)

[2] There may be other forms, e.g. as a revisionary thesis, about how we ought to think about colours.

If we characterize Colour Realism in this way it seems to be different from the one that I have described above (call that one Colour Realism (1)). Even if it were, it wouldn't detract from the significance of the sort of eliminativism/realism that I am discussing. It is surely worth wondering about, and discussing, the claim that objects do not have colours, colours that are the subject of our ordinary thought and talk. But we do not have two different problems at all: there is only one. Byrne and Hilbert are right that Colour Realism and Colour Eliminativism concern the 'various salient properties that objects visually appear to have', but their characterization of Colour Realism is incomplete: it does not tell us what sorts of properties the salient properties are. To fill it out we need to specify it as follows:

> *Colour Realism (2)*: there are certain properties, red, blue, yellow, etc., and certain physical objects, such that, at least on certain occasions, it is true that some of these objects both look red and are red; some that both look blue and are blue, etc.

But this thesis presupposes three things: that we have already identified the properties of being red, being yellow, etc.; that we understand what it is for something to *look red*, to *look yellow*, to *look purple*, and so on—and finally, that the sense of 'blue' in 'looks blue' is the same sense as that in 'is blue'; otherwise the thesis would not make sense. On the face of it, the terms 'blue', 'red', etc., are used, in the above characterization, in their ordinary way, and the properties are those ordinarily referred to, as 'red', 'blue', etc. If this is not the case, then the realist owes us an account of where the terms come from. It may be that there is some technical, non-ordinary use of colour terms. But if there is, then we should be directed to this use. Perhaps the theorist is offering us a proposal: that this is how the terms should be used. That is also fine, but the theorist owes us a justification for why s/he is using the terms, 'red', 'yellow', 'blue', 'dark blue', etc., in a way that differs from their ordinary use, and indeed why the properties s/he is giving an account of should be called 'colours' at all. I do not wish to deny that the colour terms could be used in these different ways: I am simply pointing to the need for a justification.

But in any case, the two forms of Colour Realism amount to the same thing. Let us specify Colour Realism (1) as follows:

> *Colour Realism (1)*: there are certain properties, that our colour terms 'red', 'blue', 'yellow', 'purple', etc., name; and there are certain physical objects, such that, at least on certain occasions, it is true that some of these are red; some are blue, etc.

The two forms amount to the same, for the way ordinary colour terms operate, the properties they name are certain salient properties that physical objects 'appear to have'. Our colour concepts are recognitional concepts and our use of colour names is tied to the possession of these concepts.[3] Specifically, the way our colour-naming practices

[3] See Evans (1982, 270) for discussion of the significance of colour concepts being recognitional concepts.

work, they are built around those occasions on which we identify and recognize colours. On this account, to possess the concepts of colour, of red, green, yellow, etc. one must have the capacity to recognize the colours, or defer to those who do. (This account allows that blind people can have colour concepts, but their understanding of colour is parasitic on the existence of experts who are not blind.) One's exercise of a recognitional concept involves telling that something is F from the way it looks. Hence the application of colour names will be associated with the way things look. The property 'Red' names is the same as the property certain things look to have.[4]

There is, however, an entirely different approach a Colour Realist might take, one based on a consideration of comparative colour vision.[5] It is clear, it is argued, that many non-human animal species have colour vision, and that any account of colour needs to take the facts into consideration. With this approach, there are two options open for a Colour Realist. One is to say something like the following: colours are physical properties, ones which are such that it is the function of the colour system of (each) different species, to detect. The other is to say that colours are relational properties, functionally defined, that is, defined in terms of the function played by physical properties in causing appropriate behavioural effects in different species, where the effects are mediated by the colour visual system. (These options presuppose that we can provide a stipulative, operational definition for 'colour visual system'.)

My response to this approach is to say that I admit that a fully adequate account of colour does need to include an account of comparative colour vision. Admitting this does not mean, however, that we should not concentrate on giving an account of what is the case with respect to human colour vision, and with respect to human colour terms such as *red, blue, purple*, etc. Once such an account is in place, we can give thought to how the account might be extended to other species. To anticipate what I shall argue, the sort of Eliminativist thesis that I am defending, is not a bald eliminativism, but a complex one. It is not purely negative, but has a positive component. (I am in agreement with Descartes and Locke on the necessity for each element.) We should expect both components to have a role to play if the account were extended to apply to other species.

In this paper, I will counter Colour Realism in two ways. First, I shall argue for a certain account of what our ordinary understanding of colour is, and then argue, with respect to that understanding, that Colour Realism is false. I shall connect this understanding of colour to our ordinary colour-naming practices. To do this requires arguing that the accounts of our colour-naming practices, presented by such Colour Realists as McLaughlin, Reid, and Jackson, are false. Second, I shall argue that the standard views of Colour Realism are flawed, on the grounds that they lead to a

[4] Byrne and Hilbert seem to concede this. They identify what they call *phenomenal colour*—the colour objects appear to have—and they say that our colour names are attached to phenomenal colour. And, as they also say, it is phenomenal colour that Colour Realism is concerned with.

[5] See Mohan Matthen (2005).

position that is inherently unstable, conceptually—unless, we accept a place for another concept of colour, connected to the traditional concept. I shall concentrate on accounts by Colour Physicalists (those who hold that colours are mind-independent physical properties), but the arguments are readily applicable to other forms of Colour Realism.

3. The simple argument for eliminativism

I have argued that what fixes the subject matter for the sort of colour that is to be eliminated (or not, if the argument is unsuccessful) is an account of what property it is that our ordinary colour-conceptual and colour-naming practices individuate (if any). It seems to me obvious what sort of properties colours are ordinarily understood to be, and that these are the qualities that our ordinary colour names name: *red, dark red, blue, light blue, yellow, orange,* and so on. At a minimum, such colours are (putative) qualities of the following type: they are sensuous, qualitative, mind-independent, intrinsic qualities of physical bodies. (By 'intrinsic' qualities, I mean properties that are categorical and non-relational and non-dispositional.) Call this concept of colour, the 'primitivist' concept.[6]

Knowledge of these minimal features results from phenomenological considerations, that is, by reflecting on our colour experiences: colours are experienced as certain kinds of visual qualities that physical objects possess. More specifically, this knowledge reflects the fact that colour concepts are recognitional concepts, where what it is to possess a recognitional concept—that something is F—is to be able to tell that it is F, from the way it looks.[7] (One need not have the concept of *looks F*: the point is that one can tell that the object has the property, by looking at it.)[8]

Those of us who possess colour-recognitional concepts are in a position to know other significant, and less minimal, aspects to colours. One is that colours obey what is called the 'Axiom of Unity': all yellow things have a property in common, different from all the blue things, red things, green things, and so on. A second is that colours are qualities that have a certain causal role to play in the exercise of our colour concepts. It is not that colours are experienced as playing the causal role. Rather it is that their having such a causal role is implicit in the concepts being recognitional concepts: in the presence of these qualities, we are led to recognize them.

[6] There is a group of philosophers, including Campbell (1997), who agree with this characterization of the primitivist conception, and who go further and argue that there really are such colours in the physical world. The argument in this section is, in part, against this position.

[7] Recognitional concepts, as I understand them, are similar to what Alan Millar calls 'experiential concepts'. Colour concepts are strongly experiential, in his terms.

[8] The way the thing looks may play a causal role in one's exercising the ability to tell that thing is F. I want to leave this possibility open. For the moment, I am trying to present a minimal account of recognitional concepts, which is compatible with naïve realism.)

Most important of all, we are in a position to know that colours are visual qualities that can be ordered into certain arrays, based on relationships of similarities and differences. Going further, many of us have acquired more complex colour-recognitional concepts: *that* is a richer shade of red than *that; this* is a darker (paler, blacker, whiter, richer, redder, greener . . .) shade of blue than *that*, and so on. As a result, we can determine that one of the most significant aspects to the colours putatively identified is a certain structural feature that holds between the colours, taken collectively. Colours stand in systematic relations of similarity and difference to one another: orange is more similar to red and yellow than it is to blue or green; reds become progressively closer to yellow, on one side and to blue on the other; and so on. To summarize: colours, as a group, have an internally related 4+2 structure, built on the four unique, primary hues—green, red, blue, and yellow—and related to the black/white pair.

Accordingly, we can say that, assuming the ordinary or common-sense understanding of colour, colours are properties of the following sort:

(1) Colours are: sensuous, qualitative, perceiver-independent, intrinsic (categorical, non-relational) qualities of physical bodies.
(2) Colours obey the Axiom of Unity.
(3) Colours are qualities that play a causal role in the perception of objects as having those colours.
(4) Colours taken collectively stand in certain structural relationships, of similarity and difference.

The first stage of the argument for Colour Eliminativism is now complete. The second stage is short and easy. There just are no properties which satisfy all of these principles (1) to (4). In particular, there are no properties which satisfy both (3) and (4). There are, as K. Nassau 1997 points out, many and varied physically complex properties of physical bodies that are systematic causes of our colour perception, but they do not as a group satisfy (4). This is true whether we take the physical properties to be properties intrinsic to surfaces or volumes of physical bodies, or to be modifications of light, such as spectral reflectance profiles. (See Hardin 1988: 66; Thompson 2000: 168; Pautz 2006.)

If there are simple emergent properties that satisfy (4), then they do not satisfy (3)—the properties that satisfy (3) are the physical properties that Nassau describes as causing the perception of colours. But, if they don't satisfy (3) it is hard to see how we could know that physical bodies had them. (See Maund 2006b: 266–267.) Nor would it help to say that the colours are supervenient on physical features such as spectral reflectances. Lacking an explanation of the nature of the supervenient relation, how would we know, for example, whether one physical object had the supervenient quality, and another with the same physical structure, lacked it.

It seems to me therefore that there is good reason to accept Colour Eliminativism. I realize that that there are Colour Realists who would deny that colours do have to satisfy the four principles that are crucial to my argument. In the sections to follow, I shall argue against their alternative accounts.

To forestall a possible objection to the line of thought I have been pursuing, let me point out that the idea behind this simple argument is that our colour experiences reveals to us that colours are certain kinds of visual qualities, qualities about which we can make important claims. It is similar to the thought which John Campbell has expressed, in a recent paper 'Transparency vs. Revelation in Colour Perception' (Campbell 2005). Campbell writes specifically of an idea of 'transparency', the idea that colour vision gives us knowledge of *which property* colour is, contrasting this with 'the idea that colour experience reveals the colours to us, in the sense that it provides knowledge of a number of necessary truths about the colours'. (Campbell 2005: 1). Campbell explains this *knowledge which* in terms of Russell's knowledge by acquaintance rather than knowledge by description:[9]

> Colour vision provides you with knowledge of that thing. This sort of knowledge is not to be explained as a type of propositional knowledge. Rather your knowledge of truths about the colours depends on this kind of non-propositional knowledge of the colours themselves.
>
> (2005: 5)

This point helps anticipate a related objection: that my argument rules out an externalist account of the content of colour language. My response in brief is twofold. First, the arguments, based on the Putnam-Kripke twin earth cases at best, establish only that the meanings of certain terms, and not all, lend themselves to an externalist construction.[10] Secondly, and most importantly, my account does not depend on a pure internalist interpretation of colour terms. Rather, the emphasis on recognitional concepts, lends itself to adopting a hybrid account of meaning, with internalist-externalist components. This is in keeping with Gareth Evans's account of Fregean sense, which has both internalist and externalist components. I should add that if it turns out that there the external component is empty then, as Frege and Evans point out, a fictionalist account is called for. (Evans 1982: 30–33)

4. A realist proposal for how the colour names name

The argument that I have set out is open to an important objection, namely, that I have misrepresented the way our ordinary colour-naming practice works, and that I have mis-characterized the role and character of our ordinary concept of colour. Once we have in place the right account, so the objection runs, we will see that the colours do not have to have the structural feature that I, and the others, place so much store on.

[9] Russell writes: 'The particular shade of colour that I am seeing... may have many things to be said about it... But such statements, though they make me know truths about the colour do not make me know the colour itself better that I did before: so far as concerns knowledge of the colour itself, *as opposed to knowledge of truths about it,* [my emphasis] I know the colour perfectly and completely when I see it and no further knowledge of it itself is even theoretically possible.' (Russell 1912, 47).

[10] Lewis, Jackson, Searle, and Segall argue that the externalist arguments do not establish even this much.

In particular, Colour Realists such as Brian McLaughlin, Thomas Reid and Frank Jackson offer a different account of our colour-naming practices from the one that I have set out. The core idea is that there is an important distinction to make between the property that constitutes colour and our way of conceptualizing it. This idea undermines my argument that colours are properties that have to satisfy two constraints, the causal constraint and the structural relations constraint. On the realist account, the causal constraint applies to the colours themselves, but the structural relationships only relate to the way of conceptualizing the colours.

To fix our ideas, I shall concentrate on McLaughlin's presentation of the view, which he sets out, in the form of a proposal:

> Basic proposal: redness is that property which disposes its bearers to look red to standard visual perceivers in standard conditions of visual observation and which must (as a matter of nomological necessity) be had by everything so disposed. (McLaughlin 2003, 479)

McLaughlin explains that we can identify something that he calls 'the looks-red role', the capacity of things to look red. He claims that this role is central to our conception of colour (and our use of colour terms): 'red' names the quality that is the causal basis for the looks-red role; red is whatever occupies the looks-red role. With the distinction in place, between the role and the occupant of the role, the causal constraint and the structural constraint may be separated. Colours have the right causal powers: they are occupants of the looks-red role, but they do not have to conform to the structural relations constraint. The latter is explained by reference to the looks-red role.

McLaughlin draws attention to the similarity between his views and those of the eighteenth-century Scottish philosopher Thomas Reid. Reid's writings have the advantage of making very explicit what is implicit in McLaughlin's account, namely the supposed role of our concepts in fixing the reference for colour names. Reid wrote that

> All people who have not been tutored by modern philosophy understand by colour, "not a sensation of the mind, which can have no existence when it is not perceived, but a quality or modification of bodies, which continues to be the same whether it is seen or not. (T.Reid 1970: 99)

In itself, this remark seems no more than an expression of the common sense for which Reid was famous. What is more striking is what Reid goes on to say, by way of explanation. Reid says that when we perceive the colour of body,

> The idea, which we have called the appearance of colour, suggests the conception and belief of *some unknown quality* in the body which occasions the idea, and *it is to this quality* and not the idea, that we give the name of colour. [my emphasis] (Reid 1970: 100).

Our colour names, thus, are held to apply to the unknown qualities and not to 'the appearances for which we do not have names'. Hence, if Reid is right, the concept of colour contains a component that can be thought of as a placeholder: to be filled by the essential definition, for example, by scientific investigation.

We might wonder how the users of the common language of mankind can distinguish, or even think of, red and blue, if both terms name unknown qualities. Reid's answer to this question is implicit in the following:

> when we think or speak of any particular colour . . . it is really in some sort compounded. It involves an unknown cause, and a known effect. The name of colour belongs indeed to the cause only, and not to the effect. But as the cause is unknown, we can form no distinct conception of it, but by its relation to the known effect. (Reid 1970: 100–101)

So the answer is that the colour terms are taken to name the hidden quality that causes the object to look a certain way, but the basis for using the colour name is the effect that quality causes. And a similar answer, of course, is implicit in McLaughlin's proposal.

There are, it seems to me, two objections to the Reid-McLaughlin account of colour names. The first is that the account is simply too implausible—it does not capture our use of colour names and colour concepts. The second is that it cannot accommodate certain features central to an adequate account of visual perception.

The first problem stems from the fact that the Reid-McLaughlin account assumes that ordinary language-users conceptualize colours in a certain way. The thought behind the account is that the looks-red role plays a central part in our conceptualizing colours. Two things are required of ordinary language-users, that is, of those who are expert in the use of colour terms (which includes most of us who have colour concepts). One is that they have the concept of 'looks red', 'looks blue', etc., and the other is that they think of colours themselves as unknown or hidden qualities. Reid explicitly claims that we, the folk, conceptualize the colour as an 'unknown' quality (I prefer the term 'hidden quality'). This account has the implication that our *looks*-concepts are prior to the colour concepts. This seems to me to get things entirely around the wrong way. We teach the colour terms first, and it is quite a sophisticated task to acquire 'looks concepts'. In practice, with respect to our many 'looks concepts'—*looks rusty, looks hostile, looks square, looks tired*—we first learn and apply the concepts—*rusty, hostile, square, tired,* etc.—first. Our colour terms and concepts are no different.

Now Reid and McLaughlin might have a point if what they are doing is recommending that this is how we should think of colour: that is, if they were recommending a revision to our colour naming practices. But I take it that they are not recommending, but describing. As a description of our everyday colour-naming practices and colour concepts, their account is totally implausible.

My criticism assumes that the account of what it is for something to have the 'looks-red role' explains the role in terms of the perceptual subject's having, and exercising, concepts 'looks red', 'looks yellow', etc. There is, however, an alternative way of understanding what is meant by 'the looks-red role', a way that does not place such emphasis on having such concepts. It may be pointed out that it is one thing for something to look yellow to S, and another for S to have the concept 'X looks yellow to me'. (The sense of 'looks' is a phenomenal, non-conceptual sense.) Accordingly, the property, *looks yellow to S,* may play a causal role in the subject's making colour judgements, say, that something is yellow, without the subject exercising a 'looks yellow' concept (or any equivalent). The experience with the relevant phenomenal character plays a causal part in the subject making the perceptual judgement, but the subject need not be aware of the experience (certainly not *as an experience*).

The idea behind this alternative proposal is that our ordinary colour concepts—*blue, purple, orange, yellow,* etc.—are recognitional concepts. That something looks blue (looks purple, etc.,) plays a causal role in the exercise of such concepts, but the subject does not exercise the concept *looks blue, looks purple,* etc. There are several problems with this alternative proposal. The first is that it is hard to see how ordinary perceivers can conceptualize colours as 'unknown', or 'hidden', qualities which are causes of certain effects or the realizers of certain roles, unless they conceptualize those effects or the functional role, and, on the new proposal, they do not conceptualize these things.

The second, and more important, problem with the proposal is that it fails to give an adequate answer to a question to which it had better give an answer—and this applies whether the proposal is considered as providing a descriptive account of how our colour-naming practices work, or a revisionary account. It cannot provide an adequate account of what it is *to look red,* without making implicit appeal, either to a subjectivist notion of colour or to the ordinary, 'primitivist', concept that is presupposed in my eliminativist account. In the next section, I shall defend this claim.

Before I do so, this is an opportune moment to say something about a different kind of functionalism, one which identifies colour, not with the realizer, or occupant, of the functional role, but with the role itself. (For a recent discussion, see Jonathan Cohen 2005.) That is to say, it holds that what it is to be yellow is for the object to have some property by virtue of which the object looks red—to appropriate observers and in the right kind of circumstances. (I am prepared to accept, for the sake of argument that is also a version of Colour Realism.) Given that it shares with the first type of account, its dependence on the looks-red role, it will be faced with the same problems that the realizer/occupant version (including the Hardin-Kuehni objection which I discuss below in section 7).

5. Representation, transparency and the way things look

On the account of colour names subscribed to by Reid and McLaughlin, our colour names name qualities that are the causal bases for how things look (with respect to colour). The structure, which I attribute to the colours, is supposed to be captured in the way things look. I shall argue that this account founders because it fails to give an adequate answer to a question to which it had better give an answer. The question is what exactly is it for something to *look red, to look yellow, to look blue,* and so on?.

Let us begin with McLaughlin's attempt to deny the problem of finding physical properties that participate in the right pattern of relationships of similarities and differences, 'the problem of unity'. 'The alleged problem is, I maintain, no problem whatsoever for colour physicalism, and our functional analysis will do as it stands' (McLaughlin 2003: 487). He considers relational facts such as 'Red is more similar to orange than it is to blue', 'Blue is more similar to purple than it is to yellow', and so on. The important point, he says, about the relational facts in question is, in the first instance, 'about what it is like for things to look the colours in question, and only derivatively about the colours themselves. These derivative facts about the colours are, moreover captured by our functional analysis.'

All else being equal, what it is like for something to look red is more similar to what it is like for something to look orange than what it is like for something to look blue. That is to say, all else equal, visual experiences of red are more similar to visual experiences of orange than they are to experiences of blue—more similar, that is, in their phenomenal characters. (McLaughlin 2003: 488)

But this 'solution' to our problem raises the question of which sort of features of visual experiences comprises this phenomenal character (and which stands in the relevant relations of similarity and difference). On the face of it, the physicalist has two options: either they are intrinsic features of the experiences or they are representational features.

There is reason to think that the relevant features are representational features. (This is certainly not to deny that there are intrinsic features of brain process that might also stand together in the right relations.) The reasons for choosing representational features has to do with a well-known feature of visual experiences, called 'the transparency of perceptual experience'. G. E. Moore seems to have been the first to discuss it, but recently a number of writers have made use of it (e.g. P. F. Strawson, G. Harman, S. Shoemaker, J. J. Valberg). Michael Tye, indeed, uses the phenomenon to argue for the claim that the phenomenal character of perceptual experiences is determined by the representational content of the experience. Tye describes the transparency of perceptual experiences by asking us to reflect on our typical visual experiences when we see something:

Focus your attention on the scene before your eyes and on how things look to you. You see various objects by seeing their facing surfaces. (Tye 2000: 45)

In seeing these surfaces, he holds, you are immediately and directly aware of a whole host of qualities.

You experience these qualities as qualities of the surfaces. You do not experience any of these qualities as qualities of your experience. There are no qualities of the experience that one is aware of; one is simply aware of the qualities of the objects seen. The experience of seeing is transparent. (Tye 2000: 45)

The point may be put in the following way: Try as we might, when we try to describe the experience—that is, apart from the objects in the scene represented—there seems nothing to describe. The description of the scene itself exhausts our descriptions. The visual experience, it seems, is transparent. We see through it, to the objects in the scene themselves, and their qualities.

Let us return to McLaughlin's proposal to solve the problem of 'unity', that is, of finding physical properties that participate in the right structural pattern of relationships. For him, the relevant features of experiences are intrinsic features of those experiences: 'neuroscientific properties' (McLaughlin 2003: 478). This choice spells trouble, for it runs directly counter to the transparency of perceptual experience that we have just considered.

The significance of the transparency of perceptual experience lies not in the 'fact' that we need to accept it at face value. It is important in that if we do not accept it at face value, we need to provide some plausible explanation for why it seems to be true. To accept it at face value is to endorse naïve realism, with respect to perceptual experience (see M. G. F. Martin 2000:218). To avoid naïve realism, the most plausible explanation for the physicalist to adopt is to appeal to the representational content of the experience. That is to say, the features that we are aware of when we introspect our perceptual experiences are features the object is represented as having. (An anti-physicalist can appeal to sensa, whose properties the perceptual subject takes to be properties of physical objects, but a physicalist cannot adopt this theory.)

What makes McLaughlin's proposal problematic is that it does not explain why visual experiences seem to be transparent. When we introspect our experiences and try to describe them, then there are things we can say, but these things seem to make reference only to external objects and their qualities. It is this aspect that the representationalist seems to explain, by arguing that our experiences represent there being objects with certain qualities.

Thus, it would seem to be more plausible for the physicalist to do as Tye, and others, do and adopt the other option, that is, to explain the phenomenal character of experiences in terms of representational content, that is, in terms of physical qualities that the external objects are represented as having (Tye 2000: 51–54). This option, however, fares no better than the first, in solving the problem of 'unity'. To satisfy the condition of transparency, the physical features have to be perceiver-independent features of the external objects, and to solve the structural relations problem, the features have to stand together in the right relationships of similarity and difference. And the problem is, as we have already seen, that there are no physical qualities that satisfy both constraints.

Thus, neither account of phenomenal character works. There is, however, a modification that might just work. The physicalist may concede that there is not any intrinsic, physical property of the object such that it stands in the right sorts of relations to other intrinsic properties, nor are there reflectance profiles that stand together in the right way. However, there is another type of property that is relevant: the disposition associated with reflectance profiles, to cause the perceiver's visual system to respond in the appropriate ways. Hence, it may be argued, the visual experience represents the presence of a physical property in the external object that causes a physical visual state with the right character. Byrne and Hilbert (2003) and Tye (2000) have presented variants of this position.

This solution is supposed to work by appealing to a certain theory of the computational-neural mechanisms, commonly thought to underpin colour vision: the opponent processing theory. According to this theory, there are computational mechanisms in the visual system which take as input, the output of the major types of cones in the retina: those maximally sensitive to long wavelength light, medium wavelength light, and short wavelength light respectively (L, M and S cones). It is believed that there are opponent information channels, where the activity in one channel inhibits activity in an opponent channel. Our various experiences of colour are related to the outputs of two pairs of such channels, which may be called the RED and GREEN opponent channels and the BLUE and YELLOW opponent channels, respectively.

Given the state of our knowledge, this description of the opponent-processing model is over-simplified. However, if we accept the model, it allows the physicalist to say that there are two kinds of visual states that stand in the right relations of similarities and differences that ostensibly hold between the way things look. One kind comprises the neural states that, by hypothesis, underpin the experiences of colour. Another kind consists of visual states that occur at an earlier stage of the causal process resulting in those experiences.

To solve the problem posed by the conjunction of the transparency problem and the structural relations problem, we might now claim that the experiences represent the objects as having some property which affects the visual system in the right way, so as to produce certain visual states (which occur earlier in the process), and those visual states have properties that stand together in the right sorts of relations. As a result, we are not committed to saying that the perceiver is aware of intrinsic features of their experiences. Tye, it seems to me, makes this kind of positive proposal—and so do Byrne and Hilbert. According to this view, the relevant colour-part of the representational content is specified in terms of the light produced by the object and, more particularly, in terms of the lights' intensity relative to the L-, M- and S-cones: the light's L-intensity = the degree to which it stimulates the L-cones (and analogously for the M- and S-cones) (Byrne and Hilbert 2003, 19).

Even with this modification, transparency will be a problem. There are two aspects to transparency. One aspect is that the experience is 'invisible': we are not aware of any intrinsic qualities of the experience; the other aspect is that we are aware of properties of the external objects, including relational properties. The colour-physicalist's 'solution' to the transparency problem is not a solution at all—for, it turns out, we are aware of the qualities of the object only by being aware of relations to features of one's visual system, and hence of these features as well. If the phenomenology of our perceptual experiences is meant to be captured in the thought that we are aware of independent features of external objects (including relative features), then the same phenomenology will be also captured in the thought that we are aware of independent qualities, not qualities of our visual system.

There is a response that the physicalist might make to this argument. It might be objected that I have misunderstood the nature of the representational content. I have assumed, it will be said, that the relevant physical property, which the perceived object is represented as having, is the exercise of a power to affect the visual system in a certain way. The true position is that the property is something like: having a property which disposes the object to cause the relevant visual state.

My rejoinder to this response is that it misunderstands my objection. The problem with what we are offered as comprising the representational content is that it does not explain what the explanatory hypothesis was meant to explain, namely, that our experiences appear to be transparent. The original hypothesis did seem to provide an answer: it said that the content comprises external qualities of external objects. But now, the content refers to a power to cause visual states of a certain type, and that makes transparency a mystery. It is well to recall how Tye described transparency in the first place.

> You see various objects by seeing their facing surfaces. . . . Intuitively, the surfaces you see directly are publicly observable physical surfaces. . . . In seeing these surfaces, you are immediately and directly aware of a whole host of qualities.

Before he concludes that we do not experience any of these qualities as qualities of our experience, he makes the following remark:

> You may not be able to name or describe these qualities but they look to you to qualify the surfaces; you experience these qualities as qualities of the surfaces. (Tye 2000: 45–46)

Since I am not directly aware of any qualities of my inner experiences, my experience is said to be transparent to me. Tye then presents the representationalist thesis as providing the best explanation for the phenomenon. What is the explanation? It is that the phenomenal character of experiences is explained by the representational content of the experiences, where the content is spelled out in terms of qualities of external objects. So far, so good. But now it turns out that the qualities in the content are very special qualities: they are properties which have the power to cause visual states of a certain type, visual states that stand together in the right sort of structural relations. But these properties are different from the ones we were told about at first. In the description of transparency, we were told that those qualities are 'ones that we *experience as qualities of the surfaces*'. Later we are reminded that we 'are immediately and directly aware of a whole host of qualities', and told 'you are directly aware of a range of qualities that you experience as being qualities of surfaces at varying distances away and orientations' (Tye 2000: 47).

Given that this is so, how can the representationalists now say that they have an explanation of transparency? The 'explanation' had some plausibility when the content was one that specified physical properties of the surface. With the new sort of physical property, all plausibility has been lost. On the new account of what the representational content has explained, it is not clear why the experience should seem transparent.[11]

6. Projectivism, transparency, and representation

The colour physicalist, I have argued, is faced with a choice between explaining the phenomenal character of a colour experience in terms either of the intrinsic features of the experience, or of the representational content. Neither possibility will work. There is, however, a better solution to the question of what it is for something to look red (and hence of phenomenal character), one that an eliminativist, with subjectivist leanings, can propose. The solution is given by a third option to the two already canvassed: the phenomenal character of a visual experience is explained in terms both of intrinsic features and representational content of the experience.

Our perceptual experience, I claim, contains sensory representations. We are presented in perceptual experience with subjective qualities, that is, qualia, which are both intrinsic qualities of the representation and which also form part of the content of the experience. The subjective features of the experience are both features intrinsic to the experience and features that make up part of the representational content. The transparency is explained as follows: although the subjective features are intrinsic features of the experience, the subject is not aware of them as such. The subject takes these features to be features of the external object. The subjective features are 'projected' on to the external object: they are taken to be properties of those objects.

A representation can share features in common with the object represented. We can illustrate how this is supposed to work, by examples of how some paintings and pictures represent. Now we know that a picture of a pipe is not a pipe, and a picture of a horse is not a horse. Nevertheless, a print or painting, of a map, is such that the picture could function as a map as well as representing a map. And there are many examples where the picture or the thing that is doing the representing has the very same qualities as the thing it is representing, for example, a picture of a square may contain a square. An actor on stage may represent a character's action by doing the same type of action: Othello both kisses Desdemona and strangles her. I have never heard of any actor actually strangling the actress; however, when characters are supposed to kiss each other, I have never heard of any actors who do not actually kiss each other.

Similarly, with colour: our visual experience has (phenomenal items with) sensuous qualities which they represent the grapes and billiard tables and ladies' dresses and hairstyles as having. There is an objection that is sometimes levelled at theorists who appeal to subjective qualities to explain what the representational content of experiences is (Millikan 1991: 440). It is alleged that the theorist conflates qualities of the

[11] For further arguments attacking the representationalist account of phenomenal character, see M. Nida-Rumelin (2006), and A. Pautz (2006).

representation with qualities of what is represented. The objection is that it is a fallacy to think that because the property represented is F, that the representation must have the quality F. Yes, that is a fallacy. It is not fallacious, however, to think that, in some cases, the representation shares the quality that it represents the object as having. Our examples of maps and pictures of squares, and actors illustrate just this possibility. So, I claim, do experiences of colour.

Not only does the projectivist solution solve the transparency problem but, importantly, it also solves the problem facing the colour-physicalist of explaining why it seems that colours stand together in the appropriate pattern of similarities and differences. It is the features of the sensory representations that satisfy this condition and that are 'projected' onto physical objects (and form part of the representational content).

Let me illustrate the strength of projectivism by reference to the work of Sidney Shoemaker (1997). Shoemaker canvasses the possibility of explaining phenomenal character in terms of projectivism. He distinguishes between two forms of projection—literal projectivism and figurative projectivism—before dismissing each. He goes on to argue for his own complex theory of phenomenal character, conceding, however, that it is unsatisfactory in certain respects. This result, he contends, is acceptable since, in the area of colour experience, the best we can hope for is to achieve the least unsatisfactory theory (Shoemaker 1997, 239–243). But such an ending should lead us to think about his reasons for rejecting projectivism in the first place. If we look at what he says, it seems that the only substantial reason is that projectivism requires us to admit the existence of sense data, with all of their notorious difficulties. In resting his case on the alleged difficulties of sense data, Shoemaker is in good company. Harman (1997), Tye (2000), Byrne and Hilbert (2003) and Dretske (1995), are all representationalists who make the same claim.[12] None of these authors give any good argument against sense data: at best they refer to alleged refutations by authors such as Austin, Sellars, and others. I have argued elsewhere that these historical arguments do not succeed (Maund 2003, chs. 5 and 6). They are either bad arguments or they work only against a restricted version of the thesis. Sellars, for example, distinguishes between sense data and sensa. Sense data are defined epistemologically, whereas sensa are metaphysical entities. Sensa have the properties usually associated with qualia, and are, in Searle's terms, 'ontologically subjective'. Sellars (1971), argues against sense data but for sensa! I am not alone in my arguments (see Tim Crane 2001; A. D. Smith 2002). For better arguments for sense data, see H. Robinson (1994), E. J. Lowe (2008).

There is a further consideration in favour of Projectivism. There are a number of authors who have defended a relational view of colour, and who, in defence of this theory, argue in terms of how the relational theory fits well with evolutionary theory of how colour vision has evolved. The Projectivist theory is at no disadvantage here.

[12] I should add that the account of sense data (or rather, sensa) that I defend is different from the accounts considered by Byrne and Hilbert in this volume. See Maund (2003, 116–117, 173–178).

Indeed, this is no surprise, since Projectivism is compatible with (though it does not require) a relational theory. The evolutionary advantage that colour vision bestows on the organism operates through the way colours appear, that is, by virtue of the fact that some objects look red, others green and so on. The Projectivist theory can give as good an explanation of the biological function as any other theory, since central to it is an account of how things look. This is a point Cosmides and Tooby have made, in support of their version of Projectivism:

> That objects seem to be coloured is an invention of natural selection, which built into some species, including our own, the specialized neural circuitry involved. (1995, xi)

7. Colour Realism, revisionism and the Hardin-Kuehni objection

The thrust of the argument in the past two sections has been that Colour Realists cannot sustain an adequate account of the crucial 'looks-red role'. There is another damaging objection to the reliance Colour Realists place on this role, one that I shall call 'the Hardin-Kuehni objection'. Again, to fix our ideas, let us apply it to McLaughlin's account. This restriction is harmless since the feature of his account that is problematical is typical of realist accounts.

McLaughlin's account of colour was originally expressed in the form of a proposal, but as a proposal for consideration as the right account of how our colour names operate:

> Basic proposal: redness is that property which disposes its bearers to look red to standard visual perceivers in standard conditions of visual observation and which must (as a matter of nomological necessity) be had by everything so disposed. (McLaughlin 2003: 479)

Central to this proposal is the reference to standard conditions and normal observers. There is a problem, however, as C. L. Hardin and R. Kuehni have pointed out, in identifying 'normal observers', and 'standard conditions' (Hardin 2004, 2006; Kuehni 2001). For example, there is no uniform, homogeneous class of normal observers. Among the class of competent observers, there is a large set of different sub-classes within which there is widespread agreement on colour names, but between which there is systematic disagreement. All the competent observers will agree that say 'unique' blue falls within a certain range of colours, but the different sub-classes disagree on which of the colours is unique blue. And they disagree on which colour is blue5green; blue10red, and so on.

This means that the hue circle is skewed with respect to different groups of observers. It would be completely arbitrary to select one group as the normal group. To this problem we should add another, a related problem. This problem concerns the circumstances associated with the phenomenon of simultaneous surround. A given chip will change its colour appearance very dramatically when the colours of the background change. There seems to be no non-arbitrary way to select one background over another as the standard one. (It also changes its appearance as it is made larger.)

It would seem that McLaughlin accepts that there is something wrong with his initial proposal. This is shown in his response to the objection raised by Hardin and Kuehni. McLaughlin offers a solution to this problem. Rather than embracing colour irrealism, he says, 'we should handle the problem of standard variation by radically relativising the colours: that is we should relativize them to kinds of perceivers and [kinds of] circumstances'. The new proposal is:

> Relativised colours: redness for a visual perceiver of type P in circumstances of visual observation C is that property which disposes its bearers to look red to P in C, and which is had by everything so disposed. (McLaughlin 2003: 493)

But given that we are being offered a proposal, we have to ask for what purpose it is being proposed. The answer he seems to give is that it will avoid colour irrealism (colour eliminativism). But if the question, of whether Colour Realism or colour irrealism is true, is a question concerning the standard understanding of colour, then it has already been conceded that Colour Realism, in this sense, is false.

The proposal, therefore, has to be understood as a proposal for what concept we should put in place of the standard concept, so as to avoid colour irrealism. But now we need to ask three questions: (1) why should we bother relativising? (2) Why should we prefer this proposal to others on offer? (3) why shouldn't we accept more than one proposal?

The point about question (1) is that we might very well accept eliminativism, in the sense of ontological eliminativism, but reject conceptual eliminativism. We may, for example, preserve our concepts and language, and adopt a fictionalist attitude towards them: make believe they are true, treat them 'as if they are true', for certain purposes.

The point behind question (2) is that if we are considering the physicalist account as a revisionary proposal, then we should compare it with other available proposals. And we have good candidates available. An excellent candidate is a relational theory: colour is a relational quality constituted in part by the object's capacity to look red (blue, yellow, etc.). There are two reasons for favouring this theory as a revisionary proposal. The first is that a relational view, according to which colours are relativized to standard observers and conditions, is well suited to be modified by the further relativization, as required by the Hardin-Kuehni objection. The second reason is that if we think about what reasons there are for being interested in colour, and thus for having colour concepts (and language), then those interests are built around the colours objects *appear to have*—and only very minimally about, the intrinsic features of objects that cause them to appear in the way they do. Think of the application of colour in industry, commerce, art, and everyday life, and the central role the concept plays in colour science. It is the colour objects appear to have that counts.

These revisionary proposals are, in effect, claims that there are certain properties that deserve to be called 'colours'—intrinsic features and relational properties. And if it should turn out that there are different groups of people for whom their appearances are systematically different, there is all the reason in the world to have such a concept, a concept which individuates a property, part of which is constituted by the capacity to look the characteristic way, albeit that the property is relativized.

Once we are in the business of introducing new concepts, we should note that there is, in addition, strong reason to think that there is another quality, that deserves to be called 'colour': a type of subjective quality. These are qualities inherent in the experiences: *qualia.* The reason for postulating these qualities is tied up with solving the previous problem for the physicalist account of colours. As I argued in the last section, the best solution for the transparency phenomenon and the representational content of perceptual experiences, is a projectivist account. According to that account, perceptual experiences contain subjective qualities that form part of the representational content of perceptual experiences. The subjective qualities have a phenomenal character that contributes to the representational content, and explain why we take the colours to stand in the appropriate structural relations. The subjective qualities are not colours, but they deserve to be called colours', using the term in a different *but related* sense.

Michael Tye has a different response to the Hardin-Kuehni objection. He makes a distinction between 'coarse-grained' and 'fine grained' colours. The former colours, presumably, are bluish, reddish, orange, purple, green, etc. The second include more determinate shades for example, yellow20red, blue60green, and so on. Our colour detection system, he argues, was 'designed' by evolution to detect, and discriminate between, coarse colours, but not the determinate shades. 'Mother Nature' saw adaptive benefits associated with the coarser colours, but not with the determinate colours.

Suppose we have Jane and John, two equally proficient colour observers. Each has a colour detection system that is accurate on the coarse colours. John and Jane each describe chip 527 as bluish. Tye says that 'since the chip is bluish, it must have a determinate shade of blue'. However, John's detection system 'says' it is true blue, while Jane's that it is blue tinged with green. 'But it would be an accident if either system were accurate at this level of precision.'

> Neither of our two perceivers was designed to get the determinate shade just right. To suppose that chip 527 really is exactly as it looks to either John or Jane . . . is something that could happen; but it if it did, it would be by luck. For neither [system] is designed for such precision. (Tye 2006: 343)

The solution to our problem is, therefore, that there is some fact of the matter which determinate shade chip 527 has but we do not currently know which, and indeed we may never know. Hence, it is supposed, Colour Realism is consistent with the facts described by Hardin and Kuehni.

There are several objections to this response. The first is that it is hard to see how any experiences can represent an object as true blue or as having any determinate shade. Tye explains the representational content of an experience in terms of the 'experience being the sort that would causally co-vary with the presence of true blue, were optimal conditions to obtain'. But the optimal conditions for perceptual experiences of fine-grained hues are taken 'to require that the perceiver's visual system be operating as it was designed to operate with respect to the detection of such hues'. But then, as the visual system is said to be designed only for detection of coarse-grained hues, and not fine-grained ones, it follows that there are no optical conditions for fine-grained hues. Hence, no experience will represent any fine-grained hue.

There is a more important objection. Tye's response misses the point of the Hardin-Kuehni objection. First of all, note that it is simply not true that John and Jane's visual systems are inaccurate or unreliable, with respect to determinate shades of colour. They are excellent at discriminating the shades.[13] What they disagree about is which shade is true blue. What Tye's response overlooks is that there may well be evolutionary advantage in discriminating determinate shades without there being any advantage on whether the particular one is true blue or not (see Matthen 2005, Thompson 2000). Moreover, on the physicalist's claim that colours are spectral reflectances, the visual systems are excellent at discriminating reflectances (with the exception of metamers which are not at issue here). The point of the Hardin-Kuehni objection is that, given the existence of a number of distinct groups of 'Normal Observers', who purportedly identify several 'true blues', there are no grounds for identifying one of the shades as really true blue. The point is that there is no important different physical difference that marks the difference between one of the shades ('true blue') and the neighbouring shades—apart from the effect on visual systems and experiences. Each shade, and each reflectance, of course, is special in its own way—but there is no significant physical difference between all the unique shades and the binary ones.

8. Eliminativism vindicated

I have conceded that there is a place in our thinking about colour, for introducing new concepts of colour—relational colour and subjectivist colour. These kinds of colour are not colours as ordinarily understood and named. There are no colours of that sort. There is no inconsistency in adopting this position. Even if there is a place for identifying certain properties which deserve the name 'colour', there is an important question to ask about the ordinary concept: whether there are still some useful purposes the concept serves, albeit that it is not instantiated. Colour Eliminativism, as I have explained it, goes with projectivism, and projectivism explains why the concepts of colour, even if uninstantiated, serve a useful purpose.

There is a general point here, that applies to any sort of eliminativism. For, with respect to any concept for X, we might want to preserve the concept for X, while admitting that there are no Xs. For example we might want to adopt a fictionalist attitude towards talk of Xs. Take, for example, the concepts of Newtonian mechanics, for example, Newtonian mass. An engineer who accepts that Relativistic mechanics is true, would believe that there

[13] Byrne and Hilbert overlook this point in their response to Tye's paper. See Tye (2007) for his excellent rebuttal.

is no such thing as Newtonian mass. That does not stop her, however, retaining the concept of Newtonian mass and of adopting a fictionalist attitude: treating statements about Newtonian mass, 'as if they are true'. The engineer 'makes believe' that Newtonian mechanics is true. Of course, to adopt this attitude allows one to acknowledge that there are contexts in which one adopts a different attitude: one treats the statements as false.

The possibility of adopting the fictionalist attitude undermines an otherwise insightful paper that Mark Johnston has presented on the topic of eliminativism vs revisionism. (Johnston 1997). The fact that colours are not as we may have thought them to be does not establish the more important claim that there are no colours *tout court*. It leaves open the possibility that there are colours, but we should think about them in different ways. Johnston stresses the importance of the ordinary concept of colour, but argues that this concept is a 'cluster concept', and that, in view of this, some of the core principles central to that cluster can come to be rejected without forcing us to conclude that there are no colours. (In stressing that colour concepts are recognitional concepts, I reject the view that the colour concept is a cluster concept.)

There is an objection to Johnston's approach to colour, which can be put this way. Johnston is operating with a false dichotomy. What Johnston ignores is the possibility that we retain the traditional concepts but adopt a special attitude towards them. For example, even if the concepts are not actualised, we can treat them 'as if they are actualised'—for certain purposes, and in certain contexts. What makes this attitude significant, is that these contexts are either numerous or of special importance. Colour concepts are a case in point. I have defended a projectivist account of colour experience, which implies that the representational content of the experience contains illusory colours. Accordingly, this theory implies that there are no colours, as traditionally conceived, in the physical world, but it does not say that we should drop the use of the concept, or of ordinary colour language. What it says is that we should retain the concept, but treat a wide range of statements employing the concepts 'as if they are true'.

The point of having the ordinary concepts of colour remains much as it was, before the philosophical and scientific inquiries. The concept of colour is embedded in a vast range of conceptual practices, built around the perception of colour. What is crucial for these practices is that objects in the world are perceived as having the range of various colours. It is the way things appear that is crucial to the functioning of the folk concept. Objects will appear to have the same colours as they always have, even if it is not true that they really have them—but it is only 'as if they are coloured'. And of course, the extent to which 'it is as if they are coloured' is that the objects *look coloured*. This means that, for most purposes, we treat tomatoes, oceans, fires, dresses, lips, etc., 'as if they are red, blue, yellow, etc.'.

In vindicating eliminativism in the way, I feel that I have provided a vindication of the approach of Descartes 1644/1988 and Locke 1688/1961. Their theory of colour is complex, containing like mine a positive part and a negative part, which is a form of eliminativism. Descartes' view is neatly captured in this passage:

It is clear then that when we say we perceive colours in objects, it is really just the same *as though we said*, that we perceived in objects something as to whose nature we are ignorant but which produces in us a very manifest and obvious sensation, *called* the sensation of colour.

(*Principles of Philosophy*, Para. 70; see also Paras. 68–70)

In this highly significant remark, he is doing two things. He is telling us how we should think about colours, (i.e. 'think philosophically' about colours). He is also saying something about our ordinary everyday use of colour language: that we should continue using our ordinary colour talk—about the colours of material bodies—but we should give it a novel interpretation: when we say 'X', then it is as though we said... In saying this, he is clearly implying that there is something defective to our ordinary talk, understood literally. Locke has similar views, for example, as set out in the Essay [esp. II, XXXI, 2]. Each is recommending the practice, as it was traditionally described, that 'we continue to speak with the vulgar but think with the learned'.

As the quote above illustrates, Descartes (and Locke) can be taken as recommending, as far as our 'philosophical thinking' is concerned, *a dual reference principle* of colour naming. According to this proposal, colour terms should be used in two distinct, though related ways: (i) to refer to qualities in external bodies, which are powers to cause sensations of colour; (ii) to refer to qualities in sensations. Their eliminativism comes in with respect to our ordinary use of colour terms. Consider this quote from Descartes:

we easily fall into the mistake of judging that the feature of objects *that we call colour* is something *just like the colour in our sensation*; i.e., of thinking that we clearly perceive something which in fact we do not perceive at all. (*Principles,* 70)

Thus, our colour terms would seem to follow a principle of dual reference though, in a crucial way, different from the principle he is recommending that we follow: the two principles differ in how colours are thought of, when attributed to physical bodies. Thus, Descartes clearly thinks that material bodies do not have the colours that we ordinary folk naïvely, and unphilosophically, take them to have. On my way of thinking, both he and Locke are right in this matter, but for not quite the right reasons. I have argued that our ordinary colour talk is univocal, employing a concept that is not instantiated in material bodies. I agree with them on their prescription for 'thinking philosophically' about colour, though I would replace their concept of colour as a quality in sensations, by the primitivist concept, explained on projectivist lines, as I have argued in this paper. (For further discussion, see Maund 2006b, 253–256).[14]

[14] I wish to acknowledge for helpful comments: my colleagues Miri Albahari, Nic Damnjanovic, and Nin Kirkham; and audiences at the Australasian Association of Philosophy Conference 2008, and Glasgow University, Colours and Language Conference 2008.

Bibliography

Boghossian P. A. and J. D. Velleman. 1997. 'Physicalist Theories of Color', in *Readings on Color*, Vol. I, ed. A. Byrne and D. R. Hilbert, 105–36, Cambridge, Mass.: M.I.T Press.

Broackes, Justin. 1997. 'The Autonomy of Colour', in *Readings on Color*, Vol. I, ed. A. Byrne and D. R. Hilbert, 191–226, Cambridge, Mass.: M.I.T Press.

Brown, Derek H. 2006. 'On the Dual Referent Approach to Colour Theory', *The Philosophical Quarterly*, 56: 96–105.

Byrne, A. and D. R. Hilbert. 1997a. 'Colors and Reflectances', in *Readings on Color*, Vol. I, ed. A. Byrne and D. R. Hilbert, 263–288, Cambridge, Mass.: MIT Press.

—— 2003b.'Color Realism and Color Science', *Behavioural and Brain Sciences*, 2003, 26: 1–44.

—— 2007. 'Truest Blue', *Analysis*, 67: 87–92.

Campbell, John. 1997. 'A Simple View of Colour', in *Readings on Color*, Vol. I, ed. A. Byrne and D. R. Hilbert, 177–90, Cambridge, Mass.: MIT Press.

—— 2005. ' "Transparency vs Revelation", in Color Perception', *Philosophical Topics*, 105–115.

Cohen, Jonathan. 2004. 'Color Properties and Color Ascription: A Relationalist Manifesto', *The Philosophical Review*, 101: 551–88.

—— 2005. 'Colors, Functions, Realizers, and Roles', in *Philosophical Topics* 33: 117–40.

—— Hardin C. L. and B. McLaughlin. 2006. 'True Colours', *Analysis*, 66: 335–339.

Cosmides, L. and J. Tooby. 1995. Foreword to S.Baron-Cohen, *Mindblindness*, Cambridge, Mass.: MIT Press.

Crane T. 2000. 'The Origins of Qualia', *History of the Mind-Body Problem*, T. Crane and S. Patterson (eds), 169–94, London: Routledge.

—— and S. Patterson. 2000 (eds.). *History of the Mind-Body Problem*, London: Routledge,

Descartes, Rene. 1644/1988. *Principles of Philosophy*, in John Cottingham, Robert Stoothoff and Dugald Murdoch (eds), *Descartes: Selected Philosophical Writings*, Cambridge: Cambridge University Press.

Dretske, Fred. 1995. *Naturalizing the Mind*, Cambridge, Mass: MIT Press.

Evans, Gareth. 1982. *The Varieties of Reference*, Oxford: Clarendon Press.

Gatzia, Dimitria. 2007. 'Color Fictionalism: Color Discourse Without Colors', Unpublished Ph.D.

Hardin, C. L. 1988. *Colour for Philosophers*, Indianapolis, Ind.: Hackett.

—— 2003. 'A Reflectance Doth Not a Color Make', *The Journal of Philosophy*, 100: 191–202.

—— 2004. 'A Green Thought in a Green Shade', *The Harvard Review of Philosophy*, 12: 29–39.

—— 2008. 'Color Qualities and the Physical World', in *The Case for Qualia*, ed. E. Wright, 143–54, Cambridge, Mass: MIT Press.

Harman, G. 1997. 'The Intrinsic Quality of Experience', *The Nature of Consciousness*, Ned Block, Owen Flanagan, and Gven Gzeldere (eds), Cambridge, Mass.: MIT Press.

Jackson, Frank. 2000, 'Philosophizing about Color', in *Color Perception*, ed. Steven Davis, Oxford: Oxford University Press, 152–162.

—— 2007. 'Colour For Representationalists', *Erkenntnis* 66: 169–85.

Johnston, Mark. 1997. 'How to Speak of the Colors', in *Readings on Color*, Vol. I, ed. Byrne A. and D. R. Hilbert, 137–76, Cambridge, Mass.: MIT Press.

Kuehni, R. G. 1997. *Color: An Introduction to Practice and Principles*, New York: Wiley.

—— 2001. 'Determination of Unique Hues Using Munsell Color Chips', *Color Research and Application*, 26: 61–66.

Locke, John. 1688/1961. *Essay Concerning Human Understanding*, ed. J.Yolton, London: Dent.

Lowe, E. J. 2008. 'Illusions and Hallucinations as Evidence for Sense Data', in E. Wright (ed.) *The Case For Qualia*, 59–72.

McLaughlin, B. 2003. 'The Place of Color in Nature', in R. Mausfeld and D. Meyer, *Colour Perception: Mind and the Physical World*, 475–507.

Martin, M. G. F. 2000. 'Beyond Dispute', in *History of the Mind-Body Problem*, T. Crane and S. Patterson (eds), 195–231, London: Routledge.

Matthen, Mohan. 2005. *Seeing, Doing, Knowing*, Oxford: Clarendon Press.

Maund, B. 2006a. 'Color', Entry: Stanford Encyclopedia of Philosophy, http://plato.stanford.edu/entires/color.

—— 2006b. 'The Illusory Theory of Colours': An Anti-Realist Theory', *Dialectica*, 60: 245–68.

—— 2008. 'A Defence of Qualia in the Strong Sense', E. Wright (ed.), *The Case For Qualia*, 269–84, Cambridge, Mass: MIT Press.

Millar, Alan. 1991. *Reasons and Experience*, Oxford: Oxford University Press.

Millikan, Ruth. 1991. 'Perceptual Content and Fregean Myth', *Mind*, 100: 439–59.

Nassau, K. 1997. 'The Causes of Color', in *Readings on Color*, Vol. I, ed. A. Byrne A. and D. R. Hilbert, 3–30, Cambridge, Mass.: MIT Press.

Nida-Rumelin, Martine. 2008. 'Phenomenal Character and the Transparency of Experience', *The Case For Qualia*, ed. E. Wright, 309–24, Cambridge, Mass.: MIT Press.

Noe, Alva. 2004. *Action in Perception*, Cambridge, Mass.: MIT Press.

Pautz, Adam. 2006. 'Can the Physicalist Explain Colour Structure in Terms of Colour Experience?', *Australasian Journal of Philosophy*, 535–64.

Reid, T. 1970. *An Inquiry into the Human Mind*, ed. T. Duggan, Chicago: Chicago University Press.

Robinson, H. 1994. *Perception*, London: Routledge.

Russell, B. 1912. *The Problems of Philosophy*, London: Oxford University Press.

Sellars, W. 1971. 'Science, Sense Impressions and Sensa', *Review of Metaphysics*. 23: 391–447.

Shoemaker, Sydney. 1997. 'Phenomenal Character', in *Readings on Color*, Vol. I, ed. A. Byrne and D. R. Hilbert, 227–245, Cambridge, Mass.: MIT Press.

—— 2000. 'Introspection and Phenomenal Character', *Philosophical Topics*, 28: 247–73.

Smith, A. D. 2002. *The Problem of Perception*, Cambridge. Mass: Harvard University Press.

Thompson, Evan. 2000. 'Comparative Color Vision: Quality Space and Visual Ecology', in *Color Perception*, ed. Steven Davis, Oxford: OUP, 163–86.

Tye, M. 2000. *Consciousness, Color and Content*, Cambridge, Mass. : MIT Press.

—— 2006a. 'The Puzzle of True Blue', *Analysis*, 66: 173–78.

—— 2006b. 'The Truth about True Blue', *Analysis*, 66: 340–44.

—— 2007. 'True Blue Redux', *Analysis*, 67: 92–93.

Valberg, J. J. 1992. *The Puzzle of Experience*. Oxford: Clarendon Press.

Wright, E. 2008 (ed.). *The Case For Qualia*, Cambridge, Mass: MIT Press.

Bibliography of Secondary Literature

The following bibliography aims toward a comprehensive list of the secondary literature on primary and secondary qualities (and provides a representative list of the literature on the nature of color). Please see individual chapter bibliographies for references to the primary texts and to literature on related topics.

Adams, E. M. 1948. "Primary and Secondary Qualities," *Journal of Philosophy* 45, 435–42.

Adams, Robert. 1994. *Leibniz: Determinst, Theist, Idealist*, Oxford: Oxford University Press.

Alexander, Peter. 1974a. "Boyle and Locke on Primary and Secondary Qualities," *Ratio* 16: 51–67.

—— 1974b. "Curley on Locke and Boyle," *Philosophical Review* 83: 229–37.

—— 1977. "The Names of Secondary Qualities," *Proceedings of the Aristotelian Society* 72: 203–20.

—— 1985. *Ideas, Qualities and Corpuscles: Locke and Boyle on the External World*, Cambridge: Cambridge University Press.

Allais, Lucy. 2007. "Kant's Idealism and the Secondary Quality Analogy," *Journal of the History of Philosophy* 45: 459–84.

Allen, Keith. 2008. "Mechanism, Resemblance and Secondary Qualities: From Descartes to Locke," *British Journal for the History of Philosophy* 16: 273–91.

Ameriks, Karl. 2003. *Interpreting Kant's Critiques*, Oxford: Clarendon Press.

Anstey, Peter. 2000. *The Philosophy of Robert Boyle*, London: Routledge.

Armstrong, D. M. 1961. "Problems about the Secondary Qualities," *Perception and the Physical World,* London: Routledge & Kegan Paul, ch. 14.

—— 1968a. "The Secondary Qualities: An Essay in the Classification of Theories," *Australasian Journal of Philosophy* 46: 225–41.

—— 1968b. "The Secondary Qualities," *A Materialist Theory of the Mind*, London: Routledge, ch. 12.

—— 1969. "Color Realism and the Argument from Microscopes," in *Contemporary Philosophy in Australia*, eds. R. Brown and C. D. Rollins. London: Allen & Unwin.

—— 1987. "Smart and the Secondary Qualities," in *Metaphysics and Morality: Essays in Honour of J. J. C. Smart*, eds. P. Pettit, R. Sylvan, and J. Norman, Oxford: Blackwell.

—— 1993. "Reply to Campbell," in *Ontology, Causality and Mind: Essays in Honour of D. M. Armstrong*, eds. J. Bacon, K. Campbell, and L. Reinhardt, Cambridge: Cambridge University Press.

—— 1996. "Dispositions as Categorical States," in *Dispositions: A Debate*, ed. Tim Crane, London: Routledge.

—— 1998. "Qualities: an Excerpt from *Consciousness and Causality*," in *Metaphysics: The Biq Questions*, eds by Peter van Inwagen and Dean W. Zimmerman, 272–81, Oxford: Blackwell.

Atherton, Margaret. 1990. *Berkeley's Revolution in Vision*, Ithaca: Cornell University Press.

—— 1992. "'Ideas in the Mind, Qualities in Bodies': Some Distinctive Features of Locke's Account of Primary and Secondary Qualities," in *Minds, Ideas, and Concepts: Essays on the*

Theory of Representation in Modern Philosophy, eds. Phillip D. Cummins and Guenter Zoeller, 111–24, Atascadero, California: Ridgeview.

—— 2004. "'Green is like Bread': The Nature of Descartes' Account of Color Perception," in *Perception and Reality*, ed. Ralph Schumacher, Paderborn: Mentis.

Averill, E. W. 1982. "The Primary–Secondary Quality Distinction," *Philosophical Review* 91: 343–62.

—— 1985. "Color and the Anthropocentric Problem," *Journal of Philosophy* 82: 281–303.

—— 1992. "The Relational Nature of Color," *Philosophical Review* 101: 551–88.

Ayers, Michael. 1975. "The Ideas of Power and Substance in Locke's Philosophy," *Philosophical Quarterly* 25: 1–27.

—— 1991. *Locke: Epistemology and Ontology*, 2 vols, London: Routledge.

Baxter, Donald. 1990. "Hume on Virtue, Beauty, Composites, and Secondary Qualities," *Pacific Philosophical Quarterly* 71: 103–18.

Beck, Lewis White. 1946. "Secondary Quality," *Journal of Philosophy* 43, 599–609.

Bennett, Jonathan. 1965. "Substance, Reality, and Primary Qualities," *American Philosophical Quarterly* 2, 1–17.

—— 1971. *Locke, Berkeley, Hume: Central Themes*, Oxford: Clarendon Press.

—— 2003. *Learning from Six Philosophers*, 2 vols, Oxford: Oxford University Press, ch. 25.

Boghossian, Paul A. and J. David Vellemen. 1989. "Colour as a Secondary Quality," *Mind* 98: 81–103. (reprinted in Byrne and Hilbert 1997, vol. 1).

—— 1991. "Physicalist Theories of Color," *Philosophical Review* 100: 67–106.

Bolton, Martha Brandt. 1976. "The Origins of Locke's Doctrine of Primary and Secondary Qualities," *Philosophical Quarterly* 26, 305–16.

—— 1983. "Locke and Pyrrhonism: The Doctrine of Primary and Secondary Qualities," in *The Skeptical Tradition*, ed. Myles Burnyeat, Berkeley: University of California Press, 352–76.

Bolton, Martha. 2001. "Sensible Qualities and Sufficient Reason: Can Qualities Like Heat, Cold, Colors, Odors be Explained?," in *Nihil Sine Ratione*, VII, Internationaler Leibniz Kongress, ed. Hans Poser, Hannover: Gottfried-Wilhelm-Leibniz-Gesellschaft.

Bracken, Harry M. 1976. "Berkeley: Irish Cartesian," *Philosophical Studies* (Ireland) 24: 39–51.

Broackes, Justin. 1992. "The Autonomy of Color," in *Reduction, Explanation and Realism*, eds. David Charles and Kathleen Lennon, Oxford: Clarendon Press, 421–66.

Byrne, Alex. 2001. "Do Colours Look Like Dispositions? Reply to Langsam and Others," *Philosophical Quarterly*: 238–45.

—— 2009a. "Sensory Qualities, Sensible Qualities, Sensational Qualities," in *The Oxford Handbook of Philosophy of Mind*, eds Brian McLaughlin and Ansgar Beckermann, 268–80, Oxford: Oxford University Press.

—— 2009b. "Experience and Content," *Philosophical Quarterly* 59: 429–51.

Byrne, Alex and David R. Hilbert eds 1997a. *Readings on Color*, Vol. I: *The Philosophy of Color*, Cambridge, Mass.: MIT Press.

—— 1997b. *Readings on Color*, Vol. II: *The Science of Color*, Cambridge, Mass.: MIT Press.

—— 2003a. "Color Realism Revisited," *Behavioral and Brain Sciences* 26: 791–4.

—— 2003b. "Color Realism and Color Science," *Behavioural and Brain Sciences* 26: 3–21.

—— 2004. "Hardin, Tye, and Color Physicalism," *Journal of Philosophy* 101: 37–43.

—— 2007a. "Color Primitivism," *Erkenntnis* 66: 73–105.

—— 2007b. "Truest Blue," *Analysis* 67: 87–92.

—— 2008. "Basic Sensible Qualities and the Structure of Appearance," *Philosophical Issues* 18: 385–405.

Campbell, John. 1972. "Primary and Secondary Qualities," *Canadian Journal of Philosophy* 2: 219–32.

—— 1980. "Locke on Qualities," *Canadian Journal of Philosophy* 10: 567–85.

—— 1993. "A Simple View of Colour," in *Reality, Representation, and Projection*, eds. John Haldane and Crispin Wright, Oxford: Oxford University Press, 257–68.

Clark, Austen. 1993. *Sensory Qualities*, Oxford: Oxford University Press.

Cohen, Jonathan. 2003. "Color: A Functionalist Proposal," *Philosophical Studies* 113: 1–42.

—— 2004. "Color Properties and Color Ascriptions: A Relationalist Manifesto," *The Philosophical Review*, 113: 451–506.

—— 2009. *The Red and the Real: An Essay on Color Ontology*, Oxford: Oxford University Press.

—— and Mohan Matthen. 2010. *Color Ontology and Color Science*, Cambridge, Massachusetts: MIT Press.

Cottingham, John. 1990. "Descartes on Colour," *Proceedings of the Aristotelian Society*, New Series 90: 231–46.

Crockett, Timothy. 2009. "The Fluid Plenum: Leibniz on Surfaces and the Individuation of Body," *British Journal for the History of Philosophy* 17: 735–67.

Cummins, Phillip. 1963. "Perceptual Relativity and Ideas in the Mind," *Philosophy and Phenomenological Research* 24: 202–14.

—— 1986. "Sections Nine and Ten of Berkeley's *Principles*," Berkeley Newsletter 9: 1–5.

Cummins, Robert. 1975. "Two Troublesome Claims about Qualities in Locke's Essay," *The Philosophical Review* 84: 401–18.

Curley, Edwin. 1972. "Locke, Boyle, and the Distinction between Primary and Secondary Qualities," *The Philosophical Review* 81: 438–64.

Davidson, Arnold L. and Norbert Hornstein. 1984. "The Primary/Secondary Quality Distinction: Berkeley, Locke, and the Foundations of Corpuscularian Science," *Dialogue* 23: 281–303.

Dennett, Daniel. 1981. "Wondering Where the Yellow Went," *Monist* 64: 102–8.

Dicker, Georges. 1977. "Primary and Secondary Qualities: A Proposed Modification of the Lockean Account," *Southern Journal of Philosophy* 15: 457–71.

—— 2001. "Berkeley on the Impossibility of Abstracting Primary from Secondary Qualities: Lockean Rejoinders," *Southern Journal of Philosophy* 39: 23–45.

Downing, Lisa. 1998. "The Status of Mechanism in Locke's Essay," *The Philosophical Review* 107: 381–414.

Edwards, Jim. 1992. "Secondary Qualities and the A Priori," *Mind* 101: 263–72.

Egan, Andy. 2006. "Secondary Qualities and Self-Location," *Philosophy and Phenomenological Research* 72: 97–119.

Flage, Daniel E. 2003. "Berkeley's *Principles*, Section 10," *Journal of the History of Philosophy* 41: 543–51.

Fogelin, R. J. 1984. "Hume and the Missing Shade of Blue," *Philosophy and Phenomenological Research* 45, 263–71.

Ganson, Todd Stuart. 1997. "What's Wrong with the Aristotelian Theory of Sensible Qualities," *Phronesis* XLII/3: 263–82.

——1999. "Democritus against Reducing Sensible Qualities," *Ancient Philosophy* 19: 201–15.

Gibson, James J. 1969. "Are There Sensory Qualities of Objects?" *Synthese* 19: 408–09.

Goldstick, Daniel. 1987. "Secondary Qualities," *Philosophy and Phenomenological Research* 48: 145–46.

Hacker, P. M. S. 1976. "Locke and the Meaning of Colour Words," *Royal Institute of Philosophy Lectures* 9, ed. G. Vesey, New York: St. Martin's Press.

—— 1986. "Are Secondary Qualities Relative?" *Mind* 95: 180–97.

—— 1991. *Appearance and Reality,* Oxford: Blackwell.

Hardin, C. L. 1993. *Color for Philosophers: Unweaving the Rainbow* (expanded edition), Indianapolis, IN: Hackett.

—— 2003. "A Reflectance Doth Not a Color Make," *The Journal of Philosophy* 100: 191–202.

—— 2004. "A Green Thought in a Green Shade," *Harvard Review of Philosophy* XII: 29–39.

—— and Luisa, Maffi. 1997. *Color Categories in Thought and Language*, Cambridge: Cambridge University Press.

Harman, Gilbert. 1996a. "Explaining Objective Color in Terms of Subjective Reactions," *Philosophical Issues* 7: 1–17.

—— 1996b. "Qualia and Color Concepts," in *Philosophical Issues* 7: 75–9.

Harrison, Bernard. 1973. *Form and Content,* Oxford: Blackwell.

Hatfield, Gary. 1992. "Color Perception and Neural Encoding: Does Metameric Matching Entail a Loss of Information?" *Proceedings of the Philosophy of Science Association* 1: 492–504.

—— 1998. "The Cognitive Faculties," in *Cambridge History of Seventeenth Century Philosophy*, eds. Michael Ayers and David Garber. Cambridge: Cambridge University Press, 953–1002.

—— 2003. *Descartes and the Meditations*. London: Routledge.

Heyd, Thomas. 1994. "Locke's Arguments for the Resemblance Thesis Revisited," *The Locke Newsletter* 25: 13–28.

Hilbert, D. R. 1987. *Color and Color Perception: A Study in Anthropocentric Realism*, Stanford: CSLI.

—— 1992. "What is Color Vision?", *Philosophical Studies* 68: 351–70.

—— 2005. "Color Constancy and the Complexity of Color," Philosophical Topics 33: 141–158.

Hill, Benjamin. 2004. "'Resemblance' and Locke's Primary–Secondary Quality Distinction," *Locke Studies* 4: 89–122.

Hill, James. 2009. "Primary Qualities, Secondary Qualities and Locke's Impulse Principles," *British Journal for the History of Philosophy* 17: 85–98.

Hyder, David Jalal. 1999. "Helmholtz's Naturalized Conception of Geometry and his Spatial Theory of Signs," *Philosophy of Science* 66, Supplement. *Proceedings of the 1998 Biennial Meetings of the Philosophy of Science Association.* Part I: Contributed Papers, S273–S286.

Ierodiakonou, Katerina. 2005. "Plato's Theory of Colours in the *Timaeus,*" *Rhizai: A Jounal for Ancient Philosophy and Science* 2: 219–233.

Jackson, Frank. 1977. *Perception: A Representative Theory*, Cambridge: Cambridge University Press.

—— 1996. "The Primary Quality View of Color," *Noûs* 30 (Supplement: *Philosophical Perspectives* 10), 199–219.

Jackson, Reginald. 1929. "Locke's Distinction between Primary and Secondary Qualities," *Mind* 38: 149, 56–76.

Jacovides, Michael. 1999. "Locke's Resemblance Theses," *The Philosophical Review* 108: 461–96.

—— 2007a. "Locke on the Propria of Body," *British Journal for the History of Philosophy* 15: 485–511.

—— 2007b. "Locke on the Semantics of Secondary Quality Words: A Reply to Matthew Stuart," *Philosophical Review* 116: 633–45.

—— 2007c. "Locke's Distinctions between Primary and Secondary Qualities," in *The Cambridge Companion to Locke's Essay*, ed. Lex Newman, Cambridge: Cambridge University Press.

Johnson, Kent and Wayne Wright. 2006. "Colors as Properties of the Special Sciences," *Erkenntnis* 64: 139–168.

Johnston, Mark. 1992. "How to Speak of the Colors," *Philosophical Studies* 68: 221–63.

Jolley, Nicholas. 1999. *Locke: His Philosophical Thought*, Oxford: Oxford University Press, ch. 4.

Keating, Laura. 1993. "Un–Locke–ing Boyle: Boyle on Primary and Secondary Qualities," History of Philosophy Quarterly 10: 305–23.

—— 1998. "Reconsidering the Basis of Locke's Primary–Secondary Quality," *British Journal for the History of Philosophy* 6: 169–92.

Kienzle, Bertram. 2003. "Locke's Qualities," in *Perception and Reality: From Descartes to the Present*, ed. Ralph Schumacher, Paderborn: Mentis, 122–143.

Kulvicki, John. 2005. "Perceptual Content, Information, and the Primary/Secondary Quality Distinction," *Philosophical Studies* 122: 103–31.

Landesman, Charles. 1993. *The Eye and the Mind: Reflections on Perception and the Problem of Knowledge,* Dordrecht: Kluwer.

—— 1989. *Color and Consciousness: An Essay in Metaphysics*, Philadelphia: Temple University Press.

Langton, Rae. 1998. *Kantian Humility: Our Ignorance of Things in Themselves*, Oxford: Clarendon Press.

—— 2003. "*Problems from Kant* by James Van Cleve," *Philosophy and Phenomenological Research* 66: 211–18.

Lee, Mi-Kyoung. 2005. *Epistemology After Protagoras: Responses to Relativism in Plato, Aristotle, and Democritus*, Oxford: Clarendon Press.

Lehrer, Keith. 1978. "Reid on Primary and Secondary Qualities," *Monist* 61: 184–91.

Lennon, Thomas. 1983. "Locke's Atomism," *Philosophy Research Archives* 9: 1–28.

—— 1993. *The Battle of the Gods and Giants*, Princeton: Princeton University Press.

Levey, Samuel. 2005. "Leibniz on Precise Shapes and the Corporeal World," in *Leibniz: Nature and Freedom*, eds Jan Cover and Donald Rutherford, Oxford: Oxford University Press, 69–94.

Levin, Janet. 1987. "Physicalism and the Subjectivity of Secondary Qualities," *Australasian Journal of Philosophy* 65: 400–11.

Lewis, David. 1997. "Naming the Colours," *Australasian Journal of Philosophy* 75: 325–42.

LoLordo, A. 2007. *Pierre Gassendi and the Birth of Early Modern Philosophy*, New York: Cambridge University Press.

—— 2008a. "Epicurus and Galileo in Gassendi's Physics," *Philosophy Compass* 3.2: 301–14.

—— 2008b. "Locke's Problem Concerning Perception," *Philosophy and Phenomenological Research* LXXVII.3 (November 2008), 705–204.

Lowe, E. J. 1995. *Locke on Human Understanding*, London: Routledge.

McCann, Edwin. 1994. "Locke's Philosophy of Body," in *The Cambridge Companion to Locke*, ed. Vere Chappell, Cambridge: Cambridge University Press.

McDonald, Patrick J. 2002. "Helmholtz's Methodology of Sensory Science, the Zeichentheorie, and Physical Models of Hearing Mechanisms," in *Vienna Institute Yearbook*, vol. 9, eds. Michael Heidelberger and Friedrich Stadler, Dordrecht: Kluwer, 159–83.

McDowell, John. 1985. "Values and Secondary Qualities," in *Morality and Objectivity*, ed. Ted Honderich, London: Routledge and Kegan Paul, 110–29.

McGinn, Colin. 1983. *The Subjective View: Secondary Qualities and Indexical Thoughts*, Oxford: Clarendon Press.

—— 1996. "Another Look at Color," *Journal of Philosophy* 93: 537–53.

Macintosh, J. J. 1976. "Primary and Secondary Qualities," *Studia Leibnitiana* 8: 88–104.

Mackie, J. L. 1976. Problems from Locke, Oxford: Clarendon Press.

McKitrick, Jennifer. 2002. "Reid's Foundation for the Primary/Secondary Quality Distinction," *Philosophical Quarterly* 52: 478–94.

Mandelbaum, Maurice. 1964. *Philosophy, Science and Sense Perception: Historical and Critical Studies*, Baltimore: The John Hopkins University Press.

Matthen, Mohan. 2010. "Color Experience: A Semantic Theory," in *Color Ontology and Color Science*, eds. Jonathan Cohen and Mohan Matthen, Cambridge, Massachusetts: MIT Press.

Maund, Barry (J. B.). 1981. "Colour: a Case for Conceptual Fission," *Australasian Journal of Philosophy* 59: 308–22.

—— 1991. "The Nature of Color," *History of Philosophy Quarterly* 8: 253–63.

—— 1995. *Colours: Their Nature and Representation*, Cambridge: Cambridge University Press.

—— 2003. "Tye: Consciousness, Color and Content," *Philosophical Studies* 113: 249–60.

—— 2006. "The Illusion Theory of Colour: An Anti-Realist Theory," *Dialectica* 60: 245–68.

Menn, Stephen. 1995. "The Greatest Stumbling Block: Descartes' Denial of Real Qualities," in *Descartes and His Contemporaries: Meditations, Objections, and Replies*, eds. Roger Ariew and Marjorie Grene, Chicago: The University of Chicago Press.

Miller, Michael. 1998. "William of Auvergne on Primary and Secondary Qualities," *Modern Schoolman* 75: 265–77.

Miscevic, Nenad. 1997. "Secondary and Tertiary Qualities: Semantics and Response-Dependence," *Pacific Philosophical Quarterly* 78: 363–79.

Morreall, John. 1982. "Hume's Missing Shade of Blue," *Philosophy and Phenomenological Research* 42: 407–15.

Mortley, Raoul. 1967. "Primary Particles and Secondary Qualities in Plato's *Timaeus*," *Apeiron* 2, 15–17.

Mundle, C. W. K. 1971. *Perception: Facts and Theories*, London: Oxford University Press.

Nadler, Steven. 1990. "Berkeley's Ideas and the Primary/Secondary Distinction," *Canadian Journal of Philosophy* 20: 47–61.

Nelson, Alan. 1996. "The Falsity in Sensory Ideas: Descartes and Arnauld," *Interpreting Arnauld*, ed. Elmar Kremer, Toronto: University of Toronto Press, 13–32.

Nelson, J. O. 1989. "Hume's Missing Shade of Blue Re-viewed," *Hume Studies* 15: 353–63.

Nolan, Lawrence. "Malebranche on Sensory Cognition and 'Seeing As,'" forthcoming in the *Journal of the History of Philosophy*.

—— and John Whipple. 2006. "The Dustbin Theory of Mind: A Cartesian Legacy?" *Oxford Studies in Early Modern Philosophy*, vol. 3, eds. Daniel Garber and Steven Nadler.

Novitz, David. 1975. "Primary and Secondary Qualities: A Return to Fundamentals," *Philosophical Papers* 4: 89–104.

O'Keefe, Timothy. 1997. "The Ontological Status of Sensible Qualities for Democritus and Epicurus," *Ancient Philosophy* 17: 119–34.

O'Shaughnessy, Brian. 1986. "Secondary Qualities," *Pacific Philosophical Quarterly* 67: 153–71.

Palmer, David. 1974. "Locke and the 'Ancient Hypotheses,'" *Canadian Journal of Philosophy* (suppl.), 41–48.

—— 1976. "Boyle's Corpuscular Hypothesis and Locke's Primary–Secondary Quality Distinction," *Philosophical Studies* 29: 181–89.

Pasnau, Robert. 1999. "What is Sound?" *Philosophical Quarterly* 49, 309–24.

—— 2000. "Sensible Qualities: The Case of Sound," *Journal of the History of Philosophy* 38: 27–40.

—— 2004. "Form, Substance, and Mechanism," *Philosophical Review* 113: 31–88.

—— 2006. "A Theory of Secondary Qualities," *Philosophy and Phenomenological Research* 73: 568–91.

—— 2007. "Democritus on Secondary Qualities," *Archiv für Geschichte der Philosophie* 89: 99–121.

—— 2009. "The Event of Color," *Philosophical Studies* 142: 353–69.

Pitson, A. E. 1982. "Hume on Primary and Secondary Qualities," *Hume Studies* 8: 125–38.

Priest, Graham. 1989. "Primary Qualities are Secondary Qualities Too," *British Journal for the Philosophy of Science*, 29–37.

Rickless, Samuel C. 1997. "Locke on Primary and Secondary Qualities," *Pacific Philosophical Quarterly* 78: 297–319.

Nichols, Ryan. 2003. "Reid's Inheritance from Locke, and How He Overcomes It," *Journal of the History of Philosophy* 41: 471–91.

Schmaltz, Tad. 1995. "Malebranche's Cartesianism and Lockean Colors," *History of Philosophy Quarterly* 12: 387–403.

Schumacher, Ralph, ed. 2004. *Perception and Reality*, Paderborn: Mentis.

Shoemaker, Sydney. 1990. "Qualities and Qualia: What's in the Mind?" *Philosophy and Phenomenological Research* 50 (Supplement): 109–31.

Silverman, Allan. 1989. "Color and Color-Perception in Aristotle's *De Anima,*" *Ancient Philosophy* 9: 271–92.

Simmons, Alison. 2003. "Descartes on the Cognitive Structure of Sensory Experience," *Philosophy and Phenomenological Research* 67: 549–79.

Smart, J. J. C. 1961. "Colours," *Philosophy* 36: 128–42.

—— 1963. "The Secondary Qualities," *Philosophy and Scientific Realism*, London: Routledge, ch. 4.

—— 1987. "Reply to Armstrong," in *Metaphysics and Morality: Essays in Honour of J. J. C. Smart*, eds. P. Pettit, R. Sylvan, and J. Norman, Oxford: Blackwell.

Smith, A. D. 1990. "Of Primary and Secondary Qualities," *Philosophical Review* 99: 221–54.

Smith, Rene. 2006. "Van Cleve and Putnam on Kant's View of Secondary Qualities," *Graduate Faculty Philosophy Journal* 27: 83–102.

Sorell, Tom. 1985. "Values and Secondary Qualities," *Ratio* 27: 178–88.

Stout, G. F. 1903–04. "Primary and Secondary Qualities," *Proceedings of the Aristotelian Society* (New Series) 4: 141–60.

Stroud, Barry. 1980. "Berkeley vs. Locke on Primary Qualities," *Philosophy* 55: 149–66.

—— 2000. *The Quest for Reality: Subjectivism and the Metaphysics of Color*. New York: Oxford University Press.

Stuart, Matthew. 2003. "Locke's Colors," *The Philosophical Review* 112: 57–96.

Thompson, Evan. 1992. "Novel Colours," *Philosophical Studies* 68: 321–349.

—— 1995a. "Colour Vision, Evolution, and Perceptual Content," *Synthese* 104: 1–32.

—— 1995b. *Colour Vision: A Study in Cognitive Science and the Philosophy of Perception*. New York: Routledge.

—— 2000. 'Comparative Color Vision: Quality Space and Visual Ecology,' in *Color Perception*, ed. Steven Davis, Oxford: Oxford University Press, 163–186.

Troyer, John. 1976. "Primary Qualities and the Corpuscular Philosophy," *Southern Journal of Philosophy* 14: 203–211.

Tully, R. E. 1976. "Reduction and Secondary Qualities," *Mind* 85: 351–70.

Tye, Michael. 1994. "Qualia, Content, and the Inverted Spectrum," *Noûs* 28: 159–83.

—— 2000. *Consciousness, Color, and Content*, Cambridge, Mass.: MIT/Bradford.

Valberg, Eugene. 1980. "A Theory of Secondary Qualities," *Philosophy* 55: 437–53.

Van Cleve, James. 1995. "Putnam, Kant, and Secondary Qualities," *Philosophical Papers* 24: 83–109.

Vinci, Thomas. 1985. "A Functionalist Interpretation of Locke's Theory of Simple Ideas," *History of Philosophy Quarterly* 2: 179–194.

Vision, Gerald. 1982. "Primary and Secondary Qualities: An Essay in Epistemology," *Erkenntnis* 17: 135–70.

Walmsley, Jonathan. 2003. "The Development of Locke's Mechanism in the Drafts of the *Essay*," *British Journal for the History of Philosophy* 11, 417–49.

Wells, Norman J. 1998. "Descartes and Suárez on Secondary Qualities: A Tale of Two Readings," *Review of Metaphysics* 51: 565–604.

Westphal, Jonathan. 1991. *Colour: A Philosophical Introduction*, 2nd ed., Blackwell: Oxford.

Wilson, Margaret D. 1979. "Superadded Properties: The Limits of Mechanism in Locke," *American Philosophical Quarterly* 16: 143–50. Reprinted in Wilson 1999.

—— 1982. "Did Berkeley Completely Misunderstand the Basis of the Primary–Secondary Quality Distinction in Locke?" in *Berkeley: Critical and Interpretive Essays*, ed. Colin Turbayne, Minneapolis: University of Minnesota Press 108–23. Reprinted in Wilson 1999.

—— 1987. "Berkeley on the Mind-Dependence of Colors," *Pacific Philosophical Quarterly* 68: 249–64. Reprinted in Wilson 1999.

—— 1992. "History of Philosophy in Philosophy Today; and the Case of the Sensible Qualities," *Philosophical Review* 101: 191–243.

—— 1993. "Descartes on the Perception of Primary Qualities," in *Essays on the Philosophy and Science of René Descartes*, ed. Stephen Voss, Oxford: Oxford University Press, 162–76. Reprinted in Wilson 1999.

—— 1994. "Descartes on Sense and 'Resemblance,'" in *Reason, Will, and Sensation: Studies in Cartesian Metaphysics*, ed. John Cottingham, Oxford: Clarendon Press. Reprinted in Wilson 1999.

—— 1999. *Ideas and Mechanism: Essays on Early Modern Philosophy*, Oxford: Oxford University Press.

Wilson, Robert A. 2002. "Locke's Primary Qualities," *Journal of the History of Philosophy* 40, 201–28.

Winkler, Kenneth P. 1989. *Berkeley: An Interpretation*, Oxford: Clarendon Press, ch. 8.

—— 1992. "Ideas, Sentiments, and Qualities," in *Minds, Ideas, and Concepts: Essays on the Theory of Representation in Modern Philosophy*, eds Phillip D. Cummins and Guenter Zoeller, Atascadero, CA: Ridgeview, 151–65.

Wittgenstein, Ludwig. 1977. *Remarks on Colour*, ed. G. E. M. Anscombe, trans. L. L. McAlister and M. Schttle, Berkeley: University of California Press.

Wolf-Devine, Celia. 1993. *Descartes on Seeing: Epistemology and Visual Perception*, Carbondale: Southern Illinois University Press.

Woolhouse, R. S. 1983. *Locke*, Minneapolis: University of Minnesota Press.

Wright, Crispin. 1988. "Moral Values, Projection and Secondary Qualities," *Proceedings of the Aristotelian Society*, suppl. Vol. 62, 1–26.

Wright, Wayne. 2003. "Projectivist Representationalism and Color," *Philosophical Psychology* 16: 515–529.

Yim, Dan. 2004. "The Irrelevance of Resemblance for Lockian Perception of Bodies," *Locke Studies* 4: 123–44.

Yolton, John. 1970. *Locke and the Compass of Human Understanding*, Cambridge: Cambridge University Press.

Name Index

Subject Index

Note: to maximize the utility of this index, some instances of terms such as "body," "color," and "extension" have been omitted if they are incidental to the context, such as in lists of qualities, etc.